Character Education THROUGH Story

K–6
Lessons to Build Character through Multi-Cultural Literature

Patty Smith, Patricia Maurer, Betsy Shepherd, Lucinda Windsor

Jo Anna Aguilar	Sally Cooke	Chrissie Mee	Bonnie Resley
Jill Arthur	Marta Ehrlich	Sandy Moore	Sylvia Salcido
Maggie Artley	Peggy Hailes	Lilia Nanez	Becky Sanders
Judy Buckalew	Joan Helmer	Melissa Nunez	Wendi Sanz
Melissa Burkett	Carole Jacobs	Rita Parrett	Brandi Segovia
Nancy Burney	Debby Kovacich	Susan Peery	Patricia Stevens
Dixie Burns	Susan Lillard	Priscilla Perales	Debbie Tubbs
Donna Byerlotzer	Jan Lodle	Patricia Pruitt	Lucille Vaughan
Kerry Kay Cook	Judy Lusby	Jane Rambo	Mary Wood

Edited by Joseph P. Hester, Ph.D.

Character Education through Story: K–6 Lessons to Build Character through Multi-Cultural Literature

For information, contact:
Character Development Publishing
P.O. Box 9211
Chapel Hill NC 27515-9211
(919) 967-2110, fax (919) 967-2139
E-mail: respect96@aol.com
www.CharacterEducation.com

Cover and text design by Sara Sanders

Edited by Joseph P. Hester, Ph.D.
Dr. Hester is a curriculum specialist with over 30 years of experience with public schools and colleges. His focus has been on integrating critical thinking and problem-solving techniques into the curriculum. He has trained teachers throughout the United States and Canada and has authored many books and journal articles. Among these are the following: *Philosophy For Young Thinkers* series, with Dr. Philip Vincent; *Teaching For Thinking*; *Bridges: Building Relationships and Resolving Conflicts*; and *Encyclopedia of Values and Ethics*. Dr. Hester was named the 1995 E. Paul Torrance Lecturer, University of Georgia.

ISBN 1-892056-17-8
$34.95

Quantity Purchases
Companies, schools, professional groups, clubs and other organizations may qualify for special terms when ordering quantities of this title. For ordering information, contact the Customer Service Department of Character Development Publishing at the numbers listed above.

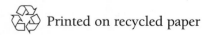 Printed on recycled paper

Table of Contents

ELEMENTARY LESSONS

Introduction

Members of the Midland Independent School District (MISD) Elementary Social Studies Curriculum Committee, in Midland, Texas, invite teachers and students to explore a wondrous world illuminated by cultural studies. Using children's literature as a catalyst for investigating representative cultures, curriculum writers crafted multicultural, integrated, thematic lessons for the K-6 classroom that can be used throughout the school year. Can you imagine the delight of children when a remote spot on the globe's surface crystallizes in their minds' eye or when an isolated character solves an insurmountable problem? Integrating social studies and literature with an emphasis on character development promises to warm children's hearts as well as enlighten their minds to the struggles and achievements of others.

In this manual, 256 books have been used to assist teachers in making character connections through reading, writing, and extensive integration with the ongoing curriculum. Teachers from the MISD have used their experience and expertise to bring character education to the forefront of their teaching.

The writers urge teachers to examine the thought questions embedded in each activity. Because critical and creative thinking are essential lifetime skills, teachers are encouraged to devote time to infusing thinking processes into content activities. For children in primary grades, teachers need to break questions into parts and rephrase them in developmentally appropriate terms. If teachers need assistance with formulating developmentally appropriate thinking skills activities or questions, *Teaching For Thinking*, published by Carolina Academic Press, 700 Kent Street, Durham, North Carolina, is an excellent resource. This book provides a developmentally appropriate sequence of thinking and creativity skills for grades K-12, a chapter on teaching abstract concepts to children, and many examples for skills understanding.

> **FOCUS:** The authors ask teachers to be especially attentive to hints which supplement specific activities. Some hints provide suggestions for skills development or for content enhancement, while other hints signal a need to either alter activities or contact parents about their children's participation in the activities.

If writers label an activity as an "alternate activity," this means that participation by children of Jehovah's Witnesses is inappropriate. Thus, teachers need to quietly plan another activity. If writers label an activity as "alternate activity, parental discretion," teachers may need to contact parents of these children about their preferences.

In both cases, the label alerts teachers to another opportunity to discuss the concept of diversity. Although children may differ from one another in the ways that they believe, speak, and/or look, from a global perspective they are much more similar than different. They are obviously all children. The writers encourage teachers to use the following ideas for open-ended discussions: Sharing leads to understanding, understanding leads to respect, respect leads to acceptance.

BELIEFS:

This manual is based on five core beliefs:

1. Celebrations are integral parts of many children's lives.

2. Individuals, groups, institutions, cultures, and nations celebrate or honor those people, events, or values that they cherish most.

3. Over time, human behaviors—such as celebrating or honoring special people, events, or values—may change.

4. When people begin to understand other individuals and their beliefs, respect and acceptance often follow.

5. Studying similarities and differences among people usually leads to the recognition that human beings are more alike than different.

GOALS:

The over-arching goal of this material is the presentation of a balanced curriculum to students. A balanced curriculum will stimulate students' intellectual growth as well as their development as democratic citizens. Specifically, this curriculum nurtures students' ability to view the world from many different perspectives, an ability which is especially critical for successful living in a rapidly changing world. This curriculum will include emphasis on the following universal themes: (1) The Democratic Ideal, (2) Cultural Diversity, (3) Economic Development, (4) A Global Perspective, and (5) Participatory Citizenship. (Walter Parker, University of Washington, Seattle)

By participating in reading/writing connections based on carefully selected examples in children's literature, students will demonstrate through various products an increased understanding of other cultures as well as their own. Given the breadth of this material and the intensity of teacher/student involvement, it is also a goal that increased understanding leads to lives that are lived with an ethical purpose. As noted above, studying similarities and differences among people usually leads to the recognition that human beings are more alike than different. Because of this, respect and acceptance often follow when people begin to understand other individuals and their beliefs.

Many of the instructional activities in this book are related to celebrations and holidays and seek a balanced cultural perspective as teachers and students pursue investigations from more than a single point of view. Literary selections, teaching strategies, instructional activities, and student grouping patterns change. However, seeking a balanced curriculum and making cultural connections through character traits remains constant throughout this manual. Teachers will determine time schedules for teaching the units and also will choose the literary selections that best fulfill students' instructional needs.

CELEBRATIONS

The primary and elementary lessons in this book are divided into six parts, each of which takes its theme from a type of celebration common to most human cultures. Each connection refers to the theme of the part in which it occurs, providing a link between every lesson and giving teachers the opportunity to have students make connections across each unit. These themes are:

Part 1: Making Lifetime Memories: Celebrating/Honoring Special Times with Family (primary lessons), or **Making Lifetime Memories: Celebrating/Honoring Life and History** (elementary lessons). In this unit, students explore celebrations, traditions, and relationships common to families (primary grades) or common to families and to cultures as they respond to their history (elementary grades).

Part 2: Harvest: Celebrations of Thanksgiving. Giving thanks for the harvest is an ancient custom maintained in most countries around the world. Some customs mark the harvest of a specific crop while others are celebrations of thanksgiving for the year's harvest and of hope for good crops in the years to come. In this unit, students explore celebrations of thanksgiving and harvest from around the world.

Part 3: Masquerade: Celebrations of Frolic and Fantasy. Masquerade explores the world of imaginative play, ranging from the practical play of the actor to the whimsical play of the prankster. Masquerading or acting out new roles may be a spiritual celebration or a means to escape daily demands. In this unit, students explore these concepts through encounters with various masquerade and carnival celebrations. Note that the masquerade sections include Halloween stories. Curriculum writers urge teachers to invite parents to preview children's literature and instructional activities related to this specific celebration. If parents object to their child's participation in the activities, offer a theme-related option.

Part 4: Festivals of Light: Celebrations of Illumination. Light is a universal symbol of the human spirit and its connection with the divine. Candles, fireworks, colored lights, and stars are common to many festivals. The custom of candles on birthday cakes, for example, comes from the association of birth and light. As teachers use the lessons in this unit, the writers recommend that they create a classroom calendar using die-cut paper candles to mark a variety of festivals of light. Use a different color of candle for each celebration. Include each student's birthday on the calendar. Display the menorah, the kinara, a lantern, a string of lights, a picture of fireworks, or an advent wreath as sources of light for celebrations.

Part 5: New Year: Celebrations of Optimism and Hope. Welcoming the New Year and saying goodbye to the old year crosses cultural boundaries throughout the world. The beginning of a new year is always a time to emphasize rejuvenation, reassessment, and resolutions. The New Year truly embodies hope for the future.

Part 6: Spring: Celebrations of Birth and Rebirth. Spring signals the beginning of new life as well as the renewal of existing life. Each year, nations, religions, racial and ethnic groups, and individuals celebrate the arrival of spring.

CONNECTIONS

In this manual, two types of connections are emphasized: content-character connections and content-skills connections. Making connections among the literary selections in this manual, character traits, and the ongoing school curriculum will assist students in building meaningful connections in their own experiences and greatly broaden their knowledge about their own and other cultures. Building content-skills connections is a developmental process. This entails using prior knowledge and skills and transferring these to new learning experiences.

Writers suggest that teachers emphasize the following processes:

- Analyzing literary selections and questioning why writers chose them.
- Using developmentally appropriate story maps and time lines for story background.
- Posting story maps to enable students to plot geographical locations described in the stories.
- Examining the character traits of the main characters in the stories and the nuances inferred from them.
- Challenging all students to develop their critical thinking and questioning skills.
- Integrating stories and concepts with social studies curriculum requiring cross-curriculum planning.
- Searching for additional books that can be added to this curriculum.
- Integrating lesson plans by using broad-based content themes, varied processes, and product options.

Patty Smith
Director of Social Studies &
  Character Education, K-12
Midland Indpendent School District
Midland, Texas

MIDLAND INDEPENDENT SCHOOL DISTRICT AUTHORS:

Patty Smith, Director of Social Studies, K-12
Patricia Maurer, Curriculum Advisor
Betsy Shepherd, Curriculum Advisor
Lucinda Windsor, Curriculum Advisor
Jo Anna Aguilar
Jill Arthur
Maggie Artley
Judy Buckalew
Melissa Burkett
Nancy Burney
Dixie Burns
Donna Byerlotzer
Kerry Kay Cook
Sally Cooke
Marta Ehrlich
Peggy Hailes
Joan Helmer
Carole Jacobs
Debby Kovacich
Susan Lillard

Jan Lodle
Judy Lusby
Chrissie Mee
Sandy Moore
Lilia Nanez
Melissa Nunez
Rita Parrett
Susan Peery
Priscilla Perales
Patricia Pruitt
Jane Rambo
Bonnie Resley
Sylvia Salcido
Becky Sanders
Wendi Sanz
Brandi Segovia
Patricia Stevens
Debbie Tubbs
Lucille Vaughan
Mary Wood

Primary Lessons

1

Making Lifetime
Memories:
Celebrating/Honoring
Special Times
With Family

CONNECTION #1:
Nina Pellegrini.
Families Are Different

Descriptions of traditional as well as nontraditional families introduce students to concepts such as stepparents, adoption, and extended families.

ALTERNATE SELECTION :

Joan Drescher. *Your Family, My Family.* Enjoyment comes from living in a variety of family structures, not just the traditional family circle of a father, a mother, a boy, and a girl.

CHARACTER TRAITS: Compassion, respect, and responsibility.

1. Ask each student to draw the people who live in his or her home on a 12" x 18" sheet of manila paper. As students finish their drawings, direct them to label people in the pictures. **Hint:** Students may need assistance in labeling people with names. When students finish, encourage them to share their family drawings with classmates.

2. Read *Families Are Different* or *Your Family, My Family* aloud. Remember to set the stage with appropriate pre-reading activities that capture students' interest. Clarify vocabulary terms necessary for understanding the text. Define clearly a purpose for reading and/or listening.

3. Ask students to compare and contrast the family in their pictures to the family in the story in a teacher-led discussion. **Hint:** Read the whole story first, discuss new vocabulary terms such as adopted, divorced, half-sister, half-brother, and then invite students to apply terms to family situations in the story.

4. Select one character trait (e.g., compassion, respect, or responsibility) and talk about how characters in the story and/or in students' pictures demonstrate the trait. Ask students to tell why they selected a particular character and how the character exemplifies the trait. Suggest that students think about their own lives, and share examples that illustrate the trait.

   Hint: For interest and variety, alternate discussions on character traits between the benefits of possessing the traits and the consequences of not possessing the traits.

EVALUATION:

Determine the level of student understanding by observing student drawings, by assessing ways they compare and contrast characters in the drawings to those in the story, and by listening to responses in class discussions. Ask students to explain what they learned from the stories and the activities in this lesson. Encourage students to connect the message in the story to the theme of celebrating or honoring special times with families.

CONNECTION #2:
Laura Krauss Melmed.
The First Song Ever Sung

Inquisitive children from around the globe question what their lives were like when they were babies.

CHARACTER TRAIT: Compassion.

1. Set the mood for the lesson by playing music that may be familiar to students such as the lullaby "Hush, Little Baby" or nursery rhymes as they enter the classroom. Copy the lyrics on the board for students to learn. Find out whether or not students have ever heard the music played anywhere else. List on a chart where they have heard the music. **Ask:** Why are there many similarities and few differences among student answers? Ask students to name other favorite childhood songs. **Hint:** Collect taped music for continuous playing before class. If students name songs other than those in teachers' collections, try to locate and add these favorites to the tape.

2. Read *The First Song Ever Sung* aloud. Remember to set the stage with appropriate pre-reading activities that capture students' interest prior to reading. Clarify vocabulary terms necessary for understanding the text. Define clearly a purpose for reading and/or listening. Discuss how the music in the book makes students feel (e.g., happy, sad, want to cry, laugh, yell, whisper).

3. Reread the story. After pairing students and allowing partners to select one section of the story, encourage them to act out the situation they chose.

4. Ask students to match colors or symbols with certain types of music and tell why they connect (e.g., rap = bright colors; lullaby = soft colors; marches = straight lines).

5. Select the character trait of compassion. Encourage students to identify how their behavior in the classroom, on the playground, or at home shows that they care about the well-being of others. Link the trait to the story by pointing out to students that caring is a learned behavior. Discuss ways that babies and children learn to care about themselves as well as others.

Hint: For interest and variety, alternate discussions on character traits between the presence and benefits of possessing the traits and the absence and consequences of not possessing the traits.

EVALUATION:

Determine the level of student understanding by studying the music list students brainstorm and by observing the socio-dramas student partners perform. Ask students to explain what they learned in this lesson. Encourage students to connect the message in the story to the theme of celebrating or honoring special times with families.

CONNECTION #3:
Mem Fox. *Shoes from Grandpa*

Through the eyes of the youngest family member, readers gain insights about how much all family members care for one another.

CHARACTER TRAIT: Compassion.

1. Ask students who buys things for them and if these items are usually tied to special occasions such as birthdays, holidays, or the beginning of school. Make a list of children's responses. **Hint:** Nudge students into discussion with questions such as: Who goes with you to get new clothes? What are some of the things you think about when you consider purchasing a new dress or a new shirt?

2. Read *Shoes From Grandpa* aloud. Remember to set the stage with appropriate pre-reading activities that capture students' interest. Clarify vocabulary terms necessary for understanding the text. Define clearly a purpose for reading and/or listening.

3. Compare persons who buy things for the little girl in the story to those who appear on the list that children generated. **Hint:** Allow similarities and differences on the list to guide the discussion.

4. Ask children to think about favorite items that other people have given them in the past, the givers' names, and the reasons for the gift. Show children how to look through magazines or newspapers and find pictures of the same or similar items. Allow students to construct collages by cutting out pictures of these highly prized gifts and gluing them randomly on a piece of manila paper. Ask for volunteers to share their finished products with classmates.

   Hint: Just for fun, talk about a time when teachers received a gift that they really didn't want but wanted not to hurt the giver's feelings. Talk about the meaning of compassion and how to apply the trait to the situation of an unwanted gift.

5. Make a class list with two headings: things bought and things made. Ask students to think of favorite things that someone either bought or made for them. Tell students to point to the side of the chart where the item should be listed and why they chose that side. **Hint:** This activity gives teachers opportunities to discuss purchasing items, what stores they would visit to buy certain items, prices of items, making items at home, remaking items that belonged to someone else, and differences between needs and wants.

EVALUATION:

Determine the level of student understanding by observing student-made lists and collages, by listening to students' oral sharing with classmates, and by assessing how students categorize items. Ask students to explain what they learned from this story and the activities. Encourage students to connect the message in the story to the theme of celebrating or honoring special times with families.

CONNECTION #4:
Eve Bunting. *Flower Garden*

A little girl assisted by her father plants a special birthday gift as a surprise for her mother.

CHARACTER TRAITS: Talk about the meaning of diligence and responsibility in terms of the classroom garden.

1. Discuss activities that families do together. If students do not mention gardening, talk about outdoor activities that families may do together. List all student responses and ask children to draw their favorite family activity on manila paper. **Hint:** Script-write what families are doing in each picture.

2. Read *The Flower Garden* aloud. Remember to set the stage with appropriate pre-reading activities that capture students' interest. Clarify vocabulary terms necessary for understanding the text. Define clearly a purpose for reading and/or listening. After reading the story, ask students to list family activities in the story and then compare the lists of family activities in the story with real-life family activities in the pictures. Invite students to predict why many similarities on the two lists exist.

3. Make a classroom garden in a planter box. **Hint:** Check local nurseries for discount prices and share the stories about bargains with students. Talk about all of the jobs necessary to make a garden grow. Assign students specific duties and keep records of how the students perform them.

4. After discussing the meaning of the character traits, diligence and responsibility, lead students into applying these traits to the garden experience. **Ask:** If you work hard and do your assigned tasks faithfully each day, what will be the results? What will happen if you neglect your tasks? Explain to students how to draw conclusions from their answers.

EVALUATION:

Determine the level of student understanding by listening to students' responses, by observing their drawings, by assessing the accuracy of their comparisons, and by watching their eagerness to participate in a class project. Ask students to explain what they learned from the story and lesson. Encourage students to connect the message in the story to the theme of celebrating or honoring special times with families.

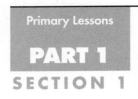

CONNECTION #5:
Caroline Castle and Peter Bowman. *Grandpa Baxter and the Photographs*

Through the process of sharing photographs, Benjamin learns about Grandpa Bear's past.

CHARACTER TRAIT: Respect

1. Send a letter home with children about a week before starting this activity. Ask to borrow about five pictures of each child for a class project. Suggest that parents write the student's name on the back of the photographs or on a separate piece of paper. Set up a classroom album that has one page for each child in the room. Entitle the page with the child's name, and then tape the pictures in the album. Share and discuss each child's pictures with the class.

   Hint: If a child does not have pictures to share, allow him to draw or cut out pictures that might represent important events in his life. Lead students in searching for similarities in the pictures such as brothers and sisters, family vacations, grandparents and other relatives, pets, or picnics.

2. Read aloud the story, *Grandpa Baxter and the Photographs*. Remember to set the stage with appropriate pre-reading activities that capture students' interest. Clarify vocabulary terms necessary for understanding the text. Define clearly a purpose for reading and/or listening.

3. Introduce the word "scenery." Talk about what types of scenery they see in the story. Make distinctions between various landforms. Compare scenery in the story to scenery in the album pictures. Decide on words that best describe the scenery such as country (rural) and city (urban). Construct a graph on the chalkboard that shows types of scenery in both the story and in the class album. Record how many times students see the type of scenery in either the story or the album. Shade in areas on the graph that show comparisons among examples of scenery. Help students draw conclusions about favorite spots for photographs and/or what events get recorded on film.

4. Discuss what it means to have pride in one's family. Explain to students that being proud of the accomplishments of family members also means that we respect what they have done. Explain the meaning of respect to the class and give examples of how we can respect each other.

EVALUATION:

Determine the level of student understanding by assessing how students compare pictures in the story and in the album, by observing how they categorize types of scenery, and by watching how they transfer graphic data drawn from pictures and stories to verbal conclusions. Ask students to explain what they have learned from the story and lessons. Encourage students to connect the message in the story to the theme of celebrating or honoring special times with families.

CONNECTION #6:
Nicola Moon. *Lucy's Picture*

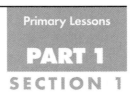

Responding to the special needs of her grandfather, Lucy creates a touching picture as a surprise gift.

CHARACTER TRAIT: Discuss the meaning of compassion.

1. Read *Lucy's Picture* aloud. Remember to set the stage with appropriate pre-reading activities that capture students' interest. Clarify vocabulary terms necessary for understanding the text. Define clearly a purpose for reading and/or listening.

2. Ask students why Lucy chooses certain materials to use in her picture. Stop the reading at a time before the author reveals the surprise and ask children to predict what the surprise will be. If children do not understand that Lucy chooses certain materials so that her blind grandfather can feel the picture instead of see the picture, reread the story and point out clues during the second reading. **Hint:** Make use of the technique of predicting in similar readings with surprise endings.

3. Fill a sack with different types of materials and fabrics. Ask students to feel different pieces and to suggest what feature each might represent in a picture and why. **Hint:** Work terms that describe various disabilities (physical challenges) such as blindness or deafness into the discussion. Be especially sensitive to handicaps of any children in the classroom. Determine whether or not to personalize the discussion by judging students' sensitivity to the topic of handicaps.

4. Invite children to make textured pictures. Give each child a paper sack and take the class on a walk around the schoolyard to gather materials. Talk about who will receive the gift of a textured picture and about construction details. Provide glue, tape, and staples. Display pictures before students present the pictures as gifts to special people.

5. Discuss the meaning of compassion. Ask students how Lucy exhibited the trait and then how they might demonstrate the trait in everyday life. Discuss how displaying the trait rewards a compassionate person.

Hint: For interest and variety, alternate discussions on character traits between the benefits of possessing the traits and the consequences of not possessing the traits.

EVALUATION:

Determine the level of student understanding by observing how quickly students recognize the clues in the story about Lucy's grandfather's blindness, by listening to student responses in the discussion on disabilities, and by assessing how students apply their understanding of the term "tactile" to their own pictures. Ask students to explain what they have learned from the story and activities. Encourage students to connect the message in the story to the theme of celebrating or honoring special times with families.

CONNECTION #7:
Pat Mora.
A Birthday Basket for Tia

Family members pack a basket full of memories that represent stages in Tia's ninety-year-old life.

CHARACTER TRAITS: Discuss the character traits of compassion and respect.

1. Discuss what happens in children's families when someone's birthday approaches. **Examples:** preparing foods, writing invitations, buying gifts, gathering family and friends together for a special occasion. Ask students to draw their favorite birthday memory and then share the story with classmates. (Alternate Activity)

2. Read *A Birthday Basket for Tia* aloud. Remember to set the stage with appropriate pre-reading activities that capture students' interest. Clarify vocabulary terms necessary for understanding the text. Define clearly a purpose for reading and/or listening.

   Hint: Find items the story mentions and assemble them in a place clearly visible to all children. Encourage students to listen carefully to the second reading of the story and pay close attention to the order in which individuals place objects in the basket. **Ask:** Who does what, when? Ask students to role-play the actions of the characters in the story by placing items in the basket in the same sequence that the author presents them in the narrative.

3. Show children how to make their own basket by weaving a pattern through slits in brightly colored 9" x 12" construction paper, bringing up three corners and stapling these together, then using the free corner as the top of the basket. Ask children to select a person to receive the basket and to decide what special items will match the person's appearance and personality, i.e., how they look and how they act. **Ask:** What pops into your minds when you think about your special person? Suggest that children find actual objects, clip pictures of objects from magazines, or draw pictures, all of which remind them of special persons. Talk about how children will present gift baskets to special persons and allow children to practice presentations.

4. Through discussion and examples drawn from the story, lead students to the understanding that Tia's family showed her both compassion and respect. Invite children to show how their gift of a basket shows compassion to and respect for a special person in their lives.

EVALUATION:

Determine the level of student understanding by observing the variety of responses on student lists about birthdays, by watching how quickly students sequence events from the story, and by listening to how students apply the meaning of Tia's basket to their own real-world situations. Ask students to explain what they learned from the lessons and story. Encourage students to connect the message in the story to the theme of celebrating or honoring special times with families.

CONNECTION #8:
Patricia Polacco.
Babushka's Doll

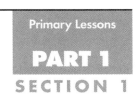

A doll that becomes real teaches her owner a valuable lesson in life.

CHARACTER TRAITS: Talk about the meaning of courage and responsibility.

1. Read *Babushka's Doll* aloud. Remember to set the stage with appropriate pre-reading activities that capture students' interest. Clarify vocabulary terms necessary for understanding the text. Define clearly a purpose for reading and/or listening. Discuss what happens between Babushka and her doll in the story. Ask students to think about similar situations in their lives and share. **Hint:** Perhaps some of these situations cause problems. If this is true, ask children to share how they solve the problems.

2. Make two headings on a large chart tablet: "real" and "make-believe." Ask students to retell the story. As each event in the story occurs, ask them to think about the event and decide if it is real or make-believe and why. Help them look for clues in the narrative and in the illustrations. List events under the appropriate heading on the chart. Then review both sides of the chart and name the clues that placed the event on one side or the other.

3. Discuss ways in which Babushka demonstrates courage and responsibility. In the story, Babushka finds out that she cannot always have her own way. Ask students to think about their classmates and their family circle. **Ask:**

> *Can you think up examples when you, just like Babushka, cannot always have your own way?*
> *What prevents people from doing everything that they wish to do?*
> *What decisions must people make in the interest of others as well as in their own interest?*

Encourage students to share examples of how they or classmates demonstrate acts of courage or of responsibility. Lead students into linking courage and responsibility to Babushka's and to their own behaviors.

Hint: For interest and variety, alternate discussions on character traits between the benefits of possessing the traits and the consequences of not possessing the traits.

EVALUATION:

Determine the level of student understanding by listening to events students share with others, by assessing ways they identify and solve problems, by observing children's reasoning as they categorize real and make-believe events, and by evaluating how children apply the story of Babushka to personal experiences. Ask students to explain what they learned from this story and from the activities. Encourage students to connect the message in the story to the theme of celebrating or honoring special times with families.

CONNECTION #9:
Ann Herbert Scott.
On Mother's Lap

In an Eskimo family, just as in any family, siblings exhibit jealousy. Mother resolves this common problem by proving she has enough love for everyone.

CHARACTER TRAITS: Talk about the traits of compassion and fairness in relationship to the story.

1. Pose the question: Who makes students feel better when they do not feel good? Make a list of persons (e.g., mother, father, sister, brother, grandmother) whom students mention. Turn the list into a graph that shows which person students mention most often.

2. Read *On Mother's Lap* aloud. Remember to set the stage with appropriate pre-reading activities that capture students' interest. Clarify vocabulary terms necessary for understanding the text. Define clearly a purpose for reading and/or listening. Discuss with students the events that happen within the family circle and why they occurred.

3. Ask students to compare what occurs in the story to what happens to them when they don't feel good. Help them make a class recipe of ingredients for making a child feel better. Post the recipe on the classroom wall so that all students know where it is and can use the recipe when a class member does not feel good or is sad.

4. **Ask:** How did the Eskimo mother show her children compassion and fairness? Extend the discussion to what students can do to make all classmates or family members feel better.

    Hint: For interest and variety, alternate discussions on character traits between the presence and benefits of possessing the traits and the absence and consequences of not possessing the traits.

EVALUATION:

Determine the level of student understanding by listening to examples students volunteer, by observing what ingredients students choose for their class recipe, and by thinking about how children apply the actions of the Eskimo mother to the actions of persons in their lives. Ask students to explain what they learned from this story. Encourage students to connect the message in the story to the theme of celebrating or honoring special times with families.

CONNECTION #10:
William T. George.
Fishing at Long Pond

Readers not only experience the excitement of the natural world but also observe a loving relationship between grandfather and granddaughter.

CHARACTER TRAITS: Talk about the meaning of citizenship, diligence, and honesty.

1. Introduce the concepts of hobbies, leisure time, and/or recreation to children. Ask if anyone has ever been fishing. By a show of hands, construct a graph on the chalkboard that shows the number of children who have been fishing and those who have not. **Hint:** A week before starting this activity, send a letter home with children and ask that families share fishing equipment and/or pictures of fishing trips. **Caution:** Ask students to leave any potentially harmful equipment, such as fishing lures with hooks, at home. Ask children how their family uses this equipment and where they go fishing.

2. Arrange fishing gear, fishing nets, and books on fishing in a table display. Talk to students about why people display items for others to see. Ask children to think up a title for their display. **Hint:** Tell children that these are the same reasons why people in communities build museums: to collect and display items special to them as well as interesting to others. Inquire what they will tell visitors to the class about the display. Introduce the concept of docents as people who share their knowledge about displays with others. Ask students in another class to visit the museum for a docented tour led by students. When students design collections, encourage them to use the language of museums such as telling stories about certain objects and describing their use.

3. Talk about the places where families living in your community might go fishing. Look at the geographic features surrounding the area and determine what features are necessary if people want to go fishing. Read *Fishing at Long Pond* aloud. Set the stage with appropriate pre-reading activities that capture students' interest. Compare pieces of equipment and fishing experiences in the story to those in students' families.

4. Divide students into pairs. Ask them to consider what they know about fishing after the discussion and story reading. Direct them to use this information to plan a fishing trip: where they are going, what they are going to take, how long they will stay, what they hope to catch, what they will do with the catch of the day. Have students act out their fishing trip for classmates.

5. Invite a person who loves to fish to class. Ask the person to tell children about lake fishing versus stream fishing, common fish in your area, fishing baits guaranteed to get the catch of the day, and their favorite fish story. **Hint:** Ask the guest to tell or make up a tall fishing tale. Apply the real and make-believe technique described in Connection #8 to the fish story.

6. Ask children to think about the story, the activities, and the guest's comments. Remind them that when they raised their hands, their actions were similar to what their parents and teachers do when they vote. Ask them to consider what happens if no one or only a few participate in class. **Ask:** Is the same thing true if no one or only a few participate in a democratic government? Why or why not? Switch to a lighter discussion and ask how working hard and being persistent apply to fishing. **Ask:** Is honesty s-t-r-e-t-c-h-e-d when a person tells a tall tale about anything?

EVALUATION:

Determine the level of student understanding by listening to fishing stories students share, by observing how they relate the hobby of fishing to existing area resources, by watching the socio-dramas about fishing trips, and by seeing how students separate the real and make-believe in fishing stories. Encourage students to connect the message in the story to the theme of celebrating or honoring special times with families.

CONNECTION #11:
Eve Bunting.
A Perfect Father's Day

Susie plans the perfect Father's Day in the way she thinks her daddy will most enjoy the celebration.

CHARACTER TRAITS: Discuss the meaning of compassion, fairness, and respect.

1. Ask children what they would do to make a day special for a favorite family member. Graph favorite family members mentioned by children. **Ask:** How many times are fathers, mothers, sisters, and grandfathers named? Show responses on a graph. **Hint:** Make sure that students have the option of any family member rather than limiting choices to only one role such as a father or a mother.

   Teachers may substitute "A Day with Dad" as an alternate activity to planning a perfect Father's Day. (Alternate Activity)

2. Read *A Perfect Father's Day* aloud. Remember to set the stage with appropriate pre-reading activities that capture students' interest. Clarify vocabulary terms necessary for understanding the text. Define clearly a purpose for reading and/or listening. Compare the activities in the story to the activities students listed in Activity #1. Ask students to look at the graph and see how many children listed fathers as favorite family members. Lead students to the understanding that they may honor anyone who is special in their lives. Allow students to plan a day of activities that will please the person of honor and share plans for a perfect day with classmates.

3. Make a pictorial book sequenced by the events that happen in the story. Use the words: first, next, and last. **Hint:** Fold a piece of paper into halves, then into fourths. Use the first square as a title sheet, the next squares for sequenced events in the story. After students write and illustrate their books, display the books in the classroom.

4. Give examples of how considerate, fair, and respectful persons treat each other. Ask students to think about how they treat classmates, neighbors, and/or family members. Ask for volunteers to share one example. **Hint:** For interest and variety, alternate discussions on character traits between the presence and benefits of possessing the traits and the absence and consequences of not possessing the traits.

EVALUATION:

Determine the level of student understanding by listening to students' responses on which family members deserve a special day and why, by observing how they compare and contrast events in the story to their plans for a special day, and by evaluating the skills quality of sequencing and illustrating pictorial books. Encourage students to connect the message in the story to the theme of celebrating or honoring special times with families.

CONNECTION #12:
Pat Lakin. *The Palace of Stars*

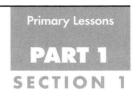

Every Saturday Amanda's uncle takes her on an outing. Because Amanda wants to surprise her uncle, she saves for weeks and weeks to take him to her special place.

CHARACTER TRAITS: Compassion, fairness, integrity, and respect.

1. Read *The Palace of Stars* aloud. Remember to set the stage with appropriate pre-reading activities that capture students' interest. Clarify vocabulary terms necessary for understanding the text. Define clearly a purpose for reading and/or listening.

2. Ask children to respond to this question: If you had all of the money in the world, how would you spend it, and with whom or for whom would you spend it? **Hint:** Show them play money and give each student some paper bills to hold during the activity. Set up a sentence pattern on the flip chart with certain parts omitted for the children to fill in with their answers to the question.

Example: If I had all the money in the world, I would buy or spend it on _____
to _____.

Example: If I had all of the money in the world, I would spend it on a family vacation to Washington, D.C., to see the most famous monuments in America.

3. Ask students to draw a picture of how they would complete the sentence. **Hint:** Pictures must visually answer the question: If you had all of the money in the world, how would you spend it, with whom or for whom would you spend it? Help children put the words on their pictures or write the words on pictures as students dictate them. Post children's stories around the classroom walls. Invite children to go on a print walk, and ask each author to share her picture and story as class members pause in front of each picture. Encourage children to clap for each story. Post the geographic location of each child's story on a wall map.

4. Play another twist with "what if" situations. Change the question to this: If you had no money but really wanted to surprise someone special to you, what might you do? **Hint:** Lead students to an understanding that acts of kindness do not always depend upon money. Connect this twist to the traits of compassion, fairness, integrity, and respect. Pick out indicators that deal with how one person treats another person.

EVALUATION:

Determine the level of student understanding by observing how students complete sentence patterns, by watching how students tell stories based on drawings, by listening to how they react to the statement that money is not necessary for doing acts of kindness, and by evaluating how they apply selected character traits to the learning. Encourage students to connect the message in the story to the theme of celebrating or honoring special times with families.

CONNECTION #13:
Harriet Rohmer.
Uncle Nacho's Hat

Uncle Nacho receives a new hat. He keeps trying to rid himself of the old hat, but his considerate friends and family keep returning it.

CHARACTER TRAITS: Discuss the meaning of honesty, integrity, fairness, and citizenship.

1. Use the book-walk technique, i.e., read the pictures. Explain the concept of patterns and ask children to watch the pictures closely to find patterns in illustrations. **Hint:** If children do not detect that Uncle Nacho's hat appears on every page, give them clues so that they will see the pattern. Talk about other visible patterns in the classroom or in children's clothing.

2. Read *Uncle Nacho's Hat* aloud. Remember to set the stage with appropriate pre-reading activities that capture students' interest. Clarify vocabulary terms necessary for understanding the text. Define clearly a purpose for reading and/or listening. For example, discuss events in the story and transfer these events to students' lives. Ask them if they have ever thrown away or given away any article. Ask also if they have never done either one of these. Then, request children to think a moment and record responses on the chalkboard by marking one of three headings: "Thrown Away," "Given Away," "Neither One." Ask students what they observe when they look at the numbers recorded on the chalkboard. **Ask:** Do most of you have similar experiences? Why or why not?

3. Encourage students to draw pictures of items either thrown away or given away. For students who recorded answers under the column entitled "neither one," suggest that they draw an item that they wore out. Ask all students to draw the item that replaced what they threw away, gave away, or wore out. **Hint:** Fold a piece of paper in half and label one side "old" and the other side "new." Teach or review the concept of opposites before students draw. Encourage children to share their pictures with classmates.

4. Discuss the concept of garage sales. Ask children to pretend that they are planning a garage sale for the classroom. Ask them to decide which items they will place in the sale and what items they will be looking for in the sale. Relate the discussion to why garage sales are popular, i.e., because people can replace goods at a garage sale for less money than they can buy goods at a store. Talk to students about pricing goods for the sale. **Ask:**

What happens to the price if a lot of customers want the item and only a few of these items are in the sale? Hint: The price increases.

What happens to the price if no one wants an item and customers see a whole table of the items stacked up high in the corner of the garage/classroom? Hint: The price decreases.

Use the exercise as an opportunity to introduce the concepts of supply and demand.

5. Discuss the meaning of honesty, integrity, and/or fairness. Remind students of the simulated garage sale in the classroom. Tell them the following story. One student placed an item in the sale that was nearly worn out and too small for anyone in her family to use. She placed the original purchase price on the item and hoped to trick someone into buying the item. Ask students to share opinions on what the girl did in terms of any or all of the character traits.

Talk about the meaning of citizenship, and relate the discussion to recording students' responses on the chalkboard in activity two. **Hint:** Remind them that their participation in class is essential to learning just as their parents' participation in elections is essential to making American government work. Compare students' choosing among three options, e.g., thr0w away, give away, or wear out, to their parents' and teachers' choosing among three candidates running for the same office. Extend the discussion to how parents and teachers record their choices among candidates. **Hint:** Ballots.

EVALUATION:

Determine the level of student understanding by observing how quickly students detect patterns in the story's illustrations, by listening to how they transfer Uncle Nacho's dilemma to personal situations, by looking at children's drawings that compare old and new items, by listening to responses on the meaning of opposites, and by watching how they comprehend points in the discussion on the garage sale. Ask students to explain what they learned from this story and activities. Encourage students to connect the message in the story to the theme of celebrating or honoring special times with families.

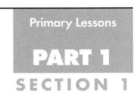

CONNECTION #14:
Judy Blume.
The Pain and the Great One

Because of the story's close-to-home truths, the topic of sibling rivalry becomes a source of chuckles for young readers as well as for adult readers.

Hint: Delay reading this story aloud until the end of the school year.

CHARACTER TRAITS: Talk about the meaning of compassion, fairness, respect, and citizenship.

1. Divide students into manageable cooperative groups. Review the types of behavior that make groups work smoothly. Assign roles and clearly explain the tasks. Ask children to follow these steps in each group:

> *Think about their own brothers and sisters or themselves and classmates;*
>
> *Decide whether groups want to show a "pain" or a "great one";*
>
> *Talk quietly in groups and make up a play that shows typical behavior of either a "pain" or a "great one"; and*
>
> *Perform the play for classmates, then ask the class to vote on whether the play showed a "pain" or a "great one." Ask students to tell why they chose one answer over the other answer.*

2. Ask students what they remember from the last time that they talked about compassion, fairness, respect, and citizenship. Suggest that they give an example from another story or from their lives that shows persons exhibiting one or more of these traits. Transfer the discussion to *The Pain and The Great One*. Take one trait at a time and discuss how the "pain" or the "great one" demonstrated the trait in either a negative or positive way. Encourage children to consider if reading this story causes them to think about their behavior in the classroom, in the neighborhood, or in the family circle and why.

3. Explain also to students that working in groups, talking to one another, and making decisions are all ways that adults participate in the democratic form of government. Ask children to share examples of their participation in decision-making. Base a discussion on the following questions:

Does the teacher ask for their opinions?

Do student opinions change the teacher's plans?

Does the teacher give students choices of activities? If so, make children aware that these activities train good citizens. Why?

Hint: Activities teach ideas such as the importance of participation, majority rule, and making choices.

EVALUATION:

Determine the level of student understanding by observing how cooperatively students work in groups, by watching students perform their original plays, and by assessing how they relate the behaviors of the "pain" and the "great one" to model behaviors. Encourage students to connect the message in the story to the theme of celebrating or honoring special times with families.

Primary Lessons

PART 1

SECTION 1

CONNECTION #15:
Ann Morris. On the Go

On the Go clearly shows the variety of ways to go from one place to another and also stimulates discussion of factors that determine how people travel.

CHARACTER TRAITS: Talk about the meaning of citizenship.

1. Read *On the Go* aloud. Remember to set the stage with appropriate pre-reading activities that capture students' interest. Clarify vocabulary terms necessary for understanding the text. Define clearly a purpose for reading and/or listening.

2. Use both a world map and a globe to locate places on the earth's surface that appear in the story. Mark these sites with peel-off stickers or construction paper stars. Use a string or a piece of yarn to measure the distance between your school and the places described in the story. Ask children if they have ever been to any of these places or read about the people who live there.

Hint: Extend this lesson over time and use the story to explain basic geographic terms such as miles, distance, and features. Ask students to look at physical features and predict what kind of transportation people are likely to use in that area and why.

3. Reread the story. Talk about means of transportation. Ask students how they would feel traveling in the ways that the pictures in the story show people traveling. Urge students to use descriptive words about various means of transportation (e.g., smooth, rough, fast, slow, smelly). Prompt students with clues until they are able to verbalize relationships among traveling modes, individual choices, and personal feelings.

Hint: Capitalize on the opportunity to point out that many times factors such as income, availability of different modes of transportation, geographic location, and cultural traditions determine the method of transportation rather than the personal choices of travelers.

4. Ask students to complete this statement:

Because I like to _____, _____ is my favorite way to travel.

Example: Because I like to travel over many miles in a short amount of time, flying is my favorite way to travel.

Hint: Extend the discussion by reviewing reasons why some people have many choices related to ways they travel while others have only one.

5. Talk about the meaning of citizenship from the point of view of having to make choices. In the American government and economy, people make choices about who is president by casting ballots and what to buy by spending dollars. Ask students to share with classmates a choice that they make as young citizens.

EVALUATION:

Determine the level of student understanding by observing how students work with maps and grasp the concept of the globe, by listening to elaboration students use in their responses to modes of transportation, and by looking at reasons why students choose one means of transportation as their favorite. Ask students to explain what they learned from the story and activities. Encourage students to connect the message in the story to the theme of celebrating or honoring special times with families.

CONNECTION #1:
Leo Politi. *Three Stalks of Corn*

A young girl learns about family traditions by preparing foods, telling stories, and making a necklace. These experiences teach her the value of family relationships and cultural heritage.

CHARACTER TRAITS: Review the nine character traits used in this manual and provide examples of each.

1. Read *Three Stalks of Corn* aloud. Remember to set the stage with appropriate pre-reading activities that capture students' interest. For example, locate Mexico on a map. Choose a city in Mexico from which the young girl's family may have originated. Encourage students in groups of three or four to finger-trace a path from that city to the city in California (Pico River) where the little girl lives now. Allow time for each group to share and to justify the path chosen. Clarify vocabulary terms necessary for understanding the text. Define clearly a purpose for reading and/or listening.

   Hint: Point out how much easier travel is through some physical features than through others. Use the exercise to teach how mapmakers show differences among geographic features on maps.

2. Chart responses to questions that relate to how families prepare for breakfast. **Ask:** Who helps? What kinds of foods do families prepare? Divide students into pairs to plan a breakfast menu. Use pictures either cut from magazines or drawn by children to illustrate breakfast menus. Encourage partners to share menus with classmates and note similarities and differences. **Ask:** What are reasons why all menus are not the same?

3. Prepare breakfast in class including foods from both Mexico and America. Allow students to discuss and to negotiate items on the menu. Use the occasion to talk about availability of foods, expense of foods, and favorite foods. Ask student volunteers to bring ingredients necessary for preparing breakfast. **Hint:** An electric frying pan, a burner and skillet, and a toaster oven will make preparing a classroom breakfast easy.

   Decorate the room with streamers and a piñata to reflect the fiesta setting in the story. In the background, play Mexican music. After talking through the rules of a Mexican game, e.g., Loteria, involve children in a lively game. **Ask:** How does participation in activities help you learn and remember important cultural ideas?

   Hint: This occasion will be an ideal celebration to invite grandparents or adult friends to attend. Model for children the proper way to introduce a guest to the teacher and classmates, then allow students to practice with partners.

4. Ask students to write about or draw something a grandmother or grandfather taught them. Invite children to bring either their grandparents or a photograph of grandparents or special older friends to share with the class. **Ask:** What does sharing experiences with others teach us? How do experiences such as bringing guests or photographs to class create a sense of family?

5. Discuss the concept of a legend. Ask students if they know any legends like the one told in the story. If children need more examples of the genre, bring in other legends such as Pecos Bill, Paul Bunyan, and Johnny Appleseed. Invite students to share legends their families or friends tell and retell. **Hint:** Make sure to point out what features legends have in common (e.g., characters, setting, problem, solution, language such as "a long, long time ago," and how legends pass on culture from older to younger generations).

6. Discuss corn as a plant. **Ask:** How does it grow? What are its parts? Trace the growth cycle of corn as a plant and the process of going from a plant to a consumable product. Encourage students to draw and chart this process on 12" x 18" construction paper sheets or model the process during discussion. Brainstorm, as a class, a list of foods made from corn. Record responses on a large stalk of corn made from chart paper. Invite students to sign up to bring a product made from corn for a "Corn Feast." Solicit parent participation as well as the participation of all students. Help students understand that one crop produces many products in different forms. **Ask:** Why? **Hint:** Explain in appropriate primary terms that in America producers make what consumers want, i.e., producers respond to market demand.

7. Pair students, then give one character trait to each partnership. Ask partners to find an example of the trait in the story. **Hint:** *Three Stalks of Corn* is an excellent story for exploring character, because characters in the story demonstrate all nine character traits. Lead students in debriefing the story and in sharing examples of character traits.

   Hint: For interest and variety, alternate discussions on character traits between the benefits of possessing the traits and the consequences of not possessing the traits.

EVALUATION:

Determine the level of student understanding by listening to student responses related to breakfast preparations, by observing the degree of cooperation among students on class projects, and by assessing the depth of answers to thought questions. Ask students to explain what they learned from the story and from activities, then tell what, how, and why they learned. Encourage students to connect the message in the story to the theme of celebrating or honoring family traditions.

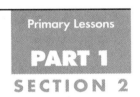

CONNECTION # 2:
Patricia Polacco. *Thunder Cake*

Primary Lessons

PART 1

SECTION 2

What better way to overcome the fear of thunderstorms than making a Thunder Cake? A wise Russian grandmother helps her granddaughter deal with fear by shifting her thoughts from Mother Nature to warm, yummy Thunder Cake.

CHARACTER TRAITS: Review the nine character traits used in this manual and provide examples of each.

1. Read *Thunder Cake* aloud. Remember to set the stage with appropriate pre-reading activities that capture students' interest prior to reading. For example, focus on the word "Babushka," i.e., the Russian name for grandmother. Ask students to brainstorm other names used for grandmothers (e.g., grandma, abuela, abuelita, nana, sitti). If possible, cite the cultural origins of the names suggested by children. Help students understand that the feeling between grandparents and grandchildren is usually one of love. Clarify vocabulary terms necessary for understanding the text. Define clearly a purpose for reading and/or listening.

2. Discuss the child and her grandmother baking a cake together. Have children sequence the steps in making a Thunder Cake. **Ask:** What ingredients and utensils do you gather? How do you use the utensils and mix the ingredients? In what order are the ingredients used?

   Invite students to draw and to write about something they enjoy doing with their grandmother or a special adult. Suggest that they write about how their grandmothers or other older adults helped them overcome a fear. Encourage students to watch carefully for sequence in their original stories and to double-check finished stories for first, next, and last events. Allow time for sharing, and then post the pictures and stories around the room in a display entitled "Making My Own Thunder Cake."

3. Discuss the little girl's fear of thunderstorms and the concept that fear often comes from not knowing. Using a K-W-L chart, list what children know and what children want to know about storms. Take a poll in the class to indicate who is afraid of thunderstorms and who is not. Graph the results. Repeat the poll and see if there are any changes in opinion at the end of the study. Discuss reasons for the changes and/or reasons for unchanged opinions. **Hint:** Use this exercise as a lead-in to a study of weather.

4. List students' responses to the question: What are fears students may have? Ask students to think about times when they feel afraid. Then think about how family members help soothe those fears. Tell children to divide a piece of drawing paper in half. Label one side of the paper, "I'm afraid," and the other side, "I feel better." Ask students to illustrate a fear on one side and who or what makes them feel better on the other side. Provide opportunities for volunteers to share products.

Hint: Because some children may choose to keep their fears to themselves, offer one-on-one conferences with the teacher as an option to sharing fears with classmates.

5. Determine where the story takes place. Discuss how the story would be different if the grandmother lived in a city. Group children into pairs and ask them to rewrite the story as if it takes place in the city where all the differences previously discussed exist. Encourage partners to share their rewritten stories with classmates.

6. Locate Russia on the map. Put a pushpin in the map to show a location children visit through literature. Use direction words (north, south, east, west) and ask students to tell a friend where Russia is in relationship to their school. Allow for thinking and planning time before students share the learning with classmates.

7. Prepare Thunder Cake according to the recipe in the back of the book. **Hint:** Keep ingredients on hand for a stormy day so that students can see how working together to accomplish a goal will take their minds off a fear of storms. Encourage students to predict if they will like the cake or not, especially since one of the ingredients is tomatoes. Using egg cartons as a graph, label one row, "I will like it," and label the other, "I will not like it." Make markers from candy eggs, red hots, beads, or stones and graph students' predictions. Graph again after tasting the cake and note any changes.

Ask: Do before-eating-cake and after-eating-cake opinions match? What factors cause changes in predictions? What does that tell students about making judgments before they know the facts?

8. Select one character trait (e.g., compassion or diligence) and discuss how these traits are important in the story. Discuss how these traits are important in students' lives. Refer to the illustrations of students' fears and who or what helps them feel better. Ask students to reflect on what character traits the person who makes them feel better possesses and to share opinions with classmates.

EVALUATION:

Determine the level of student understanding of similarities and differences among individuals and families by reviewing the list of grandmothers' names; by observing students' reactions to the use of different terms with the same meaning (e.g., grandmother); and by assessing students' drawings and/or writings. Ask students to explain what they learned from the story and from activities. Encourage students to connect the message in the story to the theme of celebrating or honoring family traditions.

CONNECTION # 3:
Marissa Moss. *In America*

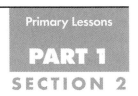

During a walk to the post office, Grandpa tells Walter about the places various people left behind to come to America and about his reasons for coming to the United States. Grandpa's inspiring story gives Walter a lifetime gift.

CHARACTER TRAITS: Review the nine character traits used in this manual and provide examples of each.

1. Read *In America* aloud. Remember to set the stage with appropriate pre-reading activities that capture students' interest. Clarify vocabulary terms necessary for understanding the text. Define clearly a purpose for reading and/or listening.

2. Pass out prunes to taste as reminders of the birthday present sent to Grandpa in the story. Determine if anyone knows the origin of prunes. Discuss birthdays with students and make a list of special days people recognize by sending gifts (e.g., birth of a new baby, weddings, various religious and ethnic holidays, and other events such as graduation). Also, extend the discussion to why gift giving relates to how people celebrate or honor special occasions. **Ask:** How does the giving of gifts make people feel special? What acts other than gift giving make people feel special? (Alternate Activity, Parental Discretion)

   Hint: Accept either general or specific responses from children. Children may also compose individual lists, and then compile one class list.

3. Talk about the tradition of and reasons for sending birthday presents through the mail. Ask students to stand for "yes" or "no" answers to this question: Have students ever received presents in the mail? Discuss procedures for sending gifts in the mail. As a class, brainstorm important details for choosing and sending gifts through the mail. If possible, arrange a field trip to the post office or invite a postal employee to the classroom to find out answers to questions that arise during brainstorming.

   Instruct students on the mechanics of addressing an envelope or package (e.g., address and return address). Incorporate math by equating weights with postage and allow students to weigh different packages to determine the postage. **Hint:** Request a weight-and-cost chart at the post office.

   Invite students to compose a how-to piece on selecting and mailing a gift that incorporates information gained from brainstorming, field trips, and/or classroom guests. **Ask:** How will you use the information learned in this activity?

4. Discuss reasons why people come to the United States. In a "long ago and far away" framework, discuss why the Pilgrims of Plymouth Colony came to America. Talk about other examples of emigrants in different time frames, i.e., Chinese leaving their homeland and coming to work in railroad construction in the 1800s, Mexicans leaving their homeland and coming to work as migrant farm workers in the 1900s. Point out the difference between an emigrant and an immigrant. Link racial/ethnic groups together with the idea that they left their native lands to seek better lives in America.

   Home Activity: In a letter to parents, inquire if any family member or friend emigrated from his or her native land. Ask if they will share a story of emigration with the class in either oral or written form. Lead students in matching reasons why people in the story leave homelands and reasons guests cite for leaving homelands. **Ask:** Are reasons the same or different? Why?

5. Locate Lithuania on a map and place a pushpin as another location children visit through literature. Ask boys and girls to finger-trace how Grandpa probably crossed all of Europe and the Atlantic Ocean to come to America. Make a list of countries through which he passed. Allow students to share the routes they trace, and then predict what Grandpa records in a travel journal.

6. Discuss Grandpa's reasons for leaving Lithuania and talk with children about the character traits he exhibits when he leaves his native land. **Ask:** What event shows Walter exhibiting the same trait?

   Extension: Extend the learning further by discussing the importance of citizenship, especially as it applies to immigrants moving to America. **Ask:** Why is knowledge about citizenship important? **Hint:** Compare a person having citizenship to a person owning "a piece of the rock" and explore reasons why the comparison is valid.

EVALUATION:

Determine the level of student understanding about giving and receiving gifts for various occasions by studying the chart of students' responses, by observing how students transfer concepts in fiction to their own lives, and by assessing how-to compositions. Encourage students to connect the message in the story to the theme of celebrating or honoring family traditions.

Primary Lessons

PART 1

SECTION 2

CONNECTION # 4:
Peter Spier. *People*

Although cultures differ in how members look, dress, act, play, live, celebrate, and believe, their shared humanity binds them together.

CHARACTER TRAITS: Review the nine character traits used in this manual and provide examples of each.

1. Read *People* aloud. Remember to set the stage with appropriate pre-reading activities that capture students' interest prior to reading. For example, discuss how classmates possess likenesses and differences. **Hint:** Graph differences in traits and/or preferences such as eye colors, favorite sports, kinds of pets, or favorite foods. These examples provide graphic pictures for seeing similarities as well as differences. Clarify vocabulary terms necessary for understanding the text. Define clearly a purpose for reading and/or listening.

2. Encourage children to publish a "Me Book" with features similar to *People*.

   Examples:
   Self-portrait
   Favorite games
   Family house
   Just-for-fun activities
   Favorite foods

   Let children get in pairs or groups to share, discuss, and compare their "Me Books." **Ask:** What does an exercise such as a "Me Book" cause you to do? **Hint:** Lead students to the understanding that the exercise causes them to reflect about themselves and to get to know themselves better.

3. Invite students to create individual paper dolls dressed like themselves. Ask students to write short autobiographies to go with the paper dolls. Ask students to share with each other and arrange paper dolls and writing samples in a display entitled "Getting to Know Me Better."

4. Using the book *Hopscotch Around the World* by Mary D. Lankford and the pages on games in *People*, discuss with students similarities and differences in the games people play around the world. Request that students draw pictures of their favorite games to play and display them on a bulletin board entitled "Play: A Learning Activity." **Ask:** Why is playing a learning activity, not just a fun-filled activity? **Hint:** Point out that play crosses all cultural lines and that people throughout time have devised ways to amuse themselves.

5. Talk about the uniqueness of fingerprints with students. Explain that fingerprints provide one way through which people in authority (e.g., police) can tell one person from another even if they look exactly alike.

   Extension: Using *The Great Thumbprint Drawing Book* by Ed Emberley, provide opportunities for children to use stamp pads to make their fingerprints and then turn fingerprints into drawings. Encourage students to share their pictures with the class. Allow students to observe one another's fingerprints and to search for markings that make the prints unique. **Ask** students to put on their thinking caps: Why are fingerprints important pieces of information?

6. Call attention to the last page in *People*. Lead students to the following understanding: While all people have many likenesses, students are glad people are different. Make a list of the reasons students give for being glad people are different. Introduce students to the word "diversity," and ask them to think up all the ways human beings are different. **Examples:** race, ethnicity, religion, language, ability, talents, gender, physical characteristics.

   Hint: Review the differences between problem solving and decision making. Use the exercise to teach the difference between the two processes (e.g., thinking up and thinking through options) as well as how to solve the problem.

7. Discuss the character trait of respect. **Ask:** Why is it important to respect other people's feelings, rights, and property? How may you apply the character trait of respect every day in the classroom and at home?

   Hint: For interest and variety, alternate discussions on character traits between the benefits of possessing the traits and the consequences of not possessing the traits.

ALTERNATE SELECTION:

Sheila Hamanaka. *All the Colors of the Earth*

EVALUATION:

Determine the level of student understanding of similarities and differences among individuals and families by studying graphs, by reviewing "Me Books," by observing creative projects such as paper dolls, and by listening to students' responses to the issue of diversity. Encourage students to connect the message in the story to the theme of celebrating or honoring family traditions.

CONNECTION #5:
Susan Kuklin.
How My Family Lives in America

Through the stories of three children, readers gain insights into African-American, Hispanic American, and Chinese American family traditions.

CHARACTER TRAITS: Review the nine character traits used in this manual and provide examples of each.

1. Read aloud the story, *How My Family Lives in America.* Remember to set the stage with appropriate pre-reading activities that capture students' interest prior to reading. Clarify vocabulary terms necessary for understanding the text. Define clearly a purpose for reading and/or listening. Group students into triads and invite them to make paper dolls that correspond to the three children in the story. Use details from the story to encourage students to create paper dolls that reflect the uniqueness of the three cultures.

Ask group members to talk about how the three children are similar to and different from one another. Provide an opportunity for each group to share conclusions with classmates and to display paper dolls.

Hint: Use the cartoon characters on the insert pages in the celebrations units as examples of similarities and differences among children. Make a transparency from one of the pages so that children can see distinct features clearly. **Ask:** What does the story tell you about the population of America?

2. Discuss the origin of each character's name. Send home a family sheet to ask the origin of each child's name. Distribute 9" x 12" pieces of construction paper on which students may write their names and the origins of their names. Encourage students to make designs or self-portraits to add to the name sheets.

During sharing time, sort names by their origin, i.e., a family member's name, a biblical name, a famous person's name, or simply a favorite name of parents, grandparents, or siblings. Discuss other ways to sort names. Compile pages to make a class book. Place the book in the Reading Center for children to read, to check out, to enjoy, and to learn about classmates.

3. Discuss unique customs and traditions of the three cultural groups highlighted in the story. Use butcher paper divided into three equal sections and chart notes from the discussion under the appropriate cultural group ("African-American," "Hispanic-American," and "Chinese-American"). Note taking may include grandparents' names, songs sung at bedtime, foods eaten, and games played. Ask students to draw conclusions about similarities and differences among the three cultures. **Hint:** Although each culture is unique, the shared experience of being American unites all three.

Hint: Provide opportunities for students to work with tangrams, a favorite game of Chinese-American children. An excellent resource to introduce tangrams is the story, *Grandfather Tang's Story,* by Robert Andrew Parker.

Hint: Extend multicultural experiences by printing the Spanish poem from the story on large chart paper to read as a class, and then talk about the meaning of the words. Use the poem as a lead-in to teach students Spanish number and color words. **Ask:** How does learning about other cultures' customs and traditions help you understand one another better?

4. Lead students in making a family tree for each child in the story. Explain the relationship between branches on the tree and branches in the family. Transfer the idea of story characters' family trees to students' family trees, then invite students to label family members and places of residence on a teacher-made tree-and-branch outline, using their parents' help. Post students' and story characters' family trees on a wall with a tree-shaped silhouette.

Extensions: Use the exercise to talk about such concepts as generations and legacies. **Ask:** What feelings do you have when you are able to share information about your families with classmates? As a further extension, use the exercise as a lead-in to a geography lesson. Engage students in searching every tree for places of residence and in making a list of these locations. Assist students in placing pushpins or stickers on a wall map for every location mentioned on the family trees. **Ask:** What does the map show you about the population of their community?

Hint: If families prepared the trees carefully, widely scattered geographic locations of family members' places of residence should appear. Visiting among family members even from widely scattered locations, a result of improved transportation and increased income, makes one's community more culturally different than a few decades ago. Talk with students about factors that make their community attractive to members of many cultures.

5. Read the story aloud for the second time. Define listening for geographic terms as the purpose for reading. In advance, review the text and select a few geographic terms to develop, (e.g., directions, island), and then develop the meaning of the terms with students before reading the story. Encourage students to raise their hands every time they think the author mentions a geographic term. **Ask:** What is the name of the geographic term? How does the story's usage of the word meet the definition of the term?

6. Discuss two or three of the nine core character traits. Pair students and ask each pair to listen for examples of the two or three traits as the teacher reads the story for the third time. Encourage students to volunteer examples of the chosen traits and suggest ways that students may apply the traits at school, at home, and in the neighborhood.

Hint: For interest and variety, alternate discussions on character traits between the benefits of possessing the traits and the consequences of not possessing the traits.

EVALUATION:

Determine the level of student understanding of how children are alike and different by studying the class book, by assessing the quality of individual research into family heritage, and by listening to the depth in student responses to thought questions. Encourage students to connect the message in the story to the theme of celebrating or honoring family traditions.

CONNECTION #6:
Tricia Brown. *Hello, Amigos!*

Brown paints a picture of a lively Mexican-American celebration that will foster comparative cultural discussions on birthdays. (Alternate Activity)

CHARACTER TRAITS: Review the character traits of diligence and respect. Discuss these before reading the story and provide appropriate examples of each.

1. Read *Hello, Amigos!* aloud. Remember to set the stage with appropriate pre-reading activities that capture students' interest. Clarify vocabulary terms necessary for understanding the text. Define clearly a purpose for reading and/or listening.

2. Invite children to brainstorm different ways to celebrate a birthday. **Ask:**

> *Do you have special foods that you like to eat?*
> *Do you plan a party or go somewhere special to celebrate?*

Lead students into understanding that many similarities as well as differences exist among cultures in the ways that they celebrate the same special occasion such as a birthday.

3. Put students into groups of four. Ask them to make a list of different places around their community where people celebrate birthdays. Compose a class list of places to celebrate a birthday. Have students list reasons why certain places are popular locations for birthday parties. Ask students to determine what factors are common to most of the places listed and if these factors guarantee a fun-filled celebration.

Talk to students about the skill of analysis, i.e., taking a topic apart and examining each piece. Ask small groups to analyze birthday-party planning, decide what things are most important to a party, and determine whether or not going to a special place makes the difference in having fun.

Hint: Monitor groups and extend students' level of thinking beyond a special place for a party. Include people who share the celebration with the honoree in the discussions. Encourage groups to report what their members feel are the most important ingredients for a successful party and why. **Caution:** Be sensitive to the cost factor and emphasize that having fun on a birthday does not depend on spending a great deal of money.

4. Make a Venn diagram in the shape of two birthday cakes and ask students to compare and contrast birthday celebrations from activities one and two with the boy's celebration in the story. Lead students in drawing valid conclusions from information recorded on the diagrams.

5. List the Spanish vocabulary and their meanings found in the story. Write the words on the chalkboard and invite students to read in chorus. Discuss the meaning of each word and use it in an appropriate context:

feliz cumpleaños	happy birthday
leche	milk
corona	crown
delicioso	delicious
fiesta	party
arroz	rice
frijoles refritos	refried beans

Reinforce the vocabulary words by playing the cakewalk game:

1. Write words on index cards.
2. Place vocabulary words face down in a circle.
3. Ask students to go around the circle.
4. When the music stops, ask students to pick up a word card and give its meaning.
5. Go around the circle and read the words in chorus.

Ask: How do choral reading and game playing help you learn?

6. Ask students to make a list of family members who live in the home and family members who do not live in the home. **Ask:**

Which special days do you celebrate with your live-in (immediate) family?

Which special occasions do you celebrate with (extended) family members who do not live with them?

Pair children and ask them to share answers with one another or with the large group. **Ask** students to put on their thinking caps: What factors appear to make the difference in whether or not family members travel to a location for a celebration?

Hint: Prompt students into understanding that many factors play a role in the decision to travel for a celebration (e.g., expense, weather, importance of the celebration, closeness of family members, work schedules, state of health).

7. Make a birthday book written by the class for each child's birthday. Cut out individual birthday cake shapes, one per child. Ask children to write on cake-shaped paper cutouts, "I will give (child's name)..." and to illustrate the gift. Encourage the birthday child to decorate the cover. Then bind the cake shapes into a class book for the birthday child to take home.

Hint: Another idea is to make a paper chain for the birthday child. Write birthday wishes on links and assemble into a chain for the birthday child to take home.

Hint: Remember to recognize children with summer birthdays with similar activities, perhaps by planning an end-of-school day of birthdays.

8. Discuss the character traits of diligence and respect. **Ask:** How does the main character in the story model these traits? Encourage students to compare themselves to the main character. **Ask:** How may you, in your everyday lives, show diligence and respect at school as well as at home?

EVALUATION:

Determine the level of student understanding by studying student-generated lists and by listening to comments, questions, and discussions. Ask students to provide relevant definitions and applications for the character traits, diligence and respect. Have them share these with the class and discuss for clarification and improvement. Encourage students to connect the message in the story to the theme of celebrating or honoring family traditions.

CONNECTION #7:
Margy Burns Knight.
Welcoming Babies

Knight's story celebrates life and diversity. From a global perspective, children and adults explore various traditions of welcoming babies.

CHARACTER TRAIT: Discuss the character trait of compassion and challenge students to not only define this word but to come up with three or four different applications of its usage.

1. Read aloud the story, *Welcoming Babies*. Remember to set the stage with appropriate pre-reading activities that capture students' interest. Clarify vocabulary terms necessary for understanding the text. Define clearly a purpose for reading and/or listening.

   Extension: Make a language experience chart of different traditions from the story as well as from children in the class. Ask students to brainstorm a set of interview questions to find out about the day they were born. Questions children may ask parents include the following examples:

   1. Who was present when I was born?
   2. What were some gifts that were given to me before I was born?
   3. Who was waiting for me at home?
   4. How was my name chosen?
   5. Were there any family celebrations in my honor?
   6. Did family members sing any songs to me?
   7. Did parents send out birth announcements?

   Provide opportunities for children to share. **Hint:** Two to five children each day can share or students may make a class book in which they write or draw about the day they were born. Place in the Reading Center for checkout purposes.

2. Invite children to bring items from their birth such as baby bracelets, announcements, stuffed animals, blankets, pictures, and/or baby books. Arrange a corner display area with place cards of student names. Ask children to explain additions to the display and to show classmates visible signs of welcoming babies. **Hint:** Help students observe objects closely and make valid conclusions (e.g., a worn, ragged stuffed animal indicates high use over an extended time period).

3. Ask students to write a response to this sentence starter: "My parent/guardian tells me that when I was a baby…" **Hint:** Children may share orally and/or choose to take the piece through the writing process during writing time. Allow time for children to talk to their parent/guardian about their babyhood before they start on a rough draft or "sloppy copy." When students finish writing and/or are ready to share responses, ask them what they learned as a result of the activity. **Ask:** How does an interview with a person help you learn about a subject?

4. Provide opportunities for students to read, reread, and sing familiar songs or nursery rhymes. Record these in large print on chart paper for the purpose of shared reading. **Ask:** How do songs and rhymes help you learn and remember information?

5. Discuss the character trait of compassion and its importance in welcoming a new baby.

EVALUATION:

Determine the level of student understanding about universal traditions by listening for insight in responses and by assessing learning from various reading/writing experiences. Ask students to debrief the learning from the story and from activities, then tell what, how, and why they learned. Encourage students to connect the message in the story to the theme of celebrating or honoring family traditions.

CONNECTION #8:
Ingrid Mennen. One Round Moon and a Star for Me

A young African boy watches excitedly as people bring gifts for the new baby. However, fears and insecurities surface when he sees his father's joy over the youngest family member.

CHARACTER TRAIT: Define and provide examples of the character trait of compassion.

1. Read *One Round Moon and a Star for Me* aloud. Remember to set the stage with appropriate pre-reading activities that capture students' interest. Clarify vocabulary terms necessary for understanding the text. Define clearly a purpose for reading and/or listening.

Discuss the tradition from the story and the country of origin. Find the country on a map or globe and place a push-pin on the spot as evidence of another place children visit through literature and also as evidence of how reading globalizes or broadens thinking, i.e., reading makes students think in global pictures rather than in community pictures. Alert students that they can become world travelers through reading.

2. Invite students to participate in making a chart divided into three sections entitled: "American Names" - "African Names" - "What They Brought to the New Baby." Lead class members in looking at the data recorded on the chart and in drawing valid conclusions.

Hint: Explain that the term "valid" means that the information is true and can be backed up with evidence. Show students that data on the chart are clues to much bigger ideas, and that like detectives they are looking for ways to connect the clues. Connected clues will lead to valid conclusions.

Encourage children to make individual charts folded into thirds entitled: "Family Members"— "What I Call Them"—"Something They Gave to Me." Share and compare charts in small groups. Allow students to assist one another in drawing valid conclusions from data on personal charts.

Ask: How does working in small groups help you learn?

3. Discuss the moon and stars and their significance in the story. **Ask:**

Do the people in Africa see the same moon that we see?

How does the moon affect the night sky?

What is the sky like when there is no moon? Relate this to feelings of joy and sadness.

Extension: Have children draw the moon and stars. Use crayon resist (yellow or white crayons with a thin coat of black paint brushed over) or white crayons on black construction paper. After engaging students in pre-writing activities, encourage children to write about personal experiences while viewing the night sky. Invite students to share experiences with classmates.

4. Discuss the character trait of compassion and decide which characters demonstrate the trait in the story. Invite students to role-play the father's reaction of showing no compassion. **Ask:**

Can anyone exhibit model behavior or must they be a certain age? Why?

Who is the model of good behavior in the story?

What may you learn from the story about setting models of behavior?

Hint: For interest and variety, alternate discussions on character traits between the benefits of possessing the traits and the consequences of not possessing the traits.

EVALUATION:

Determine the level of student understanding by studying class and personal charts of student responses and by listening for insights in discussions. Study the conclusions that they make in this lesson and keep a portfolio of their responses to check for future improvements in their thinking. Encourage students to connect the message in the story to the theme of celebrating or honoring family traditions.

Primary Lessons

PART 1
SECTION 2

CONNECTION #9:
Cynthia Rylant.
The Relatives Came

Traveling all day to reach the home of relatives proves how much family members enjoy time together.

CHARACTER TRAIT: Define and provide examples of the character traits of compassion, diligence, fairness, and respect

1. Read *The Relatives Came* aloud. Remember to set the stage with appropriate pre-reading activities that capture students' interest. Clarify vocabulary terms necessary for understanding the text. Define clearly a purpose for reading and/or listening.

Make a web to promote an understanding of relatives as a concept. Brainstorm words relating to relatives such as aunt, uncle, and cousin. Ask each child to web their own relatives and share with classmates. Invite students to make comparisons. Examples: Who has the largest family? Smallest? Most males? Point out that differences in family size as well as in language, race, ethnic group, and religion are examples of diversity. Talk about the meaning of diversity and invite students to think up other examples of how people differ from one another.

2. Discuss this question with children: What do you like to do when relatives come? As a prewriting exercise, brainstorm favorite activities in your community. Issue the writing prompt: If relatives come for the day, what plans will families make for an enjoyable visit? Invite students to write responses to the prompt, to share responses with partners, and to place the piece in writing folders. **Hint:** Delay grading writing pieces of students who wish to revise copy and publish polished pieces at a later date.

3. Ask students to fold art paper into fourths, one section for each season of the year. Brainstorm activities that families enjoy in each season. Invite students to draw pictures of their family and visiting relatives on each of the four panels. Remind students to think about the season and remember which activities match which season. Encourage students to share their drawings, and then hang pictures in a "When the Relatives Came…" display.

Extension: Extend the learning by talking about peak seasons for visiting, how weather affects travel, what celebrations draw the largest numbers of relatives, and changes around the household when relatives come to visit.

4. Discuss the character traits of compassion, diligence, fairness, and respect as they relate to large groups of people staying together. Encourage students to apply these character traits to the classroom situation.

Hint: For interest and variety, alternate discussions on character traits between the presence and benefits of possessing the traits and the absence and consequences of not possessing the traits.

EVALUATION:

Determine the level of student understanding by studying the family webs, by viewing students' pictures, and by listening to students' stories. Encourage students to connect the message in the story to the theme of celebrating or honoring family traditions.

CONNECTION #10:
Patricia Polacco.
The Keeping Quilt

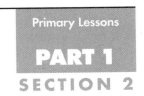

A homemade quilt, a symbol of love and faith, binds together four generations of an immigrant Jewish family.

CHARACTER TRAITS: Discuss the character traits of compassion, diligence, integrity, and respect.

1. Read *The Keeping Quilt* aloud. Remember to set the stage with appropriate pre-reading activities that capture students' interest. Clarify vocabulary terms necessary for understanding the text. Define clearly a purpose for reading and/or listening.

2. Discuss how the quilt plays an important role in family events. Use a story web to record student responses so that students will see how the quilt symbolizes family heritage. Suggest that students ask parents about quilts in their families and about the stories the quilts tell. Lead students to an understanding that stitches in cloths, like words in books, tell family and cultural histories.

3. Ask students to design their own quilt square on newsprint. **Hint:** Examples of designs for quilt squares include self-portraits, family traditions, classroom events, and "I am thankful for...." statements. Make a genuine quilt by inviting students to bring from home a fabric piece that may come from a favorite piece of outgrown clothing.

Ask volunteers to sew squares together to make a classroom quilt, display the finished quilt in a prominent place, and ask boys and girls to tell the personal stories of their own quilt square to guests from another classroom. Lead students in a discussion of how the story of making a classroom quilt relates to the story told in *The Keeping Quilt*.

4. Discuss traditions associated with new babies and weddings. Reread parts of the story that reflect these traditions. Extend the concept of family traditions by reading additional sources such as *Carry Go Bring Come* from the Houghton Mifflin anthology and *My Mother's Getting Married*. Lead students to the understanding that although cultures differ in some ways, they celebrate or honor similar events such as births and weddings.

Extension: Extend the learning by inviting students to respond to the question: What is your favorite family tradition? Allow children to write about, draw about, or act out favorite family traditions.

5. Discuss the character traits of compassion, diligence, integrity, and respect in relationship to the characters in the story. Discuss how and why the quilt symbolizes these traits.

EVALUATION:

Determine the level of student understanding by studying the creativity expressed on quilt squares and by listening for insights in student responses. Ask students to provide examples of each character trait from what they have experienced at home or at school. Encourage students to connect the message in the story to the theme of celebrating or honoring family traditions.

Primary Lessons

PART 1

SECTION 2

CONNECTION #11:
Sandra S. Yamate.
Char Siu Bao Boy

A Chinese boy uses his love for a traditional food as a means of promoting cultural understanding among his friends.

CHARACTER TRAITS: Discuss how characters in the story exhibit the traits of compassion, diligence, integrity, and respect.

1. Read *Char Siu Bao Boy* aloud. Remember to set the stage with appropriate pre-reading activities that capture students' interest. Clarify vocabulary terms necessary for understanding the text. Define clearly a purpose for reading and/or listening.

2. Ask the class to brainstorm a list of favorite foods. Record responses on a chart and graph favorite foods. Encourage students to vote on four or five favorites as a class. Construct a picture-graph that shows personal favorites. **Ask:** How and why do picture-graphs help you organize information? How and why do picture-graphs help you remember information?

3. Discuss different ways the boy likes to eat char siu bao (e.g., steamed, baked, or cold). Ask students to identify other foods that can be eaten steamed, baked, or cold. Record student responses on a chart. Using old magazines or drawings, show students how to make collages of their favorite foods. **Ask:** How do people develop favorites (e.g., favorite foods, favorite colors, favorite places, favorite friends)? Over time, do favorites change? Why?

4. Put students in groups of four and ask them to sequence how to make char siu bao. Tell them to think about what is done first, next, then, and last or first, second, third, and fourth. Invite students to share and compare recipes. **Ask:** How important is the skill of sequencing in making char siu bao? How important is the skill of sequencing in organizing information? Why?

5. Display pictures of different facial expressions on the board. Ask students to label each face with the correct word. Encourage students to mimic the expressions. **Hint:** Teachers may conduct the activity like a game in which students guess the meaning of each expression. **Ask:** Why are reading facial expressions and observing body language important skills to develop?

6. Discuss the concept of sharing and why the behavior is important to learn. Request that students tell how sharing affects their everyday lives at school and at home. Invite students to write how sharing experiences, games, objects, and stories with friends makes them feel. Tell students that they may put their words into action by sharing their writing with classmates.

7. Ask students to locate China on a map and place a push-pin on the class map as evidence of another location children visit in literature and also as evidence of how reading globalizes or broadens thinking, i.e., reading makes students think in global pictures rather than in community pictures. Remind students that they can become world travelers through reading.

8. Bring in sandwich ingredients and ask students to prepare a sandwich. Using a Venn diagram, ask students to compare and contrast their sandwich to the Chinese sandwich. Extend the activity by having students write a how-to paper that shows how to make an American sandwich. Pair students and ask each student to read the how-to paper to his partner. Instruct students to read the paper the second time to his partner while the partner draws the sandwich described in the paper. **Ask:** How does drawing an American sandwich improve the writing of a how-to paper?

9. Discuss how characters in the story exhibit the traits of compassion, diligence, integrity, and respect. Ask students how class members might exhibit these same traits at school, at home, or in the neighborhood.

Hint: For interest and variety, alternate discussions on character traits between the benefits of possessing the traits and the consequences of not possessing the traits.

EVALUATION:

Determine the level of student understanding by listening to oral responses, by assessing written responses, and by observing students' ability to transfer situations in the story to real-world situations. Encourage students to connect the message in the story to the theme of celebrating or honoring family traditions.

CONNECTION #12:
Gary Soto. *Too Many Tamales*

Primary Lessons

PART 1

SECTION 2

A Mexican-American girl wears her mother's diamond ring while making traditional Christmas tamales. When she realizes that she lost the ring, panic ensues.

CHARACTER TRAITS: Discuss the nine basic character traits associated with this manual and challenge students to provide examples of each of them.

1. Read *Too Many Tamales* aloud. Remember to set the stage with appropriate pre-reading activities that capture students' interest. Clarify vocabulary terms necessary for understanding the text. Define clearly a purpose for reading and/or listening.

2. Make a web to promote understanding of the diversity of family holiday traditions. Brainstorm these topics with students: decorations, foods, events/activities, and relatives who visit. Use student responses to complete the web and to work toward the conclusion that cultural traditions vary. **Ask:** How does drawing a web of students' answers help all students better understand an idea?

Hint: Lead students to the understanding that students learn in multiple ways. Presenting information in more than one way, i.e., talking about the information (verbal) and seeing the information (visual), helps many students understand more ideas.

3. Discuss with children how Maria reacts to losing her Mother's ring. **Ask:** What might you do if you lost your mother's ring? Ask students to write how they might solve the problem. Ask students to read their solutions to a circle of four classmates.

Extension: Talk about the author's use of "glitter" words. i.e., words that enable the reader to see or feel. Read the story again and ask students to say "glitter" when they hear one. Record these words on a chart. Encourage students to revisit their writing pieces and add some "glitter" words. Suggest that students read the improved piece to the same circle of classmates and explain to others how the use of glitter words adds sparkle to their writing.

4. Discuss eating tamales as a family tradition. As a class, sequence steps related to making tamales. Invite children to bring tamale recipes to class, then compare and contrast them. Decide on one recipe and/or write one as a class. Provide ingredients and make tamales as a cooking experience. After tasting tamales, ask for a show of hands on who likes the tamales and who does not. Explore the reasons why boys and girls who share the same experience react in different ways.

5. Call attention to the pages in the story that describe children looking through magazines and wishing for things. Invite students to write a wish list or make a collage of things they want for Christmas or other gift-giving celebrations. Invite boys and girls to share their lists with classmates. Provide envelopes to students who express an interest in taking their wish lists home.

Talk about the meaning of wishes and factors that affect whether or not wishes come true. Lead students in a discussion that causes them to consider factors beyond what money can buy, such as spending time with family members or friends and helping others in need.

6. Talk about the decorations in and around Maria's house. Ask who in the class decorates and who does not. Lead students to an understanding that decorating reflects many factors such as personal preferences, family choices on how to spend money, number of small children in the family, and cultural traditions. Invite students to draw a picture of their houses as they appear during any special celebration or family occasion. Request that children share their pictures.

Extension: Lead students in a discussion of comparing, contrasting, and classifying examples so that every child feels that he has a contribution to make to the discussion. For example, cite the name of the occasion and signs of the occasion (e.g., Christmas: lights, tree, Santa pictures, and wreath). Extend discussions further by pointing out that some families choose not to celebrate or decorate and why.

7. Discuss how the character trait of honesty applies to this story. **Ask:** How does Maria feel when she exhibits honesty? Ask students to choose another trait that a character exhibits in the story. **Hint:** Develop the trait of compassion Maria's mother shows when Maria confesses what she did. Invite students to share their thoughts about other characters and other traits.

Hint: For interest and variety, alternate discussions on character traits between the presence and benefits of possessing the traits and the absence and consequences of not possessing the traits.

EVALUATION:

Determine the level of student understanding about different ways families celebrate special occasions by assessing students' oral as well as written responses. Have students keep a notebook of their examples and definitions of the nine basic character traits associated with this manual. From time to time, check these for accuracy and relevancy. Encourage students to connect the message in the story to the theme of celebrating or honoring family traditions.

CONNECTION #13:
Cynthia Rylant. When I Was Young in the Mountains

A young girl tells a personal story of everyday life, family traditions, and growing up in the mountains with her grandparents.

CHARACTER TRAITS: Discuss the character traits of courage and compassion and challenge students to provide examples of each of them.

1. Read *When I Was Young in the Mountains* aloud. Remember to set the stage with appropriate pre-reading activities that capture students' interest. For example, brainstorm a class list in response to the question: What are activities that students enjoy doing with their families? Clarify vocabulary terms necessary for understanding the text. Define clearly a purpose for reading and/or listening.

Tell students that they will compare and contrast their class list of family activities with the main character's favorite family activities after the story reading. Thus, listening closely for family activities becomes the main purpose for the first reading. Following the first reading, lead students in a comparison-and-contrast discussion of favorite family activities from the perspective of children in the mountains and of children on the prairie. Explore with children why some of the activities among families are similar while some are different.

2. Invite an older citizen from the community to come to class. Encourage students to ask interview questions about growing up and about favorite family traditions. **Hint:** Assist students in composing interview questions. Inform students that writing good interview questions is similar to writing good descriptions: talking about what they want to know, writing the questions clearly, revising the questions, and then publishing the questions for the classroom visitor, teacher, and students.

Ask: How do prepared questions help you learn more from classroom visitors? How do prepared questions help a visitor present information?

3. Ask students to compare and contrast what children in the story do with their families and what students do now. Use pictures in the book to prompt students about various family activities. **Ask:** What are important similarities? What are important differences? List responses on two charts entitled "Then" and "Now." Ask students to put on their thinking caps and to look for similarities and differences on the two lists. Talk about reasons for similarities and differences among families. **Ask:** How important are time periods and geographic locations when one talks about family activities? Why?

4. Give the class a jar with whipping cream. Students will shake the jar until it turns to butter. While class members are making butter, let children retell a favorite story drawn from their everyday lives. **Ask:** How and why does churning butter relate to the "Then" and "Now" charts?

5. Discuss the character traits of courage and compassion. **Ask:** What characters and actions show signs of either or both traits? Allow students to volunteer examples of when they or family members demonstrated courage and/or compassion.

EVALUATION:

Determine the level of student understanding that family activities, then and now, may be the same or different by listening to the insight and reasoning expressed in their oral as well as written responses. Ask students to tell what and how they learned. Encourage students to connect the message in the story to the theme of celebrating or honoring family traditions.

CONNECTION #14:
Kristine L. Franklin.
The Shepherd Boy

A young Navajo boy of the Southwest spends the summer caring for sheep. Because he behaves responsibly, his family entrusts him with fifty sheep.

CHARACTER TRAITS: Discuss the character traits of diligence, courage, and responsibility, and challenge students to provide examples of each of them.

1. Find the Southwest on a map or globe. Give students a blackline copy of the United States and instruct them first to finger-trace around the borders of the Southwest and then to shade in the entire region on their maps. Lead students in comparing and contrasting the size and features of the Southwest to other regions in the United States. **Hint:** Call attention to geographic clues that classroom maps provide about the region. Encourage teams of students to participate in a map exercise of pointing out how their geographic area is similar to and different from other specific regions of the United States.

2. Read *The Shepherd Boy* aloud. Remember to set the stage with appropriate pre-reading activities that capture students' interest. For example, discuss Ben and his role within the family. Suggest to children that they share ways they help their families. In addition, clarify vocabulary terms necessary for understanding the text and also define a clear purpose for reading and/or listening.

3. Talk about the setting and the characters in *The Shepherd Boy*. Make sure that students understand that the season is summer and that the story portrays a sheep-raising family. Invite students to brainstorm their favorite summer activities, then to compare and contrast their activities to Ben's activities. **Ask:** What reasons account for similarities and differences between Ben's summer activities and their summer activities?

4. Pair students or put them into cooperative groups to draw or construct a map marking the way that Ben leads the sheep. Instruct students to show geographic features if the author or the classroom map provides clues about the region. Ask students to share their products with classmates. **Ask:** How and why does plotting a course on a map help students understand the story setting better?

5. Discuss reasons why Ben's family has so many sheep and what products come from sheep. Remind students that Ben's family cares for 50 sheep. Ask students to write math story problems in which certain numbers of sheep get lost.

6. Let students solve each other's story problems either individually or in pairs. They will explain both the process of solving the problem and the answer to the problem, and then suggest alternative ways of solving the problem. Students will also count the sheep by twos, fives, and tens. **Ask:** Does turning math problems into math stories help you find answers easier? Why? Why not?

7. Discuss the character traits of diligence, courage, and responsibility. Describe situations in which Ben exhibits these traits. Ask students to decide if Ben would make a good friend and why.

EVALUATION:

Determine the level of student understanding about ways families spend summers by assessing the quality of oral and written responses. Encourage students to connect the message in the story to the theme of celebrating or honoring family traditions.

CONNECTION #15:
Naomi Shihab Nye.
Sitti's Secrets

A young girl of Arabic ancestry visits her sitti (grandmother) in a village on the West Bank and thus fulfills a family tradition of spending time with elders.

Note: Clarify for students that the geographic location of Palestine mentioned in the story may date the time of the story prior to 1948 when world leaders renamed the area Israel OR that the author of Arabic ancestry still uses the land's old name because of her cultural background. The author mentions no specific date in the story. Because of continued conflicts in the area, a 1967 accord divided the same geographic area into the nation of Israel (Jewish) and of two Arab areas occupied by Israel, the Gaza Strip and the West Bank. (Update political information regularly.)

The story provides teachers an excellent opportunity to introduce students to the concept of point of view or perspective in a simplified way and how the concept shapes attitudes as well as opinions.

CHARACTER TRAITS: Discuss the character traits used in this manual and challenge students to provide examples of each of them.

1. Read *Sitti's Secrets* aloud. Remember to set the stage with appropriate pre-reading activities that capture students' interest. For example, discuss Sitti's family traditions such as baking bread, playing marbles, gathering food, saving favorite things. Inquire if any of Sitti's traditions exist in students' families. Clarify vocabulary terms necessary for understanding the text. Define clearly a purpose for reading and/or listening.

2. Talk about community helpers (e.g., farmers) and places (e.g., villages) the story mentions. Review how the family in the story gets their milk, then compare and contrast the family's method with how students' families get their milk. **Ask:**

> *What are the differences?*
> *Why are there differences?*

3. Point out Mona's letter to the President. Use the letter as a lead-in to discussing the President of the United States. **Ask:** Where does he live? What important jobs does he perform? Invite students to write the President about something that concerns them. Ask parents to send a stamp to school so that teachers may actually mail the letters to the President.

Ask students to put on their thinking caps:

> *What does writing the President of the United States tell students about the American government?*
> *Who has the power?*
> *What do Americans call their form of government?*

Hint: Look up the origin of the word "democracy" to show students that the idea of power of the people is one that has passed through many generations and nations over centuries of time. In addition, use *The Alphabet Tree* by Leo Lionni as a complementary story to *Sitti's Secrets*.

4. Draw a Venn diagram on a transparency. Lead students in comparing Sitti's breakfast to Angelica's grandmother's breakfast in the story, *Three Stalks of Corn*, and then complete the diagram by using student responses. Link both stories to other grandparent stories in primary lessons.

Extension: Extend the discussion about similarities and differences in meals to additional cultural traditions grandparent characters tell in other stories (e.g., dress, beliefs, respect from family members, love of grandchildren). **Ask:** Do grandparents or older citizens play important roles in your lives today? How?

5. Conduct a poll on how many children play with their cousins:

> *Often?*
> *Sometimes?*
> *Rarely?* or
> *Never?*

Ask students to share activities they enjoy doing with cousins in either large or small groups. **Ask:** How and why are some activities similar and some different? Request that groups choose one activity, and then act out cousins participating in fun-filled activities for classmates.

6. Locate Palestine (present-day Israel) on a classroom map and place a push-pin in the map as evidence of another location children visit through literature and also as evidence of how reading globalizes or broadens students' thinking, i.e., reading makes students think in global pictures rather than in community pictures. Alert students that they can become world travelers through reading.

Discuss the country's relative location. **Ask:** Where is Palestine (Israel) in relationship to the United States? Invite students to finger-trace the route on a classroom map and suggest different ways that travelers may reach the location. Ask students also about factors that determine which way people choose to travel to the country. **Ask:** Are these factors the same ones that determine how families travel to other locations in the United States or overseas?

7. Choose a faraway place in the world that children express interest in visiting. Simulate trip planning by engaging students in these activities: withdrawing money from a bank, purchasing tickets at an airport, and boarding the plane. Arrange chairs in a mock airplane position. Serve beverages and almonds on the flight. If possible, watch a video highlighting the destination. Incorporate passports into the "pretend trip."

Link the experience to the story of the young girl and her trip to see her sitti in faraway Palestine (Israel). **Ask:** Does the airplane experience help students understand better how the young girl must feel? What lesson does the story teach us about the way they treat newcomers in our community?

Hint: Introduce other lessons involving travel with simulated flight or story-related means of getting from one place to another. As an extension to the flight experience, encourage cooperative groups to make mobiles that reflect different means of transportation including the way that the young girl visits her sitti. **Ask:** How can you connect geographic features and means of transportation?

8. Talk about Mona's letter to the President. **Ask:** What character traits does Mona exhibit in the letter? Make a list of the traits students mention and the clues or examples that appear in the letter.

Hint: Cut the letter apart by sentences and match sentences to character traits. Ask students to explain how and why they link sentences and traits. Extend the discussion by asking students about times that they, a family member, or a close friend exhibited the same trait, and then invite them to share the example with classmates.

EVALUATION:

Determine the level of student understanding by listening to the depth of oral responses and by assessing the quality of written responses. Encourage students to connect the message in the story to the theme of celebrating or honoring family traditions.

CONNECTION #16:
Nigel Gray.
A Country Far Away

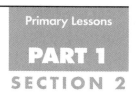

Pictures that focus on the daily lives of two boys, one in Africa and the other in America, create a remarkable photographic story of comparison and contrast.

CHARACTER TRAITS: Discuss the character traits of diligence and responsibility and provide examples for discussion.

1. Read *A Country Far Away* aloud. Remember to set the stage with appropriate pre-reading activities that capture students' interest. Clarify vocabulary terms necessary for understanding the text. Define clearly a purpose for reading and/or listening. Discuss the activities portrayed on each page over a period of days. Point out significant similarities and differences between activities in Africa and in America. Keep a list of these similarities and differences and assist students in drawing valid conclusions about activities in two cultures on two continents.

2. Invite students to rewrite the text individually or as a class. Allow time for each child to illustrate a personal version of an ordinary day's activities in his own world. Encourage children to share finished pieces with classmates.

3. Pull out examples of family traditions mentioned in the story and discuss each one. Make sure that students realize that traditions reflect beliefs and activities important to families, cultures, and nations. **Ask** students to put on their thinking caps and think up examples of family, cultural, and national traditions in America.

Extension: Invite students to work with a partner and plan how to start a tradition at school, one that will be repeated this year and in the future. Prompt students with examples such as morning announcements, flag raising, and fall festivals. **Ask:** What tradition would you like to introduce to your school? **Hint:** Determine students' interest in the project. If students express a high level of interest, involve the principal, make an action plan, and implement a new tradition.

4. Use *Toby in the Country, Toby in the City* from the Houghton Mifflin anthology in conjunction with this story. Make comparisons between the two Tobys and/or between the two stories. **Ask:** What must be true about most stories? **Hint:** Lead students to the conclusion that characters, settings, problems, and solutions exist in all stories.

5. Invite students to write about a country or place they would like to visit. Ask them to give reasons for their choices. Encourage students to share choices, and then plot each location on a map as students share with classmates. **Hint:** Try to find high-interest materials that will hook students on making geographic inquiries about countries and places. Ask the assistance of the media specialist in finding picture stories of places students select to visit in National Geographic. Use the resource as an ongoing travel study shaped by student interest.

6. Discuss the character traits of diligence and responsibility as they apply to characters in the story. **Ask:** Will model character traits be the same or different for the two boys? Why? As a related activity, ask students to make a list of ways that show how they are diligent and responsible in the classroom. Compile a class list and post as a ready reference.

Hint: For interest and variety, alternate discussions on character traits between the benefits of possessing the traits and the consequences of not possessing the traits.

EVALUATION:

Determine the level of student understanding of similarities and differences among people by studying and listening to the quality of written and oral responses and by assessing the degree of creativity in planning a new tradition for the elementary school. Encourage students to connect the message in the story to the theme of celebrating or honoring family traditions.

Primary Lessons

PART 1

SECTION 2

CONNECTION #17:
Joan Drescher.
My Mother's Getting Married

A little girl whose mother is getting married expresses her concerns and also confronts her fear about changes the marriage may bring to the mother-daughter relationship.

CHARACTER TRAITS: Discuss the character traits of compassion and honesty and provide examples of each.

1. Read *My Mother's Getting Married* aloud. Remember to set the stage with appropriate pre-reading activities that capture students' interest. For example, ask students about their wedding experiences by talking about what traditions one may expect to see at wedding celebrations, who the main characters are, and who may attend. **Hint:** Allow students to explore diversities associated with wedding celebrations (e.g., church versus civil ceremonies, formal versus informal ceremonies, large versus small ceremonies). Clarify vocabulary terms necessary for understanding the text. Define clearly a purpose for reading and/or listening.

2. Invite people who have knowledge of traditional weddings to class—perhaps an Anglo, African-American, Hispanic, or Jewish person—who can describe weddings within their culture to children. Let children interview the guests with carefully planned questions prepared in advance. Lead children in making valid conclusions about the diversity among wedding ceremonies based upon data from the storybook and from the interview.

3. Encourage each child to ask their parents about the most important day of their lives. Some parents may mention weddings or other special occasions. Ask children to illustrate the event, and then write one sentence describing the milestone in their parents' lives. Provide opportunities for children to share the events with classmates.

4. Give each child two tongue depressors, a white doily, and black construction paper. Let them create bride-and-groom puppets. Allow time for students to role-play wedding ceremonies with their puppets. If students decide they need a puppet to perform the ceremony, introduce terms such as minister, priest, rabbi, and justice of the peace.

Hint: For extension of the learning, encourage the librarian to investigate wedding ceremonies in different cultures and share interesting customs with children. Lead children to the understanding that weddings are examples of cultural traditions.

5. Discuss the character traits of compassion and honesty. Talk about how Katy resolves her feelings about her mother's wedding and what character traits enable her to solve the problem. **Hint:** For interest and variety, alternate discussions on character traits between the benefits of possessing the traits and the consequences of not possessing the traits.

EVALUATION:

Determine the level of student understanding of weddings as traditions by assessing the maturity expressed in both oral and written responses to various activities and discussions. Ask students to provide examples of the traits of compassion and honesty and explain why these traits are important to our lives. Encourage students to connect the message in the story to the theme of celebrating or honoring family traditions.

CONNECTION #1:
Sandra S. Yamate.
Ashok by Any Other Name

Yamate weaves a story of Ashok, an American Indian boy who wishes for a less ethnic, more "American" name. His experiments with new names create a variety of mishaps until he finally discovers just the right name for himself.

CHARACTER TRAITS: Discuss the meaning of integrity and its importance in friendship.

1. Read aloud the story, *Ashok By Any Other Name*. Remember to set the stage with appropriate pre-reading activities that capture students' interest. For example, ask students to discuss with their parents how and why they got their names and what their names mean. Encourage students to bring research to class and to compile information into a class book about names. Assist students in researching the origins of names in a name-the-baby book. **Hint:** If students mention the topic of christening, discuss the fact that many, not all, parents want babies christened and why. Discuss the meaning of the "the ceremony of christening" and similar ceremonies in other cultures. Clarify vocabulary terms necessary for understanding the text. Define clearly a purpose for reading and/or listening.

2. With student help graph the data gathered from research including how many parents named students after grandparents, other family members, friends, or famous people. **Hint:** Parents may choose names for students, because they like the name or the meaning of the name. Discuss names that result from cultural traditions: boys' names, girls' names, boy/girl names, naming of first sons after fathers and grandfathers and attaching Jr. (Junior) and III (the Third) to names.

3. Discuss names from other cultures. Using student responses, list common names of persons living in India or China. Use examples from literature or experience to contribute to the list. **Ask:** How may a culturally linked name affect a person? Will this practice increase a person's loyalty to his/her own culture?

4. With student assistance, construct a bulletin board entitled "What Is Special About My Name?" Invite students to display self-portraits and writing samples on the board. **Hint:** This would be a good activity to accompany the story, *The Portrait*, by Ivar Da Coll.

5. Ask students to respond in writing to the prompt, "If students could change names, what would their new names be and why?" Add these names to the bulletin board display of self-portraits and writing samples.

6. Encourage students to complete an art activity focusing on symmetry:

    1. Fold paper in half lengthwise, "hot-dog style," then open.

    2. Write name in chalk on fold line.

    3. Refold and press so chalk is also on the other side.

    4. Trace over both sides with marker.

    5. Use colors to fill in.

Add these names to the bulletin board display of names. At this point, boys and girls will see multiple examples of their names in the display: self-portraits, writing samples, name reflections.

7. Assist students in graphing the letters of names by putting one letter per square on large graph paper. Show students how to analyze the graph by determining the longest and shortest names, vowels and consonants in names, and names that begin and end in vowels or consonants. If students choose to add one more name example to the display, allow them to rearrange their special space.

8. Have students find at least two examples in the story that prove Ashok acts with integrity.

Hint: For interest and variety, alternate discussions on character traits between the presence and benefits of possessing the traits and the absence and consequences of not possessing the traits.

EVALUATION:

Determine the level of student understanding of this conclusion—names originate from family members, friends, and cultural traditions—by assessing the quality of students' writing and of creative products. Ask students to write a short narrative of what they have learned from this story. Encourage students to connect the message in the story to the theme of celebrating or honoring community and cultural traditions.

CONNECTION #2:
Virginia Kroll. Masai and I

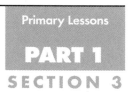

Primary Lessons

PART 1
SECTION 3

Linda, a little girl who lives in the city, learns about East Africa and the Masai in school, then imagines what her life might be like if she were Masai.

CHARACTER TRAITS: Discuss the meaning of respect and why respectful behavior is important to living with others.

1. Read *Masai and I* aloud. Remember to set the stage with appropriate pre-reading activities that capture students' interest. For example, assist students in locating East Africa and Kenya on a map or globe, and then trace with fingers an imaginary line from your school to East Africa and Kenya. Clarify vocabulary terms necessary for understanding the text. Define clearly a purpose for reading and/or listening.

2. Encourage students to celebrate ethnic heritage by interviewing family members. Suggest to students that they ask these questions:

> *Where did the family originate?*
> *Who is in the immediate family?*
> *Who is in the extended family?*
> *How did students get their names?*

Encourage students to compile a class newspaper using information from interviews.

3. Invite students to write their family history or to create a family tree with the help of family members.

4. Invite students to join the teacher in a storytelling circle. Demonstrate how to tell an interesting family story by telling a story and then retracing the events with boys and girls to establish characters, problems, and solutions. Encourage students to analyze the teacher's story and then to share a family story. Provide prompts for stories such as my little brother, my little sister, my pet rabbit. After each story, lead the students in analyzing stories from the standpoint of the major characters, their problems and solutions. **Ask:** Why does having something to look for help you understand stories better?

5. Show students how to create family heritage scrapbooks by collecting photos, drawing pictures, writing stories about the photographs or drawings, and binding the stories into one volume. Display scrapbooks in a prominent place in the classroom.

6. Invite students to discuss how Linda develops a new sense of respect for her cultural heritage. Ask students to cite examples from the story and perhaps their own lives.

   Hint: For interest and variety, alternate discussions on character traits between the presence and benefits of possessing the traits and the absence and consequences of not possessing the traits.

EVALUATION:

Determine the level of student understanding of family heritage by observing participation in activities such as tracing family histories, making scrapbooks, and telling stories. Ask students to explain what they have learned from the story and activities of this lesson. Encourage students to connect the message in the story to the theme of celebrating or honoring community and cultural traditions.

Primary Lessons

PART 1

SECTION 3

CONNECTION #3:
Arthur Dorros.
This Is My House

Text and illustrations depict different types of houses lived in by children all over the world. On each page, "This is my house..." will appear in appropriate native languages.

CHARACTER TRAITS: Discuss the meaning and importance of citizenship with students. Teach them that respect for others, even though they are different and may live in different kinds of houses, is an important citizenship trait.

1. Read *This Is My House* aloud. Remember to set the stage with appropriate pre-reading activities that capture students' interest. Clarify vocabulary terms necessary for understanding the text. Define clearly a purpose for reading and/or listening.

2. Encourage students to brainstorm and chart the kinds of houses in the United States (e.g., single-family dwellings, apartments, garden homes, duplexes), then discuss similarities and differences among the various house plans.

4. Share with students examples of several kinds of houses, i.e., an envelope is a house for a letter; a shoe is a house for a foot. Ask student partners to make up more analogies by using examples of other houses and objects.

5. Invite students to draw a picture of their house in the neighborhood. Show students how to make a model of the neighborhood. **Hint:** Use shoeboxes, construction paper, recycled materials. Ask students to include street names (e.g., cul-de-sac, avenue, court, drive, boulevard). Request that students talk about favorite neighborhood personalities (e.g., neighbors, pets, the mailman).

6. Use magazine pictures to show students examples of various types of shelters, then explain how the economy, availability of materials, and climate influence shelters. Invite students to consider the same influences and design an original collage that is different from the model but shows proof of students' understanding of shelters.

7. As a math activity, give students a ditto copy of a pre-measured house and ask them to measure the parts of the house.

> The house is _____ inches wide.
> The house is _____ inches long.
> The house is _____ inches tall.

Show students how to draw a one-inch square window on the left side of the house. Use the example as a means to discuss the concept of scale.

8. Encourage students to participate in creating a diorama of their room at home and use doll furniture or paper furniture in the model. Use the diorama experience as a writing prompt by inviting students to write a story telling what they like about their room, what they do not like, and what they would change. Extend students' understanding with the book *Home: A Collaboration of Thirty Distinguished Authors* (a collection of poems) or *A House Is a House for Me* by Mary Ann Hoberman.

EVALUATION:

Determine the level of student understanding that many factors affect types of shelters by assessing the quality of student models and explanations. Ask students to explain what they have learned from these stories and activities. Encourage students to connect the message in the story to the theme of celebrating or honoring community and cultural traditions.

CONNECTION #4:
Ann Grifalconi. *The Village of Round and Square Houses*

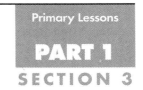
Primary Lessons
PART 1
SECTION 3

A grandmother whose village is located on the side of a volcano explains to her listeners why men live in square houses and women live in round houses.

CHARACTER TRAITS: Talk about the meaning of the character trait, respect, and how the trait threads throughout the story.

1. Read *The Village of Round and Square Houses* aloud. Remember to set the stage with appropriate pre-reading activities that capture students' interest. Clarify vocabulary terms necessary for understanding both the text and the celebration. Define clearly a purpose for reading and/or listening.

2. Invite students to tell stories to the class following the model set by Gran'ma Tika. Since she is the best storyteller in the village, request that students follow her model of storytelling. Ask students to comment about the elements they like best in classmates' stories.

3. Remind students that the little girl in the story believes all men in the world live in square houses and all women live in round ones until she leaves the village. Encourage students to list different kinds of homes. Invite students to cut pictures from magazines of different dwellings and make a home collage. Ask students to state the big idea that they learned from reading the story and making a collage so that a person not familiar with the project will understand its purpose. **Hint:** Stress how exposure to new ideas outside one's community and culture expands learning. Over time, learning leads to understanding of others, then respect of others, and acceptance of others.

4. Extend the concept of home by reading *Who's in Rabbit's House?* by Verna Aardema. Ask students to make idea connections between this story and *The Village of Round and Square Houses*. **Ask:** What ideas are common to both stories?

5. Show children the approximate location of Tos in central Africa's Cameroon Mountains. Trace with fingertips an imaginary line from your school to the Cameroon Mountains in Nigeria on a globe or world map. **Ask:** Using map colors as clues, what differences do you think might exist between the two areas? How can you use color clues in other environments?

6. In Tos, the villagers consider the oldest people very special, so they always eat first. **Ask:**

   Who will eat first in students' homes if family members eat according to age?

   Who will eat last? How do you feel about this custom? Why?

   How might you feel if they were sixty years old?

   What character trait does this practice support?

   Talk about the meaning of the character trait, respect, and how the trait threads throughout the story. Cite examples of respect in the story and in students' everyday lives.

EVALUATION:

Determine the level of student understanding that people are similar to as well as different from one another by listening to responses and by watching participation in activities. Ask students to write a narrative explaining how they can encourage respect for teachers and parents. Encourage students to connect the message in the story to the theme of celebrating or honoring community and cultural traditions.

Primary Lessons

PART 1
SECTION 3

CONNECTION #5:
Alice McLerran. Roxaboxen

Roxaboxen *is the story of a group of children who build a community from sand, rocks, and old wooden boxes. Roxaboxen becomes an imaginary town for Marian, her sisters, and their friends.*

CHARACTER TRAITS: Encourage students to examine how children in the story demonstrate the trait of citizenship.

1. Read *Roxaboxen* aloud. Remember to set the stage with appropriate pre-reading activities that capture students' interest. Clarify vocabulary terms necessary for understanding the text. Define clearly a purpose for reading and/or listening. After reading the story, discuss the characteristics that make up a community, then seek examples from Roxaboxen.

2. Enlist students in brainstorming and in webbing people, places, and things that make up the community of Roxaboxen. Lead students in categorizing the list into people, buildings, things, and rules, (e.g., government). Ask students to construct a city such as Roxaboxen by using materials such as beans, pipe cleaners, art supplies, and raisins. Encourage students to draw a class mural

showing a community with buildings, homes, streets, and neighborhoods. **Ask:** How do hands-on activities assist you in learning and remembering important ideas?

3. Show students how to create a classroom community by using the democratic process of electing officials such as a mayor and a city council. Prior to the election, make sure that all candidates know their responsibilities if elected by fellow students. Allow students to campaign for office, then elect officials. Talk students through the process of how the mayor and city council members make decisions on issues. Use the election as a lead-in to discuss such concepts as town meetings, decision-making, and majority rule. Suggest a high-interest issue so that student citizens may practice taking the issue to the mayor and council and seek to make a change for the better in their community.

4. Enlist the help of community leaders and helpers in making a floor map of a business street in the community. **Hint:** Use boxes for stores; label each box to tell what kind of store it represents. Ask students to make one observation about the community that they can support with data from the model (e.g., location of residences, location of business district, location of shopping center).

5. Ask: What are some ways that you can be good citizens at school, at home, and in other places that you go?

Hint: For interest and variety, alternate discussions on character traits between the benefits of possessing the traits and the consequences of not possessing the traits

EVALUATION:

Determine the level of student understanding of what makes up a community and what roles community helpers play by assessing the quality of the mural, of the model community, and of the ideas that students generate. Give each student a 3x5 card. On each card have them write the meaning of citizenship. Read these aloud and discuss their similarities and differences. Encourage students to connect the message in the story to the theme of celebrating or honoring community and cultural traditions.

CONNECTION #6:
Byrd Baylor.
The Best Town in the World

Primary Lessons

PART 1
SECTION 3

Many times people choose a community in which to live because it meets their specific needs. In the story, the author explains to readers what makes this community the best town in the world.

CHARACTER TRAITS: Remind students that people think their communities and towns are the "best" because of the character of the people who live in them. Discuss the nine character traits associated with these lessons and their importance to community living.

1. Read *The Best Town in the World* aloud. Remember to set the stage with appropriate pre-reading activities that capture students' interest. Clarify vocabulary terms necessary for understanding the text. Define clearly a purpose for reading and/or listening.

2. Enlist children's help in completing the web that answers this question: What makes this town the best in the world?

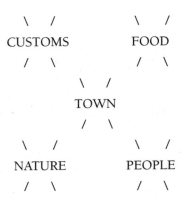

3. Demonstrate how to bake chocolate cupcakes. Let children decorate. Challenge students to make idea connections between the warm chocolate cupcakes and the warm glow that comes from living in the best town in the world. Lead students to the conclusion that warmth translates into security, i.e., a feeling that all is right in the world.

4. Show children how to construct a movie strip of pictures displaying characteristics that make a town the best in the world. Encourage children to write a movie script drawn from the movie strips. Ask students to use language that encourages visitors to stay and to live in the community. Allow students to share scripts in small groups.

5. Pair students, model how to pantomime an event in the story, then assign roles such as:

> *jumping into icy water;*
> *crawling into a blackberry thicket;*
> *climbing a tree to eat milk and bread;*
> *playing a dog growling at a rattlesnake; or*
> *mimicking a firefly lighting up.*

6. Suggest the creation of a class book. Ask each child to contribute a page with a sentence and illustration about what makes their town the best in the world. Display the book in the classroom.

7. Discuss with children the traits characters exhibit throughout the story. Extend the discussion by talking about how the story causes students to remember friends and other people they know. Ask students to name specific characters and tell why these characters remind them of other people.

EVALUATION:

Determine the level of student understanding of the community and its citizens by assessing the quality of children's contributions to the class book and children's dramatic interpretations. Encourage students to connect the message in the story to the theme of celebrating or honoring community and cultural traditions.

CONNECTION #7:
Jane Cowen-Fletcher.
It Takes a Village

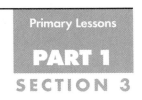
On market day in a small village in Benin, Yemi tries to care for her little brother Kokou and discovers that the entire village is also watching out for him.

CHARACTER TRAITS: Discuss the importance of compassion and responsibility in building human relationships.

1. Read *It Takes a Village* aloud. Remember to set the stage with appropriate pre-reading activities that capture students' interest. Clarify vocabulary terms necessary for understanding the text. Define clearly a purpose for reading and/or listening.

2. Using a Venn diagram, ask students to compare and contrast Yemi's village to your community or town. Lead students in developing and applying a set of criteria to use as a basis for comparing and contrasting. **Ask:** How do criteria help you in finding out about any subject?

3. **Inquire:** Where do you go when you are hungry, thirsty, frightened, hot, tired, or lost? Why? (Remember to ask these questions one-at-a-time. Do not cluster your questions because this confuses children and their answers will be unclear.)

4. Place these words in mixed-up order on a chart tablet: hungry, thirsty, frightened, hot, tired, lost. Ask students to sequence the words in the order of their introduction in the story by citing examples of feelings from the story; then ask students to demonstrate the correctness of word order by making a flipbook featuring both words and pictures.

5. Encourage students to roleplay a day at the marketplace. Ask them to construct, weave, design, mold, or invent three products to sell in the market. Show students how to trade products on market day and give tips on bargain hunting. **Ask:** How do you and your families get the goods they need? Does the size of the village determine what goods are available to people? Why?

6. Demonstrate how to write a story problem about buying products at the market. Allow student partners to write an addition or subtraction story and share with classmates. **Ask:** Did you understand the problem better after you wrote about it? Why? Why not?

7. Have students write a story using the prompt, "If a brother, sister, and/or pet wanders off, where will I look for them?" Ask them to share stories and to tell why their plan shows good common sense.

8. Have students make a map of their school and use a compass rose to indicate directions. Have them explain how this activity relates to *It Takes a Village*.

9. Read aloud *The Train to Lulu's* by Elizabeth Fitzgerald Howard. Ask for student assistance in comparing and contrasting this story with *It Takes a Village*.

10. Divide students into cooperative groups. Ask each group to hide something and then make a map that will lead someone to the hidden object. Request that groups trade maps, then search for other groups' hidden objects.

11. Discuss with children how people in the village demonstrate the traits of compassion and responsibility. Ask children to talk about specific characters who exhibit one or both traits. Then ask them to think about their lives and their opportunities to exhibit compassion and responsibility. Call for volunteers to share examples.

EVALUATION:

Determine the level of student understanding related to interactions among people at the market place by observing their participation in a simulated market day. Ask students to write a narrative explaining the importance of compassion and responsibility to community building. Encourage students to connect the message in the story to the theme of celebrating or honoring community and cultural traditions.

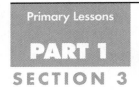

CONNECTION #8:
Marjorie Barker. *Magical Hands*

William secretly does the morning chores for each of his three good friends on their birthdays. When his own birthday arrives, he finds himself rewarded.

CHARACTER TRAITS: Discuss the importance of citizenship, compassion, and responsibility.

1. Read *Magical Hands* aloud. Remember to set the stage with appropriate pre-reading activities that capture students' interest. Clarify vocabulary terms necessary for understanding the text. Define clearly a purpose for reading and/or listening.

2. Discuss with children the last sentence in the story, "It is a wonderful thing...to have magical hands." Suggest to students that something seems magic when people do not understand how it happens. Ask students to think of and perform acts of kindness for other students in the classroom without their knowledge. Instruct students to explain how these acts of kindness differ from magic.

3. Ask students to find pictures in magazines of someone acting as a good citizen or doing a good deed. Instruct them to cut out the pictures, glue them on a piece of paper, and then write a story about how to be good citizens.

4. Invite students to explore traditions associated with birthday celebrations. Encourage students to draw and display pictures about birthday traditions, favorite birthdays, or special gifts. **Ask:** What do you learn by studying similarities and differences among birthday celebrations?

5. Suggest that student partners compile a list of birthday gifts that cost no money. Encourage students to create coupon books or gift certificates to give as gifts in celebration of birthdays for family members or to honor a family member at any time. **Hint:** Coupons or certificates must promise acts that will please the receivers (e.g., washing dishes, watering the lawn, feeding the family pet). **Ask:** How does giving this type of gift make you feel?

6. Ask students to trace their hands, label each finger with an act of kindness, cut out hand patterns, and use hands to create products of choice, (e.g., mobiles, wreaths, trees). **Ask:** How does making a product help you learn and remember important ideas?

7. Talk with students about the concept of volunteerism. Discuss opportunities within the community to help others. Help students organize a class project in which all students participate in helping the community, an organization, or a person. As a class, compose a public service announcement to encourage others to volunteer in the community. **Ask:** Is helping others a part of good citizenship? Why?

8. Use these activities to introduce a discussion on how the text of the story illustrates the traits of citizenship, compassion, and responsibility. Encourage students to talk about their examples and to tell why they chose a particular character or passage as an example.

EVALUATION:

Determine the level of student understanding about the relationship between acts of kindness and improved communities by observing student participation in planned activities and by listening to their responses to thought questions. Ask students to explain what they learned from the story and activities. Encourage students to connect the message in the story to the theme of celebrating or honoring community and cultural traditions.

CONNECTION #9:
Vera B. Williams.
Cherries and Cherry Pits

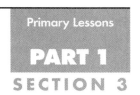

Primary Lessons

PART 1

SECTION 3

Bidemmi uses art forms such as pictures and storytelling to recount historical events.

CHARACTER TRAITS: Respect for differences among people.

1. Read *Cherries and Cherry Pits* aloud. Remember to set the stage with appropriate pre-reading activities that capture students' interest. Clarify vocabulary terms necessary for understanding the text. Define clearly a purpose for reading and/or listening.

2. Develop the concepts of history and biography as stories told by one generation to the next generation. Explain to students that people pass on their culture through art and story. Examine how Bidemmi draws and tells stories. Discuss how cherries and cherry pits thread through the story. **Ask:** Why is the practice of repeating pictures and words such as cherries and cherry pits a good story technique?

3. Encourage students to create a picture about a person they know and to introduce this person to a small group by telling a story. Model for students how minute details and colorful descriptors add interest to storytelling. **Ask:** How do drawing about and telling about a subject help you learn and remember important ideas?

Extension: Give children a cherry to use as a prompt, to tell a story about themselves. For example: "A cherry is red. I have a red shirt that Grandma made for Christmas...." **Ask:** Are you surprised that the same prompt creates so many different stories?

5. Encourage each child to contribute a picture story about himself/herself to a class book. Lead students in a brainstorming exercise to determine a common idea or theme that might be included in each picture story in the same way that the cherries and cherry pits are included in the story (e.g., a birthday cake or a pair of new shoes). Assist students in completing a theme-related picture story. **Ask:** How does brainstorming help you create ideas?

6. Show children how to set up a time line about a day at school. Prompt them with the time they get out of bed as a starting point; let them talk to a partner about sample school activities to add to the time line; set the school's dismissal time as the finish point; then ask partners to contribute to the construction of a class time line on the chalkboard. Invite students to talk about how sequencing helps organize thoughts, and then point out examples of organized thoughts on the time line.

7. Discuss the meaning of analysis, i.e., breaking a topic into small parts and investigating each one. Then analyze the story in terms of respect for likenesses and differences among people in Bidemmi's day. Ask students what changes they observe between then and now.

Hint: For interest and variety, alternate discussions on character traits between the benefits of possessing the traits and the consequences of not possessing the traits.

EVALUATION:

Determine the level of student understanding of cultural traditions by listening to stories they tell about themselves and by observing personal picture stories they construct about themselves. Ask students to list three ways they are like their best friend and three ways they are different from their best friend. Then have them write a short narrative explaining why they want respect from their friend even though they are different. Encourage students to connect the message in the story to the theme of celebrating or honoring community and cultural traditions.

Primary Lessons

PART 1
SECTION 3

CONNECTION #10:
Otto Sore Svend.
Children of the Yangtze River

Change in a community caused people to work together to save other people and their prized possessions. The story reaffirms that life goes on even in times of disaster.

CHARACTER TRAITS: Talk about the traits of courage and diligence.

1. Read *Children of the Yangtze River* aloud. Remember to set the stage with appropriate pre-reading activities that capture students' interest. Clarify vocabulary terms necessary for understanding the text. Define clearly a purpose for reading and/or listening.

2. Point out the Yangtze River on a map or globe. Ask a student to trace the imaginary line between the river and their community or town with his or her finger. Invite students to look at similarities and differences in physical features of the two areas. **Ask:** How do symbols and colors on maps provide clues about physical features of the land?

3. Invite students to practice the skill of sequencing events of the story on chain links to illustrate unity in the storybook's community. **Ask:** What changes the community? What actions do the people take? Ask students to name things that can change a community (e.g. forces, ideas, leaders, citizens) and tell why each one is capable of making changes in a community.

4. Invite a meteorologist to visit the class. Ask him or her to discuss the weather in their community or town and ways citizens can prepare for weather disasters. Allow time for student interaction with the weatherman. **Ask:** What types of disasters are most common in your town or community?

5. Model for students how to make a story cube that shows a weather disaster on each side. Roll the cube and ask children to tell how they can help their community if this disaster occurs. After students solve the problem, instruct them to work in small groups and organize a weather-related celebration for the community. Tell group members that each group will explain their celebration to the large group.

6. Talk about the traits of courage and diligence. Invite children to give examples of characters in the story who demonstrate either one or both of the traits. Ask children to reflect on their lives and cite an example of how they exhibit one or both of the traits.

   Hint: For interest and variety, alternate discussions on character traits between the benefits of possessing the traits and the consequences of not possessing the traits.

EVALUATION:

Determine the level of student understanding of how people unite when they face a common problem by listening to and assessing group presentations. Ask students to explain what they have learned from the story and activities. Encourage students to connect the message in the story to the theme of celebrating or honoring community and cultural traditions.

CONNECTION #11:
Ina R. Friedman.
How My Parents Learned to Eat

Primary Lessons

PART 1

SECTION 3

Two people from different cultures learn about the other's culture by sharing mealtimes.

CHARACTER TRAITS: Discuss the meaning of respect for parents and grandparents.

1. Read *How My Parents Learned to Eat* aloud. Remember to set the stage with appropriate pre-reading activities that capture students' interest. Clarify vocabulary terms necessary for understanding the text. Define clearly a purpose for reading and/or listening.

2. Point out the location of Japan on a map or globe. Ask a student to finger-trace an imaginary line between Japan and the place where he or she lives. **Ask:** Do you think that Japan is warmer or colder than your town or community? Why?

3. Inquire if anyone at school or in the community has visited Japan. If so, invite this person to talk to the class about Japan's island nation, the environment of Japan, and Japanese children. Prior to the visit, enlist student assistance in composing both an invitation to the guest and interview questions. Ask students what they learned by the guest's visit to the classroom. **Ask:** How does hearing the story from someone who has been to Japan help you better understand that culture?

4. Ask students to look closely at toys and playthings at home and see how many made-in-Japan labels they can find. Suggest that they bring items to exhibit in a made-in-Japan museum. Encourage students to arrange items by category and to draw conclusions about the items. **Ask:** Do the items represent only one or two categories? Do the items display detailed designs? Do you know about other items advertised and sold in the United States?

5. Help students compare and contrast the two main characters in the story on a Venn diagram. Include how they look, how they speak, how they behave, and what they eat. Ask students to look closely at the completed diagram and draw one conclusion.

6. Bring chopsticks and rice to class and allow small groups of students to practice eating rice in an Oriental fashion. Discuss with students how they feel when they eat with chopsticks. **Ask:** What does this experience with chopsticks tell you about learning the practices, (e.g., customs) of another culture?

7. Pass out paper plates on which students draw favorite foods of their families. **Ask:** How may you use foods as cultural clues? Compile students' plates into a cultural menu, and then help them make inferences about the characteristics of their local culture.

8. Remind students of how parents in the story act toward each other. **Ask:** As the story develops, does their behavior change? If so, how and why?

9. Add to students' understanding by also reading *Everybody Cooks Rice* by Norah Dooley. **Ask:** What facts in the story prove that rice is an important crop in many cultures?

EVALUATION:

Determine the level of student understanding of differences in mealtime customs by assessing each student's contribution to the class book. Encourage students to connect the message in the story to the theme of celebrating or honoring community and cultural traditions.

CONNECTION #12:
George Ancona. Powwow

This story presents a photo essay on the Pan-Indian (Native-American) celebration called powwow held on the Crow reservation in Montana.

CHARACTER TRAITS: Before the lesson, discuss the meaning of respect with the class.

1. A week before the lesson, invite students to bring any/all Indian (Native-American) artifacts, music, and stories to class. Enlist student assistance in creating a museum. Display the collection on a bulletin board/table combination around the letters P O W W O W.

2. Read *Powwow* aloud. Remember to set the stage with appropriate pre-reading activities that capture students' interest. Clarify vocabulary terms necessary for understanding the text. Define clearly a purpose for reading and/or listening. For example, define "powwow," a misunderstood French word, as a gathering of people coming together to trade. **Hint:** Original meaning: (1) a dance danced before leaving for a hunt and on return to celebrate success, (2) religious ceremonies to honor individuals, initiate members. Today's meaning: (1) to come together to celebrate and reaffirm shared heritage and traditions as Native Americans, (2) to renew old friendships and make new ones. Review the meaning of respect, and discuss the importance of respecting other cultures.

3. Ask students why the tepee was a popular form of shelter for the Plains Indians (Native Americans), (i.e., it was sturdy, portable, easy to set up and take down, packed easily as the tribe followed buffalo and other herds. Show students how to construct a tepee using 16 toothpicks, straws, sticks or cane

poles and tissue, tissue paper, paper bags, or fabric scraps. Ask students to put their models to the test: Sturdy? Portable? Easy to set up and take down?

4. Remind students of these facts from the story: parents work long and hard to make clothing used in the ceremonial dance; family members share clothes, hand down clothes, and construct ceremonial clothes from pieces of old outfits. Show students how to construct a head dress, garment, shoes, or other accessories Native Americans wear during a powwow dance. **Ask:** What clues about culture do the clothes give us? Why?

5. Remind students of these facts learned from the story: a group of singers called a "drum" sing as they beat a rhythm in unison on a large drum. Have students

   1. *Listen to Indian chants.*
   2. *Make a drum and sing powwow songs.*

Ask: What clues about culture does the music give us? Why?

6. Extend student knowledge and awareness of powwow celebrations by reading:

Powwow by June Behrens, which describes a visit to a powwow where American Indian families get together to enjoy traditional food, music, dancing, and crafts.

Cherokee Summer by Diane Hoyt-Goldsmith, which recounts Bridget's summer spent learning about her heritage during an era when kerosene lamps, oilcloth on the kitchen table, and hymns sung under the moonlight were common.

EVALUATION:

Determine the level of student understanding of powwow celebrations by observing participation in planned activities and by assessing responses to thought-provoking questions. Encourage students to connect the message in the story to the theme of celebrating or honoring community and cultural traditions.

Primary Lessons

2

Harvest:
Celebrations
of Thanksgiving

CONNECTION # 1:
Dav Pilkey. 'Twas the Night Before Thanksgiving

Sensing tragedy in the air during an excursion to a turkey farm, perceptive children cleverly thwart the annual massacre.

CHARACTER TRAITS: Talk about the traits of compassion and courage.

1. Talk about taking a field trip. **Ask:** Why is a purpose important to the success of a trip? If students wanted to know more about Thanksgiving traditions, where might they plan to go? Chart student responses to where they might go to learn more about Thanksgiving. For each answer, ask why and what children expect to see at various sites.

2. Lead a print walk through *'Twas the Night Before Thanksgiving.* **Hint:** Look only at the pictures and talk about the mini-stories in the pictures, such as seasons, fall colors, thinking bubbles, actions taking place.

3. Read *'Twas the Night Before Thanksgiving* aloud. Remember to set the stage with appropriate pre-reading activities that capture students' interest. Clarify vocabulary terms necessary for understanding both the text and the celebration. Define clearly a purpose for reading and/or listening. Ask the children if the story sounds familiar. **Hint:** Refer to *'Twas the Night Before Christmas.* Discuss the sequence of events according to the story. Divide students into pairs to cooperatively illustrate assigned parts of the story for a large class book. (Alternate Activity)

4. Divide story into 11 parts if class size is 22. **Parts to illustrate:** cover, boarding the school bus, going to a farm, arriving at the farm, playing with and learning to love turkeys, finding the ax, determining use of the ax, crying about turkeys for dinner, planning a great escape, hunting for missing turkeys, enjoying Thanksgiving dinner with family and live turkeys, authors' page. Record captions as students dictate characters' words. Connect the story about a traditional Thanksgiving to a time to give thanks. Attach all sheets together for a class book and refer to the book frequently during the season.

5. Ask students to recall the actions of the boys and girls at the turkey farm. Encourage them to think about the story and volunteer as many examples of compassion as they can by raising their hands quietly. Wait until most students raise their hands, then begin calling on students to share. Do the same with the trait of courage. Apply the actions in the story to the behavior of students in the classroom.

   Ask: Can you think of a classmate's compassionate and/or courageous act? If not, ask students how they might exhibit these behaviors at school, in the neighborhood, or at home. **Hint:** For interest and variety, alternate discussions on character traits between the benefits of possessing the traits and the consequences of not possessing the traits.

EVALUATION:

Determine the level of student understanding by assessing students' experiences with field trips and with travel of all types, by listening to their responses to the story's illustrations, by observing how accurately students sequence events in the story, by watching them prepare pages for the class book, and by observing how they link the story to the theme of harvest. Ask students to tell what they learned from the story and how they can use this knowledge in their own lives. Encourage students to connect the message in the story to the theme of harvest and celebrations of thanksgiving.

CONNECTION #2:
Kate Waters.
Samuel Eaton's Day: A Day in the Life of a Pilgrim Boy

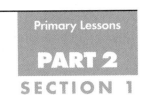

Photographs showing characters reenacting colonial life at Plimoth Plantation in Plymouth, Massachusetts, give students insight into the challenges faced by one Pilgrim boy and his family.

CHARACTER TRAITS: Talk about the meaning of diligence, especially the "work hard" example of the trait.

1. Read *Samuel Eaton's Day* aloud through page 11. Remember to set the stage with appropriate pre-reading activities that capture students' interest. Clarify vocabulary terms necessary for understanding both the text and the celebration. Define clearly a purpose for reading and/or listening.

   Hint: Make sure that students understand that the story up to this point relates to activities and chores before breakfast. Talk about the differences between what Samuel wears and does before breakfast to what students wear and do before breakfast. Clarify the meaning of any new vocabulary words in the story.

2. In a circle, ask students to give a brief response on their activities before breakfast so that all share a common understanding. Pass out 9" x 12" sheets of manila paper. Divide each sheet by folding it in half width-wise (hamburger-style). Label the sides "then" and "now." Instruct students to illustrate life before breakfast then, i.e., in the story, and now, i.e., in their own lives. Ask them to write or dictate descriptions and attach these to the illustrations.

3. Continue reading the story through page 25. **Hint:** The story will relate activities in Samuel's life including working in the fields. The time period spans breakfast to lunch. Discuss the sequence of today's story segment. Pass out 8" x 10" sheets of paper and ask students to fold in fourths. Ask students to trace the fold lines with a pencil to make four boxes. Suggest that they make four miniature pictures of Samuel's activities, one for each box, and compare/contrast their drawings with four other students in the class. Encourage them to talk to others about how they heard the same information and drew either similar or different pictures and why.

4. Continue reading the story to the end. Discuss how Samuel covers up his true feelings as he talks to his mom, a friend, his sister, and his dad. Ask students to compare Samuel's quest to be "upgrown" to their own desire to be "grownup." Then ask students if they would have enjoyed living at Plimoth Plantation. Graph answers on the chalkboard by getting students to state how they know how many responses to place in the "yes" column and how many responses to place in the "no" column, i.e., because the number recorded in each column should match the number of hands raised. Lead them to make a conclusion based on the results of the poll.

5. Ask students to apply the word, diligence, to Samuel. Discuss what being diligent cost him as well as how being diligent benefited him. Request that students think about the costs and benefits of working hard at school. Ask volunteers to share their thoughts. Encourage students to respond to one another's answers by adding their own personal examples.

EVALUATION:

Determine the level of student understanding by listening to students' answers to activities both then and now, by viewing children's drawings of a specific time period, by watching students interact with others and stay on task, and by paying attention to their expressions related to being "grownup" or working hard to accomplish a goal. Ask students to explain what they learned from this story. Encourage students to connect the message in the story to the theme of harvest and celebrations of thanksgiving.

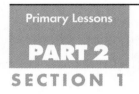

Primary Lessons

PART 2

SECTION 1

CONNECTION #3:
Gail Gibbons. *Thanksgiving Day*

A traditional Thanksgiving tale sets the stage for introducing, developing, and reinforcing the universal theme of giving thanks for blessings.

CHARACTER TRAITS: Talk about the meaning of fairness and respect.

1. Invite children to make a bulletin board around the theme of harvest and celebrations of thanksgiving. Generate words from student suggestions of what to include on the board. Find pictures to associate with the new words on the board. **Hint:** Consult reference materials in the library about how other cultures observe times for thanksgiving and tell students short stories on the name of the culture, the geographic area in which most members live, when they plan celebrations, and how they celebrate.

Expand students' understanding by locating and marking different cultures on a map as stories are told. Consider inviting local community members who represent various cultural backgrounds to the class to share their experiences related to the theme. Talk about the words on the bulletin board throughout the harvest season. Make a game using the words correctly in sentences and discussions.

2. Read *Thanksgiving Day* aloud. Remember to set the stage with appropriate pre-reading activities that capture students' interest. Clarify vocabulary terms necessary for understanding both the text and the celebration. Define clearly a purpose for reading and/or listening.

3. Discuss the sequence of events told in the story. Tape two large pieces of butcher paper to the classroom walls on opposite sides of the classroom. **Hint:** Double the paper so that crayons or paints will not bleed through on the wall. Explain to students the meaning of a mural. Excite students by saying that each of them will be an artist today and paint a mural to tell a visual story to other people.

4. Divide students into two groups. Assign these topics to partners in one group: voyaging to America, building houses, planting crops, harvesting crops, and celebrating the first Thanksgiving as related in the story. Assign these present-day topics to partners in the other group: establishing family customs, decorating classrooms and homes, gathering family and friends, traveling to homes of relatives and friends, preparing special foods, and planning the day's activities. Invite other classes to see the murals and listen to stories told by students. Make sure that students understand that this is only one of the stories in the theme of harvest and celebrations of thanksgiving. **Hint:** Divide sections on the butcher paper so that student partners know their space. Gather all materials such as crayons, markers, paints, watercolors, chalk, colored pencils, and butcher paper before the mural painting begins.

5. Is a person fair who "listens and tries to understand what others believe and feel"? Use the discussion of other cultures giving thanks as a resource base. Ask boys and girls why trying to understand what others believe and feel is important in today's world. Lead students to the realization that the more students know about others' beliefs, the more likely they are to learn to respect and accept others. Talk also about ways that students may show respect to each other in the classroom and on the playground.

EVALUATION:

Determine the level of student understanding by observing how students complete steps in creating a theme-oriented bulletin board, by listening to how they sequence events in a traditional Thanksgiving story, by watching students as they prepare murals and then tell the story to classmates and guests, and by observing how they link the story and activities to the trait of fairness.

CONNECTION #1:
Miriam Nerlove. *Thanksgiving*

Mother and son celebrate a traditional Thanksgiving at Grandma's house.

CHARACTER TRAITS: Ask students to select character traits that they feel both Pilgrims and Indians (Native Americans) exhibited. Discuss traits and reasons for selection.

1. Read *Thanksgiving* aloud. Remember to set the stage with appropriate pre-reading activities that capture students' interest. For example, brainstorm facts about the first Thanksgiving in North America with students. Involve children in setting a mood for Thanksgiving by asking them to trace around their hands and to add details to make handprints look like turkeys. Decorate the classroom with student-made turkeys. Clarify vocabulary terms necessary for understanding both the text and the celebration. Define clearly a purpose for reading and/or listening.

2. Discuss dangers that Pilgrims faced in the New (Old) World and list student responses on a chart tablet. **Ask:** Are the dangers the same as those most immigrants who enter unfamiliar lands face today? Why or why not? **Hint:** Help children understand that they may use the word pilgrim at any time in history to describe people who leave their native lands to seek a better life in another place or country.

3. Finger-trace the Pilgrims' route from England to the New (Old) World on a map. Ask students to pretend they are Pilgrims coming to America on the Mayflower. To make this experience come alive, encourage children to role-play being on the top deck of a small, swaying wooden ship and simulate different events that occur on the journey. Turn on a fan to simulate high winds on the sea and sprinkle water drops carefully to give children the taste of the sea's salt water. After the high seas adventure, ask students to abandon the ship, float to their desks, and write about how they feel being a Pilgrim in the 1600s. Encourage children to share their impressions with classmates.

4. Have students compile a list of things that the Native Americans taught the Pilgrims. Lead students through a "what if" exercise focusing on what might have happened to the Pilgrims without the Native Americans' lessons on survival. For fun, model for students how to make a Pilgrim hat and a Native American headband and allow them to choose one to make and wear while they consider the weighty "what if" question.

5. Help students compile a menu of foods eaten at the first Thanksgiving feast and a menu that reflects what they eat for Thanksgiving today. (Alternate Activity) Assist students with comparing and contrasting the two meals. Construct a graph of common or favorite foods, ask students to vote for their favorite foods at Thanksgiving, and announce the winners. Have students explain why they voted for some foods and not for others.

6. Plan a Thanksgiving feast in the classroom. Allow students to plan the menu and prepare the meal. **Hint:** Some type of vegetable stew and "friendship fruit salad" would work well. As a related creative activity, show students how to make vegetable prints on construction paper. Let them use the paper as place mats at the feast. **Hint:** Make desired designs such as leaf shapes from a potato or mushroom shapes from half a mushroom, dip in paint, and stamp designs on construction paper.

7. Draw a Venn diagram in which one circle is shaped like a Pilgrim hat and the other circle is shaped like a boy's cap. Ask students to compare and contrast the Pilgrims' Thanksgiving to the boy's Thanksgiving at Grandma's house. Lead students in making logical conclusions about the two celebrations. **Ask:** How are they different? How are they alike? The teacher should record student answers for display.

8. Ask students to make a list of things to complete this sentence: "I am thankful for…" Divide students into groups of four or five and let them choose one thing from their list to share with the group. **Hint:** One person will go first. The next person will repeat the first person's statement and tell his or her own. The third person will repeat the first two statements, and then tell his or her own. Continue until all children have a turn. **Ask:** What are the things for which you are most thankful? Can you explain why you are more thankful for some things than others?

9. Read *Happy Thanksgiving Rebus* by David A. Adler and invite students to write rebus sentences, i.e., picture writing, about the Thanksgiving celebration. Provide opportunities for sharing and displaying sentences. Refer to the dangers faced by the Pilgrims in the New World.

Alternate Selections:

William Accorsi. *Friendship's First Thanksgiving*

David A. Adler. *Happy Thanksgiving Rebus*

Bobbie Kalman. *We Celebrate the Harvest*

EVALUATION:

Determine the level of student understanding by assessing the quality of lists, sentence stems, and diagrams and by listening to the reasoning in and depth of oral responses. Ask students to explain what they learned from the story. Encourage students to connect the message in the story to the theme of harvest and celebrations of thanksgiving.

CONNECTION #2:
Aliki. Corn Is Maize: The Gift of the Indians

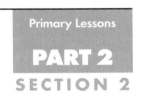

Primary Lessons

PART 2

SECTION 2

Students will learn how Native Americans discovered and utilized the versatile corn plant and how the plant later became a staple crop throughout the world.

CHARACTER TRAIT: Discuss the character trait of cooperation and how it is related to respect, compassion, and appreciation. Find out how cooperation by the Native Americans enabled the Pilgrims to survive in the New World.

1. Read *Corn is Maize* aloud. Remember to set the stage with appropriate pre-reading activities that capture students' interest. For example, ask students to name all the different products made from corn. Using chart paper, web student responses. Provide students either corn kernels to glue on yarn or macaroni to string on yarn to wear as harvest necklaces while they listen to the story and participate in various activities. Clarify vocabulary terms necessary for understanding both the text and the celebration. Define clearly a purpose for reading and/or listening.

2. Make a vocabulary bulletin board. Invite students to make drawings or find pictures of corn to c reate a collage on the bulletin board. Ask them to complete the sentence stem, "I know that corn is important because…" Add sentences to the corn display on the board. **Ask:** Why do drawing-about and writing-about activities help you learn and remember more about a subject such as corn?

3. Discuss different ways that Native Americans used corn and make a list of student responses. Ask students to work individually or in pairs to illustrate each way. Combine illustrations into a class book. Ask them to put on their thinking caps, then lead them through the process of negotiating an appropriate title for the book. **Ask:** Why does making a product such as a class book help you learn and remember more about a subject such as corn?

4. Talk about ways farmers harvest corn on farms. Compare and contrast the modern way with the ancient way Native Americans harvested corn. Enlist student assistance in completing a diagram of how corn grows. Allow students to plant corn kernels in baby food jars. Show students how to keep a class log of plant growth over a period of time. Check observable changes every day and record notes. Question students about changes that they observe in the plant and on the class log. **Ask:**

   How important is the skill of observation?
   Why?
   Is this a skill that you will use with topics other than the growth of corn plants?

   Encourage each student to think up one example of how keen observation helps all students every day and to share examples with classmates.

5. Secure materials (e.g., cornhusks, pipe cleaners, circle stickers, plastic-bead eyes) for students to make a traditional harvest toy. Emphasize step-by-step directions on a chart. **Hint:** Model the following directions for students and invite them to follow each step. First, twist the pipe cleaner around the middle of the husk. Use the ends of the pipe cleaners as arms and bend them into shape. Next, flatten out the top of the husk as the face and draw or glue on eyes. Fray the top to look like hair. Finally, separate the bottom of the husk and fluff it out to look like a skirt. Display harvest toys on a table or at individual desks.

6. Plan a classroom festival that includes feasting on foods made from corn. Invite a few parents or all parents to participate in bringing corn dishes. Encourage students to wear the Native-American "jewelry" they made in the first activity.. Sit in a circle and read a story about the first Thanksgiving. Ask students to help compile recipes into a class book or send recipes home in a newsletter format. After students sample corn foods and make decisions on personal favorites, display their favorites on kernel-shaped, yellow construction paper cutouts marked with the names of favorite corn foods and names of students. Tally the winning corn foods, then group similar foods together for the display. To further decorate the room, invite students to make cornhusk bouquets in which they peel down the husks of two or three ears of dried corn and remove the corn silk. Tie husks together at the base with yarn or ribbon and hang them from the lights.

7. Discuss character traits displayed by the Native Americans as they taught the Pilgrims to plant crops in New England. Ask students to explain how cooperation between people solves problems and prevents arguing. **Hint:** For interest and variety, alternate discussions on character traits between the benefits of possessing the traits and the consequences of not possessing the traits.

ADDITIONAL SELECTION:

Bobbie Kalman. *We Celebrate the Harvest*

EVALUATION:

Determine the level of student understanding of corn as an important food in harvest celebrations by studying the quality of the web, lists, and bulletin board display and by listening for depth of students' answers. Ask students to explain what they learned from the stories and activities. Encourage students to connect the message in the story to the theme of harvest and celebrations of thanksgiving.

CONNECTION #3:
Leslie Tryon.
Albert's Thanksgiving

An industrious duck helps school children prepare for a big Thanksgiving feast.

CHARACTER TRAIT: Select the character trait of responsibility. Talk about different ways Albert exhibits this trait towards Patsy Pig and the P.T.A. Using a large piece of paper, ask students to write down all the things Albert does for Patsy Pig. Encourage students to look at the pictures in the story and sequence Albert's actions.

1. Read *Albert's Thanksgiving* aloud. Remember to set the stage with appropriate pre-reading activities that capture students' interest. Clarify vocabulary terms necessary for understanding both the text and the celebration. Define clearly a purpose for reading and/or listening. For example, ask students to list different activities they do at home to prepare for a Thanksgiving feast, what they do during the feast, and what they do after the feast. List students' responses on a large sheet of paper with labels in three columns: "Before," "During," and "After." Look for significant similarities and differences in responses and help students draw conclusions about preparing for a feast of any kind. (Alternate Activity)

2. Discuss ways Patsy Pig communicates with Albert. Ask students how Albert feels when he receives a letter from Patsy Pig, then how they might feel if they received a letter from Patsy Pig. Record student responses. Explain the parts of a letter to students: date/heading, greeting, body, closing, and signature. Have students pretend that they are Patsy Pig and write a thank-you letter to Albert for his help during the Thanksgiving feast. Provide opportunities for students to share letters with classmates.

3. Talk about different activities that take place prior to the festive Thanksgiving feast. Encourage children to make a list of activities. Allow students to choose one of these activities to do in the classroom. For example, students may make cross-legged turkeys, pilgrim hats, or Native-American headbands. As a class, make and serve Albert's Pumpkin Pizza pies. Follow the recipe featured in the story. **Hint:** Divide ingredients among the students so that all can contribute to the product. Request parental participation in the pizza project three to five days in advance. (Alternate Activity)

4. Place two headings on a large sheet of paper: "Real" and "Make-believe." Ask students to list different events in the story that are real and ones that are make-believe. As students suggest entries, have them state reasons why a particular event goes on one side or the other, then enter responses under the correct heading. **Ask:**

What are ways to tell the difference between real and make-believe?

Why is it important for students to know the difference between real and make-believe?

5. Research library resources for additional examples of harvest festivals in other cultures. Enlist children's help in the selection of which festivals to investigate. Ask the school media specialist to find appropriate resources. Develop with children standard questions for researching all festivals such as the name of and reason for the festival, the geographic location, and common practices. Write information in the form of news bulletins and add to harvest displays in the classroom. (Alternate Activity)

8. Refer to the illustration of school children helping Albert plant a garden. Select the character trait of citizenship. Ask students to show how the school children in the illustration are modeling good citizenship. Ask them to tell about a specific time they displayed good citizenship by acting in a manner similar to the children in the story.

9. Divide students into four groups. Ask each group to illustrate one important, specific favor that Albert does for Patsy Pig on a large piece of paper and to share with classmates. **Hint:** Check student choices carefully so that each group illustrates a different favor that Albert does for Patsy Pig. Tape pictures together to form a sequenced mural and display in the classroom. Invite children to tell the story by using their group's and their classmates' illustrations as story prompts.

EVALUATION:

Determine the level of student understanding by observing how students work in cooperative groups, by listening to students' responses, and by studying lists, charts, and illustrations. Ask students to explain what they learned from the story and activities. Encourage students to connect the message in the story to the theme of harvest and celebrations of thanksgiving.

CONNECTION #1:
Michele Benoit Slawson.
Apple Picking Time

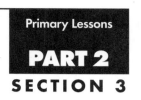

A young girl and her family spend a fall day picking apples with others from their small town. The cooperative activity reveals much about a shared sense of community.

CHARACTER TRAITS: Respect for and protection of natural resources.

1. Read *Apple Picking Time* aloud. Remember to set the stage with appropriate pre-reading activities that capture students' interest. Clarify vocabulary terms necessary for understanding both the text and the celebration. Define clearly a purpose for reading and/or listening.

2. Provide a map of the United States for each student. Use a large map or transparency to direct children in locating places where apples grow in the United States. **Ask:** Do these places show similar geographic features? What does this information tell students about the relationship between certain crops and geographic features? **Hint:** Encourage children to mark places by drawing small apples or by using apple stickers.

3. Distribute to each student a purple construction-paper ticket. Punch or stamp the ticket as children complete their assignments throughout the day. **Hint:** Emphasize that children are working to earn prizes for items they may want or need. Supply prizes such as pencils, stickers, and/or erasers from which children can choose to spend ticket punches. **Ask:** How does this activity relate to the activity of apple picking in the story?

4. Remind students that the author of *Apple Picking Time* refers to traditions passed down from generation to generation several times in the text (e.g., leaning into the ladder for balance; a lesson taught by Grandpa; wearing woolen shirts and gloves with fingers cut out, a lesson taught by Grandma). Encourage children to write family traditions on apple cutouts at school or at home. Display traditions on an apple tree silhouette in the classroom.

5. Ask students to recall the family picnics described in the story. Remind them that Grandma says food tastes better when eaten outside. Arrange an indoor/outdoor picnic. **Hint:** Find out if teachers may order sack lunches from the cafeteria. At the conclusion of the activity, ask students what makes the occasion special. Also ask if their reasons agree with Grandma's reasons and why. Encourage children to think in terms of the relationship between picnics and learning. **Ask:** When the teacher changes the place where you learn and the manner in which you learn, do these changes make learning "taste better"?

6. Talk with students about apples as a resource. Remind them that apples are abundant in the story, thus many people earn a living from one industry. Use a large wall map and locate other areas where specific products or commodities support the economy: oil in Texas, shrimp in Louisiana, corn in Iowa, and wood products in North Carolina. Ask students to predict what happens in terms of jobs, new industries, and families when the resource decreases. Talk about the skill of coping and what children can do when communities and families face economic crises.

7. Show students how to make apple prints. **Hint:** Cut an apple in half crosswise and let dry overnight. Press the apple onto a stamp pad or into very thick tempera paint, then press on paper. Arrange apple prints in a pleasing design. Explain to students that apple patterns are byproducts of an apple harvest. **Ask:** What are reasons why manufacturers and growers continue to search for new and better byproducts?

8. Participate in other apple activities:

Compare, contrast, and graph various kinds of apples;

Taste-test apples/apple products;

Cook apple recipes in the classroom; or

Make a class book of apple recipes.

ADDITIONAL SELECTION:

Steven Kellogg. *Johnny Appleseed*

EVALUATION:

Determine the level of student understanding by observing how they relate traditions to the economic base of an area. Ask students to explain what they learned from the story and activities. Encourage students to connect the message from the story to the theme of harvest and celebrations of thanksgiving.

Primary Lessons
PART 2
SECTION 3

CONNECTION #2:
Erica Silverman. *Big Pumpkin*

A favorite Halloween character tries to find and pick a perfect big pumpkin. She unexpectedly discovers the value of cooperation when she receives help from a group of monsters.

Note: The authors urge teachers to invite parents to preview children's literature and instructional activities related to Halloween. If parents object to their child's participation in the activities, offer a theme-related option.

CHARACTER TRAITS: Discuss the role of responsibility in organizing a party or field trip fun day.

1. Read *Big Pumpkin* aloud. Remember to set the stage with appropriate pre-reading activities that capture students' interest. Clarify vocabulary terms necessary for understanding both the text and the celebration. Define clearly a purpose for reading and/or listening.

2. Bring a variety of sizes and shapes of pumpkins to class. Encourage students to work in small groups to estimate weight, circumference, and number of seeds in the pumpkins. Then weigh and measure pumpkins and compare results. **Ask:** What clues or experiences help people make reasonable guesses or estimations? Invite students to volunteer examples.

3. Demonstrate how to toast pumpkin seeds. **Hint:** Wash the seeds from the pumpkin; spread them on buttered cookie sheet; bake at 275 degrees for one hour or until lightly browned; sprinkle with salt or salt substitute; serve and enjoy. **Ask:** In what other products are most parts used in some way? **Hint:** Use this as a take-home-and-bring-back-answers problem. Encourage students to involve their families in the problem-solving process whenever possible.

4. Request that students pretend that they are growing pumpkins on a pumpkin farm. Invite student partners to design and write poster advertisements to sell their pumpkins. Talk about the meaning of analysis. Ask students to analyze what attracts them to an advertisement: Is it the message? The print? The colors? A prize? A need satisfied? A want fulfilled? Post the advertisements around the classroom, invite the class next door to come and listen to a variety of sales pitches, and ask student hosts and hostesses to serve toasted pumpkin seeds to classmates and guests.

5. Introduce the concept of ghost towns. Group students in threes and have them design murals of ghost towns of the Old West. Instruct students to divide a large paper banner into six boxes and decide on a name for the ghost town. Ask them to illustrate a scene from a ghost town and to write captions and/or sentences that explain why people settled the town and why people later moved away (e.g., mining: no more ore in the mines; oil: no more oil in the basin; drought: no more water in the ground and no more rain in the sky. **Hint:** Ask the media specialist to search for picture books that show how ghost towns look, even those that independent companies presently operate for tourists. Pictures will convey the sense of abandonment characteristic of ghost towns.

6. Remind students how characters in the story cooperate with one another to solve a common problem. Discuss the concept of cooperation and its relationship to the trait of responsibility. Then explain how characters in the story were responsible in working together toward a positive end, i.e., making a pumpkin pie and planning a fun party. Encourage students to list on a class chart how they may demonstrate cooperation at home, at school, and in the neighborhood (e.g., through chores, recess, sports, scouting). Ask students to think about other positive results of cooperation with one another in the three areas of home, school, and neighborhood.

EVALUATION:

Determine the level of student understanding by observing student interaction in groups, by assessing their enthusiasm toward take-home projects, and by listening to their responses to thought questions associated with various activities. Encourage students to connect the message in the story to the theme of harvest and celebrations of thanksgiving.

CONNECTION #3:
Kristina Rodanas.
Dragonfly's Tale

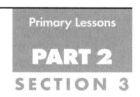

After a poor harvest, two children regain the Corn Maiden's blessings for their people with the aid of a cornstalk toy, the dragonfly.

CHARACTER TRAITS: Review the meaning of respect and compassion.

1. Read *Dragonfly's Tale* aloud. Remember to set the stage with appropriate pre-reading activities that capture students' interest. Clarify vocabulary terms necessary for understanding both the text and the celebration. Define clearly a purpose for reading and/or listening.

2. Ask students to participate in activities to develop the concepts of surplus and scarcity. Scatter a large amount of peanuts in shells on the floor and let children gather them. **Ask:** Is there enough for everyone? Is there more than enough for everyone? Explain the concept of a surplus, by using this example.

Extension: On another day, scatter peanuts in shells again and ensure that there are not enough for everyone in the room. Pose the same questions and explain the concept of scarcity by using this example.

Ask:

> *When there is more than enough to satisfy needs and wants, what is the correct term (surplus)?*
> *When there is less than enough to satisfy needs and wants, what is the correct term (scarcity)?*

Invite students to first apply these two new concepts to situations in the story and then apply them to situations in their lives. **Hint:** Seize every opportunity to connect abstract concepts such as surplus and scarcity to real-world examples in primary students' lives.

3. Remind students that the Ashiwi celebrate their rich harvest with a mock battle. They use foods as weapons to flaunt their prosperity to neighbors. Discuss their waste as well as their motive for celebration. **Ask:**

> *What does the chief want to celebrate?*
> *Why does he want to celebrate the rich harvest?*
> *How do the people celebrate?*

4. Discuss the meaning of respect and compassion. **Ask:** Do the people show that they care about their environment and harvest in the way they celebrate? Are they considerate of their neighbors' feelings by showing off their wealth? Why or why not?

5. Ask students in small groups to invent alternate ways the Ashiwi might celebrate the surplus of harvest in a manner showing respect and compassion for both their environment and their neighbors. Students may illustrate and label events in their celebrations on large pieces of paper and present them to the entire class.

Extension: If primary students appear interested in writing a plan of action through which the Ashiwi might demonstrate more compassion and respect for their neighbors, explain the process, i.e., the purpose, the intended result, a step-by-step process to accomplish the purpose. Talk them through the process with examples for each step.

6. In the story, the boy carves a butterfly to remind his sister of happier times. He paints the insect with bright colors and the "thin pigment spread out, making the eyes very large, and forming a delicate pattern of lines…." Show students how to create watercolor designs on a large coffee filter. Allow students' designs to dry, then make butterfly wings from the painted filter. Demonstrate how to paint a craft clothespin and place in the center of the watercolor wings for the body. Remind students of the statement in the book, "Although it did not look exactly like a butterfly, it was certainly a wonderful creature." Help students hang their butterflies in the classroom. **Ask:** Do art projects help students learn? How and why?

7. Help students make cornhusk dolls. Discuss with students that harvested corn provides the makings for many cornhusk toys. Distribute cornhusks to students and direct them in making cornhusk dolls. Students may also design their own cornhusk toys. **Ask:** Do art projects help students learn important ideas?

8. The boy in the story displays respect and compassion. Reread the story and ask students to listen for examples in which the boy demonstrates these traits, i.e., when he gives food to the disguised Corn Maidens and when he makes the cornhusk butterfly for his sister.

Hint: For interest and variety, alternate discussions on character traits between the benefits of possessing the traits and the consequences of not possessing the traits.

EVALUATION:

Determine the level of student understanding of the concepts and character traits by listening to their verbal and written responses, by observing their participation in multiple activities, and by assessing their ability to transfer abstract information to real-world situations. Ask students to pick a friend or favorite relative. After they have made their choice, ask them to write a response to the following: "I respect _____ because _____." Encourage students to connect the message in the story to the theme of harvest and celebrations of thanksgiving.

CONNECTION # 4:
Barbara Mitchell.
Down Buttermilk Lane

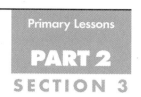

An Amish family traveling by buggy spends the day doing errands in the village and visiting before returning home in time for supper. The day's journey provides valuable insights into Amish culture.

CHARACTER TRAITS: Find out if students remember the meaning of respect. Discuss this concept with them and ask them to share real-life examples of respectful behaviors.

1. Read *Down Buttermilk Lane* aloud. Remember to set the stage with appropriate pre-reading activities that capture students' interest. Review vocabulary terms necessary for understanding both the text and the celebration. Define clearly a purpose for reading and/or listening.

2. Share with students that the Amish make most items they need and use in their daily lives. Suggest that students use strips of construction paper and strawberry baskets to weave Amish baskets. Make handles with pipe cleaners. Tell students that they may fill baskets with pictures of items that the Amish make for their families and for their communities. Ask them to listen for and look for items that may fill baskets as they participate in various activities related to *Down Buttermilk Lane*.

Extension: Lead students to the understanding that the plainness of dress and furnishings reflect the Amish belief in a simple life. Research the story of Jacob Ammann who led his Protestant group out of Switzerland to the New (Old) World in the 1700s. Put Ammann's story in primary students' language and elaborate the story in response to children's interest. Engage children in continuous dialogue about the similarities and differences between Amish and West Texas cultures during all of the activities.

3. Discuss the Amish custom of growing and preserving food. Share with students that the Amish are famous for preparing meals with many courses and with great variety. For example, demonstrate to the class how to make Amish strawberry jam.

STRAWBERRY JAM
2 quarts fresh strawberries
1/4 cup lemon juice
2 oz. package dry pectin
1 cup corn syrup
4 1/2 cups sugar

Directions: Wash, stem, and crush 2 quarts of strawberries. Mix lemon juice and dry pectin with strawberries. Stir mixture every 5 minutes for 30 minutes to completely dissolve pectin. Add corn syrup and stir well. Gradually add 4 1/2 cups sugar. Stir well to dissolve completely. Refrigerate.

Extension: Ask students to estimate the total time to make strawberry jam. Explain that strawberry jam alone does not make a meal. Suggest that class members plan a dinner meal of several meats, several vegetables, several salads, several desserts, and homemade breads. Tell them that the ingredients come from Amish fields. Work through the steps of preparing this meal and estimate the time from field to table. **Ask:** What effect does the Amish custom of preparing all foods have on leisure time? Point out the excellent cause/effect relationship between the Amish belief in a simple life and the lack of leisure time.

4. Arrange a visit to a working farm, if possible. If impossible, invite a farmer to class. Find out what the farm family produces and keeps to eat. Find out what equipment they use to cultivate crops and to raise livestock. Find out if the major purpose of raising food and/or livestock is to feed their family. Continue to point out similarities and differences between Amish farming and farming in your area.

5. Explain to students that many of the words used in Amish communities may sound quaint or strange to us. Reread the story as students listen for unfamiliar words. Discuss the words and their meaning. Test students' understanding by challenging them to take an unfamiliar word or phrase and to replace it with a common word used in their community.

   Extension: Pick an Amish pattern such as an Amish farmhouse, make a display for the bulletin board, encourage students to write the Amish words with their own words, and place on the board. Lead students to logical conclusions about the similarities and differences between cultures.

6. Make a checkerboard by using one-inch graph paper (8 squares down and 8 squares across). Color every other square. Use bottle tops, milk caps, construction paper, or tokens for checkers. Teach students the game of checkers. Explain that this game is a favorite of Amish children. Ask students to think through playing the game. **Ask:** What decisions must players make before moving checkers on the checkerboard? Talk about why using a certain skill such as predicting improves the chance of winning. Also, point out that the skills needed to win at checkers are the skills we call "critical thinking skills" or "problem-solving skills."

7. Display quilts or pictures of quilts. Design a quilt pattern on a 9-inch square and arrange all patterns on a board to create a class quilt. Discuss with students that the Amish are famous for their unique quilt patterns. Locate pictures of Amish quilts, then compare and contrast them to other American quilt styles. Point out that most quilt designs reflect important cultural clues.

8. Make butter by shaking whipping cream in a baby food jar to be served on bread or crackers. Allow students to taste the buttermilk, i.e., the liquid left in the jar. Remind students that butter is another example of the Amish making everything that they need. **Ask:** What if your families decide to make everything that they need for one week? What changes will students predict in the family schedule?

EVALUATION:

Determine the level of student understanding of Amish culture by listening to responses in experiential exercises and by assessing the quality of comparisons and contrasts between Amish ways and the way their families live. Ask students to explain what they have learned in these lessons. Encourage students to connect the message in the story to the theme of harvest and celebrations of thanksgiving.

Masquerade: Celebrations of Frolic and Fantasy

CONNECTION # 1:
Babette Cole.
The Trouble with Mom

The story's bizarre, heroic main character serves as an excellent model for teaching children not to make judgments based on first impressions.

CHARACTER TRAITS: Talk about the meaning of compassion, courage, and/or citizenship.

1. Read *The Trouble with Mom* aloud. Remember to set the stage with appropriate pre-reading activities that capture students' interest. Clarify vocabulary terms necessary for understanding both the text and the celebration. Define clearly a purpose for reading and/or listening. **Hint:** Talk about or review the meaning of masquerade with students before reading the book. Discuss the events in the story in chronolgical order. List the events on a chart under two headings, real and make-believe. Ask students to look at the completed chart and decide how one of the events in either column relates to the theme of masquerade and why.

2. Invite students to tell about an average school day from the time that they get up in the morning to the time that they go to sleep. Ask students to think about all of the activities that they know mothers do. Request that children pick one favorite activity that most mothers do and draw a picture of the activity to share with classmates. **Hint:** Explain to children that when activities are similar to one another, they can group them together, i.e., several children may draw a scene of mother reading a bedtime story so they can group several drawings and reports together. Ask them to look and to listen for similarities in classmates' reports so that they can display these together after reports. **Hint:** Use the exercise to develop students' ability to categorize.

3. Encourage children to talk about the unusual mother in the story and mothers in the drawings. **Ask:** Is the unusual mother engaged in activities that are similar to those of mothers in the drawings? Ask children if they would still call the mother in the story unusual? **Ask:** What does this experience teach you about people who look different from others? Are they always unusual? Ask children if they try to find out more about another person before they attach a label such as unusual and why finding out more information is important.

4. Point out how the unusual mother demonstrates compassion by putting out the school fire and saving children's lives at the risk of her own life. Encourage children to volunteer examples of how the unusual mother exhibits courage and citizenship in the story. Ask children to think about their classmates' actions and nominate a deserving student for the "Citizen of the Week" award based on an act of courage or citizenship.

EVALUATION:

Determine the level of student understanding by listening to how students relate chart information to the meaning of masquerade, by observing how children share information with classmates, by checking how students categorize information from reports and drawings, by listening to how students express empathy for persons who appear different, and by observing how students exemplify selected character traits. Encourage students to connect the story's message to the theme of masquerade and celebrations of frolic and fantasy.

CONNECTION #2:
Pat Whitehead.
Best Halloween Book

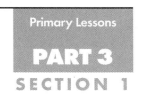

ABC-listed words portray the fun and excitement of masquerade and encourage teachers and students to apply the alphabetical technique to other themes.

Note: Teachers are urged to invite parents to preview children's literature and instructional activities related to Halloween. If parents object to their child's participation in the activities, offer a theme-related option.

CHARACTER TRAITS: Talk about the meaning of citizenship.

1. Enlist students in making an October words bulletin board by using ideas generated from students (e.g., Halloween words, fall words, autumn words). **Hint:** Add small pictures to the word display so that students can match words and pictures. The process of adding words and pictures may run throughout the season.

2. Read *Best Halloween Book* aloud. Remember to set the stage with appropriate pre-reading activities that capture students' interest prior to reading. Clarify vocabulary terms necessary for understanding both the text and the celebration. Define clearly a purpose for reading and/or listening.

Impress on students that one of the main reasons for learning to read well is to build a personal vocabulary. **Hint:** Tell students to listen closely to the reading so that they may add new words and pictures not only to the bulletin board but also to their personal vocabularies. Engage students in a discussion of the words from the story so that they explain the meaning in the context of Halloween, and then relate the words to the meaning of masquerade. Add all new words to the bulletin board.

3. Ask each student to choose a letter of the alphabet and make a masquerade mask of a person or animal that starts with the same letter (e.g., A = astronaut, P = pumpkin, S = snake). Set the stage with these directions: "Today is the official kindergarten parade. We are going to show the school that we know the alphabet and can match the letters with masks of fun-loving characters. The masks will show that we understand that people, young and old, like to play dress-up just for fun. Get ready to march in snake-like fashion around the playground." Play carnival music in the background. (Alternate Activity, Parental Discretion)

4. Talk about the meaning of citizenship from the standpoint of participation, i.e., taking part in an action although the action does not have to be the same for everyone. Make sure that children understand that participation may take several different forms, i.e., parades for some, other activities for others. Remind students that staying involved in teacher-planned activities is one way that all students can demonstrate good citizenship.

EVALUATION:

Determine the level of student understanding by watching children's responses to the bulletin-board project, by listening to their connections between words and pictures, by observing how they relate classroom activities to the theme of masquerade, by assessing their enthusiasm for the parade of masks, and by seeing how they connect class participation to the trait of citizenship. Encourage students to connect the story's message to the theme of masquerade and celebrations of frolic and fantasy.

CONNECTION #3:
Janell Cannon. *Stellaluna*

Stellaluna, a truly unique creature, must live like a bird to survive. The story unfolds when Stellaluna discovers a true identity as a bat rather than an assumed identity as a bird.

CHARACTER TRAIT: Discuss the meaning of courage.

1. Ask students to participate in the K-W-L activity related to bats: what they know, what they want to know, and what they learned at the end of the lesson. Accept all answers from students and record on chart paper. **Hint:** Do this exercise prior to reading the story.

2. Use the following information about bats to tell a story about the bat residents of Carlsbad Caverns, New Mexico. Ask the boys and girls to circle up close to the mouth of a bat cave surrounding the park ranger (teacher). Request that they listen closely for clues to the list, "what they want to know." Talk in a soft whisper as if it were time for the bats to fly from the cavern at dusk. Ron Butler, a freelance writer, describes the bat experience in *Vista USA*:

> Out of the mouth of the cave, a single bat appears, then a few more, then dozens, and finally hundreds, perhaps thousands, tens of thousands, all taking flight in an orderly swirling fashion, out of the cave and out across the darkening landscape. From the seats of the amphitheater they look like a huge swarm of bees, or an endless flock of small black birds. The only sound is the persistent noise of their wings, a hum that mounts to a steady, droning roar.

> ...No scientist has yet figured out how a bat hanging upside down in a dark cave knows when the sun has set outside. But out they come each evening at just about sunset, exiting from the natural entrance of the cave to go flying about the countryside scouting for flying insects. Using echolocation—locating an object through sound waves—they catch insects on the wing, collectively consuming more than three tons of the apparently delectable bugs per night.

> The best bat flights to watch are in August and September when the baby bats, born during the early summer, join the flight along with migrating bats from points farther north. (During the winter, the bats leave for Mexico where mosquitoes and other high-cholesterol insects are more plentiful.)

> ...Bats are the only mammals that fly. Their wings are actually extensions of their hands. Their knees bend backward, away from their bodies, enabling them to hang upside down. The size of a bat's body can vary from one inch to 15 inches long, and some bats have wing-spreads of up to five feet.

> Though certainly less lovable than furry kittens, bats ... with their hair like bones and wizened wings ... are among the most maligned and misunderstood of creatures. They shun humans and are less likely to cause rabies by biting than skunks or feral cats. Along with eating pesky insects, they sip plant nectar and pollinate flowers, are rarely dangerous and mind their own business.

> ...Once a year—on the second Thursday of August—bat-lovers gather at the early hour of 5 a.m. for a sit-down breakfast at the entrance to Carlsbad Caverns. They come to watch the thousands of bats—who've just been out for the night feeding on insects—fly back into the cave.

> Ron Butler. "Carlsbad's Batty Celebrities," *Vista USA*, Summer 1995: 25-29.

3. Check to see if the story around the entrance to the bat cave answers any of the children's questions. Invite children to stay with the park ranger to meet a special baby bat, Stellaluna. Allow time for children to talk about the questions and how the "Batty Celebrities" answers some of their inquiries.

4. Read *Stellaluna* aloud up to the part in the narrative where Stellaluna exclaims, "How embarrassing!" Remember to set the stage with appropriate pre-reading activities that capture students' interest prior to reading. Clarify vocabulary terms necessary for understanding both the text and the celebration. Define clearly a purpose for reading and/or listening. **Hint:** Check with the media specialist to see if a Stellaluna puppet is available. Ask students to predict what will happen next when Stellaluna finds it impossible to behave in typical bird-like fashion. Request that students write or dictate captions related to Stellaluna's solution to the problem. This activity may take more than one session for all students to participate in making logical and/or whimsical statements about their new bat friend. Group similar responses together and graph on a chart tablet so that students may benefit from the thinking of all students. Continue reading the story and compare the ending of the actual story with the children's predictions.

5. Review the meaning of masquerade and help students understand that people and animals can behave in ways that are different from their nature just as they can change their physical appearance by dressing up or by shedding an outer layer.

6. Ask students to show how Stellaluna exhibits courage once her un-bird-like features become known to her companions. Also talk about situations that come up in school and in neighborhoods that require courage to solve once differences arise. Ask students to volunteer examples.

7. End discussion by referring to the chart on bats and asking if students have answers to what they wanted to learn about bats. Correct misinformation. Write the National Park Service for more information about bat creatures if students appear eager for more knowledge. Use *ZOO BOOK* magazine (Bats issue, 1994) for illustrations and text on bats including such topics of interest as different types of bats according to facial features, wingspans, skeletons, and food preferences (e.g., blood, fruit, and insects).

EVALUATION:

Determine the level of student understanding by listening to student responses to K-W-L, by observing children's willingness to participate in simulated situations, by listening to the logic of student predictions, and by assessing how students link the story to the theme of masquerade. Encourage students to connect the message in the story to the theme of masquerade and celebrations of frolic and fantasy.

CONNECTION #1:
Loreen Leedy.
The Dragon Halloween Party

A group of dragons playfully plan, decorate, and prepare for a Halloween party.

Alternate Selection:

Alexandra Day. *Carl's Masquerade.* Mother accepts an invitation to a masquerade party. Lovable, amiable, trustworthy Carl unexpectedly adds two more guests to the party list.

Note: Teachers are encouraged to invite parents to preview children's literature and instructional activities related to Halloween. If parents object to their child's participation in the activities, offer a theme-related option.

CHARACTER TRAIT: Review and discuss the meaning of diligence. Provide examples for student understanding.

1. Read *The Dragon Halloween Party* aloud. Remember to set the stage with appropriate pre-reading activities that capture students' interest. For example, talk about Halloween and its origin. Consult *Childcraft*, Volume 9, "Holidays and Birthdays," pages 284-287, as an excellent resource for Halloween. Make a time line showing how the celebration of Halloween changes over the years. Clarify vocabulary terms necessary for understanding both the text and the celebration. Define clearly a purpose for reading and/or listening.

2. Ask students to design a costume. Talk about the importance of following directions. Provide colorful materials and simple patterns. Designate a day for students to wear their finished products. **Ask:** How do craft activities help you learn and remember important facts and ideas? (Alternate Activity, Parental Discretion)

3. Brainstorm a list of Halloween symbols and activities with the class. Use the stories as well as children's personal experiences to make the list. Encourage students to use suggestions from the list and create fun-type decorations as seasonal symbols for classroom display. **Ask:**

   Why does listening to the stories of others help you understand one another better?
   How do craft activities help you understand celebrations better?

4. Use suggestions in the story as guidelines for carving a pumpkin in class. Invite family members to participate in a classroom pumpkin-carving contest, "The Great Pumpkin-Carving Contest." Using an electric skillet or toaster oven, fry or toast pumpkin seeds. Enjoy eating pumpkin seeds while contestants carve pumpkins. Allow children to vote on the best pumpkin and award a special prize or recognition. Make sure that children connect the contest to the text of the stories. Invite children to explain the connection to classroom guests. (Alternate Activity)

5. Use a Venn diagram to inquire about students' Halloween plans. Entitle one circle: "Are you going to a Halloween party?" Entitle the other circle: "Are you going trick-or-treating?" If students are doing both, place their names in the middle of both circles. In addition, for students not participating in Halloween activities, ask them to share a favorite form of play with classmates. Suggest that students use data from the diagrams and from shared experiences as writing prompts on the value of play. Ask students to respond in writing to why they think that play is an important part of their lives.

Hint: Talk about reasons such as learning to share, learning to cooperate, learning to follow directions, learning about others' families and experiences, learning to appreciate the interests and talents of others. Invite children to share their writing with classmates. **Ask:** Why do active learning experiences help you remember important ideas?

6. Discuss the character trait of diligence. **Ask:** What examples of this trait can you find in the story? Review the games in *The Dragon Halloween Party*. Talk about the importance of fairness, honesty, and respect when playing games. Choose one or both of the games to play in class so students can practice fairness, honesty, and respect with classmates. **Hint:** For interest and variety, alternate discussions on character traits between the benefits of possessing the traits and the consequences of not possessing the traits.

EVALUATION:

Determine the level of student understanding by observing the quality of the time line, costumes, decorations, class lists, and Venn diagram and by listening to insights revealed by comments, questions, and responses. Ask students to explain what they have learned from the story and the lessons. Encourage students to connect the messages in the story to the theme of masquerade and celebrations of frolic and fantasy.

CONNECTION #2:
Matthew Gollub.
The Moon Was at a Fiesta

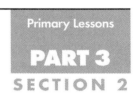

Primary Lessons

PART 3

SECTION 2

Through story, native people in Oaxaca, Mexico, explain the phenomenon of the moon and sun together in the morning sky. One delightful story contends that the moon's and sun's unusual placement results from the moon attending a fiesta all night.

CHARACTER TRAITS: Ask students to make a connection statement between the trait of citizenship and the classroom celebration of fiesta. Have them link what they learned from *The Moon Was at a Fiesta* to their behavior in the classroom as well as to their behavior at home. **Hint:** Lead students into connecting active participation and good citizenship.

1. Read *The Moon Was at a Fiesta* aloud. Remember to set the stage with appropriate pre-reading activities that capture students' interest. For example, ask students to define the term, fiesta, and to list characteristics of a fiesta by using information in the story. Clarify vocabulary terms necessary for understanding both the text and the celebration. Define clearly a purpose for reading and/or listening.

2. Use an outline to record details about the fiesta celebration in the story. Address the following topics: title of the celebration, religion, origin, and customs. Talk about why this particular fiesta fits under the masquerade theme. Extend the discussion to other celebrations that fit naturally into the same theme. **Hint:** Stress the idea that people wear festive clothes and wooden masks and also assume different roles during fiestas.

3. Remind students that most celebrations in the masquerade theme encourage participants to wear masks. Let students design masks by using poster board and crayons. Show students how to weather masks by brushing watered-down brown tempera paint over the masks, which simulates a wooden look. Give students a creative option by modeling how to make bright-colored construction paper lanterns to hang from the ceiling and by inviting them to decorate the classroom. **Ask:** How do art projects such as making masks and lanterns help you to learn important ideas?

4. Talk about the story as one explanation of why the moon joins the sun in the morning sky. Research a simplified scientific explanation of the movement of the sun, moon, and earth and phrase the research-based story in language appropriate for primary students. **Hint:** Tell students that people throughout history often made up stories, i.e., myths, to explain things that they did not understand about their world.

5. Discuss the character trait of citizenship and why it is important to be good citizens when planning an event like a fiesta. **Ask:** In what ways did each person or each group contribute to the task?

EVALUATION:

Determine the level of student understanding by observing insights expressed in both oral and written responses; by assessing the quality of masks, lanterns, and stories; and by determining the accuracy in linking participation and citizenship. Ask students to explain what they have learned from these activities and this story. Encourage students to connect the message in the story to the theme of masquerade and celebrations of frolic and fantasy.

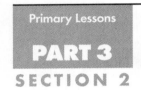

CONNECTION #3:
Miriam Nerlove. *Purim*

Students gain basic understandings of Purim by following a Jewish family's observance of the celebration at the Temple and by listening to the Rabbi read the story from the Book of Esther.

CHARACTER TRAITS: Discuss the character trait of courage and ask how Queen Esther in the *Purim* story exemplifies the trait.

1. Read *Purim* aloud. Remember to set the stage with appropriate pre-reading activities that capture students' interest. Clarify vocabulary terms necessary for understanding both the text and the celebration. Define clearly a purpose for reading and/or listening.

2. As a lead-in to the activities and as a check on students' attentiveness, ask students to contribute details from the story to make an outline by using this frame:

Title of holiday: _____

Origin: _____

Religion: _____

Customs: _____

Hint: Point out that people around the world dress up for masquerade celebrations. Invite students to name examples of other celebrations.

3. Suggest that children research other masquerade festivals or celebrations and fill in a frame (outline) for each occasion. Encourage children to choose their favorite among the examples and to illustrate their choice. Combine the illustrations in a reference book on the theme of masquerade.

Hint: Make sure that students understand that the theme of masquerade links similar celebrations throughout a calendar year.

4. Encourage student partners to plan a day of masquerade and create theme, origins, and customs. For example:

Title of celebration:	The Wonders of Story
Origin:	Celebrate that we love to read
Religion:	None
Customs:	Dress up like a favorite storybook character

Method: Each set of partners tells about their special day while all students sit in a storytelling circle. Teachers lead students to a decision by allowing them to vote on one day of masquerade in which students participate according to the plans of the winning student partners.

Hint: Invite another class to attend a special masquerade day and devise ways that children may share their learning with visitors.

5. Lead children through a discussion of important scenes in the story, then pass out names of characters in various scenes. Invite students to act out the Purim story. So that all students are involved in the drama, divide students into two groups and create additional assignments including both acting out parts and designing and making scenery. Encourage children to perform the Purim story first for classmates, then for invited guests. Request that one student in the final scene explain to the audience how the celebration of Purim links to the theme of masquerade.

6. Invite a member of the Jewish community to speak about the Purim celebration. Prior to the visit, assist children in listing topics of interest and share these with the invited guest. **Hint:** Read the story again while the visitor and children listen, and then ask the visitor to compare and contrast the Purim celebration in the story to the Purim celebration in their community. **Hint:** Simulate the treat of hamantaschen (three-cornered pastries filled with poppy seeds or fruit jam) by serving jelly doughnuts.

7. **Ask:** What other traits did Queen Esther possess and how did her actions match the behaviors on the character trait chart? Can you give reasons for your answers? **Hint:** For interest and variety, alternate discussions on character traits between the presence and benefits of possessing the traits and the absence and consequences of not possessing the traits.

EVALUATION:

Determine the level of student understanding by reviewing students' frames (outlines) and by assessing their creativity in planning a special masquerade celebration. Ask students to explain what they have learned by this story and by participating in these activities. Encourage students to connect the message in the story to the theme of masquerade and celebrations of frolic and fantasy.

CONNECTION # 1:
James Howe.
Harold and Chester in Scared Silly: A Halloween Treat

The Monroes, who are unaware that a mysterious figure will visit their cat and dogs, leave the pets alone on Halloween night.

Note: The authors urge teachers to invite parents to preview children's literature and instructional activities related to Halloween. If parents object to their child's participation in the activities, offer a theme-related option.

CHARACTER TRAITS: Talk about the meaning of courage and compassion.

1. Read the story aloud. Remember to set the stage with appropriate pre-reading activities that capture students' interest. For example, explain to children that people often feel the desire to pretend to be someone or something else. Explore with students why people assume other roles, wear costumes, or don masks (e.g., acting in a play, role playing a storybook character, playing dress-up, celebrating holidays such as Mardi Gras, Carnival, and Halloween). Clarify vocabulary terms necessary for understanding both the text and the celebration. Define a purpose for reading and/or listening.

2. Use the author's words to develop the concept of figurative language. Encourage children to think about the rich pictures that these words create, for example: "Hurt to the bone…crawling with clouds…voice full of gravel…light poured into the room…."

Ask children to fold a piece of paper in half. Invite students to illustrate the figurative meaning of their favorite phrase on one half and then illustrate the literal meaning on the other half. **Ask:**

> *Which words convey more meaning and why?*
> *When are people more likely to use figurative language and why?*
> *How does this exercise help students understand figurative language?*

3. Assemble and label parts of a skeleton. Encourage students to comment on how all connected parts make a human machine. **Ask:** Will the human machine function smoothly if some of the bones are missing? Why? Why not?

Extension: Discuss the concept of balance. **Ask:** Are all of the bones necessary for balance? Locate music that playfully teaches the skeletal parts (e.g., the African-American spiritual "Dry Bones"). Ask students to point at the correct skeletal part and to move musically from the foot bone to the head bone or vice versa. As an added treat, plan a Dry Bones Party and serve warm apple cider made with a handful of melted red hots and little doughnuts. Assist students in linking the skeleton and activities to the story about Harold and Chester, then to the theme of masquerade.

4. Show children how to make a character flap book by folding paper lengthwise, "hot-dog" style, dividing the paper into three sections, and cutting the top flap into three sections. Demonstrate how to label the front with Chester, Howie, and Harold, the three family pets. Instruct students to lift each flap and to list traits of each pet under the appropriate flap. Remind them of the power of figurative language and encourage them to think up vivid words to describe the family pets. **Ask:** How can this activity improve your writing?

5. Invite students to join a discussion on how characters demonstrate courage and compassion in the story. Ask students how they may demonstrate these traits when someone is scared. **Hint:** For interest and variety, alternate discussions on character traits between the benefits of possessing the traits and the consequences of not possessing the traits.

EVALUATION:

Determine the level of student understanding about playful masquerading by observing them in various interactive activities and by listening to their applications of courage and compassion to everyday lives. Ask students to keep a log for one week and list acts of courage and compassion that they witness at school, home, or play. Encourage students to connect the message in the story to the theme of masquerade and celebrations of frolic and fantasy.

CONNECTION #2:
Mary Blount Christian.
Swamp Monsters

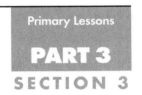

Two swamp monsters dress up like children and join real children at play.

CHARACTER TRAITS: Talk about the concept of citizenship and its importance to a safe school.

1. Read *Swamp Monsters* aloud. Remember to set the stage with appropriate pre-reading activities that capture students' interest. Clarify vocabulary terms necessary for understanding both the text and the celebration. Define clearly a purpose for reading and/or listening. Remind children that the swamp monsters put on masks and pretend to be children in the story. Provide the same opportunity for children to play dress-up in class. Bring a variety of hats or costumes to class (e.g., chef, nurse, cowboy) and encourage children to play the part of the character who matches the hat. Ask children to explain the term masquerade based on the experience of wearing various characters' hats and of assuming their roles.

2. Discuss the meaning of reality and of fantasy. Ask children to recall the story, choose one example of reality and one example of fantasy, then write a brief explanation of the difference between the two terms for a classmate. Encourage students to deliver the explanation to the classmate who will share the explanation with the whole class if the author grants permission. Check randomly to see if students can clearly and simply communicate the difference between reality and fantasy.

3. Talk to students about the differences between literal and figurative meanings of words, i.e., "take your seats," "the principal will straighten you out," "put on the T.V." Ask children to generate more phrases with literal and figurative meanings. Use the *Amelia Bedelia* Series by Peggy Parish as additional resources. Relate the exercise to the theme of masquerade. **Ask:** Can words wear masks? How?

4. Divide students into three groups. Assign one task to each group:

Create masks representing playful characters, write a scene in which the characters come to the rescue of a frightened person, and present to classmates;

Draw a Venn diagram, compare/contrast the activities of the family in the story to students' families, and draw conclusions; or

Concoct a delicious recipe that uses ingredients—just like the swamp creatures when they made snail stew and mud pie—then draw conclusions about how local resources influence eating habits.

5. Discuss how children treat each other in the story. Invite students to write how a child in school can be a good citizen, i.e., follow rules, help others, and treat others fairly. Invite students to relate the trait of citizenship to the characters in *Swamp Monsters*.

   Hint: For interest and variety, alternate discussions on character traits between the benefits of possessing the traits and the consequences of not possessing the traits.

EVALUATION:

Determine the level of student understanding by observing their participation in various activities related to the theme of the story and by listening to their distinctions between reality and fantasy. Ask students to list the qualities of good citizenship and post these in the hallway for all to see. Encourage students to connect the message in the story to the theme of masquerade and celebrations of frolic and fantasy.

Primary Lessons

PART 3

SECTION 3

CONNECTION #3:
Marjorie Thayer.
The April Foolers: A Play

Children attempt to stage a practical joke on April Fool's Day. The prank backfires, and the jokesters become victims of their own tomfoolery.

CHARACTER TRAITS: Discuss the importance of taking responsibility for your actions.

1. In March, read *The April Foolers* aloud. Remember to set the stage with appropriate pre-reading activities that capture students' interest. Clarify vocabulary terms necessary for understanding both the text and the celebration. Define clearly a purpose for reading and/or listening.

2. Discuss with students the concept of a play. Assign reading parts to students. Allow time for them to practice reading parts of the play to small groups several times. Show students how to make a play come alive by adding movements, props, and costumes. Talk about each one of these additions and ask for student suggestions.

3. Point out how different characters act when certain events happen. Allow them to practice acting out a full range of emotions. Then encourage them to talk about their assigned characters, the emotions displayed, and how they will portray the character. Present the play to an audience. Allow students to vote on whether or not they wish to invite guests to the performance. Allow students to discuss the meaning of their acting experience with the class.

4. April Fool's Day begins National Laugh Week, a time for comedians to tell jokes. Plan a comedy hour in class and invite students to tell a funny April Fool's trick, spoof, or story. Relate this activity to the theme of masquerade.

5. Tell students that traditionally the French called April Fool's pranks April Fish, which refers to the way a fish gets tricked into biting a baited hook. Talk about French bakeries today and the practice of decorating bakery shop windows with chocolate fish. Share with students that French people mail postcards covered with fish drawings to each other as jokes. Encourage students to write fish jokes on fish-shaped paper cutouts. Example: "Why are fish so smart?" Answer: "Because they are always in schools." Post the fish jokes swimming in a school on the bulletin board. Model or post only fun-type pranks for children.

6. Demonstrate the trait of responsibility, specifically the indicator of accepting the consequences of personal actions, by putting a squirt of toothpaste on a plate. Ask students to pretend that the squirt of toothpaste represents each hurtful word or deed the class can recall. **Ask:** Will the squirt of toothpaste fit back into the tube? Explain to students that just as toothpaste cannot be put back in the tube, hurtful words and deeds cannot be taken away. Suggest that just as bandages may soothe wounds, apologies may soothe unkind acts. Add drama to the moment by tearing open a bandage while explaining the analogy.

Hint: For interest and variety, alternate discussions on character traits between the benefits of possessing the traits and the consequences of not possessing the traits.

EVALUATION:

Determine the level of student understanding about the positive and negative impact of jokes by observing student participation in the play, by listening to the tone of jokes in the comedy hour, and by reading questions and responses in the fish jokes. Ask students to explain why taking responsibility for their actions is a part of being a good citizen. Encourage students to connect the message in the story to the theme of masquerade and celebrations of frolic and fantasy.

Primary Lessons

Festivals of Light:
Celebrations
of Illumination

CONNECTION #1:
B.G. Hennessy. *The First Night*

Hennessy recounts the traditional Christian story of the birth of Jesus.

CHARACTER TRAITS: Discuss respect and fairness with students. Point out other stories where these two character traits were emphasized.

1. Read *The First Night* aloud. Remember to set the stage with appropriate pre-reading activities that capture students' interest prior to reading. Clarify vocabulary terms necessary for understanding both the text and the celebration. Define clearly a purpose for reading and/or listening.

Talk about the historical and cultural setting: when and where the event occurred, circumstances surrounding the birth, and why the celebration is important to Christians. Define key terms necessary for understanding the text (e.g., stable, field, and shepherds). Invite children whose families honor the Christian tradition to share stories of how they acknowledge the birth of Jesus. **Hint:** Use the discussion as a springboard for talking to children about significant figures and their roles in other belief systems.

2. Ask students to share any family stories they might know that relate to their own birth (i.e., location, trip from hospital to home, searching for the perfect name, and relatives who came to see the new baby). On a chart table, record student responses. Discuss the preparations for a new family member. Talk about the changes when a new baby comes home. Compare and contrast students' stories to the story told about Jesus' birth.

3. Discuss with children the meaning of respect and fairness, especially the indicators of "be considerate of other people's feelings and rights" and "listen and try to understand what others believe and feel." Review the story in *The First Night* and encourage students to relate the story and its message to the stated indicators under each character trait. Talk about the fact that being born is one thing that binds all humans together despite differences in beliefs. Remind students that showing respect and fairness in discussions of all beliefs leads to understanding other people and their values.

Hint: For interest and variety, alternate discussions on character traits between the benefits of possessing the traits and the consequences of not possessing the traits.

EVALUATION:

Determine the level of student understanding by listening to students' shared stories about family beliefs, by watching students' responses to shared stories, and by listening to how they relate the Christian story of Jesus to the character traits of respect and fairness. Ask students to explain what they have now learned about respect and fairness. Encourage students to connect the message in the story to the theme of festivals of light and celebrations of illumination.

CONNECTION #2:
Jane Breskin Zalben.
Papa's Latkes

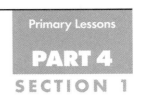

Zalben's text provides insights on how latke making during Chanukah passes on cultural traditions to the younger generation.

CHARACTER TRAIT: Review the meaning of respect. Have students give examples of behaviors that are characterized as respectful.

Note: The authors searched for cultural celebrations in which light represents a central focus. In order to develop the theme, they highlighted major as well as minor celebrations in various racial, ethnic, and religious contexts. The authors feel that children need to understand that various traditions regard some celebrations as more important than others. For example, many people in the Jewish community in America emphasize the importance of Hanukkah to a greater degree than do those in the Jewish community in Israel. The writers urge teachers to make children aware that not all celebrations are equal in importance or celebrated in the same manner around the world. Teachers are therefore critical in helping students learn sensitivity toward others' traditions, celebrations, and beliefs.

1. Invite a member of the Jewish faith to the classroom to talk to children about the celebration of Chanukah (also spelled Hanukkah and Hanukah). Lead students through a K-W-L (what they know, what they want to learn, what they have learned) before the visitor arrives. Share with the visitor what students say they want to learn so that the guest may respond directly to students' questions.

2. Read *Papa's Latkes* aloud. Remember to set the stage with appropriate pre-reading activities that capture students' interest. Clarify vocabulary terms necessary for understanding both the text and the celebration. Define clearly a purpose for reading and/or listening. Invite children to discuss specific parts of the celebration described in the story. Ask them to compare this information to information that the visitor shares with them. Refer to the recipe for latkes at the back of the story and talk about ingredients necessary for making them. Gather utensils and ingredients and make the recipe.

3. Discuss the meaning of respect. Encourage children to recall how children in *Papa's Latkes* show respect for their culture. Use the discussion to point out that understanding the beliefs of all cultures leads gradually to respecting and accepting members of all cultures.

EVALUATION:

Determine the level of student understanding by watching children's response to a visitor and to traits of the visitor's culture, by observing their enthusiasm for talking about and making a traditional Jewish recipe, and by listening to students link the lesson to the trait of respect. Ask students to explain what they learned from this story. Encourage students to connect the message in the story to the theme of festivals of light and celebrations of illumination.

CONNECTION #3:
Phoebe Gilman.
Something from Nothing

This Jewish folk tale focuses on an act of love, as a grandpa makes a most special gift for his progeny.

CHARACTER TRAITS: Discuss the meaning of diligence and persistence. Ask students to give examples of people from stories or from their own lives displaying these two character traits.

1. Do a print walk by showing each illustration and by encouraging children to tell what is happening in the story. **Hint:** Make special note of the mice at the bottom of the pages.

2. Read *Something from Nothing* aloud. Remember to set the stage with appropriate pre-reading activities that capture students' interest. Clarify vocabulary terms necessary for understanding both the text and the celebration. Define clearly a purpose for reading and/or listening.

3. Stop several times in the story and ask students to predict what will happen next. Compare these predictions to the story as it unfolds. Ask students if their experiences are similar to those in the story. **Ask:** Have students had an item that became worn and that someone thought should be thrown away? What happened to the item? Did they store it, give it away, or make it into something else?

4. Involve students in making a sentence flip book from the following sentence pattern:

_____ favorite _____ was _____.

Example: Susie's favorite dress was made into a quilt.

Ask students to share their completed sentences with classmates.

5. Provide students with an assortment of materials such as lace, ribbons, material scraps, pipe cleaners, buttons, beads, string, and yarn to make something from nothing. Ask them to share ideas that shaped their something-from-nothing projects and then to describe the how-to steps they followed to get from abstract ideas to concrete products.

6. Talk about the meaning of diligence. Ask students how the little boy shows persistence in keeping a piece of his memory. Encourage children to think of other ways that children and adults keep memories alive (e.g., photograph albums, tape recordings, music, childhood toys, holiday decorations).

EVALUATION:

Determine the level of student understanding by listening to insights children express during the print walk, by analyzing their logic as they predict events in the story, by observing how they complete sentence patterns, by evaluating their creativity in something-from-nothing products, and by listening to how they link the little boy's actions in the story to the trait of diligence. Encourage students to connect the message in the story to the theme of festivals of light and celebrations of illumination.

CONNECTION #1:
Deborah M. Newton Chocolate.
My First Kwanzaa Book

The rituals of Kwanzaa, a seven-day celebration of African-American heritage, come alive through the author's clear, concise explanations and examples.

Alternate Selection:

Denise Burden-Patmon. *Imani's Gift at Kwanzaa.* Friendship between two girls blossoms as they celebrate Kwanzaa together.

CHARACTER TRAITS: Select one character trait—either compassion, respect, or fairness—and discuss how people in the story or in students' drawings demonstrate the trait.

Note: Kwanzaa may be placed in either the harvest section or the festivals-of-light section of the unit. Kwanzaa, patterned after African harvest festivals, now celebrates pride in African-American heritage by lighting a symbolic candle on each of seven successive nights.

1. Invite children to draw how their home looks, inside and outside, at Christmas or at any period of celebration in which family members decorate homes. Ask boys and girls to describe special decorations, gift-giving traditions, and invited guests. Encourage them to share drawings with classmates.

2. Read aloud one of the stories listed, *My First Kwanzaa Book* or *Imani's Gift at Kwanzaa*. Remember to set the stage with appropriate pre-reading activities that capture students' interest. Clarify vocabulary terms necessary for understanding both the text and the celebration. Define clearly a purpose for reading and/or listening.

3. Ask students to make a model of the black, red, and green African flag. Cut construction paper in the three colors in strips at least two inches wide. Glue all three together on a poster board approximately six inches in size. Add a dowel stick to make it flag-like or shape the three colors as a banner to hang from the ceiling. Point out and discuss the meaning of the colors in the flag: black = heritage, red = hard work, and green = faith. Talk about how the meaning of the colors in the African flag connects to the character traits used in this manual.

4. Help children make a graph on the chalkboard that shows what principles are honored on the seven days of Kwanzaa. Extend the potential of children's learning from this activity by adding other activities that focus on the basic principles of Kwanzaa, i.e., December 26: African Americans honor Umoja (unity), and participants show unity by dressing in African clothing.

5. Invite student partners to make a seven-page Kwanzaa booklet, one page for each principle. Suggest that students use a color scheme of black, red, and green; draw pictures illustrating each principle; and share completed booklets with class members. **Ask:**

> *How does making an art project increase your understanding of Kwanzaa?*
> *Does making a product help you learn and remember important ideas about any subject?*
> *Why or why not?*

6. Ask students to point to north, south, east, and west on a map of Africa. Talk about the shape of the continent and facts already known about Africa. Use the geographic tools on a large classroom map to measure the length of Africa. Ask the media specialist to assist class members in finding pictures of various nations in Africa so that children realize the vast diversity on the huge continent. Help students show their pictures to classmates and point out unique features of nations or regions. Encourage children to choose a nation or region and either draw or cut out pictures to attach to the large map of Africa.

Hint: Make sure that children draw or select a wide range of pictures, such as geographic features, animal life, rural and urban life, citizens of tribes, and nations, so that children see a visual image of an extremely diverse continent. Teachers may emphasize the diversity of the continent and its people through fine arts projects such as an introduction to African-American music or a study of distinctive African clothing and jewelry.

7. Select one character trait (e.g., compassion, respect, or fairness) and discuss how people in the story or in students' drawings demonstrate the trait. Remind students to tell why they selected a character and how the character exhibits the trait.

EVALUATION:

Determine the level of student understanding by assessing the quality of various creative products and by listening for insight expressed in response to thought questions and to problem-solving activities. Ask students what they have learned from this story and activities. Encourage students to connect the message in the stories to the theme of festivals of light and celebrations of illumination.

Primary Lessons

PART 4

SECTION 2

CONNECTION #2:
Roni Schotter. *Hanukkah!*

Teachers and students will gain basic information about the Jewish holiday and traditional practices from this source.

ALTERNATE SELECTIONS:

Sylvia A. Rouss. *Sammy Spider's First Hanukkah.* A spider surreptitiously watches the Shapiro family celebrate Hanukkah and finally fulfills his wish to participate in the celebration.

Leslie Kimmelman. *Hanukkah Lights, Hanukkah Nights.* Primary teachers and students will enjoy the sequenced account of the eight special days and nights of Hanukkah.

Donna Bailey. *Where We Live in Israel.* Teachers and students will find this source helpful in providing a general overview of Israel.

CHARACTER TRAITS: Apply the ideas of freedom and responsibility to the characters of these stories.

Note: The authors searched for cultural celebrations in which light represents a central focus. In order to develop the theme, they highlighted major as well as minor celebrations in various racial, ethnic, and religious contexts. The authors feel that children need to understand that various traditions regard some celebrations as more important than others. For example, many people in the Jewish community in America emphasize the importance of Hanukkah to a greater degree than do those in the Jewish community in Israel. The writers urge teachers to make children aware that not all celebrations are equal in importance or celebrated in the same manner around the world. Teachers are therefore critical in helping students learn sensitivity toward others' traditions, celebrations, and beliefs.

1. Read aloud *Hanukkah!, Sammy Spider's First Hanukkah, Hanukkah Lights, Hanukkah Nights,* or *Where We Live in Israel.* Remember to set the stage with appropriate pre-reading activities that capture students' interest. Clarify vocabulary terms necessary for understanding both the text and the celebration. Define clearly a purpose for reading and/or listening.

2. Choose any one or a combination of the four books. Provide background information about the geographic location of Israel and about interesting details such as the people and the flag of Israel. Invite students to make a small Israeli flag and to find out if the colors stand for certain traits. Ask the school media specialist to assist students in finding details so that they may compare and contrast new information to knowledge they already have. **Ask:** Can you think of other examples of flag colors meaning something special to a group of people?

3. Ask Jewish students and their parents or a Jewish community member to compare and contrast items of clothing worn by characters in any of the stories with those worn in their own homes during Hanukkah. **Ask** students to put on their thinking caps: What determines the way we dress? **Hint:** Prompt children into considering many factors such as cultural traditions, geographic location, climate, peers, and income.

4. Ask parents to help by preparing samples of traditional foods served during Hanukkah. Invite students to sample such foods as latkes (potato pancakes). Ask students to compare traditional Jewish foods to foods served in their homes during festivals-of-light celebrations. **Ask:** Why do people link special foods with special celebrations?

5. Show children a picture or a model of a dreidel. Ask boys and girls to shape a dreidel out of clay and compare the shape to a traditional toy, i.e., a top. Talk about how the two toys are alike and different as well as the meaning attached to the symbols on the dreidel. Summarize the story behind the dreidel so that children understand the history behind the toy. **Ask:** Does the story make playing with a dreidel more interesting? more fun?

6. Assist students with applying the formula Who? What? When? Where? Why? and How? to the celebration of Hanukkah. As students answer these questions, write them on the board or on a chart for easy viewing.

7. Discuss with students the idea of freedom. Remind them that freedom does not mean that a person can do anything he or she pleases. Rather, freedom means being responsible for your actions and being careful not to infringe on the rights of others. Freedom means respecting the rights of others as they also respect your rights. Help them apply the concept of freedom to the characters in the stories and the celebration of Hanukkah.

8. Have students design a comfortable home for Sammy Spider. Instruct children to show in the drawing how Sammy feels about the Shapiros and how the Shapiros feel about Sammy. Remind them that they will be asked to explain story clues that lead to certain conclusions about Sammy and the Shapiros. Plan a sharing time, compare the feelings between Sammy and the Shapiros to the feelings between pets and owners in the real world, then post drawings on a yarn web in the corner of the classroom.

9. Encourage children to talk about how a character in a story exhibits one of the character traits (e.g., compassion, respect, or responsibility). Make sure that students respond with a specific example of how the character acts and how the action serves as an example of the trait. Suggest that children make an illustrated booklet showing how one character in the literature or in everyday life exhibits one of the character traits.

EVALUATION:

Determine the level of student understanding by assessing the quality of various creative products and by observing the insight expressed in response to thought-provoking questions. Ask students to explain what they have learned and to write several words that mean the same as freedom. Encourage students to connect the message in the stories to the theme of festivals of light and celebrations of illumination.

CONNECTION #3:
Tomie de Paola.
The Legend of Old Befana

On the Feast of the Three Kings, January 6, Old Befana visits all the children of Italy, leaves them treats, and continues her search for the Christ child.

Alternate Selection:

Olga Zharkova. *We Three Kings.* Beautiful illustrations bring new meaning to the traditional Christmas song.

CHARACTER TRAITS: These stories emphasize the traits of respect, diligence, and fairness. Be sure to define these words and help students apply them in their daily lives.

1. Read *The Legend of Old Befana* and *We Three Kings* aloud. Remember to set the stage with appropriate pre-reading activities that capture students' interest. For example, invite students to listen to the musical version of *We Three Kings.* Tell students to listen carefully to know what happens in the story. Prompt students with clues if they experience difficulty in understanding the lyrics. Discuss the meaning of light in Christian beliefs. Invite students to share knowledge about the meaning of light in other belief systems. Clarify vocabulary terms necessary for understanding both the text and the celebration. Define clearly a purpose for reading and/or listening.

2. Discuss the meaning of the light in the Old Befana legend. **Ask:** Why is the light important to the story and to Old Befana? Use the discussion to introduce, develop, and/or reinforce children's understanding of a symbol. Allow children to work with partners, to suggest examples of other symbols in their everyday lives, and share these examples with classmates.

3. Talk about the beginning, middle, and end of the Old Befana story. Explain to children different ways to show the beginning, middle, and end of a story, (e.g., booklets folded in thirds, mobiles with three scenes, and scripts of conversations between characters). Allow groups of three children to choose one product option and illustrate the beginning, middle, and end of the Old Befana story. Plan a time for children to share their projects with classmates. **Hint:** Use the activity to teach or reinforce the skill of sequencing.

4. Copy or sketch a map of Italy on an overhead transparency and point out details such as the shape of the country to students. Show students Italy on a large classroom wall map and talk through the meaning of the colors (physical features) on the map. Trace around the sides and sole of Italy's boot in the midst of a large puddle of water, i.e., the Mediterranean Sea. **Ask:** Can you remember any geographic clues about Italy from Old Befana?

5. Ask students to sketch the shape of Italy. Have them invent a new name for boot-shaped Italy and design a flag for the new country. **Ask:** How do creative activities help you learn and remember important ideas?

6. Talk about the meaning of miracles in some people's beliefs. **Ask:** Can you describe a miracle in the Old Befana story? **Hint:** Make distinction between miracles in belief systems and the Old Befana story and "miracles" misnamed, i.e., "It's a miracle that he arrived five minutes early."

7. Select a character trait (e.g., respect, diligence, or fairness) and discuss how a person in the story demonstrates the trait. Ask students to transfer examples in the story to examples in the classroom. **Ask:** How may you exhibit respect, diligence, or fairness in the classroom, on the playground, or at home?

EVALUATION:

Determine the level of student understanding by assessing the quality of creative products and by listening to the insights expressed in response to thought-provoking questions. Ask students to explain what they have learned in this story and give examples of each character trait used in the lessons. Encourage students to connect the message in the story to the theme of festivals of light and celebrations of illumination.

CONNECTION #1:
Eric A. Kimmel.
The Chanukkah Guest

On the first night of Chanukkah, Old Bear wanders into Bubba Brayna's house, mistakes him for a rabbi, and receives a delicious helping of potato latkes.

Alternate Selections:

Fran Manushkin. *Latkes and Applesauce: A Hanukkah Story*. When a blizzard leaves a family housebound during Hanukkah, they share what little food they have with some starving animals. These creatures later return the favor.

Bobbi Katz. *A Family Hanukkah*. Rachel and Jonathan join their aunts, uncles, and cousins at their grandparents' house for a traditional celebration of Hanukkah.

CHARACTER TRAITS: Discuss the meaning of compassion and courage. Ask students to give examples of people displaying these traits.

1. Read *Latkes and Applesauce: A Hanukkah Story* aloud. Remember to set the stage with appropriate pre-reading activities that capture students' interest. Clarify vocabulary terms necessary for understanding both the text and the celebration. Define clearly a purpose for reading and/or listening.

2. Instruct students on how to make a dreidel, i.e., a square top with a Hebrew letter on each side that translates to "a great miracle happened there" (Jerusalem). Talk about the historical origins of the dreidel. Encourage students to play the dreidel game by using nuts or raisins according to the directions in the back of *Latkes and Applesauce*. Invite students to participate in a dreidel tournament. At the conclusion of the game, ask students why playing games are important to both adults and children. **Ask:** What purpose other than fun does game playing fulfill?

3. Gather ingredients for latkes and make the potato treat. Follow the directions in the back of *Latkes and Applesauce*. As a substitute, buy Tater Tots with onions. Allow students to sample the latkes and suggest cultural recipes with which they are familiar. Talk about students' favorite potato recipes. **Ask:** What ingredients and processes do all recipes have in common?

    Traditionally, Jewish families make latkes during the Festivals of Light celebration. Ask students to think of celebrations of light in their belief systems and name specific foods that are characteristic of the celebration. **Ask:** What are examples of traditional foods during Christmas and Kwanzaa?

    Organize a cultural tasting day for which students and parents volunteer to bring traditional recipes for sampling. Talk about why celebrations and foods go hand-in-hand. (Alternate Activity, Parental Discretion)

4. Explain to children that a lively dance, the hora, reflects traditional Jewish culture. Play music such as "Hava Negillah" and form a circle with the children by holding hands. Model the moves and allow children to practice: raise both hands above the head, hop and kick to the left, and then hop and kick to the right while keeping time with the music. If desired, extend the activity by making costumes and by adding musical instruments. Talk to students about what kind of mood the dance creates and check out their answers by researching the history of the hora. (Alternate Activity)

5. Read *Potato Pancakes All Around: A Hanukkah Tale*, by Marilyn Hirsh. With student help, draw a Venn diagram to compare and contrast this simple Hanukkah folktale with one of the stone soup stories. **Ask:** What common elements appear in both folktales? Might these elements be in other folktales? **Ask:** Can you think of other folktales in which these common elements are present?

6. Display a menorah. Explain to students the meaning attached to the menorah. Suggest that students work in small groups to make a menorah. Keep the menorahs until the culmination of the Festivals of Light unit in order to compare different ways of depicting the symbol of light. (Alternate Activity)

7. Invite a person of the Jewish faith to visit the classroom to share traditions and customs. Talk to children about what they especially want to ask the visitor. Send the invited guest a list of high-interest topics in advance of the visit. Ask the guest to phrase information in language appropriate for primary students and allow time for questions from students.

8. Invite a person of the Jehovah Witness faith to visit the classroom and explain why most followers of this faith do not celebrate special holidays. Prepare for the visit in the same manner as for the Jewish visitor. Explain to students that knowledge about beliefs similar to and different from their own increases their understanding about other people. **Hint:** Understanding leads to respect and acceptance.

9. Show students how to create an accordion book in which they write and illustrate four facts about the Jewish celebration of Hanukkah. Invite children to sit in a circle and "play" accordions by sharing information. Talk about why some facts children choose are different from those other children choose and why some facts are similar, i.e., interest level, experience level.

10. Discuss the compassion and courage that characters demonstrate in *Latkes and Applesauce*. Invite students to share specific examples from the story and tell why they link the act to the trait. **Ask:** How can you demonstrate these traits at school, in the neighborhood, or at home?

EVALUATION:

Determine the level of student understanding of Hanukkah traditions by observing students' presentations, by listening to their comments related to various activities, and by assessing the connections they make between abstract character traits and real-world examples. Ask students to explain what they learned from the story. Encourage students to connect the message in the story to the theme of festivals of light and celebrations of illumination.

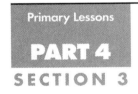

CONNECTION #2:
Marie Hall Ets and Aurora Labastida. Nine Days to Christmas: A Story of Mexico

The time for five-year-old Ceci to participate in her own posada and to choose a special piñata finally arrives. Ceci, however, appears reluctant to break the piñata.

CHARACTER TRAIT: Discuss the character trait of courage and ask if anyone in the class knows a courageous person. Have them explain why they think that person is courageous.

1. Read *Nine Days to Christmas* aloud. Remember to set the stage with appropriate pre-reading activities that capture students' interest. Clarify vocabulary terms necessary for understanding both the text and the celebration. Define clearly a purpose for reading and/or listening.

2. Ask students to role-play a posada. Enlist the participation of other classrooms in a door-to-door reenactment of the first Christmas as celebrated by members of the Mexican culture. Engage students in a conversation about important cultural clues the posada experience reveals. **Ask:** What must be important to members of the Mexican culture about celebrating Christmas? (Alternate Activity)

3. Make a class piñata in the shape of a star. Use papier-mâché, balloons, and tissue paper. Emphasize the use of geometric shapes, cones, and circles. Ask children to bring fruit, nuts, and wrapped candy to stuff the piñata. Have students write how-to paragraphs explaining the sequence of steps in making a piñata. As a class, reinforce the process by composing a sequence of steps. When disagreements over the sequence of steps occur, ask students to listen to other children's explanations, then respectfully disagree and state why. Allow class members to talk about logical answers and choose the best sequence of steps.

3. Show students how to make lanterns to carry in the posada. For a variation, use flashlights wrapped in construction paper with a hole punched for the light. Keep these lanterns until the culmination of the Festivals of Light unit when students will compare different ways of using light. (Alternate Activity, Parental Discretion)

4. Suggest that students write an illustrated newspaper article that describes events in La Posada by using the reporter's formula: Who? What? Where? When? Why? and How? Place a newspaper headline in large letters on the bulletin board, then ask students to read aloud and file their copy on the board. Conduct a student evaluation of newspaper copy by asking students to listen for answers to the reporter's formula and to watch for high-interest items to attract readers. Enlist students in the processes of nominating and voting on the three best articles measured by the criteria. The teacher should recognize students for excellent writing skills and creative theme development.

5. Examine the courage Ceci displays as she allows her piñata to be broken for the celebration, i.e., she allowed an act for the benefit of all rather than an act for the benefit of herself. Ask students to think about the time they spend at school and when they make decisions for the benefit of all students rather than for themselves. Encourage students to volunteer examples of courage from their own lives.

Hint: For interest and variety, alternate discussions on character traits between the benefits of possessing the traits and the consequences of not possessing the traits.

EVALUATION:

Determine the level of student understanding of La Posada by observing students' participation in a simulated posada, by evaluating the quality of artistic and written products, and by assessing the connections between the abstract character trait of courage and students' real-world experiences. Ask students to explain what they learned from this lesson and activities. Encourage students to connect the message in the story to the theme of festivals of light and celebrations of illumination.

CONNECTION #3:
Louise Borden.
Just in Time for Christmas

A young boy living in rural Kentucky looks forward to the annual Christmas festivities, especially the family's traditional candy making. When his favorite dog disappears, however, he realizes the deeper meaning of tradition and family.

CHARACTER TRAIT: Discuss the character trait of compassion and why it is important.

1. Read *Just in Time for Christmas* aloud. Remember to set the stage with appropriate pre-reading activities that capture students' interest. Clarify vocabulary terms necessary for understanding both the text and the celebration. Define clearly a purpose for reading and/or listening.

2. Discuss traditions the Bryan family follows in the story. Ask students to compare and contrast their family traditions to those of the Bryan family. Encourage students to think of reasons why both similarities and differences among family traditions exist.

Hint: Lead students to the understanding that multiple factors such as time periods, geographic areas, rural versus urban environments, and belief systems affect the way that families celebrate holidays and perpetuate traditions. Mention to students that multiple factors usually affect the outcome of any historical issue. Phrase examples in terms appropriate for primary students and invite students to illustrate the generalization about historical issues with other examples from the real world.

3. Engage students in prewriting activities about writing letters to a specific audience and for a specific purpose. Encourage students to write letters to senior citizens in retirement and/or nursing homes. Model for students how to ask senior citizens to share a tradition from their family celebrations and to mail a written response to the student in care of the school. Plan a special sharing time for responses from senior citizens. Use the information about traditions from *Just in Time for Christmas*, from senior citizens, and from student responses to draw conclusions about traditions.

4. Bring taffy or other candy recipes from home to compare ingredients and measurements. Use these recipes to create a class recipe book. Make taffy in the classroom and host a taffy-tasting, taffy-pulling party. While students taste taffy samples, encourage them to informally share what they learned about the family tradition of candy making.

SALT WATER TAFFY

l cup sugar	2/3 cup water	1 tablespoon cornstarch
2 tablespoons butter **or** margarine	1 teaspoon salt	2 teaspoons vanilla
3/4 cup light corn syrup		

Directions:
Butter square pan, 8" x 8" x 2". In a two-quart saucepan, combine sugar, corn syrup, water, cornstarch, butter, and salt. Cook over medium heat and stir constantly to 256 degrees on candy thermometer (or until small amount of mixture dropped into very cold water forms a hard ball). Remove from heat. Stir in vanilla. Pour into pan. When cool enough to handle, pull taffy until satiny, light in color, and stiff. If taffy becomes sticky, butter hands lightly. Pull into long strips 1/2" wide. With scissors, cut strips into 1" pieces. Wrap pieces individually in plastic wrap or waxed paper. Candy must be wrapped to hold its shape. Recipe makes one pound.

5. Research, then tell the story of St. Lucia to students. On a wall map, mark geographic locations such as Sicily and Scandinavia with miniature paper crowns. Create the "long-ago-and-far-away" setting of the story as a time of conflict between Christians and Romans. Tell students about the meaning of the advent crown and show students how to construct one similar to the one worn by St. Lucia.

   Hint: Keep crowns until the culmination of the Festivals of Light unit. (Alternate Activity)

6. Explore the compassion characters demonstrate in *Just in Time for Christmas*. Review their concern for one another and for the lost dog. Encourage children to talk about similar situations in their own families. Discuss the idea that crises often bond family members closer than day-to-day, uneventful experiences.

EVALUATION:

Determine the level of student understanding of family traditions by observing their participation in research activities focusing on similarities and differences among families and by assessing the connections they make between abstract concepts and concrete examples from their own experiences. Encourage students to connect the message in the story to the theme of festivals of light and celebrations of illumination.

Primary Lessons

PART 4
SECTION 3

CONNECTION #4:
Andrea Davis Pinkney.
Seven Candles for Kwanzaa

A young girl describes how her family celebrates the special traditions associated with Kwanzaa.

Note: The authors placed Kwanzaa in both the harvest section and the festivals of light section of the unit. Kwanzaa, patterned after African harvest festivals, now celebrates pride in African-American heritage by lighting a symbolic candle on each of seven successive nights.

CHARACTER TRAITS: Compare and contrast the character traits used in this manual to the seven principles of Kwanzaa

1. Read *Seven Candles for Kwanzaa* aloud. Remember to set the stage with appropriate pre-reading activities that capture students' interest. Clarify vocabulary terms necessary for understanding both the text and the celebration. Define clearly a purpose for reading and/or listening.

2. Discuss general reasons for holidays. Explain to students that Kwanzaa, a Swahili word meaning first fruit of harvest, began as a celebration of harvest. Assist students in recalling other holidays based on harvest such as Thanksgiving. **Hint:** Over time, the rituals and complexities associated with Kwanzaa increased to the degree that many authorities classify this celebration as one of light rather than one of harvest. **Ask:** Why do celebrations change over time?

3. Explore traditions by talking about and perhaps by tasting different foods associated with cultural celebrations. Chart foods mentioned in *Seven Candles for Kwanzaa* and holiday foods served during other Festivals of Light celebrations (e.g., Christmas, Hanukkah).

4. Play a "just suppose" game with children in which they create a special national holiday to honor foods that they enjoy,(e.g., pizza, chicken nuggets, nachos). Ask small groups to select a food, develop a holiday name, adopt colors, select songs, and create traditions to pass on to future generations. Have students explain the skills they used to organize a new national holiday. **Ask:** Are these skills that will transfer to other tasks in the future? Why? (Alternate Activity, Parental Discretion)

5. Review the practice of gift giving during various festivals of light. Talk about the type of gifts that students might make in the classroom in honor of the Kwanzaa celebration. Instruct students how to make gifts from art materials, recycled materials, and materials brought from home. Ask students to distribute Kwanzaa gifts to a special friend or family member. Discuss the gift-giving experience from the standpoint of how receiving an unexpected gift from a friend or family member makes you feel. **Ask:** Do gifts always need to be in a concrete form that you can taste, touch, or smell? Why or why not?

6. Read aloud various African folktales. Talk to students about common story elements (e.g., characters, settings, problems, and solutions). In small groups, encourage students to write folktales they pattern after those read in the classroom and act out their tale for classmates. **Hint:** This activity presents an excellent opportunity to illustrate commonalities that exist among folktales from cultures around the globe.

7. Show children how to make a kinara (candleholder) with colored candles out of egg cartons, tissue rolls, and construction paper. Discuss with children the meaning of the colors. Encourage children to investigate additional symbols of Kwanzaa and relate them to symbols used in other festivals of light. Encourage primary students to put on their thinking caps. **Ask:** Why are symbols important in celebrations and holidays? (Alternate Activity, Parental Discretion)

8. Lead students through an examination of the seven principles of Kwanzaa (The Nguzo Saba), one each day. Talk with students about the meaning of each principle, provide examples of each principle, and encourage students to compare the principles to the list of character traits used in this manual. Encourage students to practice the sounds and rhythms of Kiswahili words.

THE SEVEN PRINCIPLES OF KWANZAA

Day 1: *Umoja* - Unity

Day 2: *Kujichagulia* - Self-determination

Day 3: *Ujima* - Collective Work and Responsibility

Day 4: *Ujamaa* - Cooperative Economics

Day 5: *Nia* - Purpose

Day 6: *Kuumba* - Creativity

Day 7: *Imani* - Faith

Ask: Why is it important for celebrations to have guiding principles? Why is it important for individuals to have guiding principles?

9. Provide a day of projects designed to teach more about African culture. Allow students to choose one of these projects and share their learning with other groups:

(1) Weave a place mat by using strips of red, green, and black construction paper and tell classmates the meaning of each color;

(2) Listen to African music, then compare and contrast African rhythm to American rock 'n roll rhythm and demonstrate the differences to classmates; or

(3) Draw a pattern of a kinara and write a fact learned about Kwanzaa on each candle. Report your information to classmates in news-flash fashion.

10. Use the photographs in *Celebrating Kwanzaa* by Diane Hoyt-Goldsmith that show Americans of African ancestry practicing the rituals of Kwanzaa. Invite children to take a photo journey through seven days and nights of Kwanzaa. Prompt students that every time they see or hear a practice similar to one they know to raise their hands and share their insights with classmates. **Ask:** Why do many similarities exist among celebrations of different racial, ethnic, and religious groups?

EVALUATION:

Determine the level of student understanding by assessing comparisons and contrasts among Kwanzaa, Hanukkah, and Christmas and by observing participation in activities designed to extend knowledge about African culture. Ask students to explain what they have learned from these stories and lessons. Encourage students to connect the message in the story to the theme of festivals of light and celebrations of illumination.

Primary Lessons

5

New Year:
Celebrations
of Optimism
and Hope

CONNECTION # 1:
Helen Lester. *Tacky the Penguin*

The author illuminates startling differences between Tacky and his penguin friends. Tacky's differences, however, become blessings in disguise for his companions.

CHARACTER TRAITS: Review the meaning of compassion, courage, and integrity.

1. Read *Tacky the Penguin* aloud. Remember to set the stage with appropriate pre-reading activities that capture students' interest. Clarify vocabulary terms necessary for understanding both the text and the celebration. Define clearly a purpose for reading and/or listening. Use a Venn diagram technique to give ways that Tacky and his companions are similar or different. Instead of the traditional circle, draw two overlapping penguins to chart similarities and differences. Place the outline of penguins on butcher paper to make the responses visible.

2. Invite students to sit in a circle on the floor. Take tangible objects such as a soccer ball and a basketball and talk about the likenesses and differences between the two. Compile a list on the chart tablet of likenesses and of differences. Point out which list is longer, likenesses or differences, and tell students that they will use this information throughout the activity. **Hint:** The list of likenesses will be longer.

3. Continue the game by using students' characteristics instead of balls. Play the game "I'm Like You, I'm Not Like You." **Hint:** Ask students to put their names on an index card and turn the card face down inside the circle. Show students that they can hit one index card each time they throw a beanbag. Turn the card over and read the name. Ask the beanbag thrower to state one way that he or she is like the person and one way that he or she is different. Proceed until all children have at least one opportunity to participate.

4. Ask students to select one of the penguins in the story; to choose their favorite medium (e.g., paints, markers, crayons) to draw the penguin, label the penguin with a name, and then place drawings around the outline of the penguin diagram. Invite students to write a descriptive sentence about their penguin, i.e., "My friend can't fly, loves water, walks on webbed feet, and waves flipper-like wings." Encourage students to share sentences with classmates, then tell why they chose a particular bird.

5. Reread the story and ask students to imitate the actions of their bird as the teacher reads the story.

6. Review the meaning of compassion, courage, and integrity. Pick indicators that clearly relate to Tacky's behavior. These may include "show that you care about others." Talk about Tacky's acts and ask the students to show how Tacky's acts are true blessings for his friends.

EVALUATION:

Determine the level of student understanding by observing how students differentiate between likenesses and differences; by watching their participation in the game as well as their sensitivity toward others; by assessing their drawings, sentences, and reasons for choosing a particular penguin; and by seeing how they relate Tacky's behavior to selected character traits. Encourage students to connect the message in the story to the theme of the New Year and celebrations of optimism and hope.

CONNECTION #2:
Frank Modell. Goodbye Old Year, Hello New Year

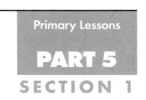

Retiring the old year and ringing in the New Year give cause for celebration to these party planners, a delightful group of happy children.

CHARACTER TRAITS: Talk about the meaning of citizenship.

1. Talk about the concept of a new year. Explain the differences among the calendar year, the school year, and the new year. Ask children what they already know about ways families and friends' families "ring in the new year."

2. Read *Goodbye Old Year, Hello New Year* aloud. Remember to set the stage with appropriate pre-reading activities that capture students' interest. Clarify vocabulary terms necessary for understanding both the text and the celebration. Define clearly a purpose for reading and/or listening.

3. Compare and contrast the events in the story to student experiences. Make two lists: story events, home events. Record the events under the appropriate heading as students volunteer information. Talk about similarities and differences on the lists.

4. Plan a New Year's celebration parade after the winter holiday break. Choose a day with good weather and involve school administrators in the parade. Decorate the classroom with student-made items such as bells for ringing in the New Year. Construct colorful noisemakers and share with students that people around the globe often use objects that make noise as a way of celebrating a special event. Consult reference sources in the library, and then research other cultural celebrations of a new year. Tell students about these practices as they are preparing for the parade. (Alternate Activity)

Examples of noisemakers and decorations: sticks to beat, horns to blow, hats to wear, balloons to carry, pots and tambourines to strike. **Hint:** Make noisemakers from toilet tissue rolls, brightly colored tissue paper, beans, rice, or rocks. Wrap the roll with tissue paper, fill the inside with noise-makers, fasten ends with rubber bands or paper-covered wire twists, and glue stickers and stars on the covers. Use paper plates for making tambourines: decorate sides of two paper plates and staple three-quarters around the two plates. Fill with noisemakers and finish stapling to close the edges. Students should practice shaking the noisemakers and clapping the tambourines. Remind students that noisemaking is a common celebratory behavior associated with some holidays.

5. Point out ways students can practice good citizenship at school. One way is participating enthusiastically in activities. Talk also about the meaning of respect. Remind children that their merrymaking must be on the playground so that the activity will not disturb others. Use the example as one of being considerate of people's rights.

Hint: For interest and variety, alternate discussions on character traits between the presence and benefits of possessing the traits and the absence and consequences of not possessing the traits.

EVALUATION:

Determine the level of student understanding by listening to students talk about the different uses of the term, year; by observing how they discriminate between story events and home events; by noting how they respond to preparations for a parade; and by assessing how they link classroom activities and behaviors to character traits. Ask students to explain what they learned from this story and about practicing good citizenship. Encourage students to connect the message in the story to the theme of the New Year and celebrations of optimism and hope.

CONNECTION #3:
Marcus Pfister.
The Rainbow Fish

Rainbow Fish discovers that sharing with less endowed fish friends improves the quality of life for all.

CHARACTER TRAITS: Discuss the meaning of compassion and respect.

1. Read *The Rainbow Fish* aloud. Remember to set the stage with appropriate pre-reading activities that capture students' interest. Clarify vocabulary terms necessary for understanding both the text and the celebration. Define clearly a purpose for reading and/or listening. Discuss what happens in the story. Ask students how they feel about Rainbow Fish's behavior. Make sure that children understand that Rainbow Fish not only makes a resolution to change behavior but also gives up extraordinary beauty in exchange for friends.

2. Talk about the custom of making resolutions or turning over a new leaf at the beginning of a new year. Ask children why they think people try to make changes for the better at the beginning of the year. **Hint:** Develop the idea that the New Year represents an opportunity for a fresh start and that people continue to make statements that they will do better (e.g., read more, work harder, relax more, develop a hobby, be kinder to the less fortunate, and lose weight). Encourage students to discuss what they would put on a list of New Year's resolutions.

3. Prepare before class a model of a large fish similar to the one on the storybook's cover and hang it in a prominent place in the classroom. Make the fish large enough to tape scales of iridescent sequins or shiny wrapping paper to the fish frame. **Hint:** Children will remove sequin scales of the Rainbow Fish in a later activity.

   Hint: Remember to tape one more sequin or shiny scale than the number of children so that Rainbow Fish will have one scale left. **Caution:** Remember that using heavy aluminum foil paper for shiny fish scales often results in cut fingers.

4. Make a 9" x 12" fish pattern for students to trace on construction paper. Encourage children to decorate their fish with beautiful colors and swirls like scales. Ask students upon completion of their projects to come to the Rainbow Fish display and ask politely if they may each have one shiny scale. Remind them that since Rainbow Fish lives up to his resolution to change, they probably will receive one shiny scale to add to their own fish.

5. Ask students to write about or dictate one thing that they can share with someone else. **Examples:** a favorite eraser, a story about their pet, a frequent smile. Invite students to sit in a circle and share their drawings and their writings with other classmates. Make sure that students recognize that Rainbow Fish's changed behavior results in a happy ending to the story.

6. Use Rainbow Fish as an example of compassion and respect. **Ask:** What does he learn when he starts to show kindness to others? What changes occur when he starts to consider fish other than himself? Are the same type of changes predictable if students show consideration for others? If everyone works together and shares with one another each day, what will be the result?

EVALUATION:

Determine the level of student understanding by listening to children's discussion about New Year's resolutions and what they will put on personal resolution lists; by noting children's interpretations of Rainbow Fish's actions; by observing children's drawing of, writing about, and sharing of their own special fish; by listening to their requests for one shiny scale from Rainbow Fish; and by assessing how boys and girls link Rainbow Fish's compassion and respect to their own behavior in the classroom. Encourage students to connect the message in the story to the theme of the New Year and celebrations of optimism and hope.

CONNECTION #1:
Jama Kim Rattigan.
Dumpling Soup

Marisa, a young girl, helps her Grandma make dumplings for the family's annual New Year's gathering.

CHARACTER TRAIT: Select the character trait of compassion and stress its importance for understanding this story.

1. Read *Dumpling Soup* aloud. Remember to set the stage with appropriate pre-reading activities that capture students' interest. Talk about how students' families celebrate the New Year. Ask students to illustrate their family's annual celebration, then tape pictures together to form a class mural.

Also talk about the geographic location of Hawaii, the residence of the relatives in the story and assist students in marking the map with a sticker or pushpin as evidence of one more world location children learn through literature. Clarify vocabulary terms necessary for understanding both the text and the celebration. Define clearly a purpose for reading and/or listening.

2. Help students write New Year's resolutions about what they can do to help their families. Encourage children to think through resolutions carefully and to plan ways to keep their resolutions. Invite boys and girls into a "good intentions" circle, request that they share their resolutions with classmates, and explain how they will turn good intentions into positive actions. **Ask:** Does sharing with others cause you to try harder to live up to your resolutions?

3. Bring canned biscuits to school and let children make dumplings in soup or broth. Talk about traditional New Year's Eve foods, list foods on the chalkboard, ask students to raise their hands if the food is a family favorite, and record the number of votes by each food. Have students study the chart and look for the most popular New Year's Eve foods that were mentioned. **Hint:** Make the point that food plays an important role in family traditions and celebrations.

4. Discuss games students play with their families, cousins, and other relatives during family gatherings. Talk about the game children play in the story. Remind children of ways that families work together as well as play together. Choose one game (let students vote on it.). Divide the class into small groups of three and ask each group to write the rules for this game. Let each group read their set of rules and make a composite set on the board. Discuss with them the concept of first, second, third, etc. when writing rules for a game. This will teach them to sequence more efficiently.

5. Invite students to share information about family trips to visit relatives for a celebration or for a reunion. Discuss who travels out of the community or state or out of the United States to see family members. List destinations and distances on the chalkboard. Assist students in taping yarn lines marking trips from their community to various destinations. **Ask:** What do the yarn lines tell us about families and about where family members live? What factors make family gatherings possible on special occasions?

6. Encourage students to tell how Marisa exemplifies compassion. Students may use either the illustrations or the story as evidence. Suggest that students think about their own lives and share examples that illustrate compassion, i.e., empathy for the feelings of others, care of self and others.

EVALUATION:

Determine the level of student understanding by studying the quality of creative projects and by listening to the insight expressed in responses and in comments. Ask students to tell what they have learned. Have them give examples of compassion to check their understanding. Encourage students to connect the message in the story to the theme of the New Year and celebrations of optimism and hope.

CONNECTION #2:
Kate Waters and Madeline Slovenz-Low. *Lion Dancer: Ernie Wan's Chinese New Year*

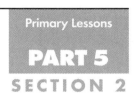

The ancient celebration of Chinese New Year unfolds through the adventures of one resourceful Chinese boy.

CHARACTER TRAIT: Select the character trait of diligence. Explain to students that Ernie learns to read and write Chinese at a special school and later learns Kung Fu at his father's school. Ask students how Ernie models diligence by studying his culture at different schools.

1. Read *Lion Dancer: Ernie Wan's Chinese New Year* aloud. Remember to set the stage with appropriate pre-reading activities that capture students' interest. Clarify vocabulary terms necessary for understanding both the text and the celebration. Define clearly a purpose for reading and/or listening.

Point out the emotions Ernie feels as he waits to perform his Lion Dance. Ask students to share experiences and/or situations in which they felt like Ernie. Talk about Ernie and the story of the most important day in his life. Ask students why this day is special for Ernie. Suggest that students write about and illustrate the most important day in their lives, assist the teacher in binding a class book of most-important-day stories, and display the book in a prominent place in the classroom.

2. Discuss the importance of family honor in Chinese culture. Talk about how Ernie brings honor to his family (e.g., by doing the Lion Dance well). Tear off a long sheet of butcher paper for a class mural, and then assign each student a space on the mural. Suggest that students draw themselves performing deeds that bring honor to their families and tell the story of their act to classmates. If students prefer to make clay figures for a diorama of good deeds, they may choose this option.

Ask: How does the performance of good deeds make you feel? How do families show pride in the accomplishments or deeds of a family member?

3. Students will examine the picture of the lion head Ernie used for his dance. Discuss specific features. Divide the class into four groups. Distribute cardboard boxes, markers, glue, and collage materials (e.g., glitter, egg cartons, pieces of fabric, construction paper). Ask groups to design a lion head. Encourage creativity in all groups. After each group completes the project, attach a long piece of cloth or a sheet to the head. Invite students to follow Ernie Wan's example and perform a lion dance. **Hint:** Make sure that each child gets a chance to wear the lion head. **Ask:** How do creative activities such as making a lion head and dancing help you understand cultural practices?

4. Discuss how students and their families celebrate the New Year. Share with students the Chinese tradition of giving and receiving red envelopes filled with money during this celebration. Explain to students that the Chinese call these special envelopes Lai See. The envelopes carry good wishes. Show students how to make Lai See. Give students a 6" square of red construction paper. Encourage them to write a good luck wish in the middle of the square. Show students how to fold up the corners of the squares to the center. Have them place gold stickers in the center to secure the corners and seal the message. Suggest that students decorate the envelopes. Collect all envelopes and distribute them randomly. Let them open the envelopes and read their good luck wishes to classmates. **Ask:** How does the Chinese custom of Lai See make you feel? Why?

5. Focus on the character trait of diligence. Give students an opportunity to identify with Ernie's actions by trying to learn some Chinese words or sayings. Make two headings on large chart tablet and label them:

ENGLISH	CHINESE
How are you?	*Ni hao* (nee.how)
Good-bye	*Sai jian* (sai.jien)
Thank you	*Xie Xie* (shei.shei)
Please	*Qing* (cheeng)

Also encourage students to practice Chinese writing. Give them sheets of drawing paper, black paint, and paintbrushes. Model strokes on an easel or chart for the numbers 1-10. Ask students to write the numbers 1-10. Talk about the major differences between writing in English and writing in Chinese. **Ask:** What does speaking and writing in Chinese teach you about diligence?

EVALUATION:

Determine the level of student understanding by observing students working in cooperative groups, by assessing various creative projects, and by listening to responses to thought questions. Ask students to explain what they have learned from the story and activities. Encourage students to connect the message in the story to the theme of New Year, celebrations of optimism and hope.

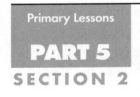

Primary Lessons

PART 5
SECTION 2

CONNECTION #3:
Diane Hoyt-Goldsmith.
Hoang Anh:
A Vietnamese-American Boy

A Vietnamese-American boy describes daily activities including traditional culture and customs like TET, the Vietnamese New Year.

CHARACTER TRAITS: Select the character traits of citizenship and courage as the major character focus of this lesson.

1. Read *Hoang Anh: A Vietnamese-American Boy* aloud. Remember to set the stage with appropriate pre-reading activities that capture students' interest. Clarify vocabulary terms necessary for understanding both the text and the celebration. Define clearly a purpose for reading and/or listening.

2. Ask students to compare/contrast their New Year's celebration to Hoang Anh's New Year's celebration. Chart similarities of and differences between the two celebrations on a Venn diagram. **Ask:** How does charting information in visual form help you learn and remember important information?

3. Tell students that the Vietnamese think of TET as a new beginning. Explain the word, resolution, and ask students to write one New Year's resolution to begin the New Year. Display the resolutions on a bulletin board entitled "A New Beginning." **Ask:** Do writing and posting resolutions make you more likely to keep them than keeping the resolutions secret? Why?

4. Share with children that during the Vietnamese TET celebration relatives come from far away to spend time with family members. Invite students to remember times when relatives came to visit them. Talk about students' favorite times that relatives visited their families and why these times are special memories. List responses and lead students into drawing conclusions about relatives, travel, and special times. **Ask:** Why do family members travel long distances to spend a short time together?

5. Read the legend in the story that explains why Vietnamese eat rice cakes during the New Year. Invite students to compare the Vietnamese legend with an American legend such as Pecos Bill and/or Paul Bunyan. **Ask:** What are similarities of and differences between the Vietnamese and American legends? Invite students to celebrate their good thinking Vietnamese-style by eating rice cakes.

6. Tell students that the Vietnamese celebrate TET by wearing their best clothes. Ask students to think of a time when someone asked them to wear their best clothes. Give children an opportunity to make paper dolls and dress them. Distribute materials (e.g., wallpaper scraps, fabric scraps, lace scraps, construction paper, wrapping paper) to make best clothes for their paper dolls. Encourage students to dress their dolls in fancy clothes. Ask students to write to the prompt, "For this special occasion, I got dressed up...." Display dressed-up paper dolls with students' writing samples around the room.

7. Tell students that relatives and friends often exchange gifts during TET. Enlist the help of children in making a list of times people exchange gifts in the United States. Review the Chinese custom of giving red envelopes to special people mentioned on page 109. Ask student partners to create a surprise to send a friend that will bring as much pleasure as the red envelopes. **Ask:** Is your surprise gift similar to the red envelopes? How and why? Why is the custom of red envelopes an example of compassion?

8. Select the character traits of citizenship and courage. Ask students how Hoang Anh and his family display the trait of citizenship and courage. Talk about why Hoang Anh and his family leave family members and flee Vietnam in a flimsy boat.

EVALUATION:

Determine the level of student understanding by observing the quality of responses, by evaluating the creativity in various art projects, and by assessing connections between TET and other New Year's celebrations. Ask students what they have learned from this story and activities. Encourage students to connect the message in the story to the theme of New Year, celebrations of optimism and hope.

CONNECTION #1:
Rachel Sing.
Chinese New Year's Dragon

Something special always happens for the Chinese at the Lunar New Year, and something positively magical happens in this particular year.

CHARACTER TRAIT: Discuss the meaning of responsibility at home and at school.

1. Read *Chinese New Year's Dragon* aloud. Remember to set the stage with appropriate pre-reading activities that capture students' interest. Clarify vocabulary terms necessary for understanding both the text and the celebration. Define clearly a purpose for reading and/or listening.

2. Invite students to trace with their fingers an imaginary line from their school to China and Taiwan, then to Singapore and Hong Kong. Point out the differences in size of the geographic examples. Use the descriptions in the story to enhance the meaning of region, nation, and island. Lead students in a geographic investigation of how to classify the locations of Singapore and Hong Kong. Enlist students in drawing up a set of clues to geographic terms so that they may apply the clues to future studies. **Ask:** How will you know that an area is an island? How can you identify a geographic region?

Hint: Avoid detailed political explanations. Use examples to illustrate these facts: students may classify geographic areas with more than one political or geographic term (e.g., nation and island); students need to look at any topic in several ways (i.e., from multiple perspectives); and students need to recognize that independent people inhabit large as well as small geographic areas.

3. Remind students that the family in *Chinese New Year's Dragon* receives calendars "from faraway places." Assist students in exploring both the data and the symbols on various calendars. Compare and contrast the dates of the Chinese New Year to the traditional American New Year. **Ask:** Why are calendar dates, data, and symbols not the same worldwide?

4. Refer to a Chinese superstition such as not cutting noodles while eating, because long Chinese noodles represent long life. Remind students that the Chinese believe that cut noodles shorten one's luck, destroy a friendship, or reduce one's lifespan. Use Chinese superstitions to lead into a discussion about superstitions in America, i.e., if your hand itches, you will come into money; if your nose itches, you will have company; if you walk under a ladder, you will have bad luck; if a black cat crosses in front of you, you will have bad luck. Ask students to put on their thinking caps. **Ask:** Why do members of any culture develop superstitions?

5. Lead students in making "chunlian" banners. Use red for China and blue for the United States. Ask students to write American New Year's traditions on index cards and tape them to the blue banner. Compare these to Chinese traditions the author describes in *Chinese New Year's Dragon*. Remind students that in the story the teacher and class wrote New Year's traditions on the red banner. Point out the differences between the two celebrations and have students compare and contrast them on a Venn diagram. **Ask:** What factors account for differences between the two celebrations?

Remind students that they learned in a previous lesson that issues in history, also in cultures, usually stem from multiple causes. (Alternate Activity, Parental Discretion)

6. Show students how to make Chinese dragons by using paper plates and tissue paper. Give each child five paper plates to decorate individually and then connect as sections of a dragon. Talk about the color and covering of most dragons pictured in storybooks. Encourage students to share dragon stories written and sequenced from head to tail on the inside of paper plates. Following story time, allow students to march in a parade of dragons around the classroom. (Alternate Activity, Parental Discretion)

7. Remind students that in China the color red represents good fortune and happiness. Tell them that Chinese children receive money in red envelopes for luck in the coming year. Show children how to make good luck envelopes by using square sheets of red paper. Fold and stuff envelopes with play money, then decorate the outside with glitter, sequins, or stickers. Ask children to take the envelopes home to present to a special person and to tell what they know about a Chinese tradition. (Alternate Activity)

8. Ask students to remember that in *Chinese New Year's Dragon*, all family members assume responsibility for a task to ensure that the New Year is "just like any other year." Talk with students about the characters, tasks, and preparations for the New Year in the story. Discuss the meaning of responsibility. **Ask:** How does each character accept responsibility? How does responsible behavior make the tasks of the celebration easier? Invite students to think quietly about the tasks that they need to accomplish at school. **Ask:** What lesson does the story teach about responsibility? How may students transfer the lesson to the classroom, the neighborhood, or the home?

9. Encourage students to choose *one* high-interest activity set up at four classroom centers:

   Paint in calligraphy style with brushes and black ink.
   Make fortune cookies with good wishes, i.e., fortunes or friendship notes enclosed in the cookies.
   Create a new recipe of dried fruits pleasing in taste.
   Cook long Chinese noodles to eat without breaking.

   Permit students to participate in the activity of their choice. Clearly state, however, that each person in the small group assumes responsibility for reporting to the large group what they learn about Chinese culture. **Hint:** This lesson presents an excellent opportunity to teach the difference between rights and responsibilities, i.e., the right to choose an activity, responsibility to report the learning.

EVALUATION:

Determine the level of student understanding by observing their use of map and globe skills, by listening to their explanations related to calendars, by measuring their enthusiasm for art and craft activities, and by assessing their insights about Chinese and American traditions. Encourage students to connect the message in the story to the theme of the New Year and celebrations of optimism and hope.

CONNECTION #2:
Anisha Kacker.
Ravi's Diwali Surprise

Primary Lessons

PART 5

SECTION 3

As preparation for the Diwali celebration begins, sadness overtakes Ravi. She longs to see her brother, a college student away from home.

CHARACTER TRAITS: Discuss the meaning of integrity as it relates to friendship and love for brothers and sisters.

1. Read *Ravi's Diwali Surprise* aloud. Remember to set the stage with appropriate pre-reading activities that capture students' interest. Clarify vocabulary terms necessary for understanding both the text and the celebration. Define clearly a purpose for reading and/or listening.

2. Show students samples of Rangoli patterns used to decorate for Diwali. Share with students some of the practices of the Hindu celebration, i.e., Hindus begin the religious celebration by cleaning house, painting the house, scrubbing tile floors, and decorating floors and doorsteps with Rangoli patterns. Ask students to study the patterns of these designs, list three distinct features of the patterns, and share with partners. **Ask:** What designs appear to be most common in Rangoli designs?

3. Remind students of prior lessons that tie festive celebrations and special foods together. Encourage students to practice saying the words, "gulab jamuns," a special treat Hindus prepare for Diwali. Ask for assistance in mixing cottage cheese, raisins, almonds, and syrup, the ingredients for gulab jamuns that Ravi's mother makes for a Diwali surprise. Refrigerate while students prepare traditional Diwali decorations. (Alternate Activity, Parental Discretion)

4. Model for students how to make Ravi's favorite part of the celebration, the hanging lights. The lights represent the diyas or clay oil lamps from long ago. Suggest that students check the illustrations in *Ravi's Diwali Surprise* and hang the lights in a similar fashion to create a Diwali atmosphere. Ask students to think about the beautiful scene that the diyas create on a dark night. **Hint:** Give students an image of the diyas by dotting glue on black construction paper and sprinkling the glue with glitter.

5. Request that students sit in a circle on the floor under the hanging lights and wait for a student host and hostess to serve gulab jamuns. Ask the music teacher to assist by finding a cassette tape of Indian music to play in the background. **Hint:** Music featuring Indian string instruments, such as the sitar, truly create an Indian ambiance. (Alternate Activity)

6. Extend the Diwali celebration by telling boys and girls about a special ceremony for sisters and brothers in which they pledge to love one another and be good friends. Talk about these tokens of the sister-brother pledges: a sister ties rakhi (bracelets) on her brother's (or father's or special male friend's) wrists, a practice which means she trusts him to protect and look after her; in return, a brother gives his sister flowers, candy, or money.

7. If students wish to make rakhi bracelets to share with a brother, sister, or friend, show them a basic pattern and allow them to be creative with their designs. If some students prefer to write dialogues rather than design bracelets, encourage them to write scripts of what a sister or brother might say to one another during the pledge. Ask students to act out the original scripts. (Alternate Activity, Parental Discretion)

8. Suggest that students make a Diwali card wishing a friend a happy new year. Help students search for designs as authentic to the Hindu religion as possible. Encourage them to seek the legends that accompany many designs and share with classmates. Ask students if they can think of American symbols with matching stories (e.g., cherry tree=George Washington) to tell their classmates. (Alternate Activity)

EVALUATION:

Determine the level of student understanding about a Hindu celebration by observing the quality of various art and craft projects; by noting how quickly they transfer information about Diwali to their general knowledge of celebrations; and by assessing their eagerness to share new information with classmates. Encourage students to connect the message in the story to the theme of the New Year and celebrations of optimism and hope.

CONNECTION #3:
Debra Frasier.
On the Day You Were Born

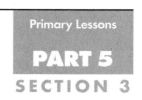

Residents of the entire earth universally celebrate the birth of newborn babies.

CHARACTER TRAITS: Discuss the meaning of respect.

1. Read *On the Day You Were Born* aloud. Remember to set the stage with appropriate pre-reading activities that capture students' interest. Clarify vocabulary terms necessary for understanding both the text and the celebration. Define clearly a purpose for reading and/or listening.

2. Discuss the sequence of events in the natural world that lead up to the child's birth in the story (e.g., migration of animals, moon pulls, rising tides, sun flares, and earth spins). Use examples from the story to introduce, develop, and/or reinforce basic geographic concepts such as revolution, rotation, and movement in primary language. Ask students to verbalize meanings of geographic concepts and support statements with examples from the story.

3. Encourage students to write a paragraph about the day they were born or the day they joined their families. Provide interview questions for students to take home and ask family members. Instruct students to use the answers to compose the paragraphs, then to share the paragraphs with classmates. Give students the following questions but also suggest that they ask other questions that interest them:

> *When and where was I born? OR When and where did I join this family?*
> *What time was I born? OR What time did I join this family?*
> *What did people say when they first saw me? (Stays the same)*
> *What did I wear home? OR What was I wearing when I joined my new family?*
> *How did I get home? OR How did I get to my new family's home?*

Hint: Encourage children to respond to the questions that fit their personal situations. Questions accommodate adopted or foster children who join families as well as children born into families.

4. Build students' interest in making a penny book for which they will collect a penny for each year of their lives. Show students a penny and point out where the year's date is located. Explain that they must enlist parents, grandparents, relatives, and/or adult friends to assist them with special events, e.g., learning to talk, learning to walk, birthday parties, getting a pet, learning new skills. Instruct students to glue one penny on each page, then write about and illustrate events that happened that year.

5. Encourage students to create a collage of the day they arrived on the planet. Point out the unusual illustrations in *On the Day You Were Born* and show students how to cut or tear, not draw, similar figures from brightly colored construction paper and sample wallpaper books. Invite them to post their colorful, simple collages on a bulletin board entitled: "I Have Arrived on Planet Earth!" **Ask** students to put on their thinking caps: Why are the simplest designs the best ones for newborn babies? **Hint:** Newborns, who must learn all of the ways of culture including art forms, must first learn simple ideas and skills, and then proceed to the more complex ones.

6. Show students how to design a personality cube. Encourage students to write, draw, cut out, and glue pictures on the cube that give clues about their personalities. Suggest to students that they include favorite colors, books, sports, heroes, pets, and photographs. Allow time for students to share information on their cubes with small groups. Tell them that the cubes are conversation starters.

Ask students to put on their thinking caps: What factors affect the way students think, the things that students learn, the things that interest students, the way students feel, the friends students seek? **Hint:** Most of the answers will relate to either environment or heredity. Make sure students understand that a person's personality is a composite of multiple influences. Phrase definition and examples in language appropriate for primary students.

7. Read the story *Owen,* by Kevin Henke. Ask if students remember a special blanket or toy when they were babies. Bring items to school for Show and Tell. In advance of this sharing activity, discuss the respect that students should display for other students' public acknowledgement of precious child-hood keepsakes. Make students aware of the importance of being considerate of other people's feelings, rights, and property. **Hint:** For interest and variety, alternate discussions on character traits between the benefits of possessing the traits and the consequences of not possessing the traits.

EVALUATION:

Determine the level of student understanding by assessing their written products, by evaluating their personality cubes and penny books, and by observing their willingness to share personal experiences with others. Encourage students to connect the message in the story to the theme of the New Year and celebrations of optimism and hope.

6

Spring:
Celebrations
of Birth
and Rebirth

CONNECTION #1:
Ruth Krauss. *The Happy Day*

Awakening after a long winter's sleep, hibernating animals discover the sprouting of a new season.

CHARACTER TRAITS: Talk about the meaning of respect.

1. Lead a print walk by encouraging students to read the pictures, not the text, up to the last two pages. During the print walk, discuss how animals live in the winter. Pass out sheets of paper to student partners and ask that they predict what animals see when they open their eyes to spring. Encourage student partners to share their predictions.

2. Read *The Happy Day* aloud. Remember to set the stage with appropriate pre-reading activities that capture students' interest. Clarify vocabulary terms necessary for understanding both the text and the celebration. Define clearly a purpose for reading and/or listening.

3. Compare and contrast what happens in the story to partners' predictions. Discuss the meaning of spring and the visual changes that take place between the seasons of winter and spring.

4. Ask students how animals show respect for one another in the story. Encourage students to respond to this statement:

> DISPLAYING RESPECT TO OTHERS
> REWARDS THE RESPECTFUL PERSON.

5. Remember that celebrations and holidays do not cease when the school year ends. Search for ways to observe cultural and/or national holidays (e.g., Memorial Day, Emancipation Day, Independence Day) that occur during summer months and also to celebrate or honor days of personal accomplishment that occur throughout the year (e.g., new learning, new skills, new roles, new responsibilities). Extend the scope of lessons taught during the school year by using theme-related examples from all twelve months of the year.

EVALUATION:

Determine the level of student understanding by listening to the logic in students' predictions, by observing the degree of accuracy in students' descriptions of spring, and by assessing how students transfer the meaning of respect to their own lives. Ask students to explain what they learned by reading this story. Encourage students to connect the message in the story to the theme of spring and celebrations of birth and rebirth.

CONNECTION #2:
Dom DeLuise.
Charlie the Caterpillar

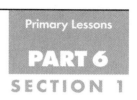

Charlie's story begins with acts of discrimination committed against him, because he is ugly. Charlie, however, emerges as a beautiful creature, and the story ends with a heartwarming example of true friendship.

CHARACTER TRAIT: Discuss the meaning and importance of compassion.

1. Order a butterfly garden from a science materials catalog prior to this activity. Help students keep track of the visual changes occurring in the butterfly cycle. Record changes on a calendar. Have students keep a personal log of changes by writing what they observe each day in their own words. Give students responsibilities for caring for the about-to-be-butterflies.

   Hint: Check directions for care in the kit. For the calendar activity, put changes on post-it notes and attach to squares on the calendar. For personal logs, staple half sheets of paper into booklet form with enough room for a three-week project. Seek good weather conditions for the butterfly garden.

2. Read aloud the story, *Charlie the Caterpillar.* Remember to set the stage with appropriate pre-reading activities that capture students' interest. Clarify vocabulary terms necessary for understanding both the text and the celebration. Define clearly a purpose for reading and/or listening.

3. Discuss the sequence of events in the story. Use student responses to map events on butcher paper. If possible, compare and contrast the observed changes in the butterfly garden to the changes in the story.

4. Pass out finger-paint paper and finger paints. Instruct students to completely cover the surface of the paper with paint. Allow sheets to dry overnight. Show students how to fold sheets in half, how to place the pattern of a large butterfly wing on the fold of the sheet, and then how to trace and cut out wings. Model these steps for students: open up cut wings, pinch in the middle, use an extra long pipe cleaner to wrap around the center of the butterfly, shape ends of pipe cleaner into antennae, spread wings open, and allow butterflies to fly.

5. Talk about the trait of compassion and how Charlie exhibits the trait in spite of being treated in a discriminatory way. Encourage children to respond to how their behavior in the classroom, on the playground, or at home can show that they truly care about the well-being of others.

   Hint: For interest and variety, alternate discussions 'on character traits between the benefits of possessing the traits and the consequences of not possessing the traits.

6. Remember that celebrations and holidays do not cease when the school year ends. Search for ways to observe cultural and/or national holidays (e.g., Memorial Day, Emancipation Day, Independence Day) that occur during summer months and also to celebrate or honor days of personal accomplishment that occur throughout the year (e.g., new learning, new skills, new roles, new responsibilities). Extend the scope of lessons taught during the school year by using theme-related examples from all twelve months of the year.

EVALUATION:

Determine the level of student understanding by watching students' participation in the three-week butterfly garden project, by assessing the quality of their personal logs, by listening to children as they compare and contrast what happens in the butterfly garden to what happens to Charlie, by observing children making their butterflies for display, and by analyzing how they link the trait of compassion to Charlie's and their own behaviors. Encourage students to connect the message in the story to the theme of spring and celebrations of birth and rebirth.

CONNECTION #3:
Mary Q. Steele.
Anna's Garden Songs

By using all or selected poems in Anna's Garden Songs, teachers may easily illustrate the visual emergence of a budding, blossoming season.

CHARACTER TRAITS: Talk about the trait of courage and how important it is to have courage even when we are afraid.

1. Collect pictures of vegetables that show the whole plant. Point out the edible parts of the plant to students. Ask students to bring one sample of a vegetable to class. Invite students to set up a display of samples with name labels. **Hint:** Seek vegetables that are different from the everyday, ordinary kind for the display since students will probably bring the more common varieties. Ask local nurseries and feed stores for seed catalogs. Laminate pictures of vegetables to add to the display.

2. Read poems aloud from *Anna's Garden Songs*. Remember to set the stage with appropriate pre-reading activities that capture students' interest. Clarify vocabulary terms necessary for understanding the poems as well as the celebration. Define clearly a purpose for reading and/or listening.

3. Compare the vegetables in the poems to those in the classroom display. Direct students to choose their favorite vegetable, draw it on an 8" x 10" sheet of paper, and make up whimsical slogans for the pictures either individually or as a class. **Example:** Carrot, Share It!

4. Prepare the sample vegetables for a sampling party. **Hint:** Check with a produce employee at the grocery store to find out which vegetables may be eaten raw. Also check with the nurse on common allergies to certain vegetables.

5. Talk about the trait of courage, especially the indicator of overcoming fear. Tell students that trying samples of unfamiliar vegetables will help them in overcoming the fear of the unknown. **Hint:** Stress that these vegetables are familiar to the teacher and safe to eat. Make certain that students understand that if the vegetables are unfamiliar to an adult that sampling is an unsafe practice. Invite students to participate in the sampling by linking the activity to the trait of courage. Following the strictly voluntary sampling, ask students about their reaction to the unfamiliar and unknown vegetables, then how they feel about their courage to try something new.

Hint: For interest and variety, alternate discussions on character traits between the benefits of possessing the traits and the consequences of not possessing the traits

6. Remember that celebrations and holidays do not cease when the school year ends. Search for ways to observe cultural and/or national holidays (e.g., Memorial Day, Emancipation Day, Independence Day) that occur during summer months and also to celebrate or honor days of personal accomplishment that occur throughout the year (e.g., new learning, new skills, new roles, new responsibilities). Extend the scope of lessons taught during the school year by using theme-related examples from all twelve months of the year.

EVALUATION:

Determine the level of student understanding by assessing their level of interest in the bring-from-home activity and in setting up a classroom display, by observing their creativity in making up whimsical slogans, by watching their willingness to participate in vegetable sampling, and by listening to how they link courage to the sampling activity. Encourage students to connect the message in the story to the theme of spring and celebrations of birth and rebirth.

CONNECTION #1:
Natalie Kinsey-Warnock.
When Spring Comes

In the early 1900s, a child describes seasonal activities that mark the beginning of spring.

ALTERNATE SELECTION:

Lucille Clifton. *The Boy Who Didn't Believe in Spring.* Weary of acquaintances' excitement over spring, King Shabazz and his friend, Tony Polito, set out to find reasons why spring brings joy to hearts as well as minds.

CHARACTER TRAITS: Compassion and respect.

1. Read aloud either story, *When Spring Comes* or *The Boy Who Didn't Believe in Spring.* Remember to set the stage with appropriate pre-reading activities that capture students' interest. Clarify vocabulary terms necessary for understanding both the text and the celebration. Define clearly a purpose for reading and/or listening.

2. Discuss the meaning of compassion and respect with students. Ask for examples that demonstrate understanding of either of these important character traits. Encourage students to find a story character who exemplifies one of the traits. Encourage students to tell who, how, when, and why in their explanations. **Hint:** For interest and variety, alternate discussions on character traits between the benefits of possessing the traits and the consequences of not possessing the traits. Current authorities in character education often refer to the absence of traits as character flaws.

3. Demonstrate for students how to make a diorama of one of the story scenes. Use only natural items for materials. Examples: grass, leaves, twigs, cotton for clouds, pebbles, and a sunflower to represent the sun. Lead children on a science-and-litter walk around the campus so that they may gather natural items for the diorama. Before and during the walk, talk informally about the purpose of recycling items and specifically about how students will use recycled products to construct a diorama. Link the activity to compassion and caring for the environment. **Ask:** What are the consequences to Planet Earth if citizens do not recycle items?

4. Have students make a list of all items they see and find on the walk. Find out which items represent spring to them and why. Lead students in comparing and contrasting their items to spring-type items King Shabazz and Tony Polito find in *The Boy Who Didn't Believe in Spring.* Ask boys and girls to label items on the list as either living (L) or non-living (NL) materials. **Ask:** How many items are living? How many items are non-living? How do labeling and separating, i.e., categorizing, help you learn and remember important ideas?

5. Ask children to put on their detective hats and search the scenes for clues about the time and place of the story. Without any advance discussion about clues, let students observe, ponder, and talk among themselves when they think they spot important details. Show the scenes slowly and remind children that they are trying to identify the when and where of the story. Examples: time of year, style of clothing, town or country, objects in scenes. Ask for volunteers to give clues related to time and place and make sure that students support their ideas with a specific detail from a scene. **Ask:** Could the story happen in your community? Why or why not?

6. Model how to make a pictorial storybook sequenced by events that occur in the story. Use the words: first, next, and last. **Hint:** Fold a piece of paper in halves, then in fourths. After students write and illustrate their books, display student projects in a prominent place in the classroom.

Invite another class to visit, lead student guests on a print walk around the classroom, and encourage authors to tell about their storybooks.

7. Remember that celebrations and holidays do not cease when the school year ends. Search for ways to observe cultural and/or national holidays (e.g., Memorial Day, Emancipation Day, Independence Day) that occur during summer months and also to celebrate or honor days of personal accomplishment that occur throughout the year (e.g., new learning, new skills, new roles, new responsibilities). Extend the scope of lessons taught during the school year by using theme-related examples from all twelve months of the year.

EVALUATION:

Determine the level of student understanding by observing the quality of various creative projects and by listening to the insight in students' responses to thought-provoking questions. Ask students to explain what they have learned from the story and the activities. Encourage students to connect the message in the story to the theme of spring and celebrations of birth and rebirth.

Primary Lessons

PART 6

SECTION 2

CONNECTION #2:
Patricia Polacco.
Rechenka's Eggs

Babushka, an egg painter, rescues an injured goose who inadvertently breaks the painted eggs intended for Easter. The remorseful, resourceful goose lays thirteen colored eggs to replace them, a true miracle in egg form.

Alternate Selection:

Mary Jane Auch. *The Easter Egg Farm.* Pauline's talents rest with her ability to lay unusual eggs. Pauline's profit-minded owner, Mrs. Pennywort, abuses her hen in order to start an Easter-egg farm.

CHARACTER TRAITS: Discuss with students the character traits of responsibility and courage. Encourage students to give examples from the story. Refer to *Rechenka's Eggs*, and discuss ways in which Rechenka demonstrates the two character traits.

1. Read both *Rechenka's Eggs* and *The Easter Egg Farm* aloud. Remember to set the stage with appropriate pre-reading activities that capture students' interest. Clarify vocabulary terms necessary for understanding both the text and the celebration. Define clearly a purpose for reading and/or listening.

2. Put two headings, "Real" and "Make-believe," on a large chart. Read either story again and ask children to retell the story in their own words. As each event in the story occurs, request that children think about the event and determine if it is real or make-believe and why. Have students look for and listen for clues in the story. Invite boys and girls to list events under the more appropriate heading on the chart. Ask students to name the clues that lead them to a decision between real events and make-believe events.

3. Ask students to think about their own classroom and perhaps their own family members. Encourage them to cite examples of how they or their family members demonstrate the traits of responsibility and courage.

4. Model for students how to design a new egg pattern for Pauline. When students complete the original egg patterns, ask them to share what thoughts they think occupied Pauline's mind when she laid the various patterned eggs. **Ask:** What decisions do you make in order to develop new patterns? **Examples:** ideas, how to picture ideas, how many times to repeat patterns, what colors to use.

5. Suggest that students make a list of places where Mrs. Pennywort might store Pauline's unusual eggs to protect them, then ask students to analyze each place in terms of safety. Lead students to consensus on the safest place. **Ask:** Does your choice match the author's script?

6. Talk about why eggs need some form of protection, i.e., protection from weather, people, and animals. Assign student partners the task of creating the best-ever egg protector. After partners complete their design, request that they write a brief how-to description of the design so that other students may follow the directions and produce the same design. **Hint:** Point out to children how important placing directions in sequential order is to good writing as well as to other children's ability to follow directions.

7. Remember that celebrations and holidays do not cease when the school year ends. Search for ways to observe cultural and/or national holidays (e.g., Memorial Day, Emancipation Day, Independence Day) that occur during summer months and also to celebrate or honor days of personal accomplishment that occur throughout the year (e.g., new learning, new skills, new roles, new responsibilities). Extend the scope of lessons taught during the school year by using theme-related examples from all twelve months of the year.

EVALUATION:

Determine the level of student understanding by observing how quickly students demonstrate higher order thinking skills and by assessing how accurately they apply abstract character traits to real-life situations. Ask students to explain what they have learned from the story and activities. Encourage students to connect the message in the story to the theme of spring and celebrations of birth and rebirth.

CONNECTION #3:
Ana Consuelo Matiella.
Mother's Day,
El Día de las Madres

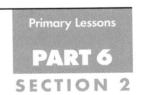

A Mexican-American girl gives her grandmother a very special gift for Mother's Day.

CHARACTER TRAITS: Select the character trait of diligence.

1. Determine what students already know about Mexico and Mexican culture by brainstorming and recording a list on the chalkboard. Invite children to survey items listed and construct a thematic web. Encourage students to suggest categories in which several items on the brainstorming list will fit, then web the category (e.g., geography, clothing, customs, foods, music, and activities).

   Extension: As another pre-reading strategy, show students how to make a piñata. Inflate a balloon and seal the opening. Mix one and one-half cups of flour with the same amount of water in a large bowl to form glue. Cut newspapers into small strips. Soak the strips in glue. Cover the surface of the balloon with layers of overlapping strips of newspaper. Use the strips to form any desired shape. Let the piñata dry for several days. Paint the piñata, let it dry thoroughly, and add banners and other decorations as finishing touches.

2. Read the story, *Mother's Day, El Día de las Madres*. Clarify vocabulary terms necessary for understanding both the text and the celebration. Define clearly a purpose for reading and/or listening. Suggest that students list ways that Sara's family celebrates Mother's Day and compare them to ways their families honor special women such as mothers, stepmothers, grandmothers, aunts, or godmothers.

Hint: Make a greeting card with a special message for the honored person. Encourage students to draw a picture on the front of the card representing what services the person provides for them. Suggest that students might write the card's message in poetry.

3. Discuss the character trait of diligence. Ask students how Sara shows diligence in the story, i.e., she learns to sing in Spanish. Invite students to learn and practice some Spanish words.

Extension: Make two headings on a large piece of chart paper:

ENGLISH	SPANISH
grandmother	*Abuelita*
aunt/uncle	*tía/tío*
Mother's Day	*día de las madres*
come on	*andale*
paper flowers	*flores de papel*
grill	*comal*
fresh	*fresca*
mornings	*mañanitas*
spinning top	*pirinola*

4. Use a wall map of the United States and ask students to find five states, cities, rivers, or mountain ranges with Spanish names. Lead students into drawing conclusions based upon the geographic exercise. **Ask:** Are the locations mainly in one region? If so, what clue does that fact give about the region's history?

5. Brainstorm ways Sara and her grandmother spend time together. Ask students to list things they do with their grandmothers or older adults. Remind students that in the story Sara makes paper flowers with her grandmother.

Extension: Help students make paper flowers. Cut strips of tissue paper 4" wide and 12" long in several different colors. Flower petals of different sizes can be cut from the paper. Wrap the lower ends of petals of each color in layers around a pipe cleaner and glue them. Cut a small hole in the center of a doily, fit several flowers through the hole, and tie them with a ribbon. Put a drop of vanilla in the center of each flower. Invite students to set up a display of bouquets in one corner of the classroom. **Ask:** Why do flower bouquets remind us of special occasions?

6. Tell students that fiestas are a way of life in Mexico. Locate Mexico on a map for students. Talk about the fiesta in the story. **Ask:** Do you know about similar celebrations? How? When? Where?

Gauge students' excitement about a fiesta. If the level of excitement is high, plan a special fiesta for Mother's Day. Help students prepare Mexican dishes for the fiesta such as tortillas, guacamole, chile con queso, and sopapillas. Invite students' mothers to come and eat with their child. Station students at the door to present cards and flowers to visiting mothers. (Alternate Activity, Parental Discretion)

Extension: As an extension, show students how to make fiesta clay figures. Give students modeling clay, toothpicks, and newspaper for materials. Demonstrate for students how to make a ball of clay about 3" in diameter. The clay should be rolled sideways into a cylinder and set upright on the newspaper. Students will make a ball about the size of a walnut for the head. Students will make arms, hat, shoes, and a nose from construction paper. Show students how to use a toothpick to carve details. Create a fiesta scene with clay figures as a classroom exhibit.

7. Share the Spanish words of the song, "Las Mañanitas," with the class so that they can sing along. After students feel comfortable singing the Spanish lyrics, share the English translation.

Discuss with them the purpose of the song. Ask students to identify other songs that compare with "Las Mañanitas." Ask students to listen to a recording of "Las Mañanitas" and share how the music makes them feel with classmates.

LAS MAÑANITAS

Estas son las mañanitas
que cantaba el rey David.
Hoy que es día de tu
te las cantamos así.

We are singing morning songs
as King David used to do.
Since today it is your cumpleaños birthday
we are here to sing them to you.

CORO

Despierta, mi bien, despierta,
mira que ya amaneció,
ya los pajarillos cantan,
la luna ya se metió.

CHORUS

Awaken, my love, awaken,
and see that the day has dawned,
that the little birds are singing
and that the moon is long gone.

Si el sereno de la esquina
me quisiera hacer favor
de apagar su linternita
mientras que pasa mi amor.

If the friendly corner watchman
might consent to be so kind
and put out his hanging lantern
as I watch my love pass by.

Despierta, mi bien...
Ahora sí, señor sereno,
le agradezco su favor,
prenda ya su linternita
que ya ha pasado mie amor.

Awaken, my love...
It's all right now, Mr. Watchman,
thanks a lot for being so nice,
you may now relight your lantern,
my love already passed by.

Despierta, mi bien...

Awaken, my love...

8. Read stories to students about Mexican Americans whose achievements in various fields earn recognition. Choose three facts about each person and then ask students to illustrate the life of one of the spotlighted persons for a class book. Display the completed product in the classroom.

9. Remember that celebrations and holidays do not cease when the school year ends. Search for ways to observe cultural and/or national holidays (e.g., Memorial Day, Emancipation Day, Independence Day) that occur during summer months and also to celebrate or honor days of personal accomplishment that occur throughout the year (e.g., new learning, new skills, new roles, new responsibilities). Extend the scope of lessons taught during the school year by using theme-related examples from all twelve months of the year.

EVALUATION:

Determine the level of student understanding of the country of Mexico and Mexican traditions by observing the quality of various creative products and by assessing the level of enthusiasm toward cooperative projects. Ask students to explain what they have learned from the story, the song, and from the other activities. Encourage students to connect the message in the story to the theme of spring and celebrations of birth and rebirth.,

CONNECTION #1:
Sherry Garland. *The Lotus Seed*

A young Vietnamese girl saves a lotus seed as a reminder of a brave emperor and of her native land. Through the years, the seed becomes a cultural symbol for her as well as a legacy for future generations.

CHARACTER TRAITS: Ask students the meaning of leadership and the character traits of a good leader.

1. Read *The Lotus Seed* aloud. Remember to set the stage with appropriate pre-reading activities that capture students' interest. Clarify vocabulary terms necessary for understanding both the text and the celebration. Define clearly a purpose for reading and/or listening.

2. Read the story a second time and list every term that represents a geographic location. Instruct students to listen closely and to raise their hand each time they think they hear a geographic location. Assure students that they will receive assistance from the teacher. Next, locate Vietnam and the United States on a map and a globe. Ask a student to finger-trace a line of cities en route from the United States to Vietnam. **Ask:** What factors determine the location of major cities and international airports? Does the text of *The Lotus Seed* give clues that match students' reasons for the location of major cities and international airports?

3. Talk about the meaning of leadership. Tell students that the emperor in *The Lotus Seed* possesses powers quite different from those of the President of the United States. Excite students with the game that they are going to play: first they must assume roles as detectives; then they must look for the differences between the Emperor of Vietnam and the President of the United States. Suggest that they search for answers to these questions in the story and in interviews with adults:

> *Who is in power?*
> *How does a person get into power?*
> *How long does a person stay in power?*
> *What is the difference between power by birth and power by vote?*
> *Does anyone or anything place limits on the powers of the leader?*

4. Ask that students join teachers in constructing a chart that clearly shows differences between two types of leaders and their powers. Tell students that they also uncover major clues about differences between two types of government when they research the powers of leaders. Expand students' understanding of the power of an emperor by reading aloud *The Empty Pot* by Demi. **Hint:** If appropriate, extend discussion by telling students that if they can locate the source of power, they often will be able to identify the type of government. Ask students to express how they feel about a type of government in which the people have guaranteed powers. Ask them what they must do to protect these powers.

5. Read aloud *The Wall* by Eve Bunting. Find out if any student's relatives or friends served in the armed services during a war or military operation. Take time for students to share stories about their family or friends who answered a call of duty. Investigate the background of Memorial Day, an occasion when Americans honor those who died in service to the nation. Request that students put on their thinking caps. **Ask:** In what ways are the two book selections linked?

Hint: Students will mention war, death, and leaving one's homeland. Probe deeper by giving students clues such as the type of sacrifices that characters in the stories make so that future generations will enjoy freedom. Invite students to offer examples of people who made sacrifices for others and for future generations.

6. Plan a day in which students enjoy enrichment activities related to *The Lotus Seed* and/or *The Wall*. Announce to students that they may choose *one* of the following activities the day before the actual enrichment day:

> *Bring a keepsake from home that reminds them of a person who made a sacrifice for others and share the story with classmates.*

> *Classify and sort a variety of seeds, draw the plant that grows from one seed, then explain the process of growth for one plant from seed to plant to seed.*

> *Gather a variety of leaves, identify each type, make leaf rubbings that show the structure of leaves, and explain to classmates why such a structure is necessary.*

> *Prepare a list of questions to ask a florist about plants, especially any variety related to the lotus plant, then assist the teacher in contacting a florist to visit the class.*

> *Choose one trait that characters in both books exhibit, cite concrete examples of behaviors, then apply the trait to everyday life.*

Ideas: Remember that celebrations and holidays do not cease when the school year ends. Search for ways to observe cultural and/or national holidays (e.g., Memorial Day, Emancipation Day, Independence Day) that occur during summer months and also to celebrate or honor days of personal accomplishment that occur throughout the year (e.g., new learning, new skills, new roles, new responsibilities). Extend the scope of lessons taught during the school year by using theme-related examples from all twelve months of the year.

EVALUATION:

Determine the level of student understanding of sacrifices that people make for others by listening to their responses to thought questions and by observing their participation in activities. Ask students what they learned from these stories and activities. Encourage students to connect the message in the story to the theme of spring and celebrations of birth and rebirth.

CONNECTION #2:
Patricia Polacco. *Chicken Sunday*

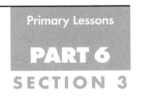

Primary Lessons

PART 6

SECTION 3

To thank old Eula for her wonderful Sunday chicken dinners, the children sell decorated eggs and buy her a beautiful Easter hat.

CHARACTER TRAITS: Review the nine character traits emphasized in this manual before reading this story.

1. Read *Chicken Sunday* aloud. Remember to set the stage with appropriate pre-reading activities that capture students' interest. Clarify vocabulary terms necessary for understanding both the text and the celebration. Define clearly a purpose for reading and/or listening. Talk about the many names for grandmother and connect the name activity to Chicken Sunday.

2. Ask children to bring hats from home to participate in a Hat Day. Help students categorize hats and allow them to write a descriptive paragraph about hats. Discuss also the tradition of wearing hats at Easter. Lead children in explaining why the hat emerges as an important symbol in the story.

3. Discuss how the children decorate eggs in the story. Ask children to share their egg-decorating traditions. Suggest that students decorate eggs and write a how-to story about decorating eggs. **Hint:** Allow students to freely design but also to observe classmates' finished products to identify cultural traditions as well as personal preferences. Lead students in a discussion of what factors influence students' designs. Allow students to taste poppy seed cake and tea during the egg-designing exercise. Link the activity to the owner in the hat store sharing cake and tea with children in the story. Talk to students about what gifts the owner of the store gives to children other than a tasty treat. **Ask:** Does the owner encourage children to pursue their goal? Invite special guests such as children's parents, adult relatives, or friends to class for this activity.

4. Engage children in additional egg activities. Link activities to incidents in the story or to personal experiences:

Make a chart showing anything associated with eggs, and then divide into categories and label.

Cook eggs three different ways (e.g., scrambled, fried, hard-boiled); then make a Venn diagram to show similarities and differences.

Soak eggs in vinegar; then predict what will happen.

Conduct egg-and-ball races by rolling or pushing with noses the two objects in straight lines and, prior to races, allow students to predict which object will reach the finish line first.

Design, as a family homework project, a method to drop an egg without breaking.

Make meringue in the classroom and use observation skills to describe changes as one person whips the egg white, then talk about or write about the process.

5. Review Miss Eula Mae's tradition of always frying chicken on Sunday. Ask students to name one special activity their family does together every week. Talk with children about how repeated activities or traditions bind people together as a family or as a culture or as a nation. Invite children to put on their thinking caps and give examples of each tradition.

6. Remind students that in this story children want to earn money to buy a hat for Eula Mae and that they sell eggs to accomplish their goal. Invite students to think of persons they want to recognize and ways they may earn money for the recognition. Lead students in a sequenced discussion of the person, approximate cost of the item, ways to earn money, purchase of the item, and presentation of the gift. **Hint:** Develop the economic concept of opportunity cost with this activity, i.e., one must give up one thing (time) to get another thing (money). Ask students to apply opportunity cost to their own lives.

7. Read aloud *Something from Nothing*, by Phoebe Gilman. Invite student partners to select one character and show how and why the character exhibits at least one character trait. Encourage students to answer these questions: Does the character use the trait to solve a problem? Does a character in *Chicken Sunday* demonstrate the same trait? How and why? Will the trait help students solve problems in their lives? How and why?

8. Remember that celebrations and holidays do not cease when the school year ends. Search for ways to observe cultural and/or national holidays (e.g., Memorial Day, Emancipation Day, Independence Day) that occur during summer months and also to celebrate or honor days of personal accomplishment that occur throughout the year (e.g., new learning, new skills, new roles, new responsibilities). Extend the scope of lessons taught during the school year by using theme-related examples from all twelve months of the year.

EVALUATION:

Determine the level of student understanding by observing their participation in various activities and by listening to their responses to higher order thinking skills questions. Ask students to choose one character trait, define what it means, and illustrate the type of behaviors characters exemplify in this story or other stories. Encourage students to connect the message in the story to the theme of spring and celebrations of birth and rebirth.

CONNECTION #3:
Jillian Wynot.
The Mother's Day Sandwich

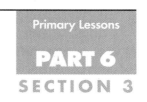

Ivy's and Hackett's plan to give their mother a Mother's Day breakfast in bed almost turns into disaster until mother finds a way to save the day.

CHARACTER TRAITS: Discuss the meaning of responsibility.

1. Read *The Mother's Day Sandwich* aloud. Remember to set the stage with appropriate pre-reading activities that capture students' interest. Clarify vocabulary terms necessary for understanding both the text and the celebration. Define clearly a purpose for reading and/or listening.

2. Encourage students to watch closely while the teacher webs the word, mother, on the chalkboard. Tell students that the information about the word comes from the teacher's memory. Show children that on the web one may place physical traits, character traits, favorite childhood memories, and any descriptor that reminds a person of the special relationship between mother (or significant caregiver) and child.

Invite children to make individual webs about their mothers. **Ask:** What physical traits appear on webs? What character traits appear on webs? What terms describe the relationship between caregivers and children? How and why? Tell students that the lists under broad headings are not only categories of related facts but also beginnings of most special gifts for mothers and caregivers.

3. Show students how to take webs and turn information into lovely mobiles, collages, or greeting cards. Pass out brightly colored construction paper, demonstrate patterns and directions of all three items— mobiles, collages, or greeting cards—and suggest that students illustrate their Mother's Day products with freehand drawings or pictures cut from magazines. Invite students to change the information on the web into an acrostic by using one of the words: mother, mom, or mother's first name.

> **Example**: **M**arvelous
> **O**riginal
> **M**erry

4. Research the origin of the celebration and ask students why this day set aside for mothers and caregivers continues to rate high as one of Americans' favorite celebrations as well as one of extraordinary profits for greeting card companies, candy companies, and florists. (Alternate Activity)

5. Model how to sequence a story by making story aprons. **Hint:** Use permanent markers to write abbreviated phrases that refer to main events of the story, arrange them in the right sequence, and add illustrations to make the words come alive. Use paper garment bags, plastic garbage bags, plastic aprons, or plastic grocery bags with the handles for shoulder straps. Cut out neck and armholes, if necessary. Stage a parade when students finish and allow each child to tell the story on the apron front from a simulated speakers' stand.

6. Reread the story and ask children to listen for items found in the kitchen. Divide children into small groups. Have students write each item on a separate index card and arrange these cards in categories. Display these on a large piece of paper. Label the categories (e.g., "Things in the Refrigerator," "Things in a Drawer"). **Ask** students to put on their thinking caps and explain to classmates why organizing small things into larger categories helps people. **Hint:** Use a classification graphic to organize these cards).

7. Discuss how families and sandwiches are different. Remind students that in the story children make the Mother's Day sandwich with mother as the cheese and with children as slices of bread. Assemble small squares of construction paper that match the color of sandwich ingredients (e.g., green square =lettuce, red square=tomato). Ask students to make a Mother's Day sandwich by using the names of family members as various sandwich ingredients.

8. Encourage children to tell about or write about their sandwich the next day. **Hint:** Lead the discussion to the generalization that although sandwiches (families) are different, they are tasty (meaningful) for the sandwich builders (family members). Allow students, if they wish to substitute family sandwiches for a Mother's Day sandwich. (Alternate Activity)

9. Discuss the mess that the children left in the kitchen and the meaning of responsibility. Talk about who is responsible for cleaning up the kitchen in *The Mother's Day Sandwich* and why. Invite students to share what tasks they do at home and to tell how their completion of these tasks assists family members. Suggest that students put on their thinking caps and talk about dividing tasks in the classroom or at home among several people. **Ask:** Does dividing the tasks make them easier, quicker, and more pleasant for everyone? Tell students that this is a big idea, or concept, called division of labor and ask them to cite other examples from the world of a primary student.

EVALUATION:

Determine the level of student understanding by assessing how students construct webs and apply information to creative products and by evaluating how students accept differences among family structures. Encourage students to connect the message in the story to the theme of spring and celebrations of birth and rebirth.

Primary Lessons

PART 6

SECTION 3

CONNECTION #4:
June Behrens. *Fiesta*

The Cinco de May celebration commemorates the victory of the Mexican Army over the French Army on May 5, 1862, a victory that marked the end of foreign invasions of North America.

CHARACTER TRAITS: Respect for differences in people and their holiday celebrations.

1. Read *Fiesta* aloud. Remember to set the stage with appropriate pre-reading activities that capture students' interest. Clarify vocabulary terms necessary for understanding both the text and the celebration. Define clearly a purpose for reading and/or listening.

2. Ask students to locate Mexico on a map and globe. Request that a student volunteer trace an imaginary line from Mexico City to their school. Talk to students about how colors on physical maps and globes give clues to geographic features. Ask students what colors, i.e., geographic features do students cross on their imaginary journey from Mexico City to their school?

3. Discuss why we should respect the holidays of other people.

4. Tell the story of the Cinco de Mayo celebration. Discuss why this celebration is important to Mexican Americans. Invite a local resource person to tell students how this holiday is observed. Discuss with the students why this celebration is important.

5. Demonstrate to students how to classify the parts of a fiesta, then how to make an accordion book of pictures and captions explaining elements such as costumes, music, food, play, and activities. Lead students to an understanding that no single activity expresses the spirit of fiesta as well as all of the activities together express the spirit.

   Hint: Alert students to the idea that people plan parts of any celebration as carefully as a music director rehearses different sections of an orchestra. People orchestrate parts of a celebration just as people orchestrate sections of a symphonic group to create a whole effect. A director must then put the pieces of the celebration or the sections of the musical selection together and lead a public presentation of the product.

6. Show students how to make individual piñatas: stuff small paper sacks or two styrofoam cups taped together with shredded newspaper, newsprint, or candy; cover the outside with fringed tissue paper; use tissue paper and construction paper to create animal features on the piñatas. Talk to students about the origin of the custom and why children as well as adults enjoy the custom. (Alternate Activity, Parental Discretion)

7. Plan a Mexican luncheon for the class. Request that students bring recipes for their favorite Mexican food. Ask parents if they will prepare the recipe for the luncheon.

   Assign a small group of students to compile recipes into a recipe book which hosts and hostesses may distribute as party favors. Discuss again why festive celebrations and special foods go hand in hand.

   Assign another group to decorate tables for the luncheon by using student-made products. Assign the third group to locate tapes or records of Mexican music to play during the luncheon. Assign a fourth group to contact a person who can teach students traditional Mexican dance steps for luncheon entertainment.

   Relate planned activities to *Fiesta*. Lead students in linking student-planned activities to fiesta descriptions in the story. **Ask:** What factors account for similarities between the two celebrations; for differences?

8. Remember that celebrations and holidays do not cease when the school year ends. Search for ways to observe cultural and/or national holidays (e.g., Memorial Day, Emancipation Day, Independence Day) that occur during summer months and also to celebrate or honor days of personal accomplishments that occur throughout the year (e.g., new learning, new skills, new roles, new responsibilities). Extend the scope of lessons taught during the school year by using theme-related examples from all twelve months of the year.

EVALUATION:

Determine the level of student understanding of Cinco de Mayo by observing student participation in and enthusiasm for the activities. Ask students to explain what they have learned from these activities. Encourage students to connect the message in the story to the theme of spring and celebrations of birth and rebirth.

Elementary Lessons

1

Making Lifetime Memories: Celebrating/Honoring Life and History

CONNECTION #1:
Joseph Bruchac. *Fox Song*

Grama Bowman opens up a new world to her granddaughter, Jamie, on their long walks through the woods. Time spent together establishes ties that bind two generations of Abenaki Indians (Native Americans) closely together. One morning Grama is gone, but Jamie feels her presence as she walks through familiar places in the woods.

CHARACTER TRAITS: Discuss the meaning of citizenship, respect, or responsibility with the class and have them provide examples of each.

1. Read *Fox Song* aloud. Remember to set the stage with appropriate pre-reading activities that capture students' interest. Clarify vocabulary terms necessary for understanding the text. Define clearly a purpose for reading and/or listening.

2. Ask students to use their imagination to describe a walk through the woods. **Ask:** What might you see, smell, or hear on a walk in the woods? Ask students to use their senses of seeing and hearing to listen for descriptive phrases as the teacher reads the story the second time. Encourage them to list examples, using descriptive phrases, such as the following:

> *"Footsteps crunching on the snow;"*
> *"Nothing as light and subtly sweet a taste as that of the syrup from a maple tree;" and*
> *"Warmth of the sun on her face."*

Invite student partners to write colorful descriptive phrases that describe their own "walk through the woods" and then share the colorful language with classmates. **Hint:** Point out the richness of descriptive language as well as the importance of using colorful words to hook the interest of both readers and listeners.

3. Explain the concepts of ecology in the story. Lead students in discovering ecological examples in the story. Show students how to divide a 9" x 12" sheet of manila paper into thirds. Ask students to draw pictures of how Grama shows respect for nature in each section. **Ask:** How can you show respect for nature every day at school, at home, and in the neighborhood?

Extension: Extend the learning by asking students to list examples of ecology in the story that show the importance of preserving the earth for future generations.

4. Discuss with students the dreamcatcher legend; i.e., according to the legend, dreams are messages from sacred spirits. Wise people say that the hole in the center of the web allows good dreams through while the web traps bad dreams until they disappear in the morning sun. People believe that dreamcatchers bless sleeping ones with pleasant dreams, good luck, and harmony throughout their lives. **Ask:** Do you know other practices that assure sweet dreams?

Extension: Talk with students about the circle of life, which is the wall hanging pictured in the story. The skin in the center represents the first kill of the young brave, usually a rabbit. The young man attaches symbols of his "firsts" (e.g., first arrowhead carved, first feather acquired) around the circle of life as he grows older.

Extension: Discuss the meaning of content-related mnemonic devices that assist students in remembering important ideas and details. Provide product options to students by allowing them to create either a dreamcatcher or a circle of life.

Extension: Students making dreamcatchers should write on brown paper sacks about special dreams they want to keep forever. Students' personal statements will be the inside of the dreamcatchers. Make rings by gluing two circles of poster board together. Wrap the rings with yarn and attach personal statements to the rings with yarn. Decorate dreamcatchers with feathers and beads.

Extension: Students making circles of life should jot down on brown paper the firsts in their lives that they wish to record for public viewing. Show them how to construct wall hangings that illustrate firsts in symbol form. Display both dreamcatchers and circles of life in a corner designated as a Native-American center that contains storybooks, artifacts, and student writings on Native-American culture.

5. Provide musical opportunities prompted by the story *Fox Song*. Lead all students in singing songs from the story. Help student volunteers make drumsticks for beating a rhythm to the songs. Sing the selection a second time with the addition of drumbeats. **Ask:** What do drumbeats add to the songs? **Hint:** Use popsicle sticks, pencils, or dowel rods for drumsticks and tie cotton-stuffed cloth on one end with yarn.

Extension: Listen and discuss the meaning of the song *Circle of Life* by Elton John. Review the process of analysis with students: analyzing means breaking something into small parts and investigating each part. Ask students to analyze how the lyrics in *Circle of Life* relate to their lives. Invite them to volunteer where one can see examples of the song lyrics in action.

6. Develop the concept of "special memories" as a capacity shared by all humans. Plan a visit to a nursing home or invite a group of grandparents or senior citizens to the classroom to tell stories about special memories of their childhood or about meaningful times spent with children and/or grand-children. Prior to the visit, assist students in developing questions that will prompt or cue a person talking about their life stories to tell more details. Equip students with a list of questions before the visit. Emphasize how important courtesy and patience are when visiting with residents in a nursing home or hosting classroom guests.

Hint: Stress the relationship between the preparation for a visit and the quality of information gathered. Ask students if this relationship exists in any of their other activities. **Ask:** How does advance preparation make a difference in product quality?

7. Use *Fox Song* as the basis for a writing prompt. Encourage students to write about and illustrate special times spent with a grandparent or another special person. Label a section of the Native-American corner as "Just Like Grama and Jamie...." and suggest that students exhibit finished pieces of writing, and then invite a partner or a small group to the corner for story sharing.

8. Select segments of a video approved for viewing such as *Land Before Time* or *The Lion King*. Request that students view segments of the video for the purpose of finding customs similar to the circle of life depicted in *Fox Song*. Encourage students to choose one scene from the video to act out, then explain to classmates how the customs on the video and on the project, circle of life, relate to one another.

9. Select one character trait (e.g., citizenship, respect, or responsibility). Talk about how people in the story demonstrate the trait. Ask students to refer to specific characters. Suggest that they think about their own lives and share examples that show how they apply these traits in daily life.

Hint: For interest and variety, alternate discussions on character traits between the benefits of possessing the traits and the consequences of not possessing the traits.

EVALUATION:

Determine the level of student understanding by assessing lists of descriptive phrases about special dreams, by observing drawings on ecological subjects, by evaluating dreamcatchers or circles of life, and by listening to reactions to interviews with senior citizens. Ask students to explain what they learned from the story and the activities in this lesson. Encourage students to connect the message in the story to the theme of celebrating or honoring life and history.

CONNECTION #2:
Miska Miles.
Annie and the Old One

A Navajo girl tries to cope with the impending death of her grandmother in this touching story.

CHARACTER TRAITS: Discuss the meanings of compassion, honesty, respect, responsibility, and integrity. Have students provide examples of each of these from their own experiences.

1. Read *Annie and the Old One* aloud. Remember to set the stage with appropriate pre-reading activities that capture students' interest. Clarify vocabulary terms necessary for understanding the text. Define clearly a purpose for reading and/or listening. For example, introduce the story to students by looking at the pictures to determine the geographic setting. Use a map to find the southwestern region of the United States. **Ask:** How does your geographical region fit into this picture? Help students identify typical geographic landforms of the area. Use the story setting as a springboard to help students learn and apply the meaning of three of the five geographic themes: location (Where is it?), place (What is it like?), region (What section of the nation or world is it in? What are the area's common characteristics?).

Extension: Apply geographic understanding to the other two themes, interaction (How do people interact with their environment?) and movement (Do people move from one area to another and why?), whenever stories present natural examples of the concepts.

2. Ask students to compare Annie's chores to their chores by making two lists. **Hint:** Explain to students that chore is a word related to responsibility; whenever they complete a chore, they fulfill a responsibility. Look at the similarities and differences between Annie's chores and students' chores. **Ask:** What factors cause differences between Annie's chores and students' chores? Will the same factors cause differences in other situations? Why?

3. Talk about things of importance to Annie and to Grandmother revealed in the story. As a lead-in to the thought questions, web with students the things that Annie and the Old One share. Then ask students to respond to these questions: What makes these things important to Annie and Grandmother? If students make a list of the most important things to them, will their lists match Annie's and Grandmother's list of important things? Why or why not?

4. Ask students to compare and contrast Navajo ways of life with their own, e.g., homes, living conditions, uses of land, means of income, children's chores, hardships, and thoughts about death. Use a classroom chart for student work. Talk to students about using data collected to form general statements. Help students understand that generalizations are statements that show a relationship between at least two concepts or two big ideas. Ask students to look at the data on the chart and then make general statements about similarities of and/or differences between Navajos' and students' lives.

5. Extend the comparison-and-contrast exercise by suggesting that students draw pictures of a hogan and their own homes that show marked differences in materials, size, and construction. Discuss how availability of materials, costs, and climates affect the type of homes people build. Invite students to use the drawings and to show classmates why the two types of shelters differ in obvious ways.

6. Encourage students to list reasons why they feel a grandparent or another significant older adult plays a special role in their lives. Ask students to describe their grandparent or special person in writing and then invite them to share tributes with classmates.

Extension: Enrich the written tribute assignment by engaging students in a card design project. Model how to fold a sheet of paper into fourths, how to decorate the front and back as a thank-you card, and then how to write a message of appreciation inside the card. **Hint:** Use sample cards as guidelines for students.

7. Revisit the story, *Annie and the Old One*, with a new purpose. Look at the facial features and expressions of both Annie and the Old One. Divide students into small groups with the task of comparing and contrasting the two characters' faces. Ask students to list similarities and differences between the two faces and then suggest reasons other than age for differences. **Ask:** In what other times and situations may one find the same factors at work that make such differences between young and old? Make sure that students reinforce their answers with reasonable examples.

8. Talk to students about the meaning of synthesis, i.e., a process through which one puts together ideas in new, creative ways. Ask students to synthesize knowledge about the Navajo culture gained from the story by weaving, e.g., drawing a story rug. Model for students how to use different colors and textures to show feelings and to mark changes in the story's characters and events. Invite students to explain how they made design decisions in either written or oral form. **Hint:** Weavers may depict good times by smooth threads and soft colors, and unpleasant times by lumps, loosely woven threads, or knotted sections. They may show the loss of a loved one by a big space. Stress to students that although each product will be different, students will be responsible for explaining how their choices of colors, weaving styles, and open and closed spaces tell personal stories.

9. Have students plan how to tell a grandparent or another special person the most interesting comparisons and contrasts between Navajo and their own cultures, and then weave potholders as artifacts for their stories. Allow students to practice stories and to explain purposes of artifacts to partners. Encourage children to tell stories and to give potholders to special persons on Grandparents' Day in September or on any other occasion of celebration or honor agreed upon by teachers and students.

10. Assign one character trait to each of five small groups (e.g., compassion, honesty, respect, responsibility, or integrity). Distribute lists of each trait's indicators and lead students in group discussions about their meanings. Allow students to discuss indicators in small groups. Ask groups then to talk about how people in *Annie and the Old One* and/or how students' projects, such as greeting cards and chants, demonstrate the trait.

    Extension: Encourage groups to respond with their observations and reasons. Suggest that students transfer the traits to examples in their own lives that illustrate the trait and then share within the small group setting. Make sure that students form the habit of thinking about their responses before they answer, then supporting their answers with specific examples.

    Hint: For interest and variety, alternate discussions on character traits between the benefits of possessing the traits and the consequences of not possessing the traits.

EVALUATION:

Determine the level of student understanding by assessing how students compare and contrast Navajo culture to their own culture and by reading the greeting cards to senior citizens. Designs for and written explanations of the story rug clearly show students' analysis and synthesis of the events and emotions in the story. Participatory activities indicate student understanding of the important relationships between Navajo children and their elders. Encourage students to connect the message in the story to the theme of celebrating or honoring life and history.

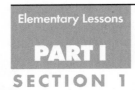
CONNECTION #3:
Bill Martin, Jr., and John Archambault. *Knots on a Counting Rope*

Boy-Strength-of-Blue-Horses and his grandfather share memories of the boy's birth, his first horse, and his first horse race. Each time Grandfather tells the story, the young boy becomes better able to face his blindness. Grandfather carefully prepares his grandson for the time when he will no longer be the boy's companion.

CHARACTER TRAITS: Discuss the meaning of courage, diligence, respect, and integrity. Provide examples of these character traits and have students give their own examples.

1. Read *Knots on a Counting Rope* aloud. Remember to set the stage with appropriate pre-reading activities that capture students' interest. Clarify vocabulary terms necessary for understanding the text. Define clearly a purpose for reading and/or listening.

2. Give students the opportunity to reread the story by using two readers instead of only one. Instruct two good oral readers to practice reading the parts of the grandfather and grandson with appropriate feelings and gestures. Request that they first read to one another and then read to classmates. **Ask:** How do two readers instead of one add to the quality of the story? Are these the same reasons why some people prefer to see stories acted out on a stage or on a television screen rather than to read stories in written form? Does variety in the way storytellers present tales add to the enjoyment of stories? Why or why not? Does variety in the way teachers present lessons add to the enjoyment of learning? Why or why not?

3. Encourage students to write stories about special times spent with grandfathers or with other special relatives. Lead students through a prewriting discussion so that every student feels a sense of contribution to the project. In small story circles, allow students to share their written stories.

Give each student a piece of rope or yarn. Instruct students to tie a knot on the ropes each time they share their writing with a small group or with the class. **Caution:** Remind students to keep their counting ropes in a safe place. When most students show several knots tied on the ropes, ask them to analyze the process of tying knots on counting ropes. **Ask:** How does tying knots on a counting rope help students learn? gain confidence?

4. Remind students of the name of the main character, Boy-Strength-of-Blue-Horses. Encourage individual students to list words that describe their own characteristics. Ask students to choose one characteristic to rename themselves. **Example:** Good-Spelling-Girl. Instruct students to explain why they chose the new name, to share names only with the teacher, and to keep new names a secret from classmates.

Ask students to bring one of their baby pictures to display on a "Who's Who?" bulletin board with the students' new names under each picture. Number the pictures and encourage students to guess identities. Ask students to talk about the characteristics used to select new name, such as physical traits and special talents. **Ask:** Does the process used by students in selecting new names match the process used by parents in selecting names for newborn babies? Why or why not?

5. Select one character trait (e.g., courage, diligence, respect, or integrity) and talk about how characters in *Knots on a Counting Rope* and/or in students' new names demonstrate the trait. Ask students to tell why they selected a character and how the character exemplifies the trait. Suggest that students think about their own lives, think up examples of the traits in their own lives, and share examples with classmates.

EVALUATION:

Determine the level of student understanding by reading stories about special times with relatives, by analyzing how students attach value to tying knots on a rope in terms of learning, and by listening to reasons how and why students chose new names. Assess observation skills by the way students match classmates' physical traits evidenced in baby pictures, present appearances, and special talents. Encourage students to connect the message in the story to the theme of celebrating or honoring life and history.

CONNECTION #4:
Joseph Bruchac.
Gluskabe and the Four Wishes

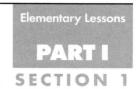

Elementary Lessons

PART I

SECTION 1

Gluskabe, helper of the Great Spirit, performs many tasks to make the world a better place, and then he travels to an island far away to rest. He grants anyone who comes to him one wish. Four Abenaki men, each with a different wish, decide to make the journey. Gluskabe tests the four men by giving them pouches with instructions not to open them until they arrive home. Subsequent events that happen to the four men carry a valuable lesson for all readers.

CHARACTER TRAITS: Review the character traits of courage, integrity, or responsibility, and provide examples of each one.

1. Read *Gluskabe and the Four Wishes* aloud. Remember to set the stage with appropriate pre-reading activities that capture students' interest. Clarify vocabulary terms necessary for understanding the text. Define clearly a purpose for reading and/or listening.

2. Encourage students to make a wish, and then discuss what may happen if the wish comes true. Give students options to change their wishes at this point. Review the meaning of artifacts. Ask students to write their special wishes on pouches made with brown paper bags tied with colorful yarn strips. Request that students place pouches in a safe holding place until they complete the second part of the activity. Create a wall mural by cutting a large canoe from brown butcher paper. Suggest that students float the canoe down a tree-lined river. Instruct students to draw themselves in native costume and position themselves inside the canoe. Display pouches by hanging them around each person's neck. **Ask:** Why is attaching the pouch to the person necessary? Is the reason similar to the one why teachers use artifacts to trigger memories about important ideas, people, or events?

3. Model for students the construction of a story line (e.g., characters, setting, events) by sequencing important happenings in the story. Place students in cooperative groups and assign the task of charting the adventures of the four men in the story. Request that students attach storylines to the bottom of the murals. **Ask:** What and how do storyline exercises teach students about Abenaki culture? About the multiple roles braves play in Abenaki culture?

4. Invite students to create group stories by using story events and student wishes as storyline patterns. Talk about how story characters change as a result of their experiences. Discuss the meaning of the words, transform and transformation. Ask students to analyze the transformations of the men in the story. **Ask:** Why do the men become what they do? Instruct students to apply what they learn about character transformations to the group stories. As groups share stories with classmates, request students to listen for examples of character transformations.

Extension: Encourage students to create another transformation by giving each child a canoe shape made from a 6" x 3" strip of paper. For one minute, ask individual students to brainstorm a list of as many unusual, varied ideas into which they can transform the canoe. Set a timer to increase the excitement. Count the number of ideas to find out who is the most productive thinker in the one-minute exercise.

Ask them to choose the most unusual idea for creating a transformation, then request that they offer suggestions for transforming one canoe into an entirely different object. Glue the transformed canoe on a 9" X 12" piece of construction paper and display for students to observe a student-generated transformation.

5. Invite students to research the location, traditions, and lifestyle of the Abenaki tribes. Use the school media specialist as a resource. When students complete the research class period, talk with them about how much cultural information students learned from the story and then about how much cultural information reference materials added to their knowledge. Lead students to appreciate the use of multiple sources in research. Most importantly, guide students into concluding that much cultural learning in addition to sheer entertainment will occur from listening closely to stories read in class.

6. Talk with students about the meaning of the moral of a story. Have students pretend that they journey to the island to seek one wish from Gluskabe. Ask students to use the situation as a prompt to write a creative story. Instruct children to describe the events that take place once they receive one wish. Challenge them to focus the story on this moral: Be careful what you wish for! Allow students to form story circles so that each student may perform for a small audience.

7. Select one character trait (e.g., courage, integrity, or responsibility), then ask students to respond to how people in the story and/or in students' wishes demonstrate the trait. Explore with students the reasons why they selected a specific character and how the character exemplifies the trait. Suggest that students think about their own lives and share examples of how they can exhibit the trait at school as well as at home.

EVALUATION:

Determine the level of student understanding by assessing various products: wall murals, storylines, student wishes, group stories, transformations, and research conclusions. Ask students to share what they learned from the story and activities that followed. Encourage students to connect the message in the story to the theme of celebrating or honoring life and history.

CONNECTION #5:
Joseph Bruchac.
The First Strawberries

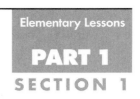
In a Cherokee legend, strawberries resolve a disagreement between a husband and wife. Additionally, the legend proves that anger causes people to miss the sweet strawberries of life such as friendship and respect.

CHARACTER TRAITS: Discuss and provide examples of the following: compassion, fairness, or respect.

1. Read *The First Strawberries* aloud. Remember to set the stage with appropriate pre-reading activities that capture students' interest. Clarify vocabulary terms necessary for understanding the text. Define clearly a purpose for reading and/or listening.

2. Invite students to listen to the story the second time for the purpose of creating a story element chart. Divide children into partners, then ask them to jot notes during the reading when they hear context clues related to setting, characters, problem, and solution. Encourage them to volunteer examples after the reading. **Ask:** Can you apply these elements to any story? Ask partners to think of a favorite story, apply the elements, and share their thinking with classmates. **Hint:** Lead students to the conclusion that story elements are excellent tools of analysis to apply to any story.

3. Talk about roles and chores that students observe family members doing at home. Ask students if males perform certain roles while females perform other roles. Ask also if one person does certain roles and chores all the time or if family members help each other by rotating chores. Talk with them about changes in traditional male and female roles. Help them make conclusions about roles and chores in today's families compared to roles and chores in past times. **Hint:** Ask students to put what they learned about present-day roles in statement form (e.g., "roles are flexible and continue to change as family life changes").

Extension: Use the activity to introduce the concept of stereotyping, i.e., the practice of applying a standard or typical image to all members of a certain group such as males and females. Select story facts that illustrate other injustices in the Cherokee legend. Lead students to the understanding that stereotyping doesn't allow for any individual differences among people. **Ask:** Is stereotyping fair? Why or why not?

4. Remind students about the purpose of artifacts. Serve strawberry slices to students, then share "sweet as a strawberry" memories. Distribute red, strawberry-shaped papers and request that students record their favorite "sweet as a strawberry" memories. Create a strawberry patch of memories on a bulletin board by inviting each student to share their memory, and then place their strawberry in the patch. **Ask:** How do "sweet as a strawberry" memories make students feel? Why?

5. Review with students how the Cherokee legend starts with a conflict between a man and a woman. Talk about the specific reasons for the conflict, how the man and woman resolve the conflict, and then proceed to a discussion of conflicts in general and various methods for resolving conflicts.

Hint: Point out to students that when they break a topic into parts and investigate each part, they are analyzing the topic, and when they put the parts together in a new, creative way, they are synthesizing the topic. Ask small groups to put the processes of analysis and synthesis into practice by writing a new beginning for the legend in which characters avoid conflict. Invite student actors from each group to act out the new beginnings to the legend.

6. Select one character trait (e.g., compassion, fairness, or respect) and talk about how characters in either version of the legend demonstrate the trait. Ask students to tell why they selected a character and how the character exemplifies the trait. Suggest that students volunteer examples from their own lives that illustrate one or more of the traits.

Hint: For interest and variety, alternate discussions on character traits between the benefits of possessing the traits and the consequences of not possessing the traits.

EVALUATION:

Determine the level of student understanding by observing story element charts and by listening to discussions on family roles and on "sweet as a strawberry" memories. Use their written and oral work to evaluate their progress. Encourage students to connect the message in the story to the theme of celebrating or honoring life and history.

Elementary Lessons

PART I

SECTION 1

CONNECTION #6:
Nancy Van Laan.
Buffalo Dance

A Blackfoot legend portrays the special bond existing between the buffalo and the Blackfoot people. A young woman's courage not only saves her people but also reinforces the importance of the buffalo dance in Blackfoot culture.

CHARACTER TRAITS: Discuss the meaning of the following character traits with students: responsibility, compassion, or courage.

1. Read *Buffalo Dance* aloud. Remember to set the stage with appropriate pre-reading activities that capture students' interest. Clarify vocabulary terms necessary for understanding the text. Define clearly a purpose for reading and/or listening.

Choose the following viewing/listening purposes for the second reading of *Buffalo Dance*: tell students to find visual patterns in the story, such as border designs and Indian picture writing, and to listen for the moral of the story and verbalize ideas about the meaning of the moral. Distribute feathers as artifacts prior to the second reading to assist students in remembering important details. Lead students in an informal discussion related to both purposes.

2. Extend the discussion to the moral of the legend by asking students how they may apply the lesson to their lives today. Ask students to describe the circumstances under which they may save other people from disaster. Have students think about examples of sacrifice in today's world. **Inquire:** Do people make sacrifices today? If so, how? Is sacrifice always an object or thing? What else may sacrifice be? Ask students to describe how a person sacrifices himself or herself for others.

3. Study picture writing in the story. Suggest to student partners that they devise a short story and communicate the story in picture writing. Have students record the story on a piece of brown paper for authenticity and decorate the story with a culturally appropriate border pattern. Use students' stories as lead-ins to discuss people's need to communicate with others. Send a research team to the library to investigate and to report different ways people throughout history have communicated with others. Informally talk about the role of computers and mass media in today's communications.

Hint: Advise students not to limit their investigations to written symbols. Include the language of signing and drum beating as well as various alphabets. Ask students to put on their thinking caps.

Ask: Why are people usually eager to communicate with other people in the present world and also leave messages (e.g., letters, diaries, journals, photo albums, personal mementos, time capsules) for future generations?

4. Provide performance options for students to increase their understanding of Native-American culture. Based on students' interests, give these activity options: learning and singing the song in *Buffalo Dance*, choreographing a dance consistent with the clues about dance styles in the story, creating a Native-American design pattern, or writing a Native-American legend by following the pattern set in *Buffalo Dance*. Have students to help in planning a sharing time around the tribal fire.

5. Select one character trait (e.g., responsibility, compassion, or courage) and talk with students about how characters in the story demonstrate the trait. Ask students to tell why they selected a character and how the character exemplifies the trait. Suggest that students think about their own lives and share examples in which they, their friends, or their family exhibit the trait.

6. Encourage students to read a story listed in the section entitled Additional Selections. Suggest that they read with the purpose of comparing and contrasting the story to *Buffalo Dance*. Ask students to share their learning with classmates. **Hint:** Use the experience to show that reading more than one source about any topic increases one's knowledge by adding other perspectives.

EVALUATION:

Determine the level of student understanding by observing their responses to thought questions and by assessing their creativity in optional activities. Ask students to explain what they have learned in this lesson. Encourage students to connect the message in the story to the theme of celebrating or honoring life and history.

ADDITIONAL SELECTIONS:

Olaf Baker. *Where the Buffaloes Begin*

Tomie dePaola. *The Legend of the Bluebonnet*

Tomie dePaola. *The Legend of the Indian Paintbrush*

Paul Goble. *Buffalo Woman.*

Paul Goble. *Her Seven Brothers*

Susan Jeffers. *Brother Eagle, Sister Sky: A Message from Chief Seattle*

Rafe Martin. *Rough-Face Girl*

Angela Shelf Medearis. *Dancing with the Indians.*

Audrey Osofsky. *Dreamcatcher*

Te Ata. *Baby Rattlesnake*

Joan Weisman. *The Storyteller*

CONNECTION #7:
Sylvia Fair. *The Bedspread*

Two sisters approach the same task in totally different ways; however, they gradually learn to appreciate each other's opposite way of thinking.

CHARACTER TRAITS: Discuss the following character traits with students and ask them to give examples of each one: diligence, compassion, and fairness.

1. Read *The Bedspread* aloud. Remember to set the stage with appropriate pre-reading activities that capture students' interest. For example, use pieces of hand-stitched patchwork or quilting to show students the intricacies of handcrafted items and to illustrate that handiwork is similar to signatures, i.e., that both are unique. Clarify vocabulary terms necessary for understanding the text. Define clearly a purpose for reading and/or listening.

2. Create a transformation by giving each student a yellow circle approximately 3" in diameter. For one minute, ask students to brainstorm individually a list of as many unusual, varied patterns into which they can transform the circle. Tell students that people who craft patterned work first start with basic lines and shapes such as circles or squares or rectangles, and then test different combinations until the pattern pleases them. Count ideas to find out who the most productive thinker is in one minute.

Talk with students about which suggestions will create the most unusual, pleasing pattern for transforming a circle. Allow the student who created the winning suggestion to place the design on a circle, then glue the circle onto a 9" x 12" piece of manila construction paper and display the product. As the student finishes the model, show other students pictures of various quilt patterns and allow them to identify how patternmakers change simple shapes into complex designs. **Hint:** Use pictures or kaleidoscopes as concrete examples of transformations.

Extension: Extend the learning according to the interest expressed by students. If the interest level appears high, the subject lends itself to introducing and/or developing concepts such as symmetry, congruency, and texture in relationship to patterns.

3. Have students draw a brick house with the following parts on a piece of 9" x 12" manila construction paper: a front door, five steps leading to the door, three windows, two chimneys, and a garden. As the sisters in the story paired pieces for one bedspread, pair drawings to make one piece. Point out that interpretation of any task rests with the individual's thinking patterns. Ask students to make a generalization about what they learned about the sisters and their thinking patterns from this activity. Challenge boys and girls to apply the generalization to classroom situations.

Extension: Extend the comparison-and-contrast exercise to the sisters' homes. Ask students to use clues in the story or in the illustrations that show examples of the sisters' similar and different thinking patterns.

4. Read *The Bedspread* a second time. Request that partners assume roles of the two sisters; one listens for characteristics of one sister while the other listens for characteristics of the other sister. Ask student partners to analyze what motivates each of the sisters and what clues in the story lead them to these conclusions. **Ask:** Are family members supposed to think and act alike? How does looking exactly like or acting exactly like someone else make people feel? Lead students in a discussion about the value of each person's uniqueness.

Find the poem "Everybody Says," by Dorothy Aldis, and share with students how she expresses her desire to be unique.

5. Give students a pattern of a plain house. Ask them to decorate the house in a manner pleasing to them. Explain to students that elaboration in writing is similar to decoration in housing. Tell students that both processes, elaboration and decoration, make reading and viewing more pleasant and more interesting than plain varieties. Challenge students to write a descriptive account of how they decorate their house. Ask partners to listen for examples of elaboration (decoration) in each other's descriptive writing.

6. Explain to students, in simple language, the theory of multiple intelligences: linguistic, logical-mathematical, visual-spatial, kinesthetic, musical, intrapersonal, and interpersonal. Explain that most people have one or two areas of strength. Encourage students to take clues from the story and decide what strengths the sisters demonstrate and why. **Hint:** Note that certain characteristics are not better than others. Note also that differences in personal strengths add variety to life.

7. Select one character trait (e.g., diligence, compassion, or fairness) and talk about how characters in the story demonstrate the trait. Ask students to tell why they selected a character and how the character exemplifies the trait. Suggest that students think about their own lives and share examples that illustrate any of the three traits.

   Hint: For interest and variety, alternate discussions on character traits between the presence and benefits of possessing the traits and the absence and consequences of not possessing the traits.

EVALUATION:

Determine the level of student understanding by assessing the quality of creative and written products, by listening to the analysis of characters, and by observing the application of multiple intelligences theory to fictional characters. Encourage students to connect the message in the story to the theme of celebrating or honoring life and history.

CONNECTION #8:
Alan Benjamin. *Buck*

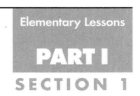
Elementary Lessons

PART I

SECTION 1

An enterprising young woman trades one possession for another until she amasses a fortune. Even so, she feels something is missing. She solves the problem by trading all of the grandeur for the return of her faithful friend, Buck.

CHARACTER TRAITS: In this lesson, begin with a discussion of fairness, compassion, and responsibility. Ask students to review the meanings of these words and give examples of them from their real-life experiences.

1. Read *Buck* aloud. Remember to set the stage with appropriate pre-reading activities that capture students' interest. Clarify vocabulary terms necessary for understanding the text. Define clearly a purpose for reading and/or listening.

2. Read aloud the story, *Buck*, the second time. After the story reading, invite students in small groups to list items traded in random order. Ask students to write names of items traded on individual index cards, and then place items in order of value from least to greatest. **Ask:** How is the value of items determined from least to greatest? Does cost determine the value of items? What other ways besides monetary ways do people attach value to items?

Hint: Explain the difference between monetary and intrinsic values. **Ask:** How did the author determine the sequence of items in the story? Is the order in terms of what items cost? If not, what are the author's criteria for sequencing items?

Extension: Encourage students to think about something in their lives that might not cost much but which they still regard as valuable, to write a descriptive statement about the item, and then to share statements with their small groups. Ask students to make a conclusion about setting the value of items and to defend the conclusion to classmates.

Hint: In addition to explaining how people set the value of items, this exercise also provides an opportunity to review the skill of sequencing. Students will learn that people must determine a reason for sequencing to establish the order of items, i.e., to place items in the order of cost or in the order of occurrence, or in the order of emotional attachment.

3. Review the purpose of artifacts. Talk with students about the main ideas in the story (e.g., bartering, value of items) Present this situation to small groups of students:

> *They are teachers of a third-grade class.*
> *They want to provide an artifact for students that will remind them instantly of the story of Buck and also the learning related to the value of items.*
> *They have no money to buy artifacts so they must create a meaningful symbol.*

They will have ten minutes to think up the idea for an artifact and make a model.

Groups will present the ideas and models to classmates by debriefing the processes group members go through to devise an artifact.

Hint: If students need assistance in starting on the artifact exercise, use a trading card as an example of an appropriate artifact for *Buck*. Talk through why the trading card is an appropriate artifact.

4. Find a copy of the song *Hush, Little Baby*. Invite students to sing this song with you. Discuss similarities between the song and the story of *Buck*. Use as many verses as students enjoy. Suggest that students work with a partner to create a poem or a song that develops two ideas: bartering or buying something that an individual believes will bring pleasure and the end result of bartering or trading. Plan a performance time and post a program in which partners sing original songs or read original poems. Perhaps enlist classmates in choral singing or reading. Display poems and songs in a special classroom space entitled "Economic Lessons from *Buck*."

5. Invite students to make a pictorial story map for display in the hallway. Review the sequence of events in the story and ask students to choose one event in which they have a special interest. Provide a long sheet of butcher paper, label sequenced events along the top or bottom of the paper, and allow small groups to work on their illustration of the event during one school week. Ask students to decide upon and write a catchy title at the beginning of the banner, then decide upon and write fictional messages from *Buck* at the end of the banner. Assist students in posting the banner in the hallway and encourage students to invite students from other classrooms to a guided print walk in the hallway.

Hint: Remind students of museum experiences in which guides tell visitors information about exhibits and answer questions.

6. Talk about the difference between fact and opinion statements. Read *Buck* aloud again one page at a time. Ask students to cite facts on each page and defend their answers, then ask them to do the same with opinions. Make sure that students explain their choices.

7. Read the poem "Smart," by Shel Silverstein. Ask students to compute the number and value of coins. Ask them to convert all currency in the poem to pennies, and then make a statement about how smart the smartest son really is. Ask students to convey what happens in the trading in graph form. After students explain how they transfer words to symbols, ask them to discuss the irony of the title. **Hint:** Talk about the difference between literal meaning and intended meaning. Ask students to think up other examples of irony.

8. Show students a picture of Buck in the story. Alan Benjamin describes Buck as a loyal and faithful companion to one master for a long time. Ask students to think about their pet or the pet of someone they know. Request that they brainstorm a list of words in addition to the words loyal and faithful that paint a colorful picture of an animal friend. Ask students to put the colorful words into descriptive sentences about a pet and share with classmates.

9. Select one character trait (e.g., fairness, compassion, or responsibility). Talk about how characters in the story demonstrate the trait. Suggest that students think about their own lives and share examples about how their actions exhibit one or more of the character traits.

EVALUATION:

Determine the level of student understanding by assessing the quality of class discussions and by observing the degree of creativity exhibited in various written, artistic, and mathematical products. Ask students to share the meaning of the emphasized character traits orally and in writing. Encourage students to connect the message in the story to the theme of celebrating or honoring life and history.

CONNECTION #9:
Barbara Cooney.
Miss Rumphius

Elementary Lessons

PART I
SECTION 1

Little Alice tells the story of her great aunt, Miss Alice Rumphius. As a child, Miss Rumphius plans to travel and to live by the sea. Her grandfather tells her that she must do something to make the world more beautiful. She fulfills his wish by scattering lupine seeds around the world.

CHARACTER TRAITS: Before the lesson unfolds, remind students of the meaning of the following character traits: citizenship, compassion, and responsibility. Tell them that these traits are important to the meaning of the story *Miss Rumphius*.

1. Show students the storybook cover. Explain that the flowers are lupine, a light purplish-blue color. Tell students that the main character of the story, Miss Rumphius, wants to do three things in her life: travel, live by the sea, and make the world more beautiful. Ask students to predict what Miss Rumphius will do to make the world more beautiful. Accept all answers and ask students to listen carefully as the teacher reads the story to see which prediction is correct or nearly correct. Discuss Miss Rumphius's actions once the story unfolds through reading.

2. Read aloud the story, *Miss Rumphius*, until almost the end, then stop. Ask students again to predict what Miss Rumphius will find when she goes for her walk. Accept all answers. Ask students to listen carefully as the teacher finishes the reading. First discuss which of the student predictions make interesting surprise endings and why, then how the author actually ends the story. Talk about the two times that students predict what will happen in the story next: how Miss Rumphius makes the world more beautiful and what she finds on her walk. **Ask:** Does the author provide clues in the story for readers to guess what will happen next? Is the element of surprise pleasing to readers? How may student writers use the same technique in their writing? Encourage partners to plot a short story in which the unexpected surprises readers. Allow time for partners to share with classmates.

3. Give students flower seeds as artifacts to keep as reminders of the story. Discuss various parts of a flower, and ask students to draw and label parts. Let students plant flower seeds and keep observation logs on growth, changes in plants, the number of seeds planted, and the number of plants sprouted. Ask students to compare the number of seeds planted to the number sprouted, and then compute the fractional number of plants that sprouted. Talk about ways of increasing the yield of the seeds planted.

Hint: Check with local nurseries to get an estimate on what professionals consider a good ratio between seeds planted and seeds sprouted. Ask professionals what they do to increase the yield of particular plants, and share insights with children.

4. Provide options for students to demonstrate their understanding of the story about Miss Rumphius. Allow students to choose *one* of the following three activities:

Draw pictures of exciting places little Alice will visit when she grows up, write one or two sentences about the pictures, and bind picture stories into a class book.

Write about a favorite event in the story and illustrate on 9" x 12" pieces of construction paper.

Create the flowers Miss Rumphius planted by painting a green stem and leaves, then sponging on lupine petals or gluing on colored popcorn. **Hint:** *To color popcorn, place popped corn in a brown bag and add 2 tablespoons of dry, blue tempera paint. Shake vigorously.*

Extension: Help students create a Miss Rumphius corner in the classroom. Talk with students about display techniques, so that visitors who are not familiar with the exhibit will understand the meaning of various projects. First, request that students surround the storybook with silk or construction-paper bluebonnets. Then, ask them to decide if some products need sequential arrangement and others need topical arrangement. Based on student decisions, ask a team of students to set up the rest of the exhibit. Request that students assume roles of exhibit tour guides or docents, and plan a script to tell visitors about Miss Rumphius's Corner.

5. Review the path of Miss Rumphius's globetrotting. Enlist student assistance in locating and marking places on a world map that Miss Rumphius visits. Model for students how to tri-fold 9" x 12" pieces of construction paper. Encourage students to select one place on Miss Rumphius's journey, research geographic facts and tourist attractions of the site, and design a travel brochure that shows why Miss Rumphius enjoys visiting this place. Add the brochures to Miss Rumphius's Corner.

6. Prepare a simple flight schedule on an overhead transparency. Use the airport nearest your home. Ask students to check the schedule to answer the following questions:

What airline has a flight to New York at 1:00 p.m.?

What time does United Airlines arrive at the airport?

How long was the flight to your airport from Chicago?

If the distance were 1500 miles and passengers arrived in three hours, how fast were they traveling?

Suggest that student groups create flight schedules, prepare transparencies, and practice the various interpretive skills with classmates. Ask students to think about Miss Rumphius's journeys. **Ask:** Which of the questions will affect her travel plans? What other questions will Miss Rumphius add to make her travels smoother?

Hint: Request a sample schedule from a travel agency or an airline office so that the examples the teacher creates are close to actual flight times.

7. Talk with students about why taking care of the earth and adding to the earth's beauty are concerns of ecologists as well as responsible citizens. **Ask:** How can you take care of the earth and add to the earth's beauty? Ask students as a class to write a letter of advice to future generations. Suggest that

CHARACTER EDUCATION THROUGH STORY

they include statements in the letter that show the consequences of ignoring the care of Planet Earth. **Hint:** Use the group experience to review letter-writing skills necessary for effective communication.

8. Read aloud Chief Seattle's poem/speech, "The Earth Is Precious," in the storybook *Brother Eagle/Sister Sky*. Ask students to participate either in a readers' theater or in choral reading of the poem.

9. Ask students to choose one of the following actions, then use the action to show how they can make the world a better place in which to live:

> *Help clean up litter.*
> *Help pass laws to preserve our earth by writing Congressmen.*
> *Plant trees, bushes, and/or flowers.*

Request that students think up reasons why Miss Rumphius and Chief Seattle agree with all of these choices.

10. Select a character trait (e.g., citizenship, compassion, or responsibility) and talk about how people in the story and/or in students' lives demonstrate the trait. Ask students to tell why they selected a character or a person and how the character or person exemplifies the trait. Suggest that students think about their own lives and share examples that illustrate the trait.

Hint: For interest and variety, alternate discussions on character traits between the benefits of possessing the traits and the consequences of not possessing the traits.

EVALUATION:

Determine the level of student understanding by listening to responses on the need to make the world a better, more beautiful place for future generations and by assessing various written and creative products. Encourage students to connect the message in the story to the theme of celebrating or honoring life and history.

CONNECTION #10:
Lauren Mills.
The Rag Coat

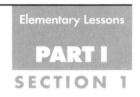

Elementary Lessons
PART I
SECTION 1

A poor Appalachian family cannot buy a coat for their daughter, Minna. Minna's father's illness forces her to stay home and help her mother make quilts to sell. Minna finally gets to go to school. She proudly wears a coat of quilt scraps made by her mother's quilting friends. Unexpected reactions from her classmates surprise Minna.

CHARACTER TRAITS: Before reading this story, review the list of nine character traits and discuss their meaning. Ask the class to provide examples. Post these on the board for all to see.

1. Read aloud the story *The Rag Coat*. Remember to set the stage with appropriate pre-reading activities that capture students' interest. Clarify vocabulary terms necessary for understanding the text. Define clearly a purpose for reading and/or listening. While students participate in preliminary activities, play Dolly Parton's song, "Coat of Many Colors," softly. Then, play the song again so that students may hear Dolly's story through the song lyrics. After the first reading of the story, compare and contrast Minna's and Dolly's stories.

2. Talk with students about the value of Minna's coat to her. Ask students to recall Minna's reactions to the rag coat that her mother's quilting friends made. Encourage students to share memorable stories of special objects either made or purchased for them. As each child volunteers a story, ask the child to tell the group about the value of the object. **Ask:** Does the object have more monetary or intrinsic value? Do other people's reactions to the object tend to increase or decrease the value of the object? What other factors may change the value of objects?

   Hint: Alert students that currently individuals and museums pay enormous sums for old, tattered examples of handiwork. These pieces often tell the story of the people who made them and of the geographic and social environment in which they lived (e.g., slave quilts, quilts of the Oregon Trail, Amish quilts).

3. Use a United States wall map or a set of desk maps to establish the story's location. Ask students to respond to the meaning of colors on the maps (e.g., the meaning of green, brown, blue). Talk about appropriate terms related to the mountainous region (e.g., "rough terrain," "rural area," "backwoods area," and "isolation"). Request that students locate the Appalachian Mountains on the maps and tell what clues the mapmakers or cartographers give about the area. Discuss the geographic clues about Appalachia the author and illustrator provide in the story.

   Extension: Extend the learning by using the geography lesson as a lead-in to discuss conservation of the environment and the value of recycling. **Ask:** Does the author write about how characters interact with their environment? Recycled products? Ask students to cite specific examples to support their answers.

4. Review the meaning of economics as a science that focuses on ways people and nations earn their living. Talk about economic clues related to Appalachia that the author and illustrator provide in the story (e.g., coal mining, farming, and logging). Invite students to think about how economic forces affect people's lifestyles. **Ask** students to put on their thinking caps, use the story of Minna and her family as the source of information, and respond to these questions:

   In Appalachia, will a small or large family give families an advantage in earning their living? Why?
   How do geographic features affect traveling to work or to school in Appalachia?
   How does poverty in the area limit children's opportunities to finish school and to choose a different way of earning a living?
   How do geographic features affect choices of how families earn a living?

   Encourage students to draw examples from Minna's family and to apply their impressions to these thought questions.

   Hint: Ask the media specialists for assistance in finding the average family income in Appalachia, and then compare the figure to the average family income in your community. Use the figures to show that poverty, like most social studies concepts, is relative.

5. Involve students in a K-W-L activity about mining. Use the story line of *The Rag Coat* to pique student interest in mining. Send a student research team with the K-W-L's "want to know" list to the library to investigate mining and mine safety. Provide the team with helpful leads such as limiting the search to coal mining in Appalachia, exploring ways workers protect themselves from harm, researching how mine owners construct tunnels that meet high safety standards, determining workers' hours and working conditions, and investigating the government's actions to improve conditions in the mines. Ask team members to watch for clues about the role of canaries in early mining ventures.

   Hint: Set up the research project with the librarian in advance so that materials are ready when students arrive. The team members should organize their report around the topics on the "want to know" list. Tell students to organize information by topic and prepare to present the information in the format of a nightly news report, i.e., fast and factual. Tell them to save the canary story until the end of the report and deliver as a human interest postscript to the story.

Extension: Extend the activity by challenging students particularly interested in the subject to write government officials and attempt to persuade them to introduce a bill for mine safety.

Hint: Advise students to tell officials what prompts their interest in mining. Suggest that the letter address one problem and include several suggestions for solving the problem. Interested students may prefer to pool their efforts, then write and mail a letter representing a committee of students.

6. Integrate a social studies and art lesson by challenging students to create their own "Coat of Many Colors" on a 9" x 12" piece of construction paper. Model different outlines of coats on the chalkboard but allow students to choose the style. Then, encourage students to design blocks that show special memories. Display the coats in a special place in the classroom.

7. Divide the class into partners. Give each pair one of the nine core character traits. Tell partners to decide if and how Minna exhibits the trait. As groups report to the class, ask a student to keep a tally on the chalkboard to determine the number of traits Minna exhibits. **Hint:** Use the exercise to point out that even in the poorest of circumstances, an individual can exhibit these traits of model behavior.

EVALUATION:

Determine the level of student understanding by listening to responses to discussions and thought questions and by assessing the quality of written and creative projects. Encourage students to connect the message in the story to the theme of celebrating or honoring life and history.

ALTERNATE SELECTIONS:

Rebecca Caudill. *Did You Carry the Flag Today, Charlie?*

Eth Clifford. *The Remembering Box*

Valerie Flournoy. *The Patchwork Quilt*

Tony Johnston. *Amber on the Mountain*

Patricia MacLachlan. *Sarah Plain and Tall*

Marcus Pfister. *The Rainbow Fish*

CONNECTION #11:
Omar S. Castañeda.
Abuela's Weave

Grandmother and granddaughter grow closer through shared experiences. The story centers on the grandmother's disfigurement and lack of confidence caused by a red birthmark. When grandmother sells her weavings at a fair, however, she learns the true value of handiwork.

CHARACTER TRAITS: Discuss what is meant by "respect for other people." Have students write a short narrative on this topic giving several examples of respect for other people.

1. Read *Abuela's Weave* aloud. Remember to set the stage with appropriate pre-reading activities that capture students' interest. Clarify vocabulary terms necessary for understanding the text. Define clearly a purpose for reading and/or listening. For the first reading, ask students to identify the story's central problem as well as the story's solution to the problem. For the second reading, ask some students to listen for clues to the Mayan culture, others to listen for clues about the history of Guatemala, and still others to listen for clues about the location (where is it?) and about the place (what is it like?) of Guatemala. Lead a discussion based on context clues on the cultural, historical, and geographic site called Guatemala.

2. Enlist the assistance of the media specialist in selecting appropriate reference materials on the Mayan ruins. Divide students into small groups with pre-selected criteria for research (e.g., location of ruins, building materials of original structures, purpose of original structures, decorations on ruins, discovery of ruins, what ruins prove about Mayan culture). Assign one topic for investigation to each group. Rotate sources so that students gain practice in scanning reference sources for specific information. Ask them to observe and to record pictorial references of their topic. Suggest that the group practice how to report the information to classmates in the most interesting way. If pictures related to the topic are unavailable, encourage students to generate a visual aid. At the conclusion of student reports, solicit reactions on the level of Mayan architectural skills. Lead students into making a generalization about Mayan architectural skills.

Extension: Extend the learning by talking about how Mayans passed these skills and also their culture on to later generations. Make the idea of cultural legacies clearer by asking students to think of traditions and/or skills passed down in their families. Invite students to share these with classmates.

Extend the learning further by talking about skills that are gradually becoming lost (e.g., weaving). Ask students to think of other lost arts, then ask students to put on their thinking caps: What are reasons why people do little individual craftsmanship today? Do some people still prefer handmade items to factory-made items? Why? Cite examples.

Hint: Some students may not have any examples of handmade items to share; thus, make this activity optional. Encourage volunteers to bring examples of handmade items to show classmates. Suggest that students investigate the stories that go with the items, so that they may share both information and products.

3. Give students a choice in making handmade items that resemble the brightly colored woven products of Guatemala: friendship bracelets or place mats. Model how to braid embroidery thread, crochet thread, or yarn into bracelets and tie ends together. Model also how to weave a place mat by drawing a picture and coloring it brightly, then folding the paper lengthwise. Show students how to cut 1" slats starting 1" from the bottom on the fold and stopping 1" from top.

Hint: Caution students to leave a 1" border on all sides of the picture place mats when cutting the slats. Instruct students to open the mats and weave in and out of the slats with bright-colored yarn or paper. Ask students what they learned about the grandmother's talents from making either a bracelet or a place mat.

4. Talk about good and bad uses of words and their effects on others. Recall and share personal situations that serve as good examples of how an unfortunate choice of words caused hurt feelings for the teacher. Lead students to the conclusion that name-calling, even in fun, most often leads to hurting someone's feelings. Challenge students to think about which character traits they will exhibit when they choose not to engage in name-calling. Invite students to tell how words play a part in the story line of *Abuela's Weave*.

5. Invite students to participate in a Market Day or Fair Day. Decide on a medium of exchange, such as beads or shells, to buy student-made items. Allow students time to make and price an item of their choice. Alert students that they must price their products in terms of how many beads are in the product. Distribute an equal number of beads or shells to every student.

Arrange desks like market stalls. Encourage visual and verbal advertisements. Appoint some students as sellers and others as buyers. Allow students to buy with beads or barter with purchased products. Continue the activity until students realize that there are more products than beads, that they must make choices in the marketplace, and that mistakes are easy to make. Introduce students to the Latin motto, Caveat Emptor (Let the Buyer Beware), and then ask students to relate the motto to the marketplace experience.

6. As a whole group activity, read each of the nine character traits with their indicators aloud and then fill in appropriate spaces with examples of the grandmother's actions in the story. Assist students in drawing the conclusion that the grandmother's actions determine the ending of the story.

Extension: Extend the learning by suggesting that students predict how changes in grandmother's actions might produce different endings for the story. **Hint:** Prompt students with "What if...?" situations to stimulate their thinking. For example, what if no one buys grandmother's weaving? How might the story end? Develop the cause (e.g., grandmother's actions) and effect (e.g., different endings, relationships with students).

EVALUATION:

Determine the level of student understanding by listening to class discussions, by evaluating responses to thought questions, and by assessing the quality of written and creative products. Pay careful attention to the character trait narratives written by each student. These are excellent indicators of student understanding. Encourage students to connect the message in the story to the theme of celebrating or honoring life and history.

ADDITIONAL SELECTIONS:

Rudolfo A. Anaya. *Farolitos of Christmas*

George Ancona. *The Piñata Maker*

Pura Belpré. *The Rainbow-Colored Horse*

Arthur Dorros. *Radio Man*

Pat Mora. *A Birthday Basket for Tia*

Robert Munsch. *Love You Forever*

Gary Paulsen. *The Tortilla Factory*

Gary Soto. *Too Many Tamales*

Jonah Winter and Jeanette Winter. *Diego*

Beatriz McConnie Zapater. *Fiesta*

CONNECTION #12:
Peter Golenbock. *Teammates*

Jackie Robinson's rise to fame in major league baseball affirms a story of atrocities toward African Americans in America. Because of the boldness of a courageous baseball commissioner, non-violent responses from Jackie, and loyal support from a teammate and friend, Pee Wee Reese, Jackie breaks through the color barrier and becomes a hero to members of his race.

CHARACTER TRAITS: Review the nine character traits and their importance.

1. Read aloud the story. Remember to set the stage with appropriate pre-reading activities that capture students' interest. **Hint:** Activities may include: singing Jack Norworth's and Albert von Tilzer's song, "Take Me Out to the Ball Game" (Silver Burdett & Ginn, World of Music, 1988); talking about why many Americans consider baseball America's favorite pastime; telling about examples of racism in the 1940s and 1950s; and showing how individuals in real life can make a difference in the treatment of all African Americans.

2. Explain the process of making a character web by placing Jackie Robinson's name in the center of a diagram and by webbing personal traits on lines from the center. Add webs as students suggest traits from the story. Invite students to reflect on the web. **Ask:** Do Jackie Robinson's traits match the traits of persons Americans label as heroes? Why or why not?

   Extension: Ask students to suggest persons in history as well as in their personal lives who are heroes and heroines. Remind students that they must support their choices with specific traits.

3. Introduce, develop, and/or reinforce the concepts of prejudice, i.e., an attitude, and discrimination, i.e., an action. In small groups, assign students the task of listing examples of unfair treatment of players in the Negro League. **Hint:** Remind students that the author draws examples in the story from American society in the 1940s and 1950s. In a large group, discuss examples, and then assign the task of noting then-and-now changes in the treatment of African Americans to the same small groups. Assist students in talking about some of the reasons why American society has changed in the last fifty years. Remind students that each person may play a role in making America a nation in which citizens treat other citizens fairly by students treating other classmates fairly.

   Hint: Draw examples from the world of elementary students in your community. If students wish to comment on other examples gained from the media or from experience, encourage them to volunteer.

   Extension: Extend the learning by suggesting that students interview either parents or grandparents to find examples of unfair treatment of African Americans that occurred when they were in school. Invite students to share the information gathered in interviews.

4. Ask students to compare and contrast the Negro League players to the Major League players on a graphic organizer such as a Venn diagram. Guide students in the activity by suggesting the following criteria for comparison and contrast:

   Exhibited extraordinary skills as players
   Adored by fans coming to see them play
   Earned a lot of money for playing
   Considered heroes
   Stayed in fancy hotels when traveling
   Earned very little money

Slept in their cars when they traveled
Ate food they brought with them
Gained public recognition with pictures on baseball cards
Enjoyed playing baseball

5. Set the stage for a letter-writing activity by reminding students of the story scene when Pee Wee Reese goes out to the playing field and puts his arm around Jackie Robinson's shoulder to show support for a friend as the crowd jeers. Ask students to assume the role of Jackie Robinson and write a friendly letter to Pee Wee Reese expressing appreciation for his courage and support. **Hint:** Use the exercise to review students on the friendly letter format.

> **Extension:** Invite students to listen to their classmates' letters to find out different ways of expressing appreciation to a friend. Suggest that students listen for words such as support and loyalty, and then compile a list of descriptors for the friendship between Jackie and Pee Wee. **Ask** students to put on their thinking caps: Are these traits common descriptors of friendship? Why or why not?

6. Select one character trait (e.g., compassion, courage, diligence, fairness, integrity) and talk about how characters in the story demonstrate the trait. Ask students to tell why they selected a character and how the character exemplifies the trait. Suggest that students think about their own lives and share examples that illustrate people exhibiting the trait. **Hint:** For interest and variety, alternate discussions on character traits between the benefits of possessing the traits and the consequences of not possessing the traits.

EVALUATION:

Determine the level of student understanding by observing the quality of character webs, letters, and comparative charts and by listening to responses in discussions. Ask students to explain what they have learned from a study of the life of Jackie Robinson. Encourage students to connect the message in the story to the theme of celebrating or honoring life and history.

CONNECTION #13:
Virginia Kroll.
Africa Brothers and Sisters

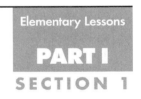

Elementary Lessons

PART I

SECTION 1

From a father-and-son storytelling session, readers gain insights into a setting where unique tribal traits establish marked differences among Africans. Valuable resources in the story include African names, phonetic spellings, and a map of tribal locations.

CHARACTER TRAITS: Focus on fairness, honesty, and respect and how the characters in the story demonstrate these traits.

1. Read *Africa Brothers and Sisters* aloud. Remember to set the stage with appropriate pre-reading activities that capture students' interest. **Hint:** Set the location of the story by locating Africa on a map and globe, by calling attention to the vastness of the continent and the diversity of geographic features, and by noting the number of countries on the continent. Engage students in an echo exercise by calling and echoing the names of countries and tribes. Clarify vocabulary terms necessary for understanding text. Define clearly a purpose for reading and/or listening.

2. Reread the story. During the second reading, ask students to listen for various jobs of tribal members mentioned in the story. Ask students also if the author talks about any form of currency. **Ask:** If there are no coins, how do tribal members get paid for their work and secure the products that they need? Use the answers to the question as a natural lead-in to discuss the concept of bartering between and among tribes.

Extension: Tear off a large sheet of butcher paper suitable in size and in shape for a pictorial map of Africa. Ask students to sketch the continent of Africa, put major geographic features on the map, place drawings of tribal members in native dress in correct geographic settings, and add pictures of goods which identify the skills of specific tribes. **Hint:** Use the exercise to introduce, develop, or reinforce the meaning of economic concepts (e.g., trade, production, consumption, distribution, interdependence, scarcity, specialization of labor, bartering, wage).

Extend the learning further by personalizing examples of bartering. Ask students to list items they possess but want to trade for new items. **Ask:** Why do you want to trade items? Why do you want new items? **Hint:** Remind students that bartering goes on continuously in most families in a "this-for-that" activity. Invite students to share humorous experiences of bartering with brothers or sisters or friends. **Hint:** If students appear quite interested in the subject of wanting new items, open the discussion up to the role of advertising in creating desire, i.e., creating consumers' demand for the most current, "up-to-the-minute" goods and services.

3. Remind students about the purpose of artifacts. Suggest creative options that reflect African crafts. Allow students to make an artifact that especially interests them: pottery (clay), jewelry (macaroni, yarn), masks (papier-mâché), or African drums (cans, construction paper, yarn for ties). Have students set up an "Out of Africa" exhibit and invite visitors (e.g., principal, intern, media specialist, counselor) to view the display and hear the artifact stories, i.e., why they chose to make a certain product, how the product represents tribal culture, how the product will help them remember Africa. **Hint:** Encourage children to link artifact stories to their knowledge base about Africa.

4. Enlist the media specialist in locating illustrated reference materials on African dress. Divide students into small groups to research the turban: turban colors, tying the turban, tie-dyeing turban cloth, tribal turban styles, turban significance. On the chalkboard, list the criteria for investigating turbans in a vertical line. Give each group one piece of chalk to record the data horizontally on each criterion. **Hint:** Use the chalkboard chart to compare and contrast African turbans. Lead students into making valid conclusions based on data about the role of turbans in African dress. Use the chart also to point out the merits of a grid in the research process.

Extension: Extend the learning by planning a demonstration of tie-dyeing cloth for turbans. Also, invite resource persons in the community to visit the classroom and demonstrate traditional African dress. **Hint:** Talk about potential questions to ask the visitor so that students may acquire maximum information from the interview. Use the interview as a link between two types of research: reference materials (secondary sources) and personal interviews (primary sources). Remind students that both types of research are valuable.

Extension: Extend the learning more by talking about other items of traditional clothing that provide clues to cultures in many movies and books (e.g., sombreros [Hispanic], buckskin suits [frontiersmen], feathered headdresses [Native Americans]). **Hint:** Caution students about making assumptions that all Hispanics wear sombreros, all frontiersmen wear buckskin suits, all Native Americans wear feathered headdresses. Although these examples of clothing became markers of cultural membership, they did not and currently do not represent all members of the culture. Point out to students that this wrong assumption exemplifies stereotyping.

5. Demonstrate how to make galimotos, a typical African push toy made by children. From pieces of old wire, sticks, cornstalks, or pieces of yams, children make cars, trucks, bicycles, trains, and helicopters. Show children that they may fashion any of these carriers by bending and shaping a piece of wire. **Hint:** Refer to *Galimoto* by Karen Lynn Williams as an additional resource. Use the craft activity as a springboard to talking about children's universal desire for toys. If toy stores and money are nonexistent, adults and children always find ways to make toys. **Ask:** What is the meaning of universal? What needs do toys fulfill? Are toys limited to children?

6. Lead students in brainstorming a list of famous, modern-day Africans and African Americans. **Ask:** What made the persons famous? Are the persons good role models? Why or why not? Must role models be famous? Invite students to name a role model in their lives and share reasons why they are role models. **Hint:** Assist students in thinking of informal ways of telling people that they are role models for them. Make students aware that people appreciate knowing that they serve as models for other people.

7. Enlist the assistance of the media specialist in collecting a variety of sources that highlight contributions of African culture to American society. Allow class time for students to scan sources that cover past and present contributions. Include traditional contributions in athletics and in the performing arts, but extend students' knowledge by showcasing other fields of accomplishment such as science, math, civil rights, politics, and military leadership.

8. Select one character trait (e.g., fairness, honesty, or respect) and talk about how characters in the story demonstrate the trait. Ask students to tell why they selected a character and how the character exemplifies the trait. Suggest that students think about their own lives and share examples of people who demonstrate the trait.

EVALUATION:

Determine the level of student understanding by listening to class discussions, by evaluating responses to thought questions, and by assessing written and creative projects. Encourage students to connect the message in the story to the theme of celebrating or honoring life and history.

CONNECTION #14:
Susan Altman and Susan Lechner.
Followers of the North Star

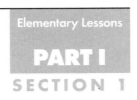
Elementary Lessons

PART I

SECTION 1

Writing in the appealing form of rhyme, Altman and Lechner relate an array of African-American accomplishments from colonial to contemporary times.

CHARACTER TRAITS: With this story emphasize the following: citizenship, compassion, courage, diligence, and responsibility and talk about how people in the story demonstrate the trait.

1. Read *Followers of the North Star* aloud. Remember to set the stage with appropriate pre-reading activities that capture students' interest. Focus students' attention on the North Star and the star's role in guiding people on water routes (e.g., early explorers), as well as land routes (e.g., runaway slaves). **Hint:** Use the excellent opportunity presented by the text in *Followers of the North Star* to talk about concepts critical to students' understanding of the society in which they live (e.g., the institutions of slavery; the processes of segregation, desegregation, integration; the Bill of Rights;

and the civil rights movement). Introduce students to the connection between how people earned a living (e.g., cotton, tobacco, sugar) and how the institution of slavery began in America. Introduce, develop, and/or reinforce concepts as they arise naturally in the text. Use a world map and globe to show students the path of human movement, forced and voluntary, between continents and between regions. **Hint:** Read each selection once, encourage students to repeat lines after they are read, so that they develop appreciation for rhyme and rhythm, then discuss the meaning and setting of the selection.

2. Give concreteness to the abstract concept, North Star, by constructing a model of Ursa Major, the constellation in which one may find the North Star. Demonstrate making the model in front of the class or allow students to construct the model in small groups. **Hint:** Follow a pattern found in a reference source to build a constellation model. Use a black construction paper circle backed with a cardboard circle, and place straight pins through the paper in the shape of the constellation. After viewing this effect, suggest that students ream out the pinholes slightly and place the black paper on an overhead projector. Darken the room and enjoy seeing the constellation pattern reflected on the wall. Students may achieve the same effect by placing a flashlight behind the black paper and projecting the image on the wall.

Enlist the media specialist in assisting a research team of students interested in finding facts about the North Star that they will present to classmates in a "Can You Believe This?" format. Ask students to search for facts on the Big Dipper, Ursa Major, Polaris, Vega, and the earth's axis. Encourage students to explain facts in language appropriate for elementary students. Talk with students about how model building and research results connect to the North Star in the story of human movement.

3. Review students over the purpose of a K-W-L chart, i.e., defining what students know, identifying what students want to know, and then assessing what students learned as a result of research and experiences. Ask students to think about the topic of African Americans; to reflect on what they know from experiences, activities, and friendships; and suggest entries on a classroom chart under K (what students know). Request that students complete the same exercise for W (what students want to know). Post the chart in the room and refer to points under W (what students want to know) as research reveals plausible answers. Delay the completion of L (what students learned) until they complete the activities for *Followers of the North Star*.

4. Review the poems and the stories they tell in *Followers of the North Star*, and then ask students to choose one favorite poem as a model. Invite students to choose a person who makes a difference in their lives, to write descriptors in terms of that person's traits or what that person does for the students, then to put descriptors together in the form of an original poem.

Extension: Distribute large, gold, construction-paper stars and allow students to glitter the edges. Ask students to write poems on the stars. Encourage students to read their poems and to cluster stars together in constellation patterns on a bulletin board or wall display entitled "Following My Own Star." **Hint:** Discuss with students the double meaning of words, i.e., the North Star as a bright star in the heavens guiding travelers throughout history and also as a greatly admired person who models exemplary character.

5. Divide students into small groups and review the meaning of cause-and-effect statements by talking through several examples and by asking students to describe the process. Distribute two sentence strips to each group, and then instruct students to write one cause-and-effect statement about a person in the story. Remind students to put the cause statement on one strip, the effect statement on the other, and to share the matched statement with the large group. Collect all of the strips, mix strips up, and give groups only one strip. Ask students to read the statement, to determine whether the statement is a cause or an effect and why, then to wait to raise their hands until the teacher reads the strip that logically matches their half.

Remind students that they need to confer with group members before they collectively raise their hands, i.e., decisions on correct matches of cause-and-effect sentence strips need to reflect group consensus. Continue the exercise until students match all sentences correctly several times. **Example:** Because Rosa Parks refused to give up her seat on the bus, African Americans won the right to sit anywhere on public vehicles.

Hint: Students may notice the use of terms other than African Americans in the text (e.g., "Blacks," "Negroes"). Explain to students that authors and historians use different terms in different historical periods. The time period as well as the geographic area influences the use of specific terms. The term currently in greatest favor is African American.

6. Enlist the assistance of the librarian in finding materials on the Bill of Rights appropriate for elementary students. Request that the librarian search for references that state specific amendments in original form with interpretations of the amendments.

Hint: Review especially Amendments 13, 14, and 15 for a background to discussions on segregation, desegregation, and integration. Point out also the amazing fact that framers of the United States Constitution and the Bill of Rights created a document so flexible that citizens have made relatively few changes (e.g. only 27 amendments) in more two hundred years.

7. Place students in the role of student legislators with the power of making and changing laws for all of the people they represent. In order to protect all students' rights, the task for small groups is to make a five-to-ten-point student bill of rights. Prior to dividing students into groups, lead students first through the process of what freedoms they consider most important to protect, then allow groups to word amendments according to their beliefs.

Structure the large-group summary discussion around how different groups approach the protection of the same freedom. Remind students that working out differences in the approach to common problems and coming to agreements acceptable to all participants are the processes of consensus building. Tell students that all us must compromise on some points. As a final discussion point, guide students in connecting the actions of the characters in *Followers of the North Star* to the study of the Bill of Rights.

Hint: Suggest to students that they may write their group's Bill of Rights on parchment-paper scrolls with quill-pen decorations, then display documents in the room.

8. Ask students to tell why they selected a character and how the character exemplifies one of the above character traits. Suggest that students think about their own lives and share examples that illustrate the trait.

Hint: For interest and variety, alternate discussions on character traits between the presence and benefits of possessing the traits and the absence and consequences of not possessing the traits.

9. Revisit the K-W-L chart and invite students to complete the L section based on all discussions and activities related to *Followers of the North Star*. Lead students to conclude how a study technique such as a K-W-L chart helps them organize, learn, and retain information.

EVALUATION:

Determine the level of student understanding by assessing the quality of written and creative products, by listening to the sensitivity expressed in discussions, and by evaluating the facility with which students use higher order thinking skills. Encourage students to connect the message in the story to the theme of celebrating or honoring life and history.

CONNECTION #15:
Jeanie Adams.
Going for Oysters

When an Australian native family goes on an extended weekend journey to the beach, they find unexpected adventures far beyond traditional water sports.

CHARACTER TRAITS: Select one character trait (e.g., integrity, responsibility, or diligence) and talk about how the characters in the story demonstrate the trait.

1. Read *Going for Oysters* aloud. Remember to set the stage with appropriate pre-reading activities that capture students' interest. For example, show children the illustrations in the story as interest builders. Encourage students to predict the setting of the story by giving clues about the location of Australia:

> *This place is in the southern hemisphere.*
> *This place is surrounded by water.*
> *This place is a country as well as a continent.*
> *This is a place where students may hear these phrases: down under; G'day, mates; Crocodile Dundee.*

Clarify vocabulary terms necessary for understanding the text. Suggest that students record unfamiliar words during the reading of the story, and then use context clues as helpers for learning unusual words. Define clearly a purpose for reading and/or listening.

2. Assist students in learning the geographic connection between Australia and the United States by finger-tracing a "straight-as-an-arrow" path between the two locations on a wall map. Ask students to find the latitude markings for both locations and note similarities and differences between the two (e.g., climates [similar], seasons [different]).

Extension: Extend the discussion to other concepts (e.g., topography, people, diversity, lifestyles, customs). Tell students to watch for examples of these concepts while they engage in activities related to *Going for Oysters*. Introduce, develop, and/or reinforce concepts as they emerge naturally either from the text or from the activities. **Ask:** What geographic clues give students the best information about a location? Are the same clues good starting points for investigating other locations? Why? **Hint:** Students may suggest numerous clues, but the question is a natural lead-in for talking about two of the five themes of geography: location (where is it?) and place (what is it like?).

3. Talk with students about the role that different types of fish and sea animals play in *Going for Oysters*. Ask students to name and to describe as many examples as they can remember from the story. Review the wide variety of creatures by showing illustrations for the second time. Distribute large sheets of manila paper to students and ask them to draw a fish shape. Challenge students to sequence events in the story inside the fish shape. Suggest that they add pictures of fishing tools used to catch fish in the story. Encourage students to share any humorous or exaggerated fish stories that their families or friends have told. Display the fish stories in the hallway and suggest that students tell members of other classes about *Going for Oysters*. **Ask** students to put on their thinking caps: How do making fish patterns and placing events in order help students get a hook on learning?

4. Divide students into small groups to talk about differences in foods in the story and foods you find in your community. Ask recorders in the groups to list traditional foods in both areas, then to participate in compiling two lists on the chalkboard. Have students compare and contrast the two lists, then in a group setting discuss possible answers to this question: Why do so many differences between the two diets exist? Request that one student from each group give the group's best answer and the process through which the group decided on the answer. **Hint:** Link the differences in diets as one example of human interaction with the environment, one of the five major themes in geography. In large measure, diets mirror resources of the area and resources of the people. Many people throughout the world cannot choose their diets or be concerned over nutrition, because they are so poor and have no choices.

Extension: Extend the learning by using the exercise to exemplify the economic problem of scarcity. Tell children that a tug-of-war exists between unlimited human needs and wants and limited resources. This tug-of-war results in scarcity and forces people into making hard choices: What will be produced? How will it be produced? Who will get it?

5. Review students on what happens when students analyze a topic or a problem, i.e., one breaks the topic or problem into small parts and investigates each part. Project a transparency of the story graph on the wall and enlist students in analyzing each topic:

> *CHARACTERS*
> *SETTING*
> *PROBLEMS*
> *SOLUTIONS*
> *CONCLUSIONS*

Ask students to respond to this question: If students carefully analyze the story, how does putting it back together in a new way, i.e., synthesis, promote further learning?

6. Invite students to show cause-and-effect relationships by completing the following sentences:

> *She threw her casting net into the water; therefore, _____.*
> *They forgot Grandpa's warnings about the eastern coast; therefore, _____.*
> *After the oysters were steamed, they _____.*
> *The boat had a hole in it; therefore, _____.*
> *Ask students to put on their thinking caps and complete this statement: Finding cause-and-effect relationships helps students learn, because _____.*

7. Declare a Going-for-Oysters Day on which activities in all subjects revolve around aspects of the Aborigine story. Lead students in brainstorming ways the class might link topics or ideas in the story to various subjects, such as social studies, language arts, science, mathematics, and fine arts. Create classroom centers for specialized activities. Invite boys and girls to propose a topic for investigation and for sharing with classmates, or to select one of the following activities and share the products with classmates:

Watercolor a colorful sunset background. When dry, use black marker or crayon to draw an end-of-day dance scene from the story. **Ask:** In Aborigine culture, what purpose does the dance fulfill? What other cultural dances fulfill similar purposes?

Draw two typical family gathering scenes, one Aborigine and one American, on a large sheet of manila paper. **Ask:** In what ways are the families similar and different?

Sketch an oyster shape as a pattern for storybook pages and cover. Select the most important events in the story, write one sentence about each event on one "oyster," illustrate and sequence events, and string together the going-for-oysters storybook. Explain to classmates the step-by-step process from thinking up ideas to finishing a product.

Review the ending of the story. Write a new ending to the story focusing on this statement: "After hearing the exciting story of the children's adventure, Grandma and Granddad said...." In the new ending, include conversations between characters. Be prepared to explain how and why the student author used quotation marks.

Invite another class to a show-and-tell session in which a student, partners, or small groups tell about their products, the relationship between the products and the story, and the learning acquired from their chosen activities.

8. Ask students to tell why they selected a character and how the character exemplifies one of the character traits emphasized in this lesson. Suggest that students think about their own lives and share examples that illustrate the trait.

EVALUATION:

Determine the level of student understanding by assessing written and creative products and by listening closely to responses to thought questions and discussions. Encourage students to connect the message in the story to the theme of celebrating or honoring life and history.

ALTERNATE SELECTIONS:

Verna Aardema. *Why Mosquitoes Buzz in People's Ears*

Nikki Grimes. *Meet Danitra Brown*

Mary Hoffman. *Amazing Grace*

Patricia Polacco. *Chicken Sunday*

Faith Ringgold. *Tar Beach*

Robert D. San Souci. *The Talking Eggs*

John Steptoe. *Mufaro's Beautiful Daughters*

Ann Warren Turner. *Nettie's Trip South*

Karen Lynn Williams. *Galimoto*

Jeanette Winter. *Follow the Drinking Gourd*

Elementary Lessons
PART I
SECTION 1

CONNECTION #16:
Sherry Garland.
The Lotus Seed

A Vietnamese grandmother who flees her war-torn country stows away a lotus seed as a cultural keepsake. Protecting the precious seed from all harm, she finally shares her heritage with family members.

CHARACTER TRAITS: Select one character trait (e.g., citizenship, courage, diligence, or integrity) and talk about how people in the story demonstrate the trait.

Note: The first lesson plan for *The Lotus Seed* is suitable for primary students. Writers suggest these activities for older elementary students.

1. Read *The Lotus Seed* aloud. Remember to set the stage with appropriate pre-reading activities that capture students' interest. Clarify vocabulary terms necessary for understanding the text. Define clearly a purpose for reading and/or listening.

CHARACTER EDUCATION THROUGH STORY

2. Review students over the meaning of elaboration, then suggest that they adopt the topic of an average school day as a subject for elaboration. Ask students to pretend that they are describing the topic to a distant relative over the telephone and to use sentences—simple, compound, complex—that paint vivid pictures of a day in the life of an elementary student. **Ask:** How does elaboration make communication clearer? More interesting? More entertaining? **Hint:** Develop or reinforce the use of different types of sentences needed for understanding as well as for interest.

Extension: Reread aloud and slowly *The Lotus Seed.* Define listening for complex sentences as the purpose for reading. Ask boys and girls to raise their hands when they hear a complex sentence. Invite them to repeat the sentence and name specific characteristics that make the sentence complex. Divide students into small groups. Assign one complex sentence to each group. Give several sentence strips to each group. Ask group members to divide the complex sentence into logical parts or phrases, write the parts on separate strips, and then demonstrate the correct order of phrases in the sentence by standing in the appropriate place in line. Allow all groups to demonstrate their complex sentences.

Extension: Ask groups to mix up sentence strips and pass the whole sentence to the next group. Challenge group members to place sentence parts passed to them in the correct order. Continue passing sentence strips until groups practice all sentences. **Ask** students to put on their thinking caps: Why is it important to writers to know about and use different sentence types or structures?

3. Encourage students to take turns retelling the story. Invite students to sit in a circle. Give the student who begins the story a lotus flower or a flower similar to the illustration in the story (e.g., fresh, tissue paper, plastic, or silk flower). Instruct students to pass the lotus flower around the circle as each child tells the next event in the story. **Ask** students to put on their thinking caps: Why does telling events in the right sequence make better stories? Extend lotus flower activities by modeling how to make tissue-paper lotus flowers and allowing students to make their own or by planting flower seeds and keeping a growth log.

4. Place a long sheet of butcher paper on the classroom wall. Randomly assign partners or threesomes one of the events listed below and ask that they illustrate what happens on smaller pieces of butcher paper. Ask that students name the event at the bottom of their drawing. Events to illustrate and to sequence include the following:

Emperor cries
Grandmother picks lotus seed
Grandmother hides seed in a secret place
Grandmother marries
Bombs fall
People leave on crowded boats
People stare at big buildings in New York
People live in crowded apartments
Little brother plants seed
Grandmother is sad
Lotus seed blooms
New seeds sprout for all of the children
Children find secret places to hide their seeds

Define a time limit for completing the drawings. Sound a bell, tell students that the long piece of butcher paper represents the grandmother's lifeline, and then invite boys and girls to take their drawings to an approximate place in the lifeline that the event occurs.

Hint: Make students aware that placement on the butcher paper may involve talking with students over what event happens in what order and reaching agreement. Use the exercise to review the process of sequencing and to teach the concept of negotiation. Once agreement occurs, request that students tape illustrations in correct order on the large sheet of butcher paper. Invite students to take a print walk beginning at the first event and allowing students to explain the drawing and placement, then proceeding to the end of the lifeline.

5. Place Vietnam in geographic perspective by enlisting students in finger-tracing the path from the United States to Vietnam on a classroom wall map, individual desk maps, and/or classroom globe. Increase the impact of the journey from Vietnam to the United States by drawing and attaching a lotus flower to Vietnam, then spacing lotus flower seeds between Vietnam and the United States. Lead students through the identification of latitudes and longitudes of the two locations, and then extend the exercise to conclusions about similarities of and differences between the two areas.

   Hint: Compare and contrast several regions of the United States with Vietnam, then talk with students about the effect that geographic factors (e.g., location, place, region, climate, features) exert on the settlement of Vietnamese immigrants in the United States. **Ask** students to put on their thinking caps: What factors account for Vietnamese immigrants moving inland once they arrive on the West Coast of the United States and the foothill region of western North Carolina?

6. Show students illustrations of typical Vietnamese clothing such as hats or thongs. Make simple patterns of Vietnamese articles of clothing, and request that children choose one item to make from paper or from brown sacks. Review conditions in Vietnam that forced so many people to leave their homeland. Remind students that people did not know what to expect in a new land; they only knew the fear that they lived with every day in Vietnam.

   Extension: Ask students attired in their article of Vietnamese clothing to reflect on what items people most likely take with them when they flee for their lives and why. Request that students think about whether or not items are similar to those of any people emigrating under the same circumstances. Suggest that they quietly record their thoughts to share with classmates. Invite students to stand and read their recorded thoughts. **Ask** students to put on their thinking caps: How and why do creative activities and reflection time increase learning?

7. Ask students to tell why they selected a character and how the character exemplifies one of the character traits emphasized in this lesson. Suggest that students think about their own lives and share examples that illustrate the trait.

   Hint: For interest and variety, alternate discussions on character traits between the presence and benefits of possessing the traits and the absence and consequences of not possessing the traits.

EVALUATION:

Determine the level of student understanding by evaluating written and creative products and by assessing class discussions and responses to thought questions. Ask students to explain what they have learned in this lesson and from the activities. Encourage students to connect the message in the story to the theme of celebrating or honoring life and history.

CONNECTION #17:
Michele Maria Surat.
Angel Child,
Dragon Child

Nguyen Hoa recounts difficulties she faced during her first year in America as she copes with the absence of her mother as well as the teasing by her school classmates. Through friendship with a former enemy, her problems find solutions.

CHARACTER TRAITS: Select one character trait (e.g., compassion, courage, or citizenship) and talk about how people in the story demonstrate the trait.

1. Read *Angel Child, Dragon Child* aloud. Remember to set the stage with appropriate pre-reading activities that capture students' interest. Point out visible cultural differences between Vietnamese and Americans by allowing students to study the illustrations (e.g., clothing and customs). Clarify vocabulary terms necessary for understanding the text. Define clearly a purpose for reading and/or listening.

2. Discuss Nguyen Hoa's first-day-of-school jitters. Ask students to describe feelings they might experience if they went to school in a new country and were unable to understand the language. Extend students' thoughts to include problems beyond the language barrier. Advise students that they first identified problems; now challenge them to propose solutions.

Hint: Clarify for students the difference between problem solving and decision making, i.e., in problem solving, one thinks up options to solve the problem; in decision making, one thinks through options and makes a decision based on what is best under current conditions.

Extension: Invite students or community members who immigrated to a new country to share experiences and feelings with classmates. Suggest that they talk about immediate problems and about how caring people help them solve problems. Lead students in a discussion that focuses on the generalization: When people begin to understand other individuals and their beliefs, respect and acceptance often follow. **Ask** students to put on their thinking caps: What is the relationship between learning about fears of newcomers and the way students behave toward newcomers?

3. Review children on the role of the matchbox in Nguyen Hoa's life. Make certain that students understand that matchboxes are containers in which people store meaningful pictures and objects. Invite students to make matchboxes with special pictures or special objects inside. **Hint:** Make matchboxes from tape boxes, paper clip boxes, or staple boxes.

Extension: Encourage children to write about their matchboxes: how they choose pictures or objects to go inside the box, what the items mean to them, how the matchbox makes them feel. Divide students into small groups and allow each student to share their writing with three other students.

4. Ask students what ways they consider best to learn about other people. Point out to students that one of the best ways to understand others is to know about their lives and interests. Pair students and instruct them to interview one another by using the reporters' formula technique for question starters (e.g., Who? What? Where? When? Why? How?). Request that they take interview notes, then write a brief biographical sketch of their partner.

Extension: Review the use of similes and metaphors (e.g., her hair is as black as coal, she was a cat waiting to spring with right answers). Request that students use similes and metaphors in their biographies. Invite students to read their work to classmates. **Ask** students to put on their thinking caps: Predict the results of Nguyen Hoa's teacher and classmates conducting student interviews when she enters school. In addition to learning information about classmates, what else is valuable about the interview process?

Hint: Encourage students to use these processes: communicate with a purpose, record notes, organize thoughts, and report results of investigation to others in written and oral forms. Lead students to comprehend the generalization: When people begin to understand other individuals and their beliefs, respect and acceptance often follow.

5. Talk about the dragon's significance in Asian cultures as a symbol of strength and goodness. Model the making of an egg-carton dragon, and invite boys and girls to make their own models. Gather the following materials: egg cartons (bottom only), tag boards, tissue paper, bottles of glue, green and red tempera paint, brushes, staplers, and scissors. Cut the last two eggcups off the carton for a head. Cut the bottom section in half lengthwise and slit down the middle. Cut a strip of tag board for the dragon's back, and place the strip in the slit. Cut half of the eggcup for the head and glue or staple on one end of the dragon. Paint the dragon green and red. Fringe tissue paper 30" x 1 1/2" and fold three times. Glue tissue around edge of carton and around dragon's head. Cut and glue large eyes, tongue, nose, and any other details desired on the dragon's head. **Hint:** Display dragons on classroom shelves in a mini-parade of dragons.

6. **Ask** students to put on their thinking caps: If a teacher in Vietnam wants her Vietnamese students to make an important American symbol, what symbol might she choose? Why? Why are symbols clues to culture?

7. Pass a basket of fortune cookies around the classroom for students to open and taste. Invite students to read their fortunes to classmates. Talk about the characters in the story and the circumstances in which they live. Ask students to place themselves in the role of a friendly writer of fortunes. Request that they write a fortune guaranteed to make a character in the story happy, then read the fortunes to classmates. (Alternate Activity, Parental Discretion) **Hint:** Advise boys and girls that first they must analyze the character to know what the character wants most, and then write a fortune that matches the character's wish. **Ask** students to put on their thinking caps: Might the process of character analysis, i.e., knowing what individuals want to hear most, influence people who write fortunes for a living? Why?

8. Ask students to tell why they selected a character and how the character exemplifies one of the character traits selected for this story. Suggest that students think about their own lives and share examples that illustrate the trait.

EVALUATION:

Determine the level of student understanding by evaluating the quality of written and creative products, class discussions, and responses to thought questions. Encourage students to connect the message in the story to the theme of celebrating or honoring life and history.

CONNECTION #18:
Bette Bao Lord.
In the Year of the Boar and Jackie Robinson

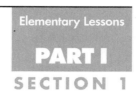
Shirley Temple Wong, full of hope for the future, leaves China for America, the land where anyone can succeed. Not knowing any English, she experiences difficulty in making friends. Because Jackie Robinson, a baseball star, stands for all that America offers to her citizens, he becomes her hero and helps her adjust to a new life in Brooklyn, New York.

CHARACTER TRAITS: In this lesson emphasize the traits of fairness, citizenship, courage, integrity, and respect.

1. Read *In the Year of the Boar and Jackie Robinson* aloud. Remember to set the stage with appropriate pre-reading activities that capture students' interest. For example, use geography as a hook by enlisting selected students to finger-trace the route from Shirley's hometown in China to Brooklyn, New York, on a classroom map and also by talking about how many geographic changes she encounters on her journey. Clarify vocabulary terms necessary for understanding the text. Define clearly a purpose for reading and/or listening.

2. Declare a Year-of-the-Boar-and-Jackie-Robinson Day on which activities in all subjects revolve around aspects of Shirley Temple Wong's story. Encourage students to brainstorm ways the class might link topics or ideas in the story to various subjects such as social studies, language arts, science, mathematics, and fine arts. Create classroom centers for specialized activities. Invite boys and girls to propose topics for investigation or to select one of the following activities, then to share the products with classmates:

Decide on what characteristics make a hero or heroine. Sketch a picture of a favorite sports hero and complete this statement at the bottom of the picture: My hero is _____, because _____. Challenge students to use the markers (e.g., characteristics) they identify as heroic in the sentence.

Assume the role of Shirley Temple Wong and write a friendly letter to a fourth cousin in China describing a new life in America. Make sure that letters follow guidelines for friendly letters (e.g., heading, greeting, indentation, closing, and signature).

Make an oriental screen by folding a piece of 9" x 12" manila paper in fourths and alternating the direction of the paper, e.g., ∧∧. Draw pictures of four favorite characters from the story, one in each section of the screen, then write two descriptive sentences about each character at the bottom of the section.

Design a book jacket to lure readers to the story of Shirley Temple Wong. Include on the front of the jacket the title, author, illustrator, and publisher. Write a "grab 'em and hold 'em" summary of the story for the back of the book jacket.

Research the life of the American movie star, Shirley Temple Black, with the assistance of the librarian. Choose important childhood and adult accomplishments of the heroine to share with classmates. Predict why Mrs. Wong named her daughter Shirley Temple Wong.

Invite another class to a show-and-tell session in which individual students, partners, or small groups tell about their products, the relationship between the products and the story, and the learning acquired from their chosen activities.

3. Share with students the story of how a Jewish playwright, Israel Zangwill gave birth to the term, Melting Pot in 1908. This term refers to the fact that people from all over the world came to America and because they lived close together in large cities, and intermarried, they began to lose many of their unique cultural traditions—they became "melted down" into new, Americans with American traditions.

Because people were unable to keep their unique cultural identity, belief in the theory and actions taken in the name of the theory (e.g., discriminatory laws) caused problems over the years. Today the preferred theory is the Salad Bowl Theory, which allows all people to be in the same bowl (e.g., America) yet keep their identity as lettuce, tomatoes, celery (e.g., Poles, Russians, Chinese).

Ask students to put on their thinking caps: Why is the Salad Bowl Theory fairer than the Melting Pot Theory? Use the indicators under the character trait of fairness to make a decision.

Hint: People in power, i.e., White Anglo-Saxon Protestants (WASPs), defined what Americans coming out of the Melting Pot would look like, act like, be like; thus, anyone not like a WASP was less than an American. **Ask:** How do WASP attitudes and actions conflict with indicators under the character trait of fairness?

4. Select one character trait (e.g., citizenship, courage, integrity, or respect) and talk about how people in the story demonstrate the trait. Ask students to tell why they selected a character and how the character exemplifies the trait. Suggest that students think about their own lives and share examples that illustrate the trait.

EVALUATION:

Determine the level of student understanding by assessing the quality of written and creative products, class discussions, and responses to thought questions. Ask students to write an essay in which they develop the generalization, "Respecting all people, no matter who or what they are, is the proper thing to do." Encourage students to connect the message in the story to the theme of celebrating or honoring life and history.

ADDITIONAL SELECTIONS:

Keith Baker. *The Magic Fan*

Molly Bang. *The Paper Crane*

Eleanor Coerr. *Sadako and the Thousand Paper Cranes*

Peggy Goldstein. *Lóng Is a Dragon*

Ai-Ling Louie. *Yeh-Shen*

Arlene Mosel. *Tikki Tikki Tembo*

Lensey Namioka. *Yang the Youngest and His Terrible Ear*

Matti A. Pitkänen. *The Children of China*

Allen Say. *Grandfather's Journey*

Ann Tompert. *Grandfather Tang's Story*

Kate Waters and Madeline Slovenz-Low. *Lion Dancer: Ernie Wan's Chinese New Year*

Blia Xiong. *Nine in One, Grr Grr*

Ed Young. *Lon Po Po: A Red Riding Hood Story from China*

CONNECTION #1:
Istvan Banyai. Zoom

Through a wordless picture story, Banyai shows a series of scenes, each one progressing farther and farther away from the original scene (e.g., a girl playing with toys that is part of a picture on a magazine cover, which is part of a sign on a bus). Teachers will delight over the visual explanation of perspective.

CHARACTER TRAIT: Ask the class to define diligence and give examples of diligent people they have known or about whom they have read.

1. Show the pictures in the story and discuss each one. Remember to set the stage with appropriate previewing activities that capture students' interest. Clarify scenes and subjects necessary for understanding the text. Define clearly a purpose for viewing.

2. Ask students to draw "Where Am I in the World?" Model for students how to fold a large piece of paper into eight squares. Instruct students to draw themselves:

1. At the desk	6. In the state
2. In the room	7. In the country
3. In the school	8. On the continent
4. On the street	9. On the earth
5. In the city	10. In the universe

Hint: Lead students into verbalizing that their place in the world is relative to other places. Ask students to relate the exercise to the pictorial story of *Zoom*. Discuss with students the meaning of perspective, how perspective applies to the exercise, to the story, and to life. Tell them how one needs to develop the habit of viewing any picture, issue, or topic from more than one perspective.

3. Explain to students that they may organize this project involving magnification around three topics: "Guess What?" "What Do Students See," and "*Zoom* In." Tell students to fold a paper in half. On the inside of the paper, ask students to draw an object of their choice. On the outside of the paper, request students to enlarge or magnify one small part of the same object. Encourage students to show a magnified version of their object to classmates who will guess the item by using a twenty-question format. **Ask:** What happens to the object when one "zooms in"? How does the project relate to the questions: Guess what? What do students see? What does the exercise show about perspective?

Extension: As an optional activity, tell students to draw an object, then on a cover sheet cut a small hole so that one sees only a little of the object. Instruct students with the same directions given above. Ask students questions ranging from the specific on the picture to the general on perspective. Also, ask for volunteers to research a science-related project about the relationship between sight and perspective. With student assistance, draw up two lists: 1) various animals; and 2) how they see. Talk about these questions before students go to the library for answers:

Do the animals have broad or limited vision?
Do the animals see fuzzy shapes or clear images?
Do the animals see black-and-white or color images?
How does the sight (e.g., view) of animals affect their perspective?
Does animals' sight influence their behavior?
Are any of the answers showing sight/perspective relationships that might apply to humans?

Hint: Seek the media specialist's help in finding examples of animals with assorted sight and behavior patterns. Lead students to a reasonable conclusion about sight and perspective in animal as well as human life.

4. Select the character trait of diligence. Discuss how the author exhibits diligence by completing the pictorial story of *Zoom*. Encourage students to respond with an example of when they demonstrate diligence by completing a task.

Hint: For interest and variety, alternate discussions on character traits between the presence and benefits of possessing the traits and the absence and consequences of not possessing the traits.

EVALUATION:

Determine the level of student understanding by assessing their responses to questions and activities focusing on the concept of perspective. Include teacher observations and rubrics in evaluating student success. Ask students to write a short narrative about one person whom they believe has displayed the character trait of diligence. Encourage students to connect the message in the story to the theme of celebrating or honoring a sense of place.

ADDITIONAL SELECTION:

Charlotte Zolotow. *The Moon Was the Best*. A mother visiting Paris brings back all of her best visual memories of beautiful fountains, sparkling rivers, and parks.

Elementary Lessons
PART I
SECTION 2

CONNECTION #2:
Dyan Sheldon.
Under the Moon

After finding an arrowhead in her backyard, a young girl dreams about what the area was once like when others lived there.

CHARACTER TRAITS: Define the meaning of compassion and respect. Ask students to give examples from their experiences with these two traits.

1. Read *Under the Moon* aloud while sitting on the playground. Remember to set the stage with appropriate pre-reading activities that capture students' interest. Clarify vocabulary terms necessary for understanding the text. Define clearly a purpose for reading and/or listening.

2. Encourage students to search the playground for artifacts. **Hint:** Plant artifacts to build a high degree of student interest as well as to lead students to important conclusions. Speculate with students about who were the owners. What were their lives like? Ask students to journey into the past and think about what happened at the time of the Folsom people, the Indians (Native Americans), and the buffaloes. **Hint:** Verify students' responses so that they leave this activity with correct data related to time, inhabitants, changes, and reasons for change, i.e., geographic as well as cultural reasons.

3. Talk about how the playground area may have looked long ago. Ask students to draw their ideas on paper, and post drawings in the classroom display entitled "Once on the Ground Where We Now Stand...." Suggest that students share with others why they chose certain physical features or animal life for their pictures. Encourage them to accurately link items in the drawings to broad periods of history.

Hint: Seek pictures and references on drawings left by Early Man, and lead students to the understanding that many times Early Man recorded in pictures those things most familiar in his life.

4. Demonstrate how to develop a class time line for your community from prehistoric to current times. Instruct students to draw pictures for each segment of the time line on index cards and post pictures above dates. **Hint:** Point out changes in the environment over time including effects of the railroad stopping or not stopping in their town or community or boats docking or not docking in their town or community.

5. Talk about the meaning of the traits of compassion and respect. Ask students to explain how the main character in *Under the Moon* exhibits the character traits of compassion and respect. Suggest that student partners discuss the traits and volunteer one example of how they or classmates may show one of the traits to another person.

Hint: For interest and variety, alternate discussions on character traits between the benefits of possessing the traits and the consequences of not possessing the traits.

EVALUATION:

Determine the level of student understanding that a sense of place changes over time by assessing the quality of class discussions, participation, and writing and by studying the development of a class time line. Include teacher observations and rubrics in evaluating student progress. Encourage students to connect the message in the story to the theme of celebrating or honoring a sense of place.

ALTERNATE SELECTIONS:

Jeannie Baker. *Window*. Wordless scenes observed from a window of a young man's house convey changes not only in his stages of life, babyhood to adulthood, but also in his environment.

Bonnie Pryor. *The House on Maple Street*. During the course of three hundred years, many people passed by or lived on the spot that a house numbered 107 Maple Street occupies. Items uncovered on site will forever remain a secret.

CONNECTION #3:
Crescent Dragonwagon.
Home Place

While hiking in the woods, a family discovers the site of an old house and finds clues about the people who once lived there.

CHARACTER TRAITS: On note cards have students put the words compassion, respect, and responsibility on one side. On the other side, have them write the name of a friend/relative/teacher that displays these characteristics. Let them share with the class and explain their choices.

1. Read *Home Place* aloud. Remember to set the stage with appropriate pre-reading activities that capture students' interest. Clarify vocabulary terms necessary for understanding the text. Define clearly a purpose for reading and/or listening.

2. Talk to students about the advantages of using preplanned research questions when investigating historical events or personalities. Assist them in developing a set of questions that will give strong clues about a time period, such as the materials used in making certain items and the clothing worn by people in pictures. Put artifacts such as a basket, music box, vase, brooch, quill, fountain pen, picture, and/or bill of sale in bags. In cooperative groups, ask students to reconstruct the family who owned the artifacts and the period of time they represent. Alert students that they must tell why they identify a particular period of time and what clues led them to a certain conclusion.

3. Ask students to bring an artifact to put in a classroom museum. The museum will feature items that reflect student interests or times in which they are living (e.g., soda can, Nintendo package, movie ticket, and newspaper headlines). Instruct students to group and label items by categories. Then, invite students to write about the significance of the artifact that they brought for the museum. Prompt students by asking: How does the artifact fit into the visual description of an elementary student's life in their community?

4. Invite students to participate in an archaeological dig prepared in advance with meaningful clues to the past. **Hint:** Plant artifacts in layers that represent different periods in time. Show students how to grid the area and record the finds by describing the artifact, the artifact's features, and logical conclusions. Lead students to the conclusion that archaeologists identify periods of time by the artifacts they uncover.

5. Discuss the meaning of the character traits of compassion, respect, and responsibility and how characters in the story demonstrate the traits. Then, invite students to share how these traits are integral parts of their lives and/or influence their behavior.

Hint: For interest and variety, alternate discussions on character traits between the presence and benefits of possessing the traits and the absence and consequences of not possessing the traits.

EVALUATION:

Determine the level of student understanding that a sense of place changes over time by assessing class discussions, participation, and writing and by studying responses to an archaeological dig. Include teacher observations and rubrics in evaluating student progress. Ask students to share orally what they have learned in this lesson. Encourage students to connect the message in the story to the theme of celebrating or honoring a sense of place.

CONNECTION #4:
Nadia Wheatley and Donna Rawlins.
My Place

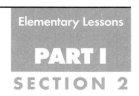

Viewing life in Australia by looking backward through time, 1988 to 1788, creates an innovative approach for teaching students about the concept of change.

CHARACTER TRAITS: Discuss the character traits of citizenship, courage, and respect.

1. Read *My Place* aloud. Remember to set the stage with appropriate pre-reading activities that capture students' interest. Clarify vocabulary terms necessary for understanding the text. Define clearly a purpose for reading and/or listening.

   Hint: Use this story prior to visiting a historical museum in your area.

2. Ask students to find out through a visit to a historical museum or by talking to an older adult how much their community has changed. If possible, they should find pictures or other artifacts that demonstrate this change. **Ask:** Why is evidence essential to the recording of history?

3. Remind students that change is inevitable. Discuss the location of students' homes and the school. Using a time machine approach, ask students to return to the past of one hundred years ago or project into the future one hundred years, and then suggest what might have been on the sites. **Hint:** Prior to predictions, talk about factors that affect changes in homes and schools, i.e., what factors keep structures relatively the same or change them dramatically. Encourage students to use discussion points in clarifying what thinking steps students must use to make good (e.g., logical), reasonable predictions.

4. Ask students to bring pictures of places where they lived in the past and show or tell how the places changed over time. Plot locations on a map. Ask students what factors caused the family to move, and discuss how many students moved for similar and for different reasons. Ask students if they find any patterns in how and why people move. **Hint:** Use this lesson as an opportunity to introduce or develop the meaning of the concept of mobility.

5. Select the character traits of citizenship, courage, and respect and relate them to characters in the story. Invite students to share examples of how they or classmates demonstrate one of the traits.

EVALUATION:

Determine the level of student understanding by assessing class discussions, participation, and writing, all of which reveal students' sense that over time significant changes take place. Include teacher observations and rubrics in evaluating student progress. Encourage students to connect the message in the story to the theme of celebrating or honoring a sense of place.

CONNECTION #5:
Linda Granfield.
Cowboy: An Album

Teachers and students will welcome a treasure trove of information about cowboy lifestyles, celebrities, and portrayals, romantic as well as true-to-life versions.

CHARACTER TRAITS: Discuss the meaning of the character traits of courage, diligence, fairness, and responsibility.

1. Read *Cowboy: An Album* aloud. Remember to set the stage with appropriate pre-reading activities that capture students' interest. Clarify vocabulary terms necessary for understanding the text. Define clearly a purpose for reading and/or listening. Stress the historic, economic, and social significance of the cowboy in Texas and the West.

2. Find pictures or diagrams of cowboy clothing and talk with students about the purpose of each item. **Ask:** How did the cowboy's lifestyle influence the style of his garments and the amount of clothing he owned?

3. Discuss the cowboy menu with students. **Ask:** Why were certain items staples of a cowboy's diet? What factors limited choices on a cowboy's menu? How does a cowboy's menu match up with what health authorities label as a balanced diet? Encourage students to link environment, job, and diet. **Hint:** Cook a favorite cowboy treat such as stew or beans to illustrate a typical cowboy meal and to emphasize the absence of fresh fruits and vegetables.

4. Show students examples of how the Spanish language influenced the English language with words associated with a cowboy's life, clothing, and skills (e.g., rodeo, lariat, corral, Amarillo, Rio Grande, and San Antonio). Invite students to seek more examples of Spanish influence on English words. **Ask:** Can one consider words as well as things historical legacies? Why? Do words and meanings, just like places, change over time? Search for examples to support your answers.

5. Invite local cowboys and cowgirls to demonstrate clothing, tack, roping, horseshoeing, branding irons, music, and cowboy poetry to culminate the place of the cowboy in community and western history. **Hint:** Ask students to state the importance of the cowboy's role in community and western history. Support statements with facts learned in the lesson.

6. Discuss the meaning of the character traits of courage, diligence, fairness, and responsibility. Talk with students about how cowboys exhibited each of the traits in their fulfillment of jobs. **Ask:** Are ways that a successful cowboy fulfilled his job similar to ways that a successful student learns at school? Why?

EVALUATION:

Determine the level of student understanding of cowboys, their lives, and their influence by assessing class discussions, participation, and activities and by studying how students identified items and purposes of cowboy clothing. Include teacher observations and rubrics in evaluating student progress. Encourage students to connect the message in the story to the theme of celebrating or honoring a sense of place.

ALTERNATE SELECTIONS:

Martin W. Sandler. *Cowboys.* Teachers and students will acquire a sense of the Old West by reading the illustrated overview of cowboy lives and legends.

Ann Herbert Scott. *Cowboy Country.* An "old buckaroo," who shares his passion for cowboy culture with readers, observes changes over time in cowboys' lifestyles.

CONNECTION #6:
Margaret Wild.
Space Travelers

Homeless in the big city, Zac and his mother reside in a rocket in the park until they can find a real home.

CHARACTER TRAITS: Discuss the meaning of the character traits of compassion, courage, and diligence.

1. Read *Space Travelers* aloud while sitting on the playground. Remember to set the stage with appropriate pre-reading activities that capture students' interest. Clarify vocabulary terms necessary for understanding the text. Define clearly a purpose for reading and/or listening.

2. Discuss basic human needs and how one might live in a rocket in the park. **Ask:** What would life in a play rocket be like? What kinds of foods would people eat? **Extend** by asking: How do people become homeless? What are ways they can personally correct the problem of being homeless? Is being homeless a part of the world in your community?

3. Connect class discussions to economics and mathematics. **Ask:** What are Zac's and his mother's needs and the needs' approximate costs? How much income does mother need to live in an apartment? **Hint:** Give students approximate costs by calling several apartment complexes to find out rental costs for the smallest units of furnished and unfurnished apartments. Remind students that sometimes it costs more to rent in a large city than in a small town or community.

4. Connect class discussions to science by encouraging students to study the solar system and identify, perhaps plot, places where Zac and his mother journey in their rocket. **Hint:** Remind students that Zac's and his mother's journey is a defense against their state of being homeless. **Ask:** What message does their journey send to people facing crises in real life?

5. Call students' attention to the pictures in the book that show a bird's-eye view and a panorama. Remind them that many mapmakers use these views or perspectives when they are designing maps. Ask students to select a scene and draw a picture from the perspective of a bird's-eye view or a panorama. **Ask:** What does the exercise teach about perspective in terms of size and attention to detail?

6. Discuss the meaning of the character traits of compassion, courage, and diligence and relate the traits to Zac and his mother. Invite students to cite examples of how they exhibit any one of the traits in their daily lives.

Hint: For interest and variety, alternate discussions on character traits between the benefits of possessing the traits and the consequences of not possessing the traits.

EVALUATION:

Determine the level of student understanding by assessing drawings from a bird's-eye view, class discussions, participation, role playing, and problem-solving ideas. Include teacher observations and rubrics in evaluating student progress. Encourage students to connect the message in the story to the theme of celebrating or honoring a sense of place.

CONNECTION #7:
Cynthia Rylant.
An Angel for Solomon Singer

A lonely New York City man finds companionship at the Westway Cafe where dreams come true.

CHARACTER TRAITS: Discuss the meaning of the character traits of compassion, respect, and responsibility.

1. Read *An Angel for Solomon Singer* aloud. Remember to set the stage with appropriate pre-reading activities that capture students' interest. Clarify vocabulary terms necessary for understanding the text. Define clearly a purpose for reading and/or listening.

2. Remind students of Solomon's favorite foods and the purposes that they serve. **Ask:** Do Solomon's favorite foods serve more purposes than to satisfy his hunger? Then, ask students to write out orders for their favorite foods without revealing information on the lists to any other student. Ask for student volunteers to record favorite foods on the chalkboard, so that students can see the many similarities as well as differences in food preferences among elementary students.

Ask: Do certain foods remind students of happy times with families or friends? When and why? Is there a connection between the way students feel and the foods they want to eat? Encourage students to give examples from their own lives. **Hint:** Lead students toward making a conclusion on the relationship between special foods and special times, i.e., good foods and good times are close friends.

3. Invite students to write their wishes and dreams for the future. Discuss with students whether or not they think that these wishes and dreams will change in the future and why. Relate the wishes and dreams to those of Solomon in *An Angel for Solomon Singer*. **Ask:** How are students' and Solomon's wishes and dreams similar? Different?

4. Suggest that the class study reflections, what makes reflections, and where one may see reflections. Relate the study to the reflections shown in the paintings in *An Angel for Solomon Singer*. **Ask:** Why does the artist use the technique of reflections for this story? Is the technique effective as far as explaining the meaning of the story? Why or why not?

Extension: Extend the learning by studying the phases of the moon after reflections. **Ask:** What is the significance of moon phases in the paintings? Is the technique effective as far as explaining the meaning of the story?

5. Discuss the meaning of loneliness, alone, and lonely in relationship to Solomon. Ask students what clues the author gives that prove that Solomon is indeed a lonely man. Encourage students to share their feelings about loneliness and ways that they cope with the feelings. Tell students to put their thinking caps on, then **ask:** Who are the lonely?

6. Relate the story to *Random Acts of Kindness,* and invite students to make a list of acts that they can do to cheer the lonely. **Hint:** Seek examples from stories in local papers and encourage students to move from talking about it to doing something about a lonely person. Teachers need to monitor students' plans for reasonableness and feasibility.

7. Encourage students to design a greeting card to send to someone (e.g., a neighbor, a shut-in, a person in a nursing home or retirement center) who might be lonely. Talk about why students selected persons and arrange a student sharing time for showing greeting cards before distribution of the cards. **Ask:** What effect does making cards for lonely people have on students? Why?

8. Discuss the meaning of the character traits of compassion, respect, and responsibility and then suggest to students that they cite characters in the story and in their lives who exemplify these traits.

EVALUATION:

Determine the level of student understanding by assessing the following: class discussions, class participation, activities, and greeting cards and by listening to students' expressions of empathy for the lonely. Include teacher observations and rubrics in evaluating student progress. A part of the evaluation might be a short quiz that requires students to match certain character traits with examples and/or definitions. Encourage students to connect the message in the story to the theme of celebrating or honoring a sense of place.

CONNECTION #8:
Linda Jacobs Altman.
Amelia's Road

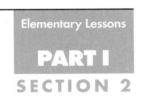

Elementary Lessons

PART I
SECTION 2

Amelia, the daughter of migrant farm workers, dreams of a stable home. The discovery of an old tree helps her create a special place as a substitute for a permanent home.

CHARACTER TRAITS: Discuss the meaning of the character traits, diligence and responsibility.

1. Read *Amelia's Road* aloud. Remember to set the stage with appropriate pre-reading activities that capture students' interest. Clarify vocabulary terms necessary for understanding the text. Define clearly a purpose for reading and/or listening. Begin class discussions related to this story by talking about different places students or their friends have lived and about general factors that cause families to move.

2. Invite students to speculate about putting treasures, i.e., items special to each child, in a box. **Ask:** What will students choose? Why? How does hiding special treasures in a box relate to *Amelia's Road*? Suggest that students draw items for the treasure box and then write about why these items are special. If students are willing to share their treasures with classmates, ask them either to post their drawings on a bulletin board with a large treasure-box cutout or to place the drawings in a decorated treasure box.

3. Discuss the meaning of the character traits diligence and responsibility. Lead students in talking about how characters in the story and in students' lives demonstrate either trait and why.

Hint: For interest and variety, alternate discussions on character traits between the benefits of possessing the traits and the consequences of not possessing the traits.

EVALUATION:

Determine the level of student understanding by assessing their writing samples and by listening to their discussions with classmates. Writing samples will reveal an understanding of what and why students treasure certain items. Discussions will indicate student awareness that a sense of place is more dependent on human relationships than geographic locations. Encourage students to connect the message in the story to the theme of celebrating or honoring a sense of place.

CONNECTION #9:
Gloria Jean Pinkney.
Back Home

Ernestine returns to visit her relatives on a North Carolina farm where she was born eight years ago.

CHARACTER TRAITS: Discuss the character traits of responsibility and respect.

1. Read *Back Home* aloud. Remember to set the stage with appropriate pre-reading activities that capture students' interest. Clarify vocabulary terms necessary for understanding the text. Define clearly a purpose for reading and/or listening.

2. Direct students to compare and contrast city life and country life by using examples drawn from the story and from personal experiences. On a T-bar chart, record student examples. Generate conclusions that students can verify with evidence on the T-bar chart. **Hint:** Lead students into revising their conclusions if evidence does not exist to support the conclusions. Talk with students about the importance of supporting conclusions with evidence and also about the value of revising thoughts, attitudes, and behaviors whenever necessary.

3. Ask students to talk with family members and to select one family memory that they treasure and are willing to share. Remind students that the memory may be a favorite person, a special time with family members, a family pet, or anything that is meaningful to their family. Invite students to volunteer to exchange stories by telling about a family memory, then writing about what makes the memory special. **Ask:** What learning takes place when class members share family memories?

4. Discuss the character traits of responsibility and respect. Encourage students to show how characters in the story and people in their lives demonstrate one or both traits.

Hint: For interest and variety, alternate discussions on character traits between the presence and benefits of possessing the traits and the absence and consequences of not possessing the traits.

EVALUATION:

Determine the level of student understanding by assessing the quality of class discussions, participation, activities, and T-bar charts, all of which highlight differences between life in the city and life in the country. Ask students to transfer their knowledge of making T-bar charts to another lesson to test their learning. Encourage students to connect the message in the story to the theme of celebrating or honoring a sense of place.

CONNECTION #10:
Frank Asch and Vladimir Vagin.
Dear Brother

Joey and Marvin find letters in the attic, then stay up all night reading an interesting collection of correspondence.

CHARACTER TRAITS: Discuss the nine basic character traits and their importance when communicating with others.

1. Read *Dear Brother* aloud. Remember to set the stage with appropriate pre-reading activities that capture students' interest. Clarify vocabulary terms necessary for understanding the text. Define clearly a purpose for reading and/or listening.

2. Ask students to write a letter to a family member that tells about their life in their community. Encourage students to make the text interesting so that someone reading the letter many years later will know about them. Instruct students to include descriptions of their home, school, family, friends, city, jobs, and hobbies. Place letters in a time capsule, open the capsule periodically, and read a student's letter without revealing his or her name.

Hint: Tell students that they should recognize classmates by the descriptions in the letter; if they do not identify the student, use the letter to stress the importance of one of the unit's generalizations: When people begin to understand other individuals and their beliefs, respect and acceptance often follow. **Ask:** How does sharing letters lead to understanding?

3. Ask students to write and mail a letter to a relative or friend who lives away from their community or town. Have students inquire about the same topics as the ones addressed in their autobiographies and later placed in a time capsule. Use the activity to teach or review correct letter form. Keep the activity alive by allowing students to read responses they receive to their letters. Also, post geographic locations of return letters so that students may see their network of correspondence grow.

EVALUATION:

Determine the level of student understanding by assessing class discussions, participation, and letters showing that multiple factors (e.g., jobs, homes, geography, hobbies) contribute to differences between students' lives in their community and lives in other places. Encourage students to connect the message in the story to the theme of celebrating or honoring a sense of place.

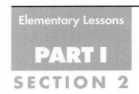
CONNECTION #11:
Jan Andrews. *The Auction*

A grandfather reveals memories of the past to his grandson as family members prepare the farm for auction.

CHARACTER TRAITS: Discuss the meaning of the character trait, compassion.

1. Read *The Auction* aloud. Remember to set the stage with appropriate pre-reading activities that capture students' interest. Clarify vocabulary terms necessary for understanding the text. Define clearly a purpose for reading and/or listening.

2. Encourage class members to make a list of crops the family raises, why family members lose the farm, why the family auctions the farm, and what changes in farming methods occur over time. Lead students through the process of collecting data from the story and drawing reasonable conclusions based on data.

3. Ask students in small groups to compare and contrast life on that farm in *The Auction* to students' lives today. As a class, decide on topics (criteria) that all groups will discuss such as time period, location, and pace of life. Remind students that using pre-selected criteria to investigate subjects often improves the quality of research.

   Hint: Review with students that comparing and contrasting means that students search for similarities and differences. Alert all groups that they will share the results of their research with classmates. **Ask:** Are the similarities and differences barely noticeable, moderately noticeable, or extremely noticeable? Why?

4. Request that class members create a time line that reflects a history of the farm over the same time period that the story covers. Assign different periods of time to class groups. Ask each group to illustrate index cards that show mini-snapshots of the farm at a given time and post cards by the correct date on the time line. Once students complete the project, ask them to draw conclusions from the data on the timeline, on the cards, and in the story. **Hint:** Use the story as an opportunity to show cause-and-effect relationships through concrete examples.

5. Help students understand the concept of auction by simulating an auction in the classroom. Talk about details such as the role of the auctioneer, the fast pace, the method of bidding, and who gets the auction items. Bring the concept closer to home by inviting a local auctioneer to demonstrate the art in the classroom. Assist students in composing a set of interview questions prior to the auctioneer's visit.

6. Discuss feelings about moving and leaving a place called home. Encourage students to share personal experiences with moving and ways they adjusted to new environments. Talk about the roles of family, relatives, and friends during times of change. Ask for volunteers to make conclusions from the discussion.

7. Discuss the meaning of the character trait, compassion. Ask students to cite characters in the story and persons in their lives who demonstrate compassion with specific acts.

Hint: For interest and variety, alternate discussions on character traits between the presence and benefits of possessing the traits and the absence and consequences of not possessing the traits.

EVALUATION:

Determine the level of student understanding of how economic factors, the passage of time, and the process of aging alter a sense of place by assessing class discussions, participation, activities, and time lines. Include teacher observations and rubrics in evaluating student progress. Ask students to explain what they learned in this lesson and its importance. Encourage students to connect the message in the story to the theme of celebrating or honoring a sense of place.

CONNECTION #12:
Thomas Locker. *Family Farm*

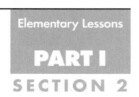
Elementary Lessons

PART I
SECTION 2

A farm family nearly loses their home until they decide to grow and sell pumpkins and flowers to supplement the corn and milk sales. Exquisite illustrations assist teachers in creating a rural scene for urban children.

CHARACTER TRAITS: Discuss the meaning of the character traits of courage, responsibility, and diligence.

1. Read *Family Farm* aloud. Encourage students to listen for problems as the teacher reads the story and to predict how characters in the story will resolve the problems. Remember to set the stage with other appropriate pre-reading activities that capture students' interest. Clarify vocabulary terms necessary for understanding the text. Define clearly a purpose for reading and/or listening.

2. Engage students in making vivid word descriptions that demonstrate their sense of home and place. Extend the discussion by talking about their fears related to changes in home and place including their fear of changing schools. **Ask:** Who and what create a sense of place at school? How may an individual create a sense of place at school? In a new school?

3. Ask students to generate a list of chores and responsibilities at home and in the classroom. **Ask:** How do chores help to establish a sense of place? Invite students to share their lists with classmates. **Hint:** Lead students to the conclusion that participation increases a sense of ownership. Request students to interpret the adage: One gets out of something what one puts into something. **Ask:** How does the adage apply to the discussion?

4. Encourage a team of students to research what crops farmers grow locally and what factors affect short-term and long-term crop production. Advise students how to interview personnel with the local County Extension Office for answers to their agricultural questions. Assist them with preparing telephone interview questions. Allow time for team members to informally share information organized around interview questions and answers.

Extension: If possible, invite a cotton farmer to visit the classroom as a guest speaker. Review with students the conclusion that good data result from asking good interview questions. Assist students in developing questions that likely will yield data that they are seeking. **Hint:** Take advantage of the excellent opportunity to introduce, develop, or reinforce the meaning of diversification. Since the family cannot make a living from only corn and milk sales, they added the production of pumpkins and flowers to supplement their farm income, i.e., four crops instead of two crops for the purpose of making a profit.

5. Discuss the meaning of the character traits of courage, responsibility, and diligence. Ask students to show how these traits apply to the family in the story and how these traits also apply to their lives. **Hint:** For interest and variety, alternate discussions on character traits between the benefits of possessing the traits and the consequences of not possessing the traits.

EVALUATION:

Determine the level of student understanding by assessing class discussions, participation, activities, research, and writing. Note especially how students apply problem-solving techniques required in the activities. Include teacher observations and rubrics in evaluating student progress. Encourage students to connect the message in the story to the theme of celebrating or honoring a sense of place.

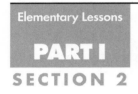

CONNECTION #13:
Diane Siebert. *Heartland*

As a literary form, poetry energizes the spirit of the land, people, and animals of the Middle West.

CHARACTER TRAITS: Review the meaning of the character traits of courage, integrity, diligence, and responsibility.

1. Read aloud the poetry in *Heartland*. Set the class mood by using George Strait's toe-tapping song about the Heartland before reading the poems. Invite students to describe the Heartland based on the song lyrics. Remember to set the stage with other appropriate pre-reading activities that capture students' interest. Clarify vocabulary terms necessary for understanding the text. Define clearly a purpose for reading and/or listening.

2. Talk with students about the visual scenes *Heartland* creates while they listen to the poems. Lead a structured discussion focusing on a comparison and contrast of the Heartland to your area. Use a Venn diagram to make the comparisons and contrasts obvious. For each entry, ask students to explain their answers. **Ask:** Based on the comparison-and-contrast exercise, can one apply the poems in *Heartland* to our community? Why or why not?

3. Encourage students to research and record differences in farming over the years including the amount of land farmed, machinery used, workers employed, and crops produced. Enlist the assistance of the school media specialist in selecting appropriate reference materials. Pair students to research differences in farming.

Model note-taking skills for students, then spend time talking about good note taking during this activity. **Ask:** Does the data reveal any trends in farming? Allow partners time to organize their notes and plan interesting, creative ways to share the data with classmates.

4. Ask students to cite the differences between crops of the Heartland and crops in their area by compiling lists of each. Talk about how geographic differences in the two areas affect the types of crops farmers grow.

Extension: Divide the class into two groups; one group paints or draws a mural of farming in America's Heartland in the 1800s and the other group makes a mural about farming today. Use research findings and the poetry as the bases for illustrating differences in farming through the years. Assist students in preparing a script that they will use to explain different scenes in the murals. Invite other elementary students to the classroom for a picture/print walk while student docents explain the murals.

5. Suggest that students write a poem about their area in the style of poetry used in *Heartland*. Ask authors to read their selections at sharing times. Either add the individual poems to the mural displays or compile poems in a class book.

6. Review the meaning of the character traits of courage, integrity, diligence, and responsibility and talk about how Diane Siebert addressed these traits through poetry. Ask students to share examples of persons in their lives who demonstrate the traits.

EVALUATION:

Determine the level of student understanding by assessing the quality of discussions, participation, activities, poems, research, and murals. All examples of assessment will show the degree of knowledge about major differences in farming between the 1800s and the present time. Include teacher observations and rubrics in evaluating student progress. Encourage students to connect the message in the story to the theme of celebrating or honoring a sense of place.

CONNECTION #14:
Tricia Brown and the Junior League of San Francisco.
The City by the Bay: A Magical Journey Around San Francisco

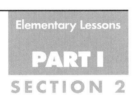

Lively narrative and attractive illustrations lead readers on a fascinating tour of one of America's gems: San Francisco, the sparkling city by the bay.

CHARACTER TRAITS: Review the meaning of the character traits of citizenship, respect, and responsibility.

1. Read *The City by the Bay* aloud. Note points of interest, the descriptions of sights, and the history of San Francisco. Remember to set the stage with other appropriate pre-reading activities that capture students' interest. Clarify vocabulary terms necessary for understanding the text. Define clearly a purpose for reading and/or listening.

2. Lead class members in a discussion of points of interest in your community and encourage students to further investigate its history. Suggest that class members design a book or brochure about their community, county, parish, or state. Ask students to answer these questions: What information holds readers' attention? How do illustrations add to the book or brochure? What are the attractions that make people want to go to San Francisco? How can the class design a book or brochure as attractive as *The City by the Bay*? Allow students to guide the production of a book or travel brochure about their community for others in the school.

3. Review the meaning of the character traits of citizenship, respect, and responsibility and encourage students to cite examples of one or more traits from *The City by the Bay*.

Hint: For interest and variety, alternate discussions on character traits between the presence and benefits of possessing the traits and the absence and consequences of not possessing the traits.

EVALUATION:

Determine the level of student understanding by assessing the quality of discussions, participation, activities, and student-designed books or brochures. Include teacher observations in evaluating whether or not students understand that smaller communities as well as larger communities boast points of interest that foster a sense of place among citizens. Encourage students to connect the message in the story to the theme of celebrating or honoring a sense of place.

CONNECTION #15:
Chris K. Soentpiet.
Around Town

Elementary Lessons
PART I
SECTION 2

A joyful celebration of city life promises to make even the most devoted suburbanite ready to take a trip to town.

CHARACTER TRAITS: Review the meaning of the character traits of citizenship, respect, and responsibility.

1. Read aloud the story *Around Town*. Remember to set the stage with appropriate pre-reading activities that capture students' interest. Clarify vocabulary terms necessary for understanding the text. Define clearly a purpose for reading and/or listening.

2. Engage students in comparing and contrasting the big city as described in *Around Town* and the community where they live. Predict the changes in daily lives that an overnight move to the city will make in such activities as going to school, getting groceries, playing outside after school hours. Ask students whether or not they see these changes as advantages or disadvantages of large city life and why. **Ask:** Is one place "better" than the other or does "better" derive its meaning from one's perspective or preferences? Talk about the reasons why some large cities such as New York and Washington continue to grow. **Ask:** What points about the city will they use to attract tourists and residents to the city? Why?

3. Facilitate face painting, portrait painting, or landscape painting happening on the streets in the story. Place student artists, easels, and materials outside the school and encourage them to draw or paint things they observe. Just as city artists paint cityscapes, tell student artists that they will paint schoolscapes to display in the school's corridors.

Suggest that as students paint, they also think about a crowd-pleasing name for their exhibit and about a crowd-attracting public service announcement to make on the school's public address system. **Hint:** Work hard on the crowd-pleasing, crowd-attracting aspects of publicity. Earned recognition of students from their peers will reinforce the learning of the entire activity.

4. Talk about street vendors as described in the story. Explain to students that the vending fair depicts aspects of a large city where people live, work, and play in a downtown setting. Ask students what they will choose to sell. Invite them to role-play a vending fair in the classroom. Allow students to choose items to make and advertise for a vending fair (e.g., paper flowers, food items, art items, face painting, or others listed in the story). Simulate booths by arranging desks in squares and encourage students to decorate the booths to attract customers.

Discuss with students how they may turn this experience into a practical lesson in economics by illustrating concepts such as supply, demand, opportunity cost, production, consumption, and distribution. Invite other elementary students to visit the vending fair. Prepare students to not only sell items with play money but also to explain important economic concepts to classmates, i.e., why they charge a certain price for an item with the explanation related to supply and demand.

5. Encourage students to write a letter of inquiry to the mayor of their city or to a county commissioner. Ask in the letter when fire departments turn on fire hydrants for a routine check, and if the mayor or the commissioners can announce times when and locations where children may play in the water. Have students consider the request from the perspective of the adults in authority and what the community and parents might think about it. What factors must the authorities consider before granting the request? Granting permission one time may lead to what action in the future?

Lead students in a decision-making activity related to how the authorities will respond to the students' request. In small groups, ask students to prepare a brief television announcement explaining the decision to others. For added interest, explain to students that this is an election year. Ask an anchorperson from each group to make the announcement to classmates.

6. Discuss the meaning of the character traits of citizenship, respect, and responsibility and provide examples of citizens exhibiting the traits in *Around Town*. **Ask:** How might citizens in your community exhibit these same traits in their everyday lives?

Hint: For interest and variety, alternate discussions on character traits between the benefits of possessing the traits and the consequences of not possessing the traits.

EVALUATION:

Determine the level of student understanding of how a large city and their community are similar and different by assessing the quality of class discussions and the degree of participation in a vending fair. Ask students to explain a decision made by their parents in response to students' requests from the parent's point of view. Encourage students to connect the message in the story to the theme of celebrating or honoring a sense of place.

ALTERNATE SELECTION:

Kathy Jakobsen. *My New York*. Becky, a young New Yorker, takes a Midwesterner as well as the readers on a tour of her favorite places in New York City.

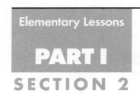

CONNECTION #16:
Eileen Spinelli.
If You Want to Find Golden

A trip through city streets reveals a full array of colors from gloriously bright construction signs to subtly grayed pigeons. Colors and verses extol the urban experience.

CHARACTER TRAITS: Review the meaning of the character traits, citizenship and responsibility.

1. Read *If You Want to Find Golden* aloud. Ask students to think about their favorite color, write about that color, determine what kinds of things they associate with that color, and decide how the color affects the mood of a place or a person. Remember to set the stage with other appropriate pre-reading activities that capture students' interest. Clarify vocabulary terms necessary for understanding the text. Define clearly a purpose for reading and/or listening.

2. Divide students into cooperative groups. Allow each group to draw a color from a box, then direct their discussions to the four actions cited in the activity above (e.g., think, write, determine, decide about one color). Ask students to include positive and negative associations with the color. Encourage groups to share their color thoughts with classmates and verify their conclusions with other groups in a round-robin style. If differences of opinions occur, suggest that student leaders allow time for all students to express opinions. **Hint:** Lead students to the conclusion that differences of opinion often occur because of different experiences.

3. Make a large color wheel. Request that students cut out magazine pictures that show items and emotions usually associated with certain colors (e.g., lipstick = red, sadness = blue). Place pictures in appropriate spots on the wheel. Informally talk about the many factors that develop word associations in people's minds and cultures. Make sure that for every idea a student suggests, he also provides a reason for the thought.

4. Demonstrate how to discover different colors within one color. Use coffee filter chemistry: cut a strip of filter paper, put a drop of ink near one end, and allow the strip to dry. Punch a hole in the other end of the strip and put a pencil through it to support the strip from the top of a jar or a glass. Fill the jar with enough water so that the end of the paper below the ink spot touches the water.

Hint: The paper absorbs water, and water climbs upward. When water reaches the spot, the liquid dissolves the ink and carries it up the paper. Some of the components in the ink are deposited at various distances from the original ink spot. The process, in effect, takes the ink apart and shows that each color is made up of many other colors. Lead students into verbalizing both the process and conclusion.

5. Ask students to draw or paint a picture in monochromatic hues that show the dramatic effect of the intensity of one color from the darkest to lightest hues. Talk about when students might use shades of a single color most effectively. Ask a student team with the assistance of the school's media specialist to search in the media center for examples of monochromatic pictures to show classmates.

6. Review the meaning of the character traits of citizenship and responsibility and discuss how these traits relate to the story and to the lives of students.

Hint: For interest and variety, alternate discussions on character traits between the benefits of possessing the traits and the consequences of not possessing the traits.

EVALUATION:

Determine the level of student understanding of colors in everyday life by listening to student discussions, by watching their eagerness to participate in the science experiment, and by assessing student writing about colors, associations, and feelings. Include teacher observations and rubrics in evaluating student progress. Encourage students to connect the message in the story to the theme of celebrating or honoring a sense of place.

CONNECTION #17:
Bernard Wolf.
Beneath the Stone

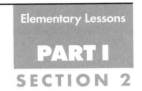

Readers view the daily life and customs of a small village in Oaxaca, Mexico, through the eyes of a young Indian boy.

CHARACTER TRAITS: Review the meaning of the character traits of citizenship, courage, and responsibility.

1. Read *Beneath the Stone* aloud. Talk about the similarities between Leo's life and students' lives by comparing such topics as foods, holidays, housing, markets, and schooling. Remember to set the stage with other appropriate pre-reading activities that capture students' interest. Clarify vocabulary terms necessary for understanding the text. Define clearly a purpose for reading and/or listening.

2. Locate Oaxaca on a classroom map by using an atlas index, longitude, and latitude. Use the story and the location of Oaxaca to practice locating other sites. **Ask:** If the class takes a trip to Oaxaca, then decides to go to _____, what is its exact geographic location? What physical features mark the way between two points? What clues do maps and globes provide about physical features? **Hint:** Relate answers to conclusions about colors students reached in *If You Want to Find Golden*.

3. Review the meaning of the character traits of citizenship, courage, and responsibility and relate the traits to characters in the story and also to persons in students' lives.

Hint: For interest and variety, alternate discussions on character traits between the presence and benefits of possessing the traits and the absence and consequences of not possessing the traits.

EVALUATION:

Determine the level of student understanding by assessing student discussions and the class-generated list of similarities and differences among children's lives. Ask students to explain what they have learned in this story and activities. Encourage students to connect the message in the story to the theme of celebrating or honoring a sense of place.

CONNECTION #18:
Anne Marie Linden.
Emerald Blue

Childhood memories of the author's life with her brother and grandmother on a Caribbean island generate the plot for a delightful child's story.

CHARACTER TRAITS: Review the meaning of the character traits, responsibility and courage.

1. Read *Emerald Blue* aloud. Ask students to compare and contrast Barbados and their home town in terms of foods, play, clothing, wildlife, weather, and land. Lead students to valid conclusions about the two areas at the end of the discussion. Remember to set the stage with other appropriate pre-reading activities that capture students' interest. Clarify vocabulary terms necessary for understanding the text. Define clearly a purpose for reading and/or listening.

2. Locate Barbados on a classroom map by using an atlas index, longitude, and latitude. Use the story and the location of Barbados to practice locating other sites. **Ask:** If the class takes a trip to Barbados, then decides to go to _____, what is the exact geographic location? What physical features mark the way between two points? What clues do maps and globes provide about physical features? **Hint:** Relate to conclusions about map/globe colors reached in *If You Want to Find Golden* and *Beneath the Stone*.

3. Ask students to identify typical foods of Barbados and Midland. List foods, and then invite students to bring samples for tasting. Request that students use only the foods as evidence from which to draw conclusions about cultures and also regions. Remind students to base conclusions on factual evidence.

4. Encourage groups of students to investigate thatched roofs in the story and roofs of their homes, then construct models of both roofs. **Ask:** What geographic clues to the two areas do roofs provide? **Hint:** Lead students to the understanding that roofs may reflect the use of certain materials and type of construction common in their geographic area.

5. Encourage students to research the wildlife of Barbados and of their surrounding community or state. Allow students to choose a way to show results of their research (e.g., drawing, diorama, poster, story, or poem). Enlist students in designing a display entitled "Two Wild Kingdoms."

6. Review the meaning of responsibility and courage. Ask students to relate the traits to the story and to their lives.

EVALUATION:

Determine the level of student understanding of similarities and differences between Barbados and their home state by assessing the quality of discussions, participation, activities, research, and roof construction designs. Include teacher observations and rubrics in evaluating student progress. Encourage students to connect the message in the story to the theme of celebrating or honoring a sense of place.

CONNECTION #19:
Catherine Stock.
Where Are You Going, Manyoni?

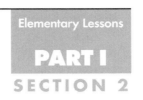
A Zimbabwe child living near the Limpopo River observes several wild animals on her way to school. These adventures shape a lively story and form the basis for interesting comparisons and contrasts between African and local students.

CHARACTER TRAITS: Review the meaning of the character traits, responsibility and courage.

1. Remember to set the stage with appropriate pre-reading activities that capture students' interest. Clarify vocabulary terms necessary for understanding the text. Define clearly a purpose for reading and/or listening.

2. Read *Where Are You Going, Manyoni?* aloud. Ask students to listen carefully for clues about the two areas during story reading. Use overlapping maps of their community and Africa to form a Venn diagram. Ask students to write on sticky notes comparisons and contrasts of a walk to school in their community and in Africa, then to place notes in the appropriate place on the diagram. Request that students read all the evidence other students post and work with a partner to make valid conclusions about going to school in two different geographic areas. **Hint:** Remind students that they must support conclusions with evidence.

3. Locate Zimbabwe on a classroom map using latitude and longitude, then compare the location with their community's latitude and longitude. Ask the school librarian to assist a student team in researching geographic features, climate, and resource base of the two areas. Request that the team provide geographic snapshots of the two areas. **Hint:** Use the activity to point out the differences in the geographic/political terms of nation and state. **Ask:** Does the geographic information influence the way that boys and girls go to school in the two areas?

4. Invite students to write about their walk or ride to school including the sights and the sounds. Provide time for students to share stories, then draw conclusions about the student population of the school. Lead students to verbalize their understanding of diversity in terms of cultures and geographic areas. **Hint:** Extend the discussion by explaining that the school population generally reflects the total community in which they live.

5. Review the traits of responsibility and courage. Encourage students to relate the traits to characters in the story and to persons in their lives.

EVALUATION:

Determine the level of student understanding of the similarities and differences between their home state and Africa by observing students' Venn diagrams and by assessing students' writing about their walks to school. Include teacher observations and rubrics in evaluating student progress. Ask students to tell what they learned through these activities. Encourage students to connect the message in the story to the theme of celebrating or honoring a sense of place.

CONNECTION #20:
Ingrid Mennen and Niki Daly.
Somewhere in Africa

Ashraf, who lives in a large city in Africa, checks out his favorite book at the library that tells about Africa outside the city. Although he finds adventure in an urban environment, he experiences different adventures through reading.

CHARACTER TRAITS: Review the meaning of the character traits of responsibility, respect, and compassion.

1. Remember to set the stage with appropriate pre-reading activities that capture students' interest. Clarify vocabulary terms necessary for understanding the text. Define clearly a purpose for reading and/or listening.

2. Read *Somewhere in Africa* aloud. Discuss with students that even though Ashraf knows about one African city, he lacks knowledge about a whole continent named Africa. Request that students apply this idea to their experiences. Ask students if they know all they want to know about their state and the United States.

Show students the wealth of knowledge that awaits them in the media center. Ask students to select a place in their state about which they want to know more. Enlist the assistance of the media specialists to help children in their research. Have students research one site by finding a good source, scanning the information, and taking notes on five important facts to report. Suggest to students that they entitle reports "Crossing the Miles Through Research" and plot the locations on a classroom map. Draw attention to the locations chosen by students. Assess reasons for variety or lack of variety. **Ask:** What does the research experience prove to students about traveling to near and faraway places?

3. Talk about the differences between similes and metaphors. Note in class discussion the many similes and metaphors used in *Somewhere in Africa*. Encourage students to revisit the texts of their reports and incorporate similes and metaphors in appropriate places. Show students how valuable the classroom map and globe can be when making reports on geographic places. Set aside a special time for "Crossing the Miles Through Research" reports.

4. Suggest that each student illustrate and caption a page for a book that will serve as a memory book of "Crossing the Miles Through Research." Bind and display the book in a prominent place in the classroom.

5. Review the meaning of the traits of responsibility, compassion, and respect and encourage students to relate them to Ashraf in the story and to their lives.

EVALUATION:

Determine the level of student understanding that one can travel vicariously through books by assessing class discussions, participation, illustrations, and reports. Include teacher observations and rubrics in evaluating student progress. Encourage students to connect the message in the story to the theme of celebrating or honoring a sense of place.

ADDITIONAL SELECTION:

Gregory Scott Kreikemeier. *Come with Me to Africa: A Photographic Journey.* A journey to Africa through Kreikemeier's comments and photographs unravels many of the continent's mysteries.

CONNECTION #21:
Anita Lobel.
Away from Home

Alliteration applied to both proper and place names brings new life to the alphabet.

CHARACTER TRAITS: Review the meaning of the character trait, responsibility.

1. Read *Away from Home* aloud after discussing the alliterative style with students. Ask them to listen for examples of alliteration. Remember to set the stage with other appropriate pre-reading activities that capture students' interest. Clarify vocabulary terms necessary for understanding the text. Define clearly a purpose for reading and/or listening.

2. Choose for each student a country to research that begins with the same letter of his/her first name. Enlist the school media specialist in the project. Suggest to students that they select five important facts about the country that they believe other boys and girls will enjoy knowing. Ask each student to write an alliterative phrase about the country similar to ones in the story, draw a picture showing unique features of the chosen country for a class book, and report information to classmates. Bind and display the class book in a prominent place.

EVALUATION:

Determine student understanding of a specific country by assessing the quality of class discussions, participation, research, writing, and illustrations for the class book. Include teacher observations and rubrics in evaluating student progress. Ask students to explain what they learned about responsibility from attending to accurate research and reporting to classmates. Encourage students to connect the message in the story to the theme of celebrating or honoring a sense of place.

CONNECTION #22:
Jacob Lawrence.
The Great Migration

A series of sixty paintings chronicle the journey of African Americans from the rural South to the industrial North about the time of World War I.

CHARACTER TRAITS: Review the meaning of the nine character traits associated with this manual.

1. Remember to set the stage with appropriate pre-reading activities that capture students' interest. Clarify vocabulary terms necessary for understanding the text. Define clearly a purpose for reading and/or listening.

2. Read *The Great Migration* aloud. Discuss reasons for the migration of African Americans from the rural South to the industrial North and hardships faced at points of destination. Send a team to the media center to research problems faced by immigrants to the United States between 1880 and 1910. Ask students to determine if immigrants, regardless of race, ethnicity, or religion, faced similar experiences to African Americans moving north after the turn of the twentieth century. Request that team members report to classmates and lead them to valid conclusions.

3. Ask students to discuss with their families when and why they came to live in their community and to share information with classmates. **Ask:** Did they face hardships as a result of the move? How did the family as a unit or individual family members resolve the hardships? Find locations on a classroom map from which each family moved and connect the locations to their school location with a line. Quiz students about the lines between old homes in other locations and new homes today. **Ask:** Are any patterns of migration obvious? If so, what are they?

4. Review the nine character traits associated with this manual and determine what character traits are needed for families to overcome hardships.

5. Reread the story and ask students to note colors in the paintings. Discuss the significance of color choices with the class. Ask students if they remember any other paintings that use similar color effects to accomplish a specific purpose. Lead students to the conclusion that artists utilize a variety of ways, including color choices, to send messages to viewers. Talk about other communications methods of artists in addition to color choices (e.g., size of figures and objects, perspective, facial expressions).

EVALUATION:

Determine the level of student understanding of purposes for migration and problems encountered in new places by listening to class discussions and to the sharing of personal experiences. Sharing stories about a move reveals student understanding of difficulties faced with any change of place. Encourage students to connect the message in the story to the theme of celebrating or honoring a sense of place.

CONNECTION #23:
Riki Levinson. *Soon, Annala*

Anticipating the arrival of her two younger brothers from the old country, Annala tries to speak less Yiddish and more English.

CHARACTER TRAITS: Review the meaning of the character traits of courage, compassion, and citizenship.

1. Remember to set the stage with appropriate pre-reading activities that capture students' interest. Clarify vocabulary terms necessary for understanding the text. Define clearly a purpose for reading and/or listening.

2. Read *Soon, Annala* aloud and encourage students to share anxious times associated with waiting for special family events. Ask students to compare their feelings to Annala's feelings. Share with classmates how they personally calmed anxious feelings.

3. Ask students to make two album pages, one page for Annala and the other page for themselves. On one page, instruct students to draw a picture that shows Annala's anxious feelings as she awaits the arrival of her two brothers; on the other page, instruct students to draw a picture of themselves in any situation in which they experience anxious feelings such as giving an oral report in class, moving

to a new classroom, going to a new school, running for a classroom office, or assuming leadership of a student group. Assemble a class book and invite students to refer to the album whenever they need assurance in stressful situations.

4. Reread the book to students as they take notes on the feelings of Annala: (1) at school; (2) concerning family responsibilities; (3) when the letter arrives; (4) at the docks; and (5) after they are at home. Ask students to make five diary entries related to the five topics and invite them to share their writing with a partner.

5. Plot the brothers' journey from Poland to New York by using longitude and latitude and the index of an atlas. Ask students to finger-trace the journey on a classroom map; then, in small groups, request that students write scripts that describe the journey in the conversational style of two brothers sharing attitudes, hopes, dreams, and fears.

6. Review the character traits of courage, compassion, and citizenship; then invite students to discuss how these traits relate to the characters in the story and to their lives.

Hint: For interest and variety, alternate discussions on character traits between the presence and benefits of possessing the traits and the absence and consequences of not possessing the traits.

EVALUATION:

Determine the level of student understanding of and empathy for feelings of immigrants moving from place to place by assessing class discussions, participation, diary entries, and album pages. Include teacher observations and rubrics in evaluating student progress. Encourage students to connect the message in the story to the theme of celebrating or honoring a sense of place.

ALTERNATE SELECTIONS:

Roslyn Bresnick-Perry. *Leaving for America.* A young Jewish girl recalls her early years, especially the last days, in a small Jewish village in western Russia prior to joining her father in America.

Riki Levinson. *Watch the Stars Come Out.* Grandma shares a story about her mama's journey from Europe to America by boat.

Bud Howlett. *I'm New Here.* A young Salvadoran girl faces her first day in an American school with worry but adjusts to an alien society when peers accept her prowess on the soccer field.

CONNECTION #24:
Muriel Stanek.
We Came from Vietnam

Black-and-white photographs poignantly illustrate the efforts of a Vietnamese refugee family to adjust to life in Chicago.

CHARACTER TRAITS: Review the meaning of the character traits of respect, courage, and diligence.

1. Remember to set the stage with appropriate pre-reading activities that capture students' interest. Clarify vocabulary terms necessary for understanding the text. Define clearly a purpose for reading and/or listening.

2. Read *We Came from Vietnam* aloud. Ask students to cite examples of Vietnamese customs, food, and holidays. Have students compare and contrast Vietnamese and students' lifestyles. Talk about adjustments that immigrants must make in moving to a new place. Encourage students to use examples from other stories about immigrants coming to America from different parts of the world and in different time periods. Lead students to conclusions related to similarities and differences among immigration experiences spanning various time periods and cultural backgrounds.

3. Point out the limited number of Vietnamese citizens' last names in comparison to the wide variety of other citizens' last names in the United States. Check the telephone directory to verify the small number of Asian names in comparison to other last names. **Hint:** Remind students that Vietnamese parents often give children names with specific meaning. Ask students to discuss their names with their families by applying the reporter's formula to the research topic, names and their origins: Who? What? Where? When? Why? How? Ask students to complete a name chart with this information and share the information with classmates. Encourage students to decorate their name chart with a design created by using the letters of their first name. **Hint:** Offer this activity as a cooperative project for family members.

4. Locate Vietnam on a classroom map. Provide a historical overview of Vietnam and tell why many Vietnamese citizens fled to the United States and other countries. Ask students to relate reasons for Vietnamese immigration to what they learned from stories about European immigration and African-American migration.

5. Review the meaning of the traits of respect, courage, and diligence and invite students to discuss how characters in the story and persons in their lives demonstrate these traits.

Hint: For interest and variety, alternate discussions on character traits between the presence and benefits of possessing the traits and the absence and consequences of not possessing the traits.

EVALUATION:

Determine student understanding of how every immigrant must establish a new sense of place by assessing the quality of class discussions, participation, designs, and reports. Include teacher observations and rubrics in evaluating student progress. Encourage students to connect the message in the story to the theme of celebrating or honoring a sense of place.

CONNECTION #25:
Sook Nyul Choi.
Halmoni and the Picnic

A Korean-American girl's third-grade class helps her newly arrived grandmother feel more comfortable with a new life in the United States by letting her share special talents.

CHARACTER TRAITS: Review the meaning of the character traits of respect, courage, and compassion.

1. Remember to set the stage with appropriate pre-reading activities that capture students' interest. Clarify vocabulary terms necessary for understanding the text. Define clearly a purpose for reading and/or listening.

2. Read *Halmoni and the Picnic* aloud. Compare and contrast Korean customs and foods with those of students' families. Use a Venn diagram to chart information. Lead students to the conclusion that food, as well as music, art, and holidays, are like windows to a culture. All markers give insights into unique cultural features. **Ask:** What other topics will make useful windows for learning more about other cultures?

3. Invite students to host a tasting event by:

> *Bringing a taste of special foods representing their family's ethnic heritage;*
> *Sharing ethnic family recipes and discussing ingredients, their origins, and measurements; and*
> *Making an illustrated ethnic recipe booklet to distribute to classmates and their families.*

Hint: Reinforce the conclusion that special foods and special times are good friends.

4. Review the meaning of the traits of citizenship, compassion, courage, and respect and invite students to apply the traits to the characters in the story and the persons in students' lives.

Hint: For interest and variety, alternate discussions on character traits between the presence and benefits of possessing the traits and the absence and consequences of not possessing the traits.

EVALUATION:

Determine the level of student understanding that families and customs are different yet alike; both assist individuals in establishing a sense of place. Assess the quality of class discussions, participation, and products. Include teacher observations and rubrics in evaluating student progress. Encourage students to connect the message in the story to the theme of celebrating or honoring a sense of place.

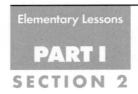

CONNECTION #26:
Staton Rabin. Casey over There

When his older brother, Casey, leaves to fight in World War I, worry overpowers Aubrey. He writes a letter to Uncle Sam and asks him to send Casey home.

CHARACTER TRAITS: Review the meaning of the character traits of citizenship, courage, and compassion.

1. Set the mood by playing the song and discussing the lyrics of George M. Cohan's rousing World War I tune, "Over There." Read *Casey over There* aloud. Remember to set the stage with other appropriate pre-reading activities that capture students' interest. Clarify vocabulary terms necessary for understanding the text. Define clearly a purpose for reading and/or listening.

2. Ask students to listen for geographic locations mentioned in the war story, and then locate the places on a classroom map. **Ask:** What clues do geographic locations give on the course of the war, the Allied positions, and the location of fighting?

3. Request students in small groups to compare and contrast pictures of uniforms, swimming wear, cost of theater tickets in the story to today's counterparts. Lead students to factual conclusions based on evidence.

5. Ask local recruiters for armed services' posters of today to compare with recruiting pictures in *Casey over There*. Lead students in comparing and contrasting one item at a time. Develop student understanding about the generalization: Over time, change occurs. **Ask:** Why?

6. Discuss with class members how letter writing ties a person to home during peacetime as well as wartime. Letter writing affirms that a person recognizes his sense of place and wants to share that place with others. Assign students to write a letter to a real or fictional person living away from his or her home place. Remind students to write about familiar sights, sounds, and smells typical of where they live. Invite students to read letters to classmates. Post letters on a bulletin board entitled "Signed, Sealed, and Delivered." Put a silhouette of a post office box on the bulletin board as well.

7. Invite students to write a letter to the President, Mayor, or other official with a request. Refer to Aubrey's letter to Uncle Sam as an example. Add letters to the bulletin board created in the previous lesson. Ask boys and girls to share the contents of their letters with classmates and predict the answers they will receive from the persons receiving the letters. **Hint:** Stress the power of words in working for changes.

8. Review the meaning of the traits of citizenship, courage, and compassion and request that students apply the traits to characters in the story and to persons in their lives.

EVALUATION:

Determine the level of student understanding that over time changes take place and that a sense of place establishes continuity in people's lives. Assess the quality of discussions, participation, and letter writing. Include teacher observations and rubrics in evaluating student progress. Encourage students to connect the message in the story to the theme of celebrating or honoring a sense of place.

CONNECTION #27:
Karen Williams.
When Africa Was Home

After returning to the United States, Peter's whole family misses life in Africa. Peter's father, therefore, seeks another job in the place the family calls home.

CHARACTER TRAITS: Review the meaning of the nine character traits used in this manual and ask students to provide definitions and examples of each of them.

1. Read *When Africa Was Home* aloud. Ask students to compare and contrast America and Africa (e.g., animals, weather, clothing, and food). Discuss, list, or diagram comparisons and contrasts. Remember to set the stage with other appropriate pre-reading activities that capture students' interest. Clarify vocabulary terms necessary for understanding the text. Define clearly a purpose for reading and/or listening.

2. Ask students to write an ad for Peter's dad to apply for a job. Encourage students to write a high-interest, right-to-the-point newspaper ad that makes Peter's dad a strong applicant (e.g., skills, experience, permanence, love of Africa). Talk about the qualities of advertisements that catch and hold people's attention. Invite students to share ads with classmates and tell how ads meet the set criteria.

3. Help students create designs similar to the designs on Peter's hat by using a variety of materials. Use a standard size of construction paper suitable for making a bulletin board border when stapled together, i.e., strips of 3" construction paper. Tell students that they may use vegetable prints, watercolors, or make their own stencil as long as the design reflects the African culture in which Peter lives.

   Hint: Make vegetable prints by cutting vegetables such as onions, cabbages, or apples in half, dipping them in paint, and pressing them on paper to produce prints. Students may carve potatoes or turnips into various shapes or designs for special effects. Show students how to cover the entire bulletin board with bright paper, how to attach the colorful African border, and then how to post the ads in an attractive manner.

4. Apply the character trait of citizenship to Peter in the story. Ask students to volunteer ways that they might exhibit any of the indicators associated with citizenship in their daily lives.

EVALUATION:

Determine the level of student understanding of geographic and cultural differences between Africa and America by assessing the quality of class discussions, voluntary participation, student-generated lists, and creative designs. Include teacher observations and rubrics in evaluating student progress. Encourage students to connect the message in the story to the theme of celebrating or honoring a sense of place.

CONNECTION #1:
Florence Parry Heide and Judith Heide Gilliland.
The Day of Ahmed's Secret

A young, industrious boy in Cairo carries heavy responsibilities in the family business. Ahmed pushes himself beyond job requirements in order to accomplish a personal goal. Because the author, as well as the illustrator, skillfully build suspense about Ahmed's secret, readers eagerly anticipate its revelation throughout the story.

CHARACTER TRAITS: Review the nine character traits associated with this manual. Ask students to define and give examples of each trait. Discuss these for clarity and understanding.

1. Remember to set the stage with appropriate pre-reading activities that capture students' interest. For example, use the Egyptian setting as a basis for comparing and contrasting the world of Ahmed in Egypt and the world of students in your community.

   Hint: Use this excellent opportunity to enlarge elementary students' horizons by emphasizing that students can become world travelers by paying close attention to geographic clues in stories, then by comparing and contrasting the story site to the world in which they live. Post locations of stories on a story map in the classroom so that students can literally see their horizons expand throughout the year. Keep a legend that shows the name of the story, main characters, and geographic sites for the purpose of building bridges between literature and geography.

   Talk about common criteria that compose settings. **Hint:** Connect the worlds of Egypt and your community by encouraging student input on a list of criteria, then check against the following list: geographic features, climate, location, people, sounds, sights, transportation, clothes, foods, architecture, space. List the criteria in the middle of the chalkboard.

   Clarify vocabulary terms necessary for understanding the text. Divide students into partners and ask that they listen for clues to the Egyptian setting during the reading of *The Day of Ahmed's Secret*. **Hint:** Read aloud the story while partners listen carefully.

   After reading, excite students about creating two word pictures of Cairo and their home town. Ask students to volunteer impressions of Cairo, as a recorder transfers word pictures to a list on the left side of the criteria on the chalkboard. Next, ask students to follow the same process for their community, and use a student to transfer word pictures to a list on the right side of the criteria. Ask students to compare and contrast the similarities of and differences between the two settings. **Ask:** How does a story help you become world travelers? What else can stories teach students?

2. Set listening for assorted tasks that Ahmed performs in his job as the purpose for the second reading of the story. Allow the same partners to take notes during story reading on every job task that they hear. Invite students to list Ahmed's multiple tasks, to compare Ahmed's responsibilities to those of many elementary students in your school, then to draw a conclusion about the degree of responsibility that Ahmed carries every day.

   Hint: Lead students in a discussion of the concept of childhood shared by most Americans, i.e., as a society, most parents generally try to protect children for as long as possible from a world filled with job responsibilities. Many adults respect the years of childhood as times to learn essential knowledge and skills for productive adult lives as democratic citizens. Most adults also seek appropriate matches among children's ages, developmental levels, and assignment of responsibilities.

Ask: How does this view of responsibilities during childhood conflict with the view in the story? What are the short-term and long-term advantages of delaying employment? What advantages do many American children enjoy that Ahmed does not? Over a lifetime, how do these advantages help American children live a better quality of life than the life Ahmed leads?

3. Revisit the story with students for the purpose of tracing Ahmed's steps in reaching his personal goal. **Ask:**

> *What evidence can you cite that Ahmed gives up anything to achieve his goal?*
>
> *What evidence can you cite that shows that Ahmed believes that sacrifice is worthwhile?*
>
> *Does the story give clues that Ahmed may have an opportunity to learn more skills in the future?*
>
> *Can you cite examples in which they give up something in the present to achieve a goal in the future?*
>
> *Why does anyone give up pleasure or reward in the present for something in the future?*

Encourage students to cite examples.

Hint: Use the discussion as a natural lead-in to the concept of opportunity cost or "give-up" cost. In order to achieve certain goals in the future, individuals usually must sacrifice certain things in the present (e.g., time, effort, immediate rewards versus future rewards).

4. Challenge students to take inspiration from Ahmed and think up a time that they set and met a personal goal. Invite students to talk about the specific time within a small group.

Extension: Model for students how to make theme-related book jackets. Work through the steps of one personal goal by showing students how the selection of a goal and the steps to accomplish the goal can take visual form on book jackets. Allow time for students to illustrate the front of book jackets and to write brief biographical sketches on the back that tell about setting and meeting personal goals. Enlist student assistance in displaying the book jackets in a prominent place in the classroom. Plan a sharing time for students to tell about choosing and accomplishing personal goals.

5. Select one character trait (e.g., responsibility or diligence) and talk about how Ahmed or individual students demonstrate the trait in meeting personal goals. Ask students to tell why they selected a character or person and how the character or person exemplifies the trait.

Hint: For interest and variety, alternate discussions on character traits between the presence and benefits of possessing the traits and the absence and consequences of not possessing the traits.

EVALUATION:

Determine the level of student understanding by observing how they shift from concrete to abstract thinking processes, by assessing the maturity they exhibit when discussing their concept of childhood, by listening to how they set personal goals, and by evaluating how they relate accomplishment of personal goals to specific character traits. Ask students to share through written or oral responses what they have learned from this story and lessons. Encourage students to connect the message in the story to the theme of celebrating or honoring coming-of-age.

CONNECTION #2:
Sheldon Oberman.
The Always Prayer Shawl

Adam, a young Jewish Russian, and his family flee Czarist Russia and journey to a new country. In an unfamiliar environment, Adam learns the critical importance of older family members passing down traditions to younger members.

CHARACTER TRAITS: Review the nine character traits associated with this manual. Ask students to define and give examples of each trait. Discuss these for clarity and understanding.

1. Read *The Always Prayer Shawl* aloud. Remember to set the stage with appropriate pre-reading activities that capture students' interest. For example, use the Russian background as a basis for comparing and contrasting the world of Adam in Russia, his new home in the United States, and the world of elementary students in their own community.

2. Ask the media specialist to locate reference sources on Jewish traditions such as the prayer shawl introduced in the story. Share the research with students and lead them into connecting the meaning of the tradition to the development of the story line. **Ask:** What is the meaning of the prayer shawl in the story?

Invite a Jewish guest to the classroom to discuss traditions mentioned in the story. Supply the guest with a copy of *The Always Prayer Shawl* and a list of practices about which boys and girls may question. Ask the guest to comment on similarities of and differences between Jewish traditions in the story and traditions in their community.

Hint: Use the opportunity to develop and reinforce the unit generalization: Over time, human behaviors such as celebrating or honoring special people, events, or values may change. Talk with the guest and students about factors that may cause either worldwide similarities and/or regional differences in the observance of traditions. **Ask:** How do classroom visitors increase your understanding beyond the standard information found in print materials?

3. Review the purpose of time lines. With the class, create a time line of the special events in Adam's life. Students will cite events in Adam's life, then place them in sequential order on the time line.

Ask students to reflect on the years from their birth to the present, to determine major events, to sequence the events, then to design illustrated personal time lines. Practice a warm-up activity with students by talking about milestones such as learning to walk, learning to talk, adjusting to the birth of a new brother or sister, taking a first trip, or going to camp. Allow time for students to check with parents on important dates of events so that time lines reflect accuracy.

Plan a sharing time for students to tell about personal markers on their time lines and to share why they believe time lines depict the unit theme of coming-of-age. **Hint:** Lead students to the understanding that most children, regardless of race, ethnicity, or religion, share many similar life events.

4. Explore with students why the interview process is a valuable historical tool. Discuss the importance of advance planning for successful interviews. Tell students they will learn about changes in America during the past two generations through personal interviews. Ask them to formulate five standard interview questions to retrieve specific information they need. **Hint:** Questions may reflect topics of special interest such as changes in the environment, society, politics, cultural trends or fads, and technology. Talk with students also about how to put the interviewee at ease so that the experience is pleasant for both parties.

Encourage students to interview an older adult about how things changed and how things remained the same during his or her lifetime. Plan a sharing time within three days of the assignment, ask students who interview people under forty to report first, then ask students who interview people over forty to report next. **Ask:** Based on the interview data, what things changed in America? What things stayed the same? Is the data between two generations similar or different? Why? Lead students in predicting reasons for similarities and differences.

As a class project, check the interview data against matching time periods in students' textbooks. **Ask:** Does the interview data support and extend the information in textbooks? What is the real value of the interview process to historians?

Connect the interview process to Adam and *The Always Prayer Shawl* by inviting students to participate in a simulated interview between the interviewer and Adam or various family members. Prompt students to use the same interview questions with Adam and his family that they asked older adults. In addition to the standard questions, ask them how immigration causes changes in some things and at the same time keeps other things the same? Use the story and the interview process as a means of developing students' understanding of change and continuity. Link traditions to the efforts of Adam's family to maintain continuity after major life changes such as immigration.

5. Talk with students about the art of drawing cartoon characters. Tell them that even though the characters may be humorous, they often convey a serious message. Ask students to design a multiframed, captioned cartoon strip that represents a tradition passed to them by a member of the older generation and one they hope to pass on to the future generation. Remind students that they are illustrating cultural continuity in cartoon form. Allow students to share cartoons with classmates and then display in an exhibit entitled "Much More Than a Laugh!"

6. Divide students into small groups. Request that students choose three character traits that will serve immigrants well as they adjust to life in a strange, new land. List nine traits on the chalkboard, ask student groups to enter their choices on the list, and explain why group members think that these traits will be most valuable to immigrants. Enlist students in surveying the completed list to detect any patterns in choosing certain traits over others in this situation.

EVALUATION:

Determine the level of student understanding by observing their responses to varied instructional techniques, by watching how they interact with classmates in small group work situations, and by listening to their responses to thought questions. Encourage students to connect the message in the story to the theme of celebrating or honoring coming-of-age.

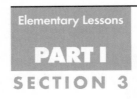

CONNECTION #3:
Mary D. Lankford.
Quinceañera: A Latina's Journey
to Womanhood

A photo journal portrays a Latina's ceremonial passage from childhood to young womanhood in Austin, Texas.

CHARACTER TRAITS: Review the nine character traits associated with this manual. Ask students to define and give examples of each trait. Discuss these for clarity and understanding.

1. Remember to set the stage with appropriate pre-reading activities that capture students' interest. For example, ask the media specialist to assist student partners in researching coming-of-age celebrations in Spanish-speaking countries around the world. As bases for geographic inquiries, ask students to bring all references to the classroom to research the quinceañera celebrations.

   Hint: Use this excellent opportunity to enlarge the horizons of elementary students by emphasizing that students can become world travelers when they pay close attention to geographic clues in stories and reference materials and then by comparing and contrasting the story sites to the world in which they live. In an informal research discussion, invite partners to summarize the celebrations, to place a marker for the countries on the story map, and to compare and contrast the settings of their countries to their own community. **Hint:** Use the activity to show the global importance of coming-of-age celebrations among Spanish-speaking people and also to illustrate that celebrations vary in different cultural settings as well as in different geographic areas.

   Read *Quinceañera: A Latina's Journey to Womanhood* aloud. Clarify vocabulary terms necessary for understanding the text. Challenge student research partners to listen carefully to the story to detect and record customs associated with the celebration (e.g., dress, invitations, guests, and ceremony). After the reading, ask students to join the teacher in webbing a quinceañera.

   If possible, invite a person whose family celebrated her fifteenth birthday in this way to come to class for the story reading. Request the visitor to comment on similarities between the young woman's celebration in the story and her own celebration, then to share photographs, artifacts, plans, and memories with boys and girls. **Ask:** Are Hispanics unique in celebrating the coming-of-age of young women? Why or why not?

2. Ask for student volunteers to research other coming-of-age observances such as sixteenth birthdays, Native-American rites of passage, bar mitzvahs, and bat mitzvahs. With the assistance of the media specialist, challenge students to locate information and report findings to classmates. On Venn diagrams, record how the ceremonies compare and contrast to the quinceañera. Lead students to the generalization that in some, not all, cultures, formal recognition of the passage from childhood to adulthood occurs.

   Ask: In the story or in the research, do students find a connection between coming-of-age celebrations and increased responsibilities? Survey the nine character traits and talk about which traits complement the research findings related to coming-of-age ceremonies. **Ask:** What observations can you make about the relevance or appropriateness of the nine character traits?

3. Lead boys and girls in planning one coming-of-age celebration from invitations through ceremonies. As a large group, instruct them to choose a celebration, to brainstorm details, and to prioritize the

details in the order that details need attention. **Hint:** Engage students in the planning stages so that they appreciate the complexities of large celebrations. The object of the activity is to fill the chalkboard with details, not to resolve arguments over precise details. **Ask:** What proves to you that many cultures value coming-of-age celebrations?

EVALUATION:

Determine the level of student understanding of quinceañera and other cultures' ceremonies marking passage from childhood to adulthood by assessing the quality of class discussions and responses to thought questions, by determining their interest in the guest speaker's comments, and by observing their willingness to participate in research projects and group tasks. Use their research and other written work for evaluating their understanding and participation in this lesson. Encourage students to connect the message in the story to the theme of celebrating or honoring coming-of-age.

ALTERNATE SELECTION:

Eric A. Kimmel. *Bar Mitzvah: A Jewish Boy's Coming of Age.* Using real-life bar mitzvah stories, Kimmel explains the historical background as well as the objects and rituals associated with the coming-of-age ceremony.

CONNECTION #4:
Lisa Larrabee.
Grandmother Five Baskets

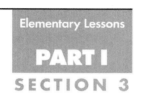

Elementary Lessons

PART I

SECTION 3

An elderly American Indian (Native American) teaches young girls to make baskets according to time-honored, traditional ways. Interwoven with her craft instructions are gentle coming-of-age lessons about the value of life, love, and family.

CHARACTER TRAITS: Review the nine character traits associated with this manual. Have students to define and give examples of each trait. Discuss these for clarity and understanding.

1. Read *Grandmother Five Baskets* aloud. Remember to set the stage with appropriate pre-reading activities that capture students' interest. For example, request students to look at the illustrations to identify geographic features in the setting. Use the illustrations to make tentative statements about location (Where is it?) and place (What is it like?). Define the geographic setting for the story from textual and visual clues as the purpose for the first reading.

Students will take notes on clues related to this one topic and jot down reminders to seek answers about unfamiliar geographic features. Following the first reading, talk about unfamiliar features and how they fit into the setting. Put a research scout on alert; once students complete story activities, send the scout to the library to find additional information on unfamiliar features and report to classmates.

Conduct a class discussion in which students volunteer and defend their best clues on the setting, then locate the setting of the story. Invite students to place a marker on the story map.

2. Locate five straw baskets and label them with the following concepts (e.g., big ideas: birth, maturity, death, outer beauty, and inner beauty). Divide students into partners and challenge them to listen for Grandmother Five Baskets' views on important life issues during the second story reading. **Hint:** Share with students that a person's views on critical life issues represent a person's philosophy.

Following the second reading, allow time for partners to talk about Grandmother Five Baskets' beliefs on the issues. Distribute small pieces of paper to partners, request that they write descriptive words about each issue, and place them in the appropriate basket. Encourage students to use their most colorful vocabulary.

Extension: Invite students to assume the role of Grandmother Five Baskets who wants to leave future generations a statement of philosophy. Model for students a simplified, yet genuine, "I believe...." philosophy statement. **Example:** I believe that people should govern themselves, thus I support a democratic form of government. Ask a student to turn over one basket at a time, starting with birth and to read the written descriptors inside. Lead individual students in their role as Grandmother Five Baskets to work toward one "I believe..., thus I support...." statement about birth, maturity, death, outer beauty, and inner beauty. Invite individuals to share their philosophies with classmates. **Hint:** Remind students to listen courteously to other students' belief statements. Emphasize that in a democracy such as America, citizens may freely and openly express their beliefs unless the statements threaten the safety of other citizens.

Ask students to quietly reflect on Grandmother Five Baskets' philosophy. **Ask:** Are any of her beliefs applicable to life in the 1990s in our community? Why or why not? What does the exercise show you about what you can learn from literature?

3. Introduce, develop, and/or reinforce the concept of legacy as something that a person wants to leave future generations. Ask students to think about a skill or a lesson or a trait that they want to leave a child in the future. Challenge students to think through the steps in developing a valuable skill, lesson, or trait. Ask students to write a legacy statement that includes the steps for acquiring and perfecting a valuable skill, lesson, or trait for a child in the future. Invite students to informally share legacies with classmates.

As an extension, talk about how different cultures leave legacies to future generations. Make sure that students grasp that legacies come in many forms such as children, gifts, ideas, and beliefs. **Ask:** Why do most people want to leave a legacy to future generations?

4. Request that students reexamine their legacy statement and decide which of the character traits will assist them in developing a skill, lesson, or trait worthy of willing to a child of the future. On a voluntary basis, encourage students to share their reasoning with classmates.

Hint: For interest and variety, alternate discussions on character traits between the benefits of possessing the traits and the consequences of not possessing the traits.

EVALUATION:

Determine the level of student understanding of *Grandmother Five Baskets*' coming-of-age lessons by assessing how insightfully they apply problem-solving thinking skills to the development of Grandmother's philosophy and by evaluating how carefully they think through the steps necessary for contributing legacies to future generations. Encourage students to connect the message in the story to the theme of celebrating or honoring coming-of-age.

CONNECTION #5:
Leigh Casler. *The Boy Who Dreamed of an Acorn*

A young boy, who dreams of acorns instead of the more traditional eagles and bears, gradually understands the wisdom of a Native-American elder's statement: "Be happy with your gift and be at peace with your dream."

CHARACTER TRAITS: Review the nine character traits associated with this manual. Ask students to define and give examples of each trait. Discuss these for clarity and understanding.

1. Read *The Boy Who Dreamed of an Acorn* aloud. Remember to set the stage with appropriate pre-reading activities that capture students' interest. For example, request that student partners listen for geographic clues to the setting so that students may add another literature-based location to the story map.

In addition, talk with students about the meaning of symbols, ask them to think up examples of symbols in their lives, and explain that dreams are symbols in the story. Request that students pay close attention to how the author describes the dreams, then challenge students to talk with their partner and agree upon the meaning of each dream in the story. **Ask:** Does a relationship between the dreams and coming-of-age exist in the story? Why or why not?

2. Discuss the thought that people other than Native Americans often link animals and objects with certain traits. **Examples:** bears with strength, rocks with endurance, and feathers with free spirits. Point out that often people connect other people, especially those in leadership roles, with certain traits.

Divide students into groups and assign the task of identifying one person in a leadership role whom the group admires. Explore reasons why the person earns the group's vote of confidence. Invite groups to share their admirable persons with classmates. Ask the following questions:

What traits does the person exhibit?

Are any of the character traits the same as the ones used in this book?

What is the meaning of the term universal?

Is there universal agreement on admirable traits? Why or why not?

How can students connect this exercise with The Boy Who Dreamed of an Acorn?

Why is the young boy's understanding of the elder's advice a sign of coming-of-age?

Hint: Gauge student interest in the activity; if interest runs high, suggest that students bring objects or pictures from home, label the items with corresponding traits, and set up a classroom corner display so that students may view multiple examples of connections between objects and traits. Entitle the exhibit "Now I See the Connections!"

EVALUATION:

Determine the level of student understanding of the wisdom taught by an elder and of the concept, coming-of-age, by assessing their interpretations of the young boy's dreams; by evaluating their connections among people, animals, objects, and/or traits; and by observing their enthusiasm for creating a classroom display. Encourage students to connect the message in the story to the theme of celebrating or honoring coming-of-age.

CONNECTION #6:
Elisa Bartone.
Peppe the Lamplighter

A young Italian immigrant struggles to help his impoverished family and unexpectedly discovers the importance of his lowly job.

CHARACTER TRAITS: Review the nine character traits associated with this manual. Ask students to define and give examples of compassion, diligence, and responsibility.

1. Read *Peppe the Lamplighter* aloud. Remember to set the stage with appropriate pre-reading activities that capture students' interest. For example, use the concept of immigration as a geographic connection between Peppe's native land, his adopted land, and your community. Ask student partners to listen for geographic clues to Peppe's native and new environments. Following the reading, discuss clues in the story, then ask students to post markers for Peppe's native and new lands on the classroom story map. Lead students into appreciating how their horizons are expanding through literature.

2. Ask students to listen carefully for Peppe's assorted jobs during the second story reading. Ask partners to record every job and set of responsibilities that they hear. Lead students in creating a story map on the chalkboard that sequences Peppe's first-to-final jobs. When students complete the story map, ask them to revisit the jobs and prioritize the jobs in order of importance to other people. When students reach consensus on the order of jobs, then ask them what factors they considered in prioritizing jobs. **Ask:** What other criteria may you use to prioritize the list of jobs? Is this process similar to the one people use when making a career choice? Why or why not?

3. Remind students of Peppe's conflict: Peppe's desire to earn money to help his family immediately and Peppe's father's desire for his son not to seek jobs beneath his ability or jobs that bring his family shame. Divide students into groups of four or five. Assign half of the groups the task of developing a strong case supporting Peppe's decision to seek lowly jobs in order to add to the family income. Assign the other half of the groups the task of developing a strong case supporting Peppe's father's decision to only take jobs that match his ability and that do not bring discredit to his family. Allow groups assigned to the same task to choose a leader who will assist group members in combining small-group decisions into large-group position statements.

Encourage spokespersons for each group to present their positions. **Ask:**

> Is Peppe's dilemma the problem the author presents in Peppe the Lamplighter?
>
> What is the solution to Peppe's problem?
>
> How do the story's problem and solution connect to short-term and long-term goals?
>
> Can you think of a problem they solved by setting a short-term goal? Long-term goal?

Hint: Lead students into thinking about jobs they hold or seek such as babysitting, pet sitting, delivering papers, caring for lawns. Suggest that they categorize the jobs as fulfillment of either short-term or long-term goals; point out that the same job can be either one depending on a person's needs and wants at the time.

4. Ask students to return to their original small groups and assume roles as employees in a newspaper advertising office. Have them recall clues from the story that relate to the job of lamplighter, such as hours, skills, public service, job commitment, job satisfaction. Distribute pieces of manila paper, and assign the task of designing an ad that will attract applicants for the job of lamplighter. Since applicants will be people who live in Peppe's world, review the historical setting of the story with students.

Select several models for newspaper ads from current newspapers, make transparencies, and lead students through the development of criteria for an effective ad, i.e., one that will attract applicants. Suggest that students brainstorm ideas for words and illustrations on scratch paper before transferring their designs to manila paper. Because lackluster ads get lost in a sea of print, encourage students to use creative lettering and pictures to attract lookers. Invite students to post their ads and to recruit applicants. **Ask:** Why do art-related projects increase your understanding of fictional and real-life situations?

5. Select one character trait (e.g., compassion, diligence, or responsibility) and talk about how Peppe or another character demonstrates the trait. Ask students to tell why they selected a character and how the character exemplifies the trait. Suggest that students think about their own lives and share examples that illustrate the trait.

EVALUATION:

Determine the level of student understanding of issues related to the job market by assessing their ability to analyze, prioritize, synthesize, and transfer information between fictional and real-life worlds; by observing their cooperation in and task commitment to a group; and by evaluating their creativity in advertisements. Encourage students to connect the message in the story to the theme of celebrating or honoring coming-of-age.

CONNECTION #7:
Jim Haskins and Kathleen Benson. *Space Challenger: The Story of Giuon Bluford*

Elementary Lessons
PART I
SECTION 3

Because of his performance in Vietnam, the Air Force considers Giuon Bluford one of its best pilots. African Americans have participated in the space program since 1962, but Bluford earns the distinction as the first African-American astronaut in space. Giuon Bluford perceives his mission of role model as important as his mission of space traveler.

CHARACTER TRAITS: Review the nine character traits associated with this manual. Have students define and give examples of each trait.

1. Ask students to read *Space Challenger: The Story of Giuon Bluford* independently in the Houghton Mifflin anthology. Remember to set the stage with appropriate pre-reading activities that capture students' interest. For example, preview the story by scanning the photographs and discussing the captions. Use the exercise as a lead-in to introduce, develop, or reinforce the concepts of permanence and mobility as they apply to Giuon's life and places of residence.

Students will list every geographic location where Giuon lives as they read. They will also give the reason for Giuon living in these places. Following the reading, discuss locations of and reasons for residences, and then post markers for Giuon's places of residence on the classroom story map.

Ask:

> *How can you apply the concepts of permanence and mobility to Giuon's life?*
>
> *Is the pattern of and reasons for Giuon's movement similar to many lifestyles today?*
>
> *Is there a connection between personal goals and mobility?*
>
> *What are the exceptions to the connection between personal goals and mobility?*
>
> *Do you believe the pattern of mobility will continue in the future? Why?*
>
> *What effect will recent technological advances, such as computers and the Internet, exert on permanence and mobility?*

Lead students into appreciating how their horizons are expanding through literature.

2. Utilize Giuon's story as an excellent example of the value of personal goal setting. Have students survey the story to find specific events and dates that chart Giuon's desire to become an astronaut. As students find examples in the text, list the information on either an overhead transparency or on a chalkboard story map.

Ask the following questions:

> *Does the goal-setting process make Giuon's dream or goal more possible? Why or why not?*
>
> *Do setbacks mean that people give up their dreams or goals?*
>
> *Why do some people have to exert more effort in reaching their dreams or goals than others?*
>
> *Does having to work harder than others to reach dreams or goals mean that people should give up?*
>
> *What character traits help Giuon accomplish his dream? Why?*
>
> *How can you apply Giuon's example to your own lives?*
>
> *How does goal setting relate to coming-of-age?*

3. Invite students to the newsroom of a major television network. Have them assume the role of scriptwriters for a popular anchorperson. Advise scriptwriters that their assignment is a news release on Giuon's success story from childhood to adulthood. Ask them to read and reread their scripts to a partner and use the partner's "I want to know more about...." statements as guidelines for revision. Invite students to share their scripts with classmates.

Hint: Extend this assignment over two days. On the first day, ask students to view several stories on a telecast of the national news. Have them apply the reporter's formula Who? What? Where? When? Why? How? to the stories and watch for techniques that make news stories snappy, pertinent, and interesting. On the second day, lead students in a group discussion on how professionals report the news by reading stories from the teleprompter.

Ask: How do professionals generate personal excitement about stories they do not write? What might be advantages and disadvantages of a newscaster not being involved in the writing process?

As an alternate activity, offer students the option of designing a T-shirt or jacket patch that celebrates Giuon Bluford's accomplishments in the space shuttle program. The design option must show the same degree of advance planning, keen observation, peer conferencing, and enthusiastic presentation as the television scripts.

EVALUATION:

Determine the level of student understanding of Bluford's challenges and opportunities by assessing their abilities to transfer specific facts to abstract concepts, by listening to their responses to questions, and by evaluating their creativity in story-related projects. Encourage students to connect the message in the story to the theme of celebrating or honoring coming-of-age.

CONNECTION #8:
Barbara Winslow.
Dance on a Sealskin

In honor of her deceased grandmother, Annie performs her first ceremonial dance at potlatch in her Yupik Eskimo village.

CHARACTER TRAITS: Review the nine character traits associated with this manual. Ask students to define and give examples of each trait.

1. Read *Dance on a Sealskin* aloud. Remember to set the stage with appropriate pre-reading activities that capture students' interest. For example, challenge students to listen for story clues related to the geographic site and to the description of Annie's village, as well as for ways geography shapes Annie's and her tribe's lifestyles.

Following the reading, discuss clues to the village site (e.g., location [Where is it?]), and to the village description (e.g., place [What is it like?]). Request a volunteer to post markers for Annie's tribal home on the classroom story map. Lead students into appreciating how their horizons are expanding through literature.

Hint: Alert two scouts to search in the media center for information about and illustrations of unfamiliar geographic features to share with classmates after the story activities.

Use the discussion on location and place as a lead-in to an exploration of how geography shapes tribal lifestyles. Ask relevant questions about the environment, climate, isolation, survival, and maturity. Project with students how geographic conditions that citizens in students' communities describe as harsh affect relationships, i.e., how people treat other people, within the tribe. Invite students to suggest examples of the concepts from the story.

2. Check other sources for descriptions of the potlatch ceremonial feasts. Common to potlatch ceremonies in Washington, British Columbia, and Alaska are two practices: at the end of the ceremony, the host often gives valuable gifts to guests from other kin groups or purposely destroys goods to show that he can afford the luxury of property destruction.

Remind students that Annie's way of honoring her grandmother is to perform a ceremonial dance. She chooses an important person in her life and conveys esteem in a creative way. Request that students select a greatly respected person in their lives and devise a creative way to express admiration. **Examples:** poems, songs, dances, eulogies, illustrations. Students must incorporate into the project the person of honor and the traits that make him/her special. Allow time for students to share their projects and place them in a Hall of Honor display.

3. Select one or more character traits and encourage students to show how Annie or other characters demonstrate the trait. Ask them to tell why they selected a character and how the character exemplifies the trait. Suggest that students transfer the traits of fictional characters to real-life characters and then share examples that illustrate the traits.

Hint: For interest and variety, alternate discussions on character traits between the benefits of possessing the traits and the consequences of not possessing the traits.

EVALUATION:

Determine the level of student understanding of honoring ancestors by assessing how quickly they develop conceptual knowledge from factual information and how creatively they interpret a story-related assignment. Encourage students to connect the message in the story to the theme of celebrating or honoring coming-of-age.

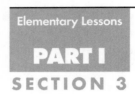

CONNECTION #9:
Rhoda Blumberg. *Bloomers!*

Blumberg's Bloomers! delightfully traces a cause-and-effect relationship between suffrage and fashions. Political participation by women gradually pushes their hemlines upward!

CHARACTER TRAITS: Review the nine character traits associated with this manual. Ask students to define and give examples of each trait.

1. Remember to set the stage with appropriate pre-reading activities that capture students' interest. For example, look for portraits, photographs, and illustrations of women, children, and fashions in different historical periods. Seek assistance from the librarian in locating these sources, then reproduce and laminate copies so that students in several classrooms may use the materials this year and also in the future. Try to find typical as well as outlandish fashions of representative periods.

Hint: Number the materials and keep a key to the correct chronological order of the visuals at the teacher's desk. Use the activity as an opportunity to discuss how historians value authenticity, the "real thing," and to stress why teachers searched for authentic historical representations for classroom materials.

Lead students in defining a fashion statement for today. Challenge students to arrange the materials in what appears to be a logical order from then to now, past to present. Ask students what criteria they used to sequence the fashions. Define the purpose for listening closely to the story as gathering data on women's growing political activity and women's changing fashions. Ask students to make defensible generalizations after they complete all story activities.

2. Read *Bloomers!* aloud. Ask student partners to list every geographic location mentioned in the story. For the second reading, request partners to note the event and date of important happenings in women's suffrage by the correct geographic location recorded in the first part of this exercise. Make a time line on the chalkboard and assign partners the task of entering specific landmark events, dates, and geographic sites in chronological order, i.e., the women's suffrage movement from the Seneca Falls Convention in 1848 to the attainment of the right to vote through the constitutional amendment process in 1920.

Remember to ask students to post locations of every event significant to the women's movement on the story map. **Ask:** Are the locations of significant events tightly clustered or widely scattered? What clues do locations give you about the success of the movement? Remind students how their horizons are expanding through literature.

3. Make paper puppet patterns of women and children from heavy, durable paper. Return to the fashion illustrations mentioned in the first activity above, recruit volunteers to take one distinctive style of dress, and encourage them to dress a paper puppet. Prior to the activity, gather fabric swatches, laces, braids, buttons, construction paper, tissue paper, glue, and scissors. **Hint:** Send a letter to parents; explain the project; and request donations of leftover craft materials. Guide students in dressing puppets for a variety of events such as attending a birthday party, going to the beach, and petitioning the government. Encourage students to match their designs to the teacher's historically accurate portraits, photographs, and illustrations. Ask students to print information about their puppets on 3" x 5" index cards.

Select a bulletin board to set up a Functional Fashions Museum and cover the background with a neutral color that will not clash with the multi-colored fashions. Request students to arrange puppets with cards of explanation in chronological order, then to stand back and think about what message the visual display sends about an interesting relationship in history (e.g., suffrage and fashion. Lead students in an informal discussion about the relationship between women's political activities and women's fashions, assist them in phrasing the generalization, and invite them to add the statement to the display.

Extension: As an extension of the lesson, talk to students about what they want to share with others about the lesson. **Ask:** What is the learning? What is the learning's importance? How does active participation help students learn? What learning activities are most enjoyable? What information causes students to investigate issues in more depth? **Hint:** Demonstrate for students how the answers to the questions make an entertaining, informative script. Invite students in neighboring classrooms to take a print walk along the bulletin board as student docents explain the project.

4. Tell students to use their imaginations and to take themselves back in time. They are now in the midst of the women's movement. Review the nine character traits and determine which three traits will serve a staunch supporter of the women's movement best. Ask one student to list all nine traits on the chalkboard, to call for a straw vote, and to tally the votes by traits.

Ask:

> *What factors caused similarities in voting patterns?*
> *What factors caused differences in voting patterns?*
> *Do you predict that these same factors influence elections of all kinds? Why or why not?*
> *Do you predict that these same factors influence decisions other than voting? Why or why not?*

EVALUATION:

Determine the level of student understanding of the interaction between women's political lives and women's fashions by observing how readily they move from examining primary sources to formulating generalizations; by assessing how quickly they identify cause-and-effect relationships; by noting how perceptively they connect the women's movement to the concept of coming-of-age; and by evaluating how effectively they transfer learning from a history activity to a public presentation. Encourage students to connect the message in the story to the theme of celebrating or honoring coming-of-age.

CONNECTION #10:
Martin W. Sandler.
Immigrants

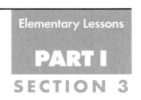

Elementary Lessons

PART I

SECTION 3

An album of photos, paintings, and posters from the Library of Congress collection graphically portrays the immigrant experience over the past two centuries. Expressions on faces, young as well as old, clearly display emotions of hope, anticipation, despair, and disappointment.

Hint: Make transparencies for the overhead projector from selected photos or show enlarged pictures with the opaque projector. Either technique will produce the dramatic, traumatic images of the story of human movement.

CHARACTER TRAITS: Review the nine character traits associated with this manual. Ask students to define and give examples of each trait.

1. Remember to set the stage with appropriate previewing activities that capture students' interest. For example, introduce, develop, or reinforce the concept of demography as the study of human populations (e.g., where they live, where they stay or move, what their racial/ethnic background is, what their present numbers are, what their growth rate is). Ask students to check with parents or guardians to identify their racial/ethnic heritage, to determine when their ancestors immigrated to America, and to search for data on decades of high immigration numbers such as the 1870s. Make students aware of other entry points in addition to Ellis Island such as Angel Island on the west coast, the Canadian border, the Mexican border, and southern Florida.

   On the next class day, ask students to take sticky, peel-off dots, write their names and years of ancestors' immigration on the dots, and stick the dots on their ancestors' native lands on a world map. Request students to study the map and to look for immigration patterns.

   Ask:

   > *Do you see clusters of immigrants coming from one area?*
   >
   > *If there are clusters, are the immigrants coming to America within two or three decades of one another?*
   >
   > *As the date moves closer to the present time, does the location of most immigrants' native lands shift to other geographic areas of the world?*
   >
   > *What reasons might account for these shifts?*
   >
   > *What was the government's response to waves of immigrants pouring into America?*
   >
   > *Do surnames provide clues about native lands? Cite examples.*
   >
   > *What does the data show you about the demographics of your community?*

   Extension: Introduce, develop, and/or reinforce students' understanding of the concept of diversity. Historians call America "a land of immigrants." Suggest that students reflect on discussions, map exercises, and thought questions, and then complete the following statement: I now understand why historians call America a land of immigrants, because _____.

   Invite students to informally share their reasoning with classmates. Ask students to verify or correct the answers to the thought questions as the teacher slowly reads aloud the story *Immigrants*.

2. Suggest that a team of four student volunteers research information on the Statue of Liberty. Encourage volunteers to solicit "I want to know" questions from classmates such as the designer's name, inspiration for design, height, weight, construction, shipping, unique features, then to search the media center for the basic facts in response to classmates' requests. Charge these students with the responsibility of getting the facts, then presenting the information to class members in an interesting, informative, and entertaining manner. While the research team works in the media center, allow students to choose among the following activities related to the immigrant experience:

   > *Draw a three-panel cartoon showing changes in sea travel across the Atlantic Ocean from sailing ships to steamships;*
   >
   > *Prepare a skit dramatizing a poor, non-English-speaking family going through customs at Ellis Island;*
   >
   > *Make a clothespin doll or paper puppet dressed in authentic clothing of the student's ancestors' native land; or*
   >
   > *Use modeling clay to craft a miniature scale model of the Statue of Liberty, then explain research and computation to classmates.*

   Require students who choose any one of the activities to link the exercise to the immigrant experience by telling how methods of transportation, customs, and native clothing affected their adjustment to a new homeland. Plan a sharing time for presentations in honor of millions of courageous immigrants.

   Hint: Alert the media specialist in advance about the projects. Ask the media specialist to select references for students to use either in the classroom or in the library.

3. Read the poem, "The New Colossus," by Emma Lazarus slowly, then ask students to interpret Miss Liberty's message.

Hint: Point out to students after they complete the research, projects, presentations, and interpretations that the vast majority of immigrants were pitifully poor and downtrodden with few exceptions. Mention to students that valid reasons for limited as well as unlimited immigration exist. Point out to students that listening to both sides of the argument will provide necessary data for making personal judgments on the issue.

4. Request students to reflect on what traits enable immigrants in any time period to confront problems inherent in leaving native lands and adjusting to life in new lands. Ask students to reference traits to the list of nine core character traits. Invite students to transfer immigrants' situations to situations in their own lives. Ask how and why specific character traits might assist students in meeting challenges in present-day lives.

EVALUATION:

Determine the level of student understanding of immigration by assessing how they apply information acquired through interviews and research, by evaluating how they interpret and use various demographic data, and by observing how they respond to creative activities designed to increase knowledge about the immigrant experience. Encourage students to connect the message in the story to the theme of celebrating or honoring coming-of-age.

CONNECTION #11:
Carolyn Reeder.
Shades of Gray

Elementary Lessons

PART 1

SECTION 3

War exacts heavy costs on civilians as well as soldiers. As a result of the Civil War, Will faces life as an orphan, the son of a slain Confederate soldier. He struggles to adjust not only to the loss of family but also to living with an uncle who did not support the war. Will's personal trials tell his story of a journey to maturity.

CHARACTER TRAITS: Review the nine character traits associated with this manual. Ask students to define and give examples of each trait.

1. Read *Shades of Gray* aloud. Remember to set the stage with appropriate pre-reading activities that capture students' interest. Clarify vocabulary terms necessary for understanding the text.

Use the following activity as an interest builder. Declare learning about the relationship between geography and history as the purpose for listening. Allow student partners to listen for geographic clues, to respond to teacher-suggested geographic topics, and to answer critical thinking questions such as How? Why? and What if...?

For example, suggested topics might include the following:

> *Using the setting of the story to establish boundaries of the North and the South;*
> *Discussing the relationship between geographic features and the role of the West in the Civil War;*

Talking about the importance of waterways in the course of the war; and

Predicting how geographic features of areas affect outcomes of battles.

Ask: Do the answers to these questions confirm or deny a close relationship between geography and history? Why?

2. Talk with students about ways they know how people feel about different subjects. Develop students' understanding that people indicate how they feel by words expressed, by words not expressed but inferred, and by body language exhibited. Connect the term, attitude to the discussion on feelings. Then, ask the same partners to reflect on story characters' expression of attitudes on subjects such as the North and the South and Will's journey to maturity.

Explain the concept of a seminar to students, i.e., everyone studies the issue, everyone offers research-based contributions, and everyone reaches reasonable conclusions in round-table discussions. If possible, arrange the setting for the seminar in a circle so that all partners share the circle, thus share the responsibility for making a contribution to the discussion. Name a story-related, age-appropriate discussion topic, encourage students to offer research-based opinions, and lead them to logical conclusions based on *Shades of Gray*.

Ask: How does literature such as the story about the North and the South increase students' understanding of complex issues such as civil wars? How does literature add to the excitement of historical events? Does literature help students link events of long ago to events of the present day? Why?

3. Retrace Will's story with students. Divide students into small groups of three or four. Ask students to consider Will's position as an orphan and to list his alternatives to living with relatives whom he does not respect. Request that students further consider the times and dangers in which Will lives, then analyze expected as well as unexpected consequences of his decision.

Remind students that Will reluctantly chooses to live with his uncle and consequently learns an important life lesson. Invite students to identify and to state what Will learns. **Ask:** Does the life lesson represent an example of Will's coming-of-age? Connect the activity to the present by asking students to volunteer similar turning points in their own lives, i.e., times that they opposed some action, acted on their beliefs, and learned much from the experience.

4. Use Will's button collection to develop an understanding of how powerful a story's recurring motif can be in terms of characterization and meaning, i.e., what the button collection tells readers about the character of Will and what the button collection reveals about tragedies associated with war. Remind students that one of Will's few, prized possessions is his collection of uniform buttons, that the button collection threads through characters' dialogue in the story, and also that the button collection enables Will to demonstrate his knowledge to curious friends. Ask students to recall the following scenes in the story and to listen for clues about uniform buttons:

1) "Let me show you the buttons." Hank dropped to his knees. "Look at 'em all!" he said, picking up a button embossed with an eagle and the letter C.

   "That's a Yankee button," said Will. "I found that one on the battlefield at Kernstown." He thought of how he and his friend Matt had begged Charlie to take them along to look for battle souvenirs.

   "If it's Yankee, how come it's got a C on it?"

   "For 'Cavalry,'" Will explained, sorting through his collection. "See this one with the I. It's off a Yankee infantry officer's uniform."

   "How d'you know he was an officer?"

   "'Cause except for the artillery, Yankee enlisted men just had the number of their regiment on their buttons," Will said.

2) To his relief, Hank shrugged and picked up a button showing a woman warrior with her foot resting on a vanquished foe.

"Which side's this one from?"

Will was amazed that Hank didn't recognize the Virginia State Seal. "That's from a Virginia militia uniform. Lots of men that volunteered at the beginning of the war went in their militia uniforms. My father did."

Ask: What clues does the dialogue reveal about the importance of the button collection to Will? What clues does the dialogue reveal about button designs?

Examples: letters, ranks, and symbols. Challenge students to assume a historically accurate role in the Civil War and to create a button design that might be on their uniform or that might reveal their homelands, their branches of service, or their ranks. Remind students that the task involves research on both the Union and Confederacy from the perspectives of both Union and Confederate soldiers engaged in battle. Allow time for students to share completed designs with classmates, then post the designs in geographically correct locations on a United States map.

5. Request students to reflect on what traits enable Will to confront problems and find solutions in his life situation. Ask students to reference traits to the list of core character traits. Suggest that students analyze how the same traits might enable them to meet a challenge or to solve a problem in their own lives.

EVALUATION:

Determine the level of student understanding about Will's reactions to war by assessing how they affirm the relationship between geography and history; by evaluating how they state the correlation among feelings, attitudes, words, and body language; by judging the creativity of their button designs; and by observing how they transfer problems and solutions in Will's life to their own life situations. Encourage students to connect the message in the story to the theme of celebrating or honoring coming-of-age.

CONNECTION #12:
James Houston.
Tikta'liktak

In response to his starving family's need for food, an Inuit teenage boy undertakes a precarious hunting trip in the Canadian Arctic. He courageously fights the isolation of the wilderness, miraculously survives the ordeal through his own cleverness, and proudly returns to his village after an absence of many months.

CHARACTER TRAITS: Review the nine character traits associated with this manual. Ask students to define and give examples of each trait.

1. Read *Tikta'liktak* aloud. Remember to set the stage with appropriate pre-reading activities that capture students' interest. For example, challenge students to listen for story clues about the geographic site, the boy's village, and examples of how geography shapes the boy's and tribe's lifestyles.

Following the reading, discuss clues related to the village site (e.g., location [Where is it?]), and to the village description (e.g., place [What is it like?]). Request a volunteer to post markers for the boy's tribal home on the classroom story map. Lead students into appreciating how their horizons are steadily expanding through literature.

Clarify vocabulary, such as habitat, necessary for understanding the text. Use the story line and the boy's hunting experiences to build understanding of one of five important geographic themes: human/environment interaction.

Ask:

> *How do humans change the environment?*
>
> *How do humans adapt to the harshness of the Arctic?*
>
> *In this culture, why is it critical for young boys to become good hunters?*

Hint: Remember to incorporate the other four geographic themes, i.e., location, place, movement, region, into explanations related to the literature and to activities whenever natural connections among themes, literature, and activities exist.

2. Talk to students about how they may visually show the relationship between humans and their environment in the Arctic. Since hunting occupies an important role in the survival of the Inuit, suggest that students listen to the story and also view the illustrations again for the purpose of identifying essential weapons and tools. After reading the story, lead students in brainstorming a list of weapons and tools such as chisels, harpoons, bows and arrows, short knives, and falling-stone traps. Encourage students to choose one and draw an attractive, authentic model. On a bulletin board or in a tabletop museum entitled "Inuit's Survival Kit," request that students group similar weapons and tools together.

Ask students illustrating short knives to join together, discuss how short knives contribute to the ability to survive, and compose one sentence that explains the importance of the weapon or tool in the Arctic. Instruct other students to place the name of their products with explanations on index cards, and then add to the display.

Ask:

> *Based on the activity, what is the relationship between humans and their environment in the Arctic?*
>
> *What is at stake if humans do not develop a relationship with their environment?*
>
> *Can you think of high-stakes relationships in other geographic areas?*
>
> *If humans fail to work out a relationship with their environment, are the stakes the same as in the Arctic?*
>
> *Do you now have a better understanding why geographers chose human/environmental interaction as one of the five major themes of geography? Explain.*

3. Review with students the reasons why Tikta'liktak wants to become a great hunter. Talk to students about other reasons that go beyond survival. For example, discuss tribal members' opinions of a great hunter and privileges that accompany the role of a great hunter. Encourage students to cite specific examples from the story.

Have students transfer Tikta'liktak's choice of hunting as a career in the Arctic to a discussion of students' career choices in their community. **Ask:** What factors will influence your career choices?

Hint: Lead students in discussing factors such as areas of interest, funds, patterns set by parents and influential adults, importance of other people's feelings about various career choices, amount of training, tools of the vocation, and market forces such as supply and demand.

Extension: Encourage students to analyze each one of these or additional forces that are suggested, so they realize that career choices are extremely serious decisions and ones that truly affect every aspect of their lives. **Ask:** Can you find similarities between factors that affect Tikta'liktak's career choice and factors that will affect your career choices in the future?

4. Request students to reflect on what character traits enable the main character in the story to confront problems and find solutions. Invite students to transfer traits of the fictional character to their own lives. Ask how and why the same character traits might assist students in meeting everyday challenges.

Hint: For interest and variety, alternate discussions on character traits between the presence and benefits of possessing the traits and the absence and consequences of not possessing the traits.

EVALUATION:

Determine the level of student understanding of reasons for Tikta'liktak's survival by observing the degree of enthusiasm for creating an authentic classroom display, by assessing the relationship established between the display and a major geographic theme, and by evaluating career choice connections in the main character's and students' lives. Encourage students to connect the message in the story to the theme of celebrating or honoring coming-of-age.

CONNECTION #13:
Marc Bernheim and Evelyne Bernheim.
The Drums Speak: The Story of Kofi, a Boy of West Africa

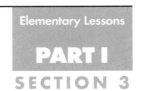

Elementary Lessons

PART I

SECTION 3

A young boy in a primitive, West African village dutifully learns tribal customs and traditions as part of his cultural education. His success in school rather than his tribal training, however, merits his selection as a future leader.

CHARACTER TRAITS: Review the nine character traits associated with this manual. Ask students to define and give examples of each trait.

1. Read aloud the story, *The Drums Speak*. Remember to set the stage with appropriate pre-reading activities that capture students' interest. For example, challenge students to listen for story clues related to the geographic setting, to the description of the boy's village, and to ways geography shapes the boy's and the tribe's lifestyles.

Following the reading, discuss clues to the village site (e.g., location [Where is it?]), and to the village description (e.g., place [What is it like?]). Use the story as the means to review latitude and longitude. Point out to students the importance of lines such as the Equator and the Prime Meridian, and then encourage them to target the locations of Ghana, the Ivory Coast, and Kofi's village by applying their knowledge of latitude and longitude to a world map. Request a student volunteer to post markers for the boy's tribal home on the classroom story map. Lead students into appreciating how their horizons are steadily expanding through literature.

2. Talk about qualities of tribal leaders. **Ask:** Does the story provide clues for traits that make strong tribal leaders? Suggest that students reflect on the tribe's environment, on their most critical needs as a group of people, on their established tribal customs and traditions, and on the amount of contact with other tribal groups. **Ask:** How does a discussion on a tribe's setting, needs, traditions, and contacts assist you in defining desirable qualities for a tribal leader? Is a similar discussion appropriate for defining desirable qualities for leaders of your community today?

Extension: Extend the activity by inviting a community leader to the class, by requesting the leader to listen to students' explanation of their investigation into tribal leadership traits, and by soliciting the community leader's opinion to the thought question: Is a similar discussion appropriate for defining desirable qualities for leaders of your community today? Lead students to a thoughtful conclusion about the exercise on tribal and community leadership.

Extension: Extend the activity further by suggesting that boys and girls prepare a page for a do-it-yourself leadership book. Request that students decide on one gift for Kofi and one gift for a community leader that will help them lead people wisely and justly. Instruct students to illustrate the gifts on one page, to write captions about both gifts, to share their work with classmates, and to assist the teacher in compiling and binding a leadership book. Display the book in a prominent place in the classroom.

3. Review with students the important story events in sequence. Alert students that they will recreate the story in dramatic form by acting out story events. To the degree possible, allow students to choose scenes of special interest. Encourage students to make props that will add realism to their dramatizations:

> *Harvesting cacao pods (cocoa) and yams*
> *Performing the warriors' dance*
> *Studying for the school entrance exam*
> *Working together for survival in activities such as building canoes, clearing fields, dedicating and launching canoes*
> *Sending drum messages such as "make it ring so sweetly that even the crocodiles will weep for joy"*
> *Mastering the coming-of-age test*
> *Participating in a celebration festival*

Ask: Is each scene necessary to paint a picture of tribal culture? **Hint:** Lead students to the understanding that "culture" means a total way of life. **Ask:** How do participatory activities help you learn and remember important ideas?

4. Have students reflect on the traits that enable Kofi to confront problems and find solutions. First, identify the problems and then analyze what traits assist him in solving the problems. Invite students to transfer how Kofi uses traits to solve problems to how they use the same traits to solve problems.

EVALUATION:

Determine the level of student understanding of tribal life by observing how correctly they connect geographic and political concepts presented in literature; by assessing how thoughtfully they compare essential leadership traits in unfamiliar and familiar settings; by evaluating how enthusiastically they recreate scenes from the story; and by judging how insightfully they respond to questions. Encourage students to connect the message in the story to the theme of celebrating or honoring coming-of-age.

CONNECTION #14:
Yoshiko Uchida. *Takao and Grandfather's Sword*

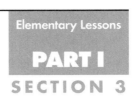

In mid-twentieth-century Japan, children must exhibit traits that demonstrate that they are ready to assume adult responsibilities. Takao undertakes the task of proving his maturity so that he may learn, practice, and perfect his father's craft of pottery making.

CHARACTER TRAITS: Review the nine character traits associated with this manual. Ask students to define and give examples of each trait.

1. Read *Takao and Grandfather's Sword* aloud. Remember to set the stage with appropriate pre-reading activities that capture students' interest. For example, challenge students to listen for story clues related to the geographic setting of an island nation. Ask student volunteers to exhibit their knowledge of latitude and longitude by correctly locating the island of Honshu, the largest of the four islands of Japan. **Ask:** Will an island nation encourage or discourage contact with other people? Why? What must happen to encourage the free flow of people and ideas?

Hint: Lead students to an understanding that people must develop a level of technology so that they can cross bodies of water or fly to another nation. If student interest runs high, encourage a team of students to investigate Japan's history to support the relationship between technology and human interaction. Request student volunteers to post markers for Takao's home on the classroom story map. Lead students into appreciating how their horizons are steadily expanding through literature.

2. Tell students to think about Takao's attitudes, i.e., how he feels, and behaviors, i.e., how he acts, in the story. Allow partners to compose a list that shows clues in the story and reasons why the clues represent signs of maturing. Ask partners to contribute data to a two-column chalkboard chart entitled "Clues" and "Reasons." Use data on the chart as a prewriting activity. Request students to assume the role of Takao and to write his father a letter asking that training as a pottery maker begin immediately. Encourage students to use data on the chart to justify the request.

Extension: Extend the activity so that students may examine their own lives, think of a responsibility they are ready to assume, and write parents or guardians a persuasive letter stating the responsibility with evidence that proves they are mature enough to accept greater responsibility. Allow time in class for students to share writing with classmates. **Ask:** How does writing personal letters to parents or guardians help you better understand Takao's request to his father?

3. Suggest that students think about the character traits that enable Takao to confront a problem and to seek a solution. Invite students to consider how a person they admire exhibits the same traits in meeting everyday challenges.

Hint: For interest and variety, alternate discussions on character traits between the benefits of possessing the traits and the consequences of not possessing the traits.

EVALUATION:

Determine student understanding of coming-of-age by assessing how accurately they relate geographic factors to human interaction and by observing how insightfully they contribute to a cause-and-effect chart on maturation. Ask students to develop a problem-solving flow chart that explains how they or the main character in the story solves problems. Encourage students to connect the message in the story to the theme of celebrating or honoring coming-of-age.

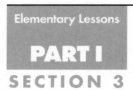

CONNECTION #15:
Patricia Polacco. *Pink and Say*

A happenstance event during the Civil War bonds two young soldiers in friendship. Together they face danger and death in this heroic adventure. Recalling stories passed down through generations of her family members, Polacco shares a powerful tale that crosses racial lines and focuses on humanity.

CHARACTER TRAITS: Review the nine character traits associated with this manual. Ask students to define and give examples of each trait.

1. Read *Pink and Say* aloud. Remember to set the stage with appropriate pre-reading activities that capture students' interest. For example, use the story to review basic facts related to the Civil War (e.g., causes, time period, leaders, players, effects). Ask students to listen carefully to the first reading for geographic descriptions of the area where Pink finds Say or of the area where Pink's mother lives. **Ask:** Do geographic factors play a role in Say's survival on the battlefield or in Pink's success in transporting Say to his home? If so, how?

2. Remind students that deeds such as those the story recounts often earn lasting tributes by people who value traits such as heroism, freedom, justice, and liberty. Tell students that people plan lasting tributes (e.g., monuments, plaques, museums, speeches, songs, and poems) to honor exemplary deeds and models of ideal behavior for other citizens.

Challenge student partners:

> *To select a deed of heroism from the story or from their lives;*
>
> *To research the person, heroic act, and setting;*
>
> *To plan a tribute to the person; to prepare an interesting way to share the deed of heroism with classmates;*
>
> *To tell classmates what model the person sets for them; and*
>
> *To add the tribute to a classroom museum entitled "Enduring Qualities of Heroes and Heroines."*

Assist students in attractively and colorfully exhibiting various tributes. Encourage students to practice their explanations with a partner, and then invite other elementary students to take a picture-and-print walk through the museum as students explain their tributes to guests.

3. Request students to reflect on what traits enable Pink and Say to confront problems and to find solutions. Ask students how and why these character traits might assist them in meeting everyday challenges.

EVALUATION:

Determine the level of student understanding of the effect of crises on human relationships and also on the coming-of-age process by assessing the insightfulness expressed in class discussions. Evaluate the quality of tributes and presentations in the classroom museum. Encourage students to connect the message in the story to the theme of celebrating or honoring coming-of-age.

CONNECTION #16:
Sid Fleischman.
The Whipping Boy

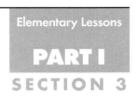

A royal family searches for a suitable whipping boy to take punishment for the spoiled young prince's misdeeds. They select an impoverished orphan boy whose family were rat catchers. After a short time filled with humiliation and beatings at the castle, Jemmy makes an important decision to flee. Haughty Prince Brat demands the right to accompany him. Thrilling adventures and narrow escapes surprisingly teach Jemmy and Prince Brat how to understand and respect each other.

Note: Point out to students that even though the story and characters are fictional, the practice of someone else taking punishment for the heir to the throne is true. In past times, laws forbad the punishment of royal heirs.

CHARACTER TRAITS: Review the nine character traits associated with this manual. Ask students to define and give examples of each trait.

1. Read *The Whipping Boy* aloud. Remember to set the stage with appropriate pre-reading activities that capture students' interest. For example, remind students that historians diligently research details related to historical times so that they may describe personalities and events accurately and place them in settings correctly. Set the purpose for reading the story as a search for context clues that enable student partners to place Jemmy and Prince Brat in a historical period. Following the reading, recruit volunteers to construct a chart of clues on the chalkboard. Encourage partners to state the clue and the reason why the clue leads to correct placement of the characters in a time period. **Hint:** Leave the chart on the chalkboard during later story activities in case students want to add new clues that surface in discussions or to reexamine clues already listed.

Ask:

How can an exercise of searching for context clues help you become better historians?

Will the skill of searching for context clues transfer to other tasks and to other subjects?

Will the skill be a helpful research tool for people other than elementary students? Why or why not?

2. Talk with students about the role of family crests, especially in the setting of *The Whipping Boy*. Explain that crests serve more than one purpose: for example, as signs of identification for all family members and as the public proclamation of values important to family members.

Extension: Gather a team of researchers to investigate crests: purposes, shapes, colors, symbols, and mottoes. Suggest that researchers look for clues that link the use of crests to certain classes of people. Ask that researchers return to the classroom with visual examples of crests to present to classmates. Remind researchers to point out specific examples that show a variety of purposes, shapes, colors, symbols, mottoes, and other unique features. After students question researchers, mention that they may invite family members to participate in these projects and to visit the family crest display center. Allow students to choose one of the following options related to family crests:

Design a crest that matches important values of students' present-day families, then write a brief explanation of the meaning of the crest symbols on the back of the crest; or

Design a crest that reflects important values of Prince Brat's royal family at the beginning of The Whipping Boy, *then write a brief explanation of the meaning of the crest symbols on the back of the crest; or*

Design a crest that reflects important values of Prince Brat's royal family at the end of The Whipping Boy *after his adventures with Jemmy, then write a brief explanation of the meaning of the crest symbols on the back of the crest.*

Set up a family crest display center. Review the three product options with students, ask students to group together all crests and explanations by types, and then share their crests with classmates. Exhibit crests by categories in a display entitled "Decoding the Meaning of Family Crests."

Ask: How do creative activities such as making family crests help you learn and remember important ideas? Why were family crests more popular in past times than in present-day times?

Hint: Talk with students about technological advances, such as those in transportation and communication, that enable family members to stay in close contact with one another and thus to informally exchange ideas. Closer contacts often reduce the need for formal family symbols. Also, in many areas of the world, federal governments assume the role as protector of citizens and reduce the need to rally around a family leader to provide defense for all family members. Today, many families use crests in decorative ways such as framed crests and stationery emblems.

3. Discuss the meaning of the term, reformer. Lead students to understand that usually a reformer looks at a current situation and works to make the situation better for people. Divide students into small groups and ask them to discuss the formal as well as the informal rules by which people in Prince Brat's world live. Point out the groups with special privileges and opportunities.

Ask student groups to assume roles as reformers of Prince Brat's world. Suggest that their main purpose for reform will focus on making the world more just and more equitable for all citizens. Tell students they first must identify characteristics of Prince Brat's world, and then propose ways to make that world better. Alert students that proposals for a better world will take form in a set of royal rules proclaimed by Prince Brat. Encourage a spokesperson from each group to publicize the reformed royal rules.

Request students to analyze which of Prince Brat's royal rules might make their classroom more just and more equitable and why. If student interest runs high, allow an artistic student to print a set of royal rules to post in the classroom. Take the opportunity to remind students that new class rules reflect democratic principles. **Ask:** If they lived in a nation where one person controlled all decisions, how might the class rules differ from the set they developed for their classroom? Why?

4. Ask students to reflect on the character traits that enable Jemmy and Prince Brat to survive dangerous ordeals and to develop respect for one another. Lead students in comparing and contrasting the traits Jemmy and Prince Brat demonstrate at the beginning and the end of the story and in suggesting logical reasons for changes. For example, ask students to revisit the story, look for examples that support the spoiled, pampered behavior of Prince Brat, and show how that behavior changes by the end of the story.

Extension: Have students transfer the traits of fictional characters to situations in their own lives in which they demonstrated the same traits. Invite students to share their stories with classmates.

EVALUATION:

Determine the level of student understanding that respect and acceptance of one another mark a turning point in coming-of-age by assessing how sensitively they respond to thought questions, by observing how skillfully they use context clues to establish the correct setting, and by judging how enthusiastically they approach individual and group tasks. Encourage students to connect the message in the story to the theme of celebrating or honoring coming-of-age.

CONNECTION #17:
Sue Alexander.
Nadia the Willful

Set in the desert, a land of drifting sands, Nadia the Willful proves that coming-of-age as a stage in life applies to adults as well as children. The experience of grief unexpectedly reverses the traditional roles of adults and children facing crises.

CHARACTER TRAITS: Review the nine character traits associated with this manual. Ask students to define and give examples of each trait.

1. Read *Nadia the Willful* aloud. Remember to set the stage with appropriate pre-reading activities that capture students' interest. For example, talk about and list on the chalkboard or on a transparency what students already know about deserts, a geographic feature that forces many people to lead nomadic lives. Discuss vocabulary terms such as desert, oasis, sheik, nomad, and lifestyle so that students realize how geographic features shape people's lives.

Suggest that student partners listen for geographic clues and take notes about Nadia's homeland that will assist them in creating a more complete picture of desert lands. After reading the story, encourage students to add geographic understandings gained from the story to the list. Ask volunteers to locate Nadia's homeland by latitude and longitude, then place a marker on the classroom story map. Lead students into appreciating how their horizons are steadily expanding through literature.

2. Challenge student partners to look at illustrations in the story and listen for textual clues that paint a picture of Bedouins' life in the desert during the second reading: how they dress, why they dress that way, how they live, who is in authority, how they survive the harshness of daily life, what values are important to tribal members, and what religion influences their lives. Urge students to make conclusions that Bedouin life sharply contrasts with the life most of them lead.

Extension: Extend students' understanding by conducting a mini-lesson on the religion of Islam: geographic location of the Muslim world, present-day expansion of the Muslim world beyond the Middle East, the role of Allah, the moral code, and the estimated number of Muslims living in the world today. Compare and contrast these to other religions. Invite a Muslim visitor to class to review basic Islamic beliefs. **Hint:** Make sure that the guest receives a list of suggested topics prior to the visit. Encourage students to ask questions that clarify the story line and add to an understanding of Islam.

3. Explore the topic of grief with students sensitively. Invite students to share brief stories of personal loss in their lives, perhaps the loss of family members, friends, or pets, and ways students learned to cope with loss. Transfer the discussion to the story of Nadia, and suggest that students talk within small groups about different characters' response to grief, then to recovery. Ask student groups to discuss these questions and prepare answers to share with classmates:

> *In the story, who exhibits the most adult or mature behavior? Why?*
> *What do students think about Nadia's strategy for dealing with grief?*
> *When the sheik realizes his error, how does he correct it?*
> *Do renaming ceremonies occur in other cultures? Where, when, and why?*
> *Does the story mention any type of memorial service acknowledging the death of Nadia's brother?*
> *How do ceremonies or memorial services help the living deal with loss and start the healing process?*
> *What does the story illustrate about the quality of children's decisions?*

Allow students to exchange ideas after each group's spokesperson reports their responses. **Ask:** What learning takes place when you investigate customs and traditions of other cultures? Ask students if they agree that studying similarities and differences among people usually leads to the conclusion that human beings are more alike than different.

4. Request students to reflect on what character traits enable Nadia to assist her father in dealing with his loss and what traits enable her father to forgive Nadia for her willfulness. Invite students to think up examples in which they observed these same traits used to solve a problem, then to share the experiences with classmates.

Hint: For interest and variety, alternate discussions on character traits between the benefits of possessing the traits and the consequences of not possessing the traits.

EVALUATION:

Determine the level of student understanding that age and maturity do not always match by assessing how sensitively they respond to thought questions, by observing how accurately they link geographic features and tribal lifestyles, and by evaluating how productively they work in group settings. Check their comparing and contrasting activity for information of what they have learned. Let them discuss these openly in class. Encourage students to connect the message in the story to the theme of celebrating or honoring coming-of-age.

Elementary Lessons

PART I

SECTION 3

CONNECTION #18:
Jim McGugan.
Josepha: A Prairie Boy's Story

The story of Josepha, an immigrant boy of the 1900s, recounts the plight of thousands of young people who struggle to adjust to a strange land, a strange language, and a strange institution called school. In spite of daily humiliations in primary row, genuine bonds form between Josepha and younger students at school.

CHARACTER TRAITS: Review the nine character traits associated with this manual. Ask students to define and give examples of each trait.

1. Read *Josepha: A Prairie Boy's Story* aloud. Remember to set the stage with appropriate pre-reading activities that capture students' interest. For example, open a discussion by asking students to describe in their most colorful words the concept of a prairie: what a prairie looks like, what crops grow on prairies, how families earn a living on prairies in the 1900s, what responsibilities children might carry in a farm family, where prairie lands still exist in America today. **Hint:** Lead students to the understanding that farming on the prairie in the 1900s involved the labor of all family members. Preview the illustrations with students and ask them to use details in the pictures to support descriptions of life on the prairie.

2. Point out that daily life on the prairie confronted people with problems such as survival, sacrifice, hardship, discomfort, and loneliness. Ask students to add immigration to the list as another force that increased the harshness of prairie life, then request that they explain why immigration might cause problems for people of the prairie.

Extension: Divide students into research teams. With the assistance of the media specialist, assign teams the tasks of finding out about and taking notes on European immigration in the 1870s, European immigration in the 1890s, cultural differences between the two waves of immigrants, and reasons why immigrants moved from urban centers to the prairie. Allow students time to compile notes in a format that illuminates the story-between-the-lines about Josepha's life on the prairie. Request groups to report research findings to the class. **Hint:** Make sure that all groups end their reports with how the research information makes Josepha's struggle clearer.

3. Recruit two students during the research project above to seek information about schools on the prairie. In advance of the project, ask the media specialist to search for sources of data: subjects studied, promotion policies, accommodations for students with special needs.

Ask:

How do research findings expand your understanding of Josepha's school experience?

What are short-term and long-term advantages in assisting immigrants to move into the mainstream of American life? Are there disadvantages?

Which view is more consistent with the American ideal of opportunity for all people? Why?

Do any of your answers include any of the nine character traits?

4. Talk with students about the role of gifts in Josepha's story. Remind students that age, language, and culture separate Josepha and his young friend, yet at the end of the story, they exchange precious possessions with one another. **Ask:** How can friendship cross cultural lines? Nudge students to the conclusion that understanding usually leads to respect, respect gradually leads to acceptance.

5. Discuss with students reasons why Josepha leaves school, so that they understand how economic needs accelerate the coming-of-age process for many young people. Engage students in a discussion of context or visual clues that support why Josepha's family believes he is old enough to assume adult responsibilities (e.g., full-time employment). **Ask:** Do the same reasons for leaving school affect today's students? What advice might elementary students give to discouraged or unsuccessful students who consider leaving school as soon as they are legally old enough?

EVALUATION:

Determine the level of student understanding about the relationship between immigration and opportunity by assessing how sensitively they respond to thought questions; by observing how accurately they connect geographic features, lifestyles, and immigration; and by evaluating how productively they use research findings to expand the meaning of the story line. Encourage students to connect the message in the story to the theme of celebrating or honoring coming-of-age.

CONNECTION #19:
Lois Raimondo.
The Little Lama of Tibet

Chosen as the future Dalai Lama by Tibetan Buddhists, six-year-old Ling Rinpohche gracefully and dutifully accepts his life structured around study and prayer. His exalted role in the Buddhist world mostly isolates him from childhood friends and pleasures, except during one week of vacation a year.

CHARACTER TRAITS: Review the nine character traits associated with this manual. Ask students to define and give examples of each trait.

1. Utilize the rich geographic and political contrasts between Tibet and America to capture students' interest. Refer to the geographic features of the mountainous nation called Tibet and project what effect physical features exert on contacts with other cultures. Use the information in the story to summarize the Communist invasion of Tibet and the forced exile of many Tibetans including Ling Rinpohche. Clarify vocabulary terms such as isolation, exile, and reincarnation, which are necessary for understanding the story.

Read *The Little Lama of Tibet* aloud. Show photographs of Ling so that students realize that he spends much of his day preparing for leadership responsibilities. **Ask:** What are the most striking differences between the daily lives of Ling and six-year-olds in your community? What accelerates Ling's coming-of-age? Why is every moment of Ling's life protected by adults? What does Ling represent to Tibetans?

2. Allow students to choose one of the following small group activities related to the story, then to share the results of activities with classmates:

> *Research the life and responsibilities of the present Dalai Lama.*
>
> *Research how Buddhists' belief in reincarnation influences Ling's.*
>
> *Find out the advantages and disadvantages of Ling's life, and then seek other examples in which children carry unusually heavy responsibilities because of background (e.g., Prince William of England) or of talent (e.g., athletes, artists).*
>
> *Debate the issue of whether age or responsibility or both determine when children come-of-age.*
>
> *Read Ling's message to American children, then compose your own list of "advices" to children in your school.*

3. Which character traits will serve Ling best as he prepares for leadership of the Buddhist world? Seek student opinions on which traits are already observable in Ling's life story. Encourage students to volunteer traits that assist them as elementary students in meeting their responsibilities.

Hint: For interest and variety, alternate discussions on character traits between the presence and benefits of possessing the traits and the absence and consequences of not possessing the traits.

EVALUATION:

Determine the level of student understanding about the acceleration of coming-of-age by assessing how insightfully they respond to thought questions; by observing how accurately they contrast geographic features, political situations, and childhood responsibilities; and by evaluating how productively they use research, discussion, and writing to expand the meaning of the story line. Encourage students to connect the message in the story to the theme of celebrating or honoring coming-of-age.

CONNECTION #20:
Cristina Kessler. One Night: A Story from the Desert

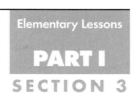

Muhamad, a young Tuareg boy in Niger, passes his coming-of-age test one night in the desert with the assistance of a fat mother goat. At sunrise, the young boy accompanied by a flock and a newborn kid, triumphantly returns to the family encampment. His father proudly orders his son's blue turban, the symbol of passage from childhood to manhood.

CHARACTER TRAITS: Review the nine character traits associated with this manual. Ask students to define and give examples of each trait.

1. Read *One Night: A Story from the Desert* aloud. Remember to set the stage with appropriate pre-reading activities that capture students' interest. For example, compare and contrast the geographic features of Niger and your community; develop an understanding of the concept, desert and why a desert promotes a nomadic life; use the geographic-feature and nomadic-life relationship to illustrate one of the five themes of geography, human-environmental interaction on the desert; and explore the role of technology in determining whether people live sedentary or settled lives, such as those in your community, or nomadic or unsettled lives, such as those in Niger.

Alert students that the story reveals many cultural clues about the nomadic Tuaregs. Use grandmother's words as an example of how Tuaregs revere the land: "Leave no path, disturb no rock," my grandmother says each day. "Make no changes on the earth, the desert is fair to someone who knows how to live with it." Lead students in deriving meaning from grandmother's words and also in comparing reverence for the land in other cultures. **Hint:** Check Native-American children's literature for similar feelings about land.

Clarify vocabulary terms such as nomads, Allah, and Ramadan, which are necessary for understanding the story line.

2. Utilize Muhamad's coming-of-age story as a way of reinforcing that education comes from many sources and can happen throughout one's lifetime.

Ask:

> *What skills does Muhamad exhibit in the story?*
> *Who are his teachers?*
> *What are the environments for his learning?*
> *How does he prove that he is ready for more responsibility?*

Categorize and chart answers to questions to serve as a model for the following group task.

Divide students into small groups. Ask that they transfer the questions from Muhamad's life to the life of a typical student in their school (e.g., skills, teachers, environments, and responsibilities). Request that a spokesperson from each group share responses with classmates.

After reports, remind students that Muhamad's test occurred in the desert, and successful completion of the test means that he receives a blue turban, tribal recognition, and increased responsibilities. Explore with students how American society recognizes coming-of-age. **Examples:** formalized religious ceremonies such as bar mitzvah or bat mitzvah, confirmation; public ceremonies such as graduation; religious and social events such as quinceañeras.

Ask students to put on their thinking caps: Does a society's level of technology affect the way that adult members protect their children's early years? Why or why not? Remind students that the higher the level of technology, the higher the level of income. In many cases, higher incomes mean that adults without children's help meet family needs and wants beyond the survival level. Thus, they may choose to postpone assignment of responsibilities to children and extend the time of relatively carefree childhood years.

Hint: Point out that the story makes no mention of coming-of-age tests for young girls. Suggest to students that the author chooses to address the story of only Muhamad or that girls occupy a less important role in tribal life. Remind students that they can often learn as much from what the author does not state as they learn from what the author does state. Allow interested students to research this issue and report to classmates.

3. Request students to reflect upon the character traits that enable Muhamad to prepare and to successfully complete his coming-of-age test. Ask students to think about these traits and decide on the traits that will assist them most in meeting responsibilities they carry as a student, a family member, and a citizen in a democracy. Suggest that students analyze whether or not the traits assist them in meeting responsibilities in all roles. Invite students to share their thoughts with classmates.

EVALUATION:

Determine the level of student understanding about one culture's acceleration of coming-of-age by assessing how insightfully they respond to thought questions, by observing how accurately they relate geographic features to lifestyles, and by evaluating how quickly they grasp that education comes from many sources and may continue throughout life. Encourage students to connect the message in the story to the theme of celebrating or honoring coming-of-age.

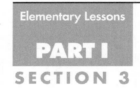

Elementary Lessons
PART I
SECTION 3

CONNECTION #21:
Deborah Kogan Ray.
My Daddy Was a Soldier:
A World War Story

The attack on Pearl Harbor on December 7, 1941, brings rapid changes to most American homes. Changes quickly sweep through American lives with the fury of a nation committed to avenging a day of infamy. Jeannie, a third grader who struggles against the "lonelies," tells the war story from the perspective of a little girl who misses her Daddy terribly.

CHARACTER TRAITS: Review the nine character traits associated with this manual. Ask students to define and give examples of each trait.

1. Read aloud the story, *My Daddy Was a Soldier.* Remember to set the stage with appropriate pre-reading activities that capture students' interest. For example, summarize important background information for students so that they understand why sacrifice was necessary on both fronts, war and home: the opponents, locations of nations at war, America's relatively isolated location, the spirit of patriotism, war years, high stakes, victory. Clarify vocabulary terms such as rationing, victory gardens, scrap drives, work force. **Hint:** Borrow World War II memorabilia from parents or members of the community. Seeing actual examples of war items will make the concepts more meaningful.

2. Reread the story, then talk about examples in the story in which the author shows Jeannie's mounting fears about her Daddy's safety. Place the examples in three categories:

> *Daddy Leaves Home;*
> *Daddy Trains in the United States; and*
> *Daddy Goes Overseas to Fight.*

Hint: Point out how examples under category headings illustrate steadily increasing apprehension in the little girl's feelings. **Ask:** What factors contribute to Jeannie's mounting fears? **Hint:** Stress that there were long time periods between reunions. These separations caused fears to increase for children as well as for adults.

3. Divide students into small groups and assign the task of recalling and listing every change in Jeannie's life that they can remember from the story. Record changes on the chalkboard.

Ask:

> *Will these changes in children's lifestyles be true in other wartime situations?*
> *Why or why not?*
> *What does this conclusion tell you about what everyone must do to win a war?*

Hint: Use student answers to introduce, develop, or reinforce the concept of opportunity or give-up cost, i.e., in order to win the war, citizens give up many peacetime needs and wants willingly.

4. Request students to reflect upon what character traits enable Jeannie to endure separation from her Daddy during World War II. Explore with students how a crisis such as war can accelerate the development of character traits as well as coming-of-age. Invite students to share examples of other crises and the effects of crises on their own coming-of-age.

EVALUATION:

Determine the level of student understanding about how crises accelerate coming-of-age by assessing how insightfully they respond to thought questions and by observing how accurately they connect wartime crises to lifestyle changes. Encourage students to connect the message in the story to the theme of celebrating or honoring coming-of-age.

CONNECTION #22:
Rosemary L. Bray.
Martin Luther King

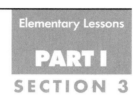

Elementary Lessons

PART I

SECTION 3

Bray skillfully intertwines the story of Martin Luther King's life with national and international events.

CHARACTER TRAITS: Review the nine character traits associated with this manual. Ask students to define and give examples of each trait.

1. Read *Martin Luther King* aloud. Remember to set the stage with appropriate pre-reading activities that capture students' interest. For example, scan the story and list vocabulary essential to the understanding of the story (e.g., civil rights movement, boycott, segregation, NAACP) on a chart tablet or the chalkboard. Ask students to define these words, as they currently understand them. Deriving meaning of words from the context of the story is one purpose for listening. After reading the story, ask students to return to the list and define the words by using context clues.

   Talk with students about patterns in the civil rights movement. Ask students to think about what elements reoccur in the movement led by Dr. King. Make sure that students understand that Dr. King focused on nonviolent strategies to accomplish his goals.

2. Provide research options from which students may choose. Permit them to work as individuals, partners, or small groups on the following projects:

   Investigate the origins of the January 15th holiday honoring Martin Luther King; contact a member of the local NAACP to explain the growth of local activities in honor of Dr. King and summarize findings for classmates.

   Investigate the 1954 Supreme Court decision of Brown versus the Board of Education, trace the events leading up to the court decision, and summarize the changes that the decision brought about in America.

   Investigate the life of Mohandas Karamchand Gandhi, known as Mahatma Gandhi; find common threads that run through the lives and the strategies of Gandhi and King; and then prepare a Venn diagram that illustrates an analysis of two leaders.

   Investigate the people who influenced Martin Luther King, try to determine how they shaped Dr. King's beliefs and, therefore, shaped the civil rights movement in America, and share information with classmates.

   Investigate the Civil Rights Museum in Memphis, Tennessee: the structure, the purpose, the exhibits; locate pictures that give fellow students a sense of visiting the museum (e.g., a picture of the bus that Rosa Parks rode); share information with classmates.

   Plan the presentations on or before January 15th. Because the civil rights movement matured under Martin Luther King's leadership, link the presentation to the theme of coming-of-age. Stress courtesy between presenters and audience members during student presentations.

3. Ask students to reflect on the life of Martin Luther King and to determine which of the character traits served the civil rights leader best. Request that students choose one world leader, decide on the person's notable accomplishments, then decide if the same traits that assisted Dr. King also helped the person reach personal goals. **Ask:** What conclusions can you draw about the use of model character traits? Why?

   Hint: For interest and variety, alternate discussions on character traits between the presence and benefits of possessing the traits and the absence and consequences of not possessing the traits.

EVALUATION:

Determine the level of student understanding about how a movement reaches maturity through the acts of one individual by assessing how insightfully they respond to thought questions and by observing how accurately they connect the civil rights movement and the lifetime of Martin Luther King. Encourage students to connect the message in the story to the theme of celebrating or honoring coming-of-age.

CONNECTION #1:
Robert J. Blake. Dog

On the edge of a small Irish village, a presumptuous stray dog chooses to live with old Peter. Dog moves freely in and out of the cottage, barks at the cottage door, and sleeps on old Peter's bed without permission. This heartwarming story of courage attests to the value of companionship when confronting the issue of survival.

CHARACTER TRAITS: Review the nine character traits used in this manual and ask students to provide examples of each of them. Tell students to keep these in a character portfolio for future reference.

1. Read *Dog* aloud. Remember to set the stage with appropriate pre-reading activities that capture students' interest. For example, distribute world atlases and lead students on a geographic investigation of Ireland: location (Where is it?); place (What is it like?); and climate, especially rainfall. Challenge students to predict how geographic influences might affect the story of a man and a dog.

Using the atlases again, compare and contrast the geographic landscape of your community to Ireland, then ask students if they see how geographic features affect lifestyles. Set a specific question as the purpose for listening to the story: How does geography influence the story of a man and a dog? After reading the story and showing the illustrations, ask students to use data to prove that relationships among geography, humans, and animals exist.

Hint: Ask students if they as elmentary students constructed a story map in their classrooms last year. Make students aware that a story map shows them the natural link between geography and literature and also allows them to become world travelers by following a simple set of directions.

Alert students that an "Around-the-world-in-180-days" journey may progress each time they post the story site of a literary selection and that by the end of the school year, they will qualify as world travelers. Encourage students to keep a class legend that notes the name of the story, main characters, and geographic site. Mark sites on the map with colored, peel-off dots or with symbols that project connections between geography and literature.

2. Explain to students that they may choose how to demonstrate their understanding of *Dog*, an Irish story of companionship and courage. Ask students to listen to the following activities; to select one that holds high interest for them; and to work individually, with a partner, or in a small group to complete the project:

Construct a diorama of a favorite scene in *Dog*; make the three-dimensional model reflect accurate details learned from the story as well as from geographic inquiries; present the favorite scene to classmates, cite the reason for choice of the specific scene, and tell how the scene fits into the story line.

Research successful advertising techniques with the help of the librarian or with the assistance of community members; use information from research to create advertising posters that lure potential buyers to purchase *Dog*; send the message on the poster that *Dog* offers something for everybody.

Assume the role of movie scriptwriters with the responsibility for turning *Dog* into an Academy Award winner; analyze the story line and illustrations of *Dog*; make production decisions such as real or animated characters, scene cuts or additions, spoken or soundless, interaction among characters, props and scenery, special effects; put design decisions on a diagram, then write one scene that shows potential moviegoers the scriptwriters' plan-in-action.

Enlist students in planning a presentation time for their projects. Use the occasion to review how respectful audience members behave during presentations.

3. Request students to reflect on what traits enable old Peter and Dog to confront the problem of survival and find a solution. Invite students to transfer the situation involving fictional characters to their own lives. Ask how and why the same character traits might assist students in meeting everyday challenges.

Hint: For interest and variety, alternate discussions on character traits between the benefits of possessing the traits and the consequences of not possessing the traits.

EVALUATION:

Determine student understanding of how companionship soothes life's pains and enables man and beast to survive in adverse situations by assessing the quality of class discussions, creative projects, written and oral assignments, and active participation. Include teacher-made rubrics and observations in evaluations.

Whenever appropriate, use literary as well as real-life examples to explore how students relate individual and collective acts of courage, diligence, and integrity to solutions of problems such as tyranny, poverty, disease, war, and/or other crucial issues. Encourage students to connect the message in the story to the theme of celebrating or honoring the human spirit.

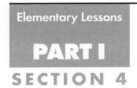

Elementary Lessons
PART I
SECTION 4

CONNECTION #2:
Ellen Levine. *I Hate English*

Because a girl's language and heritage are different from those of her classmates, she regards the English language as a symbol of their intolerance. A dedicated teacher fortunately rescues the girl from the pain of rejection by peers.

CHARACTER TRAITS: Review the nine character traits used in this manual and ask students to provide examples of each of them. Tell students to keep these in a character portfolio for future reference.

1. Read *I Hate English* aloud. Remember to set the stage with appropriate pre-reading activities that capture students' interest. For example, as a class, brainstorm and list examples of fairness and unfairness that students observe in their daily lives. Encourage students to review the list and suggest acceptable ways for elementary students to show appreciation for acts of fairness as well as to correct acts of unfairness.

For discussion purposes, distribute copies of the song "You've Got to Be Carefully Taught," from the musical *South Pacific* by Richard Rodgers and Oscar Hammerstein II (Williamson Music, Inc., 1949), and ask students to listen for types of intolerance songwriters describe in the lyrics.

Ask: How are the messages in the story and in the song connected to one another? Use the discussion as a lead-in to the differences between two important social studies concepts, prejudice and discrimination. **Hint:** Make sure that students understand that prejudice is an attitude while discrimination is a behavior. Divide students into listening partners, then ask one partner to record examples of prejudice while the other partner records examples of discrimination during the story reading.

Following the reading, encourage students to volunteer examples of both concepts based on the story line. Ask students to label the examples as either an attitude or a behavior, then to respond to the teacher's inquiry about how stydents may use this information in their daily lives.

2. Focus students' attention on how the teacher in *I Hate English* assists the main character in coping with prejudiced attitudes and discriminatory acts by classmates. Ask them to recall a time when a person exerted a positive influence in their lives by helping them solve a problem. Discuss the purpose of thank-you notes or letters, talk about words that convey appreciation to others, and then encourage students to write either notes or letters and voluntarily share the contents with classmates. **Ask:**

> *When is an appropriate time for you to send written messages of thanks to others? Why?*
>
> *Does the activity make students mindful of the importance of courtesy to others? Why?*

3. Review the story line on how the main character, with assistance from her teacher, overcomes the prejudice and discrimination of classmates. Invite students to reflect on examples of prejudice and discrimination that they have either observed or experienced. Ask that they fold pieces of manila paper in half and stand the paper up like a screen. Request students to illustrate one-half of the screen with a drawing depicting prejudice and/or discrimination and the other half with a drawing showing how the individual overcame the situation. Invite students to share their stories of triumph with classmates.

4. Display the Chinese alphabet. Challenge students to find the letters that correspond to letters in their names and practice writing names in Chinese. **Hint:** Use the activity as a means of teaching the meaning of the verbs transcribe, i.e., to write something in another language or alphabet. Divide students into partnerships, ask that they review the character traits, and select those traits that will be most helpful to a person learning a foreign language. Instruct partners to select traits and prepare to defend their choices to classmates.

Form a research team of four students to investigate unique features of the Chinese language while partners are working on the name-writing and name-the-trait projects. Ask the media specialist to assist students in finding information related to the Chinese language. Make sure the team searches for ways that the Chinese and English languages are similar to and different from one another. Examples of topics to investigate:

> *Vowels such as those in the English language;*
> *Consonants such as those in the English language; letter patterns;*
> *Necessary skills to write the language;*
> *Necessary tools to write the language; and*
> *Symbols that stand for more than one word.*

Request team members to share relevant findings, print as well as graphic, with classmates by creating a poster to show the similarities of and differences between the two languages.

5. Request students to reflect on what traits enable the story's main character to confront problems and to find solutions related to the issues of prejudice and discrimination. Invite students to transfer the situation involving a fictional character to their own lives. Ask how and why the same character traits might assist students in meeting everyday challenges.

EVALUATION:

Determine the level of student understanding of prejudice and discrimination by assessing the quality of class discussions, creative projects, written and oral assignments, and active participation. Include teacher-made rubrics and observations in evaluations.

Whenever appropriate, use literary as well as real-life examples to explore how students relate individual and collective acts of courage, diligence, and integrity to solutions of problems such as tyranny, poverty, disease, war, and/or other crucial issues. Ask students to debrief the learning from the story and activities, then tell what, how, and why they learned. Encourage students to connect the message in the story to the theme of celebrating or honoring the human spirit.

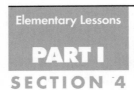

CONNECTION #3:
Katherine Paterson.
Flip-Flop Girl

Because of her father's tragic death, Vinnie Matthews's life changes completely: new town, new school, and new economic status. These dramatic changes intensify with her brother's refusal to talk; his silence makes Vinnie feel unnoticed, lonesome, and adrift. Her confusion and anger almost cost a treasured friendship with Lupe, a girl who wears bright orange flip-flops.

CHARACTER TRAITS: Review the nine character traits used in this manual and ask students to provide examples of each of them. Tell students to keep these in a character portfolio for future reference.

1. Read aloud one or two chapters of *Flip-Flop Girl* each day. Remember to set the stage with appropriate pre-reading activities that capture students' interest. For example, list important story characters and assign the tracking of one story character to small groups. Ask them to listen for clues about the character's traits, to identify what clues lead them to certain conclusions about the character, and to show how the character changes as the story progresses.

Advise students that they will develop a character profile at the end of each reading session based on what they learned from the chapters read each day. Concurrently with the profile development, lead students in predicting what will happen next in the story based on what they hear. Upon completion of the story, student partners will chart Vinnie's traits, then show causes and effects of the traits she exhibits.

Hint: Use students' character profiles as ideal lead-ins for discussions on character traits, especially the traits of courage, fairness, honesty, integrity, respect, and responsibility.

Hint: Use a story map activity to place story events and characters in correct locations after reading the story and completing the activities.

2. Write each of the nine character traits on sentence strips, and post strips in nine locations around the classroom. Ask students to write sentences on strips that demonstrate how their character exhibits or fails to exhibit a specific trait. Request that students scan the entire list of examples under each trait, and if students need further explanation, encourage them to check with the character experts. **Ask:**

> *Why do you need to analyze characters for the presence as well as the absence of character traits?*
> *How and why does the character trait identification process relate to how an author develops a story line?*

3. Request that the media specialist find critics' reviews of television shows, movies, or books to use as examples in the classroom. Ask students to listen carefully as the teacher reads four or five critiques. Lead students in identifying common factors among various critiques. Use examples as models, and invite students to write a critical review of the story recommending whether or not a friend should read the story, then explain why. Discuss similarities and differences among critiques and possible reasons for varied reactions to the same story.

EVALUATION:

Determine the level of student understanding of Vinnie's courage as she faces personal loss by assessing the quality of class discussions, written and oral assignments, and active participation. Include teacher-made rubrics and observations in evaluations.

Whenever appropriate, use literary as well as real-life examples to explore how students relate individual and collective acts of courage, diligence, and integrity to solutions of problems such as tyranny, poverty, disease, war, and/or other crucial issues. Encourage students to connect the message in the story to the theme of celebrating or honoring the human spirit.

ALTERNATE SELECTION:

Patricia Mullins. *V for Vanishing.* The beauty of illustrations calls attention to the endangerment, even extinction, of assorted animal species as well as to the value of the natural environment. Teachers and students will respond enthusiastically to Patricia Mullin's animal, plant, and geographic resource in ABC format.

CONNECTION #4:
Byrd Baylor. *The Table Where Rich People Sit*

Elementary Lessons

PART I

SECTION 4

A Native-American girl learns appreciation for nonmaterialistic elements in her life. The young girl recognizes poverty as one of life's realities; courage, diligence, and integrity, however, emerge as tools of the human spirit that enable individuals to overcome obstacles.

CHARACTER TRAITS: Review the nine character traits used in this manual and ask students to provide examples of each of them. Tell students to keep these in a character portfolio for future reference.

1. Read *The Table Where Rich People Sit* aloud. Remember to set the stage with appropriate pre-reading activities that capture students' interest. For example, ask students to consider the meaning of the story's title and predict what the story line might be. As the discussion progresses from rich people to poor people, riches to poverty, challenge students to think in terms of how many people measure wealth. **Ask:**

Do most people measure riches in terms of actual cash in the pocket or in the bank?

Do most people measure riches in terms of visible symbols such as cars and homes?

Why is money important in a society?

What are other ways of determining the wealth of people?

At the conclusion of story-related activities, return to these questions and ask students to reconsider their original answers.

Hint: Point out to students that money or some system of exchange promotes the free flow of goods and services. Most students will expand items of value far beyond money and will include family, freedom, friendship, and other intangibles important to elementary students. Use the discussion to clarify the difference between tangible and intangible items. **Ask:**

What experiences cause first answers to change?

Does the discovery of more knowledge often cause people's original answers or explanations to change slightly or completely? Why?

Invite students to talk about discoveries such as archaeological digs that change original stories either slightly or completely.

Hint: Use a story map activity to place story events and characters in correct locations after reading the story and completing the activities.

2. Explain to students that they may choose how to demonstrate their understanding that wealth comes in many forms. Ask students to listen to the following activities; to select one that holds high interest for them; and to work individually, with a partner, or in a small group to complete the project:

> Reread *The Table Where Rich People Sit*; think through the message of the story; determine who will receive an invitation to students' table of life; illustrate the guests at the table; and prepare an explanation on the who and why at the table for classmates.

> Think through the many advantages of living in a free society (e.g., of sitting at the table where rich people sit); make a list of these blessings in the form of "freedom to…"; defend freedom as a major source of wealth for democratic citizens; and prepare an explanation on why a democratic society provides the framework for citizens to find solutions to life's serious problems such as war, disease, poverty, and tyranny.

> Design a collage around the table-where-rich-people-sit theme on standard-size, colored construction paper which shows people as well as influences that students count as part of their wealth; prepare an explanation why students include these intangibles as assets; assemble collages "quilt-fashion" in a class tablecloth to display as the table where rich people sit; and prepare an explanation why the tablecloth is appropriate for class members.

Enlist students in planning a presentation time for the table-where-rich-people-sit projects. Use the occasion to review how respectful audience members behave during presentations.

3. Read *V for Vanishing* by Patricia Mullins. Explain to students that one of the most difficult thinking tasks is to find connections, i.e., to identify relationships between two or more items such as people, nations, artifacts, or stories. Set finding a connection or a common thread between *V for Vanishing* and *The Table Where Rich People Sit* as the purpose for listening. Allow students to informally discuss their thoughts with classmates. **Hint:** Emphasize how both authors stress the natural environment as a source of wealth (e.g., sunsets, mountains, rain, animals).

4. Ask students to reflect on what traits enable the story's main character to confront problems and to find solutions related to the meaning of wealth. Invite students to transfer the situation involving a fictional character to their own lives. Ask how and why the same character traits might assist students in meeting everyday challenges.

Hint: For interest and variety, alternate discussions on character traits between the benefits of possessing the traits and the consequences of not possessing the traits.

EVALUATION:

Determine student understanding of what wealth means by assessing the quality of class discussions, creative projects, written and oral assignments, and active participation. Include teacher-made rubrics and observations in evaluations.

Whenever appropriate, use literary as well as real-life examples to explore how students relate individual and collective acts of courage, diligence, and integrity to solutions of problems such as tyranny, poverty, disease, war, and/or other crucial issues. Encourage students to connect the message in the story to the theme of celebrating or honoring the human spirit.

CONNECTION # 5:
Libba Moore Gray.
Dear Willie Rudd

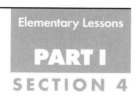
Miss Elizabeth thoughtfully reflects on society's views on race, then calls on her inner strength to challenge society's judgment.

CHARACTER TRAITS: Review the nine character traits used in this manual and ask students to provide examples of each of them. Tell students to keep these in a character portfolio for future reference.

1. Read *Dear Willie Rudd* aloud. Remember to set the stage with appropriate pre-reading activities that capture students' interest. For example, share personal stories of times when the teacher treated someone in a regrettable manner. Describe the situation and the reason for the behavior. Tell students that if the same situation occurs again, the teacher's behavior will definitely improve. Lead students in analyzing possible reasons for the change of attitude and behavior. If students wish to share similar situations, encourage them.

Lead into the story by alerting students that sometimes society, just like individuals, behaves in regrettable ways. Set the identification of society's unjust behavior as the purpose for listening. Following the reading, seek and clarify, if necessary, students' responses to the overall theme of the story.

Following the story reading, ask students how effectively the message of the story is carried through the main character, Miss Elizabeth. **Ask:**

> *Are readers more likely to listen to and understand messages if authors convey them through a story's courageous character rather than through an essay? Why?*
> *Why do students think that Miss Elizabeth chooses to address a serious problem by writing a letter and launching it in a balloon?*
> *What personal message does Miss Elizabeth send to readers about wrongful behavior?*

Invite students to select a problem that concerns them today. Write a letter to the editor on balloon-shaped, colored paper. Display letters on the bulletin board.

2. Review with students how the process of word webbing helps students analyze the contents of written and spoken words. Divide students into small groups and assign groups the task of webbing the most important elements in *Dear Willie Rudd*.

Encourage group members to talk about many elements of the story before deciding on the most important ones to place in the word web. Model the frame of a word web so that groups see that important elements compose main web lines and less important details literally attach themselves to their related element. After students finish webs, allow a group reporter to explain the word webs and reasoning behind decisions. **Ask:**

> *How does talking about a subject prior to making decisions help the quality of group products?*
> *Does compromise play a role in reaching group decisions?*
> *Why do many of the same elements appear on most of the word webs?*
> *Why do some word webs show unique elements?*
> *Why does "putting it all together," or synthesis, assist the learning of all students?*

3. Request students to reflect on what traits enable Miss Elizabeth to confront the problem of race relations and offer solutions. Invite students to transfer the situation involving a fictional character to their own lives. Ask how and why the same character traits might assist students in meeting everyday challenges.

Hint: For interest and variety, alternate discussions on character traits between the presence and benefits of possessing the traits and the absence and consequences of not possessing the traits.

Hint: Use a story map activity to place story events and characters in correct locations after reading the story and completing the activities.

EVALUATION:

Determine student understanding of an individual's role in confronting one of society's major issues by assessing the quality of class discussions, written and oral assignments, and active participation. Include teacher-made rubrics and observations in evaluations.

Whenever appropriate, use literary as well as real-life examples to explore how students relate individual and collective acts of courage, diligence, and integrity to solutions of problems such as tyranny, poverty, disease, war, and/or other crucial issues. Encourage students to connect the message in the story to the theme of celebrating or honoring the human spirit.

CONNECTION #6:
Robert Coles.
The Story of Ruby Bridges

How does an African-American six-year-old in 1960 muster sufficient courage to attend a traditionally Anglo elementary school? Amid shouting from angry protesters, Ruby Bridges starts the first grade in the recently desegregated and hostile environment of the New Orleans public schools. Personal prayer, federal marshals, and passage of time enable Ruby to survive the first year. Gradually, the mob disappears, and students return to school.

CHARACTER TRAITS: Review the nine character traits used in this manual and ask students to provide examples of each of them. Tell students to keep these in a character portfolio for future reference.

1. Read aloud *The Story of Ruby Bridges*. Remember to set the stage with appropriate pre-reading activities that capture students' interest. For example, define important terms such as civil rights, equality, segregation, desegregation, and integration, then use examples that students see in the media and/or experience in their lives to clarify the meaning of the terms.

Enlist students in researching leading personalities of the civil rights movement from the end of World War II to the present. Request the media specialist's assistance in finding a time line of personalities, events, locations of activities, and dates that emerge as landmark examples of the civil rights movement. Ask students to make a creative time line by placing each date and event on a labeled circle of brightly colored construction paper and attaching the circles to a United States map. **Ask:**

> *When and where did the civil rights movement begin?*
> *What types of protests characterize the civil rights movement after World War II?*
> *Where does the movement spread?*
> *Who are the leaders?*

CHARACTER EDUCATION THROUGH STORY

Hint: Place dates of important events in a sequenced list or on a continuum so that students detect patterns in movement. After reading the story, return to the map-and-time-line activity, and ask students if and how reading Ruby's story clarifies important definitions and events in the movement. **Ask:** Is literature an effective way to learn about historical events and personalities? Why?

Hint: Use a story map activity to place story events and characters in correct locations after reading the story and completing the activities.

2. Explain to students that they may choose how to demonstrate their understanding of *The Story of Ruby Bridges*, an example of a courageous young person's fight for equality. Ask students to listen to the following activities; to select one that holds high interest for them; and to work individually, with a partner, or in a small group to complete the project:

Research one of the heroes or heroines of the movement. By using the reporter's formula Who? What? Where? When? Why? How? prepare illustrated and captioned posters that show the individual's acts of courage to overcome the tyranny of racism; arrange a display and invite other classes to take a print walk while students explain the role of their hero or heroine in the movement.

Research one of the heroes or heroines of the movement credited as a leader in gaining legal victories. By using the reporter's formula, write the biographies in a "This Is Your Life" style; use bio-graphical clues to present the research to classmates; add the biographies to the display.

Write editorials or letters to the editor that argue the importance of desegregated schools to a democratic society; submit editorials or letters to a review board of teachers and students who will evaluate the products on content, clarity, persuasiveness, and accuracy; the board will then select the winning products for publication in your school.

Take the role of Ruby Bridges and write a week of daily journal entries; in personalized style, describe experiences with historical accuracy; share the writing and illustrations typical of a young girl's diary with classmates, then add the entries to the display collection.

Extension: Enlist students in planning a presentation time for the Ruby Bridges projects. Lead a class discussion on how Martin Luther King's statement, i.e., the statement in which he hopes that people will judge others by the "content of their character and not the color of their skin," relates to *The Story of Ruby Bridges*. **Ask:** Why do students think that Dr. King entitled the speech "I Have a Dream"? As an extension, explore with students why they might consider the racism exhibited in New Orleans as a form of tyranny. Use the occasion to review how respectful audience members behave during presentations.

Hint: Check information in the story that encourages readers to write to either Ruby Bridges about her experiences or to the author about the reason he chose Ruby Bridges to immortalize. Contact the editorial department of Scholastic, Inc., to locate their addresses.

3. Request students to reflect on what traits enable Ruby to confront problems and find solutions. Invite students to transfer Ruby's courage in New Orleans of the 1960s to their own lives. Ask how and why courage or other character traits might assist students in meeting everyday challenges.

EVALUATION:

Determine student understanding of how Ruby Bridges, a young African American, symbolizes courage in the struggle for desegregated schools by assessing the quality of class discussions, creative projects, written and oral assignments, and active participation. Include teacher-made rubrics and observations in evaluations.

Whenever appropriate, use literary as well as real-life examples to explore how students relate individual and collective acts of courage, diligence, and integrity to solutions of problems such as tyranny, poverty, disease, war, and/or other crucial issues. Ask students to debrief the learning from the story and activities, then tell what, how, and why they learned. Encourage students to connect the message in the story to the theme of celebrating or honoring the human spirit.

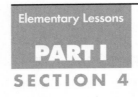

CONNECTION #7:
Nikki Giovanni.
Spin a Soft Black Song

Giovanni's contemporary poems echo the spirit of African Americans facing society's most serious ills. Because the poet addresses universal problems, particularly those associated with poverty, her poetry appeals to members of various racial and/or ethnic groups. Note: Poem titles appear in lower-case letters.

CHARACTER TRAITS: Review the nine character traits used in this manual and ask students to provide examples of each of them. Tell students to keep these in a character portfolio for future reference.

1. Divide students into eight groups. Explain that group members will read and analyze four of Giovanni's poems for classmates from various viewpoints:

> *What is the problem described in the poem?*
>
> *How does the poet give life to the problem? Choice of words? Choice of style?*
>
> *Who is affected by the problem?*
>
> *What is the root of the problem?*
>
> *Does the problem affect more people than African Americans?*
>
> *Does the poet offer hope by suggesting solutions?*

Assign each of the following poems to two groups: "mommies do" on page 15; "dreams" on page 19; "sleep" on pages 48-49; and "stars" on page 55.

Hint: Two of the eight groups will study and present the same poem for the purpose of reinforcing this idea: Poetry is an art form that encourages creative thinking, thus creative interpretation. Interpretations will vary. Separate groups working on the same poem so that interpretations are unique.

Following students' poetry reading and analysis, allow groups working on the same poem to discuss interpretations with one another. Lead all students to the conclusion that one's perspective affects one's interpretation. **Hint:** Remind students that art forms such as poetry, paintings, and sculpture evoke emotional responses from listeners and viewers, thus interpretations will vary as much as individuals do.

Ask interested students to create a visual interpretation of a poem in the form of a drawing or a collage, to present interpretations to the class, and to display in the hallway or classroom.

Hint: Giovanni's powerful poetry evokes strong feelings that citizens need to improve the quality of life for those trapped in the cycle of poverty. Lead students to an understanding that poverty is socially and economically as much a tyrant as a political dictator. If student interest runs high, curriculum writers suggest "make-a-difference" projects such as information pamphlets, editorials, and letters to elected officials.

2. Request students to reflect on what traits enable characters in poems to confront problems and find solutions. Invite students to transfer situations involving fictional characters to their own lives. Ask how and why the same character traits might assist students in meeting everyday challenges.

EVALUATION:

Determine student understanding of how society's ills, especially poverty, affect lifestyles by assessing the quality of class discussions, creative projects, written and oral assignments, and active participation. Include teacher-made rubrics and observations in evaluations.

Whenever appropriate, use literary as well as real-life examples to explore how students relate individual and collective acts of courage, diligence, and integrity to solutions of problems such as tyranny, poverty, disease, war, and/or other crucial issues. Ask students to debrief the learning from the poems and activities, then tell what, how, and why they learned. Encourage students to connect the message in the poems to the theme of celebrating or honoring the human spirit.

CONNECTION #8:
Kate Connell. *They Shall Be Heard: Susan B. Anthony and Elizabeth Cady Stanton*

Elementary Lessons
PART I
SECTION 4

The fight for feminine equality bonds two women in close friendship. By reviewing the story carefully, readers gain valuable insights into the restricted world of women in the nineteenth and early twentieth centuries, as well as into the causes of a major social movement. Connell skillfully presents the full spectrum of women's reactions to their own movement.

CHARACTER TRAITS: Review the nine character traits used in this manual and ask students to provide examples of each of them. Tell students to keep these in a character portfolio for future reference.

1. Read *They Shall Be Heard: Susan B. Anthony and Elizabeth Cady Stanton* aloud. Remember to set the stage with appropriate pre-reading activities that capture students' interest. For example, prior to reading the story, ask for volunteers to research major events in the women's movement of the nineteenth and twentieth centuries. Suggest that they enlist the librarian in helping them find a time line that chronicles the movement (e.g., dates, events, and personalities).

Hint: Remind students that they may search for information on both a national and a world level. Request that students return to the classroom and recreate the time line on the chalkboard or on a transparency, so that the time line serves as a curriculum map for the story.

Extension: Extend students' understanding by asking them to track the location of the earliest movements. **Ask:**

> *Do the earliest movements occur in locations in which some citizens already enjoyed a degree of freedom or in locations in which citizens had no freedoms?*
> *What might be the connection between the degree of freedom enjoyed and the beginning of freedom movements?*

Can students think of other examples?

Hint: The American Revolution presents an excellent example of colonists who enjoyed a degree of freedom, then gradually realized that the Mother Country was attempting to limit their freedom.

Thus, American colonists initiated a rebellious, then revolutionary movement to have freedom restored earlier than people living under tyranny with no freedom (e.g., the French, Latin Americans, Prussians, and Russians). For these reasons, historians label the American Revolution as a dynamic movement, one that continues to give life and hope to people oppressed by tyranny on a worldwide basis.

Hint: Use a story map activity to place story events and characters in correct locations after reading the story and completing the activities.

2. Develop the concept of tyranny, i.e., one group in power but making decisions for all, by allowing only the girls in the classroom to vote on all classroom procedures for the day. **Examples:** homework assignments, positions in lunchroom lines, and special activities for girls. At the end of the day, ask students:

> *Why was the learning experience of the day an example of tyranny?*
> *How do students transfer the experience to the content of Connell's story?* **Hint:** *Use the information to develop the concepts of enfranchisement and disenfranchisement.*
> *Does the story provide evidence that men always treated women with respect?*
> *Do the girls in power in the classroom today always treat boys with respect?*
> *What are democratic citizens' principal objections to tyranny?*
> *What are the principal objections of powerless boys to tyranny in the classroom today?*
> *What lessons do Connell's story and the learning experience teach students about appreciating life in a democratic society?*
> *What lessons do both sources teach students about the power of voting?*
> *How do citizens harm the system when they choose not to vote?*

3. Briefly review the issue of feminine equality as told in the story and as evidenced in student research. Share with students that one strategy for dealing with controversial issues is a modified debate, each side preparing a case for their position, and then allow audience judges to evaluate the strength of arguments. **Hint:** Notice that the teaching suggestion for group positions is not the standard format for debate but will cause students to understand the basic "pro" and "con" positions of opposing sides.

Before assigning any students to one side, lead all students in developing criteria for judging the merits of a debate. **Ask:** What are the most important items to consider when judging the quality of a debate? Allow students' ideas to form the basis for a rubric.

Divide students into three groups and ask each group to:

> *Prepare a defensible argument for this position: Susan B. Anthony and Elizabeth Cady Stanton, diligent, courageous leaders of the women's movement.*
> *Prepare a defensible argument for this position: Susan B. Anthony and Elizabeth Cady Stanton, stubborn rabble-rousers of the women's movement.*

Research details of interest to students about the two personalities; during the presentations of both positions. Three students will serve as judges and apply the criteria of evaluation, reach a decision on the stronger argument, and share the decision with students. Then, teachers will reveal the high-interest details about the feminine leaders to students and lead discussion on how closely the judges' decision matches the research findings.

Remind students on both sides and in the audience about the necessity of listening carefully to presenters and the importance of showing respect for all participants and their viewpoints.

4. Suggest that students design a Women's Hall of Fame for all sixth-grade students to view. Allow each student to choose a woman who played a significant role in the women's movement or to draw from a teacher-made pool of women important in the movement. Provide time for students to research personalities in the library, and encourage students to seek additional sources other than the school library. Instruct students to apply the reporter's formula, Who? What? Where? When? Why? How? to research sources.

Ask students to search for examples of obstacles the women overcame while making individual and collective contributions to the women's movement. Request that students transfer research information to colorful, attractive posters suitable for display in a Women's Hall of Fame. Assist students in preparing the display as well as a two-minute explanation of each woman's contribution to the movement. Invite other classes to tour the Hall of Fame.

5. Request students to reflect on what traits enabled Anthony and Stanton to confront problems and find solutions. Invite students to transfer the situation involving the historical characters to their own lives. Ask how and why the same character traits might assist students in meeting everyday challenges.

Hint: For interest and variety, alternate discussions on character traits between the presence and benefits of possessing the traits and the absence and consequences of not possessing the traits.

EVALUATION:

Determine student understanding of how Susan B. Anthony and Elizabeth Cady Stanton symbolize courage in women's struggle for equal rights by assessing the quality of class discussions, creative projects, written and oral assignments, and active participation. Include teacher-made rubrics and observations in evaluations.

Whenever appropriate, use literary as well as real-life examples to explore how students relate individual and collective acts of courage, diligence, and integrity to solutions of problems such as tyranny, poverty, disease, war, and/or other crucial issues. Encourage students to connect the message in the story to the theme of celebrating or honoring the human spirit.

CONNECTION #9:
John Cech.
My Grandmother's Journey

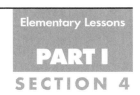

Elementary Lessons
PART I
SECTION 4

Set in pre-revolutionary Russia and based on the life of a Russian woman, My Grandmother's Journey chronicles a story of personal struggle amidst civil war, depression, World War II, Nazi invasion, and immigration to the United States. The story clearly demonstrates how acts of courage, diligence, and integrity enable people to survive in times of cruelty and destruction.

CHARACTER TRAITS: Review the nine character traits used in this manual and ask students to provide examples of each of them. Tell students to keep these in a character portfolio for future reference.

1. Read *My Grandmother's Journey* aloud. Remember to set the stage with appropriate pre-reading activities that capture students' interest. For example, talk to students about why authors choose to tell experiences of an entire group of people through the story of one person. **Hint:** Share with students that the story recounts the trials of Russian commoners through periods of political, economic, and social upheaval.

Ask student listening partners to concentrate on the series of events in Russia that the grandmother's story traces in world history. During the second reading, ask partners in a think-pair-share activity to list dates, places, and events described on paper imprints of Grandmother's feet. Remind students of the following quotes from the story:

1. *"Feet," she said. "Where haven't you been? What haven't we been through together?"*
2. *"I liked it when she wiggled her toes and talked to her feet. That's how she got comfortable."*
3. *"You are light on your feet and can dance all night, but there will come a time when your every footstep will be pain."*
4. *"She did not tell me that I would eat bread again, in a warm house, where I can rest my feet, these old friends, that have carried me halfway around the world to you."*

Following the reading, categorize the events as examples of either tyranny, poverty, disease, or war, then cite how individuals or groups survive through acts of courage, diligence, or integrity. Lead students in a focused discussion on categories and character traits.

Hint: Use a story map activity to place story events and characters in correct locations after reading the story and completing the activities.

2. Talk with students about this fact: Most adults, particularly older adults who have experienced how large forces beyond their control affect personal lives, possess interesting stories of courage, diligence, and integrity to tell. In groups of three, ask students to select individuals to interview, develop questions to ask about life stories, conduct interviews, then tell the stories in the form of illustrated children's books to share with classmates. Ask each group to link their story to *My Grandmother's Journey,* and schedule time for group presentations.

3. Request students to reflect on traits that enable Grandmother to confront problems and find solutions. Invite students to transfer situations involving Grandmother's trials and triumphs to their own lives. Ask how and why the same character traits might assist students in meeting everyday challenges.

EVALUATION:

Determine student understanding of how Grandmother, a symbol for Russian commoners, utilizes courage, diligence, and integrity in her struggle against tyranny by assessing the quality of class discussions, creative projects, written and oral assignments, and active participation. Include teacher-made rubrics and observations in evaluations.

Whenever appropriate, use literary as well as real-life examples to explore how students relate individual and collective acts of courage, diligence, and integrity to solutions of problems such as tyranny, poverty, disease, war, and/or other crucial issues. Ask students to debrief the learning from the story and activities, then tell what, how, and why they learned. Encourage students to connect the message in the story to the theme of celebrating or honoring the human spirit.

CONNECTION #10:
Robert J. Norrell.
We Want Jobs! A Story of the Great Depression

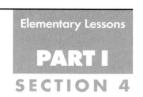

John Waskowitz and his family endure effects of the economic war of the 1930s entitled the Great Depression. Disheartened by a continuous battle with poverty, John and a group of jobless workers join a Pittsburgh priest who organizes a trip to Washington, D.C. Ignored by President Herbert Hoover and other leaders, the Waskowitzes begin to work for Franklin D. Roosevelt's political campaign.

CHARACTER TRAITS: Review the nine character traits used in this manual and ask students to provide examples of each of them. Tell students to keep these in a character portfolio for future reference.

1. Read *We Want Jobs!* aloud. Remember to set the stage with appropriate pre-reading activities that capture students' interest. For example, review with students the meaning of courage, judgment, integrity, and dedication, then talk about present-day people who exemplify the traits. Set finding examples of the traits the Waskowitzes demonstrate during the Great Depression as the purpose for listening to the story.

Following the story reading, lead students in a discussion in which they cite examples of the character traits from *We Want Jobs!* **Ask:** How does the Waskowitz story agree or disagree with stories of the Great Depression that students have viewed on television or in the movies, heard from relatives or friends, or read in other stories?

Hint: Alert students that many people during the Great Depression suffered economic setbacks in varying degrees. Point out, however, that some citizens, mostly wealthy citizens, experienced relatively few changes in their lifestyles.

Hint: Use a story map activity to place story events and characters in correct locations after reading the story and completing the activities.

2. Explain to students that they may choose how to demonstrate their understanding of *We Want Jobs!*, an example of one courageous family's fight for security. Ask students to listen to the following activities; to select one that holds high interest for them; and to work individually, with a partner, or in a small group to complete the project:

Research federal work programs of the New Deal, then design pamphlets that recruit people to a specific agency such as the Works Progress Administration (WPA), Civilian Conservation Corps (CCC), National Youth Administration (NYA), or Public Works Administration (PWA); share information with classmates and, if possible, find similar programs existing today that fulfill economic needs of citizens.

Research the effects of the Great Depression in other parts of the world, then compare and contrast ways that governments dealt with economic woes; locate countries on a world map as students share information with classmates in the form of nightly news reports.

Plan family meals from the contents of the brown box of food that the Waskowitz family receives in the story, i.e., a bag of navy beans, a slab of bacon, a square of margarine, and a five-pound sack of flour; explain menus to classmates and comment on how the menus meet or do not meet nutritional standards as well as predictable short-term and long-term effects on family members. Stretch the ingredients as far as possible.

Note: Check the following nutritional standards included in The Edible Pyramid by Loreen Leedy:

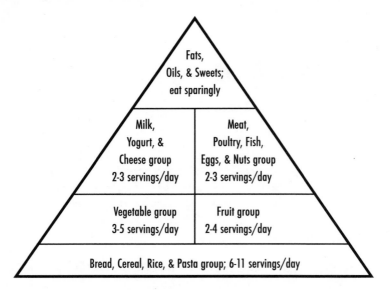

Nutritionists suggest eating a variety of foods, preferably with more servings from the bottom rows of the pyramid.

Remind students prior to any student presentations of the importance and necessity of listening courteously and of questioning respectfully.

3. Ask students to reflect on what traits enable the Waskowitzes to confront problems and find solutions. Invite students to transfer situations involving the Waskowitzes to their own lives. Ask how and why the same character traits might assist students in meeting everyday challenges.

EVALUATION:

Determine student understanding of how the Waskowitzes utilize courage, diligence, and integrity in their struggle against poverty by assessing the quality of class discussions, creative projects, written and oral assignments, and active participation. Include teacher-made rubrics and observations in evaluations.

Whenever appropriate, use literary as well as real-life examples to explore how students relate individual and collective acts of courage, diligence, and integrity to solutions of problems such as tyranny, poverty, disease, war, and/or other crucial issues. Ask students to debrief the learning from the story and activities, then tell what, how, and why they learned. Encourage students to connect the message in the story to the theme of celebrating or honoring the human spirit.

CONNECTION #11:
James Stevenson. *Don't You Know There's a War On?*

While ten-year-old Sydney's father and brother serve in World War II, he learns the meaning of sacrifice on the home front. Citizens, both young and old, willingly make sacrifices for the boys at the front and enthusiastically support the war effort.

CHARACTER TRAITS: Review the nine character traits used in this manual and ask students to provide examples of each of them. Tell students to keep these in a character portfolio for future reference.

1. Read *Don't You Know There's a War On?* aloud. Remember to set the stage with appropriate pre-reading activities that capture students' interest. For example, seek a simple definition of scarcity from students. Explain that scarcity is a situation caused by the constant tug-of-war between limited resources and unlimited human needs and wants. People wrestle with decisions related to what goods will be produced, how goods will be produced, and who will get the goods. If a crisis such as war or depression exists, a democratic government increases its role in making economic decisions in the interests of the public good.

Establish listening partners, and then request that partners listen for examples of scarcity on the home front and examples of government actions taken to address scarcity. Through discussion, develop student understanding of rationing during wartime. **Hint:** Clarify for students the differences between rationing and food stamps by comparing and contrasting the purposes, the settings, and the groups affected. Students mistakenly assume that the issuance of stamps makes the two programs the same.

Hint: Use a story map activity to place story events and characters in correct locations after reading the story and completing the activities.

2. Search for a reference such as Julie R. Strathman's thematic unit on World War II (Huntington Beach, CA: Teacher Created Materials, Inc., 1994) to locate a rationing schedule chart. Duplicate copies of the chart, then challenge students in small groups to plan three meals for a family of four by using information from the chart. **Ask:** What do students observe about the quality of meals during wartime? Why did people willingly accept rationing during World War II?

Use a pictorial Venn diagram to compare and contrast the three planned meals during World War II with three meals students might enjoy today.

Extension: Extend student learning by asking small groups to write math story problems that use the rationing chart for data and then by seeking solutions from other groups in a round-robin manner. **Ask:** Do solutions to the math story problems agree with students' first conclusions about the quality of meals during wartime? Why or why not?

3. Request students to reflect on what traits enable Sydney to confront problems and find solutions. Invite students to transfer situations involving Sydney to their own lives. Ask how and why the same character traits might assist students in meeting everyday challenges.

Hint: For interest and variety, alternate discussions on character traits between the presence and benefits of possessing the traits and the absence and consequences of not possessing the traits.

EVALUATION:

Determine the level of student understanding of Sydney's willing sacrifices on the home front during World War II by assessing the quality of class discussions, creative projects, written and oral assignments, and active participation. Include teacher-made rubrics and observations in evaluations.

Whenever appropriate, use literary as well as real-life examples to explore how students relate individual and collective acts of courage, diligence, and integrity to solutions of problems such as tyranny, poverty, disease, war, and/or other crucial issues. Encourage students to connect the message in the story to the theme of celebrating or honoring the human spirit.

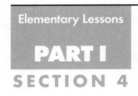

Elementary Lessons
PART I
SECTION 4

CONNECTION #12:
Michael Foreman.
War Boy: A Country Childhood

Teachers and students will welcome the high-interest, full-of-adventure account told by a young participant in World War II. The story clearly shows how wartime triggers exceptional acts of courage, thus accelerates the coming-of-age process. War Boy: A Country Childhood also affords opportunities for students to review differences between primary and secondary sources in history.

CHARACTER TRAITS: Review the nine character traits used in this manual and ask students to provide examples of each of them. Tell students to keep these in a character portfolio for future reference.

1. Read *War Boy: A Country Childhood* aloud. Remember to set the stage with appropriate pre-reading activities that capture students' interest. For example, scan the story for important geographic locations. Make sure that students comprehend that geography encompasses much more than the vast outdoors and physical features; geography includes small indoor areas such as homes and hiding places and the human relationships that occur within those spaces.

Prior to reading the story, chart important sites on the classroom map so that students may judge how war exerts a geographic impact on people and their movements. Ask students to listen closely for geographic evidence that wartime affects human life. Following the reading, use evidence in the story to support the generalization that wartime causes individuals and groups to make adjustments in their lifestyles.

2. Utilize *War Boy: A Country Childhood* as a style model to review with students the narrative style, the choice of descriptive words, the sentence patterns, and other elements that build reader interest in the historical event.

Have students choose one topic about the person, place, event, or item of highest personal interest in World War II; use the reporter's formula (e.g., Who? What? Where? When? Why? How?) to research basic facts about the topic; elaborate the topic with unique, memorable information or with illustrations; and prepare the report on a topic-related silhouette cut from construction paper. **Examples:** helmets, tanks, planes, personality profiles. Assist students in posting completed reports on "The World War II Data Bank" display board either in the classroom or hallway. Invite students to take a print walk along the display while students share information from their reports with classmates.

3. Request students to reflect on what traits enable the young boy in the story to confront problems and find solutions to life during wartime. Invite students to transfer the historical examples to their own lives. Ask how and why the same character traits might assist students in meeting everyday challenges.

Hint: For interest and variety, alternate discussions on character traits between the presence and benefits of possessing the traits and the absence and consequences of not possessing the traits. Current authorities in character education often refer to the absence of traits as character flaws.

EVALUATION:

Determine student understanding of what wartime causes for families and children by assessing the quality of class discussions, creative projects, written and oral assignments, and active participation. Include teacher-made rubrics and observations in evaluations.

Whenever appropriate, use literary as well as real-life examples to explore how students relate individual and collective acts of courage, diligence, and integrity to solutions of problems such as tyranny, poverty, disease, war, and/or other crucial issues. Encourage students to connect the message in the story to the theme of celebrating or honoring the human spirit.

CONNECTION #13:
David A. Adler.
Child of the Warsaw Ghetto

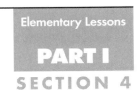

Elementary Lessons
PART I
SECTION 4

In a gripping World War II story of hardships and indignities, Froim Baum reveals the plight of Polish Jews during the Nazi occupation.

CHARACTER TRAITS: Review the nine character traits used in this manual and ask students to provide examples of each of them. Tell students to keep these in a character portfolio for future reference.

1. Read *Child of the Warsaw Ghetto* aloud. Remember to set the stage with appropriate pre-reading activities that capture students' interest. For example, talk about similarities of children's ages in the story and in the class. Lead students to understand that even though the children were Polish and Jewish, most children were interested in the same things as students today. On the first reading, request that students listen closely to the story for evidence of family, faith, friends, and fun; then after reading the story, clarify who deprives children of their normal childhood pleasures and why.

Hint: Use a story map activity to place story events and characters in correct locations after reading the story and completing the activities. Point out to students the locations of the major powers in World War II, Axis as well as Allies, and explain how Poland experiences the geographic misfortune of occupying space between two enemies, Germany and Russia.

2. Distribute an assorted collection of paper clips, popsicle sticks, pennies, pebbles, buttons, and strings to small groups of students, then request that the groups invent children's toys. Instruct students to name each toy, explain its purpose, and connect the toy to *Child of the Warsaw Ghetto*. **Ask:**

Are Polish children in World War II interested in many of the same things as children today?

What does the story say about adults throughout time trying to make life happy for children?

3. Read the story aloud a second time. Enlist the assistance of students in listening for important dates and events in the story line. Ask two students to draw a time line on the chalkboard and the other students to raise their hands when a date and event appear in the story. At the completion of the story, the time line will show not only dates and events but also changes in Nazi policies toward their enemies. **Ask:** As the war progresses in the story, how do people's attitudes—Axis and Allies, young and old—change?

Use the information on the time line as a writing prompt. Encourage student partners to choose any date and event on the time line and craft a historically accurate story of a Polish child during Nazi occupation. Instruct students to weave into the stories how various characters take risks either in an attempt to maintain normal activity or in an effort to help others. **Ask:**

Do the acts display courage, diligence, or integrity?

Can students justify labeling World War II as a fight against tyranny?

Why or why not?

Invite partners to read stories to classmates who will then evaluate the accuracy of the story lines.

Hint: For interest and variety, alternate discussions on character traits between the benefits of possessing the traits and the consequences of not possessing the traits.

EVALUATION:

Determine the level of student understanding of life in the ghetto during World War II by assessing the quality of class discussions, creative projects, written and oral assignments, and active participation. Include teacher-made rubrics and observations in evaluations.

Whenever appropriate, use literary as well as real-life examples to explore how students relate individual and collective acts of courage, diligence, and integrity to solutions of problems such as tyranny, poverty, disease, war, and/or other crucial issues. Encourage students to connect the message in the story to the theme of celebrating or honoring the human spirit.

ALTERNATE SELECTIONS:

Chana Byers Abells. *The Children We Remember*. Nothing paints a more poignant story of war than the faces and voices of children. Abells details the struggles of Jewish children during the Nazi regime.

Norman H. Finkelstein. *Remember Not to Forget*. Finkelstein compiles a concise introduction to the Holocaust, the Nazi's vicious extermination plan instigated during World War II.

CONNECTION #14:
Yoshiko Uchida. *The Bracelet*

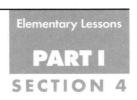

During World War II, internment camps become home for thousands of Japanese Americans. For second-grader Emi, the loss of a cherished bracelet thwarts her adjustment to life in the camp. As time passes, Emi realizes that her memories, rather than an actual bracelet, keep alive the bonds of close friendship.

ALTERNATE SELECTION:

Lois Lowry. *Number the Stars.* Through the character of ten-year-old Annemarie, readers learn about the remarkably heroic World War II story of Danes who shelter Jewish friends during the German occupation of Denmark. Danish citizens not only devise escapes to safe havens but also maintain property for their neighbors in exile.

CHARACTER TRAITS: Review the nine character traits used in this manual and ask students to provide examples of each of them. Tell students to keep these in a character portfolio for future reference.

1. Read *The Bracelet* aloud. Remember to set the stage with appropriate pre-reading activities that capture students' interest. For example, inquire about students' understanding of two concepts: prejudice and discrimination. Solicit definitions and examples of both concepts; then, if necessary, clarify misconceptions by explaining that prejudice is an attitude while discrimination is a behavior.

Share this example with students to clarify the difference between the concepts. Tell the class that only blue-eyed students might sit next to the teacher during class, only blue-eyed students might respond to the teacher's questions, only blue-eyed students might participate in activities, and only blue-eyed students might go to lunch on time. **Ask:**

> *How do blue-eyed students feel?*
> *How do all other students feel?*
> *Is the teacher's example a story of prejudice or discrimination or both? Why?*

Set listening for examples of prejudice and discrimination as the purpose for reading *The Bracelet*.

2. Read the story, *Number the Stars*, by Lois Lowry. On a Venn diagram, record the significant similarities and differences between *Number the Stars* and *The Bracelet*. **Hint:** Prompt students with questions that lead to entries related to locations, lifestyles, prejudicial attitudes, discriminatory behaviors, and survival techniques. Request that students answer these questions: How are the story lines similar? How are the story lines different? Ask students to reflect on the completed diagram and on the responses to the thought questions, then lead students into drawing defensible conclusions about the effects of war on children.

3. Inquire about the importance of friendship in students' lives, then transfer the discussion on the importance of friendship to the children in the stories. Use students' examples to develop the idea that friends in stories, historical accounts, or real lives make a difference through simple acts of kindness.

Ask:

> *What examples in the stories prove that children value their friends?*
> *How does friendship enable story characters to survive war?*
> *Does friendship as well as the human spirit give individuals strength? Why?*

4. Share the story of the man throwing a starfish back into the ocean. When asked what he was doing, the man said he was trying to save a starfish that washed ashore. He was told there were too many to save. He replied, as he threw another one back into the sea, "It makes a difference to that one." **Ask:** What is the connection between the starfish story and the other two stories, *The Bracelet* and *Number the Stars*?

On the "arms" of a paper starfish, ask students to write five acts of kindness, one from each story plus three acts the student can do for another person (e.g., a friend or relative).

Enlist student assistance in citing acts of kindness that friends do for one another in their school and in the two stories. **Ask:**

> Even though time, location, and circumstance separate the friendship stories, what are the similarities about them?
>
> What must be true about the bonds of genuine friendship?

5. Solicit volunteers to research two examples of relocation of citizens during World War II: Japanese Americans to internment camps in mid-America and Jews to concentration camps in Germany. Instruct student volunteers to use the reporters formula (e.g., Who? What? Where? When? Why? How?) in gathering data on the two examples of relocation. Request that researchers organize oral reports to classmates according to the formula. **Ask:**

> According to research data, what were the reasons for relocation?
>
> According to research data, what part did prejudice and discrimination play in the decisions to relocate citizens?
>
> What lessons may students learn from studies of citizens' relocation during World War II?

6. Request that students reflect on what traits enable children to survive the relocation process during wartime. Ask students to transfer the situation involving story characters to their own lives. Ask how and why the same character traits might assist students in meeting everyday challenges.

Hint: For interest and variety, alternate discussions on character traits between the presence and benefits of possessing the traits and the absence and consequences of not possessing the traits.

EVALUATION:

Determine the level of student understanding of children's courage during stressful times by assessing the quality of class discussions, creative projects, written and oral assignments, and active participation. Include teacher-made rubrics and observations in evaluations.

Whenever appropriate, use literary as well as real-life examples to explore how students relate individual and collective acts of courage, diligence, and integrity to solutions of problems such as tyranny, poverty, disease, war, and/or other crucial issues. Encourage students to connect the message in the story to the theme of celebrating or honoring the human spirit.

ADDITIONAL SELECTION:

Ken Mochizuki. *Baseball Saved Us.* Because of their ancestry, Japanese Americans on the West Coast find themselves uprooted from their homes, then hustled to internment camps for the duration of World War II. Humiliation represents only part of the relocation story. Adults witness the decline in traditional values such as responsibility and respect. In a moving, first-person account, Mochizuki shows how the sport of baseball unites dispirited camp residents in a productive activity.

CONNECTION #15:
Sheila Hamanaka.
The Journey

Through text and illustrations, Hamanaka traces the Japanese experience in America from the late 1800s to the 1980s. Countless examples of core character traits emerge from this story of courageous people.

ALTERNATE SELECTION:

Junko Morimoto. *My Hiroshima.* Dropping the atomic bomb on August 6, 1945, forever changes Japanese history and culture. Morimoto recounts the story through the pre- and post-bomb reactions of a little girl living in Hiroshima.

CHARACTER TRAITS: Review the nine character traits used in this manual and ask students to provide examples of each of them. Tell students to keep these in a character portfolio for future reference.

1. Read both *The Journey* and *My Hiroshima* aloud. Remember to set the stage with appropriate pre-reading activities that capture students' interest. For example, tell students that an important instructional purpose exists for reading two stories about the Japanese, one story set in Japan and the other set in the United States. Divide students into listening partners, make sure they understand that they are to discover the purpose for using two stories about the Japanese, then allow a brief time for partners to discuss the task.

Following the story reading, encourage partners to talk through ideas about the purpose of reading two sources. Lead students to the conclusion that many factors affect the way people interpret historical events (e.g., national loyalties, experiences, and consequences).

Encourage students to search for evidence in the stories that support their thoughts. Allow partners to offer ideas on the instructional purpose of using two or more sources. After partners report their conclusions, tell students that the purpose focuses once again on showing students the validity of the theme: Celebrating or Honoring the Human Spirit. Both sources demonstrate that when adversity overpowers individuals, they may call upon the human spirit for strength.

2. Explain the rules for the instructional strategy of "Taking a Stand": students hear a statement; based on their knowledge and experience, they choose one of three positions—agree, disagree, or neutral—and physically move to one of three positions; they justify the position taken through deliberation with students who take the same stand, then report to the large group. Give two examples not related to story content such as "My favorite vegetable is broccoli" or "My favorite football team is the Dallas Cowboys" (name of team optional). Caution students that statements must cause students to take a pro, con, or neutral stand.

Divide students into groups no larger than four. Instruct them to write five statements about Japanese experiences in Japan as well as in America. Ask students to base statements on information in the two stories. Allow each group to read statements that motivate students to move to the place in the room that matches their position. **Hint:** Remind students that they must defend each stand. **Ask:** What do you learn while participating in an active instructional strategy such as "Taking a Stand"?

Lead students in making a class mural or a class collage that demonstrates that they learn content, how others think, how positions change, and how to work together in groups. Display the finished product in the classroom or in the hallway.

Hint: Make sure that students support statements with facts, not emotions. The dropping of the A-bomb obviously arouses strong emotions. Students at the elementary level may have difficulty in separating fact and emotion. If students are highly interested in researching both sides of the issue and placing the data in the proper historical context, assist them in locating objective sources.

3. Ask students to reflect on the character traits, as recounted in the two stories, that enable the Japanese people to survive adversity in times of war and of peace. Invite students to transfer the situation involving fictional and/or historical characters to their own lives. Ask how and why the same character traits might assist students in meeting everyday challenges.

Hint: For interest and variety, alternate discussions on character traits between the benefits of possessing the traits and the consequences of not possessing the traits.

EVALUATION:

Determine the level of student understanding of adversities faced by the Japanese in different periods of history and in different circumstances by assessing the quality of class discussions, creative projects, written and oral assignments, and active participation. Include teacher-made rubrics and observations in evaluations.

Whenever appropriate, use literary as well as real-life examples to explore how students relate individual and collective acts of courage, diligence, and integrity to solutions of problems such as tyranny, poverty, disease, war, and/or other crucial issues. Encourage students to connect the message in the story to the theme of celebrating or honoring the human spirit.

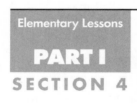

CONNECTION #16:
Walter Dean Myers.
A Place Called Heartbreak:
A Story of Vietnam

Teachers and students gain insights into the controversial war in Southeast Asia by reading a personal account of a captured pilot. The story describes his arduous trials as a prisoner of war for seven and one-half years.

CHARACTER TRAITS: Review the nine character traits used in this manual and ask students to provide examples of each of them. Tell students to keep these in a character portfolio for future reference.

1. Read *A Place Called Heartbreak: A Story of Vietnam* aloud. Remember to set the stage with appropriate pre-reading activities that capture students' interest. For example, talk with students about the meaning of the term, prisoner of war (POW). Ask them to list the freedoms that captors most likely take away from prisoners of war. Check to see if students can add to the list by recalling prisoner-of-war stories popularized by books, television, and movies. Discuss the role that courage, diligence, or integrity might play in assisting a prisoner of war to survive life in a prison camp. Students should listen carefully for the trials the captured pilot endures and the qualities that give him strength.

2. Request that the media specialist assist a volunteer research team of four in finding an illustrated time line of United States' involvement in the Vietnam War. Ask that the team either reproduce the timeline on the chalkboard or on a transparency so that students may see the length of the war and the cycles of escalation and de-escalation.

Hint: Check to see that the information on the time line includes the names of nations on opposing sides. **Ask:**

What appears to decide which side a nation joins in the Vietnam War?
Is this division of nations unique to the Vietnam War?
If not, what are other examples?

While the research team gathers information, invite other students to choose one of three writing assignments:

Write a letter of encouragement to a prisoner of war;
Write a letter of hope to the prisoner of war's family; or
Write a persuasive letter to the President of the United States to step up efforts to free thousands of prisoners of war.

Allow those students who select the same option to brainstorm potential ideas to include in letters prior to actual writing. After writing letters, suggest that students choose the best example in their category of letters to share with classmates. Plan presentation time for the Vietnam projects.

3. Prisoners of war in the story develop a tap code to communicate with each other. Challenge students to create a tap code or written code to send a message to a POW. Invite students to share codes and messages with classmates. Use codes as springboards to study the role of codes during other periods of national crisis.

4. Ask students to reflect on what traits enable the captured pilot to survive life in a prisoner-of-war camp. Invite students to transfer situations involving the story character to their own lives. Ask how and why the same character traits might assist students in meeting everyday challenges.

EVALUATION:

Determine the level of student understanding of how a prisoner of war endured more than seven years of captivity by assessing the quality of class discussions, creative projects, written and oral assignments, and active participation. Include teacher-made rubrics and observations in evaluations.

Whenever appropriate, use literary as well as real-life examples to explore how students relate individual and collective acts of courage, diligence, and integrity to solutions of problems such as tyranny, poverty, disease, war, and/or other crucial issues. Ask students to debrief the learning from the story and activities, then tell what, how, and why they learned. Encourage students to connect the message in the story to the theme of celebrating or honoring the human spirit.

ALTERNATE SELECTION:

Judy Donnelly. *A Wall of Names.* Donnelly surveys the history of the Vietnam War, chronicles the construction of the Vietnam Memorial, and reflects on the wall's meaning to many Americans.

CONNECTION #17:
Margy Burns Knight.
Who Belongs Here?
An American Story

War in Cambodia forces a young boy, Nary, and his grandmother to flee their native land for the United States. Leaving behind family, friends, and familiar surroundings exacts a heavy price from the two immigrants. Both must call on inner strengths to survive the experience.

CHARACTER TRAITS: Review the nine character traits used in this manual and ask students to provide examples of each of them. Tell students to keep these in a character portfolio for future reference.

1. Read *Who Belongs Here?* aloud. Remember to set the stage with appropriate pre-reading activities that capture students' interest. For example, tell students that the story takes place in two unique geographic environments, one in Asia and the other in North America. Enlist students in locating Cambodia and New York City on the classroom map and in comparing the two places strictly from standard data derived from lines, markings, and colors on the map. Challenge students to describe the two places from map clues. Ask two students to measure the distance between the two sites, then report to classmates in terms of miles as well as kilometers.

Ask: Based on the geographic data derived from the map, what predictions might students make about immigrants' adjustments to their new environment? Why is adjustment to the environment only part of the story?

Divide students into partners and ask that they make a list of questions that immigrants must answer immediately on arriving in a new land. **Examples:**

> *Where will they live?*
> *Where will they work?*
> *How will they buy needed goods?*
> *How will they communicate?*
> *How will strangers treat them?*
> *How will they combat loneliness?*

Tell students that the answers to these questions compose the rest of the story. Set listening for the answers to these questions as the purpose for reading. Following the reading, lead a discussion based on these questions.

Hint: Draw the experience closer to home by inviting students who have moved to your community and entered new schools to share their stories, i.e., the major concerns of elementary students when moving to a new city, a new neighborhood, and a new school. Encourage students to identify similarities and differences between classmates' and immigrants' experiences.

Hint: Use a story map activity to place story events and characters in correct locations after reading the story and completing the activities.

2. Explain to students that they may choose how to demonstrate their understanding of the immigrant experience. Ask students to listen to the following activities; to select one that holds high interest for them; and to work individually, with a partner, or in a small group to complete the project:

Construct a "This-Is-Nary's-Life" time line with events entered in correct sequence and illustrated with meaningful symbols; for each event, determine which of the character traits might provide the most assistance to an immigrant in solving a specific problem (list of nine character traits in appendix); interpret and justify entries on the time line for classmates; lead classmates in listing common experiences that many students who move to their community share with immigrants; point out the drama of the relocation experience; compare these to Nary's experiences.

Select the part of the story in which Nary and/or his grandmother as immigrants encounter the greatest challenge; identify what causes the challenge and what traits assist Nary and/or his grandmother in overcoming the challenge; retell the story in the form of poems, songs, illustrations, diary entries, or interviews between reporter and immigrants.

Enlist students in planning a presentation time for their projects. Use the occasion to review how respectful audience members behave during presentations.

3. Remind students that literary characters overcome challenges in their lives by calling on one or more sources of inner strength. Add reality to literary examples by inviting students to tell about similar situations from the real world, i.e., a person confronts and solves a difficult problem by calling on one or more of the character traits, all sources of inner strength.

Hint: For interest and variety, alternate discussions on character traits between the benefits of possessing the traits and the consequences of not possessing the traits.

EVALUATION:

Determine student understanding of the immigrant experience by assessing the quality of class discussions, creative projects, written and oral assignments, and active participation. Include teacher-made rubrics and observations in evaluations.

Whenever appropriate, use literary as well as real-life examples to explore how students relate individual and collective acts of courage, diligence, and integrity to solutions of problems such as tyranny, poverty, disease, war, and/or other crucial issues. Encourage students to connect the message in the story to the theme of celebrating or honoring the human spirit.

ALTERNATE SELECTION:

Jim Murphy. *Across America on an Emigrant Train.* Only romance could prompt a young Scottish writer to endure a stormy crossing of the Atlantic and a jostling train ride to California. Murphy weaves Robert Louis Stevenson's experiences with immigrants heading west into an exciting story focusing on the construction of the transcontinental railroad. Social history at its best!

CONNECTION #18:
Allan Baillie. *Rebel*

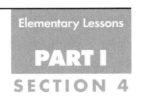

Elementary Lessons

PART I

SECTION 4

The courageous acts of a rebel unite Burmese citizens against a destructive, arrogant general whose marauding troops flatten slides, swings, and monkey bars on a school playground.

CHARACTER TRAITS: Review the nine character traits used in this manual and ask students to provide examples of each of them. Tell students to keep these in a character portfolio for future reference.

1. Read *Rebel* aloud. Remember to set the stage with appropriate pre-reading activities that capture students' interest. For example, enlist students in locating Burma on the classroom map and in describing Burma's geographic setting by using map clues. Also, call students' attention to the title of the story; invite them to define the term, rebel and ask them how one's point of view or perspective might affect the use of the term.

   Hint: Use a story map activity to place story events and characters in correct locations after reading the story and completing the activities.

2. Establish discussion-and-research partners. Challenge students to reflect on their studies in local or state history, United States history, and world culture studies, then select individuals who might be labeled rebels in their times. Students will be responsible for naming an individual, for citing the individual's cause, and for explaining why some people may view the person as a hero or heroine and others may view the person as a traitor.

   Ask students to search for data in the media center that conforms to the criteria, then construct a profile of the rebel from research data.

   Students will write pertinent information on a teacher-prepared form with spaces for the rebel's name, rebel's cause, and views on the rebel. Set a time for student presentations entitled "Rebels with a Cause." Lead students in a culminating discussion of common traits that rebels call upon when they champion a cause.

3. Challenge students to test their understanding of point of view by rewriting *Rebel* from the general's perspective. As a prewriting activity, review and list the sequence of events in the story; encourage small groups of students to assume roles of conquering Burmese generals and report the same series of events from a different perspective. Provide time for students to informally present the new versions of *Rebel* as essays, skits, poems, newscasts, or interviews. **Ask:** What skills must you draw upon to successfully complete this assignment? How will these skills assist you in viewing current news stories, television shows, and movies?

4. Remind students that rebels face challenges in pursuing their causes that they overcome by calling upon one or more sources of inner strength. Add reality to examples by inviting students to tell about similar situations, i.e., a person confronts and solves a difficult problem by calling upon one or more of the character traits, all sources of inner strength.

EVALUATION:

Determine student understanding of what the term, rebel, means by assessing the quality of class discussions, creative projects, written and oral assignments, and active participation. Include teacher-made rubrics and observations in evaluations.

Whenever appropriate, use literary as well as real-life examples to explore how students relate individual and collective acts of courage, diligence, and integrity to solutions of problems such as tyranny, poverty, disease, war, and/or other crucial issues. Ask students to debrief the learning from the story and activities, then tell what, how, and why they learned. Encourage students to connect the message in the story to the theme of celebrating or honoring the human spirit.

ALTERNATE SELECTION:

Patricia Polacco. *Pink and Say.* Neither race nor war nor imprisonment is able to weaken the bonds that tie two courageous Union soldiers together in friendship. Polacco, who strongly believes in the shared humanity of people around the globe, retells a family story with passion.

CONNECTION #19:
Zlata Filipovic. Zlata's Diary

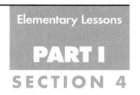

Through entries in her diary, Zlata recounts the dramatic story of Sarajevo as seen through a child's eyes. Zlata vividly reveals the turmoil war creates for families.

CHARACTER TRAITS: Review the nine character traits used in this manual and ask students to provide examples of each of them. Tell students to keep these in a character portfolio for future reference.

1. Read *Zlata's Diary* aloud. Remember to set the stage with appropriate pre-reading activities that capture students' interest. For example, ask the librarian to find an overview of the geographic setting complete with physical and cultural descriptions. Reduce the complexity of the conflict by sharing only the most essential points for student understanding of the story. On the board, show students that the regional conflict represents a clash of two different cultures.

Hint: Make further research into the issues of this conflict an optional assignment, but require that researchers share information with classmates.

In addition to setting the geographic and political stage for *Zlata's Diary*, talk with students about why they think the author chooses the literary form of a diary to tell such a complex story. Divide students into partners; instruct students to listen, discuss, and then defend their thoughts on why Filipovic selects the diary as the form to tell her story; and then allow time in class for partners to share their reasoning.

2. Explain to students that they may choose how to demonstrate their understanding of the impact of war on families. Ask students to listen to the following activities; to select one that holds high interest for them; and to work individually, with a partner, or in a small group to complete the project:

> *Research additional materials on war-torn Sarajevo, then compose interview questions to ask ordinary citizens in Sarajevo; stage interviews between a reporter and citizens that reveal what adjustments citizens who live in strife must make.*

> *Research the 1914 assassination of Archduke Francis Ferdinand in Sarajevo, connect the story to the present-day struggle in Sarajevo, then share the information in the form of a television newscast.*

> *Choose several scenes from Zlata's Diary, and then dramatize the scenes so that classmates see distinct differences between family life in peacetime and in wartime.*

> *Illustrate Sarajevo scenes before and during the war on a classroom mural; divide the mural in half so that classmates see distinct differences between peacetime and wartime.*

Set aside time for students to expand classmates' knowledge through sharing well-researched, creatively crafted interviews, newscasts, socio-dramas, and murals. Remind students how important courteous, attentive listening is to the presenters as well as to audience members.

3. Ask students to reflect on traits that enable Zlata and her family to survive conflict in war-torn Sarajevo. Invite students to transfer situations involving conflicts to their own lives. Ask how and why the same character traits might assist students in meeting everyday challenges.

Hint: For interest and variety, alternate discussions on character traits between the presence and benefits of possessing the traits and the absence and consequences of not possessing the traits.

EVALUATION:

Determine the level of student understanding of how war causes upheaval in families' lives by assessing the quality of class discussions, creative projects, written and oral assignments, and active participation. Include teacher-made rubrics and observations in evaluations.

Whenever appropriate, use literary as well as real-life examples to explore how students relate individual and collective acts of courage, diligence, and integrity to solutions of problems such as tyranny, poverty, disease, war, and/or other crucial issues. Ask students to debrief the learning from the story and activities, then tell what, how, and why they learned. Encourage students to connect the message in the story to the theme of celebrating or honoring the human spirit.

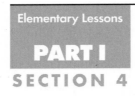

Elementary Lessons

PART I

SECTION 4

CONNECTION #20:
I dream of peace: images of war by children of former Yugoslavia

Original art works and writings by children of war-torn Yugoslavia reveal the effects of war on youth. Robbed of their carefree days of childhood and forced to play real-life games of survival, children still express hope for a better world in the future. Maurice Sendak's preface poignantly describes how war accelerates the coming-of-age process for all children.

CHARACTER TRAITS: Review the nine character traits used in this manual and ask students to provide examples of each of them. Tell students to keep these in a character portfolio for future reference.

1. Read aloud the scripts in *I dream of peace*. Remember to set the stage with appropriate pre-reading activities that capture students' interest. For example, seek clarification of students' definitions of war, poverty, and tyranny by asking that they describe each concept, and offer examples by reading reference sources, viewing media sources, or discussing similar situations with family members or family friends.

Set finding examples of war, poverty, and tyranny in the former Yugoslavia as the purpose for reading scripts and viewing art works. As examples arise naturally, quiz students about evidence that shows individuals calling upon courage, judgment, integrity, or dedication to overcome the ill effects of war, poverty, or tyranny.

Hint: Make sure that students realize that these are the accounts of eyewitnesses, thus the accounts are primary sources. Point out that many times primary sources are more graphic than secondary sources because actual participants express the emotional as well as the historical impact of an event, i.e., they are on the scene and in the midst of what is happening. **Ask:** Why do students need to seek both primary and secondary sources when researching a topic?

Hint: Use a story map activity to place story events and characters in correct locations after reading the story and completing the activities.

2. Enlist students and the media specialist in a two-week project of collecting newspaper and magazine articles that focus on citizens of all ages combating tyranny, poverty, disease, and war by using courage, diligence, and integrity.

Divide students in small groups, distribute five current examples from periodicals, then request groups to choose one and create an illustrated "I dream of peace" page for a class book. On the page, ask students to convey the message of the story in script or poetry and draw scenes that complement the message in the script or poem. Allow time for students to share their scripts and drawings with classmates before binding the book for display.

Ask: Do opportunities to exhibit courage, diligence, and integrity exist on an everyday basis in your community? Encourage students to reflect and then share their thoughts and examples with classmates.

3. Share a collection of quotes or symbols related to peace and solicit ideas on how these quotes or symbols might inspire people to work for peace. Give students two options:

Compose original quotes, or
Design symbols that will convey peace.

Provide sheets of multi-colored construction paper so that students may make attractive quotes and designs suitable for public display. Sample quotes include the following:

"Peace is the happy, natural state of man."
"If I am at war with myself, I can bring little peace to my fellow man."
"Great victories come, not through ease but by fighting valiantly and meeting hardships bravely."
"Remember there's blue sky behind the blackest cloud."

(Anonymous Quotes from Wings of Silver, compiled by Jo Petty)

Sample symbols include the following: doves, seeds of hope, dreams of peace, circles, crosses, fish, candle lights.

Once students complete quotes and symbols, enlist students in constructing a bulletin board display of their original quotes and symbols of peace. As students debrief their creation for other students, ask all students how the quote or symbol might foster courage, diligence, or integrity.

4. Ask students to brainstorm ways that innocent persons caught in the conflict of war must use courage, diligence, integrity, and/or responsibility to survive. Request that students reflect on the traits and volunteer examples of ways that they may call upon the same traits to meet challenges in their everyday lives.

EVALUATION:

Determine the level of student understanding of children's courageous responses to war by assessing the quality of class discussions, creative projects, written and oral assignments, and active participation. Include teacher-made rubrics and observations in evaluations.

Whenever appropriate, use literary as well as real-life examples to explore how students relate individual and collective acts of courage, diligence, and integrity to solutions of problems such as tyranny, poverty, disease, war, and/or other crucial issues. Encourage students to connect the message in the story to the theme of celebrating or honoring the human spirit.

ADDITIONAL SELECTION:

Christophe Gallaz and Roberto Innocenti. *Rose Blanche.* A young girl struggling daily to survive during World War II takes time to show compassion to others. Rose Blanche's mysterious, unexplained disappearance causes readers to construct the story's ending.

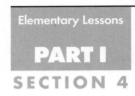

CONNECTION #21:
Mirra Ginsburg.
The Chinese Mirror

A mysterious mirror creates confusion by producing humorous, unexpected, thought-provoking images. Mirror reflections cause story characters to inquire, "Who is this stranger?" The tale provides a perfect lead-in to a discussion on how perspectives differ.

CHARACTER TRAITS: Review the nine character traits used in this manual and ask students to provide examples of each of them. Tell students to keep these in a character portfolio for future reference.

1. Read *The Chinese Mirror* aloud. Remember to set the stage with appropriate pre-reading activities that capture students' interest. For example, prepare a small, cardboard "Magic Box" with a mirror attached to the bottom. Ask students to peek inside the box and describe what they see. Undoubtedly, they will answer that they see reflections of themselves. Clarify important terms such as reflections and illusions before reading the story. Set determining the difference between reflections and illusions as the purpose for listening to the story.

   After reading the story, review each example of a character looking into the mirror, and then ask students if the example represents a reflection or an illusion and why. **Ask:**

   > *How does the unpredictable mirror carry the storyline in this Korean/Chinese tale?*
   > *What is the message of the tale? Is the message still meaningful today?*
   > *Why or why not?*

2. Explain to students that they may choose how to demonstrate their understanding of differences between reflections and illusions. Ask students to listen to the following activities; to select one that holds high interest for them; and to work individually, with a partner, or in a small group to complete the project:

   Review the ending of *The Chinese Mirror*, change the storyline to include more characters who look into the mirror, then rewrite at least two other endings to the tale.

   Reflect on how animals and humans create illusions through the use of such things as coloration, mimicry, and camouflage, and then compose a list of examples of illusions with the purposes they serve. Seek illustrations that show how animals and humans develop illusions.

   Invite students to create pictures with hidden objects, protective coloration, or camouflage. For an example refer to the "Hidden Pictures" activity in the magazine, *Highlights for Children*. Assemble students' pictures in a class book.

   Search for illustrations of optical illusions in the media center so that classmates may interpret the meaning of visual examples, then connect examples to the message of the story. **Hint:** Seek examples in references such as M.C. Escher's *Important Book* and in Larry Kettlekamp's *Tricks of Eye and Mind*.

   Set aside time for students to expand classmates' knowledge through sharing well researched, creatively crafted story endings and explanations. Remind students how important courteous, attentive listening is to the presenters as well as to audience members.

3. Request students to reflect upon what traits enable story characters to solve the mysteries of a Chinese mirror. Invite students to transfer situations involving fictional characters to their own lives. Ask how and why the same character traits might assist students in meeting everyday challenges.

Hint: For interest and variety, alternate discussions on character traits between the benefits of possessing the traits and the consequences of not possessing the traits.

EVALUATION:

Determine the level of student understanding of differences between reflections and illusions by assessing the quality of class discussions, creative projects, written and oral assignments, and active participation. Include teacher-made rubrics and observations in evaluations.

Whenever appropriate, use literary as well as real-life examples to explore how students relate individual and collective acts of courage, diligence, and integrity to solutions of problems such as tyranny, poverty, disease, war, and/or other crucial issues. Ask students to debrief the learning from the story and activities, then tell what, how, and why they learned. Encourage students to connect the message in the story to the theme of celebrating or honoring the human spirit.

CONNECTION #22:
Charlie Chin. *China's Bravest Girl*

Elementary Lessons

PART I

SECTION 4

Huo Mu Lan, a woman, defies society's stereotypical image of a heroic general and earns eternal fame in Chinese legends.

CHARACTER TRAITS: Review the nine character traits used in this manual and ask students to provide examples of each of them. Tell students to keep these in a character portfolio for future reference.

1. Read *China's Bravest Girl* aloud. Remember to set the stage with appropriate pre-reading activities that capture students' interest. Request students to define the concept of a stereotype in their own words, then challenge them to name examples of stereotypes common in the world of elementary students. Set identification of how the main character defies a stereotypical image as the purpose for listening to the story.

After reading the story, lead students in a focused discussion on how Huo Mu Lan defies an established Chinese stereotype. **Ask:** Do the times in which Huo Mu Lan earns fame make the accomplishment even more remarkable? Why?

2. Review the reporter's formula (e.g., Who? What? Where? When? Why? How?) and then lead students on a research expedition into Chinese history. Divide the period 960-1279 AD into approximately three centuries, and then assign a research group to each century. Challenge each group to find answers to the critical questions in the reporter's formula, record the information on a time line, and report to classmates. **Hint:** Use students' research to summarize the male-dominated political, economic, and social world of China.

Ask again:

Do the times in which Huo Mu Lan earns fame make the accomplishment even more remarkable? Why?

Why would accomplishments similar to those of Huo Mu Lan be easier to attain in today's world?

Does a connection exist between a nation's political system and an individual's opportunity for accomplishment?

Hint: Lead students to the understanding that a democratic system offers many more opportunities for all citizens than an autocratic system.

3. Ask students to reflect upon what traits enable Huo Mu Lan to overcome a stereotypical image. Invite students to transfer the situation involving a legendary character to their own lives. Ask how and why the same character traits might assist students in meeting everyday challenges.

EVALUATION:

Determine the level of student understanding of Huo Mu Lan's remarkable accomplishment by assessing the quality of class discussions, written and oral assignments, and active participation. Include teacher-made rubrics and observations in evaluations.

Whenever appropriate, use literary as well as real-life examples to explore how students relate individual and collective acts of courage, diligence, and integrity to solutions of problems such as tyranny, poverty, disease, war, and/or other crucial issues. Ask students to debrief the learning from the story and activities, then tell what, how, and why they learned. Encourage students to connect the message in the story to the theme of celebrating or honoring the human spirit.

Elementary Lessons
PART I
SECTION 4

CONNECTION #23:
David Barry. *The Rajah's Rice*

A strange illness befalls the Rajah's elephants. Chandra, the official elephant bather, not only saves these highly prized transporters of rice but also exacts a reward from the Rajah that secures the future of her people.

CHARACTER TRAITS: Review the nine character traits used in this manual and ask students to provide examples of each of them. Tell students to keep these in a character portfolio for future reference.

1. Read *The Rajah's Rice* aloud. Remember to set the stage with appropriate pre-reading activities that capture students' interest. For example, form a research team to investigate the best conditions for growing rice, to determine the areas in India and in the world where the ideal conditions exist, and to point out where these regions are on a classroom wall map.

Also, alert students that most people in the story are workers in the rice fields. Set finding clues about the field workers' jobs as the purpose for listening. After reading, discuss the context clues that provide insights into the lifestyle of field workers. **Ask:** Considering the lives of field workers, how important is the prize Chandra wins for her people? Why?

Hint: Use a story map activity to place story events and characters in correct locations after reading the story and completing the activities.

2. Explain to students that they may choose how to demonstrate understanding related to the worth of Chandra's prize. Ask students to listen to the following activities; to select one that holds high interest for them; and to work individually, with a partner, or in a small group to complete the project:

Distribute sheets of paper divided into squares like a chess board and also plastic bags of uncooked rice; instruct students to start counting out grains of rice to fill the chess board as recounted in the story; allow students to fill in at least eight or ten squares; discuss the difficulty of filling the entire board with rice. **Hint:** Use this activity as an excellent lead-in to teaching exponents.

Describe the unusual units used to measure the rice, then explore the reasons for measuring the crop in these ways; convert measurement to ways more common in your area (e.g., a dump truck filled with rice equals nine cubic yards).

Investigate the price of rice in today's market. Write story problems using rice as a theme, then challenge classmates to solve the problems; compile a class book with problems and illustrations.

Plan a time for students to share results of their research with classmates. Review the importance of and necessity for courtesy toward presenters by audience members.

3. Divide students into groups, each group with the assignment of investigating one agricultural crop grown in India and/or in the United States: rice, peanuts, sugar cane, tea, bananas, cotton, wheat, pepper, and jute. Prepare and distribute a chart with six spaces on which students will search for and record: 1) methods of production; 2) size of areas cultivated; 3) costs of production; 4) labor supply; 5) gross and net profits; and 6) growth in one or both nations and why.

Ask that groups report from the outline on the charts so that classmates may listen for similarities and differences among crops. **Ask:**

> *Given the information from the story, research projects, and student presentations, how might students describe the life of most farm workers?*
>
> *Given that most farm workers will not encounter Chandra or the Rajah, what are means through which they may improve their lifestyles?*

4. Lead students in reflecting upon lives of farm workers in India as well as in the United States. Ask students to examine the list of character traits and decide on traits that will serve the workers best as they face challenges of a harsh life. Invite students to transfer the same traits to their everyday lives and cite how one or more traits might assist them in confronting difficult tasks.

Hint: For interest and variety, alternate discussions on character traits between the benefits of possessing the traits and the consequences of not possessing the traits.

EVALUATION:

Determine the level of student understanding of the lasting value of Chandra's prize for her people by assessing the quality of class discussions, creative projects, written and oral assignments, and active participation. Include teacher-made rubrics and observations in evaluations.

Whenever appropriate, use literary as well as real-life examples to explore how students relate individual and collective acts of courage, diligence, and integrity to solutions of problems such as tyranny, poverty, disease, war, and/or other crucial issues. Ask students to debrief the learning from the story and activities, then tell what, how, and why they learned. Encourage students to connect the message in the story to the theme of celebrating or honoring the human spirit.

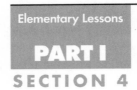

CONNECTION #24:
Susan L. Roth. *Buddha*

After extensive research, Roth guides readers on the spiritual journey of Prince Siddhartha two thousand years ago. Born to riches and power yet troubled by the plight of masses, Siddhartha forsakes family, wealth, and security to become a holy man, the first Buddha or "Enlightened One." His teachings shape the lives of millions.

CHARACTER TRAITS: Review the nine character traits used in this manual and ask students to provide examples of each of them. Tell students to keep these in a character portfolio for future reference.

1. Read *Buddha* aloud. Remember to set the stage with appropriate pre-reading activities that capture students' interest. For example, create a background for the story by pointing out to students the geographic areas in which Buddhism plays a dominant role, e.g., India, China, Japan, Korea, Vietnam, Sri Lanka, and Tibet. Also, ask students to assume roles as word detectives during the story reading and record vocabulary that they wish to clarify. Following the reading, talk about the meaning of the words in the context of the story.

2. Consider the life of a religious leader, then choose those traits that might be most helpful in meeting his or her responsibilities. Invite students to transfer the same traits to their everyday lives and cite how one or more traits might assist them in confronting problems and finding solutions.

Hint: For interest and variety, alternate discussions on character traits between the benefits of possessing the traits and the consequences of not possessing the traits.

3. Lead students in researching the major religions of the world for similarities and differences. For example: number of believers, name of their god(s), powers of their god(s), religious practices, geographical locations, and origins. Put these on a huge chart, discuss with class, and guide students to logical conclusion.

EVALUATION:

Determine the level of student understanding of one of the world's most established religions by assessing the quality of class discussions and active participation. Include teacher-made rubrics and observations in evaluations.

Whenever appropriate, use literary as well as real-life examples to explore how students relate individual and collective acts of courage, diligence, and integrity to solutions of problems such as tyranny, poverty, disease, war, and/or other crucial issues. Evaluate their research and how well they cooperated with others in their group. Encourage students to connect the message in the story to the theme of celebrating or honoring the human spirit.

CONNECTION #25:
Florence Parry Heide and Judith Heide Gilliland.
Sami and the Time of the Troubles

In Beirut, Lebanon, violence frequently resolves differences among citizens. Yet in the midst of warfare, Sami and her family strive to lead normal lives.

CHARACTER TRAITS: Review the nine character traits used in this manual and ask students to provide examples of each of them. Tell students to keep these in a character portfolio for future reference.

1. Read *Sami and the Time of the Troubles* aloud. Remember to set the stage with appropriate pre-reading activities that capture students' interest. For example, summarize the following information about Lebanon:

Lebanon has been influenced by civil war since it was given independence from France in 1943. Until 1958, Christians, who usually were better off financially than the Muslims, dominated the government. The Muslims grew tired of this dominance and rebelled for more positions in government and better living conditions. These two groups continue to fight for power with violence. Although the majority of leaders have settled differences more peacefully since 1992, this conflict has made it difficult for the government and military to unite against outside influences.

The Palestinian refugees from Israel began to settle in southern Lebanon during the 1960s. They made raids on Israel from time to time. Israel seized a strip of land from Lebanon along the southern border as protection. This strip is referred to as the security zone and is presently nine miles wide. The conflict between the Palestinian Liberation Organization (PLO) and Israel continued to break out and escalated during the 1980s with hijackings and kidnappings. However, on May 4, 1994, the two parties signed an autonomy pact. In 2000, Israel withdrew from the security zone.

During the 1980s, Lebanon turned to neighboring Syria for help in controlling the conflict in the south. By the time Syria agreed to pull out of Lebanon in 1991, Syria controlled almost two-thirds of Lebanon.

Sporadic violence still occurs in Beirut and Lebanon but periodically life returns to somewhat of a normal balance.

Utilize background information as a lead-in to the geographic study of the Middle East. **Hint:** Use a story map activity to place story events and characters in correct locations after reading the story and completing the activities.

2. Explain to students that they may choose how to demonstrate understanding related to how Sami's family deals with violence. Ask students to listen to the following activities; to select one that holds high interest for them; and to work individually, with a partner, or in a small group to complete the project:

Research the decade 1981-1991 in Lebanon; construct an illustrated time line on the chalkboard to fill in factual background to Sami's story; connect facts to story line for classmates.

Write the script for a socio-drama that shows a Lebanese family trying to live a normal life in the midst of violence; through your script and by acting it out, deliver the message to the audience that violence often leads to further violence rather than to resolution of problems.

Brainstorm different ways of resolving problems such as those described in Sami's story; form a panel with each panel member presenting one way of resolving a problem.

Plan a time for students to make presentations. Request that students discuss new insights gained as a result of classmates' research, socio-drama, and panel discussion. Remember to review the importance of and necessity for courtesy toward presenters by audience members.

3. Lead students in reflecting upon how Sami and her family strive for a normal life in the midst of violence. Ask students to examine the list of character traits and decide on those that will serve Sami and her family members best as they face violence on an everyday basis. Invite students to transfer the same traits to their everyday lives and cite how one or more traits might assist them in confronting problems and finding solutions.

Hint: For interest and variety, alternate discussions on character traits between the benefits of possessing the traits and the consequences of not possessing the traits.

EVALUATION:

Determine the level of student understanding of the quest for normalcy by Sami's family in a violent environment by assessing the quality of class discussions, creative projects, written and oral assignments, and active participation. Include teacher-made rubrics and observations in evaluations.

Whenever appropriate, use literary as well as real-life examples to explore how students relate individual and collective acts of courage, diligence, and integrity to solutions of problems such as tyranny, poverty, disease, war, and/or other crucial issues. Ask students to debrief the learning from the story and activities, then tell what, how, and why they learned. Encourage students to connect the message in the story to the theme of celebrating or honoring the human spirit.

Elementary Lessons
PART I
SECTION 4

CONNECTION #26:
Margaret Hodges.
Hidden in Sand

A caravan owner's son blessed with keen observation skills averts the disaster of being lost in the desert with no water. The experience affirms his courage and maturity.

CHARACTER TRAITS: Review the nine character traits used in this manual and ask students to provide examples of each of them. Tell students to keep these in a character portfolio for future reference.

1. Read *Hidden in Sand* aloud. Remember to set the stage with appropriate pre-reading activities that capture students' interest. For example, quiz students about how they use the word, pilot; ask them to consider the title of the story and to predict other uses of the term; then encourage students to expand their usage of the term to a person who leads others on land, sea, or air.

Next, trace the most popular caravan routes on a classroom wall map. Invite students to describe the type of route followed by heavily laden caravans. Encourage students to show how geographic features dictate the routes caravans follow. **Ask:** Considering the perils involved in piloting and staffing a trade caravan, why did people engage in this economic activity? Suggest that students think about the answer as they listen to the story, then respond after the story reading. Utilize the story as a lead-in to the concept of profit.

Hint: Use a story map activity to place story events and characters in correct locations after reading the story and completing the activities.

2. Explain to students that they may choose how to demonstrate economic understanding related to trade, past or present. Ask students to listen to the following activities; to select one that holds high interest for them; and to work individually, with a partner, or in a small group to complete the project:

Research ways of transporting goods from the East to European markets based on story clues, ways of transporting goods from Europe to America in the colonial period, and ways of transporting goods globally today; draw conclusions about the relationship among geography, technology, and market demand for goods.

Explain how Europeans' desire for Eastern goods created jobs in transporting, manufacturing, and banking industries; take classmates on a trip between points of origin and points of final sale to eager customers.

Contact airport officials to learn about the amounts and types of goods trafficked through the local or regional airports; determine the meaning of the term, international, in the name of an airport; investigate methods of security at the airport that minimize the dangers faced by trade caravans.

Plan a time for students to share results of research with classmates. Challenge students to use creative methods for presentation (e.g., maps, charts, skits, and illustrations). Review the importance of and necessity for courtesy toward presenters by audience members.

3. Lead students in reflecting upon the feelings that caravan members, such as those described in *Hidden in Sand*, surely experience if lost in a sea of sand. Ask students to examine the list of character traits and decide on those traits that will serve lost caravan members best. Invite students to transfer the same traits to their everyday lives and cite how one or more traits might assist them in staying on the right route, i.e., in making sound decisions.

EVALUATION:

Determine the level of student understanding of economic risks in pursuit of profits by assessing the quality of class discussions, creative projects, written and oral assignments, and active participation. Include teacher-made rubrics and observations in evaluations.

Whenever appropriate, use literary as well as real-life examples to explore how students relate individual and collective acts of courage, diligence, and integrity to solutions of problems such as tyranny, poverty, disease, war, and/or other crucial issues. Encourage students to connect the message in the story to the theme of celebrating or honoring the human spirit.

ALTERNATE SELECTION:

John S. Major. *The Silk Route.* Threading their way along the ancient, lucrative silk route from China to Constantinople, caravans convey Eastern treasures to covetous consumers.

CONNECTION # 27:
Margy Burns Knight.
Talking Walls

Knight becomes a travel agent for an around-the-world trip conceptually focused on walls.
Readers confront issues far beyond architectural details as they consider issues related to walls:
   Why build them? Are they always visible?
   Do they tell stories of people through the ages?
   Is there extrinsic as well as intrinsic value to wall building?

CHARACTER TRAITS: Review the nine character traits used in this manual and ask students to provide examples of each of them. Tell students to keep these in a character portfolio for future reference.

1. Read *Talking Walls* aloud. Remember to set the stage with appropriate pre-reading activities that capture students' interest. For example, photocopy Margy Knight's descriptions of fourteen walls, cut out the copied paragraphs about each wall, glue each piece to 5" x 8" colored index cards, laminate the cards, and distribute them to student partners. Explain to students that this information about a specific wall is just the beginning of the story.

Divide the class into groups. Allow time for partners to read the paragraphs and to talk about the unique features of their wall. Challenge them to listen to the stories of the other walls, and then cite ways that their wall is similar to and different from other walls. Partners will become experts on the following examples of walls:

> *The Great Wall of China*
> *Mexican Murals*
> *Aborigine Wall Art*
> *The Canadian Museum of Civilization*
> *The Lascaux Cave*
> *The Western Wall*
> *The Vietnam Veterans Memorial*
> *Mahabalipuran's Animal Walls*
> *Muslim Walls*
> *Nelson Mandela's Prison*
> *Great Zimbabwe Walls*
> *The Berlin Wall*
> *The Taos Pueblo*

Following the reading, encourage partners to volunteer three similarities and three differences between their wall and the other thirteen. **Ask:** Based on the story reading and the input of others, what reasonable conclusions about walls can you make?

2. Extend the story of fourteen walls to an exciting geography lesson. Show students the location of their wall on the world map at the back of the story, transfer the locations to a large classroom map, and invite students to attach the colored index cards to the map with masking-tape loops.

In the media center, lead students in researching the geographic setting of their wall. Prompt them into looking beyond physical features by projecting what geographic and/or economic hurdles people overcame in building their wall. Examples: accessibility of building materials, terrain of the building site, tools to build the wall, labor required to build the wall.

3. Use the story of fourteen walls as an excellent basis for a history lesson. Draw a time line on the chalkboard with the BC and AD divisions. Review basic understandings related to chronology such as the system of numbering years, i.e., large to small on the BC side, small to large on the AD side. Emphasize the meaning of time-related vocabulary words such as decade, century, and millennium, and then point out examples on the timeline.

Students will enter the time of their wall's creation and, if appropriate, the time of the wall's discovery. Once partners enter dates on the time line, ask students to reflect on messages the time line sends to them. **Ask:**

> *As a human activity, does the construction of walls span millenniums?*
>
> *What does the answer tell you about the practice of wall building?*
>
> *Can you think of times that walls serve people?*
>
> *Can you think of times that walls hinder people?*
>
> *How do you interpret these lines from the "Mending Wall" by Robert Frost?*
>> *"Before I built a wall I'd ask to know*
>> *What I was walling in or walling out*
>> *And to whom I was like to give offense."*
>
> *Invite students to write or illustrate on a large index card their interpretation of Frost's poem.*

4. Ask students to tell the second chapter of their wall story to classmates in presentations entitled "Walls Do Talk."

Ask:

> *Do reports and additional information gained through research make the walls even more remarkable than they were in the story?*
>
> *Why or why not?*
>
> *How can you transfer answers to other areas of study?*

5. Stimulate students' curiosity by telling them that they have just begun to understand the many dimensions of walls. Give small groups the following assignment: choose one of the stories listed under the section entitled "Alternate Selections"; read the story for the purpose of finding a new perspective to the topic of walls; plan a creative way to present the new perspective to classmates (e.g., models, interviews, socio-dramas) in presentations entitled "Walls Do Talk II."

Hint: Assist student groups in choosing a meaningful product or activity that helps all students broaden their understanding about walls. At the end of the unit on walls, encourage students to view walls as both external and internal structures. Challenge students to reflect upon the stories, discussions, and projects, and then cite examples in which walls serve positive as well as negative purposes. Also ask them to cite examples in which walls, like people, change over time.

6. Ask students to reflect upon what traits the wall builders in various historical periods exhibit. Invite students to transfer the situation involving wall builders to their own lives. Ask how and why the presence of or absence of the same character traits might assist students in meeting everyday challenges.

EVALUATION:

Determine the level of student understanding of the many dimensions of walls and wall building by assessing the quality of class discussions, creative projects, written and oral assignments, and active participation. Include teacher-made rubrics and observations in evaluations.

Whenever appropriate, use literary as well as real-life examples to explore how students relate individual and collective acts of courage, diligence, and integrity to solutions of problems such as tyranny, poverty, disease, war, and/or other crucial issues. Ask students to debrief the learning from the story and activities, then tell what, how, and why they learned. Encourage students to connect the message in the story to the theme of celebrating or honoring the human spirit.

ALTERNATE SELECTIONS:

Judy Allen. *What Is a Wall, After All?* Rhymed text and pictures tell how people construct walls, why they build walls, and how they climb walls. Allen describes locations of walls that play major roles in world history.

Eve Bunting. *The Wall.* By reverently touching the name of his grandfather on the Vietnam Veterans Memorial, a young boy and his father symbolize the emotions of thousands who have paid similar tributes to the courage of American men and women who served in the armed forces.

Leonard Everett Fisher. *The Great Wall of China.* Fisher traces the history of the Great Wall of China, originally constructed over two thousand years ago as a buffer against Mongol invaders.

Mary Elizabeth Haggerty. *A Crack in the Wall.* While his mother searches for employment, Carlos transforms a crack in the wall into something unique. Even vicious poverty cannot deny simple pleasures that Carlos and his mother derive from beauty in a bleak environment.

Frances Ward Weller. *Matthew Wheelock's Wall.* Matthew Wheelock erects a wall of stone that becomes a source of family strength for generations.

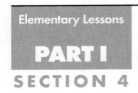

Elementary Lessons

PART I

SECTION 4

CONNECTION #28:
Robert Frost. "Mending Wall."
The Classic Hundred: All-Time Favorite Poems. William Harmon, Ed.

Hidden underneath the story of mending a wall rests a more thoughtful story of human relationships. The idea that "good fences make good neighbors" causes both young and old to reflect on how they relate to others.

CHARACTER TRAITS: Review the nine character traits used in this manual and ask students to provide examples of each of them. Tell students to keep these in a character portfolio for future reference.

1. Read the poem "Mending Wall" aloud. Prior to reading, distribute copies of the poem to listening partners so that they may follow the lines. Remember to set the stage with appropriate pre-reading activities that capture students' interest. For example, talk about the meaning of the literary term, proverb.

Hint: Lead students to the understanding that a proverb is a brief, always-to-the-point, frequently used saying which expresses a basic truth. Invite students to cite and interpret familiar proverbs drawn from their own experiences or from the following samples from *My First Book of Proverbs* (*Mi Primer Libron de Dichos*) by Ralfka Gonzalez and Ana Ruiz:

> The early bird gets the worm.
> > (*El Pájaro que se levanta temprano, agarra primero el gusano.*)
> A bird in the hand is worth a hundred in the air.
> > (*Más valle pájaro en mano que cien volando.*)
> Where there's a will there's a way.
> > (*Donde hay gan a hay maña.*)
> It's the squeaky wheel that gets the grease.
> > (*La rueda que más chilla es la que consigue la grasa.*)

A lesson well learned is never forgotten.

(Lo que se aprende bien nunca se olvida.)

Set finding the proverb in "Mending Wall" as the purpose for listening.

Hint: Remind students that the process of analysis requires students to break the whole, i.e., the poem, into smaller parts, i.e., lines. Therefore, they should separate the poem into natural thought divisions, reread the sections, and ask listening partners to discuss the meaning of the poem. Check student understanding by asking partners to describe the scene sketched by the lines read from the poem:

Who are the players?

What are they doing?

Why is the wall necessary?

Why must people be careful when building or mending walls?

Must walls be made of stones and bricks?

Are there other types of walls?

How might walls lead to an attitude such as prejudice or an emotion such as fear?

Invite students to interpret the meaning of the proverb, "Good fences make good neighbors," within the context of the poem, then to interpret the meaning of the proverb in their everyday lives.

Congratulate students on their efforts to intellectually stretch their understanding of "Mending Wall" by analyzing the poem and by responding to the thought questions. Encourage students to work with a partner and define the meaning of these three lines in words they understand:

"Before I built a wall I'd ask to know

What I was walling in or walling out

And to whom I was like to give offense."

2. Request students to reflect upon what traits the speaker and the neighbor exhibit during their annual mending of the wall. Invite students to transfer the situation involving fictional characters to their own lives. Ask how and why the presence or absence of the same character traits might assist students in meeting everyday challenges.

EVALUATION:

Determine the level of student understanding of the specific as well as the universal meaning of two neighbors' relationship by assessing the quality of class discussions, written and oral assignments, and active participation. Include teacher-made rubrics and observations in evaluations.

Whenever appropriate, use literary as well as real-life examples to explore how students relate individual and collective acts of courage, diligence, and integrity to solutions of problems such as tyranny, poverty, disease, war, and/or other crucial issues. Encourage students to connect the message in the poem to the theme of celebrating or honoring the human spirit.

CONNECTION #29:
Leonard Everett Fisher.
The Wailing Wall

Throughout history, Jewish people have faced and overcome injustices such as tyranny and war. Fisher chronicles major events and personalities in a story of faith and courage.

CHARACTER TRAITS: Review the nine character traits used in this manual and ask students to provide examples of each of them. Tell students to keep these in a character portfolio for future reference.

1. Read aloud *The Wailing Wall*. Remember to set the stage with appropriate pre-reading activities that capture students' interest. For example, select and copy pictures from the story, distribute them to small groups of students, and ask:

> *What are the problems?*
>
> *What evidence supports student assumptions?*
>
> *What human actions might moderate or solve the problems?*
>
> *What evidence supports student assumptions?*

Encourage students to respond with the results of group investigation. At the completion of the activities, reassemble the groups to review their original assumptions. Query students about their understanding of both cultural unity and cultural oppression. **Ask:**

> *How accurate are each group's original assumptions?*
>
> *How valuable are photographs as primary sources? Why?*

In addition, make certain that students comprehend the meaning of wailing as the human behavior of crying out, weeping, or lamenting in response to great sadness. Alert students to listen for clues in the story that connect the act of wailing to the structure of a wall.

2. Divide students into listening partners. Ask partners to fold a piece of notebook paper into three equal parts, to open the paper, and to head each column with one of three titles: "Dates," "Events," and "Personalities." If necessary, reread *The Wailing Wall* slowly so that partners may record factual data about major events in Jewish history.

Following the reading, lead students in a discussion on the major events students record from the story. Draw a time line on the board and select one student to enter each event in chronological order. Invite the partnership reporting the event to recap the story and the players. After students enter major events on the time line, ask partners to decide upon one big idea or concept that describes each entry. **Ask:** Is the event a story of joy, freedom, sadness, oppression, tyranny, or war?

Assign each partnership the task of creating a symbol to represent the various events. Request students to post symbols above each event on the timeline. **Ask:**

> *How do symbols add to your understanding of, interpretation of, and empathy for the Jewish story?*
>
> *Are symbols effective means for communicating and remembering messages?*
>
> *How do symbols and structures relate to one another?*

Encourage students to reflect on times in local, state, national, or world history when symbols played important roles and to share examples with classmates.

3. Clear one of the bulletin boards in the classroom or a section in the classroom. Allow students to decide on construction details of a contemporary wailing wall in two parts: rough-hewn stones? rectangular-cut bricks? concrete forms? tall? short? sturdy? graffiti-free?

Ask partners to identify two or more current problems on the world scene in need of reform and to propose two or more solutions that citizens' positive actions might effect. Instruct students to make mock building blocks (e.g., stones, bricks, or concrete blocks) labeled with either problems or solutions.

Enlist the assistance of artistic volunteers to draw a gate both imposing in size and decorative in design. The gate will artistically and symbolically link problems bricks with solutions bricks. Ask students to hang the gate in the middle of the display, and then request partners to build the wall, placing problems on one side of the gate and solutions on the other side of the gate. Challenge students to step back and view the total impact of the wall.

Ask:

Do the building blocks tell a story of long-standing, unresolved problems?

Do the building blocks tell a story that focuses on certain groups of people throughout history?

Do certain themes emerge as potential solutions?

To what degree can you become problem-solvers of world issues?

Hint: Lead students to the understanding that positive actions even by individuals or on campus promote resolution of long-standing problems. Cite citizens' efforts to address issues during national "Make a Difference Day" in October. Also invite a civic leader to the classroom to ask how participation in government by informed citizens can tear down walls of injustice.

4. Ask students to reflect upon what traits enable the Jewish people to confront problems and to find solutions throughout history. Invite students to transfer the historical examples to their own lives. Ask how and why the same character traits might assist students in solving everyday problems.

EVALUATION:

Determine student understanding of what cultural unity and cultural oppression mean by assessing the quality of class discussions, creative projects, written and oral assignments, and active participation. Include teacher-made rubrics and observations in evaluations.

Whenever appropriate, use literary as well as real-life examples to explore how students relate individual and collective acts of courage, diligence, and integrity to solutions of problems such as tyranny, poverty, disease, war, and/or other crucial issues. Encourage students to connect the message in the story to the theme of celebrating or honoring the human spirit.

Harvest:
Celebrations
of Thanksgiving

CONNECTION #1:
Myra Cohn Livingston.
Celebrations, "Columbus Day"

Livingston highlights American holidays in a collection of short, lively poems. The favorites of curriculum writers become focal points for theme-related teaching episodes.

CHARACTER TRAITS: Emphasize courage, diligence, and integrity.

1. Read the poem "Columbus Day" aloud. Remember to set the stage with appropriate pre-reading activities that capture students' interest. Talk with students about the concept of exploration:

> *What does exploration mean?*
>
> *How does exploration attract men and women to follow its call?*
>
> *What did exploration mean in the fifteenth and sixteenth centuries?*
>
> *What does exploration mean today?*
>
> *What links the concepts of exploration and frontier?*
>
> *How does the concept of exploration transfer from water routes to land and space routes?*
>
> *What links exploration and experimentation in all fields?*
>
> *What do Americans define as frontiers in the twenty-first century?*
>
> *Why do historians label explorers as risk-takers?*
>
> *How do Americans define risk-takers today?*

After class discussion, allow students to finger-trace the routes of the major explorations of the fifteenth and sixteenth centuries on a classroom wall map. Mark various routes of explorers with different colors of pens or with cutouts of sailing vessels. Assist students in viewing Columbus and other explorers as important players in an era of exploration. Connect the historical importance of a person and his or her actions to a cause for celebration and to a time to give thanks. Clarify vocabulary terms necessary for understanding both the poem and the celebration. Define clearly a purpose for reading and/or listening.

2 Present a mini-lesson on descriptive verbs. Find and discuss examples other than those in the Columbus poem. Ask students to contribute to a chalkboard list of descriptive verbs. Explore with students reasons why poets and authors use descriptive verbs.

Reread the Columbus poem slowly, and ask students to listen for and record descriptive verbs. Tell students to listen for Columbus' actions. Revisit the discussion on why poets use descriptive verbs. **Ask:** Do descriptive verbs help the poet create a "you-are-there" feeling for readers? How? Why? What message does the poet send to students about using descriptive verbs?

Ask students to volunteer one action-packed sentence that describes an exploration in their lives. Ask classmates to identify descriptive verbs as writers read their sentences.

3. Ask students to reproduce the illustration from the poem by painting light blue skies with clouds on 12" x 18" sheets of white construction paper. Suggest that students cut three ships from 4 1/2" x 4" squares of black construction paper and label ships with names.

Give students 4" x 18" strips of dark blue paper to cut ocean waves. Instruct students to glue ocean-wave strips at the bottom of the white pages and ships on the horizon. Ask students to write the Columbus poem on 3" x 3" cards as neatly as possible, write sentences about explorations in their own lives on other 3" x 3" cards, and glue both cards on the pictures. Display products on a classroom wall or in a hallway with an exhibit title of "Sailing the Ocean Blue."

4. Introduce a writing prompt to students by sharing an overview of one explorer's accomplishments: Columbus possessed the important character traits of courage, diligence, and integrity. He believed in himself and knew he could help Spain and the rest of the world if he found a new route to India. He refused to give up until he persuaded King Ferdinand and Queen Isabella to help pay for the ships and supplies. Ask students to think about the story and about times in their lives in which they demonstrated one or more of these character traits in order to accomplish a goal.

Remind students to use this process: decide on a personal goal that they want to write about, then analyze which trait helped them reach that goal and why. When finished, request that students participate in a sharing exercise entitled "Just Like Columbus, I Set My Goal."

Hint: Notice the use of "set" instead of "accomplished." Columbus never realized his primary goal of finding a route to the East but his discovery shaped the lives of millions of people. Use this information to discuss with students that sometimes goals change during the course of working toward them. Sometimes, however, results can be as good or better than the original goals. Talk with students about the benefits of goal setting:

What the does process do for individuals?
What example does the process set for others?
What traits help students reach their goals?

Use the exercise to point out that individuals in either the fifteenth century or today need many of the same character traits to face problems and to find solutions.

Hint: For interest and variety, alternate discussions on character traits between the benefits of possessing the traits and the consequences of not possessing the traits.

EVALUATION:

Determine the level of student understanding by evaluating the quality of written and creative products, by analyzing students' success in identifying and in using descriptive verbs, and by listening to responses in class discussions. Encourage students to connect the message in the poem to the theme of harvest and celebrations of thanksgiving.

CONNECTION #2:
Eve Bunting. *How Many Days to America? A Thanksgiving Story*

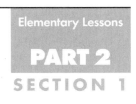
Elementary Lessons
PART 2
SECTION 1

A fearful African-American family flees from their native Caribbean homeland. After experiencing harrowing adventures on a flimsy freedom boat, they arrive safely in America on Thanksgiving Day.

CHARACTER TRAITS: In this lesson, emphasize citizenship, courage, and integrity.

1. Introduce the story by asking boys and girls to assist the teacher in telling a traditional American Thanksgiving story. Talk about the historical times of almost four hundred years ago: the main

events, the players, and the feast of celebration. Remind them that many people, just like the Pilgrims of long ago, continue to give thanks for surviving hardships of all kinds. Alert students that *How Many Days to America?* tells about a family quite different from and also quite similar to the Pilgrims of 1620. Invite student participation in locating the island of Jamaica on a classroom wall map or globe. Ask students to use geographic clues to discover what life on the island of Jamaica must be like: location, climate, vegetation, and physical features. Ask children if they consider the island a pleasant place to live. If students accept island living as pleasant, request that they predict reasons for leaving a homeland.

Extension: Extend the discussion to talking about how one packs a bag when fleeing for one's life. Talk about what guidelines a person might use in packing a survival kit. Ask students to assume the roles of a father or a mother advising children what they need to pack. Encourage small groups to act out scenarios.

Read *How Many Days to America?* aloud. Ask students if they predicted correct reasons for the family fleeing Jamaica. Explain to students that not being able to think freely accounts for many people leaving their homelands throughout history. Develop a comparison and contrast of pilgrims in different time periods after students read *N.C. Wyeth's Pilgrims* by Robert D. San Souci. **Hint:** Lead students in comparing and contrasting human experiences so that students understand that hardships accompany difficult journeys in any time period and also that family members' feelings of distress occur today as well as in 1620.

Extension: Extend the discussion by using text clues to determine how many days people in the story journey on the ocean and to point out probable landing points for immigrants.

2. Divide students into cooperative groups. Review with students the process of making a story map. Remind students that first they must decide upon major events in the story, and then place events in sequence. Next, tell students that groups must decide how to produce an attractive and accurate story map. **Ask:** Does each group member take one event and complete the illustration? Does each group member take one character and illustrate the character and his or her actions in all pictures? What are the reasons why group members decide on one method over other methods? Answers to these questions should be group decisions.

Encourage students to hang illustrations on the classroom wall and invite classmates to take a print walk to visit all illustrated story maps. Ask students from each group to explain how group members decided upon their production process and why. **Hint:** Remember that this allows students to recount the actual thinking processes used in attacking and completing an assigned task.

3. Review with students the steps in finding cause-and-effect relationships. Ask students to fold 9" x 18" sheets of manila paper into four sections. Invite students to draw pictures in each section that show a particular hardship facing emigrants in the story. **Hint:** Change the use of terms, emigrant and immigrant, to match various stages in the story characters' journey. Suggest that students write a sentence under the picture that tells how story characters responded to the hardship. Ask volunteers to describe their visual and verbal cause-and-effect relationship pictures.

Ask: Why and how do drawing about and writing about cause-and-effect relationships assist you in comprehending the meaning of a skill or in learning correct usage of words?

4. Talk about how illustrators help students understand the storyline as well as the characters. **Hint:** Point out that readers can read or listen to the story, see the pictures, and infer how a certain event or action affects a character.

Extension: Review with students the meaning of inference. Divide students into small groups. Tell them that they will practice the skill of drawing inferences by using events or actions in the story and by studying effects of events or actions on the feelings of story characters.

EXAMPLE OF FEELINGS CHART

EVENTS (Column A)	EMOTIONS (Column B)
The soldiers came to the home.	The family felt anger and sadness.
Mother left the cover, a gift from her grandmother.	Mother felt sadness.

Ask groups to pick five events from the story, enter the events on a feelings chart in Column A, show the resulting human emotions in Column B, and share with classmates the clues that led them to infer these results.

5. Discuss with students why the Jamaican family wants to come to America. **Ask:** What are the author's clues about how the family feels about America? What do they believe will be true about their life in America?

Tell students that within decades of Columbus's journey America developed a worldwide reputation as a country that welcomed all immigrants. Over the years, huge numbers of immigrants seeking a better life for themselves and their families came to what they viewed as a land of opportunity. Although immigration gave America a richness drawn from diverse populations, the thousands of people eventually caused overcrowding in many areas. Many Americans are in favor of stopping or slowing the immigration rate into this country.

Ask students to thoughtfully consider this issue, and then write the President a letter expressing personal feelings on the subject and encouraging his support of their feelings with members of Congress. Alert students that they must use factual reasons to back up feelings.

Ask: In making decisions about how one feels about a subject, what things must one consider? **Hint:** Lead students to consider what one knows about the subject, what one believes about the subject, how the subject affects family members and friends, how one balances what one believes with what one knows to be true. Assist students in posting the letters on a bulletin board entitled "Dear Mr. President..." As a culminating activity, ask students to join the teacher in stating the issue of immigration as a cause-and-effect relationship.

6. Encourage students to select one character trait (e.g., citizenship, courage, or integrity) and talk about how characters in the story demonstrate the trait. Ask students to tell why they selected a character and how the character exemplifies the trait. Suggest that students think about their own lives and share examples that illustrate the trait.

Hint: For interest and variety, alternate discussions on character traits between the benefits of possessing the traits and the consequences of not possessing the traits.

EVALUATION:

Determine the level of student understanding by assessing the quality of written and creative products, by observing their enthusiasm to participate in activities, and by evaluating the degree of cooperation and compromise among students in group settings. Encourage students to connect the message in the story to the theme of harvest and celebrations of thanksgiving.

CONNECTION #3:
Robert D. San Souci.
N. C. Wyeth's Pilgrims

Exquisite paintings depict the adventurous saga of the settling of Plymouth Colony.

CHARACTER TRAITS: Talk with students about the following traits before reading the story: courage, diligence, and respect.

1. Remember to set the stage with appropriate pre-reading activities that capture students' interest. Because students will talk about events and personalities after the teacher reads the story, encourage them to listen carefully to the following topics:

> *Reasons why the Pilgrims made the journey;*
> *Hardships the Pilgrims endured while sailing;*
> *Hardships the Pilgrims faced once they sighted land;*
> *Ways that Squanto helped the Pilgrims;*
> *Preparations for winter; and*
> *Preparations for the Thanksgiving feast.*

Read *N. C. Wyeth's Pilgrims* aloud. Clarify vocabulary terms necessary for understanding both the text and the Thanksgiving celebration.

2. Divide the class into six cooperative groups and assign one topic to each group. Distribute markers and sheets of white butcher paper to each group. Instruct students to cut out the shape of a sail.

Emphasize the importance of the brainstorming process, then invite students to participate in their groups by volunteering as many thoughts as possible on their assigned topic and by recording the thoughts on the group's sail. Ask group members to review their thoughts, decide upon the three most logical responses, and mark these with an accurate picture of a miniature sailing vessel. Encourage groups to share not only the results of brainstorming but also the results of decision-making.

Place a dark brown cutout of a ship's hull on the bulletin board or the classroom wall, then invite groups to hoist their sails above the Mayflower's hull. Engage students in a "What if..." discussion such as what if the Pilgrims had known all of the hardships that would face them on their journey before they left their homeland. **Ask:** Might prior knowledge have changed the decision to land and stay in North America? Why or why not? How strong was the Pilgrims' commitment to freedom?

Hint: Invite students to comment on the value of interacting with other students during brainstorming. Lead students to understand that they may learn valuable information from varied sources including family, school, church, organizations, friends, and people of similar or different backgrounds.

3. Ask students to recreate the first Thanksgiving by making costumes (e.g., collars and hats), weaving place mats, and brainstorming foods for the menu. Assign students in cooperative groups to plan different courses such as salads, desserts, or trimmings for a Thanksgiving feast in the 1620s. Suggest that they include cranberry sauce, pumpkin bread or pie, and churned butter, then explain to classmates the origin of the ingredients. (Alternate Activity)

RECIPES FOR A THANKSGIVING FEAST

PUMPKIN BREAD

1/3 cup oil	1/3 cup water	1-1/3 cups sugar	2 eggs
1 tsp. soda	1/2 tsp. baking powder	1 tsp. salt	1 tsp. cinnamon
1-2/3 cups flour	1 tsp. nutmeg	1/2 can pumpkin	

Preheat oven to 350 degrees. Mix oil and sugar thoroughly. Add eggs, pumpkin, and water. Mix flour, soda, salt, baking powder, cinnamon, and nutmeg. Mix all ingredients together. Pour into a well-greased loaf pan. Bake 65 to 70 minutes until a toothpick stuck into the center comes out clean.

CRANBERRY SAUCE

1 cup sugar	1 cup water	1 package cranberries

Bring water to a boil in a crockpot. Add sugar and cranberries. Cook until sauce is formed.

BUTTER

1/2 pint of whipping cream, baby food jars

Directions: To churn butter, whipping cream must be cold. Pour whipping cream into baby food jars and ask students to shake until a solid ball of butter forms. Refrigerate until time to spread over the pumpkin bread.

Encourage students to set up a feast table with place mats, decorations, and pictures of foods served in the 1620s. Ask several students to serve as class storytellers and invite younger students to the table where they receive an explanation of the first Thanksgiving feast in story form. (Alternate Activity)

Extend the discussion to Thanksgiving feasts of today and how and why they are similar to and different from the first feast. As an alternate activity, choose one or several of these options:

Use the feast as a way to talk about factors then and now that changed food production, distribution, and consumption in the last three centuries;

Use the feast experience as a way to talk about how geographic and cultural factors influenced the Thanksgiving menu of the 1620s as well as today;

Use the feast experience as a lead-in to how people throughout the world express thanks for their blessings in planned celebrations; and/or

Use the feast experience as the basis for students to write a detailed how-to piece on planning a perfect present-day family feast.

4. Invite students to participate in a choral reading of the poem, "Thanksgiving at Plymouth." (Alternate Activity, Parental Discretion)

Hint: Use the choral reading exercise as an opportunity to invite boys and girls to share their thoughts on the relationship between participation and learning. (Alternate Activity, Parental Discretion)

5. Share Lydia Maria Child's story and song, *Over the River and Through the Wood*, with children. Use information in the song lyrics to lead a comparison-and-contrast discussion on Thanksgiving celebrations of today, one hundred years ago, and the first Thanksgiving celebration. Place student responses on a triple Venn diagram, then ask students to draw logical conclusions from the data. (Alternate Activity, if teacher invites children to sing.)

6. Talk about the turkey and the bird's traditional association with the American Thanksgiving celebration. Set the stage for this activity by drawing a large bird with wattle head, skinny neck, and plump body on brown wrapping paper and by posting the bird's unfinished portrait on the bulletin board or classroom wall. Excite the children by asking them what is missing from the drawing. Cut brown paper feathers large enough for students to write a complete sentence: "I am thankful for...."

Encourage children to share their statements with classmates and then pin the feathers on the turkey's tail. (Alternate Activity)

Hints: Give importance to the figure of the turkey by outlining all of the parts including the feathers with marking pens and also by varying the shades of brown and tan for feathers. Use the exercise to emphasize that the spirit of thanksgiving connects to harvest celebrations and times for giving thanks all around the globe.

As the audience admires the display of Mr. Turkey, the traditional Thanksgiving bird, ask students to compare things for which Pilgrims were thankful to those for which they are thankful. Lead students in analyzing why answers drawn from two historical periods differ (e.g., survival for most Americans is not as critical an issue today as it was in the 1620s), and why answers are similar (e.g., Americans continue to value home and family).

Hint: Challenge students to listen to an explanation of the term, universal, as something that stays true through the ages and as something that often crosses cultural lines. Then ask students to apply the term to why answers about Thanksgiving in two distinct periods are similar. Tell students to look for other examples in which they may apply the term correctly.

7. Select one character trait (e.g., courage, diligence, or respect) and talk about how people in the story or the Thanksgiving scenario demonstrate the trait. Ask students to tell why they selected a character and how the character exemplifies the trait. Suggest that students think about their own lives and share examples that illustrate the trait.

Hint: For interest and variety, alternate discussions on character traits between the benefits of possessing the traits and the consequences of not possessing the traits.

EVALUATION:

Determine the level of student understanding by observing the reenactment of the first Thanksgiving, by assessing the quality of written and creative products, and by listening to responses in class discussions. Ask students to explain what they have learned from this story and activities. Encourage students to connect the message in the story to the theme of harvest and celebrations of thanksgiving.

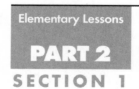

Elementary Lessons

PART 2

SECTION 1

CONNECTION #4:
Barbara Cohen. *Molly's Pilgrim*

Molly, a young Russian Jewish immigrant, encounters cultural difficulties in American schools and with American students. Strangely, an assignment of making pilgrim dolls bridges cultural barriers and teaches Molly and her classmates the true meaning of the word "pilgrim."

CHARACTER TRAITS: Review the following character traits before the story is read: compassion, courage, honesty, and integrity.

1. Read *Molly's Pilgrim* aloud. Remember to set the stage with appropriate pre-reading activities that capture students' interest. For example, use the word, pilgrim, as a discussion starter by asking students to write definitions and to share them with classmates. Tell them to keep their definitions ready to clarify during the story reading. Whenever students gain new insights into the meaning of the term, pilgrim, instruct them either to raise their hands with a "I want to clarify my definition" statement or to participate in a large-group, teacher-led discussion in which all students share changes in original definitions.

Hint: Assist students in understanding that pilgrims' journeys have occurred throughout history and that people undertake these difficult, life-threatening journeys for an opportunity to lead a better quality of life.

Hint: This exercise provides an excellent opportunity to demonstrate that more information about a subject not only increases knowledge but also sheds new light on first impressions. New light often but not always causes changes in what was originally accepted as truth. Lead students in a discussion of other times in students' lives in which new light changed first impressions about people, events, or values.

2. Invite boys and girls to a video showing of *Molly's Pilgrim*. Instruct students to watch for likenesses and differences between the video story and the storybook. Lead students through a comparison-and-contrast discussion by using a Venn diagram on the chalkboard or on a transparency. **Ask:** Why do authors and movie directors not tell stories in exactly the same ways?

Hint: This question provides an opportunity for creative thinking. Prompt students to think about issues such as examining types and ages of audiences, showing the video one time versus reading the book many times. Ask students to back up their thinking with good reasons and explanations.

3. Encourage volunteers to participate in Molly's journey by finger-tracing the route from Russia to America on a large classroom map while partners finger-trace the same route on desk maps. Give students a concrete idea of distance by breaking up the trip in segments: Russia to Alaska; Alaska to California; California to New York. Suggest that students attach the actual distances between points by using the scale on the map.

Place the length of Molly's journey in perspective by asking students the farthest distance that they have ever traveled and comparing their answers to segments of Molly's journey. Link the distance Molly's family travels, the hardships the family endures, and the adjustments they face to these discussion questions:

How are the journeys of Molly's family and of the Pilgrims similar and different?
How do Molly's feelings change between the beginning and end of the book?
How does Molly's mother help her find new meaning for the word "pilgrim"?

Ask: How does geography help you understand the feelings of an immigrant family better? **Hint:** Linking the crossing of actual distances, time zones, and cultural zones to personal experiences and feelings helps students find meaning in the story, especially when this information is transferred to other situations.

4. Declare an official Molly Day on which activities in all subjects revolve around aspects of the Jewish immigrants' story. Lead students in brainstorming ways the class may link topics or ideas in the story to various subjects such as social studies, language arts, science, mathematics, and fine arts. Enlist students in creating classroom centers for specialized activities.

Extension: Invite boys and girls to either propose a topic for investigation and share results with classmates or to select one of the following activities and share the products with classmates in a classroom Molly display:

Family in an urban environment. Explain to classmates the meaning of pilgrims living in two time periods and in two environments. **Hint:** Use wooden clothespins or toilet tissue rolls for dolls' bodies, then draw faces and dress dolls in appropriate costumes.

Make an illustrated story map of *Molly's Pilgrim* that shows the problem, main players, sequenced events, and the solution. Take classmates on the step-by-step journey by recounting the scenes on the story map.

Plan and present a socio-drama that shows how one who is different feels. Analyze first the ways in which Molly is different. Assume roles as Molly, her mother, her teacher, and her classmates. Show in the scenes how classmates treat Molly and then how understanding among the characters develops. Share with students the lessons about treatment of others learned from the story. Fashion dolls of Pilgrims and Native Americans in a colony environment or of Molly and her classmates.

Invite another class to a show-and-tell session in which individual students, partners, or small groups tell about their products, the relationship between the products and the story, and the learning acquired from their chosen activities.

5. Sing Woody Guthrie's tribute to the land and people of the United States. Ask boys and girls to quietly reflect about the meaning of "This land was made for you and me." **Ask:** Do the song lyrics say anything about the land being for only those who are alike? What do the lyrics tell you about America?

6. Select one character trait (e.g., compassion, courage, honesty, or integrity) and talk about how people in the story demonstrate the trait. Ask students to tell why they selected a character and how the character exemplifies the trait. Suggest that students think about their own lives and share examples that illustrate the trait.

EVALUATION:

Determine the level of student understanding by evaluating their definitions of pilgrims, by observing creative products, by reading examples of writing, and by listening to responses in classroom discussions. Encourage students to connect the message in the story to the theme of harvest and celebrations of thanksgiving.

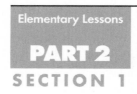

Elementary Lessons

PART 2

SECTION 1

CONNECTION #5:
Jennifer Berry Jones.
Heetunka's Harvest: A Tale
of the Plains Indians

A beautifully illustrated story about Bean Mouse gives readers a glimpse into a Sioux woman's daily life.

CHARACTER TRAITS: Review the nine basic character traits used in this manual before reading the story.

1. Read *Heetunka's Harvest* aloud. Remember to set the stage with appropriate pre-reading activities that capture students' interest. For example, use a United States wall map to focus student attention on the region of the Dakotas, the region's geographic features, and the relationship between the geographic features and the culture of the Sioux, a buffalo-hunting tribe. Clarify vocabulary terms necessary for understanding the text by reviewing important words in the glossary. Make sure that students understand the concepts of tribes, customs, and traditions.

Reread the story. Ask student partners to listen the second time for tribal customs and traditions and record examples in note form. Talk about Sioux culture by discussing children's notes on customs and traditions. Lead students in a compare-and-contrast discussion between the Sioux of past times and Native Americans today. **Hint:** Point out the vast differences between the two cultures. Also alert students that both groups of people, however different, preserve their cultures in similar ways, i.e., by passing on their customs and traditions to the next generation.

2. Lead a discussion on the concept of bartering and reasons why bartering developed. **Hint:** Talk about people not producing all of the products that they need or want. Long ago, creative people driven by the desire for more goods and services solved the problem with a system of trading for what they needed or wanted, i.e., a "this-for-that" bartering system with no currency exchange. Encourage students to find examples of the Sioux woman in the story bartering for things she needed or wanted and also to cite examples of elementary students bartering for things they need or want today. **Ask:** What are your best suggestions for successful bartering?

3. Reassemble partners/recorders who listen for a specific purpose. Review with them that the purpose for the first reading was to hear the story and that the purpose for the second reading was to listen for customs and traditions. For the third reading, challenge students to listen for and record ways the author describes the coming of winter through the use of colorful picture words. As students name the following examples, ask them to interpret the words with movements and/or sounds:

> *Nearly bare branches;*
> *Chilly breeze ran along the ground;*
> *Mouse's fur thickening;*
> *Geese flying south;*
> *Mouse's full storehouse;*
> *Dakota woman smells the hint of snow in the air;*
> *Dakota woman filling parfleche boxes with dried foods (parfleche = rawhide soaked in water and lye, then dried on a stretcher);*
> *Willows spangled with frost; and*
> *River edged with ice.*

Encourage partners to select one phrase and then illustrate the words with ideas drawn from the story on a long paper banner entitled "The Coming of Winter." **Ask:** Do picture words make stories more exciting? Why or why not? What message does the author send students about using picture words in their writing?

4. Invite students to design a parfleche box. Ask them to bring a shoebox from home. Show students how to dip brown paper bags in water, wad bags up to create a leather look, and spread them out to dry. Suggest that students use colored chalk, crayons, markers, or paint to decorate the make-believe leather when dry. Model for students how to glue leather on shoeboxes, and then allow class time for students to complete the parfleche boxes.

Encourage students to arrange a class collection of parfleche boxes along with a basket of beans, pumpkins, and squash in a display. Talk with students about the purpose of the parfleche box in the story. Lead students into thinking about containers in their lives in which they keep special, treasured items. **Ask:** Is the container more than a storehouse for a special object? What are special containers in young children's lives, teenagers' lives, adults' lives? Why do types of containers change?

Hint: Use diaper bags, toy boxes, lunch boxes, athletic bags, and safe deposit boxes as discussion starters. Mention to students that containers have become important enough in people's lives that specialty stores selling only containers now exist. This is an excellent opportunity to talk about the concept of demand. People (consumers) needed and wanted containers (demand) so the market (risk-takers) responded with containers (supply).

(Alternate Activity) As an alternate art project, allow students to make quillwork wall hangings by using scraps of make-believe leather, then gluing a Native-American design on the leather. Make design parts from colored toothpicks broken into different lengths.

5. Enlist parent or volunteer assistance in planning a "Taste the Harvest" experience. Ask that they prepare a feast of nine-bean soup and cornbread squares. **Hint:** Purchase dried beans at any grocery store. Prepare in crock-pots in the classroom or at home. Place samples in small paper cups, squares of cornbread on paper napkins, then serve and enjoy. Talk about how and why this type of feast matches what students learned in *Heetunka's Harvest*. Extend the discussion to other kinds of feasts in which people serve different foods. **Ask** students to put on their thinking caps: What factors determine menus? **Hint:** Start discussion with geographic regions, cultural beliefs, cultural traditions, family income, personal tastes, personal goals, and then explore other student responses.

6. Review this relationship with students: the Plains Indians' survival depended on the large, powerful buffalo and the small, weak bean mouse. Write the following statement on the chalkboard: "All things, regardless of size, are important in nature." Invite students to use the sentence as a writing-prompt and develop the prompt with examples from the story.

7. Ask students to explain the Indians' way of life based on living in harmony with nature. Divide students into pairs and give each partnership one of the nine character traits. Ask partners to decide if the Dakota woman exhibits the character trait. Encourage students to share examples from the story that help them make decisions. Suggest that students think about their own lives and share examples that illustrate the trait.

EVALUATION:

Determine the level of student understanding by evaluating the quality of creative and written products, by assessing the application of character traits from the story to real life, and by listening to responses in class discussions. Encourage students to connect the message in the story to the theme of harvest and celebrations of thanksgiving.

CONNECTION #1:
Verda Cross and Gail Owens. Great-Grandma Tells of Threshing Days

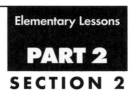

A little girl and her brother help their family on threshing day in the early 1900s. Neighbors congregate to thresh the wheat and to assist the women with the midday meal. Teachers will welcome a story that powerfully illustrates the idea that many hands lighten the workload. In addition, the story clearly exemplifies the generalization that common purposes bind people together.

CHARACTER TRAITS: Review the meaning of the character traits of diligence, citizenship, and compassion.

1. Read *Great-Grandma Tells of Threshing Days* aloud, and discuss how and why neighbors help neighbors on threshing day. Assist students in brainstorming as a class the ways neighbors help neighbors today.

Request that students ask family members or neighbors about other ways they respond to their fellow citizens' needs. Consult community organizations such as the United Way or civic clubs that conduct annual projects. Call the local newspaper or county library for stories that tell about citizens helping citizens. **Ask:** How the actions of these citizens represent the character trait of compassion?

Remember to set the stage with other appropriate pre-reading activities that capture students' interest. Clarify vocabulary terms necessary for understanding both the text and the celebration. Define clearly a purpose for reading and/or listening.

2. Reread the story. In advance of rereading, request that students listen carefully for similarities and differences between life in the 1900s and today. Enlist student assistance in constructing a large Venn diagram entitled "Then and Now" on the chalkboard or butcher paper.

Hint: Differences will outnumber similarities. **Ask** students to put on their thinking caps and talk about probable reasons why so many more differences exist than similarities. Lead students into making valid conclusions based on data they draw from the story, on data they discuss, or data the teacher introduces as evidence (e.g., increased level of industrialization, inability of small farmers to compete with agribusinesses, and many farmers' children going into other lines of work rather than the family farm). Nudge students toward the generalization: "Over time, changes occur."

Note how the farmers in the story demonstrate the character trait of diligence by working hard and by making the land produce crops. Challenge students to share examples of times that they have shown diligence in projects at school, in the neighborhood, and at home.

Hint: For interest and variety, alternate discussions on character traits between the benefits of possessing the traits and the consequences of not possessing the traits.

EVALUATION:
Determine the level of student understanding of how neighbors help neighbors throughout history and how lifestyles change over the years by assessing the quality of comparisons and contrasts between two time periods and the quality of connections between characters in the story and persons in students' lives. Include teacher observations and rubrics in evaluating student progress. Encourage students to connect the message in the story to the theme of harvest, and celebrations of thanksgiving.

CONNECTION #2:
Jean Craighead George.
The First Thanksgiving

Entertaining text enhanced with beautiful paintings describes the Pilgrims' journey to America; Squanto's trek to England and back; and the cooperative spirit between the Pilgrims and Squanto that results in a memorable feast of thanksgiving in North America.

CHARACTER TRAITS: Review the nine basic character traits used in this manual.

1. Read *The First Thanksgiving* aloud. Involve children in a discussion about Squanto's contributions to the Pilgrims that enabled them to adapt to a new, strange environment. Remember to set the stage with other appropriate pre-reading activities that capture students' interest. Clarify vocabulary terms necessary for understanding both the text and the celebration. Define clearly a purpose for reading and/or listening.

2. Lead students to research other hardships that the Pilgrims faced on their journey to America and in their efforts to establish homes in a colony. Compile a list of hardships, and then send a research team to the media center to consult other references in order to create a more complete story. Recruit the school media specialist to assist students in this project. Ask team members to summarize and share data found in the library. **Ask:** Based upon references used for finding more details about the Pilgrim's story, what is the true meaning of their first harvest in North America?

3. Invite students to write and illustrate letters from a Pilgrim's point of view to a family member left behind. Ask students to describe both the trip to America and the problems in establishing farms and homes on unfamiliar ground. Give students the option of writing and illustrating letters from an Indian's (Native-American's) point of view that express concerns over what new arrivals to the continent may mean to their tribes. **Note:** In the states we refer to today as New England, 90 to 98 percent of the Native Americans had died of diseases they had contacted from white Europeans, years before the Pilgrims arrived on their shores.

Divide the class into two groups, Pilgrims and Indians, and ask members of each group to share their letters with classmates. **Hint:** Group Pilgrims and Indians together. At the end of the letter reading, they may draw conclusions about life in America from two perspectives. Post letters on a harvest bulletin board.

4. Talk about the menus and about food preparations for Thanksgiving dinners today. Point out to students the ethnic similarities and differences in menus. Then, enlist students in a compare-and-contrast exercise related to today's menus, food preparations, and those in the story setting of *The First Thanksgiving*. **Ask:** How did geographic factors determine menus in past times? What factors enable present-day Americans to enjoy more variety in foods and more ease in food preparations in spite of existing geographic factors?

5. Ask students to consider the entire narration of the Pilgrims and the Indians in *The First Thanksgiving*, then decide which of the nine character traits were necessary for the survival of both groups and why. Remember to ask students to support their choices with specific examples.

EVALUATION:

Determine the level of student understanding of the Pilgrims' problems and hardships and the Native-Americans' contributions to the Pilgrims by assessing the quality of discussions, participation, comparisons and contrasts, and letters. Include teacher observations and rubrics in evaluating student progress. Encourage students to connect the message in the story to the theme of harvest and celebrations of thanksgiving.

CONNECTION #3:
Paulla Jennings.
Strawberry Thanksgiving

Grandmother offers insights into Native-American culture in New England by telling a legend about Strawberry Thanksgiving to Adam.

CHARACTER TRAITS: Review the meaning of the character traits of respect and responsibility.

1. Read *Strawberry Thanksgiving* aloud. Remember to set the stage with appropriate pre-reading activities that capture students' interest. Clarify vocabulary terms necessary for understanding both the text and the celebration. Define clearly a purpose for reading and/or listening.

2. Suggest that students bring cookbooks from home and research recipes using strawberries. Talk about recipes that are familiar in the South such as strawberry shortcake. Talk also about recipes that are unfamiliar to students. Invite students to select their favorite strawberry recipe, copy the recipe on strawberry-shaped paper, and compile a strawberry recipe collection for the class and perhaps for students' families. Allow students who want to duplicate the activity the story describes, i.e., painting a strawberry on a small rock, to prepare their examples during an art period, then arrange the rocks in a display with the storybook and recipe collection.

Extension: Review the time period covered in *Strawberry Thanksgiving*. Explain the process of analysis to students. Challenge students to analyze recipes that Native-American tribes in New England might make and enjoy in the time period of *Strawberry Thanksgiving*. **Hint:** Encourage students to consider geographic regions, ingredients, and equipment. **Ask:** What clues do strawberry recipes provide about changing lifestyles, then and now?

3. Brew sassafras tea for students to taste. Encourage a small research team with the assistance of the school media specialist to investigate the origins of sassafras tea, a product tribal members took to the Strawberry Thanksgiving festival.

Engage students in various tea-related activities. Talk about the popularity of teas of different flavors in their community. **Ask:** Why is iced tea more popular with southerners than hot tea? Contact various restaurants in your area and ask how often customers request hot tea on the menus. **Ask:** When customers order tea, what is the number one choice, iced tea or hot tea?

4. Invite students to review the character traits of respect and responsibility and apply traits to characters in the story and also to persons in students' lives. **Hint:** Extend the discussion to care of items students bring from home. They must exhibit responsibility in caring for their own items and also demonstrate respect for other people's property.

Hint: For interest and variety, alternate discussions on character traits between the benefits of possessing the traits and the consequences of not possessing the traits

EVALUATION:

Determine the level of student understanding that harvest celebrations and times for thanksgiving cross generational and cultural lines by assessing the quality of class discussions, participation, activities, and products. Include teacher observations and rubrics in evaluating student progress. Encourage students to connect the message in the story to the theme of harvest and celebrations of thanksgiving.

CONNECTION #4:
Deborah M. Newton. *Kwanzaa*

Readers gain basic insights into Kwanzaa, a seven-day observance that celebrates African cultural heritage and economic history as well as African harvest customs.

CHARACTER TRAITS: Review the meaning of the nine character traits used in this manual.

Note: The writers placed Kwanzaa in the harvest section and the festivals of light section. Kwanzaa, patterned after African harvest festivals, now celebrates pride in African-American heritage by lighting a symbolic candle on each of seven successive nights.

1. Read *Kwanzaa* aloud. Remember to set the stage with appropriate pre-reading activities that capture students' interest. Clarify vocabulary terms necessary for understanding both the text and the celebration. Define clearly a purpose for reading and/or listening. Then read and discuss the story with students.

2. List the seven principles of Kwanzaa on the chalkboard, practice the pronunciation of the terms with students, then ask students to practice with partners. **Hint:** Point out to students that practicing the correct pronunciation of unfamiliar terms gradually makes the flow of syllables and words easier. **Ask:** Does correct practice of all new skills make learning easier? Request that students provide examples of other situations in which they learned new skills through practicing the steps of the skill correctly.

Talk about reasons why Kwanzaa words are difficult for almost all students whether they be Anglo Americans, African Americans, Hispanic Americans, or members of other racial/ethnic groups. **Hint:** Use the discussion to introduce, develop, or reinforce the concept that most students have the common experience of being Americans born in America, so most students will experience difficulty with the pronunciation of any foreign terms unless family members practice them either in the home or in racial/ethnic celebrations. Extend the discussion to include why learning Kwanzaa terms by English-speaking students is similar to learning English terms by non-English-speaking students.

THE SEVEN PRINCIPLES OF KWANZAA

Day 1: *Umoja* - Unity

Day 2: *Kujichagulia* - Self-determination

Day 3: *Ujima* - Collective Work and Responsibility

Day 4: *Ujamaa* - Cooperative Economics

Day 5: *Nia* - Purpose

Day 6: *Kuumba* - Creativity

Day 7: *Imani* - Faith

3. Lead students in a comparison-and-contrast discussion of the seven principles of Kwanzaa and of the nine core character traits listed in the appendix (e.g., ujima—collective work and responsibility—and responsibility). Diagram student responses so that students observe the recording of similarities and differences as the discussion develops.

Hint: Choose the principles to compare and contrast on the basis of which principles appropriately match the developmental level of students. Extend the learning of the diagram exercise by asking students to identify characters in other stories who demonstrate one or more of the Kwanzaa principles and why. Lead students to an understanding that certain principles cross cultural lines.

4. Invite students to set a Kwanzaa table patterned after the one the story describes. Ask table setters to prepare short explanations related to the importance of items and of colors on the table. Talk about other occasions when families set special tables. Encourage students to participate in a discussion related to the following statement: Today's fast-paced lifestyles often prevent all family members from gathering around the table at the same time except on special occasions. **Ask:** Is the statement true? Why or why not?

5. Invite a resource person to talk about Kwanzaa and how people observe Kwanzaa traditions in your community. Seek a person who can share the growth of the tradition in the community from the first observance to the present time.

EVALUATION:

Determine the level of student understanding of the Kwanzaa celebration and principles by assessing their participation in class discussions and their ability to transfer literary examples to situations either in other stories or in the real world. Include teacher observations and rubrics in evaluating student progress. Encourage students to connect the message in the story to the theme of harvest and celebrations of thanksgiving.

CONNECTION #1:
Marcia Sewall.
The Pilgrims of Plimoth

Driven by their desire for religious freedom, Pilgrims faced external as well as internal dangers during their bold adventure in the New (Old) World. They not only encountered and befriended people they labeled as savages but they also confronted challenges of creating social order within their own community. The Pilgrims' journey to and settlement in the New (Old) World carried high stakes: survival.

ALTERNATE SELECTIONS:

Joan Anderson. *The First Thanksgiving Feast*
Stunning photographs from Plimoth Plantation, a living history museum, recreate the Pilgrims' experience in the New (Old) World. Characters' dialogue in present-day dramas reflects style and wording of accounts penned by original colonists.

Jean Craighead George. *The First Thanksgiving*
Grateful colonists celebrated their survival in the New (Old) World and the first harvest with a feast of Thanksgiving.

Note: Various spellings of Plymouth result from a lack of standardized spelling in the primary sources researched by various writers.

CHARACTER TRAITS: Review the nine character traits used in this manual and give examples of each of them. Ask students to provide other examples from their own experiences.

1. Read aloud the three accounts of the Pilgrims' experiences in the New (Old) World. Remember to set the stage with appropriate pre-reading activities that capture students' interest. For example, use historical accounts to develop or to reinforce students' geographic understanding of the Pilgrims' journey and the colony's location. Ask student volunteers to finger-trace the journey and then post the location of the colony on the story map in the classroom.

    Hint: Use this opportunity to enlarge elementary students' horizons by emphasizing that students can become world travelers by paying close attention to geographic clues in stories and then comparing and contrasting the story site to the world in which they live. Post locations of stories on a story map in the classroom so that students can literally see their horizons expand throughout the year. Keep a legend that shows the name of the story, main characters, and geographic sites for the purpose of building bridges between literature and geography. This activity reinforced throughout the year connects perfectly with world culture studies taught in upper elementary grades.

    Encourage students to record information related to the Pilgrims' thanksgiving feast on a K-W-L chart on the chalkboard (K-W-L: what students Know, what students Want to know, what students Learned). Lead students into listing information about setting, participants, and reasons for the journey to the New (Old) World, causes of celebration, results of celebration, foods, clothing, and shelter.

    As a class, suggest that students review the first two columns, select a partner, and then listen to the reading of the three selections to verify or to contradict information on the chart. Suggest that partners take notes on points they wish to discuss or points they want to add to the chart following the reading of stories. Prior to reading, clarify vocabulary terms necessary for understanding both the text and the celebration.

After reading the stories, invite partners to elaborate on or to correct the listings on the chart. At the conclusion of the activities, direct students to revisit the chart and complete the third column, i.e., What Students Learned. **Ask:** How does the use of multiple sources add to the quality of research on a single topic? Why? How does working with a partner help students acquire or correct information? In addition to information, what else do students learn from working with a partner?

2. Explain to students that they may choose one of the following three options to demonstrate understanding of the Pilgrims' daily lives or of the harvest feast:

Construct a classroom model similar to the Pilgrims' colony. Make sure that the model shows varied ways those individuals earned a living; interacted with the environment; helped one another; fulfilled different roles assigned to males, females, and children; and contributed to a Thanksgiving feast.

Paint a classroom mural showing typical harvest scenes at Plymouth Colony. Make sure that the mural shows the planting, harvesting, and use of various crops and that the artists can explain how a community spirit among Pilgrims culminated in the first harvest and in the first thanksgiving feast.

Assume the role of a Pilgrim and write an account of the first harvest and the first Thanksgiving feast. Make sure that Pilgrims write accounts in first person, study the sources, and incorporate words and phrases typical of the Pilgrims. For authenticity, write the accounts on paper weathered by the ages and found in an old trunk (rumpled beige paper with burned edges).

Select a corner of the classroom for Plymouth Colony and invite students to hang the class mural for a backdrop, to position the model in a prominent place, and to surround the display with first-hand accounts of Pilgrims. Allow groups and individuals to share their project information with classmates, and then invite students to add new information to column three on the K-W-L chart on the chalkboard.

3. Ask students to reflect on the character traits that enable the Pilgrims to survive the hardships of their experience. Invite students to talk about the traits of the Pilgrims and to volunteer examples from their lives in which they exhibited the same trait in meeting everyday challenges.

Hint: For interest and variety, alternate discussions on character traits between the benefits of possessing the traits and the consequences of not possessing the traits.

EVALUATION:

Determine the level of student understanding of the challenges at Plymouth Colony and the reasons for the harvest celebration by observing accuracy and variety on the K-W-L chart, by judging enthusiasm for content-related activities, and by assessing transfer of character traits from historical to personal situations. Ask students to explain what they learned from the stories and activities. Encourage students to connect the message in the stories to the theme of harvest and celebrations of thanksgiving.

CONNECTION #2:
Barbara Greenwood.
A Pioneer Sampler: The Daily Life of a Pioneer Family (Pages 134-239)

Teachers will welcome a source that vividly portrays life in the 1840s: how pioneers cooked food, how they slaughtered hogs, how they made maple syrup, and how they celebrated important events. For present-day adventurers interested in simulating pioneer experiences, Greenwood provides directions for churning butter, telling time by the sun, and making candles and dyes.

CHARACTER TRAITS: Review the nine character traits used in this manual and give examples of each of them. Ask students to provide other examples from their own experiences.

1. Read aloud sections of the passage from *A Pioneer Sampler*. Remember to set the stage with appropriate pre-reading activities that capture students' interest. For example, use textual as well as visual clues to determine the geographic location of the story. Talk about the association of the two concepts, frontier and pioneer, about how and why the location of the frontier changes throughout American history, and whether or not Americans still have frontiers left for exploration and also for settlement.

Hint: Utilize the frontier topic as an excellent basis for interdisciplinary discussion on different dimensions of frontiers (e.g., land, sea, and space). **Ask:** How might students define frontier for other elementary students? In students' opinions, will frontiers continue to exist in history?

Clarify vocabulary terms necessary for understanding both the text and the celebration. Define learning about frontier life in the 1840s as the purpose for reading and listening to the story.

2. Ask students to reflect on examples of weather from the story. Talk informally with students about similarities and differences between the seasons of spring and fall. Encourage volunteers to research weather-related terms such as precipitation, temperature, and daylight hours.

After student volunteers clarify the meaning of terms for classmates, ask two students to contact a television weatherman to discuss other weather factors that are especially important to farmers. Lead students in matching or verifying information about weather and farming learned from reading the story, researching weather terms, and interviewing a television weatherman.

Explain to students that a generalization states a relationship between two or more concepts. Challenge student partners to develop a story-related generalization that clearly establishes a relationship between farming and weather and to present the statement and their reasoning to classmates.

3. Explain to students that they may choose how they demonstrate understanding of pioneer life in the 1840s. Ask students to listen to the following activities; to select one that holds high interest for them; and to work individually, with a partner, or in a small group to complete the project:

Collect photographs and/or drawings of crops ready to harvest, identify crops farmers grew in *A Pioneer Sampler*, and assemble the collection in harvest collages. Highlight the cause/effect relationship between crops and weather.

Compare and contrast farm equipment used by the Robertson family in the 1840s and by present-day farmers, then share similarities and differences with classmates. Examples: hoes, sickles, scythes, cradles, winnowing trays, combines, tractors. Make sure that an explanation on visuals include how the level of technology influences the number of workers needed and the number of hours worked. Identify cause/effect relationships in the explanation for classmates.

Investigate how farmers measure various crops. Use story clues, research data, or inquiries to present-day farmers to learn accurate measurement terminology. Plan an exhibit that shows various crops, how farmers measure the yield of crops, and the correct terms for crop measurement.

Design and build a gristmill with a diagram that offers an explanation of how grain becomes flour. Include in an explanation to classmates why milling is an example of human/environment interaction, one of the five major themes of geography.

Invite students to paint a mural that portrays a harvest scene described in *A Pioneer Sampler*. In the mural, show various stages of harvest from planted fields to dinner tables. Illustrate accurate scenes depicting the number of workers needed and period tools.

Hint: For fun-related activities with a pioneer flavor, allow students to fashion hay straw and yarn or cord into a variety of typical farm animals in the 1840s. If students wish to trim animals with eyes, ears, or tails, they may cut felt scraps into desired shapes. Also, obtain wheat kernels from a health food store. Allow students to experience pioneer gum chewing. Define the word "gluten" and ask students to describe how and when kernels become gummy.

Enlist students in assembling all products in a tastefully arranged classroom display entitled "A Sampling of Pioneer Life." Invite students to spotlight their products with an explanation that connects to the story.

4. Ask students to reflect upon what traits enable the main characters in the story to confront and to solve problems of rugged pioneer life. Invite students to transfer the situation of a fictional character to their own lives. Ask how and why a specific character trait might assist them in meeting every-day challenges.

EVALUATION:

Determine the level of student understanding of early pioneers' lives and methods of earning a living by assessing experience-based and research-based responses to thought questions, by observing the enthusiasm for project options, and by evaluating the quality of projects. Ask students to explain what they learned from the story and activities. Encourage students to connect the message in the story to the theme of harvest and celebrations of thanksgiving.

CONNECTION #3:
Elizabeth King. *Chile Fever:*
A Celebration of Peppers

Reading about a chile pepper festival, the culmination of a bountiful harvest, heightens awareness of the pepper plant, a favorite of the American Southwest. Through the text and illustrations, readers gain knowledge about the chile pepper's growth cycle, cultural importance, and worldwide appeal.

CHARACTER TRAITS: Review the nine character traits used in this manual and give examples of each of them. Ask students to provide other examples from their own experiences.

1. Read *Chile Fever: A Celebration of Peppers* aloud. Remember to set the stage with appropriate pre-reading activities that capture students' interest. For example, use the story to illustrate the concept of the region, one of five themes of geography. Draw students' attention to an area called the Southwest, a region bound together by similar geographic features.

Hint: Continue to review stories as sources for teaching children about the geographic theme of region as well as the other four themes: location, place, movement, and human/environment interaction.

Refer to the story map project and ask volunteers to enter the Southwest as a story site on the map's legend. Remind students how their geographic horizons are expanding through literature. As soon as students establish the setting and demonstrate understanding of new vocabulary, invite student partners to listen carefully and to record notes on the steps between planting and tasting peppers. Discuss students' notes after reading the story. Make certain that students sequence steps from seeds to peppers in a scientifically accurate manner.

2. Excite students by announcing that their classroom will stage a chile pepper festival similar to the one described in the story. Challenge students as individuals, partners, or small groups to choose a project, one that holds special interest for them, from the following options:

Gather a wide variety of peppers from local produce markets; develop criteria for comparison and for contrast such as sizes, shapes, colors, tastes, costs, uses; then graph findings on a chart or poster. Inquire about factors that affect costs of both canned and fresh peppers. **Hint:** Lead students in an investigation of factors such as labor, packaging, marketing, distribution, life of fresh produce, supply and demand, and consumers' personal preferences.

Research and illustrate the life cycle of chile peppers in diagram form on a chart or poster suitable for classroom display.

Assume the role of a chile pepper grower, seek clues in the story or research clues in the library for ways to produce a bountiful crop, and then write a cousin living in the Northeast (USA) about tips for success in the chile pepper market.

Research and choose recipes of Southwestern favorites; copy and illustrate recipes on ditto masters that students may duplicate for recipe booklets; design a cover for the recipe collection, and then bind recipes in booklet form for classmates.

Research the origin of ristras, then prepare a model to add to the class display; write a brief summary of the origin and uses of ristras to accompany the model.

Talk with students about eye-catching display ideas as they prepare projects of their choice. Appoint a small committee composed of at least one student from each project group to plan the display. Encourage students to survey all of the projects, then plan placement of objects by considering such things as projects requiring viewers to read explanations, projects of different sizes, and projects that students will receive as favors. Assist students in arranging projects for display and in polishing explanations related to various projects, then invite teachers and students in other classes to visit "A Taste of the Southwest" exhibit.

3. Request students to reflect upon what traits enable the main characters in the story to confront problems and to find solutions. Invite students to transfer situations involving story characters to situations in their own lives. Ask how and why specific character traits might assist them in meeting everyday challenges.

Hint: For interest and variety, alternate discussions on character traits between the presence and benefits of possessing the traits and the absence and consequences of not possessing the traits.

EVALUATION:

Determine the level of student understanding of the growth, harvest, and uses of chile peppers by assessing the depth of responses in class discussions, by observing the degree of enthusiasm for personally selected projects, and by evaluating the quality of content-related products. Encourage students to connect the message in the story to the theme of harvest and celebrations of thanksgiving.

CONNECTION #4:
Gordon Regguinti.
The Sacred Harvest: Ojibway Wild Rice Gathering

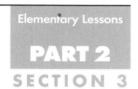

Elementary Lessons

PART 2

SECTION 3

An Ojibway family instructs their 11-year-old son how to harvest, store, and use wild rice on Minnesota's Leech Lake Reservation. Legend attributes relocation from eastern North America to Minnesota to the tribe's search for food that grows in water.

CHARACTER TRAITS: Review the nine character traits used in this manual and give examples of each of them. Ask students to provide other examples from their own experiences.

1. Read *The Sacred Harvest: Ojibway Wild Rice Gathering* aloud. Remember to set the stage with appropriate pre-reading activities that capture students' interest. For example, enlist student volunteers to finger-trace the Ojibway journey from eastern North America to Minnesota on a United States classroom wall map.

Hint: Refer to the reason for the Ojibway journey, and then point out that most movement of people throughout history involves their efforts to get away from something deemed intolerable and to get to some place where they might enjoy a better quality of life. Challenge students to think up examples in which this generalization is true.

Hint: Remind students that color on physical maps provides clues about the terrain. Ask students to retrace the journey and to identify physical features that the Ojibway encountered on their trek.

Use specific information to paint vivid pictures of the setting. Ask students to practice geographic skills by establishing the location (Where is it?) and the place (What is it like?) of Minnesota. Use the location of Minnesota for a quick review of latitude and longitude.

In addition to developing geographic inquiries into pre-reading activities, utilize the opportunity to explain the reservation system in United States history. Encourage students to view the issue from the perspective of governmental policy makers as well as from the perspective of Native Americans. After reading the story, ask students to illustrate the concepts of movement, perspective, and reservations with examples drawn from the story.

2. Divide students into small groups of three or four. Review with each group the math-related concepts in the storyline. Challenge student groups to write two problems keyed to the Ojibway story, and then pose the problems to classmates in a round-robin manner.

   Example: Harvest time is from 9 A.M. to 12 Noon. How many hours are worked per day and per week? Harvest permits are sold for $2.00 each. In 1991, one thousand people bought permits. How much money did the government receive from the sale of permits? **Hint:** Explain to students that this story problem involves elementary math skills. Encourage them to write more complex, more creative, and more story-related brainteasers.

3. Gather and display samples of various types of rice. Lead students in a compare-and-contrast exercise based strictly on observation. Use criteria such as size and color or student-generated criteria to compare and contrast unique features.

   In advance of the lesson, ask the librarian to select resource material in which students may research geographic origins of various types of rice. Request teams of students to investigate types, write names and places of origin on sticky notes, and attach notes to a classroom wall map. Ask students to reflect on the locations of the sticky notes on the map, then formulate reasonable conclusions about rice, i.e., where the crop grows, favorable growth conditions, why rice is one of the world's main staples.

   Ask: How and why do the conclusions connect to the Ojibway story?

   Extension: As an extension, show students one cup of uncooked rice, cook the cup of rice, then invite students to relate what happens to rice when cooked to their conclusion on why rice is one of the world's main staples. **Ask:** What connects cooked rice to rice's worldwide popularity?

4. Ask students to reflect upon what traits enable the Ojibway to confront problems and to find solutions. Invite students to transfer situations involving the Ojibway in the story to their own lives. Ask how and why a specific character trait might assist them in meeting everyday challenges.

EVALUATION:

Determine the level of student understanding of Ojibway wild rice gathering as well as the growth, harvest, and uses of rice by assessing the depth of their responses to thinking questions and by evaluating their ability to define, exemplify, and transfer social studies concepts from the story to other situations. Encourage students to connect the message in the story to the theme of harvest and celebrations of thanksgiving.

CONNECTION #5:
Michael Dorros. Guests

Moss, a young Native-American boy, views the entry of strangers into his village with suspicion. He struggles to cope with changes that outsiders bring to his community. Retreating to the forest to think through this troubling situation, Moss reaches unexpected conclusions about his present and future worlds.

Note: The setting for *Guests* focuses upon a feast that villagers share with strangers; thus the writers categorize the story as a harvest selection. Since the storyline recounts Moss's thinking through complex problems and reaching new understandings, the writers also encourage teachers to connect the story to the coming-of-age section. Use the story to illustrate how and why one story may fit several themes.

CHARACTER TRAITS: Review the nine character traits used in this manual and give examples of each of them. Ask students to provide other examples from their own experiences.

Read *Guests* aloud. Remember to set the stage with appropriate pre-reading activities that capture students' interest. For example, assess students' knowledge of tribes of the Eastern Woodlands:

> *The approximate geographic location of tribes (Where are they at this point in history?);*
> *A description of the geographic place (What is their environment like?);*
> *How place shaped tribal lifestyles before colonists arrived;*
> *How tribal members overcame the harshness of winters;*
> *How tribal members divided tasks; and*
> *How Native Americans bestowed names on children then changed children's names as they matured.*

Accept all answers and then divide students into listening groups assigned to one of the six topics cited above. Encourage groups to record notes on story examples that will assist members in enriching their assigned topics for classmates. Following the story reading, allow groups to discuss and organize their notes, then clarify and/or extend the topic with information from the story.

Ask: Who are the guests? What are story clues that support students' answers? How and why does seeking information from multiple sources enrich any topic of study? How does the story introduce another perspective on a traditional story?

Assist students in answering these questions by prompting them with story details from *Guests* as well as from the traditional thanksgiving story of the Pilgrims.

2. Talk about the meaning of allegory. Explain that an allegory is a story told in literary, dramatic, or picture form that parallels another story. Lead students in a discussion about the major events told in *Guests* and about reasons why the story might be an allegory.

Reread the story that Moss's father told, "How the People Lost Each Other," and the story that his mother told, "The Beaver and the Muskrat Woman." Request that students identify the major events in each of these stories. **Ask:** How and why might they classify the two stories as allegories?

Extension: Divide students into small groups, then challenge them to decide whether or not they may correctly classify any or all of the stories as allegories. Encourage students to prepare their responses to the challenge in the form of group presentations, debates, or persuasive essays. Invite students to a listening circle for presentations and for classmates' questions.

3. Reread Chapter 8 for the purpose of finding examples in which Moss thinks that the outsiders are rude. Invite students to project reasons why Moss draws the conclusion that guests or outsiders are rude. Lead students in a discussion focusing on how and why Moss's and the outsiders' cultural customs differ.

Hint: Suggest that people need to recognize that cultural customs develop and continue in practice, because they are satisfactory to members of that culture. Invite students to respond to this statement: Understanding cultural customs, their similarities as well as their differences, will improve harmony among cultures.

4. Explain to students that an epilogue takes the form of a short speech or poem at the end of a story or drama. Remind students that epilogues often deal with the future of the main characters. Invite students as individuals, partners, or small groups to write and present an epilogue to *Guests*.

5. Ask students to decide what traits enable Moss and the members of his tribe to confront problems and to find solutions. Invite students to transfer situations involving Native Americans in the story to their own lives. Ask how and why a specific character trait might assist them in meeting everyday challenges.

EVALUATION:

Determine the level of student understanding of cultural encounters by assessing the depth of their responses to thinking questions and processes, by evaluating the quality of their public presentations, and by determining their ease in transferring concepts and character traits from the story to real-life situations. Encourage students to connect the message in the story to the theme of harvest and celebrations of thanksgiving.

CONNECTION #1:
Louise Mandrell and Ace Collins. *Runaway Thanksgiving*

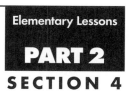

A young girl and her pet turkey run away from their log cabin home to avert the inevitable fate that awaits turkeys on Thanksgiving.

CHARACTER TRAITS: Review the nine character traits associated with this manual. Have students to check their definitions, share new insights, and provide different examples of each trait that they have discovered.

1. Read *Runaway Thanksgiving* aloud. Remember to set the stage with appropriate pre-reading activities that capture students' interest. For example, lead students in listing reasons why most people are thankful.

Encourage students to share examples of items for which they are most thankful, then direct students to categorize items under the headings "non-material" and "material." **Ask:**

Which list is longer?

What might account for one list being longer than the other?

What are items for which most elementary students express thanks? Examples: family, faith, friends, fun.

Set items for which the young girl is thankful as the first listening priority. As the second listening priority, set remembering events in a time sequence. Establish listening partnerships so that two students may listen and record notes as the teacher reads the story. Following the reading, ask students to respond to the first and second listening tasks. **Ask:** Do similarities exist between the young girl's and your "I am thankful for...." lists? Why or why not?

Hint: Use this light-hearted approach to Thanksgiving as a springboard for reviewing the traditional Thanksgiving story of the Pilgrims in Plymouth Colony, 1620, and for stressing their reasons for thankfulness (e.g., survival, religious freedom, and political freedom). Request that the media specialist search for a source that tells the story of the Spanish colonizing expedition in the Southwest led by Don Juan de Oñate in 1598. These families also staged a feast of thanksgiving in recognition of surviving an extremely harsh overland journey. Use the examples to point out to students that people of different cultures and different times, after trials and ordeals, have paused in their daily activities to give thanks to a higher power.

2. Invite students to volunteer reasons why the skill of sequencing is important to learning and remembering information. Provide options for partners to create illustrated story maps that depict sequenced events in *Runaway Thanksgiving*: 1) right-to-left or left-to-right pattern; 2) maze-like pattern; or 3) circular pattern. Request that students sketch patterns on 12" x 18" white or manila construction paper, then enter events and illustrations. Allow students to share pattern designs, then ask the introductory question again: Why is the skill of sequencing important to learning and remembering information?

3. Challenge students in small groups to create a story-related Thanksgiving acrostic. Tell students that words representing each letter in T-H-A-N-K-S-G-I-V-I-N-G may be nouns, verbs, adjectives, or adverbs, but that they must use the word correctly in a story-related sentence when they explain the acrostic. Ask students to prepare either a poster or an illustrated transparency to use during their presentation to classmates. (Alternate Activity, Parental Discretion)

4. Ask students to consider what traits the young girl demonstrates in her efforts to save the turkey from becoming a holiday fatality. Suggest that they transfer the situation involving a fictional character to one that they might encounter in the world of an elementary student. Ask how and why the same character traits might assist them in meeting everyday challenges.

Hint: For interest and variety, alternate discussions on character traits between the benefits of possessing the traits and the consequences of not possessing the traits.

EVALUATION:

Determine the level of student understanding of how a young girl protects her pet by assessing the quality of responses, the enthusiasm for research as well as creative projects, and the degree of participation. Ask students to explain what they have learned from the story and activities, then tell what, how, and why they learned. Encourage students to connect the message in the story to the theme of harvest and celebrations of thanksgiving.

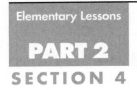

CONNECTION #2:
Andrea Davis Pinkney.
Seven Candles for Kwanzaa

A young girl leads readers through an explanation of Kwanzaa by describing how her family observes the traditional African-American celebration.

Note: The writers placed Kwanzaa in the harvest section and the festivals of light section. Kwanzaa, patterned after African harvest festivals, now celebrates pride in African-American heritage by lighting a symbolic candle on each of seven successive nights.

CHARACTER TRAITS: Review the nine character traits associated with this manual. Have students check their definitions, share new insights, and provide different examples of each trait that they have discovered.

1. Read *Seven Candles for Kwanzaa* aloud. Remember to set the stage with appropriate pre-reading activities that capture students' interest. For example, talk about the meaning of the concept and its origin, and set learning about the origin of Kwanzaa as the purpose for listening. Challenge students to come up with a list of questions so that they possess basic knowledge about the celebration by the end of the story reading. Asking the reporter's questions (e.g., Who? What? Where? When? Why? and How?) will effectively guide listening for a purpose.

On the board, list vocabulary words and meanings essential to the understanding of the storyline, then practice pronunciation of the words. Following the reading, return to the discussion of the celebration's origin. With students' assistance, trace the celebration's development from origin to the present time.

Ask: Why may students categorize the event as either a harvest or festivals-of-light celebration?
Hint: Remind students that in the beginning the celebration focused on harvest, a specific topic. As the celebration developed through the years, the theme broadened to pride in African-American heritage, a general topic.

2. Divide students into seven groups, with each group representing one of the festival days. Assign each group one principle (unity, self-determination, collective work, cooperation, purpose, creativity, or faith) to investigate. Research should focus on topics for each principle, i.e., the name of the principle, the meaning of the principle, and the activities associated with the principle.

Explain the Kwanzaa tradition of zawadi, the practice of gift giving. Invite students to participate in making a zawadi for the class in the form of a reference book on Kwanzaa. For each principle, ask students to prepare two illustrated pages that tell the principle, the meaning of the principle, and how celebrants observe the principle in either story or poetry form.

Assign the task of designing covers for the reference book to a small group of students with a special interest in art. **Hint:** Inspire artistic students by showing them the border designs on each page of *Seven Candles for Kwanzaa*. Plan a time for student groups to share knowledge about the principles of Kwanzaa: unity, self-determination, collective work, cooperation, purpose, creativity, and faith.

Extension: As an extension, review common words related to Kwanzaa traditions (e.g., mkeka [straw placemat], muhindi [ears of corn], mazao [crops], kinara [wooden candle holder], karamu [a glorious feast]). Link the use of words to their function in the celebration. **Ask:** How do authentic words add to the quality of this or other celebrations?

3. Invite students to choose an African American whose accomplishments exhibit one or more of the Kwanzaa principles. Direct students to research what acts in the person's life exhibit one or more principles, then write a high-interest television spotlight that features the person and his or her accomplishments. Select a program host who introduces the television show, "Focus on Famous Americans." Rotate around the room as students spotlight various African-American citizens. **Ask:**

Do these achievements represent a wide range of interests?
Do spotlighted personalities exhibit any of the nine core character traits?
Where do similarities exist between the Kwanzaa principles and the nine core character traits?
What is the meaning of the term, universal?
How does the term apply to the Kwanzaa principles and the nine core character traits?

4. Invite a resource person to talk about Kwanzaa and how people observe Kwanzaa traditions in your community. Seek a person who can share the growth of the tradition in the community from the first observance to the present time. Ask the resource person to comment on variations in traditional practices that might result from the relatively isolated geographic location of the community.

Ask students to put on their thinking caps and respond to this question: Do students believe that people living in other geographic regions put their unique brands or stamps on celebrations? Why? Help students cite concrete examples.

EVALUATION:

Determine the level of student understanding of Kwanzaa as a harvest celebration by judging the quality of responses, the enthusiasm for research as well as creative projects, and the degree of participation. Ask students to explain what they have learned from the story and activities, then tell what, how, and why they learned. Encourage students to connect the message in the story to the theme of harvest and celebrations of thanksgiving.

ADDITIONAL SELECTIONS:

Denise Burden-Patmon. *Imani's Gift at Kwanzaa*
Dorothy Rhodes Freeman and Dianne M. MacMillan. *Kwanzaa*
Diane Hoyt-Goldsmith. *Celebrating Kwanzaa*
Cedric McClester. *Kwanzaa: Everything You Always Wanted to Know but Didn't Know Where to Ask*
A.P. Porter. *Kwanzaa*

CONNECTION #3:
Patricia Polacco.
Tikvah Means Hope

During Sukkoth, an angry fire burns a destructive path through an Oakland, California, neighborhood. Out of the ashes, however, hope emerges.

CHARACTER TRAITS: Review the nine character traits associated with this manual. Ask students to check their definitions, share new insights, and provide different examples of each trait that they have discovered.

1. Read *Tikvah Means Hope* aloud. Remember to set the stage with appropriate pre-reading activities that capture students' interest. For example, review with students the nine core character traits and ask that listening partners record examples of one or more of the traits during the story. Clarify the literal meaning of Sukkoth as a Jewish word for booth or tent. Encourage students to replicate scenes in the story that show huts used by the Jewish people fleeing from Egypt. Suggest to students that they create three-dimensional models or dioramas.

Lead students in a discussion of how different characters exhibit these traits in the story. **Ask:**

> *Does a crisis such as a fire cause many people to demonstrate traits in a more overt way than every-day living requires? Why or why not?*
>
> *Can students remember television accounts of other disasters in which individuals exhibited instantaneous, intense courage, compassion, or any other trait?*

Hint: For interest and variety, alternate discussions on character traits between the presence and benefits of possessing the traits and the absence and consequences of not possessing the traits.

2. Talk with students about the thread that binds all harvest celebrations together despite differences in cultures and times, i.e., most people use the occasion to give thanks for blessings. Share with students that Sukkoth reminds Jewish people of their escape from slavery in Egypt, an event of thanksgiving.

Request that students reflect upon their lives and traditions, select one source for thanksgiving, and express thanks in written form such as an essays, poem, or story. Encourage students to utilize all steps of the writing process.

Plan a time during which students may present as well as listen to real-life expressions of thanksgiving. Lead students to the understanding that people share more similarities than differences. In this case, most students in class share a common bond through the act of thanksgiving.

EVALUATION:

Determine the level of student understanding of Sukkoth as a celebration of thanksgiving by assessing the quality of responses, the enthusiasm for research as well as creative projects, and the degree of participation. Ask students to explain what they learned from the story and activities, then tell what, how, and why they learned. Encourage students to connect the message in the story to the theme of harvest and celebrations of thanksgiving.

CONNECTION #4:
Lee Bennett Hopkins.
"Merrily Comes Our Harvest"
in Poems for Thanksgiving

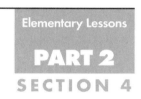

Teachers will welcome a resource of Thanksgiving poems that serves as an interdisciplinary vehicle for teaching the skills of rhyme, alliteration, and personification.

CHARACTER TRAITS: Review the nine character traits associated with this manual. Have students to check their definitions, share new insights, and provide different examples of each trait that they have discovered.

1. Read aloud one poem that illustrates important poetic elements essential for students to recognize and use. Ask students about what they enjoy most about the literary form of poetry (e.g., choice of words, sound of rhymes, patterns of words and phrases, mental pictures words create, or message).

Encourage poetry lovers to respond to the poem with personal reactions about why certain elements are particularly meaningful to them. Then encourage students who are less than enthusiastic about poetry to find at least one element in the poem that carries meaning for them.

2. Engage students in a discussion about the definitions of rhyme, alliteration, and personification. Cite several examples of each element so that students develop a working knowledge of the three elements and possess the skills to transfer the knowledge to other poetry.

Divide students into three groups. Ask each group to read the assigned poem for the purpose of determining the poet's message to the reader and to find examples of rhyme, alliteration, and personification. Each group will then present their poem with one student reading the poem to classmates, a second student expressing the poet's message to readers, and a third student identifying examples of rhyme, alliteration, and personification:

> *Group 1: "Thanksgiving" by Ivy O. Eastwick*
> *Group 2: "All in a Word" by Aileen Fisher*
> *Group 3: "I Like Fall" by Aileen Fisher*

Hint: Provide a mini-lesson to the three students who will read the poem to classmates. Help them with delivery techniques and suggestions for avoiding "sing-song" poetry reading.

3. Pass out lists of the nine core character traits to small groups. Emphasize the indicators under each trait. Remind students that indicators detail specific behaviors that are examples of a person demonstrating a general trait. Assign one trait to each group. Select sample poems from *Poems for Thanksgiving*; read each poem; ask groups to listen for examples of their trait; allow small groups to deliberate how the poem illustrates the trait; and then defend the group's reasoning to classmates.

Hint: For interest and variety, alternate discussions on character traits between the benefits of possessing the traits and the consequences of not possessing the traits.

EVALUATION:

Determine the level of student understanding of rhyme, alliteration, and personification by assessing the quality of responses, the enthusiasm for research as well as creative projects, and the degree of participation. Ask students to explain what they learned from the poems and activities, then tell what, how, and why they learned. Encourage students to connect the message in the poems to the theme of harvest and celebrations of thanksgiving.

CONNECTION #5:
Valerie Reddix. *Dragon Kite of the Autumn Moon*

By following the traditions of Kite's Day, an autumn celebration, Taiwanese believe that they may send worries soaring out of their lives. For this blessing, they are most thankful.

CHARACTER TRAITS: Review the nine character traits associated with this manual. Ask students to check their definitions, share new insights, and provide different examples of each trait that they have discovered.

1. Read *Dragon Kite of the Autumn Moon* aloud. Remember to set the stage with appropriate pre-reading activities that capture students' interest. For example, alert students that although most people recognize kite flying as a pleasurable recreation, many more obscure, fascinating details about the art of kite flying exist.

Ask for volunteers to research the following details: the origin of the word, kite; purposes of kites; materials used for construction of kites; types of kites; the scientific principles of flying a kite; and connections between kites and history such as the experiments of Benjamin Franklin and Alexander Graham Bell. Prior to reading the story, allow researchers to share new knowledge about kites with classmates.

Hint: Use a story map activity to place story events and characters in correct locations after reading the story and completing the activities.

2. Divide students into kite-building teams. Give teams the option of either building a model kite or preparing a large illustration of a kite. Alert students that they must also prepare an explanation of the kite including types, purposes, and hints for launching. After student explanations, ask students to apply their kite knowledge to the kite in the story: What is the type? What is the purpose? How does the kite connect to Taiwanese culture?

3. Review with students that many Taiwanese believe that worries may be launched out of their lives on high-flying kites. Challenge students to think about the Taiwanese custom, then contrast the kite flying with one way that most elementary students deal with worries, i.e., by identifying a problem and calling upon one or more of the core character traits to solve the problem. Use the comparison and contrast discussion as a writing prompt. Ask students to write an essay beginning, "Instead of flying a kite, I...." in which they identify and solve a problem. Invite students to share their writing.

EVALUATION:

Determine the level of student understanding of a Taiwanese custom and why members of the culture are thankful for kites by assessing the quality of responses, the enthusiasm for research as well as creative projects, and the degree of participation. Ask students to debrief the learning from the story and activities, then tell what, how, and why they learned. Encourage students to connect the message in the story to the theme of harvest and celebrations of thanksgiving.

Masquerade: Celebrations of Frolic and Fantasy

CONNECTION #1:
Barbara Diamond Goldin.
Cakes and Miracles

As a Jewish widow and her blind son prepare for the celebration of Purim, they unexpectedly find a miracle of their own.

CHARACTER TRAITS: Ask students to define the following words: compassion, courage, honesty, and integrity. Post their definitions in the room for easy viewing.

1. Read *Cakes and Miracles* aloud. Remember to set the stage with appropriate pre-reading activities that capture students' interest. Clarify vocabulary terms necessary for understanding both the text and the celebration.

For a second reading of the story, divide students into pairs and assign pairs the task of listening closely for clues about the celebration—Purim's origin, customs and traditions of merrymaking, and activities. Invite student partners to assist the teacher in completing a Purim web on butcher paper that tells a story of celebration. Invite a member of the Jewish faith to visit the classroom to elaborate on details as the teacher and/or students record them on the web, and to add information and insights on how Jewish people observe Purim in different parts of the United States.

Hint: Investigate how customs and traditions differ. Several sources indicate that customs are cultural practices while traditions are cultural practices passed down through generations. Other sources use the two terms interchangeably.

2. Give students a taste-and-sound flavor of Purim by sharing triangular-shaped cookies, Hamantashen, during the second reading of *Cakes and Miracles*. Allow students to design shapes for Purim cookies such as Hershel's birds, fish, and flowers on manila paper, then cut out shapes to use as a border for the Purim web. (Alternate Activity, Parental Discretion)

HAMANTASHEN

For dough you will need:
4 cups all-purpose flour
1 cup sugar
3 teaspoons baking powder
1/2 teaspoon salt
3 large eggs, beaten
4 tablespoons orange juice
1 cup margarine or butter,
softened to room temperature

For filling you will need:
3 ounces cream cheese,
2 teaspoons jam (any kind),
1/4 cup chopped nuts
Alternate filling: strawberry,
apricot, or purne preserves or
4-5 chocolate chips, or
peanut butter & jelly

Directions:

1. Preheat oven to 350 degrees. Grease two cookie sheets.

2. Using an electric mixer, cream the margarine and sugar together in a large bowl.

3. Add the eggs and orange juice. Mix well.

4. In a separate bowl, mix together the flour, baking powder, and salt. Add the flour mixture to the sugar and egg mixture. Mix together with a large spoon. If this mixture is too sticky, add a little more flour. (The dough will be easier to handle if refrigerated for an hour or more.)

5. Since the dough will be soft, sprinkle flour on the rolling pin and on a piece of waxed paper used to roll out the dough so it doesn't stick. Roll out the dough to 1/8"–1/4" thickness.

6. Find a round glass, mug, or cookie cutter with a rim about 2 1/2"–3" across. Flour the rim. Use it to cut the dough into circles.

7. Mix together the filling ingredients. Put about 3/4 of a teaspoon of filling in the center of each circle. Shape into triangles by bringing two sides of the circle up to the center and pinching them together. Then bring up the third side and pinch it to the other two sides. Be sure to pinch the dough firmly so the pastry will not open during the baking. Do not close the tops completely, so some filling will show in the center.

8. Place the hamantashen on the greased cookie sheets, about an inch apart. Bake for 10-12 minutes until lightly browned along the edges. Cool on wire racks. Makes about five dozen.

Tell students about the use of graggers (rattles) in association with the name of Haman, an evil advisor to the Persian King Ahasuerus. During the reading of the Purim story in the synagogue, people make sounds by twirling graggers, stamping their feet, and shouting "May his name be blotted out!" whenever the narrative mentions Haman's name.

Model steps in making brightly painted rattles called graggers. Show students how they may use tissue paper rolls filled with pebbles or beans for soft sounds or orange juice cans filled with pebbles or beans for louder sounds. Glue paper on the models and paint with fluorescent paint, then invite children to make rattles. When completed, encourage students to add products to the Purim display. (Alternate Activity, Parental Discretion)

Remind students that customs (e.g., serving Hamantashen cookies, making noisemakers, wearing costumes and masks) practiced within family circles and within religious or ethnic groups accompany most celebrations and may vary widely. Lead students in discussing other celebrations in which foods and objects play a special part.

3. Increase awareness of Hershel's accomplishments by engaging students in two sensory experiences. First, instruct students to keep their eyes closed while forming clay into animal shapes. Connect the task to how Hershel "saw" his work. Next, instruct students to keep their eyes closed while the teacher writes on the board or passes out manipulatives. Connect the task to how Hershel knew that Mama stoked the fire or kneaded the bread. Invite students to share reactions to doing tasks sightlessly.

   Ask: How do sightless experiences affect the way you feel about Hershel? How do sightless experiences affect the way you feel about physically challenged classmates? How does Hershel's courage change Mama's attitude between the beginning and the end of the story? What lessons may you learn from Hershel's courage?

4. Select one character trait (e.g., compassion, courage, honesty, or integrity) and talk about how characters in the story demonstrate the trait. Ask students to tell why they selected a character and how the character exemplifies the trait. Suggest that students think about their own lives and share examples that illustrate the trait.

   Hint: For interest and variety, alternate discussions on character traits between the benefits of possessing the traits and the consequences of not possessing the traits.

EVALUATION:

Determine the level of student understanding by observing creative and written products, by assessing their insights gained through simulated experiences, and by listening to class discussions. Ask students to explain what they learned from the lesson and activities. Encourage students to connect the message in the story to the theme of masquerade and celebrations of frolic and fantasy.

PART 3

CONNECTION #2:
Denise Burden-Patmon. *Carnival*

Rosa, a young girl from Trinidad, visits relatives in Brooklyn, New York. As a visitor far from her native land, she experiences loneliness until preparations for Carnival infuse a comforting taste of home. Glimpses of family relationships and cultural traditions as well as beautiful illustrations and actual photographs make the story an entertaining, informative resource.

CHARACTER TRAITS: Before reading the story, review the nine basic character traits with students and make sure they understand the meaning of each one. In your discussion, ask students to provide examples that demonstrate their understanding.

1. Introduce the story and characters by locating Trinidad and New York on a map, by finger-tracing the route, and by computing the distance between Rosa's and her relatives' homes. Remember to set the stage with other appropriate pre-reading activities that capture students' interest. Clarify vocabulary terms necessary for understanding both the text and the celebration. Define clearly the purpose for listening to the first reading of the story to page 6. Ask boys and girls as partners to listen for and record clues that describe Rosa's home in Trinidad and her relatives' home in Brooklyn, New York. Lead students in charting similarities and differences between the two locations, then talk about how and why the communities differ (e.g., climate, size, and population). **Hint:** Use the activity to reinforce two of the five themes in geography: location (Where is it?) and place (What is it like?).

2. Talk with students about how authors create believable, full-of-life characters. Share with students that authors paint images of characters with colorful words in a manner similar to the way that artists paint images of characters with colorful oils. Ask students what they know about Rosa's feelings after hearing only six pages of the story.

Ask students to recall the words and phrases that the author uses to make Rosa a real character. Show students how to fold a 12" x 18" sheet of manila paper in half. Encourage them to draw pictures on the left side of the paper that show Rosa's feelings at the beginning of the story. Finish reading the story, then ask students to draw pictures on the right side of the paper that show Rosa's feelings at the end of the story.

Ask: What events happen in the story that cause changes in Rosa's feelings? What are the signs visible in the pictures that show changes in Rosa's feelings? Are facial expressions and body language good clues about how people feel? Why or why not? Encourage students to share stories about how they read facial expressions and body language every day of their lives at school, at home, and in the neighborhood.

3. Enlist student assistance in setting up three centers: one for writing, one for music, and one for art. Allow students to choose one center to complete a project or to rotate through three centers to complete three projects. Focus activities in three centers by printing one set of the following instructions for each center:

Try to remember all of the fun activities of Carnival that Rosa enjoys. Jot notes on the ones that are most appealing. Write a make-believe story in which Rosa, her cousins, and class members participate in a full day of Carnival. Share stories with partners first, then with members of the class.

Create a steel band by making drums from coffee cans in different sizes. Use the plastic lids of the cans as drum tops. Paint cans and decorate with whimsical designs. **Hint:** Enlist the music teacher in finding music with a calypso beat. Encourage boys and girls to accompany calypso-taped music with rhythmic drum beats.

Make masks by drawing patterns on tag board, cutting out holes for eyes, painting the surface, and decorating with sequins and feathers.

Ask: How and why do writing stories, playing steel drums, and wearing masks help students learn and remember more? Declare a Carnival afternoon in which music center members lead all students in a march set by calypso beats, art center members wear masks, and writing center members share stories.

4. Select one character trait, and talk about how characters in the story demonstrate the trait. Ask students to tell why they selected a character and how the character exemplifies the trait. Suggest that students think about their own lives and share examples that illustrate the trait.

EVALUATION:

Determine the level of student understanding by assessing the quality of creative and written products and by evaluating the depth of thinking in compare-and-contrast, analysis, and synthesis activities. Encourage students to connect the message in the story to the theme of masquerade and celebrations of frolic and fantasy.

CONNECTION #3:
Suzanne M. Coil. *Mardi Gras!*

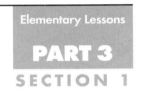

Elementary Lessons
PART 3
SECTION 1

Mardi Gras revelers lead readers through the historical background and established traditions of the popular celebration immediately preceding Lent.

CHARACTER TRAITS: Before reading the story, review the nine basic character traits with students and make sure they understand the meaning of each one. In your discussion, ask students to provide examples that demonstrate their understanding.

1. Read *Mardi Gras!* aloud. Remember to set the stage with appropriate pre-reading activities that capture students' interest. For example, invite students to finger-trace the route between their town and New Orleans, then ask them to compute the distance using the map's scale. Talk about the names and origins of the main cultural groups represented in New Orleans, then compare the diversity to the population of the students' community. Ask students if they know family members or friends who might share the Mardi Gras experience with classmates. If so, arrange for a classroom visit.

Clarify special vocabulary terms (e.g., doubloons, Comus, krewes) associated with the celebration. At a party favor shop, purchase plastic bead necklaces, preferably in the traditional colors of green, gold, and purple, so that children may see what people on parade floats throw to onlookers. In advance, tell children to listen closely to the second reading of the story so that they may gather ideas for a classroom Mardi Gras.

2. Lead students in a discussion focusing on why people celebrate Mardi Gras. Point out that the tradition dates back to ancient times when people held spring festivals to ensure the fertility of animals and crops. Alert students that over time the purpose of celebrations usually changes. **Ask:** Why do celebrations not stay the same? Why do people not observe celebrations in exactly the same ways generation after generation? **Hint:** Suggest to students that the needs, wants, beliefs, values, and locations of people change; therefore, their ways of celebrating change also.

3. Engage students in planning a classroom Mardi Gras celebration. Divide students into cooperative groups and assign the task: plan an authentic Mardi Gras celebration for the class involving the senses of seeing, hearing, tasting, smelling, and touching. (Alternate Activity)

Talk about the meaning of the word "authentic," and ask children to apply the term to their group plan. Also, take time for students to share organizational tips with one another (the overall theme, how they will plan for each of the five senses, what the unique features will be, how they will invite guests, how they will enlist needed help, what they will wear, how they will act, what entertainment they will have). (Alternate Activity)

Enlist the assistance of the media specialist to help students find information on the sights, sounds, tastes, smells, and touches of Mardi Gras. Alert students that they must be able to sell classmates on the idea that their plan does address all of the five senses and that therefore their plan obviously is the best one. Allow time for research, note taking, and collaboration. (Alternate Activity)

Talk with students about choosing a plan. Tell them that each group will have exactly three minutes to convince classmates that their plan is without question the best one. Announce that each student will vote for one plan by secret ballot. (Alternate Activity)

Hint: Make official ballots by listing groups by number, and then ask students to circle the group of their choice. Appoint election officials to collect and count votes, and then announce the winner. Publish the winning plan, assign tasks to students, and celebrate Mardi Gras. (Alternate Activity)

Hint: Celebrate Mardi Gras authentically. Encourage students to select projects of personal interest: making green, gold, and purple masks decorated with sequins, glitter, and feathers; planning a tasting party with red beans and rice and perhaps gumbo, jambalaya, or crawfish; listening to and playing music of jazz greats; planning the parade route, including crowd behavior, crowd control, and a cleanup crew; designing an attractive invitation; compiling a guest list. With each project, ask students to relate the project to the overall flavor of a New-Orleans-style Mardi Gras. (Alternate Activity)

Hint: Several of the tasks suggest input from community experts. Invite these individuals with special talents (e.g., chefs, jazz musicians) to join the celebration. Each of the projects involves an opportunity to research the cultural markers of Mardi Gras in New Orleans. Much cultural learning will take place if teachers set the quest for authenticity as the number one priority.

4. Plan a quiet time for students to reflect on the Mardi Gras experience from start to finish. Ask them to jot notes on the learning that they consider the most valuable and why. Request that they write their story on green, gold, or purple paper, share with classmates, and post stories in a New Orleans corner of the classroom. Students might enjoy decorating the corner with cutouts of ornamental iron patterns, Mardi Gras masks, and brightly colored tissue-paper flowers.

5. Select one character trait and talk about how people in the story demonstrate the trait. Ask students to tell why they selected a character and how the character exemplifies the trait. Suggest that students think about their own lives and share examples that illustrate the trait.

Hint: For interest and variety, alternate discussions on character traits between the benefits of possessing the traits and the consequences of not possessing the traits.

EVALUATION:

Determine the level of student understanding by assessing the quality of creative and written products, by observing the degree of cooperation and task commitment in a group setting, and by evaluating organizational skills. Encourage students to connect the message in the story to the theme of masquerade, celebrations of frolic and fantasy.

CONNECTION #4:
Arthur Dorros.
Tonight Is Carnaval

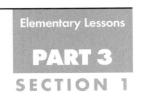

Preparing for Carnaval creates a high level of excitement for a South American family as well as for readers attracted by the festive, fun-loving spirit of celebration.

CHARACTER TRAITS: Emphasize the following traits: citizenship, diligence, and responsibility.

1. Read *Tonight Is Carnaval* aloud. Remember to set the stage with appropriate pre-reading activities that capture students' interest. Clarify English and Spanish vocabulary terms necessary for understanding both the text and the celebration. Define clearly a purpose for reading and/or listening. For example, set the purpose of reading *Tonight Is Carnaval* by asking student partners to listen for, look for, and jot notes on the following assigned topics:

> *Setting of the story;*
> *Names of the musical instruments used in Peru;*
> *Sounds words;*
> *List of preparations necessary for Carnaval; and*
> *Arpilleras used in the illustrations. (Arpilleras are wall hangings usually portraying scenes of day-to-day life, made from cut and sewn pieces of cloth. They are a popular art form especially in Chile, Peru, and Columbia. Some examples have small pockets sewn on the back to hold written stories of the scenes).*

2. Divide the class into cooperative groups. Assign each group a vegetable that story characters plant or a product they produce (e.g., potatoes, corn, onions, beans, wool). Ask students to web different products made from each item. Encourage group members to share the webs with the class, to ask for additions, and to post webs on the classroom wall for reference.

Invite students to sample vegetable bites, corn chips, or potato chips to remind them that what comes out of the ground or walks around on an animal's back often comes to the consumer in a totally different form. For example, ask students what mention the potato receives in the story and how the South American family uses the product. Then, ask students to recall a trip to a North American grocery store and how many forms of potatoes they saw. Lead students in working through the same process with corn, onions, beans, and/or wool.

Ask students to put on their thinking caps: Which group of people, South American or North American, tends to use products in a more natural way? What reasons might account for the difference in how consumers in two geographic areas use products? **Hint:** Mention ideas such as industrialization, food processing, transportation systems, higher incomes, greater demand for variety.

3. Check students' awareness of the names and sounds of musical instruments in the story. Share with students that playing simple musical instruments in the band provides relief and relaxation in villagers' work-filled lives. Invite student partners to compare and contrast Peruvian and American instruments (e.g., quena/flute; bombo/bass drum; charango/guitar; and zampoña/harmonica) and then to compare and contrast the roles that musical instruments play in people's lives. Remind students that sounds as well as decorations, colors, and parades are important parts of the Carnaval atmosphere.

Reread the story. Ask student partners to record sound words as they hear them during the reading. Encourage student partners to volunteer a sound word, and then demonstrate what sound it makes. Invite students to pantomime a Carnaval band with gestures and sounds.

Show students each illustration in the story. Ask students to look at the illustration for the purpose of finding people or objects that make sounds. Request that students imitate sounds appropriate for the persons or objects. Allow Spanish-speaking students to teach other students Carnaval greetings similar to what characters in the story might say. Transfer the use of sound words in the story to sound words in students' writing. Ask partners to brainstorm sound words that describe the celebration of Carnaval and to volunteer examples to the class. Ask students to describe Carnaval in one sentence that contains three sound words and share with classmates. Through open-ended questioning, lead students into making the conclusion that sound words improve students' writing.

Hint: Continue to reinforce the use of sound words as well as color words in students' writing and link them to specific characters or events in stories. Emphasize how much more real, interesting, and exciting sound and color words make authors' stories and students' writing.

4. Encourage students to create a scene similar to one that a bird flying high in the sky might observe in the Andes Mountains, the second highest mountain range in the world. Suggest that students locate and describe the Andes Mountains by using geographic clues on the classroom map. **Ask:** How high are the mountains? Are the mountains tree-covered? Are the mountains steep? What creatures might climb to the top? Send a team of researchers, the "Mountain Climbers," to the media center to seek answers to thought-provoking questions. Have students to report their findings to classmates.

Hint: Remind students that location (Where is it?) and place (What is it like?) are two of the five themes of geography: The other themes are interaction between people and environment, movement, and regions.

Model how to make a llama and an alpaca from construction paper. Gather the following materials: brown and white construction paper, scissors, glue, cotton balls, crayons or markers. Give each child a sheet of brown paper. Then instruct students to round the top edges into shapes of tall mountains. Next, ask students to draw a llama and an alpaca on white construction paper and cut them out. Finally demonstrate where to place the animals on the mountains.

Note: The alpaca and its beast-of-burden cousin, the llama, have made human life sustainable in the harsh reaches of the upper Andes by providing wool for clothing as well as milk and meat for consumption. To survive such inhospitable climatic conditions, the alpaca grows a thick coat of extremely fine, hollow-cored fleece. Alpacas are shorn once a year, with a yield of 6 to 12 pounds. The animal grows naturally in 22 distinct shades, and even in its finest counts, the fiber is stronger and more resilient than any other wool. Alpaca's one limitation, perhaps, is that it is even scarcer than cashmere. Once reserved for the use of Inca royalty, alpaca, because of its softness and exceptional warmth, was favored over cashmere in the courts of Queen Victoria.

Hint: Researchers will uncover some information that will affect the composition of the picture, i.e., can animals climb to the top and survive? Suggest that students cover alpacas with wool (cotton balls) and glue small bundles on llamas' backs. Make sure that students connect the project of constructing three-dimensional arpilleras to the illustrations of Andean daily life in the story.

As children complete the task and glue the animals at approximately correct elevations, talk about the uses and processing of alpacas' wool and also the function of small bundles on llamas' backs. Prompt students with the idea of small bundles by asking if the bundles give a clue about the relationship between llamas and people. Explore the topic and seek other examples of close relationships between animals and people (e.g., the buffalo and Native Americans).

Extension: Extend the art project by suggesting that students add people getting ready for Carnaval to the mountain scenes. Show them how native artists add three dimensions to their human and animal figures: modeling some methods and show them the illustrations again. **Hint:** Assemble a box of material scraps, felt, braids, beads, and yarn to make villagers in the arpilleras.

Invite students to participate in an "Isn't This Amazing?" discussion of what they learned from making one creative project, a scene in the Andes Mountains: Location? Place? Native people? Animals? Survival? Relationships?

5. Select one character trait (e.g., citizenship, diligence, or responsibility) and talk about how people in the story demonstrate the trait. Ask students to tell why they selected a character and how the character exemplifies the trait. Suggest that students think about their own lives and share examples that illustrate the trait.

Hint: For interest and variety, alternate discussions on character traits between the benefits of possessing the traits and the consequences of not possessing the traits.

EVALUATION:

Determine the level of student understanding by assessing the quality of creative and written products, by observing the degree of enthusiasm for group and research projects, and by listening to thoughts expressed in classroom discussions. Ask students to write a brief narrative explaining what they learned from this story. Encourage students to connect the message in the story to the theme of masquerade and celebrations of frolic and fantasy.

CONNECTION #5:
Myra Cohn Livingston.
Celebrations, "Halloween"

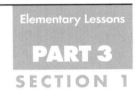

Elementary Lessons

PART 3

SECTION 1

Livingston highlights American holidays in a collection of short, lively poems. The favorites of curriculum writers become focal points for theme-related teaching episodes.

CHARACTER TRAIT: Review the meaning of responsibility and allow students to provide examples of responsible behavior.

Note: The authors urge teachers to invite parents to preview children's literature and instructional activities related to Halloween. If parents object to their child's participation in the activities, offer a theme-related option.

1. Introduce the celebration of Halloween by emphasizing strictly the fun aspects of imaginative play: costumes, masks, noisemakers, treats. Ask students to list familiar Halloween symbols (e.g., jack-o'-lanterns, ghosts, goblins, witches, broomsticks, black cats, skeletons, and spooky sounds). Lead students in practicing friendly spooky sounds, then invite boys and girls to record their choral version of sounds as one student dims the classroom lights. Explain to students that class members are creating an atmosphere for poetry just as sound and light engineers create atmospheres for radio and television shows. In a room dimly lighted with recorded sounds softly playing, read the poem, "Halloween."

Hint: Choose the verses most appropriate for elementary students. Invite students to write a poem about Halloween. Remind them about all of the Halloween symbols discussed, the poet's version of the holiday, and the effect of spooky sounds and dim lights. Set the guideline that student poems will focus on the fun aspects of celebrating imaginative play. Encourage students to join the teacher in the poet's circle and read their poems in an atmosphere created for Halloween. Lead students in clapping for each poet's performance. (Alternate Activity)

Extension: Extend the poetry project by allowing children time to illustrate and display their work in the classroom.

2. Write the words to the song, "The Farmer in the Dell," on the chalkboard. Encourage students to sing at least one verse to set the mood. Ask students to rewrite the song lyrics by substituting Halloween ideas. Lead students in brainstorming ideas, in trying out various words in the lines, then in deciding on new lyrics, and finally in singing the Halloween version of an old favorite with piano accompaniment. **Hint:** In advance, request that the music teacher assist by making a piano recording of "The Farmer in the Dell." (Alternate Activity)

   Ask: What thinking processes do you use when you write song lyrics? Why is it important for all students to regularly try new ways of thinking and learning?

3. Plan a contest to see who can design the best jack-o'-lantern on construction paper. Talk with students about the shapes of eyes, noses, and mouths conveying certain moods. Encourage students to design happy, playful, laughing jack-o'-lanterns. Give contestants an opportunity to sell the good points of their design to classmates, and then allow students to vote to determine the winner. (Alternate Activity)

   Carve the winning design on a pumpkin, then invite students to write a how-to plan for designing and carving a Halloween jack-o'-lantern. As students write their piece on pumpkin-shaped, orange paper, pass out roasted pumpkin seeds for a treat. Encourage students to share their how-to papers with a partner, then a small group. (Alternate Activity)

4. Provide each student with a small, orange paper pumpkin and a variety of materials such as felt, paint, sequins, beads, and construction paper. Instruct students to transform their pumpkins into some other Halloween symbol. Display transformations on a board entitled "Masquerade." **Ask** students to put on their thinking caps: Why is the title, "Masquerade," a correct one for a display of transformed pumpkins? (Alternate Activity)

5. Talk about the custom of trick-or-treating. Tell students that they are responsible for taking three five-year-olds who live in the neighborhood on a Halloween trick-or-treating walk. Assign partners the task of writing safety rules for the five-year-olds as well as for themselves. Encourage the sharing of these guidelines. Invite a security officer to visit the class and offer an expert opinion on the merits of students' guidelines. (Alternate Activity)

   Note: Change the holiday being discussed from Halloween to some other celebration and the neighborhood to the shopping mall, if there are objections to using Halloween. Assign partners the task of writing safety rules for the five-year-olds as well as for themselves. Encourage the sharing of these guidelines. Invite a security officer to visit the class and offer an expert opinion on the merits of students' guidelines.

   Ask: If one changes the time and the place, why do so many safety guidelines stay the same? Where does an elementary student learn basic safety guidelines? Do students need to watch out for themselves and for others? Why or why not? If a student alerts a friend about an unsafe practice on Halloween night or any other evening, what character trait(s) will he exhibit?

   Hint: For interest and variety, alternate discussions on character traits between the benefits of possessing the traits and the consequences of not possessing the traits.

EVALUATION:

Determine the level of student understanding by assessing creative and written products, by judging the level of maturity in safety guidelines, and by listening to responses in class discussions. Ask students to write a short story illustrating how someone displayed responsible behavior. Evaluate these stories for grammar, spelling, punctuation, and content. Encourage students to connect the message in the poem to the theme of masquerade and celebrations of frolic and fantasy.

CONNECTION #6:
George Ancona.
Pablo Remembers: The Fiesta of the Day of the Dead

During the three-day celebration of the Day of the Dead, a young Mexican boy and his family make elaborate preparations to honor the spirits of the dead. Readers gain valuable insights into the meaning of the celebration.

CHARACTER TRAITS: Focus on the following traits: diligence, respect, and responsibility.

1. Remember to set the stage with appropriate pre-reading activities that capture students' interest. For example, introduce the concept of a three-day celebration to honor the spirits of the dead. Explain to students that this celebration begins on October 31 (All Hallows' Eve, the eve of All Saints' Day, on which the angels of the young come to visit) and continues through November 1 (All Saints' Day, All Hallows', in honor of all saints) and November 2 (All Souls' Day, on which prayers are said for souls in Purgatory). Clarify other vocabulary terms necessary for understanding both the text and the celebration.

Read *Pablo Remembers, the Fiesta of the Day of the Dead* aloud. Ask students to listen closely for examples of each day's activities. Pass out large note cards on which student partners make three columns, "October 31," "November 1," and "November 2." Students will enter activities that they hear in the story in the correct column.

2. Place partners into cooperative groups. Instruct groups to use the information on the note cards and to discuss the activities for each of the three days: All Hallows Eve (All Hallow E'en), All Saints' Day, and All Souls' Day. Ask group members to summarize activities for each day and report findings to the large group. After the report of the first group, ask the second group if they have additions to any of the columns. Continue until all groups have an opportunity for input.

On a Venn diagram, use the data from groups to complete a compare-and-contrast picture of the three days of activities. **Ask:** How are the activities alike? How are they different? **Hint:** Lead students to the conclusion that this celebration focuses on more issues than fun, pranks, merrymaking, and masquerade. The Day of the Dead blends Halloween fun with homage to deceased family members.

Extend students' knowledge of the celebration by sharing articles, practices, and data:

Purchase pan de los muertos at a Mexican bakery and serve with cocoa and other traditional treats of the celebration; (Alternate Activity)

Remind students that family members place food at home altars for the spirits of deceased family members, then ask if leaving food for unseen guests is common in other celebrations; and

Show students pictures of skeletons, a customary symbol of the Day of the Dead; ask for assistance in identifying major bones of the body. **Hint:** *Seek a reference chart in a health book or encyclopedia, and then let students enjoy matching bones and practicing tongue-twisting words.*

3. Review Pablo's and his family's preparations for the celebration. Allow students to share times in which special preparations for a celebration or an occasion involved all family members. For the sharing session, suggest that students tell the name of the celebration or occasion, the time spent in preparation, the tasks of various family members, and the end result of family teamwork. After sharing, invite students to write about their family's team efforts to make a celebration or occasion special.

4. Select one character trait (e.g., diligence, respect, or responsibility) and talk about how people in the story demonstrate the trait. Ask students to tell why they selected a character and how the character exemplifies the trait. Suggest that students think about their own lives and share examples that illustrate the trait.

EVALUATION:

Determine the level of student understanding by assessing the quality of written products and by observing the degree of cooperation in group settings. Encourage students to connect the message in the story to the theme of masquerade and celebrations of frolic and fantasy.

CONNECTION #1:
Ian Wallace. *Chin Chiang and the Dragon's Dance*

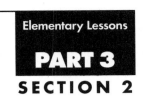

Dancing the dragon's dance with his grandfather is Chin Chiang's fondest wish. When the first day of the Year of the Dragon arrives, however, he fears that he will shame his family and bring bad luck to everyone.

CHARACTER TRAITS: Discuss the character traits of diligence, respect, and responsibility. Make sure students can define these traits as well as provide examples of each of them.

1. Read *Chin Chiang and the Dragon's Dance* aloud. **Hint:** Remember to set the stage with appropriate pre-reading activities that capture students' interest. Clarify vocabulary terms necessary for understanding both the text and the celebration. Define clearly a purpose for reading and/or listening, then read and discuss the story.

2. Invite students to volunteer for a research expedition. Set the location of the Chinese calendar as the objective of the expedition. Involve the school media specialist in the project so that he or she may reinforce media skills as students undertake a quest for the calendar.

Ask students to share the Chinese calendar with classmates. Make sure that students understand that various animals denote different years of birth. Ask the media specialist to help students research reasons why the Chinese chose particular animals. Search for clues such as whether or not these were the most familiar animals in China or whether or not they represented mythical figures in Chinese lore.

Allow partners to choose one of the animals on the calendar. Model for students how to make a basic lantern pattern, then encourage student partners to design lanterns decorated with symbols of their chosen animal. Ask students for assistance in displaying finished lanterns in the classroom. (Alternate Activity, Parental Discretion)

Make certain that students grasp the concept that each animal symbolizes certain years. Extend the discussion to the meaning of symbols in students' lives (e.g., patriotic symbols, traffic symbols, proofreading symbols, math symbols). Invite students to illustrate symbols on the chalkboard as they discuss various examples. **Ask** students to put on their thinking caps and talk about reasons why people throughout history have used symbols to communicate with other people.

3. Give student groups opportunities to do one of two art projects, either costumes or dances. For the costume group, provide colorful tissue paper and copy-paper boxes. Encourage these students to design and to decorate their own dragon costumes suitable for a Chinese parade. For the dance group, play Chinese music and ask students to choreograph a dragon dance that might accompany a Chinese parade, one in which a dragon accompanied by dancers weaves his way down a crowded street. Invite students to stage a Chinese parade in the classroom. (Alternate Activity, Parental Discretion)

Ask students to put on their thinking caps and talk about reasons why many people, children as well as adults, enjoy dressing up and becoming fictional characters for a short time.

4. Select the character traits of diligence, respect, and responsibility. Talk about appropriate indicators under each trait. Discuss how Chin Chiang demonstrates these traits and how students in their everyday lives may exhibit these same traits. Encourage students to share examples with classmates.

Hint: For interest and variety, alternate discussions on character traits between the benefits of possessing the traits and the consequences of not possessing the traits.

EVALUATION:

Determine the extent to which students understand the Chinese New Year celebration by assessing the quality of class discussions and of the level of student enthusiasm for participatory activities. Include teacher observations and rubrics in evaluating student progress. Encourage students to connect the message in the story to the theme of masquerade and celebrations of frolic and fantasy.

Elementary Lessons

PART 3
SECTION 2

CONNECTION #2:
Dakari Hru.
Joshua's Masai Mask

Fearing ridicule from classmates for playing a kalimba in the school's talent show, Joshua seeks assistance from Uncle Zambezi. By masquerading as a masked Masai, Joshua assumes different roles of interesting people. As a result of this experience, he learns to value his own identity more.

CHARACTER TRAITS: Discuss and give examples of the traits of respect, compassion, and responsibility.

1. Read *Joshua's Masai Mask* aloud. Remember to set the stage with appropriate pre-reading activities that capture students' interest. Clarify vocabulary terms necessary for understanding both the text and the celebration. Ask students to listen carefully for clues that define the relationship between Joshua and his family. After story reading, begin activities with a discussion of family relationships based on context clues.

2. Lead students in a discussion related to the characteristics of Masai masks. **Ask:** Are the masks painted with bright or dull colors? Are the masks elaborate or plain? Do the masks display similar or unique designs? After establishing parameters based on cultural accuracy, provide students with materials to make their own Masai masks. **Hint:** Materials might include paper plates, feathers, construction paper or tissue paper for feather making, crayons, and glue. **Hint:** Lead students to the understanding that masks or costuming temporarily change physical appearances, but that people retain their unique identities during periods of imaginative play.

Extension: Arrange a display for masks and encourage students to write about the design, color, and cultural accuracy of their masks. Request that they write this assignment on rectangular slips of brightly colored construction paper. Add descriptions to the mask display. Compare the exhibit of artifacts and of descriptions to children's experiences with displays in museums. **Ask:** Why are exhibits with both artifacts and descriptions more interesting, more exciting, more likely to produce learning than those with only one type of item to view?

3. Locate and play recorded kalimba music. Talk about the influence of geographic resources on the development of this African wood-and-metal instrument. Also talk about how the instrument's sounds and rhythms influence a style of dancing. Lead students to grasp the generalization that people's art forms (e.g., masks or dancing) reveal valuable clues to their cultures.

4. Connect *Joshua's Masai Mask* to *The Important Book* by Margaret Wise Brown. Through discussions about characters in both stories, move students toward the conclusion that each student possesses a unique identity. **Ask:** Why is this conclusion a cause for celebration?

5. Discuss the characters in the story and their exhibition of such traits as respect, compassion, and responsibility. Ask students to volunteer ways that they may exhibit these traits everyday in their classrooms, neighborhoods, or homes. Invite them to share examples.

EVALUATION:

Determine the level of student understanding of masquerade by assessing the quality of class discussions, writing samples, and connections among content disciplines. Include teacher observations and rubrics in evaluating student progress. Encourage students to connect the message in the story to the theme of masquerade, celebrations of frolic and fantasy.

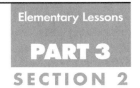

CONNECTION # 3:
Lee Bennett Hopkins.
Ragged Shadows: Poems of Halloween Night

Elementary Lessons

PART 3
SECTION 2

A collection of lively, playful poems portrays Halloween as one of children's favorite celebrations.

Note: The authors urge teachers to invite parents to preview children's literature and instructional activities related to Halloween. If parents object to their child's participation in the activities, offer a theme-related option.

CHARACTER TRAITS: Discuss and give examples of the nine character traits associated with this manual.

1. Read aloud selected poems from the collection in *Ragged Shadows*. Choose poems that paint a playful picture of Halloween. Remember to set the stage with appropriate pre-reading activities that capture students' interest. Clarify vocabulary terms necessary for understanding both the text and the celebration. Define clearly a purpose for reading and/or listening.

2. Request that students scan the illustrations in the collection and raise their hands quietly any time that they detect a character in the act of masquerading. Invite students to explain their interpretations of the pictures to classmates. Use this exercise to lead into a discussion of other times that people wear masks and pretend to be someone or something else. Use the exercise also to discuss purposes other than playful ones for using masks, i.e., to add protection (athletes), to hide identity (thieves).

Ask students to put on their thinking caps and reflect on the discussion. Review with students that purposes of masks differ because people choose to use masks for different reasons. Discuss the fact that most citizens accept some uses of masks and reject others based on personal codes of conduct. Lead students to understand the importance of making wise, informed decisions on every subject as individuals as well as members of groups. **Hint:** Request that students think about the discussion, decide on the most meaningful point to them, and tell classmates how they are going to remember and use the point in their lives.

3. Review with students the meaning of metaphors and similes. Read selected examples from poems in the collection that illustrate use of these literary forms. Start a description game on assorted, familiar subjects such as family pets or favorite relatives. Invite students to draw vivid word pictures through the use of metaphors and/or similes. Record examples as rapidly as possible on the chalkboard.

Pass out assorted general topics to partners, ask them to write colorful metaphors or similes describing the topics, and allow other students to guess the general topics from hearing only the metaphors or similes. **Ask:** What did students learn about the use of colorful words? How may the use of colorful words improve students' writing? Play this game again, but this time use the nine character traits. Ask students to write colorful metaphors or similes describing people they have observed who possess one of these traits.

Expand the lesson by talking about how words are as powerful a resource for writers as paints are for artists. Invite students to define an analogy by using the example of words and paints, then think up other analogies that extend the concept of powerful resources.

EVALUATION:

Determine the level of student understanding of masquerade by assessing student responses in class discussions, student enthusiasm for activities, and student ease or difficulty in the use of metaphors, similes, and analogies. Use teacher observations and rubrics in evaluating student progress. Encourage students to connect the message in the story to the theme of masquerade and celebrations of frolic and fantasy.

ADDITIONAL SELECTIONS:

Denise Burden-Patmon with Kathryn D. Jones. *Carnival.* In Brooklyn, Rosa celebrates Carnival, a traditional festival of her birthplace, Trinidad. Both geographic locations observe the celebration of Carnival in regionally distinct ways.

Steven Michael Harris. *This Is My Trunk.* From the perspective of an insider who earns his livelihood masquerading for the public, a circus clown provides the behind-the-scenes story of the demands as well as the rewards of continuous public performances.

CONNECTION #1:
Suzanne M. Coil. *Mardi Gras*

Coil assembles a basic Mardi Gras primer on the fanciful celebration's meaning, history, and customs. Readers will find the source entertaining as well as informative.

CHARACTER TRAITS: Review the nine character traits used in this manual and give examples of each of them. Ask students to provide other examples from their own experiences.

1. Read *Mardi Gras* aloud. Remember to set the stage with appropriate pre-reading activities that capture students' interest. For example, enlist a team of students who express special interest in the celebration of Mardi Gras to research the founding of New Orleans by Jean Baptiste le Moyne, Sieur de Bienville, in 1718, so that students connect the city's French heritage with the celebration of Mardi Gras.

Also, invite community members of different Christian faiths, Catholic and Protestant, to share with students how individual churches celebrate the time immediately prior to the beginning of the Lenten season. Make sure that students grasp the connection between and reasons for the merriment of Mardi Gras and the solemnity of Lent. **Ask:** How and why do classroom guests enrich your understanding of topics beyond the text of stories?

Prior to reading, introduce or clarify the celebration's specialized vocabulary (e.g., krewes and merrymakers). Define learning about the meaning, history, and customs of Mardi Gras as the primary purpose for the first reading.

2. Invite another class to join students in planning a Mardi Gras experience for the school. Allow students to choose project options from the following list, then group students into teams:

Research the styles and the themes of Mardi Gras floats in library resources, then design models for a miniature parade; enlist student assistance in bringing sequins, beads, braids, feathers, glitter, and felt scraps from home projects to add to classroom supplies; include brief descriptions of the krewes written on cards placed close to the models. (Alternate Activity)

Research the styles and the themes of Mardi Gras costumes in library resources, then plan a mural of life-size Mardi Gras characters decorated with sequins, beads, braids, feathers, glitter, laces, fabrics, and felt to greet visitors to Mardi Gras; include brief descriptions of the costumes written on cards placed close to the costumed figures. (Alternate Activity)

Investigate the music of New Orleans, including jazz and blues, that visitors encounter during the celebration, then research some of the musical "greats" and songs that earned them celebrity status; seek recordings of music to play during the celebration for authentic New Orleans flavor.

Design room decorations and Mardi Gras flags in the traditional colors of purple (justice), green (faith), and gold (power); place decorations in high-traffic areas of classrooms and hallways to announce the celebration. (Alternate Activity)

Write a series of brief, appealing promotional announcements to make on the public address system that spotlight the approach of Mardi Gras; focus announcements on the meaning, history, location, flavor, and merrymaking of the celebration. (Alternate Activity)

Search media center resources to locate other masquerade celebrations; seek the assistance of the media specialist; research these celebrations and highlight their similarities; post markers of the worldwide celebrations in appropriate locations on a world map.

Bake the King Cake recipe so that students and visitors may enjoy a bite of authentic Mardi Gras food. (Alternate Activity)

KING CAKE RECIPE

3 cups flour	1/4 cup warm water
1/4 cup margarine	4 teaspoons dry yeast
1 teaspoon salt	3/4 cup scalded milk
1/2 cup sugar	1 egg

Dissolve yeast in water. Add milk and sugar, salt, egg, margarine, and half of the flour. Mix until smooth. Add the rest of the flour and knead. Place in a greased bowl and cover. Allow it to rise. Divide the dough into three parts. Roll it into tubes and braid. Make a wide ring of the braid. Sprinkle with Mardi Gras colored sugar (purple, green, and gold). Insert a tiny plastic baby or bean for a prize. Bake at 375 degrees for 20 minutes. (Recipe from Social *Studies & the Young Learner*. November/December 1993).

Write a script to serve as a guideline for student presenters as they describe the Mardi Gras celebration for visitors; practice the script so that presenters will deliver the message in an informal, informative manner; plan a print walk to displays such as the model parade, mural, world map, and refreshment center.

Consider this fact: Today's population of New Orleans represents many diverse cultures. **Ask:** what effects will a celebration such as Mardi Gras produce with people of diverse cultural heritages? Can you think of a local celebration that produces the same effect on your community?

3. Ask students to reflect upon what traits enable them to stage a Mardi Gras celebration. Invite them to transfer the planning experience to other situations in their lives. Ask how and why the same character traits might assist them in meeting everyday challenges.

Hint: For interest and variety, alternate discussions on character traits between the benefits of possessing the traits and the consequences of not possessing the traits.

EVALUATION:

Determine the level of student understanding of Mardi Gras by evaluating the degree of individual and group cooperation, creativity, and enthusiasm exhibited at each stage of the celebration. Include teaacher observations and rubrics in evaluations. Encourage students to connect the message in the story to the theme of masquerade and celebrations of frolic and fantasy.

CONNECTION #2:
Brian Swann.
A Basket Full of White Eggs

Just as masks hide masqueraders, riddles hide answers. To unravel the puzzle in a riddle, readers must assume roles as word detectives and search for clues. Teachers and students will enjoy the challenge of riddles from around the world.

CHARACTER TRAITS: Review the nine character traits used in this manual and give examples of each of them. Ask students to provide other examples from their own experiences.

1. Read aloud the collection of riddles. Remember to set the stage with appropriate pre-reading activities that capture students' interest. For example, make students aware that the riddles reflect a wide variety of geographic locations and that they will assume responsibility for matching riddles and locations, then placing sticky notes labeled with the correct names of the countries on a classroom world map.

Clarify vocabulary terms necessary for understanding each riddle. Follow this pattern with each riddle: clarify vocabulary; read the riddle; identify geographic origin of the riddle; place labeled sticky note on map; then solve the riddle. Allow students to talk through clues that support their answers to the riddle. **Ask:** In addition to finding correct answers, what skills do group problem-solving exercises develop?

2. Use riddles as a basis for a geography review lesson. Reread each riddle, then ask for volunteers to cite an exact location and a relative location for the geographic home of the riddle. **Hint:** Remind students that the exact or absolute location of the riddle's home requires the use of longitude and latitude while relative location states the riddle's home in relationship to another place.

Reread selected riddles for students to identify either cultural or environmental clues that connect the riddle to a specific country. For example, practice with students on logical connections between riddles and countries, such as the link between shamrocks and Ireland, that might be woven into the riddles.

Extension: Extend the review lesson by talking about another geographic concept, cultural diffusion or cultural borrowing, i.e., whenever people move from one location to another, they spread their culture to groups with whom they have contact. Thus, locating precise geographic homes of riddles becomes more complex if members of the culture emigrated to new lands. Explain to students that they may identify geographic homes of riddles as long as they understand that riddles travel with the rest of culture when people move from one place to another. **Ask:** How does the practice of skills such as identifying and locating items in context help you learn?

3. Divide students into groups, then encourage them to write one riddle that contains cultural and/or environmental clues to one particular geographic area. Remind them to first choose the area, identify the clues they wish to spotlight, weave the clues into a riddle, and then challenge classmates to solve the riddle. **Hint:** Ask students to show classmates how their word clues serve the same purposes for riddles as masks serve for masqueraders.

4. Ask students to reflect on what traits enable them to confront the task of unraveling riddles and seeking defensible answers. Ask students to transfer the problem-solving exercise to other situations in their lives. Invite students to tell how specific character traits might assist them in meeting everyday challenges.

Hint: For interest and variety, alternate discussions on character traits between the benefits of possessing the traits and the consequences of not possessing the traits.

EVALUATION:

Determine the level of student understanding of riddles and how riddles connect to the theme of masquerade by assessing the depth of responses to thinking questions and by evaluating the degree of creativity in writing riddles that mask geographic concepts. Include both observations and rubrics in evaluations. Encourage students to connect the message in the riddles to the theme of masquerade, celebrations of frolic and fantasy.

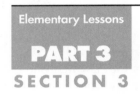

CONNECTION #3:
Phyllis Shalant. *Look What We've Brought You from Mexico:* Crafts, Games, Recipes, Stories, and Other Cultural Activities from Mexican-Americans

Teachers and students will visit and revisit this resource of crafts, recipes, activities, and stories. The source serves as a ready reference for creative activities that challenge students.

CHARACTER TRAITS: Review the nine character traits used in this manual and give examples of each of them. Ask students to provide other examples from their own experiences.

1. Show students different sections of the reference so that they are aware that they may use it to seek quick, specialized information. Give students a sampling of games, riddles, stories, words, and activities by scanning these pages in the reference.

Prepare slips of paper labeled with the names of the various activities in the reference, and then allow small groups of students to draw one slip that determines the activity of the group. **Examples:** legend of Quetzalcoatl, sea serpent game, legacies of the Aztecs and Mayans, writing in glyphs, and architecture.

Reproduce copies of the sections that students need to understand, present, and model their research topic for classmates. Encourage them to seek information in other references and prepare visuals to accompany reports on Mexico. Assemble materials necessary for making crafts such as sea serpents or Aztec masks. Allow time for research, deliberation within student groups, construction of crafts or design of visuals, and preparation of reports.

Hint: Remind students of the importance of using presentation skills that hold the interest of audience members. Suggest that students practice the report first with small groups before class presentations.

Hint: Talk with students about basic criteria for studying a group of people in any time in history. Review with them that the completed study based on *Look What We've Brought You from Mexico* mainly deals with cultural aspects and legacies left by past people for future generations.

Point out to students that a thorough study of people will also include the way they govern themselves; the way they earn a living; the way they relate to other people within and outside their culture; and the way they answer life's universal questions, i.e., belief systems. Share with students that writers organize most social studies texts and curricula around these topics.

2. Ask students to reflect on what traits enable them to complete individual and group tasks related to *Look What We've Brought You from Mexico*. Invite students to respond to how they may use the same character traits in meeting other challenges in their everyday lives.

EVALUATION:

Determine the level of student understanding of the cultural history of Mexico by observing their enthusiasm, cooperation, and task commitment within group settings and by evaluating individual contributions in public presentations. Encourage students to connect the message in the resource to the theme of masquerade and celebrations of frolic and fantasy.

CONNECTION #4:
Lulu Delacre.
Vejigante Masquerader

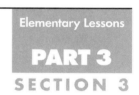

Elementary Lessons

PART 3

SECTION 3

In Puerto Rico, the vejigantes of Ponce enjoy masquerading for the entire month of February. As readers follow the story of a young boy's desire to join the vejigantes, they gain insights into Puerto Rican as well as Spanish and Latin American masquerade celebrations.

CHARACTER TRAITS: Review the nine character traits used in this manual and give examples of each of them. Ask students to provide other examples from their own experiences.

1. Read *Vejigante Masquerader* aloud. Remember to set the stage with appropriate pre-reading activities that capture students' interest. For example, establish the geographic setting of Puerto Rico, including location (Where is it?), place (What is it like?), and culture (Who lives there?).

Spend time developing the meaning of vocabulary critical to understanding the story such as the words vejigante masqueraders and carnaval. Invite students to share their carnival experiences with the class.

Look for common characteristics of carnavals that cross geographic lines. **Ask:**

> *Do carnavals focus on merrymaking?*
> *Do people dress in costumes and masks?*
> *Do music and decorations play a part in the celebration?*
> *Do the carnavals occur year after year?*
> *Do carnavals seem to unite people of several cultures in the common cause of celebration?*
> *Use student answers to the questions as criteria for investigating the carnaval in* Vejigante Masquerader.

2. Assign students to one of the following three topics or allow them to choose one special interest topic out of the three options. Explain to students that their research and presentations will increase all students' knowledge of carnavals. Build excitement about the options by reading the

CHARACTER EDUCATION THROUGH STORY

329

descriptions and by asking for students' ideas about how they might enhance each project and/or how they might increase each project's usefulness:

Search for the English/Spanish cognates (words that share the same root) in the story as the basis for making an illustrated class bilingual dictionary; assume responsibility for adding words to the dictionary as students read new literary sources.

Research the 15th- and 16th-century Spanish explorers who linked the New and Old Worlds; trace their routes on a classroom wall map and share with classmates the cultural changes brought to the island culture by Europeans, i.e., language, religion, names, customs.

Investigate global locations of carnaval celebrations; make balloon markers from brightly colored construction paper to attach to the classroom wall map; label the balloon markers with names and dates of the celebrations.

Allow time for students to complete the following tasks:

> *Talk about information found through research;*
> *Plan interesting presentations that use visuals, maps, and/or props appropriately; and*
> *Practice presentations with members of small groups before making presentations to entire class.*

> **Hint:** *Remind students that finding information is not the final step in research. Explain that using and communicating information are equally important parts of the research process.*

Following the presentations on each topic, lead students in drawing conclusions about the importance of the topic. Assist students in the process by asking them to reflect on this question: What difference does this make in the course of history? So what?

3. What character traits do the vejigante masqueraders exhibit in the story?. Ask students to identify and to cite an example for each trait. Invite students to transfer the situation to their own lives by asking how and why one or more of the character traits might assist them in meeting everyday challenges.

Hint: For interest and variety, alternate discussions on character traits between the benefits of possessing the traits and the consequences of not possessing the traits.

EVALUATION:

Determine the level of student understanding of Puerto Rico, the vejigantes, and carnaval by assessing the degree of cooperation, enthusiasm, and task commitment within group settings and by evaluating the quality of public presentations. Include teacher observations and rubrics in evaluations. In groups of three to five, have students list five things they learned in this lesson and be prepared to share their list with the class. Encourage students to connect the message in the story to the theme of masquerade and celebrations of frolic and fantasy.

CONNECTION #1:
Barbara Diamond Goldin.
Cakes and Miracles:
A Purim Tale

Youth and blindness do not discourage Hershel who yearns to assist his mother with preparations for the Jewish holiday of Purim. Fortunately, he discovers how to use a talent that earns his mother's appreciation.

CHARACTER TRAITS: Review the nine character traits associated with this manual. Ask students to check their definitions, share new insights, and provide different examples of each trait that they have discovered.

1. Read *Cakes and Miracles* aloud. Remember to set the stage with appropriate pre-reading activities that capture students' interest. For example, provide a brief background to the celebration of Purim: who and what the celebration honors and also the geographic and chronological setting of the celebration's origin.

Develop understanding of vocabulary essential to either the story or the activities such as miracles and parodies. Set making a connection between the celebration of Purim and the theme of masquerade as the purpose for reading. After reading the story, ask students to connect the story and the theme. Ask students to respond to the nature of the miracle in the story.

Hint: Use a story map activity to place story events and characters in correct locations after reading the story and completing the activities.

2. Lead all students in developing criteria to apply to any celebration. Examples include the following:

Place of origin;

Reason for celebrating;

Participants;

Features such as special dress, foods,

Colors,

Ceremonies, and

Gift giving.

Allow students in small groups to make choices among the following activities to demonstrate their understanding of Purim:

Analyze the celebration of Purim by using criteria developed by all students, then show classmates how they may use the same criteria to analyze other celebrations.

Plan and present in skit form the story of Esther as the origin of the celebration.

Research the term, parody, and show how the celebration is a parody on Haman; construct a noise-maker and demonstrate how, when, and why participants use noisemakers in the Purim celebration.

Investigate and report on the origin of Purim treats such as Hamantashen, then prepare samples for students to enjoy during Purim presentations.

Hint: Allow adequate time for researching, planning, and baking so that presentations exhibit quality work.

3. Talk about Hershel's desire to help his mother in the preparations for Purim, then transfer the discussion topic to the world of the elementary student in your community. Lead students in brainstorming ways that they may assist classmates, family members, neighbors, and/or community agencies. **Hint:** Stress that assistance comes in all forms but must be done willingly and without the expectation of receiving pay. Ask each student to select one person to help in some way, to perform the deed, and to share with classmates the rewards of volunteering assistance.

Extension: Extend the activity by requesting students to ask adults who assist others what their reasons for volunteering are and what their rewards are. **Hint:** Encourage students to find articles in the newspaper about volunteers in their community. What volunteer services do they perform? What is their reward? **Ask:** Are their reasons for offering assistance to others similar or different? Why?

Following the discussion, lead students in analyzing how the various acts of assistance demonstrate one or more character traits and why.

EVALUATION:

Determine the level of student understanding of Purim by assessing the quality of responses, the enthusiasm for service-oriented and creative projects, and the degree of participation. Ask students to explain what they learned from the story and activities, then tell what, how, and why they learned. Encourage students to connect the message in the story to the theme of masquerade and celebrations of frolic and fantasy.

ADDITIONAL SELECTIONS:

Miriam Chaikin. *Make Noise, Make Merry: The Story and Meaning of Purim*

Miriam Chaikin. *Menorahs, Mezuzas, and Other Jewish Symbols*

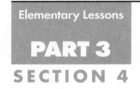

Elementary Lessons

PART 3

SECTION 4

CONNECTION #2:
Kathleen Krull. *Maria Molina and the Days of the Dead*

Throughout Mexico and in many Latin American countries, families celebrate Los Días de los Muertos as a special time to honor all of their deceased relatives. Important as a national holiday and also as a religious fiesta, Los Días de los Muertos unites families through the act of paying respects to their ancestors. Maria, a child, learns the true meaning of the celebration.

Note: The writers urge teachers to invite parents to preview children's literature and instructional activities related to Halloween and Los Días de los Muertos. If parents object to their child's participation in the activities, offer a theme-related option.

CHARACTER TRAITS: Review the nine character traits associated with this manual. Ask students to check their definitions, share new insights, and provide different examples of each trait that they have discovered.

1. Read *Maria Molina and the Days of the Dead* aloud. Remember to set the stage with appropriate pre-reading activities that capture students' interest. For example, introduce new vocabulary essential to the understanding of the story. Set finding the meaning of new vocabulary words as the purpose for listening.

   Hint: Write a passage from the story on the overhead that includes unfamiliar vocabulary. Read the passage and ask students to think of four or five substitute words. Write substitute words above the vocabulary word. Do this with the entire list of words. After the story reading, return to the first passage and ask students to decide on the best substitute word, circle it, and discuss why they chose the word. Request that students cite the context clues that lead them to the correct definitions. Complete the rest of the passages in this manner.

   VOCABULARY WORDS:

abuela:	grandmother
Los Días de los Muertos:	the Days of the Dead
angelitos:	little ones
calavera de azúcar:	sugar-candy skull
Pan de los Muertos:	bread of the dead
garbanzo:	kind of bean
el baile de los esqueletos:	the dance of the skeletons
ofrenda:	altar (offering)

2. Explain to students that they may choose how to demonstrate their understanding of Los Días de los Muertos. Ask students to listen to the following activities; to select one that holds high interest for them; and to work individually, with a partner, or in a small group to complete the project:

   Review the story about how Maria shows concern for the spirits of relatives left in Mexico, how the family soothes her concerns, and how she comes to the realization of the celebration's true meaning. Share these thoughts with classmates through a skit, then quiz them about their understanding of the author's message, the true meaning of the celebration. (Alternate Activity)

   Develop criteria for researching any celebration, and then investigate Los Días de los Muertos and Halloween. Prepare a Venn diagram on a transparency that shows the similarities and differences between the two celebrations. (Alternate Activity, Parental Discretion)

   Create a story about fun-loving spirits whose relatives forget them during Los Días de los Muertos. In the story, engage the spirits in playing tricks upon their family members. Read the story in a darkened classroom and challenge classmates to write and share stories of forgotten spirits. Alert classmates that the only stories permitted are the type with fun-loving, kindly, playful spirits. Pin finished stories to happy-spirited esqueletos similar to those pictured in the story. (Alternate Activity)

   Hint: Allow time for students to research and plan quality presentations. Ask for volunteers to bake the recipe for Pan de los Muertos listed at the back of the story and to serve the treat on the day of presentations.

3. Share a time in which the teacher encountered an unfamiliar cultural tradition. Tell students how much respect the teacher demonstrated and how much learning the teacher acquired through the encounter. Summarize the story by sharing how the experience broadened the teacher's knowledge. Demonstrate how this discussion might serve as a writing prompt, and then model a written response to an encounter with an unfamiliar cultural tradition on a transparency.

   Invite students to write to the same prompt and share their writing within small groups. Ask students to extend the small group discussions by analyzing stories of classmates and deciding if authors use one or more character traits in their encounters with unfamiliar cultural traditions.

Hint: For interest and variety, alternate discussions on character traits between the benefits of possessing the traits and the consequences of not possessing the traits.

EVALUATION:

Determine the level of student understanding of *Los Días de los Muertos* by assessing the quality of responses, the enthusiasm for research and creative projects, and the degree of participation. Ask students to explain what they learned from the story and activities, then tell what, how, and why they learned. Encourage students to connect the message in the story to the theme of masquerade and celebrations of frolic and fantasy.

ADDITIONAL SELECTION:

Jeanne M. Lee. *Bà-Nam*

Elementary Lessons

PART 3

SECTION 4

CONNECTION #3:
Kit Williams. *Masquerade*

Williams creatively explores masquerade through the themes of love, adventure, and fortune. Especially intriguing are the hares hidden in each illustration. Riddles play the role of word masks challenging readers to unmask their answers.

CHARACTER TRAITS: Review the nine character traits associated with this manual. Ask students to check their definitions, share new insights, and provide different examples of each trait that they have discovered.

1. Read the story aloud. Remember to set the stage with appropriate pre-reading activities that capture students' interest. For example, involve students in a discussion about the character traits of honesty and compassion. Use the indicators under each trait, then invite students to think up examples that illustrate any of the indicators.

Hint: For interest and variety, alternate discussions on character traits between the benefits of possessing the traits and the consequences of not possessing the traits. Talk about situations that might cause people to soften or mask a totally honest statement in order to avoid hurting another person's feelings. **Example:** Instead of saying, "Your hair is a wreck," a person mindful of the effect of harsh words might say, "Humidity causes everyone's hair to frizzle." Point out that the second statement is not dishonest; instead, the statement shows compassion for a person's feelings. Remind students about the role that good judgment plays in relationships with others.

Allow students (or groups) to think about and share comparable examples of how people soften or mask brutally honest statements that may hurt other people's feelings. Extend the discussion by explaining how the exercise exemplifies the meaning of diplomacy as the use of tact or skill in people-to-people or nation-to-nation relationships. Set finding words as masks as the purpose for listening to the story. Discuss word masks after reading the story.

Extension: Extend learning by inviting students to write riddles for their classmates to solve or unmask.

2. Ask students to bring small hand mirrors to class to assist them in drawing self-portraits. Suggest that students sketch outlines of the head and shoulders, then fill in features such as hair and eyes with accurate colors. When students finish, ask that they put three adjectives under their self-portrait that describe their personality. **Examples:** sunny, fun loving, studious, happy, and cheerful. **Hint:** Alert students that they may use only words that convey positive thoughts.

Pair students and allow them to share self-portraits. Instruct them to tell their partner about the adjectives chosen; if the partner agrees, ask the partner to draw a star by the adjective. If the partner wants to enter one or more adjectives to the self-portrait, allow them to add adjectives to the list. **Hint:** Remind students that they may use only words that convey positive thoughts.

Ask:

Do differences exist between the artist's list of adjectives and the observer's list of adjectives? Why might differences exist?

How does the activity add to students' understanding that sometimes words act as masks?

How does the activity relate to the story?

EVALUATION:

Determine the level of student understanding of the multiple dimensions of masquerade by assessing the quality of responses, the enthusiasm for research as well as creative projects, and the degree of participation. Ask students to explain what they have learned from the story and activities, then tell what, how, and why they learned. Encourage students to connect the message in the story to the theme of masquerade and celebrations of frolic and fantasy.

NOTE: In the masquerade sections of other grade levels, curriculum writers include Halloween stories. They urge teachers to invite parents to preview children's literature and instructional activities related to this specific celebration. If parents object to their child's participation in the activities, offer a theme-related option.

4 Festivals of Light: Celebrations of Illumination

CONNECTION #1:
Brett Harvey.
My Prairie Christmas

Weaving an optimistic message through a piece of historical fiction, Harvey fascinates readers with a beautiful account of new beginnings and eternal hope.

CHARACTER TRAITS: In this lesson, give attention to the traits of courage and compassion.

1. Remember to set the stage with appropriate pre-reading activities that capture students' interest. For example, introduce the story by studying the pictures, then by predicting both the place and the time of the setting. Introduce the characters in the story and their main concerns. For example, one main character, Rabbit, worries that no cranberries growing on the prairie means no decorations for the Christmas tree. Use Rabbit's worry to predict what decorations the family will use. Ask students to remember their predictions on the setting and on the decorations as they listen to the story.

Hint: After reading the story and discussing similes in the next exercise, allow students to share their predictions in a "I knew it all the time" discussion. Tell them that lucky guessing is not good enough. Students must use clues from the story to back up their predictions.

Extension: Review students on the meaning of a simile. Read *My Prairie Christmas* aloud. and ask student partners to record each simile that they hear. Talk about student examples. Invite students to share all notes on similes and point out what makes each phrase a simile. Examples of similes might include the following:

> *We put Billy in a sling like an Indian baby.*
> *Ice crystals looked like diamonds.*
> *Snow coming down so hard it looked like a white curtain.*
> *Millions of stars twinkled like tiny diamonds.*

Ask: How will the use of similes make our writing more exciting?

2. Tell students that they will take a test to measure how closely they listen and how well they match a character with the plot of the story. Hand four students one slip of paper with one of the following written quotations. Ask that they read the words with feeling and then call on one of their classmates to identify the character and the scene in which the character said the words:

> *"We'd better get started making our decorations or we won't have anything to put on our tree."* (Mama)
> *"Come on, Rabbit, let's have a look at the stars."* (Papa)
> *"Do you really think Papa will be here?"* (Rabbit)
> *"Mama, I can't see anything out the window."* (Marjorie)

Ask: Are the characters' lines critical to the development of the story? Are the characters' lines a way of predicting what will happen later in the story? Why or why not?

3. Present a mini-lesson on cause-and-effect relationships. Solicit everyday examples from students and then ask them to apply their knowledge to the storyline:

> *The days had turned cold and dark, so…*
> *They had to leave their Christmas ornaments in Maine, so…*
> *There were no turkeys on the prairie, so…*

Aunt Addie sent sacks of wheat flour and sugar, so...

There was no store and very little money to buy Christmas gifts, so...

Ask: How do cause-and-effect statements help readers understand the story? **Hint:** Cause-and-effect statements bring sense and setting to the story in a short amount of time. Because of the information that these statements provide to readers, readers can then concentrate on the main storyline.

4. Excite students about creating a prairie Christmas in the classroom. Tell students the story of how the evergreen tree as part of the Christmas celebration originated in Germany, spread to England, and came to America with immigrants who longed for a taste of home in their new country. Share with students that much of the richness of American culture stems from what immigrants brought and are still bringing to their new land from the old countries.

Hint: Tell children that they are mature enough to learn a concept, cultural borrowing, which teachers usually reserve for upper elementary grades. The term simply means one culture borrows the best of what another culture offers and absorbs it into their own culture. Thus, many Americans enjoy the German tradition of the Christmas tree.

Alternate Activities:

Lead students in brainstorming how they might create a prairie Christmas in the classroom. Once students decide on projects, seek their assistance in setting up centers to create the products. Use student suggestions or some of the following suggestions based on the story:

Construct popcorn garlands and/or cornhusk ornaments for a small evergreen tree or bulletin board. **Ask:** Why are these materials used for decorations?

Find a recipe and pattern for gingerbread men. Either bake the gingerbread men or draw them on brown construction paper and decorate, then hang on the tree or bulletin board. **Ask:** What characteristic do the gingerbread men share with popcorn garlands and cornhusk ornaments?

Assume the role of a boy or girl living on the prairie who wants to make a special gift for someone. Select a person and a gift to make, then make a decorated picture of the item and hang it on the tree or the bulletin board. **Ask:** What role do available resources play in the choice of gifts to make?

Write a friendly letter to a cousin in Maine on golden paper shaped like a cornhusk doll and explain exactly how to make the doll. Use at least one simile about life on the prairie in the letter. Hang letters on the tree or the bulletin board. **Hint:** Review the guidelines for writing a friendly letter.

Invite students to gather around the display to admire the classroom prairie Christmas. Encourage children to listen again to the story for new insights resulting from a simulated prairie Christmas. Welcome their comments about what they learn through active involvement in participatory activities.

5. Select one character trait (courage or compassion) and talk about how characters in the story demonstrate the trait. Ask students to tell why they selected a character and how the character exemplifies the trait. Suggest that students think about their own lives and share examples that illustrate the trait.

Hint: For interest and variety, alternate discussions on character traits between the benefits of possessing the traits and the consequences of not possessing the traits.

EVALUATION:

Determine the level of student understanding by assessing the quality of creative and written products, by observing the degree of enthusiasm for and cooperation in simulation experiences, and by listening to the depth of responses to thought-provoking questions. Ask students to provide definitions and examples of courage and compassion. Encourage students to connect the message in the story to the theme of festivals of light and celebrations of illumination.

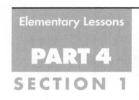

CONNECTION #2:
Eric Kimmel. *Hershel and the Hanukkah Goblins*

Wicked goblins frighten villagers of Ostropol to the degree that they no longer celebrate Hanukkah. Hershel decides to confront the problem directly by devising ingenious plans to outwit the goblins. Once Hershel breaks the goblins' stranglehold on the village, the spirit of Hanukkah triumphs again.

CHARACTER TRAITS: Review the following character traits before beginning the lesson: courage, diligence, and citizenship

Note: The authors searched for cultural celebrations in which light represents a central focus. In order to develop the theme, they highlighted major as well as minor celebrations in various racial, ethnic, and religious contexts. The authors feel that children need to understand that various traditions regard some celebrations as more important than others. For example, many people in the Jewish community in America emphasize the importance of Hanukkah to a greater degree than do those in the Jewish community in Israel. The writers urge teachers to make children aware that not all celebrations are equal in importance or celebrated in the same manner around the world. Teachers are therefore critical in helping students learn sensitivity toward others' traditions, celebrations, and beliefs.

1. Remember to set the stage with appropriate pre-reading activities that capture students' interest. Build background knowledge by summarizing the author's note on Hanukkah, a celebration of freedom of the Jewish people from Syrian rule. Make sure that children understand that the story takes place in a time long ago (two thousand years ago) and in a place far away (Palestine, now Israel). Use the wall map to show the geographic relationship between present-day Israel and the United States. Make sure also that children understand why the author calls the burning of oil for eight days in the menorah a miracle.

Clarify vocabulary terms necessary for understanding both the text and the celebration. Request that student partners listen carefully for traditions of Hanukkah. **Hint:** Alert students that the author does not present traditions in one neat list but rather weaves them into the story as clues to the celebration (e.g., brightly burning candles, merry songs, spinning dreidels, plates of potato latkes). Read *Hershel and the Hanukkah Goblins* aloud.

Review the meaning of symbols. Mention that at other times students have learned that a symbol stands for something else, i.e., the American flag stands for the loyalty and unity of all Americans. **Ask:** What does Hershel's victory over the goblins stand for? **Hint:** Hershel's victory over the goblins wins freedom for the villagers to celebrate Hanukkah and symbolizes the Jewish people's victory over the Syrians that meant freedom for Jews in Palestine (present-day Israel).

2. Enlist the assistance of boys and girls in planning a Hershel-of-Ostropol afternoon in which children experience the flavor of Hanukkah through active participation in personally chosen activities. Allow students to choose two of the following centers:

Invite one or more members of the Jewish community to share Hanukkah stories with children. Ask guests to tell students about the origins of Hanukkah and how Jewish people celebrate it today, and then let children tell the guest the story of Hershel. In the story center, let guests and students find similarities and differences between the authentic and fictional accounts of Hanukkah.

Assist students in cooking latkes (potato pancakes), then topping them with jam, applesauce, or sour cream. Serve latkes to all center participants. (Alternate Activity, Parental Discretion)

Enlist students in setting up a center for getting the best of the goblins. Allow students to choose one of the goblins in the story, illustrate the goblin on a tri-folded piece of 9" x 12" manila paper (head on one-third, body on one-third, legs and feet on one-third), fold the goblin up in thirds, and write on the outside how to out-goblin the goblin and restore the happy spirit of Hanukkah. (Alternate Activity)

Encourage students to learn how to play the dreidel game. The author, Eric A. Kimmel, shares this information about the dreidel:

> ... a square-shaped top. It has one of the Hebrew letters "nun," "gimel," "hay," and "shin" on each of its four sides. The letters stand for the words "Nes Gadol Haya Sham"—"A Great Miracle Happened There." The dreidel game is played with nuts, raisins or pennies. Everyone puts "a piece" in the center of the table or floor, and then one player spins the dreidel. If "nun" comes up, the spinner gets nothing; "gimel," the spinner takes the pot; "hay," the spinner takes half; "shin," the spinner adds a nut to the center. These are the usual rules.

> Hint: Hershel makes his own rules to outwit the goblins. (Alternate Activity, Parental Discretion)

At the end of the afternoon, assemble boys and girls into a large group. **Ask:** How do classroom guests help you learn about a subject? Why does participation in any activity help students learn about a subject?

3. Select one character trait (e.g., courage, diligence, or citizenship) and talk about how people in the story demonstrate the trait. Ask students to tell why they selected a character and how the character exemplifies the trait. Suggest that students think about their own lives and share examples that illustrate the trait.

Hint: For interest and variety, alternate discussions on character traits between the presence and benefits of possessing the traits and the absence and consequences of not possessing the traits.

EVALUATION:

Determine the level of student understanding by assessing the quality of creative and written products, by observing the degree of enthusiasm for participatory activities, and by listening to the depth in answers to thought-provoking questions. Encourage students to connect the message in the story to the theme of festivals of light and celebrations of illumination.

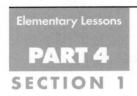

CONNECTION #3:
Tomie de Paola.
The Legend of the Poinsettia

A little girl's unselfish gift to the Christ Child elevates the position of the poinsettia to one of legendary importance: the flower of the Holy Night.

CHARACTER TRAITS: In this lesson emphasize the following character traits: compassion, integrity, and respect.

1. Read *The Legend of the Poinsettia* aloud. Remember to set the stage with appropriate pre-reading activities that capture students' interest. For example, inquire if any student's family participates in a Las Posadas procession. If so, invite the student and a family member to share the experience with other students; if not, ask children to listen closely to reading clues about the procession so that they may talk about the celebration after reading the story. Clarify vocabulary terms necessary for understanding both the text and the celebration.

   Hint: If families of children practice the tradition, plan a time during the study of the story when they may share stories with the class. If no families practice the tradition, discuss the procession after reading the story. Ask students also to listen carefully for other important ideas in the story-line, because later they will become storytellers for guests invited to the classroom.

2. Remind students about the relationship between participation and learning, then invite them to participate in creating, debating, weaving, and writing activities focused on the poinsettia:

   Create a pinwheel poinsettia by cutting a piece of red construction paper into a 4" x 4" square. Cut diagonals to about 1/2" from the center of the square. Glue the tip of each corner to the center of the square, until a pinwheel is made. Glue small, square pieces of yellow tissue paper to the center of the poinsettia. Cut five red petal shapes and two green leaf shapes to add to the pinwheel to complete the flower. **Hint:** Send a research team of student botanists to the library to find out proper names for the parts of the poinsettia plant and unique features such as color changes. (Alternate Activity)

   Weave a place mat using various colors that symbolize Christmas (e.g., red to represent the berries of the holly plant, green for the evergreen tree, and white for the snowy fields of winter). Use place mats as a decoration for a Christmas tea party. (Alternate Activity)

   Talk about the gift-giving tradition of Christmas, and then ask students to share family gift-giving customs that occur at different times during the year. **Ask** them to put on their thinking caps: In a gift exchange, who receives more—the giver or the receiver? Lead students in a discussion: "If I were a gift, I would be _____." Ask children to share why they chose a certain item.

   Pick a holiday symbol such as a holly plant or an evergreen tree, and then write an original story that explains how the holly and the evergreen became Christmas symbols. (Alternate Activity)

3. Enlist students in planning for and practicing for a Christmas tea:

   Arrange classroom desks or tables in clusters of four;
   Put place mats on desktops;
   Place poinsettias in the middle of each cluster;
   Practice telling the story of the poinsettia to others in the small group;
   Discuss the art of being hosts and hostesses;

Invite another class to the Christmas tea;

Serve cups of Christmas punch and cookies;

Encourage students to talk to guests about the decorations, tell the story of the poinsettia, and share original stories about other Christmas symbols; and

Thank the guests for coming to the tea. (Alternate Activity)

4. Remind students about the discussion on gift giving. Suggest that class members write a friendly letter to a person living in a nursing home (e.g., "Dear Friend") Write letters on poinsettia-shaped paper. Tell nursing home residents that members of the class made poinsettias for gifts and that class members enjoy sharing the gifts made at school with them. Wish new friends a happy holiday season. (Alternate Activity)

Extension: Pack letters and poinsettias in a decorated box or basket and plan delivery to residents of a nursing home. Assure students how much residents will appreciate their gifts even if personal delivery is impossible. **Hint:** Make all arrangements well in advance of delivery. Residents enjoy visits, but teachers must coordinate activities carefully and sensitively with nursing home personnel.

5. Select one character trait (e.g., compassion, integrity, or respect) and talk about how people in the story demonstrate the trait. Ask students to tell why they selected a character and how the character exemplifies the trait. Suggest that students think about their own lives and share examples that illustrate the trait.

EVALUATION:

Determine the level of student understanding by assessing the quality of creative and written products and by observing the level of enthusiasm for sharing traditions, stories, and projects with classmates and residents of a nursing home. Encourage students to connect the message in the story to the theme of festivals of light and celebrations of illumination.

CONNECTION #4:
Denise Burden-Patmon.
Imani's Gift at Kwanzaa

Elementary Lessons

PART 4

SECTION 1

Imani's excitement about Kwanzaa dulls when she thinks about an encounter with an insensitive, difficult family member. She decides to confront Enna's teasing with a gift of love.

CHARACTER TRAITS: Discuss the traits of compassion, courage, fairness and respect before the story is read. Ask students to provide relevant examples of these traits.

Note: The authors placed Kwanzaa in either the harvest section or the festivals-of-light section of the unit. Kwanzaa, patterned after African harvest festivals, now celebrates pride in African-American heritage by lighting a symbolic candle on each of seven successive nights.

1. Read *Imani's Gift at Kwanzaa* aloud. Remember to set the stage with appropriate pre-reading activities that capture students' interest. Define clearly a purpose for reading and/or listening. For example, request that students listen closely for words they do not know and how the author uses the words in the story. Tell them that success in a game they will play later will depend on how well they can remember new words from the story.

2. Explain the guidelines for the "Match Game" and invite students to play a game to test their listening skills. Randomly hand out index cards with a word on one card and a definition on another card.

Extension: Read the story the second time. Ask students with a word card to call out the word, then wait for students with definition cards to raise their hands. Explain to students that those students who raise their hands must believe that their definition matches the word. Once students make a match, invite students in the large group to recall the situation in the storyline in which the author uses the word. Ask word-and-definition partners to write and share sentences in which they use the word in the context of *Imani's Gift at Kwanzaa*.

3. Talk with students about Imani's technique of showing friendship to Enna, who teases her. **Ask:** Is this a good way to win over a new friend? Why or why not? Allow students to make and wear friendship bracelets by braiding colored yarn and by threading wooden or glass beads in pleasing designs. Use bracelets as a way of talking about friendship, the importance of friends, how one forms friendships, how friends behave toward each other, and how Enna treats Imani. **Ask:** Does Enna behave as a friend to Imani? Why or why not?

Extension: Challenge students to assume the role of Imani and write a letter to Enna. Ask students to tell Enna how she makes them feel when she says such ugly things. Request that students tell Enna that they still want to be her friend. Ask students to use the lessons of Kwanzaa as the basis of their offer of friendship to Enna. Invite students to a friendship circle to share letters with classmates.

4. Select one character trait (e.g., compassion, courage, fairness, or respect) and talk about how characters in the story demonstrate the trait. Ask students to tell why they selected a character and how the character exemplifies the trait. Suggest that students think about their own lives and share examples that illustrate the trait.

Hint: For interest and variety, alternate discussions on character traits between the presence and benefits of possessing the traits and the absence and consequences of not possessing the traits.

EVALUATION:

Determine the level of student understanding by assessing the quality of creative and written products and by listening to the sensitivity expressed in discussions about friendship. Encourage students to connect the message in the story to the theme of festivals of light and celebrations of illumination.

CONNECTION #5:
Barbara Robinson. *The Best Christmas Pageant Ever*

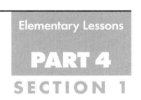

The poor, bad-mannered Herdman children not only invade the church but also take over the children's annual Christmas pageant. Who can imagine that the Herdman clan will shed light on the true meaning of Christmas?

CHARACTER TRAITS: As the story introduces characters, consult the list of traits, and tentatively label traits with character's names based upon their actions. Read the story and clarify first impressions through discussions with classmates.

1. Share with students that the activities, which accompany this story, will spread over seven days. Confide in students that characters in the story and the character traits they exhibit compose the most important ideas to understanding the message of the story. Prior to reading, lead students in brainstorming a list of character traits on the chalkboard or use the list of nine character traits in the appendix. Read *The Best Christmas Pageant Ever* aloud, one chapter each day. Enlist students in adding character traits matched to names of characters each day.

2. Explain to students the idea of a storyline scroll. Model on a 5' x 10" roll of poster paper the possibilities of showing or of concealing specific events and characters as the illustrator unrolls the scroll. Pass out blank paper scrolls to each student. Invite students to make a story scroll by listening each day, then selecting one person or one event that keeps the story moving along. Tell students that their selection of one person or one event will be what they draw on the scroll for that day and roll up until the story unfolds (unrolls) on the next day. Encourage students to share story scrolls and tell reasons why they choose people or events as ones that keep the story moving. **Ask:**

   What thinking skills do students practice as they make story scrolls? Why and how?

3. Review with students the art of headline writing: seek the most important ideas; state ideas in simple, yet startling, reader-attracting words; leave out all unnecessary words. Distribute to each student a 4" x 18" strip of paper.

   Ask students to choose the most memorable event in the story and write a headline that will interest readers in big, bold letters. Alert students that headline writers attract readers' attention by using different letter styles. Encourage students to announce their headlines and then display them on a classroom wall or hallway with the title, "EXTRA! EXTRA! READ ALL ABOUT IT!"

4. Review the steps of the writing process. Place students in roles as newspaper feature writers whose task is to excite other students about reading and enjoying *The Best Christmas Pageant Ever*. Ask students to follow the writing suggestions in the reporter's formula (e.g., Who? What? When? Where? Why? How?) Allow students to choose story assignments, to join conversation groups who choose the same writing topic, and to write feature stories following conversations:

   Talk about taking one of the Herdman children home to spend an evening and how students will introduce the child to parents. What happens is the subject of the feature story.

   Talk about colorful characters in the story and identify their strongest character trait. Write a descriptive riddle ending with "Who am I?" that will appear in the feature section of the newspaper.

   Talk about how much Mother enjoys being the pageant director and how much she wants to direct the pageant next year. Her qualifications for the job will be the subject of the feature story.

Talk about the Herdmans' behavior and why/how the behaviors of family members change. What students can learn by participation in groups will be the subject of the feature story.

Talk about how Imogene and Alice portray Mary in the pageant. The traits both girls bring to the character of Mary will be the subject of the feature story.

Talk about why Mother said, "This was the BEST Christmas pageant ever!" Mother's reasons will be the subject of the feature story.

Ask students to choose the best story in each category. Invite a reporter to class to review the stories and to give tips on writing feature stories that grab readers' attention.

5. Divide students into cooperative groups. Give each group a large sheet of poster paper and ask students to tri-fold the paper. Instruct each group to decide which event is the most important event in the story, and then draw the event in the middle section of the tri-fold. Next, instruct students to draw an event that happens earlier on the left side, then draw an event that happens later on the right side. Allow time for a group leader to explain the choice of pictures to classmates.

Ask: In choosing, illustrating, placing, and explaining events, what thinking skills do students use to complete the tri-fold project? Why and how?

6. Select one character trait and show how characters in the story demonstrate the trait. Suggest that students think about their own lives and share examples that illustrate the same trait.

Hint: For interest and variety, alternate discussions on character traits between the presence and benefits of possessing the traits and the absence and consequences of not possessing the traits.

EVALUATION:

Determine the level of student understanding by observing the originality in the tri-folds, scrolls, and headlines and by assessing the quality of feature stories. Encourage students to connect the message in the story to the theme of festivals of light and celebrations of illumination.

CONNECTION #1:
Ruth Suyenaga.
Obon

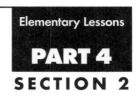

Japanese Buddhists commemorate the spirits of ancestors in the summertime celebration of Obon. Paper lanterns at the bow of miniature, rice-straw boats guide the spirits who visit Obon each year on their waterborne journey to Meido. Suyenaga compares and contrasts how Japanese Americans living in Hawaii and in Massachusetts celebrate Obon.

CHARACTER TRAITS: Discuss and give examples of respect.

1. Read *Obon* aloud. Remember to set the stage with appropriate pre-reading activities that capture students' interest. Clarify vocabulary terms necessary for understanding both the text and the celebration. Define clearly a purpose for reading and/or listening.

2. Ask children to listen closely for specific examples of similarities and differences in Obon celebrations during the second reading of the story. Remind students of the importance of understanding two unique geographic locations, both states in the United States of America yet separated by many miles. Chart similarities and differences on a large Venn diagram made of overlapping lantern shapes.

Locate Hawaii and Massachusetts on a wall map and/or globe. Talk about the similarities and differences listed on the Venn diagram and how both physical and cultural geography such as climate, location, proximity to Japan, and communities might influence the manner in which people observe the celebration. **Ask** students to put on their thinking caps and respond to this question: Will these same factors influence the observance of other celebrations? How? Why? Lead students in developing the generalization that geographic factors influence celebrations of all racial/ethnic groups.

3. Invite children to investigate the illustrations in the story that show miniature boats with lanterns on their bow. Point out structural details of the boats. Talk about how building materials determine whether or not boats float on the water's surface. Encourage partners to construct miniature boats and lanterns, and then float models in a tub of water. **Hint:** As the flotilla journeys out to sea, remind students of the connection between the floating boats and the celebration of Obon. Make sure that students understand the significance of the journey to Meido. (Alternate Activity)

4. Discuss with children the concept of ancestors. Ancestors are acknowledged in all cultures although ways of honoring them differ. Talk about the structure of trees and how trunks and branches relate to families. Introduce the concept of genealogy to children by explaining the meaning of the term. Remind students that one of the best sources for finding out about their heritage is their own family who will be able to fill in many branches and leaves on family trees.

Ask students to research their ancestors, share their findings with classmates, and draw a family tree with help from their family members. Display family trees in the classroom and suggest that students tell about the different generations in their families, where family members lived in the past, and where they live in the present. Use family trees as springboards to teach the concepts of emigration, immigration, migration, and mobility.

5. Discuss the character trait of respect and how the story and the craft of shipbuilding show Japanese respect for ancestors, and how the family-tree exercise demonstrates cross-cultural respect for ancestors. Extend the learning to a discussion of how students may show respect for their school family of classmates, teachers, and principals.

Hint: For interest and variety, alternate discussions on character traits between the presence and benefits of possessing the traits and the absence and consequences of not possessing the traits.

EVALUATION:

Determine the level of student understanding of Obon celebrations by assessing the degree of students' cross-cultural learning from classroom activities. Include teacher observations and rubrics in evaluating student progress. Ask students to tell what they have learned from the story and activities. Encourage students to connect the message in the story to the theme of festivals of light and celebrations of illumination.

Elementary Lessons

PART 4

SECTION 2

CONNECTION #2:
Arthur A. Levine.
All the Lights in the Night

In a poignant emigration story, Moses and his little brother, Benjamin, find a way to celebrate Hanukkah during a dangerous journey to Palestine (present-day Israel). Respect for family, homesickness, and miracles thread through the story of two courageous young boys.

Note: The authors searched for cultural celebrations in which light represents a central focus. In order to develop the theme, they highlighted major as well as minor celebrations in various racial, ethnic, and religious contexts. The authors feel that children need to understand that various traditions regard some celebrations as more important than others. For example, many people in the Jewish community in America emphasize the importance of Hanukkah to a greater degree than do those in the Jewish community in Israel. The writers urge teachers to make children aware that not all celebrations are equal in importance or celebrated in the same manner around the world. Teachers are therefore critical in helping students learn sensitivity toward others' traditions, celebrations, and beliefs.

CHARACTER TRAITS: Review the indicators of the character traits of courage, compassion, and responsibility.

1. Read *All the Lights in the Night* aloud. Talk with students about the boys' feelings related to leaving home without family and to traveling alone to a strange, new country. Invite students to share feelings similar to those of Moses and Benjamin that they experience when they set out on new adventures. Remember to set the stage with other appropriate pre-reading activities that capture students' interest. Clarify vocabulary terms necessary for understanding both the text and the celebration. Define clearly a purpose for reading and/or listening.

2. Engage students in a "Pack Your Bag" exercise. Describe a situation in which they are leaving home for a strange, new land. **Ask:** What will students take on their journey? What *light* will students take? Why? Encourage students to chart their journeys on a world map or globe and share experiences with one another. **Hint:** Lead students to the conclusion that most people regardless of age or culture pack a *light* that reminds them of home.

3. Invite a resource person to the classroom to compare and contrast the Hanukkah celebration of Moses and Benjamin and current Hanukkah celebrations on local, state, national, and/or global levels. Recommend that the resource person discuss the origins of the celebration, symbols of the celebration, and reasons why celebrations differ across the globe.

4. Encourage students to role-play events in the story (e.g., scenes such as hiding under the potatoes and telling the Hanukkah story). Ask students what reassuring story they might tell a younger brother or sister if they were in a strange place and homesick. **Hint:** This exercise presents an excellent opportunity to discuss how the power of stories affects people of all ages.

5. Allow students to choose any of the following potato activities to complete with a small group: make potato pancakes for the class; make potato prints; plant potato eyes; or grow grass on potato slices. Display group projects in the classroom. Encourage group members to keep track of the sequential steps in completing the project and to seek ways to link the potato activities to the story. **Ask:** Could any of these activities take place on Moses and Benjamin's journey? Why or why not?

6. Remind students of the following narrative in *All the Lights in the Night*:

> *Moses tried to be brave, but everyone was crying and waving as the potato cart pulled away into the pink skies of dawn.*
>
> *As the day wore on the two boys rumbled along, listening to the rattle of the potatoes and watching the clouds. "That cloud looks like Potemkin, the butcher," said Moses. "What do you think that one looks like?"*
>
> *"Mama," sniffed Benjamin. Then he started to cry again.*

Talk with children about clouds and pictures that the shapes appear to create. Use the narrative as a lead-in to a science activity in which students learn differences among cloud shapes, colors, compositions, and altitudes. Extend the discussion to what shapes students are most likely to see in their community and why. Over a period of time, send a team of student sky watchers to the playground to report on cloud shapes and plan mini-field trips to the playground for scientific investigations.

Extension: As students become more expert in detecting differences among clouds they observe outside, in reference sources, or on television, add an integrated art activity in which students construct and label different types of clouds with cotton balls. Back cloud designs with construction paper that matches the sky color in which certain types of clouds form. Ask students to explain how the lessons connect social studies, language arts, science, and the arts.

7. Review the indicators of the character traits of courage, compassion, and responsibility. Talk about how the brothers in the story demonstrate those traits and how students in their everyday lives have opportunities to exhibit the same traits.

EVALUATION:

Determine the level of student understanding of the celebration of Hanukkah and of important terms used in the story (e.g., emigration, homesickness) by assessing the quality of class discussions, of simulation experiences, and of creative activities. Include teacher observations and rubrics in evaluating student progress. Encourage students to connect the message in the story to the theme of festivals of light and celebrations of illumination.

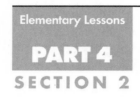

CONNECTION #3:
Flavia Weedn and Lisa Weedn.
Flavia and the Christmas Legacy

In a delightful seasonal story, the authors clearly send this message to readers: the magic of Christmas rests in the hearts of those who celebrate, not in the size of the gifts or of the tree.

CHARACTER TRAITS: Review the indicators of the character traits of compassion, respect, responsibility, and diligence.

1. Read the story aloud. Remember to set the stage with appropriate pre-reading activities that capture students' interest. Clarify vocabulary terms necessary for understanding both the text and the celebration. Define clearly a purpose for reading and/or listening.

2. Invite students to draw the name of another classmate, an activity in which students keep names a secret for two weeks. Talk about the concept of gift giving in different cultural celebrations (e.g., Christmas, Hanukkah, Kwanzaa, and/or Obon). Discuss the wide range of gift options (e.g., illustrated books, original poems, I.O.U.s for future favors) then allow students time to create personalized gifts for their secret pals. Plan special refreshments for the gift exchange day. Encourage students to express their feelings about classmates' acts of kindness at the conclusion of the exchange. (Alternate Activity, Parental Discretion)

3. Remind students of Flavia's description of foods for special times. Ask children to brainstorm foods that family members prepare and eat at special times. Talk to students about the meaning of the term, relationship, i.e., a bond that holds two or more people or things together. Then, invite children to state the relationship between special celebrations and special foods. **Hint:** Prepare cultural treats for a tasting fair or a brunch using Flavia's favorite foods (e.g., chow-chow, "crumble up" [bacon, biscuits, and gravy]).

4. Ask parents to bring Christmas, Hanukkah, or Kwanzaa picture albums for a parent/student show-and-tell exercise. Link the cross-cultural activity to the story character's eagerness to share a Christmas album. Lead students to the understanding that families in all cultures celebrate special occasions and that they usually are willing to share these in some way with others.

5. Discuss with students the value of interviewing older family members or friends about their memories of a special celebration. Assist students in making a list of interview questions that likely will gather information needed for a lively classroom discussion about favorite memories.

Ask students to write sample explanations to use prior to interviewing people, then practice with partners. Request that they explain what the project is, why they want information from a special person, and what they plan to do with the information. **Hint:** Invite partners to model interpersonal communication skills for classmates. Point out the importance of clear explanations and common courtesy to the success of the interview. Allow a week for students to interview a person of their choice about a favorite celebration, and then request that students report the results of the interviews to classmates in either oral or written form.

6. Demonstrate how to make dough ornaments similar to Mother's dough stars in *Flavia and the Christmas Legacy*. (Alternate Activity, Parental Discretion)

KITCHEN CLAY

Makes a lump of clay about the size of a softball:

1 1/2 cups flour   1/2 cup salt

1/4 cup vegetable oil   1/2 cup water (or a few drops of liquid soap)

Directions: Mix flour and salt in a mixing bowl. Slowly stir in water and oil. Squeeze the mixture for about three or four minutes, until it feels like clay. If the mixture breaks apart while students are squeezing it, tell them to moisten their hands with water and continue to squeeze. To store, place in an airtight container. Keep in refrigerator.

Models made from kitchen clay are strong. After several days, they dry to a stiff, hard finish. They can be painted with tempera paint. Use Mother's stars as design patterns. Allow students to develop designs that hold personal meaning for them. Invite students to decorate spray-painted branches or a small tree and then create a title for the display that reflects the personal and collective importance of the classroom decoration.

Hint: Connect the classroom activity to how families decorate during celebratory times and why shared experiences in classrooms or within family circles create lifetime memories for all people. Lead students in an open-ended, non-judgmental discussion related to memories of special times and talk about the differences between memories based on close relationships and those based on the things one buys.

7. Discuss how characters in the story exhibit the character traits of compassion, respect, responsibility, and diligence. Invite students to identify a family member or an acquaintance who demonstrates one of these traits and to relate an incident that shows a specific behavior associated with the trait.

Hint: For interest and variety, alternate discussions on character traits between the benefits of possessing the traits and the consequences of not possessing the traits.

EVALUATION:

Determine the level of student understanding of memories and their importance by assessing the quality of class discussions and by observing children's eagerness to participate in creative activities. Include teacher observations and rubrics in evaluating student progress. Encourage students to connect the message in the story to the theme of festivals of light and celebrations of illumination.

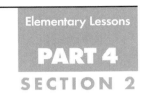

CONNECTION #4:
Patricia Polacco.
Uncle Vova's Tree

Elementary Lessons

PART 4

SECTION 2

An extended Russian family following typically Russian traditions joins together to celebrate Christmastide and Epiphany.

CHARACTER TRAITS: Review the indicators of the character traits of compassion, respect, responsibility, and diligence.

1. Read aloud the story, *Uncle Vova's Tree*. Remember to set the stage with appropriate pre-reading activities that capture students' interest. Clarify vocabulary terms necessary for understanding both the text and the celebration. Define clearly a purpose for reading and/or listening.

Talk about the author's family roots in the faraway country of Russia, locate Russia on a world map, then investigate probable geographic differences between two rural areas at Christmastide, one in Russia and the other in the U.S. Invite students whose families immigrated from other geographic areas to share family stories of celebrations in various homelands. Repeat the story-and-geography connections started by *Uncle Vova's Tree* and the location of Russia with the telling of each story.

2. Remind students of the author's description of kutya as a thick porridge of wheat or rice with honey, poppy seeds, raisins and nuts and why (geographic locations, personal preferences) recipes for kutya differ within Uncle Vova's family. Talk with students about what they might choose to put as toppings for a bowl of either thick Russian porridge or oatmeal. Lead them to link choices of toppings to family traditions, past and present, as well as to personal preferences.

3. Review with children the storyline that describes children making paper stars as a means of carrying on a family tradition. Look for pictures that show colorful examples of the paper stars. Encourage children to choose one of two activities: make paper stars similar to those in the story and place in a decorated basket (Alternate Activity) or practice telling the story of Uncle Vova with a partner (Alternate Activity, Parental Discretion). Invite students from another class to visit the classroom, allow partners to share the story with student guests, and distribute paper stars to each visiting student as a gift.

4. How did the characters in this story represent the character traits of compassion, respect, responsibility, or diligence? Give examples from the story to support your answers.

EVALUATION:

Determine the level of student understanding of different Christmas traditions by assessing the quality of class discussions and by observing the enthusiasm for various activities that students exhibit. Include teacher observations and rubrics in evaluating student progress. Ask students to write a brief narrative explaining what they have learned from reading this story and engaging in these activities. Encourage students to connect the message in the story to the theme of festivals of light and celebrations of illumination.

ALTERNATE SELECTION:

James Rice. *Cowboy Night Before Christmas.* Santa's reindeer abandon their job during a Texas storm. Fortunately, two lonely cowboys help Santa finish his Christmas Eve rounds.

CONNECTION #1:
Patricia C. McKissack and Frederick L. McKissack.
Christmas in the Big House, Christmas in the Quarters

In the antebellum South, Christmas signaled a season of joy for Christians in plantation houses as well as in slave quarters. Students gain valuable insights into customs, poems, songs, language patterns, and recipes from two cultural perspectives.

CHARACTER TRAITS: Review the nine character traits used in this manual and give examples of each of them. Ask students to provide other examples from their own experiences.

1. Read *Christmas in the Big House, Christmas in the Quarters* aloud. Remember to set the stage with appropriate pre-reading activities that capture students' interest. For example, establish the setting of the story through time and place. Remind students that more than a century has passed between the lives of the children in the story and their lives today. Remind them also that the children and adults in the story were less than two years away from the Civil War. Ask that student partners listen closely for geographic clues about Virginia in the antebellum South.

Assist partners in note taking techniques by showing students how to make a tri-fold. Instruct them to use the left side for key clues in the text or illustrations about the daily lives of children in the story, the middle column for key clues in the text or illustrations that hint of impending troubles that eventually erupt in war, and the right column for geographic clues in the text or illustrations about Virginia in 1859.

Show students a model tri-fold with the columns labeled "Children's Daily Lives," "Impending Troubles," and "Geographic Clues." Read slowly so that students can process information through listening, categorizing, and listing. Take time at the conclusion of the reading for partners to volunteer information on these three subjects. **Hint:** If time permits, use the data students collect as a foundation for comparing and contrasting these same subjects in present times.

Remind students that Virginia as a state and the South as a region share many common geographic features that affect both daily lives and conflicts in peace and also in war. Talk about the role geographic features played in the Civil War that entirely changed the setting portrayed in *Christmas in the Big House, Christmas in the Quarters*. Post the location of the story on the classroom story map so that students can literally see their horizons expand throughout the year.

2. Point out to students that the celebration of Christmas excites all residents on the plantation. Discuss the following instructional options with students and encourage them as individuals or as partners to select one project of special interest:

Design and make a slave's "Big Times" ornament for decoration. Select only natural materials, then prepare an explanation for classmates so that they see connections between the absence of income and the inability to purchase goods. End the explanation by challenging classmates to respond to the relationship between income and beauty in people's lives. **Ask:** Are the two ideas connected to one another? If so, how and why? Must the lack of income determine the amount of beauty in people's lives? How can people of little or no income express beauty? (Alternate Activity)

Research song lyrics in the story, then identify what settings, conditions, and/or attitudes they describe. Extend students' knowledge of seasonal songs and spirituals by investigating the topics in the media center. Prepare song sheets for classmates and lead them in singing popular seasonal songs and spirituals. Ask the music teacher to give students tips on how to lead group singing. **Hint:** Make sure that students recognize that songs are message carriers, then challenge students to give examples of lyrics that carry messages. (Alternate Activity)

Assume roles as family members living in the Big House nestled comfortably on a pre-Civil War Virginia plantation. Based on knowledge gained from the story, write a letter to a friend that describes the family's seasonal festivities. Catch the spirit of the celebratory season by using colorful descriptors of activities. Share letters with class members, then pick three ideas from the story that prompted statements in the letters. Show classmates how story text inspires personal writing. **Hint:** Make students aware that personal letters were and are common forms of communication among friends. **Ask:** How and why do people today prefer sending seasonal cards rather than writing personal letters? (Alternate Activity)

Join class members interested in dramatizing Christmas Eve in the Big House as well as in the slave quarters. Check the story carefully so that the script, songs, and dances project historically authentic information, then write, cast, and perform the scenes for classmates. After the performance, **ask:**

> *With so many differences in lifestyles between slave owners and slaves, what factors unify the two groups in the story?*
> *Do the same factors serve as unifiers of diverse people today?*
> *What lessons, related to human relationships, does the story teach?* (Alternate Activity)

Use the note on the abolitionist movement and the role of some slaves in the movement to enlighten classmates. Research famous abolitionists including Frederick Douglass, William Lloyd Garrison, Charles Sumner, Sojourner Truth, and Harriet Tubman and their contributions to the movement. Describe ways that these and other abolitionists sent messages of hope to slaves. Investigate ways that slaves working as drivers for plantation owners passed information to other slaves on nearby plantations. Lead classmates in a discussion of the types of information most likely exchanged by the slaves.

With the help of the media specialist, find a story that tells about the network of stations that made up the Underground Railroad and then read the story to students. Point out to students on a wall map how far Virginia slaves must travel to get to freedom and what signs told them that they were on the right route. **Ask:**

> *What risks did runaway slaves take in their freedom flights?*
> *What were the consequences of being caught?*
> *Can you think of similar situations in which people risked their lives for freedom?*

Plan a special time for performance of the product options. **Hint:** Use student performances as a lead-in to review how courteous audience members show respect for presenters.

Extension: Extend learning about pre-Civil War Christmas customs in the South by inviting students to prepare cinnamon-soaked apples to scent the room, to practice "wiggy-waggy," to demonstrate a popular children's game, to write tongue-twisters to entertain classmates, or to make masks to show how Southerners masqueraded at the New Year's ball in the Big House. **Hint:** Help students look for clues in the story text about instructions and illustrations for these activities. (Alternate Activity, Parental Discretion)

3. Talk about the practice of stuffing stockings with mini-surprises for children at times of celebration. Ask them to consider the facts that they learned about life in the Big House and in the slave quarters (e.g., income, opportunity for leisure time, availability of resources to make surprise gifts, accessibility of markets to buy gifts). In small groups, ask students to sketch two stockings, one for a child in the Big House and one for a child in the slave quarters. Request that students fill stockings with historically accurate illustrations of surprises and defend their choices of stocking stuffers to classmates. (Alternate Activity, Parental Discretion)

Extension: Extend students' thinking by asking them to think about stockings that observers might see in homes in the 1990s. Set the stage for the activity by inviting students to share family customs about stockings. **Ask:** What changes might you see in the stockings' contents then and now? What reasons account for changes in the contents?

4. Students will choose one character from the story of special interest, identify problems that the character faces, select traits that enable the character to solve problems, and share thoughts with classmates. Invite students to transfer story situations to challenges in their everyday lives, then to tell how the use of the same traits might help them confront and solve problems.

EVALUATION:

Determine the level of student understanding of plantation celebrations by assessing how quickly they grasp that multiple factors affect all aspects of organizing celebrations and by observing the degree of enthusiasm for participating in learning options. Include rubrics in evaluations. Ask students to explain what they have learned from the story and activities. Encourage students to connect the message in the story to the theme of festivals of light and celebrations of illumination.

CONNECTION #2:
Diane Hoyt-Goldsmith.
Celebrating Kwanzaa

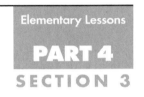

Elementary Lessons

PART 4

SECTION 3

An African-American family explains the origin, meaning, and symbols of a mid-winter cultural celebration. From its origins as a festival focusing upon African harvest traditions, the celebration has emerged today as an affirmation of pride in African heritage.

Note: The authors placed Kwanzaa in both the harvest section and the festivals of light sections. Kwanzaa, patterned after African harvest festivals, now celebrates pride in African-American heritage by lighting a symbolic candle on each of seven successive nights.

CHARACTER TRAITS: Review the nine character traits used in this manual and give examples of each of them. Ask students to provide other examples from their own experiences.

1. Read *Celebrating Kwanzaa* aloud. Remember to set the stage with appropriate pre-reading activities that capture students' interest. For example, explain that the focus of Kwanzaa continues to expand as the celebration matures. **Hint:** Use the Kwanzaa story to reinforce the meaning of the unit generalization: Over time, human behaviors—such as celebrating or honoring special people, events, or values—may change. **Hint:** Also utilize the story line of an American family living in Chicago and honoring their African roots to show that a democratic system of government provides a framework for free citizens to celebrate diversity (ethnic, racial, religious heritages) and unity at the same time.

Ask students to reflect a few moments and offer responses to the question: Why may citizens under all forms of government not enjoy the same privileges as Americans, i.e., the right to express loyaly to their native culture as well as their American culture?

Review important words associated with the celebration of Kwanzaa, especially the meanings of the seven principles of Kwanzaa. Talk to students about examples of behaviors that clearly show people following the principles. **Ask:** Why are principles to follow important to any set of beliefs? How do cultures pass on principles to the next generation?

2. Talk with students about the advantages of selecting learning options for different purposes:

> *They may choose an option that holds a special interest for them;*
> *They may choose an option in which they possess special talents; or*
> *They may choose an option in which they know they need to develop either an interest or a skill.*

Offer the following learning options to individuals or partners, and then allow time for task investigation, completion, and presentation (Alternate Activity, Parental Discretion):

> *Study the seven principles, then make an illustrated, captioned Kwanzaa book;*
> *Construct a simple, handmade kinara, then prepare a script that explains the meaning of the candle colors and of the symbol of light;*
> *Design and color a pattern for kente cloth on graph paper, then explain the inspiration for the design;*
> *Make an illustrated, captioned poster series showing one principle on each poster, then display the series in the hallway, office, or in the media center; or*
> *Plan an informative talk on basic Kwanzaa facts, then offer to present the program to other classes and/or to invited representatives of your school/community.*

Hint: Extend the learning by talking through plans for a Kwanzaa feast including foods, rituals, dress, and decorations. If student interest runs high, allow students to move from the planning stage to the celebrating stage. Point out the purpose of each participant making an "I am thankful for...." statement in which people make public statements of appreciation for ancestors, heritage, parents, and/or knowledge. **Ask:** Can you think of other celebrations in which participants thank other people for their past and present contributions? Use "I am thankful for...." statements as writing prompts for individual student responses. (Alternate Activity, Parental Discretion)

3. Students will study the meaning of the seven principles of Kwanzaa, then compare and contrast the seven to the nine core character traits. Talk about why they think similarities and differences in the two codes exist. For efficiency, divide students into groups of two or three to complete this activity.

Hint: For interest and variety, alternate discussions on character traits between the benefits of possessing the traits and the consequences of not possessing the traits.

EVALUATION:

Determine the level of student understanding of the celebration of Kwanzaa by assessing the depth of responses to thought questions and by observing the quality of various learning options. Include rubrics in evaluations. Encourage students to connect the message in the story to the theme of festivals of light and celebrations of illumination.

CONNECTION #3:
Sundaira Morninghouse.
Habari Gani? What's the News?
A Kwanzaa Story

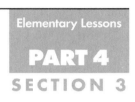

Through the character of Kia, readers acquire understanding about Kwanzaa, an African-American celebration organized around seven guiding principles.

Note: The authors placed Kwanzaa in both the harvest section and the festivals of light sections. Kwanzaa, patterned after African harvest festivals, now celebrates pride in African-American heritage by lighting a symbolic candle on each of seven successive nights.

CHARACTER TRAITS: Review the nine character traits used in this manual and give examples of each of them. Ask students to provide other examples from their own experiences.

1. Read *Habari Gani? What's the News? A Kwanzaa Story* aloud. Remember to set the stage with appropriate pre-reading activities that capture students' interest. For example, make the purpose of the first reading gathering details to construct the history of the celebration.

Talk to students about what details comprise a history (e.g., time, place, founder, purpose, personalities, traditions, symbols, growth, and changes in the celebration). Lead students in selecting criteria for constructing a history of Kwanzaa. Ask students to divide note sheets into however many columns or squares the class chooses for criteria. Challenge students to listen carefully for details and record notes in the appropriate column or square as the teacher reads slowly.

Following the reading, lead students in webbing the celebration of Kwanzaa on the chalkboard. Use student responses as opportunities to show students how one places specific details into general categories.

For the second reading, set the seven principles and their meaning as the purpose for listening. Allow students to practice the pronunciation of the Swahili words, develop meanings for the words through context clues, and contemplate the importance of using Swahili in an American celebration. Add language information to the Kwanzaa web. Then challenge students to support the following two generalizations:

Individuals, groups, institutions, cultures, and nations celebrate or honor in other ways those people, events, or values that they cherish most.

Over time, human behaviors—such as celebrating or honoring special people, events, or values— may change.

Explain that the process of scholarly writing forces people toward organizing details and weaving them into a story with meaning. Allow students to take information on the Kwanzaa web and write a brief history of the celebration to share with classmates. When they are finished sharing their original works of history, ask students what the experience of listening to the same story, constructing a web with common information, and then writing individual histories tells them about the process of writing history.

Hint: Use student answers to develop the concept of interpretation. Stress that most historians accept the responsibility of searching for the truth and of reporting events in an accurate manner. Their backgrounds and experiences, however, shape the accounts they write. Readers need to watch closely for clues that reveal writers' viewpoints in all written accounts.

2. Students will identify the character traits Kia exhibits as he recounts the story of his family and community. Invite students to transfer Kia's demonstration of traits to times in their lives in which they exhibited the same traits. If students choose to share their stories, welcome the addition of examples from the real world.

EVALUATION:

Determine the level of student understanding of Kwanzaa by assessing the quality of notes, written histories, and answers to higher-order thought questions. Include teacher-made rubrics in evaluations. Encourage students to connect the message in the story to the theme of festivals of light and celebrations of illumination.

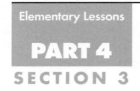

CONNECTION #4:
Michael J. Rosen. *Elijah's Angel*

Michael, nine years old and Jewish, befriends Elijah, an elderly African-American barber and Christian. By carving an angel as a Christmas gift for his young friend, Elijah unintentionally causes a dilemma for Michael. Should Michael bring a Christian angel into his Jewish home? Does the act bring conflict into the relationship between Michael and God? How will refusal of the gift affect his friend? Michael's parents ease the situation by providing enlightenment for the young boy as well as for readers.

Note: Point out to students that the spelling of the feast's name (e.g., Chanukah, Hanukah, or Hanukkah) varies with the source used.

Note: The authors searched for cultural celebrations in which light represents a central focus. In order to develop the theme, they highlighted major as well as minor celebrations in various racial, ethnic, and religious contexts. The authors feel that children need to understand that various traditions regard some celebrations as more important than others. For example, many people in the Jewish community in America emphasize the importance of Hanukkah to a greater degree than do those in the Jewish community in Israel. The writers urge teachers to make children aware that not all celebrations are equal in importance or celebrated in the same manner around the world. Teachers are therefore critical in helping students learn sensitivity toward others' traditions, celebrations, and beliefs.

CHARACTER TRAITS: Review the nine character traits used in this manual and give examples of each of them. Ask students to provide other examples from their own experiences.

1. Read *Elijah's Angel* aloud. Remember to set the stage with appropriate pre-reading activities that capture students' interest. For example, talk about the learning advantages of listening to a story for a specific purpose. Also, talk about why understanding vocabulary in any story is important to learning. Select examples of critical terms, show how the author uses them in the story, and challenge students to uncover the meanings of terms as they listen to the story.

The overall purpose for reading the story is to find commonalities in the celebrations of Chanukah and Christmas. Alert student partners to listen for story clues that define the differences and similarities between the two celebrations. Encourage students to record notes only on the two celebrations. After reading the story slowly, enlist students in completing a Venn diagram related to the two celebrations. Focus on the symbol of light.

Ask: Why does understanding the information on the diagram assist students in appreciating the story? How may understanding the story elements (e.g., setting, plot, and characters) assist you in understanding real-life situations?

4. Students will identify the major theme of the story, which extends beyond two characters with different belief systems. **Hint:** Accept all student answers, then lead students to the understanding that one major theme is friendship. Use the story as a springboard for discussions on friendship: for example, the importance of friendships; those traits that build strong friendships; why many friendships cross ethnic, racial, religious, socioeconomic, gender, and/or generation lines; and why many friendships not only last for years but also serve as symbols of light (e.g., hope, comfort, closeness) for the people in them.

Use the characters of Michael and Elijah to point out that their friendship crosses several lines. Invite students as individuals, partners, or small groups to reflect on why and how friendship exists among people of similar as well as different backgrounds, and express and present that theme in a creative way to classmates (e.g., illustrated and captioned posters, dramatic skits, greeting cards, or designs for friendship symbols).

3. Students will identify the character traits that enabled Michael, Elijah, and Michael's parents to find a solution to the story's problem. Invite students to transfer the situation involving fictional characters to their lives and to suggest traits that might assist them in solving similar problems.

Hint: For interest and variety, alternate discussions on character traits between the benefits of possessing the traits and the consequences of not possessing the traits.

EVALUATION:

Determine the level of student understanding of Chanukah and Christmas as well as the concept of friendship by assessing both the maturity and the quality of thoughts expressed in class discussions and in creative projects. Include rubrics in evaluations of student performance. Encourage students to connect the message in the story to the theme of festivals of light and celebrations of illumination.

CONNECTION #5:
Sholem Aleichem.
Hanukah Money

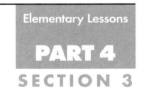

Elementary Lessons

PART 4

SECTION 3

A young boy's anticipation of receiving money gifts from relatives during the Feast of Lights illuminates the traditions of the Jewish celebration for readers.

Note: Point out to students that the spelling of the feast's name (e.g., Chanukah, Hanukah, or Hanukkah) varies with the source used.

Note: The authors searched for cultural celebrations in which light represents a central focus. In order to develop the theme, they highlighted major as well as minor celebrations in various racial, ethnic, and religious contexts. The authors feel that children need to understand that various traditions regard some celebrations as more important than others. For example, many people in the Jewish community in America emphasize the importance of Hanukkah to a greater degree than do those in the Jewish community in Israel. The writers urge teachers to make children aware that not all celebrations are equal in importance or celebrated in the same manner around the world. Teachers are therefore critical in helping students learn sensitivity toward others' traditions, celebrations, and beliefs.

CHARACTER TRAITS: Review the nine character traits used in this manual and give examples of each of them. Ask students to provide other examples from their own experiences.

1. Read *Hanukah Money* aloud. Remember to set the stage with appropriate pre-reading activities that capture students' interest. For example, use the story's setting as a geography exercise to review latitude and longitude. Ask two student volunteers to locate the story setting and their own community by pointing to the sites on a world map, then ask student partners to approach the map; to agree upon approximate geographic locations of these areas in degrees; to describe the areas by using color clues on the map; and to make logical inferences related to land forms, altitudes, and climates.

Hint: Link the activity to two of the five major themes of geography: location (Where is it?) and place (What is it like?).

Scan the text and select terms that are critical to the understanding of the story and the culture (e.g., kopeks, ruble, piatak, grivennik, chetvartak). Make the purpose for reading learning about another culture through language. Write the terms on the chalkboard, then ask students to be word detectives and listen for their use in the story. Following the first reading, lead students in a discussion about the meaning of terms by seeking definitions in the glossary and by using context clues.

Hint: Bring the real world into the meaning of terms by seeking examples of their use in people's everyday lives (e.g., compare rubles and dollars by researching the international monetary conversion chart in the business section of your local newspapers). Practice changing rubles to dollars by converting the rubles that characters received as gifts to dollars. **Ask:** Under what circumstances will information about geographic differences and international currency be useful to elementary students?

2. Remind students about the advantages of choosing a way to demonstrate learning that matches individual interests and/or strengths, then allow time for students in small groups to prepare one of the following assignments:

Research the origin of the Hebrew language, who speaks the language today, and where people speak the language; mark with sticky notes or peel-off symbols the nations where people speak Hebrew, then lead classmates in making logical conclusions about the use of the Hebrew language throughout the ages.

Research the significance of the menorah and important details that link the menorah to the symbol of light; prepare an illustrated poster to use while making a presentation to classmates; include in the presentation how other religious and cultural celebrations also use light as a symbol.

Research the custom of giving gifts in various cultures and on various occasions; review the custom of giving money as gifts; lead audience members in an analysis of reasons why many people give gifts to other people.

Prepare a skit that demonstrates how the family in the story celebrates Hanukah; contact local members of the Jewish faith, review the script with them, and ask that they add insights on how Jewish families celebrate Hanukah; include interview information in the skit. (Alternate Activity)

Encourage students to prepare assignments accurately and creatively. Talk with students about giving the gift of knowledge to other students. Suggest that students invite another class for a sharing session. Assist a master or mistress of ceremonies in writing introductory and concluding statements that summarize the generalization: Gifts reflect thoughtfulness and come in many different forms.

3. Students will identify the character traits the characters in the story demonstrate as they seek solutions to problems. Invite students to relate how fictional characters solve problems to how they solve problems in their everyday lives.

Hint: For interest and variety, alternate discussions on character traits between the presence and benefits of possessing the traits and the absence and consequences of not possessing the traits.

EVALUATION:

Determine the level of student understanding of Hanukah by how enthusiastically they complete research tasks, and by evaluating how accurately and creatively they present data to classmates. Include teacher-made rubrics in evaluations. Encourage students to connect the message in the story to the theme of festivals of light, celebrations of illumination.

CONNECTION #6:
Malka Drucker.
Grandma's Latkes

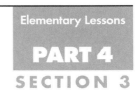

The origins and traditions of Hanukkah gradually come alive for Molly as Grandma teaches her the culinary art of latke making.

Note: Point out to students that the spelling of the feast's name (e.g., Chanukah, Hanukah, or Hanukkah) varies with the source used.

Note: The authors searched for cultural celebrations in which light represents a central focus. In order to develop the theme, they highlighted major as well as minor celebrations in various racial, ethnic, and religious contexts. The authors feel that children need to understand that various traditions regard some celebrations as more important than others. For example, many people in the Jewish community in America emphasize the importance of Hanukkah to a greater degree than do those in the Jewish community in Israel. The writers urge teachers to make children aware that not all celebrations are equal in importance or celebrated in the same manner around the world. Teachers are therefore critical in helping students learn sensitivity toward others' traditions, celebrations, and beliefs.

CHARACTER TRAITS: Review the nine character traits used in this manual and give examples of each of them. Ask students to provide other examples from their own experiences.

1. Read *Grandma's Latkes* aloud. Remember to set the stage with appropriate pre-reading activities that capture students' interest. For example, talk to students about the meaning of the term, symbol and make uncovering the story's symbol and its meaning as the purpose for the first reading. Encourage students to analyze the author's use of a symbol, i.e., latkes, as the storyline and discuss why the symbol appeals to elementary school readers.

   Ask: How may you utilize the same technique, i.e., the use of a symbol, in writing and also in storytelling? Read through the recipe for latkes and allow students to predict which of the ingredients ties to the Hanukkah story, then reread the story so that students may verify their predictions. **Hint:** If possible, serve samples of latkes during both story readings to whet student interests and appetites.

   Extension: Extend understanding of the celebration by allowing student partners to discuss how they might plan an authentic Hanukkah celebration inlcuding guest lists, invitations, menus, food preparations, and decorations. (Alternate Activity)

2. Introduce the concept of oppression by reviewing the details in the story about the Israelites and the Syrians. **Ask:** Who was in power? How did they use their power? How did they treat subject people? If subject people were oppressed, what is the meaning of oppression?

Challenge students to think through their knowledge of United States history, past and present; apply their understanding of oppression; and cite examples of oppressed people. Tell students that they may use oppression as a reason for coming to America or as a condition that occurred in America itself. Allow students to substitute examples they have seen on television news or documentaries. Use domestic or international examples where people have or are suffering under oppressive rule as a means of locating geographic sites on a classroom wall map.

Hint: Help students bring examples of oppression up to the present time, in which many oppressed people have improved the condition of their lives through various means (e.g., legislation, acquisition of skills, educational opportunities, higher standard of living, increased tolerance among American citizens). In other words, refrain from leaving a group as society's victims when in recent times the group's condition has greatly improved.

3. Students will identify the character traits Grandma and Molly exhibit in the story. Invite students to transfer situations involving fictional characters to their own lives. Ask them to volunteer how and why the same character traits might assist them in meeting everyday challenges.

EVALUATION:

Determine the level of student understanding of Hanukkah by assessing how quickly they grasp abstract conceptual knowledge and by observing how accurately they transfer meaning of concepts from one historical period to another. Include teacher-made rubrics in evaluations. Encourage students to connect the message in the story to the theme of festivals of light and celebrations of illumination.

ADDITIONAL SELECTION:

Dennis Brindell Fradin. *Hanukkah*

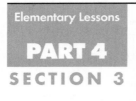

CONNECTION #7:
Marjorie Pickthall.
The Worker in Sandalwood: A Christmas Eve Miracle

A cruel master orders Hyacinthe, a young carpenter's apprentice, to either carve an intricate cabinet of precious sandalwood before Christmas morning or endure a beating. On Christmas Eve, a mysterious visitor finishes the cabinet with magical skill while he tells tales of his homeland.

CHARACTER TRAITS: Review the nine character traits used in this manual and give examples of each of them. Ask students to provide other examples from their own experiences.

1. Read *The Worker in Sandalwood: A Christmas Eve Miracle* aloud. Remember to set the stage with appropriate pre-reading activities that capture students' interest. For example, take time to talk about the author's background (e.g., English and Canadian) and about how the background of an

author may influence the text of any story. Engage students in predicting examples of how background may shape the storyline. After students volunteer examples, offer one example of language that sounds slightly stilted to elementary students, then talk about ways students may decode meaning from statements such as the following one:

> *Monsieur le curé shrugs his patient shoulders, but then he is tainted with the infidelities of cities, good man, having been three times to Montreal and once, in an electric car, to Sainte Anne.*

Use French words such as le curé (priest), monsieur (sir or Mr.), madame (madam or Mrs.), cinq (five), chateaux (inn), and Noël (Christmas) as lead-ins to a geography lesson prior to reading the story. Investigate the geographic origins of the author, any geographic place used in the text such as the Holy Land and the place in which the story takes place. Ask student volunteers to locate specific places on a classroom map, then post the story site on the classroom story map.

Extension: Extend student background by reviewing when and how the French explored Canada, how the English defeated French forces, and how and where the French left a lasting influence in the New (Old) World.

Talk with students about their understanding of the term, miracle, and set listening for the miracle in the story as the purpose for reading. **Hint:** Use language, geography, and vocabulary study as vehicles for setting the stage for the story.

2. Present the following activity options to students to explore and then share with classmates either as individuals, partners, or small groups:

Research the geographic origins of sandalwood, explain to classmates why the wood holds special value, and seek aromatic examples such as soaps or candles with sandalwood scent to familiarize students with one of the reasons why people value the wood.

Research the meaning of apprenticeship, how children and young people in North America trained under this system, and what industries commonly used the system of apprenticeship.

Use the example of Hyacinthe who "sometimes found himself able to tell in wood, not words" as a springboard for demonstrating various ways that people use to exhibit understanding (e.g., dance, poetry, art, sculpture); include models and examples in explanations to classmates.

Define lifestyles as ways people live, then show how physical and cultural geography shape lifestyles in Canada and in the Holy Land by using story examples as well as present-day examples.

Analyze the character of Hyacinthe for reasons why he experiences loneliness and despair, identify ways he copes with these feelings in the story, and lead classmates in determining whether or not these methods are sound ways to deal with loneliness and despair in today's world.

Construct a scale model of Hyacinthe's cabinet by using a shoe box, paints, and markers for classroom display, and by writing a display card that explains design principles such as choice of materials, choice of colors, and choice of scale.

3. Have students identify the character traits that Hyacinthe and the mysterious visitor exhibit in the story. Invite students to transfer traits that fictional characters exhibit in the story to situations in which they might use the same traits. **Ask:** Do some character traits endure the test of time? Why or why not?

Hint: For interest and variety, alternate discussions on character traits between the presence and benefits of possessing the traits and the absence and consequences of not possessing the traits.

EVALUATION:

Determine the level of student understanding of a miracle in a story by assessing the depth of thoughts expressed in class discussions and by observing the degree of learning gained through various research and creative projects. Include teacher-made rubrics in evaluations. Encourage students to connect the message in the story to the theme of festivals of light and celebrations of illumination.

CONNECTION #8:
Diane Hoyt-Goldsmith.
Apache Rodeo

Ten-year-old Felecia resides on an Apache reservation in Arizona. She not only pursues activities typical of children that age but also participates in cultural experiences through which she learns Apache customs and traditions.

CHARACTER TRAITS: Review the nine character traits used in this manual and give examples of each of them. Ask students to provide other examples from their own experiences.

1. Read *Apache Rodeo* aloud. Remember to set the stage with appropriate pre-reading activities that capture students' interest. For example, lead students in investigating and discussing the geographic setting of Whitewater, Arizona: the location (Where is it?), the place (What is it like?), and the symbolism of the name Whitewater. Following the first reading, inquire about how geographic factors complement the drama of the sunrise ceremony (e.g., landforms, light, and clarity of the atmosphere).

2. Enlist student input on topics they would research if they wanted to know about any ceremony (e.g., purpose, roles of participants, costumes, music, special effects, and unique features). List the student-generated topics on the chalkboard. Ask student partners to listen carefully for details on the Apache sunrise ceremony as the teacher rereads pages 18 and 19. After reading, solicit student responses under each topic and ask whether or not students need additional information to describe any of the criteria. Allow students to further research any interesting topic, then encourage students to share information with classmates. Divide the class into groups of two. Challenge each group to discuss the completed criteria, then defend why placement of the Apache sunrise ceremony in the festivals-of-light section is correct.

Hint: Listen carefully for arguments that focus on light as a symbol, then show students why the use of light makes these arguments strong. Comment on arguments that include comparisons and contrasts of the Apache ceremony with other festivals of light such as Christmas, Hanukkah, and Kwanzaa. Point out how comparison and contrast of celebrations add strength to verbal as well as written arguments.

Ask: How may you transfer this pattern of defending a position to other assignments?

If student interest runs high, invite a small group to dramatize the ceremony and videotape the student production. Enlist audience members to critique the reenactment from the standpoint of authenticity.

3. Students will identify the character traits the Apaches exhibit in the story as they plan a solemn cultural ceremony. Invite students to cite situations in their lives in which they use the same traits to meet challenges in their everyday lives.

EVALUATION:

Determine the level of student understanding of a cultural ceremony by assessing the quality of research methods and of responses to the thought questions. Encourage students to connect the message in the story to the theme of festivals of light and celebrations of illumination.

CONNECTION #1:
Lynn Joseph.
An Island Christmas

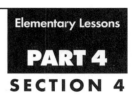

In stark contrast to Americans' preparations for Christmas, Rosie prepares for Christmas festivities in Trinidad by picking red petals for a sorrel drink, mixing up a black currant cake, and singing along with the parang band.

ALTERNATE SELECTION:

Fran O. Manushkin. *My Christmas Safari*
A cumulative counting song describes animals photographed on an imaginative safari to Africa. Manushkin's resource provides an excellent background for a compare-and-contrast activity with "The Twelve Days of Christmas."

CHARACTER TRAITS: Review the nine character traits associated with this manual. Ask students to check their definitions, share new insights, and provide different examples of each trait that they have discovered.

1. Read *An Island Christmas* aloud. Remember to set the stage with appropriate pre-reading activities that capture students' interest. For example, talk with students about the reasons that Christians celebrate Christmas and why Christians consider the birth of Jesus as a symbol of light in their faith.

Review with students the difference between the terms, sacred and secular. Explain that in public schools teachers and students may talk about various religions to learn more about other belief systems but may not talk about religion for the purpose of influencing others' beliefs. Extend the explanation by stating that this reason, supported by Supreme Court rulings, often shifts the focus of celebrations to secular issues.

Spend a few minutes in a pre-reading activity in which students share what Christmas means in their homes. After voluntary contributions, ask students to reflect upon responses and categorize responses into big ideas or concepts such as origin of the celebration, mood of the season, family traditions, and unique features. The purpose for listening to the story is to find clues about Christmas in Trinidad.

Tell students that they will be constructing a Venn diagram about the differences in Christmas celebrations in their community and Trinidad. Following the reading of the story, lead students in constructing a Venn diagram on Christmas traditions in their commnity and Trinidad. **Ask:**

> *What factors might account for the similarities in Christmas celebrations in two distinctly different geographic areas?*
>
> *What factors might account for the differences in Christmas celebrations in two distinctly different geographic areas?*
>
> *How can you connect this to one or more of the unit generalizations?*

2. Read *My Christmas Safari*. Compare and contrast the text to the lyrics of "The Twelve Days of Christmas." Find a copy of this song and review the familiar lyrics with students.

Divide students into small groups and challenge them to think about a motif for writing cumulative verses. Request that students compose, illustrate, and present cumulative verses about the

Christmas celebration in a mural or a mobile. When finished, exhibit student work in a gallery (e.g., the hallway) so that other students may enjoy the creativity of their classmates. (Alternate Activity)

Encourage students to reflect upon the thinking processes groups used to complete creative projects. **Ask:**

> *Throughout the processes of thinking up, designing, and making the project, which character traits served you the best? Why?*
>
> *Do you think that the same traits will transfer to other situations in your lives? Why? Invite students to cite examples.*

EVALUATION:

Determine the level of student understanding of the Christian celebration of Christmas by assessing the quality of responses, the enthusiasm for research as well as creative projects, and the degree of participation. Encourage students to connect the message in the story to the theme of festivals of light and celebrations of illumination.

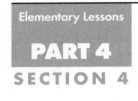

Elementary Lessons

PART 4

SECTION 4

CONNECTION #2:
David A. Adler.
A Picture Book of Hanukkah

Illustrations aid readers in capturing the essence of Hanukkah: origin, setting, personalities, diffusion, and customs.

Note: Point out to children that the spelling of the celebration's name (e.g., Hannukah, Hanukkah, Hanukah, Chanukah, Chanukkah) varies with the source used.

Note: The authors searched for cultural celebrations in which light represents a central focus. In order to develop the theme, they highlighted major as well as minor celebrations in various racial, ethnic, and religious contexts. The authors feel that children need to understand that various traditions regard some celebrations as more important than others. For example, many people in the Jewish community in America emphasize the importance of Hanukkah to a greater degree than do those in the Jewish community in Israel. The writers urge teachers to make children aware that not all celebrations are equal in importance or celebrated in the same manner around the world. Teachers are therefore critical in helping students learn sensitivity toward others' traditions, celebrations, and beliefs.

CHARACTER TRAITS: Review the nine character traits associated with this manual. Ask students to check their definitions, share new insights, and provide different examples of each trait that they have discovered.

1. Model the reading-the-pictures technique when presenting the story, *A Picture Book of Hanukkah*. Remember to set the stage with appropriate pre-reading activities that capture students' interest. For example, quiz students on what subjects they might paint into illustrations if they want to tell the story of a celebration from the time of its origin to the present.

Lead students in developing a general list of criteria such as origin, setting, personalities, diffusion, and customs. During story reading, allow listening partners to record evidence of the illustrator addressing students' criteria.

Ask:

How does listening for specific criteria assist you in learning?

After listening to the story, what criteria might you add to the list?

After listening to the story, what criteria might you delete from the list?

Do you think that additions and deletions are a standard part of any research process?

Connect your answers to the value of revision in thinking, listening, and writing processes.

2. Review *A Picture Book of Hanukkah* again. Ask a student to serve as a recorder to list on the chalk-board the names of individuals or groups of people as the teacher reviews the story. Depending upon the number of entries, divide students into research groups to find additional data on what role characters play in the Hanukkah story. Request that students take notes, organize notes around the roles that individuals or groups play in the Hanukkah story, and analyze what character traits they exhibit and why. Invite students to present deeds of individuals and groups in chronological order.

Hint: For interest and variety, alternate discussions on character traits between the benefits of possessing the traits and the consequences of not possessing the traits.

Hint: Use a story map activity to place story events and characters in correct locations after reading the story and completing the activities.

3. Ask students to research the importance of menorahs, latkes, dreidels, and gelt to the Hanukkah celebration. Suggest students make and share one of the items.

EVALUATION:

Determine the level of student understanding of the Jewish celebration of Hanukkah by assessing the quality of responses, the enthusiasm for research as well as creative projects, and the degree of participation. Ask students to explain what they have learned from the story and activities, then tell what, how, and why they learned. Encourage students to connect the message in the story to the theme of festivals of light and celebrations of illumination.

CONNECTION #3:
Wendy Wax, Editor. Hanukkah, Oh, Hanukkah! A Treasury of Stories, Songs, and Games to Share

Elementary Lessons

PART 4
SECTION 4

Teachers as well as students will delight over this treasury of Hanukkah stories, songs, and games. The resource serves as a ready reference for researching details related to the celebration.

CHARACTER TRAITS: Review the nine character traits associated with this manual. Ask students to check their definitions, share new insights, and provide different examples of each trait that they have discovered.

1. Select one story, one song, and one game to share with students. Contact the music teacher to find out if any of the songs are on tape so that students may listen to the music and lyrics. Make the purpose of listening to the story or the song or playing the game learning more about the celebration of Hanukkah. At the conclusion of the story, song, or game, question students about how the activity adds to students' understanding of Hanukkah. (Alternate Activity)

For students with high interest in learning more about Hanukkah, provide time for them to investigate other features of the celebration through research in *Hanukkah, Oh, Hanukkah!* Assist these students in condensing and reporting the new information in the form of telecasts.

2. Request that students reflect upon past festivals-of-light celebrations and choose their favorite memory as a writing prompt. Encourage students to share the assignment with their parents and to ask them to help recall some of their family's most memorable celebrations. (Alternate Activity)

Ask students to choose one memory and write why this one represents their favorite festivals-of-light celebration. Request that students take the assignment from the "sloppy-copy" step to the published-work step, then share products with classmates in a writers' circle. (Alternate Activity)

When each student finishes his or her story, invite class members to find connections between the story told and the character traits exhibited. **Ask:** Do the students' stories demonstrate that the opportunity for modeling character traits exists in every person's life? (Alternate Activity)

EVALUATION:

Determine the level of student understanding of the Jewish celebration of Hanukkah by assessing the quality of responses, the enthusiasm for research as well as creative projects, and the degree of participation. Encourage students to connect the message in their chosen activities to the theme of festivals of light and celebrations of illumination.

ADDITIONAL SELECTIONS:

Karla Kuskin. *A Great Miracle Happened There: A Chanukah Story*

Eric A. Kimmel. *The Chanukkah Guest*

Barbara Diamond Goldin. *Just Enough Is Plenty: A Hanukkah Tale*

David A. Adler. *Happy Hanukkah Rebus*

Nina Jaffe. *In The Month of Kislev: A Story for Hanukkah*

Miriam Chaikin. *Hanukkah*

CONNECTION #4:
Anisha Kacker.
Ravi's Diwali Surprise

Diwali celebrates a Hindu story of Prince Ram returning to his people. The story follows the traditional pattern of the triumph of good over evil.

CHARACTER TRAITS: Review the nine character traits associated with this manual. Ask students to check their definitions, share new insights, and provide different examples of each trait that they have discovered.

1. Prior to reading *Ravi's Diwali Surprise* aloud, lead students in a focused discussion on the importance of background research to understanding any storyline. Establish research partners to investigate the following topics in school, public, or home libraries, then report to classmates:

> *Prince Ram: details of the triumphant story that Hindus celebrate each year;*
> *Diyas (e.g., clay oil lamps) and their role in the celebration of Diwali;*
> *Geographic features of India: climate, landforms, demographics, vegetation, crops;*
> *Dominant religions in India: basic beliefs;*
> *Rangoli patterns: their role in Diwali celebrations.*

Talk about how newly acquired information on Diwali—traditional story, symbol of light, geographic features, important religions, and artistic expressions—will assist students in understanding *Ravi's Diwali Surprise*. Set finding matches between the research and the storyline as the purpose for listening to the story. Tell students that they need to listen for and then cite examples of how research information clarifies the storyline. **Ask:** When might the use of the same process, research before reading, prove useful to you? Explain your answer.

Hint: Use a story map activity to place story events and characters in correct locations after reading the story and completing the activities.

2. Lead students in comparing and contrasting Diwali with other festivals that use light as a focal point. Encourage them to include traditions such as decorations, foods, clothing, greetings, and symbols. As students volunteer information, record responses on a Venn diagram in the shape of two diyas or clay oil lamps. Challenge students to study the diagram and advance reasonable conclusions about festivals of light.

3. Suggest that students trace the story of Prince Ram in India and find specific character traits that serve him well in his struggle against evil. Lead students in a discussion about how the same traits might serve students in your community in confronting problems and finding solutions in everyday life.

EVALUATION:

Determine the level of student understanding of the Hindu celebration of Diwali by assessing the quality of responses, the enthusiasm for research and creative projects, and the degree of participation. Ask students to explain what they learned from the story and activities, then tell what, how, and why they learned. Encourage students to connect the message in the story to the theme of festivals of light and celebrations of illumination.

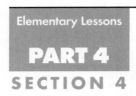

CONNECTION #5:
Maxine Rhea Leighton.
An *Ellis Island Christmas*

Landing at Ellis Island on Christmas Eve excites Krysia. Memories of Poland and of a rough ocean crossing fade temporarily as she anticipates a reunion with her father in America.

CHARACTER TRAITS: Review the nine character traits associated with this manual. Ask students to check their definitions, share new insights, and provide different examples of each trait that they have discovered.

1. Read *An Ellis Island Christmas* aloud. Remember to set the stage with appropriate pre-reading activities that capture students' interest. For example, alert the librarian that a team of students will investigate the history of Ellis Island and provide an overview about the island's relationship to immigration. Ask students to be attentive to details about immigrants' experiences on the island.

After students present a historical overview of Ellis Island, lead students in predicting what might happen to Krysia, a young immigrant from Poland, on Ellis Island. List the predictions on a chart tablet, chalkboard, or transparency. Following the reading, check the accuracy of students' predictions.

Ask:

> *Does the storyline indicate Maxine Rhea Leighton's knowledge of immigrant experiences on Ellis Island?*
> *For what reason does the author tie the place of Ellis Island and the time of Christmas Eve together?*
> *What do the place and the time represent to immigrants?*
> *How does the story connect to the theme of festivals of light and celebrations of illumination?*
> *Is the story an effective way to present history?*
> *What are the advantages of learning history through stories?*

2. Explain to students that they may choose how to demonstrate their understanding of Krysia's immigration to America. Ask students to listen to the following activities, to select one that holds high interest for them, and to work individually, with a partner, or in a small group to complete the project:

Reread the story and pay close attention to the actions of Petrowski family members. Use the core character traits to analyze how one or more traits assist family members in adapting to a new life in America. Finally, prepare a list of examples, use the list to create a poster, then present the information to classmates.

Assume the role of Krysia, then consider all of her new experiences in America; write these impressions in a letter to Krysia's closest friend in Poland; urge the friend to immigrate to America for specific reasons; share letters with classmates.

Assume the roles of Polish immigrants living in a crowded urban area; research elements of authentic Polish celebrations, then plan one for the neighborhood in the story including songs, foods, games, and dances; share demonstrations and examples with classmates. (Alternate Activity)

Hint: Remind students that both presenters and audience members share responsibilities for courteous behavior during student presentations.

EVALUATION:

Determine the level of student understanding of the immigrant experience by assessing the quality of responses, the enthusiasm for research and creative projects, and the degree of participation. Take this opportunity to assess their writing skills and their research competency. Encourage students to connect the message in the story to the theme of festivals of light and celebrations of illumination.

CONNECTION #6:
Aaron Shepard.
The Gifts of Wali Dad:
A Tale of India and Pakistan

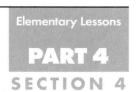

Elementary Lessons

PART 4

SECTION 4

To his surprise and dismay, a poor grass cutter discovers that gifts sometimes carry mixed blessings.

CHARACTER TRAITS: Review the nine character traits associated with this manual. Ask students to check their definitions, share new insights, and provide different examples of each trait that they have discovered.

1. Read *The Gifts of Wali Dad: A Tale of India and Pakistan* aloud. Remember to set the stage with pre-reading activities that capture students' interest. For example, talk about the geographic setting of India and Pakistan. Lead students in investigating the climate, landforms, vegetation, and population density of India and Pakistan at the time of the story and in the present. Direct students to listen for examples of how geographic features influence the storyline of *The Gifts of Wali Dad*.

As a second purpose for listening, request that students think about how the tale connects to festivals of light and celebrations of the human spirit. **Hint:** Extend students' likely response of gift giving as the connector between the tale and the theme by pointing out that light may come in the form of enlightenment to characters. Thus, Wali Dad's discovery that gifts sometimes carry mixed blessings represents his enlightenment.

Use the story as a means for students to practice the skill of predicting events based upon story clues. Select strategic spots in the story to stop, then encourage students to make predictions. Reading the story will check the correctness as well as the creativity of predictors.

2. Share with the class personal stories about times when the teacher received gifts he or she did not want or could not use. Concentrate on the humor of the situation as well as the empathy felt toward the giver.

Invite students to write about receiving a gift they did not want or could not use:

What did the student do with the gift?

How did they respond to the giver of the gift? Why?

If students volunteer to talk about examples, plan a sharing session.

3. Organize a "white elephant" gift exchange. Ask students to bring wrapped objects from home that are no longer useful to them. Stress the meaning of a white elephant. Label each gift with a number, then exchange gifts by drawing numbers. Tell students they may choose either a wrapped gift with a matching number or, after the first round, a previously opened gift already chosen by another child. Continue until all students possess a white elephant.

Hint: Allow students to take a gift back only after a full round is over. A full round means that all students have chosen one white elephant. Set a reasonable limit on the number of times that a student may choose another student's white elephant.

4. Ask students to demonstrate their understanding by giving examples of the presence of or the absence of character traits that came into play during the game. **Hint:** For interest and variety, alternate discussions on character traits between the presence and benefits of possessing the traits and the absence and consequences of not possessing the traits.

Extension: Extend students' thinking by quizzing them on the relationship between Wali Dad's gifts and white elephant gifts. **Ask:** What is the relationship? Challenge students to state the relationship in proverb form such as "Be careful what you wish for."

EVALUATION:

Determine the level of student understanding of the message from *The Gifts of Wali Dad* by assessing the quality of responses, the enthusiasm for research and creative projects, and the degree of participation. Encourage students to connect the message in the story to the theme of festivals of light and celebrations of illumination.

Elementary Lessons

PART 4

SECTION 4

CONNECTION #7:
Diana Hendry.
Christmas on Exeter Street

The house on Exeter Street bulges with aunts, uncles, friends, and even strangers in frenzied preparation for a festive Christmas celebration.

CHARACTER TRAITS: Review the nine character traits associated with this manual. Ask students to check their definitions, share new insights, and provide different examples of each trait that they have discovered.

1. Read *Christmas on Exeter Street* aloud. Remember to set the stage with appropriate pre-reading activities that capture students' interest. For example, alert students to listen for clues about the location of Exeter Street and about examples of traditional Christmas preparations. Following the first reading, seek answers to both purposes for listening.

2. Discuss the character traits necessary for the Mistletoe family to welcome and accommodate their guests during the busy holiday season. **Ask:** Based upon the behavior of Mistletoe family members, would you agree that they exhibit peace and good will to all? Why or why not?

Hint: For interest and variety, alternate discussions on character traits between the benefits of possessing the traits and the consequences of not possessing the traits.

3. Reread the story and create a chart about the Christmas Eve visitors. Include the visitors, what they brought, and where they slept. **Ask:** What conclusions about the Mistletoes, the visitors, and the celebration of Christmas can you draw from the chart?

4. Divide the students into ten groups of visitors. Enlist each group to write about their visit to the Mistletoe house. Include details about why they come, what they bring, where they sleep, and how well they sleep. Finally, describe Christmas Day from the point of view of the guests. Invite students to share their new story with the class. (Alternate Activity)

EVALUATION:

Determine the level of student understanding of the author's interpretation of the Christmas spirit by assessing the quality of responses, the enthusiasm for research and creative projects, and the degree of participation. Ask students to explain what they learned from the story and activities, then tell what, how, and why they learned. Encourage students to connect the message in the story to the theme of festivals of light and celebrations of illumination.

Elementary Lessons

5

New Year: Celebrations of Optimism and Hope

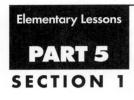

Elementary Lessons

PART 5

SECTION 1

CONNECTION #1:
Eric Kimmel. *Days of Awe: Stories of Rosh Hashanah and Yom Kippur*

Kimmel provides interesting, informative insights into traditions of the Jewish New Year.

CHARACTER TRAITS: Provide examples and definitions of the following character traits: integrity, responsibility, and respect.

1. Read the story aloud. Remember to set the stage with appropriate pre-reading activities that capture students' interest. For example, review the meaning of symbols, then call students' attention to the stained glass design of Jewish symbols on the cover of the story. Encourage students to volunteer the proper names and meanings of these symbols. If students lack knowledge of these symbols, assure them that the story will clarify many of their questions. Divide students into pairs, and then request that partners listen closely for names and meanings of these symbols, and then record notes while the teacher reads the story.

Clarify other terms (e.g., Torah, shofar, cantor, fast, synagogue) that are necessary for understanding both the text and the celebration. After reading the story, lead students in a discussion about Jewish symbols and their meanings from the context of the story and/or personal experiences.

Hint: Ask students to share names and meanings of symbols important in their belief systems. Elevate discussions to the point that the use of symbols, although different in designs and meanings, serves similar purposes for all people.

Once they reach this understanding, explain to students that they moved their thinking processes from a factual level to a conceptual level, i.e., comprehending facts and definitions about symbols to generalizing about people's use of symbols. Lead students in a round of applause for their learning accomplishment. Invite students to share their thoughts on how to transfer specific knowledge to general knowledge in future discussions.

Extension: Enlist the assistance of the media specialist in finding sources on stained glass. Invite a research team to apply the reporter's formula technique, Who? What? When? Where? Why? How? to sources on stained glass and provide classmates with a quick overview of the process. Model for students how to make a stained glass window design on a 9" x 12" sheet of black construction paper by drawing a symbol, cutting out certain parts of the symbol, and placing various colors of tissue paper over the cut-out parts. Encourage students to make stained glass windows with symbols important in their lives, and then display their designs on classroom windows. **Hint:** Talk to students about what light does to colors, how light coming through colors makes them feel, and whether or not these feelings account for people throughout centuries using stained glass in windows of houses of worship.

2. Discuss the customs of Rosh Hashanah, the Jewish New Year usually celebrated in late September or early October. Arrange for students to taste typical Rosh Hashanah foods: dip apple slices in honey to symbolize hope for a year of sweetness and/or share halla loaves—yeast-leavened, usually braided breads in the shape of ladders—which express wishes for good fortune during the coming year. (Alternate Activity, Parental Discretion) Point out to students special foods are part of special celebrations. **Ask:** What reasons account for the relationship between special foods and special celebrations?

3. Discuss customs of Yom Kippur (the Day of Atonement), the holiest day of the year, the day that follows the celebration of Rosh Hashanah, and the time of new beginnings. Invite students to join in a Yom Kippur custom by listing three personal good deeds of the past year. **Hint:** Choose the number of deeds that serve instructional purposes best.

Challenge students to volunteer examples of deeds and ask them how they might improve deeds already done and/or accomplish more good deeds in the future. **Ask** students to put on their thinking caps: How is this custom similar to other cultures' customs of making new beginnings? **Hint:** Talk with students about the custom of making resolutions and reasons why many cultures honor the practice of making new beginnings.

4. Talk with students about the K-W-L technique (what I Know, what I Want to know, what I Learned). Lead students in applying the technique to *Days of Awe*. Assist them in changing items listed under W (e.g., what I Want to know), into interview questions. Invite a member of the Jewish faith to class to answer questions and to broaden understanding about why Rosh Hashanah and Yom Kippur are important days to Jewish people.

5. Select one character trait (e.g., integrity, responsibility, or respect) and talk about how Jewish people demonstrate the trait in their observance of Rosh Hashanah and Yom Kippur. Students may use what they learned from the story, what they learned from the classroom guest, or what they learned from personal experience as a basis for responding to the discussion topic. Suggest that students think about their own lives and share examples that illustrate the trait.

Hint: For interest and variety, alternate discussions on character traits between the benefits of possessing the traits and the consequences of not possessing the traits.

EVALUATION:

Determine the level of student understanding by assessing the quality of creative projects by listening to the depth of responses in discussions and by observing the level of enthusiasm for participation in cultural studies. Ask students to explain what they have learned from the story and activities, then tell what, how, and why they learned. Encourage students to connect the message in the story to the theme of the New Year and celebrations of optimism and hope.

CONNECTION #2:
Myra Cohn Livingston.
Celebrations, "New Year's Eve"

Elementary Lessons

PART 5

SECTION 1

Livingston highlights American holidays in a collection of short, lively poems. These favorites of curriculum writers become focal points for theme-related teaching episodes.

CHARACTER TRAITS: Select either the character trait of diligence or responsibility and discuss both definitions and examples with the students prior to reading the story.

1. Read aloud the poem "New Year's Eve." Remember to set the stage with appropriate pre-reading activities that capture students' interest. Clarify vocabulary terms (e.g., resolution) necessary for understanding both the poem and the celebration. Advise students that they will become poets in one activity so they must listen closely to the poet's word choice and writing style. After reading the poem, discuss the poet's word choice as well as the writing style with students.

2. Distribute a copy of the poem to students and ask them to write the poem in their neatest hand-writing on a sheet of paper. Invite students to decorate the poem with a border made of brightly colored confetti. **Hint:** Use a hole-punch to make confetti from construction paper. Show students how to spread glue around the edge of the paper, and then sprinkle confetti on top of the glue. Enlist student assistance in making a display of poems on the classroom wall. (Alternate Activity, Parental Discretion)

Ask: How does participation in art projects help students remember the poet's words? **Hint:** Remind students that learning through physical activity, i.e., making a project with one's hands, reinforces learning by other methods, i.e., reading a story or writing a poem.

3. Ask students to memorize the poem by engaging in a cooperative learning activity. Divide the class into groups of four by counting off students. Instruct each person in the group to memorize one stanza and practice with members of the group. Present the poem to classmates as a group activity or as a chorus made up of all number ones followed by number twos, threes, and fours.

Ask: How does participation in a group help students learn? **Hint:** Remind students about the support that comes from others engaged in the same or similar project (e.g., group members become each other's cheering squad). (Alternate Activity, Parental Discretion)

Extension: Challenge students to put this theory on group work to the test by writing an original poem about the New Year. Review with students the power of the following process: brainstorming ideas, selecting one idea, describing one idea, thinking up rhyme words, matching ideas and rhyme words, making ideas flow, and testing results by reading aloud to others. Plan a sharing time for original poems. Add the poems to the wall display.

4. Review with students what a resolution means. Encourage students to cut out balloon shapes from brightly colored 9" x 12" construction paper. Ask students to think up one New Year's resolution, write it on a balloon, and attach a piece of yarn as a streamer to each balloon. Invite each student to read his or her resolution. Instruct each student or the class to clap their hands with one big CLAP as students read resolutions. Add the balloons to the wall display in a special section entitled "POP into the New Year!" **Ask** students to put on their thinking caps, reflect a few moments, and respond to the questions: What kinds of activities assist students in meeting their resolutions? Why? What is the connection between making resolutions and setting goals? (Alternate Activity, Parental Discretion)

5. Model for students how to make paper plate party hats by cutting a straight line from the edge of the plate to the center of the plate and then shaping the plate into a cone by sliding one cut edge under the other cut edge. Show students how to decorate their hats with colorful designs, sparkling sequins, and fringed tissue paper and to staple decorated plates into cone shapes. Show students how to place a brad on each side of the hat and make a rubber-band chinstrap by slipping the band around both brads.

Extension: Allow students to use the party hats as thinking caps prior to adding them to the wall display of decorated poems, original poems, and resolutions. **Ask:** If circles have 360 degrees and students remove one fourth of the circle to make a cone-shaped hat, how many degrees do they remove from the circle? Link the use of party favors to the celebration of a new year, then remind students of other cultural celebrations in which noisemaking plays a part in the festivities. Invite students to taste New Year's foods such as black-eyed peas or greens traditionally served in the South. (Alternate Activity, Parental Discretion)

6. Select either the character trait of diligence or responsibility and talk about how characters in the poem demonstrate the trait. Ask students to tell why they selected a person and how the person exemplifies the trait. Suggest that students think about their own lives and share examples that illustrate the trait.

EVALUATION:

Determine the level of student understanding by assessing the quality of creative and written products, by evaluating the feasibility of and action plans for resolutions, and by listening to the depth in responses during class discussions. Ask students to write their own poem about diligence or responsibility. Use these poems to evaluate student knowledge and understanding. Encourage students to connect the message in the poem to the theme of the New Year and celebrations of optimism and hope.

CONNECTION #3:
Myra Cohn Livingston.
Celebrations, "Presidents' Day"

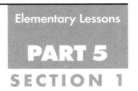

Livingston highlights American holidays in a collection of short, lively poems. These favorites of curriculum writers become focal points for theme-related teaching episodes.

CHARACTER TRAITS: Before the lesson, discuss the following character traits with students: citizenship, diligence, integrity, and responsibility.

1. Read aloud the poem, "Presidents' Day." Remember to set the stage with appropriate pre-reading activities that capture students' interest. Clarify vocabulary terms necessary for understanding both the poem and the celebration. Indicate that understanding the reason for the Presidents' Day celebration is the primary purpose for listening. After the reading, discuss this reason with students as well as the reason why planners chose a specific date for the celebration.

2. Remind students that people's memories often link together historic events and famous persons. Ask students to name and describe the historic event that took place about the time George Washington became President. Challenge students to compute the number of years between Washington's presidency (1789-1797) and the present.

Extension: Ask students to name and describe the historic event that took place during Abraham Lincoln's presidency. Challenge students to compute the number of years between Lincoln's presidency (1861-1865) and the present. Suggest that they research selected historic events and presidents such as the Spanish-American War and William McKinley, World War I and Woodrow Wilson, and World War II and Franklin Delano Roosevelt, then write word problems for classmates to describe the event and to compute the difference between the event and the present time.

As students solve classmates' story problems, ask that they sequence events on a time line drawn on the chalkboard. Request student partners to volunteer notable events other than wars and people other than wartime presidents. Encourage partners to add these to a bank of story problems and to the timeline.

3. Distribute copies of the poem to students. Ask students to write the poem neatly in the middle of a 12" x 18" sheet of white construction paper. Instruct students to glue a strip of red at the top and a strip of blue at the bottom and to cut out silhouettes of Washington and Lincoln on the sides of the poem. **Hint:** Look for a pattern of Washington and Lincoln and encourage students to make silhouettes.

Remind students that people remember Washington and Lincoln as solvers of big problems. Ask students to think about their own world and the unsolved problems they see on television newscasts. **Ask** students to put on their thinking caps: What solutions to problems might earn places in history for present and future presidents? Why?

4. Select one character trait (e.g., citizenship, diligence, integrity, or responsibility) and talk about how people in the poem demonstrate the trait. Ask students to tell why they selected a character and how the character exemplifies the trait. Suggest that students think about their own lives and share examples that illustrate the trait.

EVALUATION:

Determine the level of student understanding by assessing the quality of creative products, by observing the degree of enthusiasm for cooperative activities, and by listening to the depth of responses in classroom discussions. Encourage students to connect the message in the poem to the theme of the New Year and celebrations of optimism and hope.

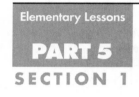

CONNECTION #4:
Myra Cohn Livingston.
Celebrations,
"Martin Luther King Day"

Livingston highlights American holidays in a collection of short, lively poems. These favorites of curriculum writers become focal points for theme-related teaching episodes.

CHARACTER TRAITS: Review the nine character traits associated with this manual and assist students with providing relevant examples of each of them.

1. Read aloud the poem, "Martin Luther King Day." Remember to set the stage with appropriate pre-reading activities that capture students' interest. For example, talk about the meaning of opposites, distribute a written copy of the poem to student partners, and ask that they circle examples of opposites on the copy during two readings of the poem (e.g., spring, winter; gray dawn, blinding light; the hawk and the dove flying together).

Request that students volunteer examples, then check to see how many students mark the same words as opposites. **Ask** students to put on their thinking caps: What effect does the poet's use of opposites have on the reader? Suggest that partners demonstrate understanding of opposites by writing five sets of opposites and sharing examples with classmates. Encourage partners to select one set of opposites, write the set into a sentence, and share the sentence with classmates.

Ask partners to write the sentence neatly in the middle of a 9" x 12" piece of manila paper. Challenge students to take their set of opposites and symbolize the meaning of the opposites into a border design for the sentence. Tell students that this technique of matching words and designs appears in many published works, like *Sam Johnson and the Blue Ribbon Quilt* (Ernst).

Ask: Why do authors and illustrators give readers a verbal as well as a visual image of the same words or ideas? **Hint:** Explain that some students will derive meaning from visual clues much more rapidly than from verbal clues; thus, authors and illustrators often team up to address the strengths of both linguistic and visual learners. Invite students to display decorated sentences on a classroom wall to reinforce this point.

2. Divide students into groups of five and ask each person in the group to memorize one of the stanzas, then practice reciting stanzas one through five within the group. Ask the ones to group together and discuss the meaning of the stanza; ask twos through fives to follow the same pattern. Request that students within each group recite the stanza in chorus to their classmates, then explain the stanza's meaning. **Ask:** What thinking skills do students use when they memorize information? Why is finding meaning in memorized lines so important for learners?

Hint: Remind students that they sometimes memorize information without understanding the meaning, and that if they do not understand the information, they certainly cannot transfer the information to new situations.

3. Talk with students about the value of using firsthand information or primary sources to make history come alive. Remind them that the poem talks about days in America in which African Americans, either by law (*de jure*) or in practice (*de facto*), received unfair treatment. Assist students in finding references in the poem that suggest unfair treatment of this group of citizens.

Extension: Ask students to assume roles as interviewers. Request that they ask parents, guardians, grandparents, and/or neighbors to think back to the years when they were growing up and to share with them the changes in laws affecting the treatment of African Americans. Ask them also how laws affecting other minorities have changed. Arrange interview information in two columns: the first from people forty or older and the second from those forty and younger. Allow students to share interview information and record in column one or two. Ask students to look at the two columns and make general statements about gains made by African Americans through the passage of laws. Suggest that they analyze the information to detect differences in the information related to the age of the person interviewed. **Ask:** What reasons might account for these differences?

Hint: Show students that over many decades, minority citizens struggled on the road toward fair and equal treatment. Check a reference source that charts the civil rights movement through the passage of laws and ask students to assist you in making a timeline on the chalkboard. Point out to students matches among the poet's words, the interview information, and the reference source.
Hint: Use the exercise to reinforce how much richer stories from history become when people spend time investigating multiple sources.

4. Model for students how to make a dream mobile. Make sure that students connect Dr. King's famous "I Have A Dream" speech and the mobile project. Instruct students to draw large clouds on 9" x 12" sheets of white construction paper, cut cloud patterns out, then write Dr. King's dream on the clouds: World Peace. Instruct students to draw and cut out three smaller clouds, and then write three words that will help this dream come true (e.g., love, cooperation, respect, and friendship). Assist students in making clouds into mobiles. Show them how to connect smaller clouds to larger clouds with 10" pieces of string. Invite students to hang the dream mobiles either in the classroom or in the hallway to serve as reminders that practicing these traits regularly will promote peace at school.

5. Select one character trait and talk about how the character in the poem demonstrates the trait. Suggest that students think about their own lives and share examples that illustrate the trait.

Hint: For interest and variety, alternate discussions on character traits between the benefits of possessing the traits and the consequences of not possessing the traits.

EVALUATION:

Determine the level of student understanding by assessing the quality of creative projects, by observing the degree of enthusiasm for original research, and by evaluating the comparisons drawn from multiple sources (e.g., poetry, interviews, reference sources). Encourage students to connect the message in the poem to the theme of the New Year and celebrations of optimism and hope.

CONNECTION #5:
Susan Miho Nunes.
The Last Dragon

During a summer visit with his great aunt, a young Chinese boy learns the importance of cultural traditions. A moving narrative accompanied by exquisite illustrations reinforces the idea that relationships with elders and with a community mold character as well as tradition.

CHARACTER TRAITS: Focus attention on the traits of compassion, courage, diligence, integrity, respect, and responsibility.

1. Read *The Last Dragon* aloud. Remember to set the stage with appropriate pre-reading activities that capture students' interest. For example, introduce the story by looking at the illustrations and establishing the setting, i.e., Chinatown in San Francisco, California. Clarify vocabulary terms necessary for understanding both the text and the celebration. Define clearly a purpose for reading and/or listening.

Extension: Encourage students to locate China and San Francisco on the classroom map and finger-trace the route across the Pacific Ocean. Talk with students about logical geographic and economic reasons for Chinese settlement on the West Coast, i.e., because San Francisco is the closest location to where most Chinese get off the boat, because they do not have money to travel about and look for an ideal place to live, because they find some comfort in being in a small community with other Chinese.

Extension: Focus student attention on the illustrations of street scenes in Chinatown. Ask students to point out what they observe about the cityscape of Chinatown (e.g., small shops, store owners living above the shops). Ask students to compare the urban environments of Chinatown and the town in which they live or near which they live. Point out differences and the reasons for these differences.

2. Remind students that in the last activity their observations focused on urban cityscapes. Explain to students that they will revisit the story's illustrations with a new purpose: to compare the faces of Great Aunt and Peter as they peer at the bedraggled dragon. Take one character at a time and record student responses on a chart or chalkboard. For example:

PETER	GREAT AUNT
Bright eyes of wonder	Tired eyes of disbelief
Neatly combed, shiny black hair	Graying, dull, scraggly hair
Let's-get-going body language	Ho-hum body language
Pretty teeth	Missing teeth

Ask students to put on their thinking caps: What factors cause different responses from Peter and Great Aunt? How do artists show emotions such as happiness, sadness, interest, enthusiasm, and tiredness in illustrations? How do authors show these same emotions in their writing? What message do the artists and authors send to students about improving their illustrating and writing skills?

3. Invite students to participate in a picture-is-worth-a-thousand-words activity. Ask students to fold 8 1/2" x 11" pieces of paper in half and then in half again. On the front and back of the booklet, ask students to label the squares with"Dragon"; on the inside, instruct students to label the squares "Peter."

Ask students to listen carefully to the description of the dragon, reread page one of the story slowly, then request that students describe and draw how the dragon might feel if he were real on the front of the booklet. Suggest that students record the emotions the dragon feels under the drawing. Reread page two of the story, follow the same process for Peter, then draw and record Peter's emotions on the inside of the booklet.

Tell students that the action of the story is about to change. Reread the page that recounts the dragon's entry into the restaurant. Invite students to show changes in the story's characters as situations change by drawing and describing the dragon on the back of the booklet and by drawing and describing the boy on the inside of the booklet. Encourage boys and girls to share drawings and descriptions with others, point out how characters change as situations change, then display booklets on the bulletin board entitled "Pictures Are Worth a Thousand Words."

Hint: Tell students that change resulting from the interaction of characters and situations shape storylines. Invite students to share other examples in the story that support the conclusion that interactions between characters and situations become the storyline in *The Last Dragon*.

4. Divide students into cooperative groups. Distribute a large sheet of butcher paper to each group. Instruct students to draw and decorate a large dragon. Ask students to decide on the most important events of the story, sequence the events, and insert a story map of events inside the outline of the dragon. Encourage students to contribute to a Wall-of-Dragons display with their decorated dragons.

Lead students in a wrap-up discussion of the processes that the groups went through to get from a blank sheet of paper to a dragon on the wall. Speculate with students what the dragon might say if he were suddenly able to talk. **Hint:** Remind students that characters will respond to situations in which authors place them and that words in the script are clues to the characters' emotions.

5. Use the story to teach a mini-lesson on inferences. Make sure that students understand the meaning of inference before starting the activity, i.e., ideas derived from the script and believed to be true but not actually stated. Reread the story slowly while student partners listen carefully for examples of inferences. Encourage partners to raise their hands when they hear an example during the reading of the story. Stop the story and invite partners to say what and why the example meets the definition of an inference. Examples of inferences include the following:

Because Peter went to spend the summer with Great Aunt even though he didn't want to go, students may assume that he respected his parents and followed their wishes.

Because Great Aunt said, "Couldn't have his mouth gaping open like a foal!" students may assume that she fixed the dragon's mouth, combed its whiskers, and polished the pearl.

Ask: Why are inferences powerful tools for authors and illustrators? What do inferences cause readers and viewers to do? **Hint:** Talk with students about how inferences keep people involved in the story and cause them to think actively and deeply.

6. Discuss how and why Peter represents a good example of the character traits of compassion, courage, diligence, integrity, respect, and responsibility. Suggest that students think about their own lives and share examples that illustrate the trait.

Hint: For interest and variety, alternate discussions on character traits between the benefits of possessing the traits and the consequences of not possessing the traits.

EVALUATION:

Determine the level of student understanding by assessing the quality of creative products, by observing the degree of enthusiasm for cooperative projects, and by listening to the depth of responses to thought-provoking questions. Encourage students to connect the message in the story to the theme of the New Year and celebrations of optimism and hope.

CONNECTION #6:
Tricia Brown. *Chinese New Year*

Brown describes how various traditions of the Chinese New Year reflect the idea of new beginnings.

CHARACTER TRAITS: Give attention to the traits of respect and responsibility. Ask students to define these words and cite examples from a wide variety of sources.

1. Read *Chinese New Year* aloud. Remember to set the stage with appropriate pre-reading activities that capture students' interest. For example, talk about the meaning of cultural traditions (e.g., activities repeated year after year). Ask student partners to make a list of traditions they hear during story reading. Remind students to listen for information on how the Chinese set the date for the New Year. Following the first reading of the story, discuss student notes on Chinese traditions and calendar dates. Clarify vocabulary terms necessary for understanding both the text and the celebration.

2. Invite students to create Chinese lanterns by asking them first to illustrate a celebration scene (e.g., perhaps a dragon on a 12" x 18" piece of construction paper). Instruct students to color scenes vividly so that scenes are identifiable after cutting.

Model the folding and cutting processes: fold pictures lengthwise; cut across the paper beginning at the fold and stopping 1" from the top, sides, and bottom; unfold and staple the top and bottom together; compress slightly to form a lantern shape; and attach yarn to the top in order to hang the lantern. Ask students to help in making yarn or ribbon strings of lanterns to hang in the classroom. Reinforce with students that the use of lanterns reflects a longstanding Chinese tradition.

Ask: Why does reading about a subject, talking about a subject, then making a product related to the subject help students learn more than just reading about the subject? **Hint:** Lead students to the conclusion that students learn in different ways. When teachers plan instruction in varied ways, more students are likely to learn. Also, actual involvement with the subject reinforces spoken and written words about any subject.

3. Remind students about the Chinese tradition of sending good wishes for the New Year to family members and friends. Model for students how to make a good-wishes scroll with the words, "May the Year Be Filled with Happiness," written in the middle: cut red poster paper in vertical banner lengths approximately 1' x 5'; splatter gold glitter over the banner; use large brushes and black paint to write the wish for the new year; glue dowel rods on the top and bottom and roll slightly to complete the scroll look; attach a string to the top dowel rod in order to hang. Allow students to work in small groups for this project. Display Chinese scrolls in the classroom or in the hallway. (Alternate Activity, Parental Discretion)

Ask students to put on their thinking caps and search through their own personal experiences. Invite them to share with classmates celebrations in which they send good wishes to family members and friends. **Hint:** Encourage students to include traditions of sending good wishes during cultural celebrations as well as on birthdays. Good wishes come in many forms (e.g., greeting cards, fortune cookies). Lead students to the conclusion that most human beings wish good things for their fellow human beings. (Alternate Activity, Parental Discretion)

4. Enlist students in organizing and in setting up learning centers for a morning of Chinese traditions. Explain activity options to students and ask that they circulate through learning stations to experience more Chinese traditions. Encourage students to seek the teacher's approval before changing centers. If students finish at one center and are waiting to go to the next center, refer them to a center where optional selections for enrichment are available.

Alert students that they will share information from the enrichment center during discussion period. Ask students to sign their names at this center. At each center, start every group with a clean sheet of paper for recording responses to the task's specific question; collect and use recorded responses as the basis for class discussion.

Extension: Show the class pictures of typical flower arrangements. Let students arrange flowers in a vase for classroom decoration by using only a few long-stemmed flowers. When the small group finishes the arrangement, ask them to discuss and record on a tablet why they think the Chinese value simple arrangements. **Hint:** Simplicity in design and in color defines beauty in Chinese culture. Simplicity allows the viewer to focus on a single object and think about its beauty.

Extension: Set up a center in which students taste the New Year's cake called Nin Go, a treat similar to a cinnamon roll that symbolizes the act of bringing sweetness to the New Year. When the small group finishes tasting the sweet cake, ask them to discuss and record other ways to experience sweetness (e.g., smiles, kindness, and cards). **Hint:** Make sure that students understand that behaving in a considerate way toward others reflects a personal decision and costs no money.

Extension: Set up a mobile center in which student groups construct a year-of-birth mobile. Ask students to decorate one side of a 2" x 24" strip of tag board with Chinese designs chosen from examples at the table. Request that they place dots at 2" intervals on the other side and staple the ends of the strip together with decorations on the outside. Dots will provide places to hang animals from the strip.

Make Chinese animal figures from patterns found in media center reference sources. **Hint:** In many student activity books related to Chinese culture, animal as well as calendar patterns are standard entries. Encourage students to show originality and draw animals freehand. Emphasize to students that the Chinese devised a calendar to keep track of time in an orderly way. **Ask:** Why is a system of accounting for time important? They probably linked character traits to animals because model behavior was most important in Chinese culture.

Direct group members to color and cut out designs, to sequence animals in the right order on the mobile, to attach 4" pieces of string to the backs of animals, and to tape the other ends of string to dots inside the mobile.

Show students how to turn the decorated strip into a mobile. Provide students with a 48" piece of string and ask students to cut it into four equal lengths. Space four lengths evenly around the strip, join the four strips at the top end, tie a knot, and hang. **Hint:** Use the exercise as an opportunity to discuss the number of degrees in a full circle, in half a circle, in a quarter of a circle.

Allow students to review a copy of the Chinese calendar. Ask the groups who tour this center to turn information on the calendar into math story problems and test other groups in a game-type format, i.e., ask each group to write two story problems, challenge other groups to solve problems in a round-robin fashion, and keep score on the chalkboard.

REFERENCE TABLE FOR CALENDAR

YEAR	ANIMAL	CHARACTER TRAITS
1979 & 1991	Sheep	Sincere & Sensible
1980 & 1992	Monkey	Intelligent & Talented
1981 & 1993	Rooster	Forgiving & Adventurous
1982 & 1994	Dog	Gracious & Responsible
1983 & 1995	Boar	Loyal & Trustworthy
1984 & 1996	Rat	Loving & Keeper of Secrets
1985 & 1997	Ox	Patient & Slow to Anger
1986 & 1998	Tiger	Cautious & Proud
1987 & 1999	Rabbit	Lucky & Gentle
1988 & 2000	Dragon	Successful & Bold
1989 & 2001	Snake	Elegant & Sensible
1990 & 2002	Horse	Clever & Capable

Allow students who visited the reading center while waiting to move to another center to share what they learned at the center. Then lead students in a discussion about which Chinese traditions are their favorites and why. Remind students that thinking through activities associated with Chinese New Year, making decisions on favorite ones, and supporting decisions with reasons are the same processes one uses in writing.

Invite students to write about their favorite activity, put a signature mark on the paper in the form of a Chinese symbol, and display their work on a bulletin board entitled "Cultural Insights Through Literature."

5. Select the character trait of respect or responsibility and talk about how people in the story demonstrate the trait. Discuss similarities between the character traits on the Chinese calendar and on the ones used in this book. Invite children to speculate on why so many similarities between the two lists exist. Ask students to tell why they selected a character and how the character exemplifies the trait. Suggest that students think about their own lives and share examples that illustrate the trait.

EVALUATION:

Determine the level of student understanding by assessing the quality of creative and written products, by observing the degree of enthusiasm for cooperative projects, and by listening to the depth in responses to thought-provoking questions. Encourage students to connect the message in the story to the theme of the New Year and celebrations of optimism and hope.

CONNECTION #1:
June Behrens.
Gung Hay Fat Choy

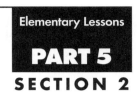
Through vivid descriptions and pictures, family and friends as well as readers enjoy the celebration of Chinese New Year (Gung Hay Fat Choy = Best Wishes and Congratulations, Have a Prosperous and Good Year). At the birth of a new year, Chinese typically plan family reunions, exchange gifts, pay homage to ancestors, and give thanks to gods for blessings.

CHARACTER TRAITS: Review the indicators of the nine character traits used in this manual.

1. Read *Gung Hay Fat Choy* aloud. Remember to set the stage with appropriate pre-reading activities that capture students' interest. Clarify vocabulary terms necessary for understanding both the text and the celebration. Define clearly a purpose for reading and/or listening.

2. Introduce students to the Chinese Lunar Horoscope calendar found on page thirteen of the story. Ask students to find the year of their birth on the calendar, then connect the year with the year's animal symbol: rat, ox, tiger, hare, dragon, snake, horse, sheep, monkey, rooster, dog, and pig.

Hint: Many Chinese believe that animal symbols on the Chinese zodiac shape their futures and fortunes. As a special treat, teachers and students may wish to write messages of good cheer, bake each one inside canned biscuits, and share these fortune cookies with others. Remind students that what they know about animals, just as what the Chinese knew at the time of creating their calendar, comes from real, read-about, or told-about experiences. (Alternate Activity)

Divide students into small groups and ask them to brainstorm descriptive words that "flesh out" the character of the animal (e.g., Cunning? Secretive? Mysterious?). Challenge students to write a brief statement about their animal symbol and share with the large group. Then ask for a volunteer team to research animal characteristics from reference sources. **Ask:**

Do the characteristics match? Why or why not?

Why might there be a mismatch between what students think about animal characteristics and what they learn from reference sources?

Could the same thing have happened to the Chinese calendar makers when they chose the animals with certain characteristics?

Lead students to conclude that research supports, clarifies, or denies commonly held beliefs such as the ones about animal characteristics. **Ask:** What does this experience teach students about how to handle information and data of all kinds?

3. Divide students into the same groups that worked on animal descriptions. Talk to children about how some animals show devotion to their masters while others serve their masters in courageous ways. Ask student groups to write five rules for animals to live by and report to the large group. Use this question as a focus for discussion: Are there similar elements in the animal codes and in the nine core character traits? Why or why not? Direct each group to share the code of rules and answers to the thought questions with classmates.

Hint: For interest and variety, alternate discussions on character traits between the benefits of possessing the traits and the consequences of not possessing the traits.

EVALUATION:

Determine the level of student understanding of the Chinese New Year celebration by assessing the quality of class discussions, by noting awareness of commonalities among cultures, and by observing enthusiasm for research and creative activities. Include teacher observations and rubrics in evaluating student progress. Encourage students to connect the message in the story to the theme of the New Year and celebrations of optimism and hope.

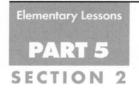

CONNECTION #2:
Emily Kelley. *Happy New Year*

The author assembles an around-the-world reference on New Year celebrations. Teachers and students may use this source as a tool for quick research.

CHARACTER TRAITS: Review the indicators of the nine character traits used in this manual.

1. Share *Happy New Year* with students and discuss how the source serves as a valuable reference for celebrations and holidays. Discuss parts of the reference source and processes for finding information quickly. Invite students to suggest a favorite celebration, and then practice the research skills necessary to find the information. **Hint:** Allow students to share information about the celebration with classmates. By the time each student finishes with a favorite celebration, they will enjoy a potpourri of around-the-world, throughout-the-year experiences.

2. Assist students in developing criteria for investigating global celebrations of the new year (e.g., parades, firecrackers, colors, tokens, promises to live better lives, unique features). Make sure that students understand the purpose of the criteria and the meaning of the examples prior to starting the research process. Then establish partners or groups so that students may research the largest number of countries and celebrations possible. **Hint:** Because group members need ready access to the information, copy each country's section from the book.

Encourage students to develop a creative project (e.g., a representation of the country's flag, to accompany the group report). Talk with students about presentation skills, allow group members to practice reports in their groups before making presentations to the large group and then invite volunteers to present the group reports. Prompt students to look for commonalities among celebrations beyond the criteria. **Hint:** Students will realize that even though criteria guide the research process, the discovery of new data requires refinement of original criteria.

3. Ask students to choose one core character trait that they wish to develop in themselves. Request that students think about a way that they may demonstrate the trait at school. Invite students to write the trait on a strip of paper in the form of a New Year's resolution, put the resolutions in a hat, and pass the hat around the room for everyone to draw one resolution. (Alternate Activity, Parental Discretion)

Challenge students to follow the resolution for the rest of the school day, and then lead students in a discussion about how they followed or did not follow their resolution at the end of the school day.

Ask:

How does it feel to follow someone else's resolution?

What did students learn about setting resolutions for themselves?

What does the experience teach students about changing habits?

If the process of change is so slow, why do people keep trying to change their attitudes or behaviors?

4. Invite other teachers, school volunteers, and/or students' parents to assist in planning a New Year's Good Luck Tasting Luncheon featuring English wassail, French pancakes, Swiss milk, Spanish grapes, Southern black-eyed peas, and Iranian rice pilaf. Prior to the luncheon, request assistance from the librarian in locating information about how relationships developed between certain foods and good luck. (Alternate Activity) Ask confident students to present the information on how these traditions started in different geographic locations for the luncheon's entertainment. Request that students draw pictures of these foods and place them in geographically correct locations on a classroom map.

EVALUATION:

Determine the level of student understanding of global new years' customs by assessing class discussions, activities, presentations, and participation. Include teacher observations and rubrics in evaluating student progress. Encourage students to connect the message in the story to the theme of the New Year and celebrations of optimism and hope.

CONNECTION #3:
Malka Drucker.
Rosh Hashanah and Yom Kippur: Sweet Beginnings

Rosh Hashanah and Yom Kippur, high holy days focusing on personal reflection rather than noisy merrymaking, represent the most solemn days of the Jewish year. Teachers will welcome this instructional resource of games, recipes, puzzles, and crafts.

CHARACTER TRAITS: Review the indicators of the nine character traits used in this manual.

1. Read *Rosh Hashanah and Yom Kippur* aloud. Remember to set the stage with appropriate pre-reading activities that capture students' interest. Clarify vocabulary terms necessary for understanding both the text and the celebration. Define clearly a purpose for reading and/or listening.

2. Review and exemplify the geographic concept of cardinal directions: north, south, east, and west. Use information from the story and other reference sources to illustrate the geographic, cultural, and symbolic link established by the Jewish practice of honoring the Temple in the East. In the story, point out various meaningful symbols commonly associated with the celebration of these holidays (e.g., animals, flowers), then encourage children to design collages to hang on the east wall of the classroom.

Hint: Review the meaning of the symbols as well as why they hang on the east wall of the classroom. Extend the learning on geographic and cultural links by asking for other examples children know about or ties between geographic concepts and religious traditions such as the role of the Star in the East in Christian tradition and the practice of facing east (e.g., Mecca) in Islamic tradition.

3. Explain that Sephardic Jews serve foods that express wishes for a happy new year. Names, parts, and shapes of foods are as important as tastes. Certain combinations of foods carry meaning: for example, an apple in honey means that a person is as good as an apple and as sweet as honey.

Extension: Review the use of similes and metaphors as ways to bring color into descriptive writing. Invite small groups of students to choose a combination of favorite foods and to create similes or metaphors similar to the above example. **Hint:** Monitor group progress closely and remind students first to select a combination of favorite foods, then devise the meaning for the combination. Ask students to write, illustrate, and display similes and metaphors. **Hint:** Group products may suggest a link between similes, metaphors, and character traits. Point out natural connections that exist in student products and use examples to emphasize the importance of looking for connections among all learning.

EVALUATION:

Determine the level of student understanding of the Jewish New Year celebration by assessing the quality of class discussions, the enthusiasm for group participation, and the creativity demonstrated in activities. Include teacher observations and rubrics in evaluating student progress. Encourage students to connect the message in the story to the theme of the New Year and celebrations of optimism and hope.

CONNECTION #1:
Barbara Greenwood. A Pioneer Sampler: The Daily Life of a Pioneer Family in 1840 (pages 230-237)

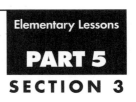

Greenwood engages readers in typical pioneer life of the 1840s through vivid accounts of daily activities and special occasions. Family customs such as New Year or Hogmanay stem from Granny's Scottish homeland.

CHARACTER TRAITS: Review the nine character traits used in this manual and give examples of each of them. Ask students to provide other examples from their own experiences.

1. Read the selection from *A Pioneer Sampler* aloud. Remember to set the stage with appropriate pre-reading activities that capture students' interest. Sweeten activities by serving samples of oatcakes or shortbread and apple juice as students listen to the story. Link geography to everyday lives by discussing pioneer recipes and availability of ingredients on the prairie. Discuss how scarcity of ingredients increases the value of holiday treats.

   Hint: Contrast how present-day systems of production, marketing, distribution, and transportation make most ingredients, even the exotic ones, available to consumers.

2. Encourage students to select a Hogmanay tradition detailed in the story and either research more information in the media center or create additional examples that extend classmates' understanding of a specific tradition:

   Investigate the tradition of sweeping the house at midnight (e.g., reason, participants, similar practices in other cultures).

   Analyze the Hogmanay greeting: "Good health and happiness to this house and all in it. And may none but friends cross the threshold." Research other cultural examples of sending friends good wishes at the beginning of a new year.

   Examine the practice of a "first-footer" bringing gifts of good fortune such as a loaf of bread or a glowing coal, then seek similar practices of gift giving in other cultures.

   Hint: After students report findings to classmates, assist them in using evidence to support these generalizations:

   When people begin to understand other individuals and their beliefs, respect and acceptance often follow.
   Studying similarities and differences among people usually leads to the recognition that human beings are more alike than different.

3. Students will identify the character traits that enabled pioneers to confront problems and to find solutions to the challenges of everyday life on the frontier. Invite students to think of examples in which they call upon the same traits to meet challenges in their lives. **Ask:** Why do many traits cross generational as well as cultural lines and continue to serve people well? **Hint:** Use the discussion to develop understanding of the term, universal, as it applies to character traits.

   Hint: For interest and variety, alternate discussions on character traits between the benefits of possessing the traits and the consequences of not possessing the traits.

EVALUATION:

Determine the level of student understanding of the pioneer family's celebration of New Years by assessing the quality of research, the presentation of research findings, and the responses to higher-order thinking questions. Include teacher-made rubrics in evaluations. Ask students to explain, through writing, the connection between possessing certain character traits and the courage to find solutions to the problems that confront them. Encourage students to connect the message in the story to the theme of the New Year and celebrations of optimism and hope.

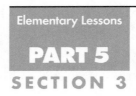

Elementary Lessons

PART 5

SECTION 3

CONNECTION #2:
Myra Cohn Livingston, Ed.
New Year's Poems

Livingston's collection presents various customs for celebrating the New Year in poetic form and thus becomes a valuable teaching tool for cultural and geographic inquiries.

CHARACTER TRAITS: Review the nine character traits used in this manual and give examples of each of them. Ask students to provide other examples from their own experiences.

1. Read aloud poems selected for cultural and geographic studies. Remember to set the stage with appropriate pre-reading activities that capture students' interest. For example, alert students to the tasks associated with the next activity. Tell them that they may choose the poem that holds the highest degree of personal interest for inquiry, illustration, and presentation. Remind them that listening to all poems, thinking about their messages, investigating unfamiliar words, and locating the geographic site of the poem are important parts of this arts-related project. Urge students to listen attentively to all poems. (Alternate Activity, Parental Discretion)

2. Allow students to select their personal poem, and then provide them with individual copies with which to work. Excite students by describing both tasks and products (Alternate Activity, Parental Discretion):

> *Select a poem;*
>
> *Locate the culture on a world map;*
>
> *Research additional information about the cultural celebration;*
>
> *Sketch the shape of the country on a sheet of manila paper, then superimpose an illustration that projects the cultural celebration;*
>
> *Write notes to serve as a basis for presenting the cultural celebration to classmates;*
>
> *Present the celebration by speaking from notes, and then post a cultural symbol of the celebration on the world map;*
>
> *Submit illustrated sheets to the teacher who will bind the pages together for a class reference on new years' celebrations as worldwide expressions of hope for the future.*

Following presentations, call students' attention to the distribution of symbols on the world map. Use symbols as evidence to reinforce the unit's generalizations:

> *Celebrations are integral parts of many, but not all, children's lives.*
>
> *Individuals, groups, institutions, cultures, and nations celebrate, or honor in other ways, those people, events, or values that they cherish most.*

Over time, human behaviors—such as celebrating or honoring special people, events, or values—may change.

When people begin to understand other individuals and their beliefs, respect and acceptance often follow.

Studying similarities and differences among people usually leads to the recognition that human beings are more alike than different.

3. Ask students to reflect on the processes used to complete and present the arts-related project. Ask them to review the total list of character traits and choose the traits that assisted them in the project, share their thoughts with classmates, and predict how the traits will help them accomplish tasks in the future.

EVALUATION:

Determine the level of student understanding of new years' celebrations by assessing the quality of class presentations and creative products and by listening to the thought processes used in support of generalizations. Include teacher-made rubrics in evaluations. Encourage students to connect the message in the poems to the theme of the New Year and celebrations of optimism and hope.

CONNECTION #3:
Miriam Chaikin.
Sound the Shofar

Jewish people mark the beginning of the year in the fall by celebrating the high holy days of Rosh Hashanah and Yom Kippur. Chaikin clarifies for readers the symbols, legends, customs, greetings, and foods associated with the celebration.

CHARACTER TRAITS: Review the nine character traits used in this manual and give examples of each of them. Ask students to provide other examples from their own experiences.

1. Read *Sound the Shofar* aloud. Remember to set the stage with appropriate pre-reading activities that capture students' interest. For example, lead students in a cultural geography mini-lesson on the original homeland of the Jewish people. Point out the location and the place of origin. With student assistance, consult atlases, maps, and other resources for geographic clues about what type of land the homeland represents (e.g., Is it flat? Mountainous? Hot? Cold? Fertile?)

Construct a geographic profile of the homeland and then challenge students to predict how geographic factors shaped Jewish culture. Ask students to verify their predictions by seeking information in the story or other sources.

Extension: Extend the geography lesson by explaining the term, Diaspora, i.e., the scattering of Jews outside their homeland. Talk about probable reasons why Jewish people emigrated from their native land, then ask student volunteers to research historical evidence for emigration. As an alternate activity, ask a community resource person to explain the movement of people and reasons for emigration.

Hint: Use the discussions in this lesson to introduce, develop, and/or reinforce the five themes of geography: location, place, human/environment interaction, movement, and region. Develop understanding of the five themes by encouraging students to cite examples from the discussion that illustrate the concepts.

2. Allow students to choose one of the following activities to complete with a partner or a small group:

Research the symbolism of foods served at a typical Jewish feast during the celebration of Rosh Hashanah and Yom Kippur, e.g., pomegranate seeds and good deeds; if possible, show classmates pictures of Jewish feasts as students report on the symbolism of the foods.

Construct an emigration/immigration timeline that shows major movements of Jewish people from their homeland; mark each movement with the reason for emigration, migration, or immigration; explain the differences among the three terms of movement to classmates.

Research examples of cultural borrowing between the Jewish culture and other cultures especially as emigration increased. **Hint:** Tell students that some sources may use the term cultural diffusion instead of cultural borrowing.

After groups report to classmates, ask students to review the topics: feasts and symbolism, movement from homelands, and cultural borrowing. **Ask:** Are these three topics common themes that thread through the histories of most cultural groups? Why or why not?

3. Ask students to give some thought to the history of the Jewish people as reflected in this story. Add research to this history from the media center, and invite a Jewish person to talk to the class about his or her religious/cultural history. When this project is completed, ask students to consider what character traits the Jews exhibited at different historical periods. Invite students to predict whether the same traits will serve them well as they confront issues in their everyday lives and why.

Hint: For interest and variety, alternate discussions on character traits between the benefits of possessing the traits and the consequences of not possessing the traits.

EVALUATION:

Determine the level of student understanding of Rosh Hashanah and Yom Kippur by assessing the quality of research, presentations, products, and responses during all phases of the literature-related activities. Include teacher-made rubrics in evaluations. Encourage students to connect the message in the story to the theme of the New Year and celebrations of optimism and hope.

Elementary Lessons

PART 5

SECTION 3

CONNECTION #4:
Roch Carrier.
A Happy New Year's Day

Carrier draws from childhood memories as he recalls his family's New Year's celebration. He vividly remembers the hustle and bustle of preparing for and participating in a special day. He fondly recounts how close ties create a sense of well being for family members.

CHARACTER TRAITS: Review the nine character traits used in this manual and give examples of each of them. Ask students to provide other examples from their own experiences.

CHARACTER EDUCATION THROUGH STORY

1. Read *A Happy New Year's Day* aloud. Remember to set the stage with appropriate pre-reading activities that capture students' interest. For example, lead students through a geographic mini-lesson focused on Canada, the city of Quebec, the winter season in Canada, and the necessity for sleighs and snowmobiles. **Hint:** Utilize the discussion to illustrate cause-and-effect relationships between geography and lifestyles.

   Use maps and atlases for data so that students may make projections based on facts. Encourage students to compare and contrast the winter season in Canada and in their community (e.g., the amount of snow and the degree to which winter conditions influence people's daily lives). Challenge student partners to make logical conclusions about the setting of the story based on the discussion about winter in two locations.

   Divide class into groups of two (reading partners) and remind them that the purposes of the reading are threefold:

   > *To verify conclusions about Canadian winters;*
   > *To affirm that geography influences people's daily lives; and*
   > *To show how the illustrations complement the text of the story.*

   Tell them to read slowly, pause frequently, and allow their reading partners to discuss thoughts that support the three purposes. Following the reading, lead a discussion directed toward the three purposes. **Ask:** How and why do stated purposes for reading help you learn?

2. Invite students to share how their families welcome in a new year. List traditions on one side of a Venn diagram or T-chart. Encourage students to revisit the diagram or chart, draw the author's traditions from the text and illustrations of *A Happy New Year's Day*, and complete the other side of the diagram or chart. Point out the similarities and differences between New Year's celebrations.

   Hint: Make sure that students recognize that political, economic, cultural, and geographic factors contribute to similarities and differences among celebrations.

   Hint: Encourage parent volunteers to prepare traditional snacks and serve them during the comparison-and-contrast exercise.

   Extension: Extend the learning by talking with students about why many cultures plan celebrations for "starting again." Use the discussion to develop an understanding of the concept of universality and then cite examples from the activities of *A Happy New Year's Day*, students' traditions, and other reference sources that illustrate the concept.

3. Ask students to reflect on the New Year's tradition of starting again and decide what traits might help a person accomplish a New Year's resolution. Lead students in using the indicators under each of the character traits as guidelines for deciding whether or not a specific trait might assist a person in keeping resolutions.

EVALUATION:

Determine the level of student understanding of new year's celebrations by assessing the degree of participation exhibited in activities and by listening for the depth of thoughts expressed in responses. Watch how quickly students move from concrete to abstract processes when prompted by higher-order thinking questions. Encourage students to connect the message in the story to the theme of the New Year and celebrations of optimism and hope.

CONNECTION #1:
Carol Levin.
A Rosh Hashanah Walk

On Rosh Hashanah afternoon, Jewish families gather on the banks of a river or a stream to recite prayers and to ask for forgiveness. Levin gives readers valuable insights into solemn times for personal reflection and resolution.

CHARACTER TRAITS: Focus on the character traits associated with this manual. Ask students to check their definitions, share new insights, and provide different examples of each trait that they have discovered.

1. Read *A Rosh Hashanah Walk* aloud. Remember to set the stage with appropriate pre-reading activities that capture students' interest. For example, talk with students about the act of walking. Ask students if they receive any benefits other than exercise as a result of walking at either a fast or leisurely pace. **Hint:** Share with students that many people report that their best problem solving and decision making result from thinking during a brisk walk. Ask students if they have experienced clearer thinking during walks. Use the informal discussion about walking to introduce the story.

Review students on the story map technique by modeling a map that outlines a story already read. Include elements such as setting, problem, solution, personalities, and any others that the teacher wishes to emphasize. Point out to students that sequenced events may fit into or substitute for the problem-and-solution section. Set the completion of a story map as the purpose for listening. Stop reading several times during the story and allow small groups to discuss what information goes into the map. At the end of the story, encourage students to volunteer information to complete the map.

Ask:

Does a clearly defined purpose for listening assist students in learning and remembering information? Why?

Does the practice of defining a purpose before beginning a task apply to other tasks? How and why?

Extension: Extend the learning by appointing a research team to investigate how Yom Kippur relates to Rosh Hashanah and then to explain the two celebrations to classmates.

2. Discuss the purpose of reflection and resolution. Invite students to reflect upon the past year and to mentally take a Tashlich walk to symbolically discard inconsiderate acts. **Hint:** Share with students that during Tashlich trips participants sing, walk, search, look, question, remember, and think. When they reach water (e.g., rivers, streams, or fountains), they dig deep into their pockets, pull out crumbs that stand for something in the past year they regret, and cast them into the water. In other words, Tashlich trips are meant to give people the opportunity to say they're sorry. Then people turn their thoughts to a new year.

Alert students that the practices of reflecting on past deeds and resolving to make amends cross many cultural lines. Invite all students to share knowledge about similar practices from their cultural perspectives. **Ask:** If similar practices occur in many cultures, what does that tell students about people's desire to do better?

Ask students to follow these steps:

Examine the past year;

Select an area they wish to improve this week;

Write their selection in the form of personal goals on a piece of paper;

Plan steps to reach their goals; and

Place the goals in envelopes with their names on the front.

Pass out the envelopes once a week for students to evaluate their progress toward their goals. Encourage students to make entries similar to those in a journal. Invite students to share what they are learning each week during the process, then collect the envelopes until the next session. Continue the process as long as student interest runs high. Talk with students about how Tashlich walks, resolutions, and goal setting share common elements. **Ask:**

How do all of the processes help you accomplish goals?

Why does the goal-setting process make goal accomplishment easier than pursuing a goal without a plan?

How can you relate goal setting to the unit theme?

3. Ask students to reflect on the goal-setting exercise, then determine what character traits assisted them most in completing their goal. Ask students how they may apply the same character traits to other situations in their lives. **Ask:** What evidence can students find that the character traits touch all aspects of their lives?

EVALUATION:

Determine the level of student understanding about how members of many cultures reflect on past deeds and resolve to do better by assessing the quality of responses, the enthusiasm for research and creative projects, and the degree of participation. Ask students to debrief the learning from the story and activities, then tell what, how, and why they learned. Encourage students to connect the message in the story to the theme of the New Year and celebrations of optimism and hope.

ADDITIONAL SELECTIONS:

Barbara Diamond Goldin. *The World's Birthday: A Rosh Hashanah Story*

Maida Silverman. *The Glass Menorah and Other Stories for Jewish Holidays*

CONNECTION #2:
Ann Grifalconi. *The Bravest Flute: A Story of Courage in the Mayan Tradition*

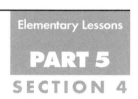

Elementary Lessons

PART 5

SECTION 4

As a Mayan boy leads the New Year's Day parade, his courage serves as an inspiration for all villagers.

CHARACTER TRAITS: Focus on the character traits associated with this manual. Ask students to check their definitions, share new insights, and provide different examples of each trait that they have discovered. Ask students to provide definitions of the trait of courage and give examples of people who have done courageous acts.

1. Read *The Bravest Flute* aloud. Remember to set the stage with appropriate pre-reading activities that capture students' interest. For example, refer to the character trait of courage. Ask students if they remember a person demonstrating any of the specific indicators of courage such as taking a stand; holding to your convictions; being willing to sacrifice self-interest for the greater good; risking failure; risking disfavor from others; and overcoming fear and adversity.

   Take the time to talk about the meaning of each indicator and categorize student examples under one or more of the indicators. As part of the discussion, mention to students that they are not born with courage or any other character trait; people learn traits as a result of informal and formal experiences. **Examples:** informal experiences such as those learned from family, friends, and neighbors; formal experiences such as those learned through churches, schools, and organizations.

   Hint: For interest and variety, alternate discussions on character traits between the benefits of possessing the traits and the consequences of not possessing the traits.

   Tie the discussion focusing upon the world of elementary students to the world described in *The Bravest Flute*. Set learning about similarities and differences in space, time, cultures, and lifestyles as the purpose for listening. After the reading, enlist students' assistance in completing a Venn diagram on the similarities and differences between the two worlds.

2. Explain to students that they may choose how to demonstrate their understanding of Mayan culture. Ask students to listen to the following activity options; to select one that holds high interest for them; and to work individually, with a partner, or in a small group to complete the project:

   Research the size of Mayan lands in ancient times, then compare the size with the size of present Mayan holdings; prepare a "then-and-now" poster or transparency.

   Research the time period of Mayan greatness in terms of accomplishment in many fields; prepare a chart or poster that shows the Mayan civilization at its height.

   Research the role of priests in Mayan culture, then plan a skit that demonstrates the amount of power priests held.

   Research class structure in Mayan society. Prepare a social pyramid on a transparency, poster, or chalkboard that shows who is at the top, middle, and bottom of society. Lead classmates in a discussion of why people were members of one class rather than another class. Lead students in an investigation of whether people moved up or down on the social pyramid and why.

   Research Egyptian culture at the time of its height in the ancient world, then compare and contrast Egyptian culture to Mayan culture; prepare a Venn diagram on the two great civilizations.

   Research Egyptian and Mayan writing, then prepare a transparency or illustration with examples of hieroglyphic or picture writing.

   Research how Mayans accounted for the passage of time, then make a T-chart or Venn diagram to compare and contrast their calendar to modern-day calendars; determine if both calendars enable people to keep an accurate account of time.

   Research the ancient city of Tikal, Guatemala, then construct a model that shows major features of the city; be able to explain the reasons for placement of structures in certain places.

   Research principles of Mayan mathematics, then determine if any of the principles will transfer to problem-solving methods used by elementary students today; demonstrate Mayan and present-day problem solving with examples.

   Research in several references how historians account for the disappearance of Mayan civilization; share as many stories as the references reveal, then lead classmates in a discussion about what might be the most probable theories and why.

   Set reasonable deadlines for the completion of Mayan projects, then plan a special time for presentations entitled "Mayan Markers: Insights into Greatness." Stress to students that knowing and organizing their subjects thoroughly enables them to present information in an informal, exciting manner. Emphasize that they may use note cards, if necessary, but that they cannot read a written report word-for-word. After presentations, lead students in a discussion of why Mayan culture is important for students to understand. **Hint:** Focus attention on contributions to American culture from the Mayan culture.

EVALUATION:

Determine the level of student understanding about Mayan contributions to American culture by assessing the quality of responses, the enthusiasm for research as well as creative projects, and the degree of participation. Encourage students to connect the message in the story to the theme of the New Year, and celebrations of optimism and hope.

CONNECTION #3:
Sothea Chiemruom.
Dara's Cambodian New Year

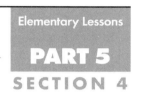

Elementary Lessons

PART 5

SECTION 4

Chiemruom transports readers to a Cambodian family's two-day springtime celebration of the New Year.

CHARACTER TRAITS: Focus on the character traits associated with this manual. Ask students to check their definitions, share new insights, and provide different examples of each trait that they have discovered.

1. Read *Dara's Cambodian New Year* aloud. Remember to set the stage with appropriate pre-reading activities that capture students' interest. For example, assist students in locating the country of Cambodia on a map, and then challenge them to paint the landscape by drawing geographic clues from concepts such as latitude and longitude, altitude, and zone on the classroom map. Request that they add to the picture by using map data to predict climate, vegetation, and landforms.

After the painting-the-scene activity, talk to students about how authors set the mood of a story. Authors create moods through skillful interplay among characters, settings, plots, solutions, illustrations, and dialogue. Set listening for the way Chiemruom creates a mood as the purpose for listening to the story.

Following the story reading, request that students comment on the mood set by the author. **Ask:**

> *What is the mood of the story?*
> *Is the mood consistent throughout the story?*
> *What factors contribute to the overall mood of the story?*
> *Does Dara use one or more of the character traits to overcome the problem?*
> *In what ways might you call upon the same character traits to solve a problem?*

2. Tell students that the author interweaves three topics with the characters and the storyline (e.g., Buddhism, immigration, and rice). Alert students that each of the topics plays an important role in the story of a Cambodian family as well as in the celebration of New Year.

Assign teams of students to one of three topics and challenge them to search for information that extends or illuminates why the topic is important to the story. After students complete their research, invite them to a story festival in which they thoughtfully analyze the storyline and creatively share why their topic of Buddhism, immigration, or rice adds to the richness of a Cambodian story.

Extension: Extend the discussion by pointing out to students how celebrations such as New Year vary among cultures and regions. Ask students to list characteristics of other new year's celebrations.

EVALUATION:

Determine the level of student understanding about why culture and geography influence how people celebrate by assessing the quality of responses, the enthusiasm for research as well as creative projects, and the degree of participation. Ask students to explain what they learned from the story and activities, then tell what, how, and why they learned. Encourage students to connect the message in the story to the theme of the New Year and celebrations of optimism and hope.

Elementary Lessons

PART 5

SECTION 4

CONNECTION #4:
Myra Cohn Livingston, Ed.
New Year's Poems

From Livingston's collection of New Year's poems, teachers may select examples that best serve instructional purposes and that enable students to teach their peers successfully.

CHARACTER TRAITS: Focus on the character traits associated with this manual. Ask students to check their definitions, share new insights, and provide different examples of each trait that they have discovered.

1. Read aloud selected poems such as "Chinese New Year," "The New Year's Journey," and "Beginning a New Year Means." Explain to students that when teachers plan lessons, they carefully choose materials that will model the main ideas or concepts they wish to teach.

2. Make transparencies of the three poems; ask students to assume roles as teachers; then ask student teachers to plan how they will use the poems to introduce, develop, or reinforce main ideas. Lead students through the analysis of each poem with questions such as the following:

> *What is the poet's message?*
>
> *What is the poem's most outstanding, most unusual, most interesting feature?*
>
> *Can student teachers use the poem to teach cultural celebrations, geographic locations, poetic elements, or grammar?*
>
> *Can student teachers plan how they want students to demonstrate understanding?*
>
> *Do characters in the poem demonstrate one or more of the character traits? How?*

3. Select other poems in the collection, then distribute copies of different poems to groups of four students. Challenge them to answer the same questions that the large group used for analyzing poetry, choose what concept they want to teach classmates, and prepare a mini-lesson. Request that each group decide how they will measure the success of their teaching. **Ask:** How will student teachers know if learning occurs? What knowledge or skills will classmates demonstrate if learning takes place?

EVALUATION:

Determine the level of student understanding about how poets convey concepts through poetry and also how teachers plan lessons to teach specific concepts by assessing the quality of responses, enthusiasm for the project, and the degree of participation. Encourage students to connect the message in the poems to the theme of the New Year and celebrations of optimism and hope.

CONNECTION #5:
Steven A. Chin. *Dragon Parade: A Chinese New Year Story*

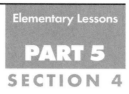
Through story and illustrations, readers acquire knowledge of the Chinese New Year celebration as well as changes in traditional celebratory practices. The author affirms one of the unit's generalizations: Over time, human behaviors—such as celebrating or honoring special people, events, or values—may change.

CHARACTER TRAITS: Focus on the character traits associated with this manual. Ask students to check their definitions, share new insights, and provide different examples of each trait that they have discovered.

1. Read *Dragon Parade: A Chinese New Year Story* aloud. Remember to set the stage with appropriate pre-reading activities that capture students' interest. For example, introduce the story by asking students how their family celebrates the beginning of a new year. **Examples:** Gatherings of family and friends? Decorations? Symbols? Special foods? Resolutions? Activities such as watching football games on television? As students suggest different customs, list the ideas on the chalkboard, then affirm that they might categorize these customs as the typical American observance of a New Year.

Divide students into partners and ask that they listen for customs similar to and different from the American celebration. Request that students record notes on a sheet of notebook paper folded in half, one column labeled "Similarities" and the other "Differences." Following the story reading, solicit student assistance in completing a Venn diagram in the shape of overlapping New Year's bells. **Ask:**

> *What other element for comparison and contrast does Chin introduce in the story?*
>
> *Is it possible to add another bell to the Venn diagram and extend the comparison-and-contrast exercise?*
>
> *If researchers add more data to topics of study, what trait must they remember to apply?*

Hint: Lead students to understand that the best trait for researchers to apply in any inquiry is open-mindedness. Encourage students to investigate all data carefully and objectively, then draw valid conclusions based on reason.

Hint: Prior to this activity, ask the media specialist to assist students in finding various New Year's customs throughout history (e.g., the legend of Janus from Roman mythology or the ringing of bells to welcome in a new year). Encourage students to share research with classmates.

2. Lead students in an analysis of how effective the criteria on the chalkboard are for judging similarities and differences in New Year's celebrations. Request that students consider the addition of other criteria, if necessary.

Divide students into six groups, then make the following story-related assignments:

> Assign four groups the task of explaining a typical American celebration (e.g., President's Day, Mother's Day, Father's Day, Memorial Day, Fourth of July, Labor Day, or Thanksgiving Day) to a group of Chinese citizens touring the United States. Apply the criteria used for analyzing *Dragon Parade: A Chinese New Year Story*. Consider the level of English proficiency of the audience when making explanations, and make adjustments in presentations. Link this activity to the unit generalization related to people celebrating or honoring in a variety of ways those things they cherish most.

Challenge one group to research the differences between the lunar and solar calendars and to explain how the information relates to the story. Show students an illustration of traditional Chinese signs attached to the calendar such as the year of the monkey, rat, or hare, and read the traits under each sign to classmates. Use the calendar and traits as natural lead-ins to those character traits that the main character in the story exhibits.

Invite two students who show special interest in science projects to assist the teacher in planting bulbs in shallow pans filled with pebbles; place pans in several different locations in the classroom and set up a system for keeping records on growth; explain to classmates that many Chinese believe that good fortune accompanies the new year if flowers bloom on New Year's Day.

Set aside time for presentations on American celebrations, research on calendars, and bulb planting.

EVALUATION:

Determine the level of student understanding about comparisons and contrasts between Chinese and American celebrations by assessing the quality of responses, the enthusiasm for research as well as creative projects, and the degree of participation. Evaluate their written and oral assignments using a variety of criteria such as organization, clarity of thought, and neatness. Encourage students to connect the message in the story to the celebrations of optimism and hope.

ADDITIONAL SELECTIONS:

Kate Waters and Madeline Slovenz-Low. *Lion Dancer: Ernie Wan's Chinese New Year*

Tricia Brown. *Chinese New Year*

Rachel Sing. *Chinese New Year's Dragon*

June Behrens. *Gung Hay Fat Choy*

Clara Yen. *Why Rat Comes First: The Story of the Chinese Zodiac*

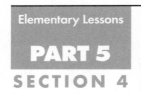

Elementary Lessons

PART 5

SECTION 4

CONNECTION #6:
James Stevenson.
Un-Happy New Year, Emma

Stevenson's trio of characters manipulates the usually honorable intentions of New Year's resolutions with surprising as well as humorous results.

CHARACTER TRAITS: Focus on the character traits associated with this manual. Ask students to check their definitions, share new insights, and provide different examples of each trait that they have discovered.

1. Read *Un-Happy New Year, Emma* aloud. Remember to set the stage with appropriate pre-reading activities that capture students' interest. For example, inquire about how students define the term, resolution, then lead them to the understanding that a New Year's resolution usually implies that a person commits to a change for the better either in attitudes or actions. Ask students to listen carefully to the story for the purpose of determining whether or not the trio of characters makes resolutions to change attitudes or actions for the better.

Prior to reading the story, talk with students about the power of cartoons in terms of messages they carry. Tell students that cartoonists often exaggerate physical characteristics to cause humorous responses in viewers and to call attention to their message. Ask students to study the cartoon illustrations as the teacher reads and holds up the pictures for view. **Ask:**

How do the resolutions of the characters match the definition of the term?

Are the characters committed to making their attitudes and actions better?

Why do students think that Stevenson chose a cartoonist to illustrate the storyline?

What messages do the cartoons carry to readers?

What character traits does the trio exhibit or fail to exhibit in Un-Happy New Year, Emma?

2. Enlist students in preparing a bulletin board entitled "New Year's Resolutions." Assist them in covering the board with colored paper and in cutting out letters for the title and symbols of the celebration. Ask them to assume the role of one of the characters, make a written resolution to improve attitudes or actions from the perspective of the character, and illustrate the resolution with a captioned cartoon. Encourage students to post their work on the bulletin board.

Next, request that students reflect on their everyday activities at school, at home, at church, in the neighborhood, or in organizations, then write a New Year's resolution related to one of the daily activities. Instruct them to think about how to improve attitudes and/or actions and to design a step-by-step plan for improvement. Schedule this activity before the winter holidays so that students may work on the resolution during vacation. After the holidays, ask volunteers to share resolutions and progress reports. Invite them to post these resolutions on the bulletin board.

Hint: Talking with students about the process of making resolutions prior to setting their personal resolutions will increase chances for all students to be successful. Encourage them to celebrate small steps toward keeping a resolution and not wait until they make dramatic changes in attitudes and actions. Applaud consistency and diligence in working toward improvement.

EVALUATION:

Determine the level of student understanding about New Year's resolutions by assessing the quality of responses, the enthusiasm for research as well as creative projects, and the degree of participation. Ask students to explain what they learned from the story and activities, then tell what, how, and why they learned. Encourage students to connect the message in the story to the theme of the New Year and celebrations of optimism and hope.

Spring:
Celebrations
of Birth
and Rebirth

CONNECTION #1:
Lynn Sharon Schwartz.
The Four Questions

Readers gain valuable insights into Jewish symbols and rituals traditionally associated with the Passover holiday.

CHARACTER TRAITS: Focus attention on the traits of respect, compassion, and responsibility.

1. Read *The Four Questions* aloud. Remember to set the stage with appropriate pre-reading activities that capture students' interest. For example, establish the focus of the study with the question: Why is this night different from all other nights? Point out to students that the questions and answers provide a framework for listening to the story and for drawing meaning from the text. Number students one through four so that students may pay special attention to the corresponding question and response during story reading:

> *Why tonight do we eat only matzoh?*
> *Why tonight do we eat only bitter herbs?*
> *Why tonight do we dip them twice into salt water?*
> *Why tonight do we all recline?*

Clarify vocabulary terms necessary for understanding both the text and the celebration.

Extension: Divide the class into cooperative groups numbered one through four. Challenge each group to discuss and phrase the meaning of the previously assigned question and response in language appropriate for elementary students. Remind students how valuable examples are to explanations and encourage them to add these to their explanations. Invite groups to share responses to the questions with classmates. Encourage members of other groups to ask questions about the explanations.

2. Assign partners to study the twelve pictures of the Passover Seder in the story and match pictures to correct descriptions. Provide partners with two index cards. Assign one picture to each set of partners with these directions: draw the picture on one card and write a matching description on the other card. Invite partners to share pictures and descriptions with classmates. Distribute pictures and descriptions randomly among students. Instruct students to find the person with the matching picture or description. When students find the correct partner, tell them to stand in the correct sequence and share the picture and description for the second time.

Ask: Why does participating in varied activities help you find meaning in any topic of study? **Hint:** Participation in different types of activities in different grouping patterns addresses students' individual talents and reinforces the lesson. Students tend to remember the lessons in which they play an active role.

3. Invite a person from the Jewish community to class to comment on the explanations of Passover that students have learned through reading, listening, and cooperative activities. Advise students in advance that they will be offering an explanation of their learning to a visitor who will add more understanding to their knowledge of Passover. Ask the guest to provide insights into the symbols and traditions of the celebration not discovered through classroom activities, especially the significance of the celebration in the Jewish religion.

Prior to the visit, discuss interview questions students want to ask, and then provide a list of questions to the guest. At the end of the visit, lead students in summarizing what they learned about Passover from varied approaches: reading, listening, cooperative activities, and a personal interview. Use student responses to reinforce the value of varied teaching/learning activities. Extend students' understanding further by sharing David Adler's story, *A Picture Book of Passover*.

4. Select one character trait (e.g., respect, compassion, or responsibility) and talk about how people in the story demonstrate the trait. Ask students to tell why they selected a character and how the character exemplifies that trait. Suggest that students think about their own lives and share examples that illustrate the trait.

Hint: For interest and variety, alternate discussions on character traits between the presence and benefits of possessing the traits and the absence and consequences of not possessing the traits.

5. Remember that celebrations and holidays do not cease when the school year ends. Search for ways to observe cultural and/or national holidays (e.g., Memorial Day, Emancipation Day, Independence Day) that occur during summer months and also to celebrate or honor days of personal accomplishment that occur throughout the year (e.g., new learning, new skills, new roles, new responsibilities). Extend the scope of lessons taught during the school year by using theme-related examples from all twelve months of the year.

EVALUATION:

Determine the level of student understanding by assessing the quality of creative projects, by observing the degree of enthusiasm for cooperative projects, by determining the receptiveness to processing information from multiple sources, and by listening to the depth of responses to thought-provoking questions. Encourage students to connect the message in the story to the theme of spring and celebrations of birth and rebirth.

CONNECTION #2:
Virginia Kroll.
A Carp for Kimiko

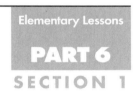

Elementary Lessons

PART 6

SECTION 1

In a delightful story, Japanese parents emphasize to children the importance of nurturing family life, of perpetuating traditions, and of celebrating life.

CHARACTER TRAITS: Review examples and definitions of respect and diligence.

1. Read *A Carp for Kimiko* aloud. Remember to set the stage with appropriate pre-reading activities that capture students' interest. For example, establish the Japanese setting for the story by seeking clues from the illustrations. Then allow students to compare and contrast the location, size, and features of Japan and your state from information on a classroom world map.

Next, review students on the idea that all cultures preserve unique customs and traditions. Focus the purpose of listening to the story on how and why the Japanese celebrate Children's Day. Prior to reading, clarify vocabulary terms necessary for understanding both the text and the celebration.

2. Invite students to make windsocks by following these directions as the teacher models each step of the process: cut a 12" x 2" strip of tag board; staple strip into a circle; use permanent markers to design a carp on a small, white trash can liner; staple the opening of the liner around the tag board circle; use a 6' to 8' length of twine and attach the twine to the tag board circle. Ask students to turn the windsock over and write why they think the Japanese use the fish symbol on Children's Day. Lead them in a discussion that links the symbol to the celebration prior to hanging the windsocks in a classroom display. In the discussion, talk about how and why Kimiko and the carp are similar.

3. Advise students that the first reading of the book focused on learning about the celebration of Children's Day. Tell them that the second reading will fulfill the purpose of learning more about the Japanese people. Add flavor to the second reading by allowing students to sit on the floor in Japanese style, sip a cup of warm tea, and taste a bite of cooked rice and/or egg-drop soup.

Divide students into five groups and assign one of the following topics to each group: the Japanese home, Japanese dress and food, the Japanese family, Japanese physical characteristics, and the importance of individual family members.

Read the story slowly and take time for all students to view the illustrations on each page. Allow time for students to talk among themselves after reading sections in the story to determine if they gathered any evidence on the assigned topic. Encourage groups to present evidence gathered on their topic and to field questions from curious classmates.

Extension: For fun, ask class members to practice in chorus the names of Japanese family members by first breaking the names into syllables and then repeating the syllables until they become easier to pronounce. Remind students that their names surely will seem as different to Japanese children as Japanese names seem to American children. **Hint:** Share with students the adage that correct practice breeds familiarity. Also remind students that diligence pays off when confronting an unfamiliar task. With practice, students can master new sounds.

Lead students in a discussion of what information they can learn from storybooks other than the story if they know how to use clues in the text as well as in the pictures. List suggested items on the chalkboard and ask students to apply the list to another story recently studied. Make sure that students cite the story and the example of learning more than the storyline.

4. Share with students the historic fact that members of the traditional Japanese culture view the birth of boy babies in a much more joyous way than the birth of girl babies. Ask boys and girls to recall clues in the story that support this idea. Query students about evidence in the story that this old cultural tradition is changing. Talk about examples that students suggest. Ask students to take a position on whether the change will be slow or fast and why, then invite them to write their viewpoint in a position statement. Encourage students to share finished pieces of writing with classmates by dividing students into two groups: slow change and why, fast change and why. **Ask:** What conflict exists between American and Japanese views on the birth of boy and girl babies? Which beliefs are more democratic and why? **Hint:** Stress the concept of equality in democratic societies. Point out also that changes in traditions, just like changes in attitudes, are usually gradual and spread over time.

5. Select one character trait (e.g., respect, diligence, courage) and talk about how people in the story demonstrate the trait. Ask students to tell why they selected a character and how the character exemplifies the trait. Suggest that students think about their own lives and share examples that illustrate the trait.

Hint: For interest and variety, alternate discussions on character traits between the benefits of possessing the traits and the consequences of not possessing the traits

6. Remember that celebrations and holidays do not cease when the school year ends. Search for ways to observe cultural and/or national holidays (e.g., Memorial Day, Emancipation Day, Independence Day) that occur during summer months and also to celebrate or honor days of personal accomplishments that occur throughout the year (e.g., new learning, new skills, new roles, new responsibilities). Extend the scope of lessons taught during the school year by using theme-related examples from all twelve months of the year.

EVALUATION:

Determine the level of student understanding by assessing the quality of creative projects, by observing the degree of enthusiasm for cooperative projects, by determining the receptiveness to processing information from multiple sources, and by listening to the depth of responses to thought-provoking questions. Encourage students to connect the message in the story to the theme of spring and celebrations of birth and rebirth.

CONNECTION #3:
Beatriz McConnie Zapater.
Fiesta

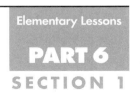
Because Chucho is three years old when his family moves from Columbia, he has no memories of celebrating fiestas in his homeland. Immigration, however, does not dampen the enthusiasm of the entire Mosquera family in planning the Fiesta de Santiago in their new country.

CHARACTER TRAITS: Review the traits of compassion, courage, diligence, and respect. Ask students to provide examples of each of these from their daily experiences.

1. Read *Fiesta* aloud. Remember to set the stage with appropriate pre-reading activities that capture students' interest prior to reading. For example, ask students to define the term, saint, i.e., a holy person who becomes a religious hero or heroine through acts of service, sacrifice, or courage. Ask students to listen closely for the reason why people celebrate the Fiesta de Santiago during the story reading. Also explore students' prior knowledge of fiestas and encourage those who have attended fiestas to share their memories with classmates. Clarify vocabulary terms necessary for understanding both the text and the celebration.

2. Tell students about a geographic tool called a gazeteer that is an index to locations. Enlist the assistance of the media specialist in finding a gazeteer or atlas for student groups to use. Divide the map of the United States into six regions, assign student groups to regions, and ask students to list the states in their region. Ask students to record the full name of a city, river, valley, or mountain range in their assigned region when they see the words, "san" in Spanish or "saint" in French. Transfer names to a laminated wall map or desk map and label them with a marking pen.

Extension: As students end the search, ask them to look for any type of pattern in the names. Ask students if they see Spanish or French names clustered or spread out in their region. **Ask** students to put on their thinking caps and speculate how Spanish and French names landed in regions of the United States. Once they speculate possible answers, ask students to complete and deliver this inquiry addressed to the media specialist:

> The research team in Room _____ investigated evidence of Spanish (or French) names on the map of the United States. The region under investigation covers the present-day states of _____. The team believes that there must be a connection between geographic names and early settlement patterns. Please help team members locate reference sources to solve this geographic mystery.

Allow students to verify connections between names and settlement patterns in multiple reference sources. When all groups finish the task, encourage each group to report findings to classmates. **Hint:** Introduce the term, legacy, along with its meaning, then reinforce the meaning of legacy with examples of Spanish and French names left on the map long after settlements disappear.

3. Remind students about the value of a K-W-L chart. For example, they start with a body of prior knowledge; then they list knowledge they wish to acquire, and then they organize a process of investigation and a process of evaluation.

Invite students to brainstorm as a large group what they already know about fiestas and record under K on the chart. Prompt responses by mentioning items such as food, music, dance, clothing, and customs. Discuss how different Hispanic cultures join together to celebrate a common heritage. Ask students to volunteer items they want to learn about fiestas. Save the chart for future reference.

Use the K-W-L activity as a lead-in to planning a mini-fiesta in the classroom. Talk to students about resource people who might visit the class and offer information on topics listed under W. **Hint:** Invite guests who can provide participatory learning experiences in dancing, singing, and cooking, such as folkloric dancers, musicians, and chefs.

Enlist students in decorating the classroom in fiesta fashion (e.g., with streamers, paper flowers, masks), for Visitors' Day. Allow students to enjoy all of the classroom activities related to fiestas. During a quiet time, ask students what they learned in planning for and participating in the classroom fiesta. Enlist students in checking the L column for unanswered topics, and then allow volunteers to research explanations in the library and report to classmates.

While researchers solve mysteries in the library, assign students in the classroom to roles as reporters. Ask them to recall students' reactions to the fiesta experience. Invite students to write eyewitness accounts of the classroom fiesta for a newspaper published by students and displayed on the bulletin board. Encourage students to capture the excitement of the celebration by using colorful descriptions of the festivities as well as the participants. Ask for student assistance in displaying articles on a "Read All About It!" bulletin board.

4. Select one character trait (e.g., compassion, courage, diligence or respect) and talk about how people in the story demonstrate the trait. Ask students to tell why they selected a character and how the character exemplifies the trait. Suggest that students think about their own lives and share examples that illustrate the trait.

Hint: For interest and variety, alternate discussions on character traits between the benefits of possessing the traits and the consequences of not possessing the traits.

5. Remember that celebrations and holidays do not cease when the school year ends. Search for ways to observe cultural and/or national holidays (e.g., Memorial Day, Emancipation Day, Independence Day) that occur during summer months and also to celebrate or honor days of personal accomplishment that occur throughout the year (e.g., new learning, new skills, new roles, new responsibilities). Extend the scope of lessons taught during the school year by using theme-related examples from all twelve months of the year.

EVALUATION:

Determine the level of student understanding by assessing the quality of creative and written products and the degree of enthusiasm for cooperative projects. Encourage students to connect the message in the story to the theme of spring and celebrations of birth and rebirth.

CONNECTION #4:
Myra Cohn Livingston.
Celebrations,
"Easter: For Penny"

Livingston highlights American holidays in a collection of short, lively poems. These favorites of curriculum writers become focal points for theme-related teaching episodes.

CHARACTER TRAITS: Ask students to define diligence and give examples of people whom they know or about whom they have read that possessed this trait. Post these on the board.

1. Read aloud the poem, "Easter: For Penny." Remember to set the stage with appropriate pre-reading activities that capture students' interest. For example, invite students to volunteer family traditions associated with the celebration of Easter. Point out that the basis of the Christian celebration is religious, but many decorations and practices of the season are secular (e.g., bunnies, baby chicks, decorated eggs, egg hunts, spring flowers, green grass).

Clarify vocabulary terms necessary for understanding both the poem and the celebration. Ask student partners to listen carefully during the poetry reading and take notes on words that serve as signs that the spring season has arrived. Following the poetry reading, encourage student partners to share words in their notes, then make a class list of signs of spring. If students present a list of religious and non-religious signs, use the opportunity to teach the difference between the terms, sacred and secular, and lead students in categorizing the class list.

2. Use the class list to reinforce the meaning of elaboration. Take an example such as green grass as a sign of spring and web ideas that students volunteer about green grass (e.g., furnishes food for animals, serves as a hiding place for animals, feels soft when one walks barefoot on the surface, holds moisture, holds dirt as winds blow).

Point out to students how the process of webbing enriches the words on the list (e.g., green grass). Reinforce the value of the webbing process by encouraging student partners to take one term from the class list, make their own web, and then write a description of the term by using information on the web. Invite students to share descriptions with classmates and to draw a conclusion about the process of webbing as an aid to thinking and writing.

3. Talk to students about their understanding of ecology, i.e., studies related to relationships between organisms and their environment. Ask students to listen carefully to a second reading of the poem for clues about the natural relationships between organisms and their environment. Extend the discussion to how boys and girls who are mindful of the relationship between people and environment can improve the classroom environment and thus student learning by knowing about classmates, caring about them, and acting responsibly.

4. Engage students in closely observing the artwork that accompanies the words. Use the opportunity to point out differences between the words obvious and subtle, and ask students to think up examples of both. Advise them that art as well as words can be obvious or subtle.

With these criteria, obvious and subtle, in mind, ask students to revisit the artwork: What is obvious? What is subtle? Lead students to an understanding that subtle means just a hint about something, not a clear statement about something.

Hint: Check the subtle shape of the bunny. Might the bunny be hiding treats? Conclude the discussion by encouraging children always to be watchful for subtle clues from authors, poets, and illustrators.

Share with students that teachers often call subtle clues by the name, inference. Review the meaning of inference and its relationship to subtle clues. Invite students to interpret this line from the poem: "Mama has a way to let us know." Ask students to identify the subtle clue or inference in the context of the poem.

5. Advise students that their diligence in searching for subtle clues is commendable. Encourage them to engage in a creative activity of decorating and hiding plastic or paper eggs. Place glitter, yarn, sequins, paints, beads, watercolors, stick-on designs, braid, and/or tiny silk or paper flowers in a central location. Allow students to decorate eggs in a personally pleasing way. If students finish early, ask them to assist other students. (Alternate Activity)

Tell students that they will put the word, subtle, into practice by contemplating good hiding places for their egg, writing subtle clues about the egg's hidden location, then giving the clues to classmates. Divide the classroom into quadrants and label each fourth. Draw the quadrant on the chalkboard and label it so that all students share a common reference point. (Alternate Activity)

Tell children that they will start their list of subtle clues by stating the quadrant location of the hidden egg and continue their list with three more subtle clues. Allow time for each child to hide the egg while others cover their eyes, then invite children to give their clues to classmates. Lead students in clapping for successful egg hunters. **Ask** students to put on their thinking caps: What common traits made egg-hunting clues subtle? (Alternate Activity)

6. Select one character trait (e.g., diligence) and talk about how characters in the poem demonstrate the trait. Ask students to tell why they selected a character and how the character exemplifies the trait. Suggest that students think about their own lives and share examples that illustrate the trait.

7. Remember that celebrations and holidays do not cease when the school year ends. Search for ways to observe cultural and/or national holidays (e.g., Memorial Day, Emancipation Day, Independence Day) that occur during summer months and also to celebrate or honor days of personal accomplishment that occur throughout the year (e.g., new learning, new skills, new roles, new responsibilities). Extend the scope of lessons taught during the school year by using theme-related examples from all twelve months of the year.

EVALUATION:

Determine the level of student understanding by observing the degree of enthusiasm for cooperative and participatory activities, by assessing the quality of creative and written products, and by evaluating the depth in responses to thought-provoking questions. Ask students to research and write about one person who displayed the character trait of diligence in his or her life. Encourage students to connect the message in the story to the theme of spring and celebrations of birth and rebirth.

CONNECTION #5:
Myra Cohn Livingston.
Celebrations, "Memorial Day"

Livingston highlights American holidays in a collection of short, lively poems. These favorites of curriculum writers become focal points for theme-related teaching episodes.

CHARACTER TRAITS: Focus on and review the traits of citizenship, courage, and responsibility.

1. Read aloud the poem, "Memorial Day." Remember to set the stage with appropriate pre-reading activities that capture students' interest. For example, review the meaning of the celebration and symbols related to the day honoring servicemen and servicewomen who have given their lives for their country: flags, bugles, poppies, parades. Ask students to listen carefully for patriotic symbols mentioned in the poem. Clarify vocabulary terms necessary for understanding both the poem and the celebration. Talk about the symbols after reading the poem.

2. Assist children in transferring abstract symbols of patriotism into concrete examples of patriotism by inviting them to participate in an art project. Divide students into partnerships or small groups and distribute 9" x 12" pieces of white construction paper. Model how to glue seven 1" strips of red paper across the width of the sheet. Then model how to glue a 4" x 4" square of blue paper in the upper left corner and dot on stars using white chalk, white crayons, or white paint. Allow time for students to complete both gluing and painting steps. (Alternate Activity)

Distribute copies of the poem. Urge students to use their neatest writing as they copy the poem on a 3" x 5" white card and attach the card to the right of the field of blue.

Suggest that poppies might be the finishing touches needed for students' patriotic symbols. Model the process of poppy making: cut 1 1/2" x 6" strips of red tissue paper; attach the end of the tissue strip to a green pipe cleaner with tape; roll and twist the pipe cleaner and paper to form a flower shape, then tape the end; place black pom-poms in the center. Encourage children to make four or five poppies to glue across the bottom of flags. Invite the students to display flags on a patriotic bulletin board entitled "In Your Honor...." (Alternate Activity)

Ask students to put on their thinking caps: What functions do patriotic symbols serve? **Hint:** Lead students to the conclusion that traditional symbols unite all citizens as Americans regardless of race, ethnicity, religion, or class.

3. Share with students that patriotic songs such as "America, the Beautiful" also unite all citizens regardless of race, ethnicity, religion, or class. Distribute copies of the song and invite students to join in singing a tribute to America.

Note: The words to the song were written in 1893 by a college professor, Katharine Lee Bates, during a visit to Colorado. As she looked at Pike's Peak, she was inspired to write a poem. The poem was eventually set to the hymn, "Materna," written in 1882 by Samuel Augustus Ward. The music and lyrics were published together in 1910. (Share the Music, Macmillan/McGraw-Hill, 1995)

Ask students to put on their thinking caps: How and why do the music and lyrics make us feel proud to be Americans? **Hint:** Lead students to the conclusion that word pictures paint scenes of beauty and portray America as a beautiful nation. Ask small groups to investigate geographic clues in the song lyrics such as "amber waves of grain" and "Purple Mountain's majesty." Challenge students to match clues in the lyrics to logical geographic locations on the United States map.

Review with students a logical pattern for investigation: find a specific clue such as "amber waves of grain"; look for a geographic setting in which grain might grow in waves; match clues (e.g., amber color, wind making waves, and land features); tell why the match is logical. Request that student groups investigate the clues in all verses and match words to geographic features. Lead student groups in reporting their findings and in debriefing their thinking processes for classmates. (Alternate Activity)

4. Share stories about brave men and women who have served in the United States' armed forces to preserve freedom for all citizens. Ask boys and girls if family members have participated in any of the nation's wars.

   Encourage students to interview parents for names, war, branch of service, and location of service of family members. Turn the veterans' story into a high-interest geography lesson by asking students to volunteer the information from home, and then attach red, white, or blue stars labeled with names of these servicemen or servicewomen to a large classroom map. Invite students to write a letter thanking either a family member or a friend for their courage and for their willingness to protect the freedom of all citizens. Request that students share the letters and post on the patriotic bulletin board. (Alternate Activity)

5. Select one character trait (e.g., citizenship, courage, or responsibility) and talk about how veterans exemplify the trait. Suggest that students think about their own lives and share examples that illustrate the trait.

   Hint: For interest and variety, alternate discussions on character traits between the benefits of possessing the traits and the consequences of not possessing the traits.

6. Remember that celebrations and holidays do not cease when the school year ends. Search for ways to observe cultural and/or national holidays (e.g., Memorial Day, Emancipation Day, Independence Day) that occur during summer months and also to celebrate or honor days of personal accomplishment that occur throughout the year. Extend the scope of lessons taught during the school year by using theme-related examples from all twelve months of the year.

EVALUATION:

Determine the level of student understanding by assessing the quality of creative and written products and the degree of enthusiasm for participatory projects. Ask students to explain what they have learned from this lesson and activities. Encourage students to connect the message in the poem to the theme of spring, celebrations of birth and rebirth.

CONNECTION #6:
Myra Cohn Livingston.
Celebrations. "Fourth of July"

Livingston highlights American holidays in a collection of short, lively poems. These favorites of curriculum writers become focal points for theme-related teaching episodes.

CHARACTER TRAITS: Review all nine of the character traits used in this manual.

1. Read aloud the poem "Fourth of July." Remember to set the stage with appropriate pre-reading activities that capture students' interest. For example, talk with students about the reasons why Americans celebrate the date, how their families typically observe the celebration, and how many years have passed since the historic signing of the Declaration of Independence. Advise students to listen to the poem carefully for previously unknown details related to the celebration. Clarify vocabulary terms necessary for understanding both the text and the celebration. Following the reading, lead students in a "Things-I-never-knew...." discussion about the Fourth of July.

2. Explain the jigsaw technique of research to students, i.e., separating a research topic into segments, assigning specific segments to groups, and putting the groups' segments of information together just like a jigsaw puzzle. Divide the class into cooperative groups and then assign each group one segment to research:

   The players in the War for Independence
   The years of the War for Independence
   The location of major naval and land battles
   The reasons why colonists fought the war

   Hint: Make sure that students understand that the first year of fighting, 1775, was a rebellion of colonists against England, the Mother Country; by 1776, the rebellion had turned into the war for independence known as the Revolutionary War.

   Once students complete their research, enlist students in putting together the puzzle parts about the War for Independence. Share with students that untrained, loosely organized colonists revolted against the mightiest empire in the world at that time. Ask them to reflect on the actions of colonists, decide which of the character traits colonists exhibited, and speculate what caused colonists to take such great risks.

   Hint: Point out to students that no colonists in the world at that time enjoyed a greater degree of freedom than American colonists. They became dissatisfied when England tried to take away some of their freedom. **Ask:**

   Which group of people might be more likely to revolt, those who had never enjoyed freedom or those who had enjoyed freedom, then felt that they were gradually losing it? Why?
   Can students apply this same idea to the life of an elementary student?

3. Invite students to a Fourth-of-July center. Allow students to choose one of the following three activities:

   Make a starburst of fireworks by using a glue, glitter, and a 9" x 12" dark blue sheet of construction paper. Write the poem on a 3" x 5" card, glue card to a sparkling sky, and post on the bulletin board. (Alternate Activity)

Assume the role of a child during the War for Independence. Write a letter to General George Washington and tell him how you are helping Mother at home while Father is fighting in the colonial army. (Alternate Activity)

Research the story of Francis Scott Key, take notes on the important points in the story, recount the story to classmates, and encourage students to join in the singing of the national anthem. (Alternate Activity)

Note: John Stafford Smith probably wrote the music for "The Star-Spangled Banner," a tune from the 1700s called To Anacreon in Heaven. Francis Scott Key, a prominent American lawyer who was aboard a captured American ship on September 14, 1814, wrote the words. As he looked out over the water at dawn and saw the American flag flying over Fort McHenry, he was inspired to write the lyrics. The Army and Navy bands played the song in the 1890s whenever a national anthem was required. It was made the official national anthem by President Herbert Hoover in 1931.
(Share the Music, Macmillan/McGraw-Hill, 1995)

Plan a sharing time in which students tell how they felt as they made sparkling fireworks, researched the life of a famous American, or wrote to General George Washington. **Ask** students to put on their thinking caps: How and why does participating in projects make students feel more a part of history than reading the story in a textbook?

4. Select one character trait (e.g., citizenship, compassion, courage, diligence, or integrity) and talk about how responsible citizens demonstrate the trait. Suggest that students think about their own lives and share examples that illustrate the trait.

Hint: For interest and variety, alternate discussions on character traits between the presence and benefits of possessing the traits and the absence and consequences of not possessing the traits.

5. Remember that celebrations and holidays do not cease when the school year ends. Search for ways to observe cultural and/or national holidays (e.g., Memorial Day, Emancipation Day, Independence Day) that occur during summer months and also to celebrate or honor days of personal accomplishment that occur throughout the year (e.g., new learning, new skills, new roles, new responsibilities). Extend the scope of lessons taught during the school year by using theme-related examples from all twelve months of the year.

EVALUATION:

Determine the level of student understanding by assessing the quality of creative and written products and the degree of enthusiasm for participatory projects. Ask students to write their own song celebrating a holiday of their choice. Encourage students to connect the message in the poem to the theme of spring, and celebrations of birth and rebirth.

CONNECTION #1:
Steven Kroll.
Mary McLean and the St. Patrick's Day Parade

The potato crop failure in Ireland forces Mary McLean, her parents, brother, and baby sister to immigrate to America. The family settles in New York City. When Mary hears that Mr. Finnegan, the local grocer, always rides in a marvelously decorated cart in the St. Patrick's Day Parade, she sets her goal on becoming Mr. Finnegan's parade partner.

CHARACTER TRAITS: Review the indicators of the nine character traits used in this manual.

1. Read *Mary McLean and the St. Patrick's Day Parade* aloud. Remember to set the stage with appropriate pre-reading activities that capture students' interest. Clarify vocabulary terms necessary for understanding both the text and the celebration. Define clearly a purpose for reading and/or listening. **Hint:** Set the historical scene by using Steven Kroll's excellent background information on the last page of the story.

2. Use the story as a lead-in to a word study lesson of the similarities and differences among emigration, immigration, and migration. Encourage students to use characters from the story and write grammatically correct examples of emigration and immigration. Ask students to finger-trace the journey from Ireland to America on a large world wall map. Talk about reasons why Mary's family in the story or other families in students' experiences immigrate to America. **Ask:** Are reasons for immigration similar? Different? What factors influence large or small numbers of immigrants coming to America? **Hint:** Make sure that students look at the issue from an American citizen's standpoint and from the standpoint of an immigrant to America.

Hint: Note that the term used correctly dictates the preposition that follows (e.g., emigrate from, and immigrate to). Ask the media specialist to help find any of the countless examples of past and present human movements in history. Point out to students that movement is so consistent in history that the concept is one of the five themes of geography (e.g., location, place, interaction, movement, and region). **Ask** students to put on their thinking caps and think about why and how immigration changes the way people plan celebrations once they come to a new land.

3. Talk about the concept of parades in observance of certain celebrations, then discuss the meaning and symbols of a St. Patrick's Day parade. Guide students to organize details associated with a special event and build models for a classroom St. Patrick's Day parade. Suggest that students use small boxes or shoe boxes as floats. Set up the parade in a display, play Irish music, and invite guests to view the parade and to hear students tell the origin of the celebration. (Alternate Activity)

Hints: Encourage students to research the meaning of traditional St. Patrick's Day markers: the color green and the shamrock symbol. Search for locations in the United States in which planners stage St. Patrick's Day parades so that students might view television coverage of these events or write chambers of commerce for parade information.

4. Plan other art-related activities that use Irish potatoes as the main material. Demonstrate to students how to carve shamrocks in potato halves and to make art prints by either using green paint or printing on green paper. (Alternate Activity) Offer an alternate activity: show students how to make Mr. Potato heads. Cut a small slice off the top of a potato; hollow out enough of the potato to insert a cotton ball. Wet the cotton ball and sprinkle with grass seeds. Grass will sprout as hair. Students then may complete decorating the rest of the potato head with felt, pipe cleaners, and paper.

Hint: Talk to students about why making projects with one's hands helps most students remember important information, i.e., students experience the learning, thus students move from abstract learning to concrete learning.

5. Find story sources about the Irish, elfin folklore creatures called leprechauns. Read aloud several passages from various stories that paint these mischievous little people as cobblers and keepers of hidden treasures. Invite children to write a make-believe adventure to share with a leprechaun, then ask them to tell their stories first to a partner, then, after revision, to all classmates. Suggest that students illustrate and display their stories. (Alternate Activity, Parental Discretion)

6. Review the immigration experiences of Mary McLean and her family. Ask the students to look at the list of character traits and decide which ones best serve persons who decide to leave their native lands and move to strange, faraway places. Ask also what traits Mary demonstrates when she sets out to ride on the parade float. Invite the students to respond to situations in their own lives in which they need these same traits.

7. Remember that celebrations and holidays do not cease when the school year ends. Search for ways to observe cultural and/or national holidays (e.g., Memorial Day, Emancipation Day, Independence Day) that occur during summer months and also to celebrate or honor days of personal accomplishments that occur throughout the year (e.g., new learning, new skills, new roles, new responsibilities). Extend the scope of lessons taught during the school year by using theme-related examples from all twelve months of the year.

EVALUATION:

Determine the level of student understanding of the concepts of immigration and of St. Patrick's Day by assessing the quality of class discussions, the enthusiasm for group participation, and the creativity demonstrated in art-related activities. Include teacher observations and rubrics in evaluating student progress. Encourage students to connect the message in the story to the theme of spring and celebrations of birth and rebirth.

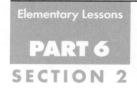

Elementary Lessons

PART 6

SECTION 2

CONNECTION #2:
Geoffrey Scott. Memorial Day

Memorial Day, observed on the last Monday in May, provides an opportunity for national recognition of those who fought and died in the nation's wars.

CHARACTER TRAITS: Review the indicators of the nine character traits used in this manual.

1. Read *Memorial Day* aloud. Remember to set the stage with appropriate pre-reading activities that capture students' interest. Clarify vocabulary terms necessary for understanding both the text and the celebration. Define clearly a purpose for reading and/or listening.

2. Play patriotic music (e.g., "Battle Hymn of the Republic," "When the Caissons Go Rolling Along," "When Johnny Comes Marching Home") and place each selection in the correct historical setting, i.e., time, place, situation. Allow students to move creatively in a way that the music dictates. If students do not march in time to the music, model for them the natural connection between the music and the movement. **Ask** students to put on their thinking caps. **Ask:** Why does music often send a message to more people than print materials? What purposes does patriotic music serve? (Alternate Activity)

CHARACTER EDUCATION THROUGH STORY

3. Talk with students about the meaning of the word, veteran. Tell students the story of Veteran Stars, those symbols that represent soldiers serving in World War II. Invite students to make a veteran star for any person who served the nation in a branch of the Armed Forces and who is a relative, a family friend, or a soldier whom they admire. (Alternate Activity)

Extension: Model the making of one star with the soldier's name, picture, and branch of service, location of service, date of birth, special recognition. Display the stars on a red-white-and-blue bulletin board dedicated to men and women in the Armed Forces and decorated with poppies and American flags. (Alternate Activity)

Hint: Extend the learning by inviting a recruitment officer to class to tell boys and girls about men and women who serve the nation in the Armed Forces today. Extend the learning further by sending a team to the media center to research Gold Star Mothers in World War II, then to report the meaning to classmates. Inquire if any student knows about military "dog tags" and why men and women wear them. **Ask** students to put on their thinking caps: Do symbols help people remember the sacrifices other people made for them? Do monuments serve much the same purpose? What is so important about linking past and present times? Use the questions and answers to develop the concept of continuity in human history.

4. Connect the character traits of respect, courage, citizenship, compassion, and fairness to the story. Suggest that boys and girls share examples of people who demonstrate these traits in their daily lives. Invite children to share how they might also exhibit these same traits.

Hint: For interest and variety, alternate discussions on character traits between the presence and benefits of possessing the traits and the absence and consequences of not possessing the traits.

5. Remember that celebrations and holidays do not cease when the school year ends. Search for ways to observe cultural and/or national holidays (e.g., Memorial Day, Emancipation Day, Independence Day), that occur during summer months and also to celebrate or honor days of personal accomplishments that occur throughout the year (e.g., new learning, new skills, new roles, new responsibilities). Extend the scope of lessons taught during the school year by using theme-related examples from all twelve months of the year.

EVALUATION:

Determine the level of student understanding of Memorial Day by assessing the quality of class discussions, the enthusiasm for group participation, and the creativity demonstrated in art-related activities. Include teacher observations and rubrics in evaluating student progress. Encourage students to connect the message in the story to the theme of spring and celebrations of birth and rebirth.

CONNECTION #3:
Linda Lowery. *Earth Day*

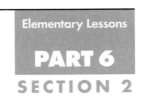

Elementary Lessons

PART 6

SECTION 2

Lowery presents a brief history of Earth Day celebrations, 1970 to 1990, in the United States as well as in the world. Teachers will welcome the source, which highlights environmental problems, and use the information as a natural connection to the environmental program and activities.

CHARACTER TRAITS: Review the indicators of the nine character traits used in this manual.

1. Read *Earth Day* aloud. Remember to set the stage with appropriate pre-reading activities that capture students' interest. Clarify vocabulary terms necessary for understanding both the text and the celebration. Define clearly a purpose for reading and/or listening.

2. Direct students in small groups to brainstorm two lists: environmental problems and possible solutions. Use student lists to create a class chart entitled "Pollution Problems and Possible Solutions." Review with students the processes of analysis and synthesis by explaining that analysis means breaking a problem into small parts and looking at each part while synthesis means putting parts back together in a new, creative way. Ask students to revisit the chart and choose one problem to analyze. Suggest that they break the problem into small parts and determine what may lead to a solution. **Ask:** Will a solution quite likely come from private citizens, corporations, government, or a combination of all three? **Hint:** Lead students to the conclusion that individual and group efforts on school campuses can play an important role in solving environmental problems. Link the discussion to the character trait of citizenship.

3. Use the activity above to encourage students to generate ideas for a class recycling project such as saving aluminum cans for a period of time, exchanging them for cash, and purchasing a tree to plant on the campus.

4. Suggest that students observe their environment on the way to and from school. Ask student partners to choose the worst example of pollution and to draw "before" and "after" pictures on newsprint. Refer to pages 30 and 31 in the story for examples. Remind partners that each illustration will show an environmental problem as well as an environmental solution. Choose a hallway in the school to exhibit student products on Earth Day with a catchy, student-generated, lead-in banner that draws attention to the display. **Ask:** What message related to future actions does the display send to students?

5. Discuss how the character traits of responsibility, diligence, and citizenship connect to the health of the environment. Focus the discussion on what every elementary student may do to protect the environment for themselves, their families, and future generations.

Hint: For interest and variety, alternate discussions on character traits between the benefits of possessing the traits and the consequences of not possessing the traits.

6. Remember that celebrations and holidays do not cease when the school year ends. Search for ways to observe cultural and/or national holidays (e.g., Memorial Day, Emancipation Day, Independence Day) that occur during summer months and also to celebrate or honor days of personal accomplishment that occur throughout the year (e.g., new learning, new skills, new roles, new responsibilities). Extend the scope of lessons taught during the school year by using theme-related examples from all twelve months of the year.

EVALUATION:

Determine the level of student understanding of the important role that individuals and community members play in protecting the environment and natural resources. Assess the learning by evaluating the quality of class discussions, group participation, and problem-solving activities. Include teacher observations and rubrics in evaluating student products. Encourage students to connect the message in the story to the theme of spring and celebrations of birth and rebirth.

CONNECTION # 1:
Barbara Greenwood.
A Pioneer Sampler:
The Daily Life of a Pioneer
Family in 1840 (pages 8-67)

Greenwood engages readers in typical pioneer life of the 1840s through vivid accounts of daily activities and special occasions. Many of the family's traditions stem from Granny's Scottish homeland. Teachers' use of A Pioneer Sampler *in previous sections as well as the spring section provides excellent opportunities to show students how to view the same story from different perspectives.*

CHARACTER TRAITS: Review the nine character traits used in this manual and give examples of each of them. Ask students to provide other examples from their own experiences.

1. Read the selections from *A Pioneer Sampler* aloud. Remember to set the stage with appropriate pre-reading activities that capture students' interest. For example, review the life cycle of plants with students: seeds, sprouts, plants, blossoms, fruits. Make sure that students grasp the meaning of the term, cycle, then set finding examples of plant cycles as the purpose for listening. Encourage student partners to take notes so that they may participate in discussions and activities related to the agrarian lifestyles of American pioneers in the 1840s.

2. Develop students' understanding of the term, agrarian, by using examples from the story. Make certain that students can verbalize the meanings of several important economic concepts, (e.g., an agrarian economy in contrast to an industrial economy, self-sufficiency in contrast to interdependence, a rural environment in contrast to an urban environment). Lead them in finding examples of the concepts from *A Pioneer Sampler* and from their own lives.

Allow students to choose one of three projects to research in the library and to report findings to classmates:

Investigate what crops the pioneer family in the story must raise to supply themselves and their livestock; tie the discussion about the life cycles of plants to the crops investigated; project amounts of crops needed to sustain the family and livestock during non-growing seasons.

Investigate how pioneers stored crops used to feed the family as well as livestock; research when and how refrigeration and freezing changed traditional means of storage; make classmates aware that even though inventions improved storage, families needed extra money to afford such luxuries.

Investigate the average size of pioneer families' farms by researching land acts of the period; look for information on how a family might divide land into living, cultivating, and/or grazing space; prepare a map or transparency that shows a typical family dwelling, how the family divided fields, what crops they grew, where they stored crops, and where livestock grazed; contrast the transparency to how present-day people in your community divide land for home gardens both inside and outside the city limits.

Following the students' reports, remind them that the pioneer family in the story led an agrarian lifestyle, and then contrast the meaning of agrarian to the term, urban. **Ask:** What economic developments happened in America that resulted in urban centers on prairie lands? **Hint:** Use the growth of industry, the increase in immigration, and improvements in transportation and communication as discussion starters.

3. Ask students to identify the character traits that enabled pioneers in the 1840s to survive on the prairie in America. Invite students to cite times in their lives that the same traits served them well in confronting a problem and/or in solving a problem.

Hint: For interest and variety, alternate discussions on character traits between the presence and benefits of possessing the traits and the absence and consequences of not possessing the traits.

4. Remember that celebrations and holidays do not cease when the school year ends. Search for ways to observe cultural and/or national holidays (e.g., Memorial Day, Emancipation Day, Independence Day) that occur during summer months and also to celebrate or honor days of personal accomplishments that occur throughout the year (e.g., new learning, new skills, new roles, new responsibilities). Extend the scope of lessons taught during the school year by using theme-related examples from all twelve months of the year.

EVALUATION:

Determine the level of student understanding of pioneer lifestyles by assessing the degree of enthusiasm for literature-related activities and by evaluating the quality of research, presentations, and discussions. Include teacher-made rubrics in evaluations. Encourage students to connect the message in the story to the theme of spring and celebrations of birth and rebirth.

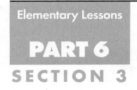

Elementary Lessons

PART 6

SECTION 3

CONNECTION #2:
Brock Cole. *The Winter Wren*

A village boy and his sister who long for the arrival of spring set out to thwart Old Man Winter. Thus, their actions hasten the coming of spring.

CHARACTER TRAITS: Review the nine character traits used in this manual and give examples of each of them. Ask students to provide other examples from their own experiences.

1. Read *The Winter Wren* aloud. Remember to set the stage with appropriate pre-reading activities that capture students' interest. Review with students the meaning of a story setting, i.e., time and place. Set listening for and looking for context clues that collectively reveal the time and place of *The Winter Wren* as the purpose for reading.

Prior to the reading, assist students in developing general criteria that may provide clues to the setting (e.g., costume styles, how people earn their living, language phrases, technological level of tools and conveniences, landscapes, streetscapes). Allow student partners to assume roles as word detectives, take notes during the reading of the story, build a defensible case for the when and the where of the story, and present it to classmates. Lead students in reaching a consensus about setting after student presentations of evidence.

Ask: Why and how do criteria agreed upon in advance of a research task assist you in finding evidence and in reaching conclusions?

2. Review the meaning of metaphor, compare the meaning of metaphor to the meaning of simile, and then ask students to find metaphors in the text of *The Winter Wren*. **Ask:**

How does Brock Cole develop the metaphors of winter and spring?

What other ways can students suggest to develop metaphors for the two seasons?

What does the story reveal about the power of using metaphors in writing?

Why is the use of the metaphor a powerful writing tool?

3. Students will identify the character traits the village boy reveals as he undertakes the quest for spring. Invite students to cite times in their lives that the same traits served them well in confronting a problem and/or in solving a problem.

4. Remember that celebrations and holidays do not cease when the school year ends. Search for ways to observe cultural and/or national holidays (e.g., Memorial Day, Emancipation Day, Independence Day), that occur during summer months and also to celebrate or honor days of personal accomplishment that occur throughout the year (e.g., new learning, new skills, new roles, new responsibilities). Extend the scope of lessons taught during the school year by using theme-related examples from all twelve months of the year.

EVALUATION:

Determine the level of student understanding of the use of metaphors as literary devices by observing the degree of accuracy in identifying the story setting and by assessing the quality of responses to higher-order thinking questions. Include teacher-made rubrics in evaluations. Encourage students to connect the message in the story to the theme of spring, celebrations of birth and rebirth.

CONNECTION #3:
Susan Kuklin. *Kodomo: Children of Japan*

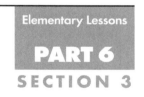

Elementary Lessons

PART 6

SECTION 3

Although Kuklin focuses upon unique Japanese traditions, readers conclude that children around the world are remarkably similar. Note: Use the storyline to support the unit generalization: Studying similarities and differences among people usually leads to the recognition that human beings are more alike than different.

CHARACTER TRAITS: Review the nine character traits used in this manual and give examples of each of them. Ask students to provide other examples from their own experiences.

1. Read aloud the story, *Kodomo: Children of Japan*. Remember to set the stage with appropriate pre-reading activities that capture students' interest. For example, use cities in the story such as Hiroshima and Kyoto as springboards to a study on Japan, the island nation.

Ask student volunteers to finger-trace the distance between Tokyo, Japan, and their community on a large classroom wall map. Encourage them to measure the distance between the two locations, to observe geographic differences between the two locations, and to research differences in time between the two locations. **Ask:** Why is geography such an important learning tool for students to use? Why does geography go hand-in-hand with cultural studies?

Hint: Use the story map activity to place story events and characters in correct locations after reading the story and completing the activities.

2. Talk with students about signs of spring in their community, then contrast them to the signs of spring in Japan. Divide students into small groups, provide them with large doubled sheets of butcher paper, and have them illustrate a typical spring scene in their community and Japan. They may use markers, torn construction-paper patterns for trees, and colored tissue paper to add three-dimensional blossoms.

Remind students to brainstorm the contents of the scenes before drawing. Ask them to talk about how geography influences spring landscapes and how both landscapes support the unit theme: Spring, the Awakening of Life. Display the drawings in a classroom or hallway exhibit and be prepared to offer explanations to other students or visitors about why spring all over the world signals an awakening of life.

3. Describe the following enrichment options to students, then allow them to choose one that they wish to pursue individually, with a partner, or in a small group. Invite students to share findings with classmates:

Select several words or a phrase in the Japanese language, imitate the brush strokes by using brushes or markers on manila paper or on a transparency, then relate four important facts about the language to classmates.

Research the art of origami, practice folding shapes such as paper cranes, demonstrate to classmates how to make an origami model, then link the paper cranes to the Japanese memorial for peace and disarmament.

Investigate traditional Japanese clothing such as the kimono and the kendo, label the parts, then illustrate the styles either on butcher paper or on a transparency.

Research the traditional tea ceremony, reenact a typical ceremony, and then invite classmates to join the researchers for tea.

Reread the story, complete a Venn diagram or a T-chart on the similarities and the differences between Japanese and American children, then review product and conclusions with classmates.

4. Ask students to identify the character traits that they use to complete the optional assignments and to present findings to classmates. Invite students to share thoughts about the traits and also to predict situations in which the same traits might serve them well in confronting a problem and/or in seeking a solution.

Hint: For interest and variety, alternate discussions on character traits between the benefits of possessing the traits and the consequences of not possessing the traits.

5. Remember that celebrations and holidays do not cease when the school year ends. Search for ways to observe cultural and/or national holidays (e.g., Memorial Day, Emancipation Day, Independence Day) that occur during summer months and also to celebrate or honor days of personal accomplishment that occur throughout the year (e.g., new learning, new skills, new roles, new responsibilities). Extend the scope of lessons taught during the school year by using theme-related examples from all twelve months of the year.

EVALUATION:

Determine the level of student understanding of Japanese children's activities by assessing how creatively they translate research data into products and presentations and by evaluating how quickly they grasp that children around the globe evidence more similarities than differences. Include teacher-made rubrics in evaluations. Encourage students to connect the message in the story to the theme of spring and celebrations of birth and rebirth.

CONNECTION #4:
Laura Whipple. Celebrating America: A Collection of Poems and Images of the American Spirit

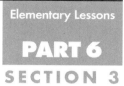
Works of American artists exhibited at the Art Institute of Chicago add richness to this collection of poetry by American poets. Teachers will welcome the collection as an excellent resource for developing students' appreciation for the literary form of poetry.

CHARACTER TRAITS: Review the nine character traits used in this manual and give examples of each of them. Ask students to provide other examples from their own experiences.

1. Select poems to read aloud that illustrate the wide diversity in poetic form and in poetic language. Remember to set the stage with appropriate pre-reading activities that capture students' interest. For example, talk with students about the processes of looking for specific qualities in each poem, then of using these qualities as the basis for small group discussions.

Suggest qualities such as the following:

> *Form in terms of the number of lines and rhyming patterns;*
> *Language in terms of richness created by the use of poetic devices (e.g., metaphors, similes, symbols, and personification);*
> *The poet's message to the reader; and*
> *Ways the poet conveys the American spirit.*

Allow students to practice on one or two poems as a large group before dividing the class into small groups for listening, deliberating, and reaching consensus.

Hint: Choose poems that show how poets use many literary devices to send messages to readers. Read carefully selected poems, and then encourage small groups to analyze the poet's form, language, message, and connection to the American spirit.

Ask: How and why are cooperative group strategies helpful when you undertake challenging learning tasks?

2. Use the exercise on American poetry as the basis for students writing original poems on the theme of spring. Review the importance of deciding upon form, language, message, and theme before starting to write. Explain that they may create poetry with the same range of diversity as the poems analyzed in class as long as the product delivers the poet's concept of spring.

Encourage students to first write the "sloppy copy" version, then to polish the draft through revision. Instruct students to print the final copy on clean paper, illustrate their work, and add the poem to a classroom display entitled "Spring, the Awakening of Life."

3. Ask students to identify the character traits that they use to write and to display original poems. Invite them to share their thoughts about the traits and also to predict situations in which the same traits might serve them well in confronting other challenges.

Hint: For interest and variety, alternate discussions on character traits between the benefits of possessing the traits and the consequences of not possessing the traits.

4. Remember that celebrations and holidays do not cease when the school year ends. Search for ways to observe cultural and/or national holidays (e.g., Memorial Day, Emancipation Day, Independence Day) that occur during summer months and also to celebrate or honor days of personal accomplishment that occur throughout the year (e.g., new learning, new skills, new roles, new responsibilities). Extend the scope of lessons taught during the school year by using theme-related examples from all twelve months of the year.

EVALUATION:

Determine the level of student understanding of poetry by assessing how well they analyze others' poems as well as how creatively they compose their own. Include teacher-made rubrics in evaluations. Encourage students to connect their poems to the theme of spring and celebrations of birth and rebirth.

CONNECTION #1:
Daisaku Ikeda.
English version by Geraldine McCaughrean.
The Cherry Tree

War in an Asian country spares a cherry tree from total destruction. An elderly man and a group of children nurture the battered tree. For them, the cherry tree becomes a promise for a better life after the war.

Note: This story can be used to supplement units about Earth Day or wars.

CHARACTER TRAITS: Focus on the character traits associated with this manual. Ask students to check their definitions, share new insights, and provide different examples of each trait that they have discovered.

1. Read *The Cherry Tree* aloud. Remember to set the stage with appropriate pre-reading activities that capture students' interest. For example, invite students to share stories about how they help family members with yard work. Focus the discussion on pruning trees, treating trees for assorted diseases, feeding trees with nutrients, and watering trees, particularly in times of drought.

Contact personnel of a local nursery so that information shared with students reflects the most current methods of care. Set listening for how story characters care for an abused tree as the purpose for listening. Following the story reading, compare and contrast methods of caring for trees in the story with methods used by families of students in your school. **Ask:**

Where do similarities exist?

Where do differences exist?

What reasons account for differences in the methods of care?

Is the tree a symbol to war-weary characters in The Cherry Tree?

What does the tree represent to them?

What are examples of symbols important in the lives of students in your school?

Do most people use symbols in their everyday lives?

What purposes do they serve?

2. Organize a tree planting on campus by leading students through a task analysis process:

Gain permission from the principal,

Check with nurseries for information about the hardiest trees for your area and their cost,

Select a site on campus,

Plan a fundraising campaign for students and parents,

Make all students aware of the project by announcements on the public address system and on signs posted in the hallways,

Seek invitations to read The Cherry Tree to other students and to explain the project, and

Plan a dedication ceremony that tells the story of how literature inspires community service.

Lead students in analyzing the tree-planting project in terms of which character traits will help students realize success. Remind them to retrace all steps from gaining permission from the principal to planning the dedication ceremony. Assist students in reaching the conclusion that the nine character traits can play important roles in their everyday lives.

3. Show students the trash pile picture in the story and ask them to recall how the illustration matches the storyline. Point out to students that trash art is one form of contemporary art that usually carries a message to the viewer. Divide students into groups; ask them to select a story-related message; then create a sculpture, poster, or mobile from trash and/or scrap materials in the classroom. Suggest that groups lead classmates on a "search-for-the-message" discussion by asking questions that cause higher levels of thinking; share the message of the project with classmates; then commend the resourcefulness of group members in finding materials.

4. Remember that celebrations and holidays do not cease when the school year ends. Search for ways to observe cultural and/or national holidays (e.g., Memorial Day, Emancipation Day, Independence Day) that occur during summer months and also to celebrate or honor days of personal accomplishments that occur throughout the year (e.g., new learning, new skills, new roles, new responsibilities). Extend the scope of lessons taught during the school year by using theme-related examples from all twelve months of the year.

EVALUATION:

Determine the level of student understanding about the relationship between symbols and people by assessing the quality of responses, the enthusiasm for service-oriented and creative projects, and the degree of participation. Encourage students to connect the message in the story to the theme of spring and celebrations of birth and rebirth.

Elementary Lessons
PART 6
SECTION 4

CONNECTION #2:
David A. Adler.
A Picture Book of Passover

Illustrations tell the story of Passover or Pesach, the eight-day holiday that celebrates God liberating the Jewish people from slavery.

ADDITIONAL SELECTIONS:

Howard I. Bogot and Robert J. Orkand. *A Children's Haggadah.*
Haggadah, a book traditionally read during the Passover holiday, recounts the Jewish story of freedom in an ancient world setting.

Lauren L. Wohl. *Matzoh Mouse.*
The excitement of Passover overpowers Sarah. Even though she tries not to succumb to temptation, she nibbles too many bites of the matzoh hidden in a box behind a living-room chair. Obviously, she must create an explanation for the missing matzoh.

Note: Because Passover occurs in the spring, curriculum writers include the celebration in this section.

CHARACTER TRAITS: Focus on the character traits associated with this manual. Have students check their definitions, share new insights, and provide different examples of each trait that they have discovered.

1. Read *A Picture Book of Passover* and *A Children's Haggadah* aloud. Remember to set the stage with appropriate pre-reading activities that capture students' interest. For example, lead students in

brainstorming criteria for investigating any celebration: place in history; geographic hearth, i.e., place of origin; religious or racial or ethnic or national origins; specific cause for celebration; symbols; customs; participants; and students' special interests.

Ask students to choose three celebrations with which they are familiar and apply the criteria. **Hint:** Spend sufficient time concentrating on skills of analysis so that students may apply those skills with ease to less familiar content. Following the reading, lead students in completing the description of Passover.

Hint: Provide an authentic touch to the activities by distributing matzoh, traditional cracker-like cakes eaten during the eight-day period, and allowing students to munch on the cakes during story reading.

2. Explain to students that they may choose how to enrich their knowledge of Passover. Ask students to listen to the following activity options; to select one that holds high interest for them; and to work individually, with a partner, or in a small group to complete the project:

> Research the site of the events that result in the Jewish celebration of Passover; tell the story while locating geographic features critical to the storyline.

> Contact the music teacher and ask for assistance; select Jewish songs for the class to learn, then weave the story into the singing; include in the script that songs as well as dialogue carry messages.

> Research characteristics of the written language of Hebrew, then demonstrate how people communicate with others in written form; predict reasons why such stark differences between the Hebrew and English languages exist.

> Read Matzoh Mouse, dramatize the story of Sarah's dilemma, then analyze her actions and also her family's actions in terms of the character traits; remember that analysis includes the presence as well as the absence of character traits.

> Plan presentation and performance times for students. Remind all students about the importance of courtesy while listening to the work of classmates.

> Reflect on the Passover story, then decide which character traits served Moses best in his leadership role. Ask students to think about how they may call upon the same traits to help solve everyday problems. Seek lively student interaction.

Hint: For interest and variety, alternate discussions on character traits between the benefits of possessing the traits and the consequences of not possessing the traits.

3. Remember that celebrations and holidays do not cease when the school year ends. Search for ways to observe cultural and/or national holidays (e.g., Memorial Day, Emancipation Day, Independence Day) that occur during summer months and also to celebrate or honor days of personal accomplishments that occur throughout the year (e.g., new learning, new skills, new roles, new responsibilities). Extend the scope of lessons taught during the school year by using theme-related examples from all twelve months of the year.

EVALUATION:

Determine the level of student understanding about Passover by assessing the quality of responses, the enthusiasm for research as well as creative projects, and the degree of participation. Encourage students to connect the message in the story to the theme of spring and celebrations of birth and rebirth.

ADDITIONAL SELECTIONS:

Barbara Diamond Goldin. *The Passover Journey: A Seder Companion*

Norma Simon. *Passover*

Leslie Swartz. *A First Passover*

CONNECTION #3:
Argentina Palacios. Viva México! The Story of Benito Juárez and Cinco de Mayo

Personalities and celebrations, often in cause-and-effect relationships, play dramatic roles in the course of human history. Palacios spotlights how the career of one individual and the celebration of one event in the 1800s influence the story of Mexico.

CHARACTER TRAITS: Focus on the character traits associated with this manual. Have students to check their definitions, share new insights, and provide different examples of each trait that they have discovered.

1. Read aloud the story, *Viva México! The Story of Benito Juárez and Cinco de Mayo.* Remember to set the stage with appropriate pre-reading activities that capture students' interest. For example, scan the story for locations important to the storyline and mark these on a classroom map with peel-off dots. Then point out to students the site and the reason for importance. During story reading, pause to locate events either in the life of Benito Juárez or the history of the Mexican government.

Review with students the meaning of storyline. Emphasize the importance of sequencing events in the storyline. For the story reading, ask partners to take notes about events critical to the development of the storyline. Ask partners to pay particularly close attention to cause-and-effect relationships between the personality of Benito Juárez and the celebration of Cinco de Mayo.

Following the reading, lead partners in plotting important events in the story on a continuum. Review these events from two standpoints: 1) Are cause-and-effect relationships evident in the storyline? 2) Are there connections among personalities, events, and geographic locations?

2. Revisit the storyline on the chalkboard and divide the story of Benito Juárez and Cinco de Mayo into major sections. Invite small groups of students to dramatize each section by assuming roles of important people and acting out events. Encourage groups to begin each segment with a narrator setting the scene, to follow introduction with actors performing the skit, and to end with the narrator summarizing cause-and-effect relationships between personalities and events.

Hint: Remind students that props and costumes add much to the drama of any presentation and capture the attention of the audience.

Lead students in summarizing the connections between the personality of Benito Juárez and the celebration of Cinco de Mayo. Encourage students to apply the criteria of the nine core character traits to the personality of Juárez and determine which traits Juárez exhibited and why.

3. Invite three volunteers to investigate story-related topics while most students prepare for the presentation of skits:

Research various types and uses of cacti; design an experiment to show how cacti can survive with very little water; relate the research to the story.

Research Aztec, Chinese, and Roman calendars; make a chart or transparency that compares and contrasts the calendars; relate the research to the story.

Research, design, make, and display a piñata; relate the research and project to the story.

Invite students who research and make individual projects to present information following the skits.

4. Remember that celebrations and holidays do not cease when the school year ends. Search for ways to observe cultural and/or national holidays (e.g., Memorial Day, Emancipation Day, Independence Day) that occur during summer months and also to celebrate or honor days of personal accomplishments that occur throughout the year (e.g., new learning, new skills, new roles, new responsibilities). Extend the scope of lessons taught during the school year by using theme-related examples from all twelve months of the year.

ADDITIONAL SELECTIONS:

George Ancona. *The Piñata Maker*

Elizabeth Silverthorne. *Fiesta! Mexico's Great Celebrations*

EVALUATION:

Determine the level of student understanding about cause-and-effect relationships between personalities and events by assessing the quality of responses, the enthusiasm for research as well as creative projects, and the degree of participation. Encourage students to connect the message in the story to the theme of spring and celebrations of birth and rebirth.

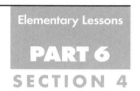

CONNECTION #4:
Janet McDonnell.
Celebrating Earth Day

In 1970, students focused the first Earth Day on the need to conserve the world's natural resources. A quarter of a century later, students on all levels still actively participate in greatly expanded, environmentally oriented programs. McDonnell describes typical Earth Day festivities on April 22 by reporting on a class party.

1. Read *Celebrating Earth Day* aloud. Remember to set the stage with appropriate pre-reading activities that capture students' interest. For example, well in advance of reading the story, send a research team to the library to investigate the origins of the celebration, the purpose of the celebration in 1970, and the purpose of the celebration at the present time. **Ask:** Based on answers to the questions, what predictions can students make about the celebration of Earth Day in the twenty-first century?

Ask research team members to wrestle with issues such as reasons for growth, for popularity among student groups, and for media appeal. Request that they, as talk show hosts, present research data in the form of television interviews broadcast live on Earth Day.

The purpose for listening will be to find consistencies between the data and the story. Suggest that students fold a piece of paper lengthwise in half, then entitle one column "Agree" and the other "Disagree." As the teacher reads the story, instruct students to record consistencies under "Agree" and inconsistencies under "Disagree."

In a round-robin discussion, ask a student to state one consistency, ask the next student to counter with one inconsistency, and ask the rest of the students to alternate between the two types of responses. Insist that students support their answers with data from research or from the story. **Ask:** How and why does a stated purpose for listening increase students' comprehension? How does the process of justifying answers improve the quality of students' responses?

2. Post a list of Earth Day projects on the bulletin board and permit students as individuals or as partners to choose one of the following:

Investigate changes between the original and present-day Earth Day celebrations, then construct a then-and-now chart for display.

Reflect on elementary students' responsibilities to Planet Earth, then take a stand on conservation by writing an editorial.

Survey the most common environments of elementary students, look for areas of careless disregard for the environment, then illustrate the scenes on posters or write a one-week series of public service announcements.

Research paper making, then make a transparency showing the tree-to-tablet process and explain why the process concerns environmentalists.

Lead classmates in listing how students use water and produce trash in one week's time, then in examining ways to reduce, reuse, and recycle resources.

Choose and research an endangered species of plant or animal, then prepare an illustrated booklet on the topic for a classroom library.

Research the world's rainforests, locate the areas on the classroom map, report reasons for conserving as well as clearing rainforest areas, then present information in a "what's-at-stake" format.

Assume the role of environmentalists, survey the list of character traits, and then justify which traits will serve the group best. Extend the presentation by predicting what the absence of specific traits will cost Planet Earth.

Plan an Earth Day party for students to present, display, and perform projects related to the celebration.

3. Remember that celebrations and holidays do not cease when the school year ends. Search for ways to observe cultural and/or national holidays (e.g., Memorial Day, Emancipation Day, Independence Day), that occur during summer months and also to celebrate or honor days of personal accomplishment that occur throughout the year (e.g., new learning, new skills, new roles, new responsibilities). Extend the scope of lessons taught during the school year by using theme-related examples from all twelve months of the year.

EVALUATION:

Determine the level of student understanding about the celebration of Earth Day by assessing the quality of responses, the enthusiasm for research as well as creative projects, and the degree of participation. Ask students to explain what they learned from the story and activities, then tell what, how, and why they learned. Encourage students to connect the message in the story to the theme of spring and celebrations of birth and rebirth.

CONNECTION #5:
Steven Kroll.
Queen of the May

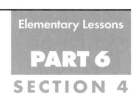

"Will good conquer evil?" never fails to grab readers' attention to the ever-popular Cinderella storyline.

CHARACTER TRAITS: Focus on the character traits associated with this manual. Ask students to check their definitions, share new insights, and provide different examples of each trait that they have discovered.

1. Read *Queen of the May* aloud. Remember to set the stage with appropriate pre-reading activities that capture students' interest. For example, take advantage of the popular Queen-of-the-May theme to show students how celebrations such as May Day evolve throughout history and also how each successive culture adds unique features.

Select a research team to investigate May Day from the ancient times of Egypt and India through present-day times in America. Alert team members to look for common characteristics in the celebrations despite wide differences in space and time. **Examples:** flowers, singing, dancing around a Maypole, gift giving, crowning the King and Queen of the May. Invite the team to report to class members prior to reading the story.

If student interest runs high, encourage students to plan May Day festivities for classmates. Enlist the assistance of other teachers and students in planning the election of a King and Queen of the May, popular games, special foods, and Maypole dancing. (Alternate Activity)

Ask students to identify the main characters of the story, then describe the characters in terms of the presence or absence of character traits. **Ask:**

> *Does Sylvie possess more of the model traits than her stepmother and stepsister possesses?*
> *What does this information imply to students?*
> *How do authors use traits in developing story characters?*

Seek copies of other Cinderella stories from the media specialist or other teachers' collections. Assign stories to small groups, encourage them to write a skit, mark the place of origin on the classroom map with a peel-off dot, and present the variations on a traditional theme to classmates. **Ask:**

> *In most of the versions, what characteristics stay the same?*
> *In most of the versions, what characteristics vary?*
> *What factors cause some of the characteristics to stay the same while others vary?*

4. Remember that celebrations and holidays do not cease when the school year ends. Search for ways to observe cultural and/or national holidays (e.g., Memorial Day, Emancipation Day, Independence Day) that occur during summer months and also to celebrate or honor days of personal accomplishments that occur throughout the year (e.g., new learning, new skills, new roles, new responsibilities). Extend the scope of lessons taught during the school year by using theme-related examples from all twelve months of the year.

EVALUATION:

Determine the level of student understanding about the celebration of May Day by assessing the quality of responses, the enthusiasm for research as well as creative projects, and the degree of participation. Ask students to explain what they learned from the story and activities, then tell what, how, and why they learned. Encourage students to connect the message in the story to the theme of spring and celebrations of birth and rebirth.

CONNECTION #6:
Astrid Lindgren.
Lotta's Easter Surprise

Children eagerly await the arrival of the Easter Bunny and the delivery of chocolate-covered Easter eggs. Adults, however, face the dilemma of where to buy the treats when the only candy store in town closes on the day before Good Friday. How will Lotta's father solve the problem?

CHARACTER TRAITS: Focus on the character traits associated with this manual. Ask students to check their definitions, share new insights, and provide different examples of each trait that they have discovered.

1. Read *Lotta's Easter Surprise* aloud. Remember to set the stage with appropriate pre-reading activities that capture students' interest. For example, use the story as a means of clarifying the terms, secular and sacred. Point out that the story represents a light-hearted, secular approach to a serious celebration sacred to Christians. Review with students why Christians consider Easter one of their most holy or sacred celebrations.

Use *Lotta's Easter* Surprise as an example of secular children's literature. Set the identification of the problem and solution as the purpose for listening. Increase the mystery of the storyline by stopping at points and inviting students to predict what happens next. Allow time for predictions and also time for checking the accuracy of predictions. **Ask:**

> *What techniques does the author use to build suspense?*
> *Are the techniques effective?*
> *How can young writers use Lindgren's techniques? (Alternate Activity, Parental Discretion)*

2. Divide students into small groups, then challenge them to solve "What if...?" issues by rewriting the storyline with creative, Lindgren-like techniques:

> *What if Lotta does not visit the candy store?*
> *What if Jonas and Maria do not go to the birthday party?*
> *What if Vasilis has no candy to give to Lotta?*
> *What if Lotta fails to exhibit courage and diligence?*

Request that students list each of the "What if...?" challenges on newsprint with space in between the entries, then insert how the group will rewrite the story line and maintain suspense for the reader. Invite student groups to share their creative storylines with classmates.

Ask:

> *Is it possible that authors play with storylines prior to making final decisions on the plot?*
> *How does their process differ from the decisions historians make when writing history?*
> *Why can students learn from both types of writing?*
> *Does literature enhance history? Why or why not?*

If possible, distribute small pieces of candy, preferably marzipan animals, as a reward for good thinking. (Alternate Activity, Parental Discretion)

Hint: Extend students' enjoyment of the highly improbable, seemingly unsolvable situation in *Lotta's Easter Surprise* by encouraging them to share similar, real-life stories with happy endings.

3. Remember that celebrations and holidays do not cease when the school year ends. Search for ways to observe cultural and/or national holidays (e.g., Memorial Day, Emancipation Day, Independence Day) that occur during summer months and also to celebrate or honor days of personal accomplishments that occur throughout the year (e.g., new learning, new skills, new roles, new responsibilities). Extend the scope of lessons taught during the school year by using theme-related examples from all twelve months of the year.

EVALUATION:

Determine the level of student understanding about the secular and sacred celebration of Easter by assessing the quality of responses, the enthusiasm for research as well as creative projects, and the degree of participation. Ask students to tell what they learned from the story and activities, then tell what, how, and why they learned. Encourage students to connect the message in the story to the theme of spring and celebrations of birth and rebirth.

Appendix

Primary Resources

NOTE: All entries listed are in English unless noted in the following manner:
(E/S) - entry includes both English and Spanish and indicates the book is bilingual;
(S) - entry is available in Spanish as well as in English.

Aardema, Verna. *Who's in Rabbit's House?* New York: Dial Press, 1977.

Accorsi, William. *Friendship's First Thanksgiving.* New York: Holiday House, 1992.

Adler, David A. *Happy Thanksgiving Rebus.* New York: Viking Press, 1991.

Aliki. *Corn Is Maize: The Gift of the Indians.* New York: Harper, 1976.

Aliki. *Christmas Tree Memories.* New York: HarperCollins, 1991.

Aliki. *Welcome, Little Baby.* New York: Greenwillow Books, 1987.

Ancona, George. *The Piñata Maker.* San Diego: Harcourt Brace Jovanovich, 1994: (E/S)

Ancona, George. *Powwow.* New York: Harcourt Brace Jovanovich, 1994.

Anno, Mitsumasa. *All in a Day.* New York: Philomel Books, 1986.

Auch, Mary Jane. *The Easter Egg Farm.* New York: Holiday House, 1992.

Aylesworth, Jim. *The Good-Night Kiss.* New York: Atheneum, 1993.

Baer, Edith. *This Is the Way We Go to School.* New York: Scholastic, Inc., 1990.

Baker, Keith. *The Magic Fan.* New York: Harcourt Brace Jovanovich, 1989.

Bailey, Donna. *Where We Live: Israel.* Austin, TX: Raintree Steck-Vaughn, 1992.

Balian, Lorna. *Mother's Mother's Day.* Nashville: Abingdon Press, 1987.

Ballard, Robin. *Carnival.* New York: Greenwillow Books, 1995. (S)

Barker, Marjorie. *Magical Hands.* Saxonville, MA; Picture Book Studio, 1989.

Baylor, Byrd. *The Best Town in the World.* New York: Macmillan Publishing Company, 1982.

Behrens, June. *Fiesta! Cinco de Mayo.* Chicago: Children's Press, 1978. (S)

Behrens, June. *Powwow.* Chicago: Children's Press, 1983.

Blaine, Marge. *The Terrible Thing That Happened at Our House.* New York: Four Winds Press, 1975.

Blume, Judy. *The Pain and the Great One.* New York: Bradbury Press, 1974.

Borden, Louise. *Just in Time for Christmas.* New York: Scholastic, Inc., 1994.

Brown, Tricia. *Hello, Amigos!* New York: Henry Holt, 1986. (S)

Bunting, Eve. *A Perfect Father's Day.* New York: Clarion Books, 1991.

Bunting, Eve. *Flower Garden.* New York: Harcourt Brace Jovanovich, 1994.

Bunting, Eve. *The Day Before Christmas.* New York: Clarion Books, 1992.

Bunting, Eve. *The Wall.* New York: Clarion Books, 1990.

Burden-Patmon, Denise. *Imani's Gift at Kwanzaa.* Cleveland, OH: Modern Curriculum Press, 1992.

Cannon, Janell. *Stellaluna.* San Diego: Harcourt Brace Jovanovich, 1993. (S)

Castle, Caroline, and Peter Bowman. *Grandpa Baxter and the Photographs.* New York: Orchard Books, 1993.

Chin-Lee, Cynthia. *Dragon Well Tea.* Chicago: Polychrome Publishing Corporation, 1992.

Chocolate, Deborah M. Newton. *My First Kwanzaa Book.* New York: Scholastic, Inc., 1992.

Christian, Mary Blount. *Swamp Monsters.* New York: Dial Press, 1983.

Clifton, Lucille. *The Boy Who Didn't Believe in Spring.* New York: Dutton Children's Books, 1973.

Cole, Babette. *The Trouble with Mom.* New York: Coward-McCann, 1984.

Cowen-Fletcher, Jane. *It Takes a Village*. New York: Scholastic, Inc., 1994.

Day, Alexandra. *Carl's Masquerade*. New York: Farrar, Strauss, and Giroux, 1992.

de Paola, Tomie. *The Legend of Old Befana*. New York: Harcourt Brace Jovanovich, 1980.

DeLuise, Dom. *Charlie the Caterpillar*. New York: Simon & Schuster, 1990.

Demi. *The Empty Pot*. New York: Henry Holt, 1990.

Dooley, Norah. *Everybody Cooks Rice*. Minneapolis: Carolrhoda Books, 1992.

Dorros, Arthur. *Abuela*. New York: Dutton Children's Books, 1991. (S)

Dorros, Arthur. *This Is My House*. New York: Scholastic, Inc., 1992.

Drescher, Joan. *Your Family, My Family*. New York: Walker and Company, 1980.

Drescher, Joan. *My Mother's Getting Married*. New York: Dial Books, 1986.

Emberley, Ed. *The Great Thumbprint Drawing Book*. New York: Little, Brown, 1992.

Ets, Marie Hall, and Aurora Labastida. *Nine Days to Christmas: A Story of Mexico*. New York: Puffin, 1991. (S)

Fox, Mem. *Shoes from Grandpa*. New York: Orchard Books, 1989.

Frasier, Debra. *On the Day You Were Born*. New York: Harcourt Brace Jovanovich, 1991.

Franklin, Kristine L. *The Shepherd Boy*. New York: Atheneum, 1994.

Friedman, Ina R. *How My Parents Learned to Eat*. Boston: Houghton Mifflin, 1984.

Garland, Sherry. *The Lotus Seed*. San Diego: Harcourt Brace Jovanovich, 1993.

George, William T. *Fishing at Long Pond*. New York: Greenwillow Books, 1991.

Gibbons, Gail. *Thanksgiving Day*. New York: Holiday House, 1983.

Gibbons, Gail. *The Missing Maple Syrup Sap Mystery or How Maple Syrup Is Made*. New York: Frederick Warne, 1979.

Gilman, Phoebe. *Something from Nothing*. New York: Scholastic, Inc., 1993.

Gleeson, Libby. *The Great Big Scary Dog*. New York: Tambourine Books, 1994.

Gollub, Matthew. *The Moon Was at a Fiesta*. New York: Tambourine Books, 1994.

Gray, Nigel. *A Country Far Away*. New York: Orchard Books, 1989.

Griego, Margot C., Betsy L. Bucks, Sharon S. Gilbert, and Laurel H. Kimball. *Tortillitas Para Mama: and Other Nursery Rhymes in Spanish and English*. New York: Henry Holt, 1981. (E/S)

Grifalconi, Ann. *The Village of Round and Square Houses*. Boston: Little, Brown, 1986.

Hamanaka, Sheila. *All the Colors of the Earth*. New York: William Morrow & Company, 1994.

Henkes, Kevin. *Owen*. New York: Greenwillow Books, 1993.

Hennessy, B.G. *The First Night*. New York: Viking, 1993.

Hirsch, Marilyn. *Potato Pancakes All Around: A Hanukkah Tale*. Philadelphia: Jewish Publication Society, 1982.

Hoberman, Mary Ann. *A House Is a House for Me*. New York: Viking Children's Press, 1978.

Howe, James. *Harold and Chester in Scared Silly: A Halloween Treat*. New York: Morrow Junior Books, 1989.

Howard, Elizabeth Fitzgerald. *The Train to Lulu's*. New York: Bradbury Press, 1988.

Hoyt-Goldsmith, Diane. *Celebrating Kwanzaa*. New York: Holiday House, 1993.

Hoyt-Goldsmith, Diane. *Cherokee Summer*. New York: Holiday House, 1993.

Hoyt-Goldsmith, Diane. *Hoang Anh: A Vietnamese-American Boy*. New York: Holiday House, 1992.

Joosse, Barbara M. *Mama, Do You Love Me?* San Francisco: Chronicle Books, 1991. (S)

Kacker, Anisha. *Ravi's Diwali Surprise*. Cleveland, OH: Modern Curriculum Press, 1994.

Kalman, Bobbie, and Tina Holdcroft. *We Celebrate New Year*. New York: Crabtree Publishing Company, 1994.

Kalman, Bobbie. *We Celebrate the Harvest*. New York: Crabtree Publishing Company, 1986.

Kajpust, Melissa. *A Dozen Silk Diapers: A Christmas Story*. New York: Hyperion Books, 1993.

Katz, Bobbi. *A Family Hanukkah*. New York: Random House, 1992.

Kellogg, Steven. *Johnny Appleseed: A Tall Tale*. New York: Morrow Junior Books, 1988.

Kimmel, Eric A. *The Chanukkah Guest*. New York: Holiday House, 1990.

Kimmelman, Leslie. *Hanukkah Lights, Hanukkah Nights*. New York: HarperCollins, 1992.

Krauss, Ruth. *The Happy Day*. New York: Harper & Row, 1989.

Keats, Ezra Jack. *The Trip*. New York: Greenwillow Books, 1978.

Kinsey-Warnock, Natalie. *When Spring Comes*. New York: Dutton Children's Books, 1993.

Knight, Margy Burns. *Welcoming Babies*. Gardiner, ME: Tilbury House, Publishers, 1994.

Kroll, Virginia. *Masai and I*. New York: Four Winds Press, 1992.

Kohn, Rita. *Spring Planting*. Chicago: Children's Press, 1995.

Kohn, Rita. Fall Gathering. Chicago: Children's Press, 1995.

Kroll, Steven. *Oh, What a Thanksgiving!* New York: Scholastic, Inc., 1988.

Kroll, Virginia. *The Seasons and Someone*. New York: Harcourt Brace Jovanovich, 1994.

Kuklin, Susan. *How My Family Lives in America*. New York: Bradbury Press, 1992.

Lakin, Pat. *The Palace of Stars*. New York: Tambourine Books, 1993.

Lankford, Mary D. *Hopscotch Around the World*. New York: Morrow Junior Book, 1992.

Leedy, Loreen. *The Dragon Halloween Party*. New York: Holiday House, 1986.

Lester, Helen. *Tacky the Penguin*. Boston: Houghton Mifflin, 1988.

Levinson, Riki. *Our Home Is the Sea*. New York: E.P. Dutton, 1988.

Lionni, Leo. *The Alphabet Tree*. New York: Dragonfly Books, 1968.

Lyon, George Ellen. *Basket*. New York: Orchard Books, 1990.

Manushkin, Fran. *Latkes and Applesauce: A Hanukkah Story*. New York: Scholastic, Inc., 1989.

Matiella, Ana Consuelo. *Mother's Day, El Dia de las Madres*. Cleveland, OH: Modern Curriculum Press, 1994. (E/S)

McDermott, Gerald. *Raven: A Trickster Tale from the Pacific Northwest*. San Diego: Harcourt Brace Jovanovich, 1993.

McLerran, Alice. *Roxaboxen*. New York: Scholastic, Inc., 1991.

Melmed, Laura Krauss. *The First Song Ever Sung*. New York: Lothrop, Lee & Shepard Books, 1993.

Mennen, Ingrid. *One Round Moon and a Star for Me*. New York: Orchard Books, 1994.

Mitchell, Barbara. *Down Buttermilk Lane*. New York: Lothrop, Lee & Shepard Books, 1993.

Modell, Frank. *Goodbye Old Year, Hello New Year*. New York: Greenwillow Books, 1992.

Moon, Nicola. *Lucy's Picture*. New York: Dial Books for Young Readers, 1995.

Mora, Pat. *A Birthday Basket for Tia*. New York: Macmillan Publishing Company, 1992. (S)

Morris, Ann. *Loving*. New York: Lothrop, Lee & Shepard Books, 1990.

Morris, Ann. *On the Go*. New York: Scholastic, Inc., 1990.

Moss, Marissa. *In America*. New York: Dutton Children's Books, 1994.

Nerlove, Miriam. *Thanksgiving*. Morton Grove, IL: Albert Whitman & Company, 1990.

Nerlove, Miriam. *Purim*. Morton Grove, IL: Albert Whitman & Company, 1992.

Nye, Naomi Shihab. *Sitti's Secrets*. New York: Four Winds Press, 1994.

Pellegrini, Nina. *Families Are Different*. New York: Holiday House, 1991.

Pennington, Daniel. *Itse Selu: Cherokee Harvest Festival*. Watertown, MA: Charlesbridge Publishers, 1994.

Pfister, Marcus. *The Rainbow Fish*. New York: North-South Books, 1992. (S)

Pilkey, Dav. *'Twas the Night Before Thanksgiving*. New York: Orchard Books, 1990.

Pinkney, Andrea Davis. *Seven Candles for Kwanzaa*. New York: Dial Books for Young Readers, 1993

Polacco, Patricia. *Chicken Sunday*. New York: Philomel Books, 1992.

Polacco, Patricia. *Babushka's Doll*. New York: Simon & Schuster, Inc., 1990.

Polacco, Patricia. *The Keeping Quilt*. New York: Simon & Schuster, 1988.

Polacco, Patricia. *Thunder Cake*. New York: Philomel Books, 1990.

Polacco, Patricia. *Rechenka's Eggs*. New York: Philomel Books, 1988.

Politi, Leo. *Three Stalks of Corn*. New York: Charles Scribner's Sons, 1993.

Raffi. *Tingalayo*. New York: Crown, 1989.

Raffi. *The Legend of Old Befana*. New York: Harcourt Brace Jovanovich, 1980.

Rattigan, Jama Kim. *Dumpling Soup*. Boston: Little, Brown, 1993.

Rodanas, Kristina. *Dragonfly's Tale*. New York: Clarion Books, 1991.

Rohmer, Harriet. *Uncle Nacho's Hat*. Emeryville, CA: Children's Book Press, 1989. (E/S)

Ross, Katharine. *Rabbit's Carnival*. New York: Random House, 1995.

Rouss, Sylvia A. *Sammy Spider's First Hanukkah*. Rockville, MD: Kar-Ben Copies, Inc. 1993. (S)

Rylant, Cynthia. *When I Was Young in the Mountains*. New York: Dutton Children's Books, 1982.

Rylant, Cynthia. *The Relatives Came*. New York: Bradbury Press, 1985.

Schotter, Roni. *Hanukkah!* Boston: Little, Brown, 1990.

Scott, Ann Herbert. *On Mother's Lap*. New York: Clarion Books, 1992.

Silverman, Erica. *Big Pumpkin*. New York: MacMillan Publishing Company, 1992.

Sing, Rachel. *Chinese New Year's Dragon*. Cleveland, OH: Modern Curriculum Press, 1992.

Slawson, Michele Benoit. *Apple Picking Time*. New York: Crown Publishers, 1994.

Soto, Gary. *Too Many Tamales*. New York: G.P. Putnam's Sons, 1993.

Spier, Peter. *People*. New York: Doubleday & Company, 1988. (S)

Stanley, Sanna. *The Rains Are Coming*. New York: Greenwillow Books, 1993.

Steele, Mary Q. *Anna's Garden Songs*. New York: Greenwillow Books, 1989.

Svend, Otto Sore. *Children of the Yangtze River*. London: Pelham Books, 1985. Out of Print

Swartz, Leslie. *A First Passover*. Cleveland, OH: Modern Curriculum Press, 1992.

Thayer, Marjorie. *The April Foolers: A Play*. Chicago: Children's Press, 1978.

Tompert, Ann. *Grandfather Tang's Story*. New York: Crown Publishers, Inc., 1990.

Tryon, Leslie. *Albert's Thanksgiving*. New York: Atheneum, 1994.

Waters, Kate. *Samuel Eaton's Day: A Day in the Life of a Pilgrim Boy*. New York: Scholastic, Inc., 1993.

Waters, Kate, and Madeline Slovenz-Low. *Lion Dancer: Ernie Wan's Chinese New Year*. New York: Scholastic, Inc., 1990.

Watkins, Sherrin. *White Bead Ceremony*. Tulsa, OK: Council Oak Books, 1994.

Weiss, George David and Bob Thiele. *What a Wonderful World*. New York: Atheneum Books, 1995.

Whitehead, Pat. *Best Halloween Book*. Mahwah, NJ: Troll Associates, 1985.

Williams, Vera B. *A Chair for My Mother*. New York: Mulberry Books, 1982. (S)

Williams, Vera B. *Cherries and Cherry Pits*. New York: Greenwillow Books, 1986.

Wynot, Jillian. *The Mother's Day Sandwich*. New York: Orchard Books, 1990.

Yamate, Sandra S. *Ashok by Any Other Name*. Chicago: Polychrome Publishing Corporation, 1992.

Yamate, Sandra. *Char Siu Bao Boy*. Chicago: Polychrome Publishing Corporation, 1991.

Zalben, Jane Breskin. *Papa's Latkes*. New York: Henry Holt, 1993.

Zapater, Beatriz McConnie. *Three Kings' Day*. Cleveland, OH: Modern Curriculum Press, 1992.

Zharkova, Olga. *We Three Kings*. New York: Scholastic, Inc., 1993. (S)

Audiovisual Materials (Primary)

America's Special Days: Arbor Day/Earth Day. Videocassette. Lincoln, NE: GPN, 1994. 14 min.

America's Special Days: Flag Day/Citizenship Day. Videocassette. Lincoln, NE: GPN, 1994. 14 min.

America's Special Days: Independence Day. Videocassette. Lincoln, NE: GPN, 1994. 14 min.

America's Special Days: Martin Luther King, Jr. Day/Black History Month. Videocassette. Lincoln, NE: GPN, 1994. 14 min.

America's Special Days: Memorial Day/Veterans' Day. Videocassette. Lincoln, NE: GPN, 1994. 13 min.

America's Special Days: Native American Day. Videocassette. Lincoln, NE: GPN, 1994. 14 min.

America's Special Days: New Year's Day. Videocassette. Lincoln, NE: GPN, 1994. 14 min.

America's Special Days: Presidents' Day. Videocassette. Lincoln, NE: GPN, 1994. 14 min.

America's Special Days: Thanksgiving Day. Videocassette. Lincoln, NE: GPN, 1994. 14 min.

America's Special Days: Women's History Month. Videocassette. Lincoln, NE: GPN, 1994. 14 min.

Celebrate 1. Videocassette. Columbus, OH: Coronet/MTI Film & Video, 1995. 24 min.

Celebrate 2. Videocassette. Columbus, OH: Coronet/MTI Film & Video, 1995. 23 min.

The Gift of the Sacred Dog. Videocassette. Lincoln, NE: GPN, n.d. 30 min.

Global Celebrations: Authentic Music from Festivals and Celebrations Around the World. 4 audiocassettes. New York: Ellipsis Arts, n.d.

It's in Every One of Us. Videocassette. Wernher Krutein and David Pomeranz. New Era Media, 1987. 5 min.

Holidays for Children: Arbor Day. Videocassette. Bala Cynwyd, PA: Schlessinger Video Productions, 1994. 30 min.

Holidays for Children: Chinese New Year. Videocassette. Bala Cynwyd, PA: Schlessinger Video Productions, 1994. 30 min.

Holidays for Children: Christmas. Videocassette. Bala Cynwyd, PA: Schlessinger Video Productions, 1994. 30 min.

Holidays for Children: Cinco De Mayo. Videocassette. Bala Cynwyd, PA: Schlessinger Video Productions, 1994. 30 min.

Holidays for Children: Easter. Videocassette. Bala Cynwyd, PA: Schlessinger Video Productions, 1994. 30 min.

Holidays for Children: Halloween. Videocassette. Bala Cynwyd, PA: Schlessinger Video Productions, 1994. 30 min.

Holidays for Children: Hanukkah/Passover. Videocassette. Bala Cynwyd, PA: Schlessinger Video Productions, 1994. 30 min.

Holidays for Children: Independence Day. Videocassette. Bala Cynwyd, PA: Schlessinger Video Productions, 1994. 30 min.

Holidays for Children: Kwanzaa. Videocassette. Bala Cynwyd, PA: Schlessinger Video Productions, 1994. 30 min.

Holidays for Children: Rosh Hashanah/Yom Kippur. Bala Cynwyd, PA: Videocassette. Schlessinger Video Productions, 1994. 30 min.

Holidays for Children: Thanksgiving. Videocassette. Bala Cynwyd, PA: Schlessinger Video Productions, 1994. 30 min.

Holidays for Children: Valentine's Day. Bala Cynwyd, PA: Videocassette. Schlessinger Video Productions, 1994. 30 min.

The Lotus Seed. Videocassette. Lincoln, NE: GPN, n.d. 30 min.

Multicultural Celebrations. (Kit with books, audiocassettes, teacher's guides, teacher's resources, and posters) Cleveland: Modern Curriculum Press, 1992.

Multicultural Celebrations II. (Kit with books, audiocassettes, teacher's guides, teacher's resources, and posters) Cleveland: Modern Curriculum Press, 1994.

Teaching in a Multicultural Society. Videocassette. Chappaqua, NY: New Castle Communications, Inc., 1994. 16 min.

TEACHER RESOURCES (Primary)

Abbott, Marti, and Betty Jane Polk. *Celebrating Our Diversity: Using Multicultural Literature to Promote Cultural Awareness, Gr. K-2.* Carthage, IL: Fearon Teacher Aids, 1993.

Allen, Judy, Earldene McNeil, and Velma Schmidt. *Cultural Awareness for Children.* Menlo Park, CA: Addison-Wesley Publishing Company, 1992.

Andreev, Tania. *Food in Russia.* Vero Beach, FL: Rourke Publications, Inc., 1989.

Anzaldua, Gloria. *Friends from the Other Side: Amigos del Otro Lado.* Emeryville, CA: Children's Book Press, 1993.

Asch, Jan. *Games for Global Awareness.* Carthage, IL: Good Apple, 1994.

Bailey, Donna. *Where We Live: Australia*. Austin, TX: Raintree Steck-Vaughn, 1992.

Bailey, Donna. *Where We Live: Canada.* Austin, TX: Raintree Steck-Vaughn, 1992.

Bailey, Donna. *Where We Live: Germany*. Austin, TX: Raintree Steck-Vaughn, 1992.

Bailey, Donna. *Where We Live: India*. Austin, TX: Raintree Steck-Vaughn, 1992.

Bailey, Donna. *Where We Live: Israel*. Austin, TX: Raintree Steck-Vaughn, 1992.

Bailey, Donna. *Where We Live: Japan*. Austin, TX: Raintree Steck-Vaughn, 1992.

Bailey, Donna. *Where We Live: Kenya*. Austin, TX: Raintree Steck-Vaughn, 1992.

Bailey, Donna. *Where We Live: Mexico*. Austin, TX: Raintree Steck-Vaughn, 1992.

Bailey, Donna. *Where We Live: Nigeria*. Austin, TX: Raintree Steck-Vaughn, 1992.

Bailey, Donna. *Where We Live: Philippines*. Austin, TX: Raintree Steck-Vaughn, 1992.

Bailey, Donna. *Where We Live: Spain*. Austin, TX: Raintree Steck-Vaughn, 1992.

Bahous, Sally. *Sitti and the Cats: A Tale of Friendship*. Niwot, CO: Roberts Rinehart Publishers, 1993.

Barr, Marilynn G. *Patterns for World Cultures: Multicultural Units for Many Lands*. Palo Alto, CA: Monday Morning Books, Inc., 1995.

Baruth, Philip E., ed. *Holiday Cooking Around the World*. Minneapolis: Lerner Publications Company, 1988.

Bauman, Toni, and June Zinkgraf. *Celebrations*. Carthage, IL: Good Apple, Inc., 1985.

Begaye, Lisa Shook. *Building a Bridge*. Flagstaff, AZ: Northland Publishing Company, 1993.

Blackaby, Susan. *One World: Multicultural Projects and Activities*. New York: Troll Associates, 1992.

Braddon, Kathryn. *Cultural Awareness Through Literature: Activities to Accompany 33 Pieces of Children's Literature*. Greensboro, NC: Carson-Dellosa Publishing Company, 1993.

"Bread: Staff of Life." *Faces*. January, 1994.

"Buddhism." *Calliope*. March, 1995.

Burstein, Chaya M. *The Jewish Kids Catalog*. Philadelphia: The Jewish Publication Society, 1993.

Butterfield, Moira, and Nicola Wright. *Getting to Know Britain: People/Places*. Hauppauge, NY: Barron's Educational Series, Inc., 1993.

Caballero, Jane, and Derek Whordley. *Children Around the World*. Atlanta: Humanics Limited, 1984.

Carroll, Joyce Armstrong. *Books for Special Days*. Englewood, CO: Teacher Ideas Press, 1993.

Cerbus, Deborah Plona, and Cheryl Feichtenbiner Rice. *Connecting Social Studies and Literature*. Huntington Beach, CA: Teacher Created Materials, Inc., 1992.

Chaikin, Miriam. *Menorahs, Mezuzas, and Other Jewish Symbols*. New York: Clarion Books, 1990.

"Christianity." *Calliope*. March, 1996.

Cohn, Janice, D.S.W. *The Christmas Menorahs: How a Town Fought Hate*. Morton Grove, IL: Albert Whitman & Company, 1995.

"Coming of Age." *Faces*. February, 1988.

Copage, Eric V. *Kwanzaa: An African-American Celebration of Culture and Cooking*. New York: William Morrow & Company, 1991.

Cuyler, Margery. *Jewish Holidays*. New York: Holt, Rinehart & Winston, 1978.

Dame, Melvina Azar. *Serving Linguistically and Culturally Diverse Students*. New York: Neal-Schuman Publishers, 1993.

DeBoer, Karen. *Multicultural Activities*. Waterloo, Ontario: Roylco Ltd., 1994.

De Saules, Janet. *Getting to Know Spain and Spanish*. Hauppauge, NY: Barron's Educational Series, Inc., 1993.

Edwards, Gerry. *Discovering World Cultures Through Literature*. Glenview, IL: Good Year Books, 1995.

Elder, Pamela, and Mary Ann Carr. *Worldways: Bringing the World into the Classroom*. Menlo Park, CA: Addison-Wesley Publishing Company, Inc., 1987.

Everix, Nancy. *Ethnic Celebrations Around the World*. Carthage, IL: Good Apple, 1991.

"Family Night: Let's Celebrate Mardi Gras." *Pack-O-Fun*. February, 1995: 42-44.

Fitzjohn, Sue. *Festivals Together: A Guide to Multi-Cultural Celebration*. Landsdown Lane, UK: Hawthorn Press, 1993.

Flora, Sherrill. *Multicultural Mini-Units.* Minneapolis: T.S. Denison & Company, Inc., 1993.

Fryar, Maridell, Patty Smith, and Lucinda Windsor. *Celebrations Throughout the Year.* Midland ISD, 1992. (Found in MISD Libraries)

Gaylord, Susan K. *Multicultural Books to Make and Share.* New York: Scholastic Professional Books, 1994.

"Getting Married." *Faces.* June, 1987.

Gomez, Paolo. *Food In Mexico.* Vero Beach, FL: Rourke Publications, Inc., 1989.

Griswold, Verra Jo, and Judith Starke. *Multi-Cultural Art Projects.* Denver: Love Publishing Company, 1987.

"Happy Holidays." *Faces.* December, 1990.

Harlowe, Joyce, and Victoria Saibara. *Holiday Story Play: Costumes, Cooking, Music and More, PreK-4.* Englewood, CO: Teacher Ideas Press, 1993.

Hayden, Carla D. *Venture into Cultures.* Chicago: American Library Association, 1992.

Heltshe, Mary Ann, and Audrey Burie Kirchner. *Multicultural Explorations: Joyous Journeys with Books.* Englewood, CO: Teacher Ideas Press (Division of Libraries Unlimited, Inc.), 1991.

Hester, Joseph P. *Teaching For Thinking.* Durham: Carolina Academic Press, 1994.

Hester, Joseph P. *Encyclopedia of Values and Ethics.* Denver: ABC-Clio, 1996.

"Hinduism." *Calliope.* March, 1995.

Holiday Cooking Around the World. Photographs by Robert L. and Diane Wolfe. Minneapolis: Lerner Publications Company, 1988.

Hopkins, Lee Bennett. *Hand In Hand, An American History Through Poetry.* New York: Simon & Schuster, 1994.

"Islamic Spain." *Calliope.* November, 1995.

"Judaism." *Calliope.* March, 1994.

Kalman, Bobbie. *We Celebrate Christmas.* New York: Crabtree Publishing Company, 1985.

Kalman, Bobbie. *We Celebrate Easter.* New York: Crabtree Publishing Company, 1985.

Kalman, Bobbie. *We Celebrate Family Days.* New York: Crabtree Publishing Company, 1986.

Kalman, Bobbie. *We Celebrate the Harvest.* New York: Crabtree Publishing Company, 1986.

Kalman, Bobbie. *We Celebrate New Year.* New York: Crabtree Publishing Company, 1985.

Kalman, Bobbie. *We Celebrate Valentine's Day.* New York: Crabtree Publishing Company, 1986.

Kaur, Sharon. *Food in India.* Vero Beach, FL: Rourke Publications, Inc., 1989.

Kollar, Judith. *An Annotated Bibliography of Multicultural Literature.* Huntington Beach, CA: Teacher Created Materials, Inc., 1993.

Linse, Barbara, and Richard Judd. *Fiesta! Mexico and Central America: A Global Awareness Program for Children in Grades 2-5.* Carthage, IL: Fearon Teacher Aids, 1993.

Lipson, Greta, and Jane Romatowski. *Ethnic Pride.* Carthage, IL: Good Apple, Inc., 1983.

Loewen, Nancy. *Food in Germany.* Vero Beach, FL: Rourke Publications, Inc., 1991.

Loewen, Nancy. *Food in Greece.* Vero Beach, FL: Rourke Publications, Inc., 1991.

Loewen, Nancy. *Food in Israel.* Vero Beach, FL: Rourke Publications, Inc., 1991.

Loewen, Nancy. *Food in Korea.* Vero Beach, FL: Rourke Publications, Inc., 1991.

Loewen, Nancy. *Food in Spain.* Vero Beach, FL: Rourke Publications, Inc., 1991.

Lopez, Barry. *Crow and Weasel.* San Francico: North Point Press, 1990.

MacDonald, Margaret Read, Ed. *The Folklore of World Holidays.* Detroit: Gale Research, Inc., 1992.

McElmeel, Sharron L. *Bookpeople: A Multicultural Album.* Englewood, CO: Teacher Ideas Press (Division of Libraries Unlimited, Inc.), 1992.

Meyer, Carolyn, and Kel Pickens. *Multicultural Sing and Learn: Folk Songs and Monthly Activities.* Carthage, IL: Good Apple, 1994.

Milord, Susan. *Hands Around the World: 365 Creative Ways to Build Cultural Awareness & Global Respect.* Charlotte, VT: Williamson Publishing, 1992.

Milord, Susan. *Tales Alive!* Charlotte, VT: Williamson Publishing, 1995.

Myers, Walter Dean. *The Story of the Three Kingdoms.* New York: HarperCollins, 1995.

Nelson, Wayne E., and Henry "Buzz" Glass. *International Playtime: Classroom Games and Dances from Around the World*. New York: Fearon, 1992.

Perl, Lila. *Piñatas and Paper Flowers*. New York: Clarion Books, 1983.

Polon, Linda, and Aileen Cantwell. *The Whole Earth Holiday Book*. Glenview, IL: Scott, Foresman and Company, 1983.

Resnick, Abraham, Margaret Pavol, and Helen Pappas. *Every Day's A Holiday: Value-Based Theme Units For Individual Calendar Days*. Carthage, IL: Fearon Teacher Aids, 1991.

Rochman, Hazel. *Against Borders: Promoting Books for a Multicultural World*. Chicago: American Library Association, 1993.

Rothlein, Liz, and Terri Christman Wild, Eds. *Read It Again: Multicultural Books for the Primary Grades*. Glenview, IL: Good Year Books, 1993.

Rozakis, Laurie. *Celebrate Holidays Around the World*. Santa Barbara: The Learning Works, Inc., 1993.

Rufus, Anneli. *The World Holiday Book*. New York: HarperSanFrancisco, 1994.

Sansone, Emma. *Getting to Know Italy and Italian*. Hauppauge, NY: Barron's Educational Series, Inc., 1993.

Schon, Isabel. *Basic Collection of Children's Books in Spanish*. Metuchen, NJ: Scarecrow Press, 1986.

Schon, Isabel. *Books in Spanish for Children and Young Adults: An Annotated Guide, Series VI*. Metuchen, NJ: Scarecrow Press, 1993.

Schon, Isabel. *Doña Blanca and Other Hispanic Nursery Rhymes and Games*. Minneapolis: T.S. Denison and Company, Inc., 1983.

Sevaly, Karen. *International Children*. Riverside, CA: Teacher's Friend Publications, Inc., 1991.

Smallwood, Betty Ansin. *The Literature Connection: A Read-Aloud Guide for Multicultural Classrooms*. Reading, MA: Addison-Wesley Publishing Company, 1991.

Soleillant, Claude. *Activities and Projects: Mexico*. New York: Sterling Publishing Co., Inc., 1977.

Spann, Mary B. *Literature-Based Multicultural Activities*. New York: Scholastic Professional Books, 1992.

Spann, Mary B. *Literature-Based Seasonal and Holiday Activities*. New York: Scholastic Professional Books, 1991.

Stepanchuk, Carol, and Charles Wong. *Mooncakes and Hungry Ghosts: Festivals of China*. San Francisco: China Books & Periodicals, 1991.

Stevens, Beth Devergsten. *Celebrate Christmas Around the World*. Huntington Beach, CA: Teacher Created Materials, Inc., 1994.

Stull, Elizabeth Crosby. *Multicultural Discovery Activities for the Elementary Grades*. West Nyack, NY: Center for Applied Research in Education, 1995.

Takeshita, Jiro. *Food in Japan*. Vero Beach, FL: Rourke Publications, Inc., 1989.

Tan, Jennifer. *Food in China*. Vero Beach, FL: Rourke Publications, Inc., 1989.

Terzian, Alexandra M. *The Kid's Multicultural Art Book: Art and Craft Experiences from Around the World*. Charlotte, VT: Williamson Publishing, 1993.

Vaughn, Jenny. *Where We Live: Russia*. Austin, TX: Raintree Steck-Vaughn, 1992.

Westridge Young Writers Workshop. *Kids Explore America's African-American Heritage*. Santa Fe, NM: John Muir Publications, 1993.

Westridge Young Writers Workshop. *Kids Explore America's Hispanic Heritage*. Santa Fe, NM: John Muir Publications, 1992.

Westridge Young Writers Workshop. *Kids Explore America's Japanese Heritage*. Santa Fe, NM: John Muir Publications, 1994.

Whipple, Laura. *Celebrating America: A Collection of Poems and Images of the American Spirit*. New York: Philomel Books, 1994.

Wright, Nicola. *Getting to Know France and French*. Hauppauge, NY: Barron's Educational Series, Inc., 1993.

Zaslavsky, Claudia. *Multicultural Math: Hands-On Math Activities from Around the World*. New York: Scholastic Professional Books, 1994.

Zaslavsky, Claudia. *Multicultural Mathematics: Interdisciplinary Cooperative Learning Activities*. Portland, ME: J. Weston Walch, 1993.

Elementary Resources

NOTE: All entries listed are in English unless noted in the following manner:
(E/S)—entry includes both English and Spanish and indicates the book is bilingual;
(S)—entry is available in Spanish as well as in English.

Aardema, Verna. *Why Mosquitoes Buzz in People's Ears.* New York: Dial Press, 1975.

Abells, Chana Byers. *The Children We Remember.* New York: Greenwillow Books, 1986.

Adams, Jeanie. *Going for Oysters.* Morton Grove, IL: Albert Whitman & Company, 1993.

Adler, David A. *Happy Hanukkah Rebus.* New York: Viking Kestrel, 1989.

Adler, David A. *A Picture Book of Hanukkah.* New York: Holiday House, 1982.

Adler, David A. *Child of the Warsaw Ghetto.* New York: Holiday House, 1995.

Adler, David A. *A Picture Book of Passover.* New York: Holiday House, 1982.

Aleichem, Sholem. *Hanukah Money.* New York: Greenwillow Books, 1978.

Alexander, Sue. *Nadia the Willful.* New York: Knopf, 1983.

Allen, Judy. *What Is a Wall, After All?* Cambridge, MA: Candlewick Press, 1993.

Altman, Susan, and Susan Lechner. *Followers of the North Star.* Chicago: Children's Press, 1993.

Altman, Linda Jacobs. *Amelia's Road.* New York: Lee & Low Books, 1993.

Anaya, Rudolfo A. *Farolitos of Christmas.* New York: Hyperion Books for Children, 1995.

Ancona, George. *The Piñata Maker.* San Diego: Harcourt Brace Jovanovich, 1994. (E/S)

Ancona, George. *Pablo Remembers: The Fiesta of the Day of the Dead.* New York: Lothrop, Lee & Shepard Books, 1993.

Anderson, Joan. *The First Thanksgiving Feast.* New York: Clarion Books, 1984.

Anderson, Joan. *Christmas on the Prairie.* New York: Clarion Books, 1985.

Andrews, Jan. *The Auction.* New York: Macmillan, 1991.

Asch, Frank, and Vladimir Vagin. *Dear Brother.* New York: Scholastic, Inc., 1992.

Ata, Te. *Baby Rattlesnake.* San Francisco: Children's Book Press, 1989.

Baillie, Allan. *Rebel.* New York: Ticknor & Fields, 1994.

Baker, Keith. *The Magic Fan.* San Diego: Harcourt Brace Jovanovich, 1989.

Baker, Olaf. *Where the Buffaloes Begin.* New York: Viking Children's Books, 1989.

Baker, Jeannie. *Window.* New York: Greenwillow Books, 1991.

Bang, Molly. *The Paper Crane.* New York: Greenwillow Books, 1985.

Banyai, Istvan. *Zoom.* New York: Viking, 1995.

Barry, David. *The Rajah's Rice.* New York: W.H. Freeman & Co., 1994.

Bartone, Elisa. *Peppe the Lamplighter.* New York: Lothrop, Lee & Shepard Books, 1993.

Baylor, Byrd. *The Table Where Rich People Sit.* New York: Charles Scribner's Sons, 1994.

Behrens, June. *Gung Hay Fat Choy.* Chicago: Children's Press, 1982.

Belpré, Pura. *The Rainbow-Colored Horse.* New York: F. Warne, 1978.

Benjamin, Alan. *Buck.* New York: Simon & Schuster Books for Young Readers, 1993.

Bernheim, Marc, and Evelyne Bernheim. *The Drums Speak: The Story of Kofi, a Boy of West Africa.* New York: Harcourt Brace Jovanovich, 1971.

Blake, Robert J. *Dog.* New York: Philomel Books, 1994.

Blia Xiong. *Nine in One, Grr Grr.* San Francisco: Children's Book Press, 1989.

Blumberg, Rhoda. *Bloomers!* New York: Bradbury Press, 1993.

Bogot, Howard I., and Robert J. Orkand. *A Children's Haggadah.* New York: Central Conference of American Rabbis, 1994.

Bray, Rosemary L. *Martin Luther King*. New York: Greenwillow Books, 1995.

Bresnick-Perry, Roslyn. *Leaving for America*. San Francisco: Children's Book Press, 1992.

Brown, Tricia. *The City by the Bay: A Magical Journey Around San Francisco*. San Francisco: Chronicle Books, 1993.

Brown, Tricia. *Chinese New Year*. New York: Henry Holt, 1987.

Bruchac, Joseph. *The First Strawberries*. New York: Dial Books for Young Readers, 1993.

Bruchac, Joseph. *Fox Song*. New York: Philomel Books/Putnam & Grosset Group, 1993.

Bruchac, Joseph. *Gluskabe and the Four Wishes*. New York: Cobblehill Books/Dutton, 1995.

Bunting, Eve. *The Wall*. New York: Clarion Books, 1990.

Bunting, Eve. *How Many Days to America? A Thanksgiving Story*. New York: Clarion Books, 1988.

Burden-Patmon, Denise. *Carnival*. Cleveland: Modern Curriculum Press, 1992.

Burden-Patmon, Denise. *Imani's Gift at Kwanzaa*. Cleveland, OH: Modern Curriculum Press, 1992.

Carrier, Roch. *A Happy New Year's Day*. Montreal: Tundra Books, 1991.

Casler, Leigh. *The Boy Who Dreamed of an Acorn*. New York: Philomel Books, 1994.

Castañeda, Omar S. *Abuela's Weave*. New York: Lee & Low Books, 1993. (S)

Caudill, Rebecca. *Did You Carry the Flag Today, Charlie?* New York: Holt, Rinehart, & Winston, 1966.

Cech, John. *My Grandmother's Journey*. New York: Bradbury Press, 1991.

Chaikin, Miriam. *Make Noise, Make Merry: The Story and Meaning of Purim*. New York: Clarion Books, 1983.

Chaikin, Miriam. *Menorahs, Mezuzas, and Other Jewish Symbols*. New York: Clarion Books, 1990.

Chaikin, Miriam. *Sound the Shofar*. New York: Clarion Books, 1986.

Chaikin, Miriam. *Hanukkah*. New York: Holiday House, 1990.

Chiemruom, Sothea. *Dara's Cambodian New Year*. Cleveland: Modern Curriculum Press, 1992.

Chin, Steven A. *Dragon Parade: A Chinese New Year Story*. Austin, TX: Raintree Steck-Vaughn, 1993.

Chin, Charlie. *China's Bravest Girl*. Emeryville, CA: Children's Book Press, 1993.

Chocolate, Deborah M. Newton. *Kwanzaa*. Chicago: Children's Press, 1990.

Choi, Sook Nyul. *Halmoni and the Picnic*. Boston: Houghton Mifflin, 1993.

Cisneros, Sandra. *Hairs*. New York: Alfred A. Knopf, 1994. (E/S)

Clifford, Eth. *The Remembering Box*. Boston: Houghton Mifflin, 1985.

Coerr, Eleanor. *Sadako and the Thousand Paper Cranes*. New York: Putnam, 1977.

Cohen, Barbara. *Molly's Pilgrim*. New York: Lothrop, Lee & Shepard Books, 1983.

Coil, Suzanne M. *Mardi Gras!* New York: Macmillan Publishing Company, 1994.

Goldin, Barbara Diamond. *The Passover Journey: A Seder Companion*. New York: Viking, 1994.

Cole, Brock. *The Winter Wren*. New York: Farrar, Straus, & Giroux, 1984.

Coles, Robert. *The Story of Ruby Bridges*. New York: Scholastic, Inc., 1995.

Connell, Kate. *They Shall Be Heard: Susan B. Anthony and Elizabeth Cady Stanton*. Austin, TX: Raintree Steck-Vaughn Co., 1993.

Cooney, Barbara. *Miss Rumphius*. New York: Viking Press, Inc., 1982. (S)

Cross, Verda, and Gail Owens. *Great-Grandma Tells of Threshing Days*. Morton Grove, IL: Albert Whitman & Company, 1992.

Delacre, Lulu. *Vejigante Masquerader*. New York: Scholastic, Inc., 1993. (S)

de Paola, Tomie. *The Legend of the Bluebonnet*. New York: Putnam, 1983.

de Paola, Tomie. *The Legend of the Indian Paintbrush*. New York: Putnam, 1988.

de Paola, Tomie. *The Legend of the Poinsettia*. New York: Putnam, 1993. (S)

Donnelly, Judy. *A Wall of Names*. New York: Random House, 1991.

Dorros, Arthur. *Tonight Is Carnaval*. New York: Dutton's Children's Books, 1991. (S)

Dorros, Arthur. *Radio Man*. HarperCollins Child Books, 1993.

Dorros, Michael. *Guests.* New York: Hyperion Books, 1994.

Dragonwagon, Crescent. *Home Place.* New York: Macmillan, 1990.

Drucker, Malka. *Grandma's Latkes.* San Diego: Harcourt Brace Jovanovich, 1992.

Drucker, Malka. *Rosh Hashanah and Yom Kippur: Sweet Beginnings.* New York: Holiday House, 1981.

Fair, Sylvia. *The Bedspread.* New York: William Morrow & Company, Inc., 1982.

Filipovic, Zlata. *Zlata's Diary.* New York: Viking Press, 1993.

Finkelstein, Norman H. *Remember Not to Forget.* New York: Franklin Watts, 1985.

Fisher, Leonard Everett. *The Great Wall of China.* New York: Macmillan Publishing Company, 1986.

Fisher, Leonard Everett. *The Wailing Wall.* New York: Macmillan Publishing Company, 1989.

Fleischman, Sid. *The Whipping Boy.* New York: Greenwillow Books, 1986. (S)

Flournoy, Valerie. *The Patchwork Quilt.* New York: Dial Books for Young Readers, 1985.

Foreman, Michael. *War Boy: A Country Childhood.* New York: Arcade Publishing, Inc., 1990.

Fradin, Dennis Brindell. *Hanukkah.* Hillside, NJ: Enslow Publishers, 1990.

Freeman, Dorothy Rhodes, and Dianne M. MacMillan. *Kwanzaa.* Hillside, NJ: Enslow, 1992.

Gallaz, Christophe, and Roberto Innocenti. *Rose Blanche.* New York: Stewart, Tabori & Chang, 1990. (S)

Garland, Sherry. *The Lotus Seed.* San Diego: Harcourt Brace Jovanovich, 1993.

George, Jean Craighead. *The First Thanksgiving.* New York: Philomel Books, 1993.

Ginsburg, Mirra. *The Chinese Mirror.* Orlando: Harcourt Brace Jovanovich, 1988.

Giovanni, Nikki. *Spin a Soft Black Song.* New York: Farrar, Strauss & Giroux, Inc., 1987.

Goble, Paul. *Buffalo Woman.* Scarsdale, NY: Bradbury Press, 1984.

Goble, Paul. *Her Seven Brothers.* New York: Bradbury Press, 1988.

Goldin, Barbara Diamond. *The World's Birthday: A Rosh Hashanah Story.* San Diego: Harcourt Brace Jovanovich, 1990.

Goldin, Barbara Diamond. *Cakes and Miracles: A Purim Tale.* New York: Viking, 1991.

Goldin, Barbara Diamond. *Just Enough Is Plenty: A Hanukkah Tale.* New York: Viking, 1988.

Goldstein, Peggy. *Lóng Is a Dragon.* San Francisco: China Books & Periodicals, Inc., 1991.

Golenbock, Peter. *Teammates.* New York: Harcourt Brace Jovanovich, 1990.

Gonzalez, Ralfka, and Ana Ruiz. *My First Book of Proverbs.* Emeryville, CA: Children's Book Press, 1995. (E/S)

Granfield, Linda. *Cowboy: An Album.* New York: Ticknor & Fields, 1994.

Gray, Libba Moore. *Miss Tizzy.* New York: Simon & Schuster, 1993.

Gray, Libba Moore. *Dear Willie Rudd.* New York: Simon & Schuster, 1993.

Greenwood, Barbara. *A Pioneer Sampler: The Daily Life of a Pioneer Family in 1840.* New York: Ticknor & Fields Books for Young Readers, 1995.

Grifalconi, Ann. *The Bravest Flute: A Story of Courage in the Mayan Tradition.* New York: Little, Brown, 1994.

Grimes, Nikki. *Meet Danitra Brown.* New York: Lothrop, Lee & Shepard Books, 1994.

Haggerty, Mary Elizabeth. *A Crack in the Wall.* New York: Lee & Low Books, Inc., 1993. (S)

Hamanaka, Sheila. *The Journey.* New York: Orchard Books, 1990.

Harmon, William, Ed. *The Classic Hundred: All-Time Favorite Poems.* New York: Columbia University Press, 1990.

Harris, Steven Michael. *This Is My Trunk.* New York: Atheneum, 1985.

Harvey, Brett. *My Prairie Christmas.* New York: Holiday House, 1990.

Haskins, Jim, and Kathleen Benson. *Space Challenger: The Story of Giuon Bluford.* Minneapolis: Carolrhoda Books, 1984.

Heide, Florence Parry, and Judith Heide Gilliland. *Sami and the Time of the Troubles.* New York: Clarion Books, 1992.

Heide, Florence Parry, and Judith Heide Gilliland. *The Day of Ahmed's Secret.* New York: Lothrop, Lee & Shepard Books, 1990.

Hendry, Diana. *Christmas on Exeter Street*. New York: Knopf, 1989.

Hodges, Margaret. *Hidden in Sand*. New York: Charles Scribner's Sons, 1994.

Hoffman, Mary. *Amazing Grace*. New York: Dial Books for Young Readers, 1991.

Hopkins, Lee Bennett. *Ragged Shadows: Poems of Halloween Night*. Boston: Little, Brown, 1993.

Hopkins, Lee Bennett. *Merrily Comes Our Harvest In: Poems for Thanksgiving*. Honesdale, PA: Boyds Mills Press, 1993.

Houston, James. *Tikta'liktak*. New York: Harcourt Brace & World, 1965.

Howlett, Bud. *I'm New Here*. Boston: Houghton Mifflin, 1993.

Hoyt-Goldsmith, Diane. *Celebrating Kwanzaa*. New York: Holiday House, 1993.

Hoyt-Goldsmith, Diane. *Apache Rodeo*. New York: Holiday House, 1995.

Hoyt-Goldsmith, Diane. *Celebrating Kwanzaa*. New York: Holiday House, 1993.

Hru, Dakari. *Joshua's Masai Mask*. New York: Lee & Low, 1993.

I dream of peace: images of war by children of former Yugoslavia. New York: HarperCollins, 1993. (available only through the United Nations) (S)

Ikeda, Daisaku. *The Cherry Tree*. New York: Alfred A. Knopf, 1991.

Jaffe, Nina. *In the Month of Kislev: A Story for Hanukkah*. New York: Viking, 1992.

Jaffe, Nina. *The Uninvited Guest and Other Jewish Holiday Tales*. New York: Scholastic, Inc., 1993.

Jakobsen, Kathy. *My New York*. Boston: Little, Brown, 1993.

Jeffers, Susan. *Brother Eagle, Sister Sky: A Message from Chief Seattle*. New York: Dial Books, 1991.

Jennings, Paulla. *Strawberry Thanksgiving*. Cleveland: Modern Curriculum Press, 1992.

Johnson, Angela. *Tell Me a Story, Mama*. New York: Orchard Books, 1989.

Johnston, Tony. *Amber on the Mountain*. New York: Dial Books for Young Readers, 1994.

Jones, Jennifer Berry. *Heetunka's Harvest: A Tale of the Plains Indians*. Niwot, CO: Roberts Rinehart Publishers, 1994.

Joseph, Lynn. *An Island Christmas*. New York: Clarion Books, 1992.

Kacker, Anisha. *Ravi's Diwali Surprise*. Cleveland: Modern Curriculum Press, 1994.

Kelley, Emily. *Happy New Year*. Minneapolis: Carolrhoda Books, 1984.

Kessler, Cristina. *One Night: A Story from the Desert*. New York: Philomel Books, 1995.

Kimmel, Eric A. *Bar Mitzvah: A Jewish Boy's Coming of Age*. New York: Viking, 1995.

Kimmel, Eric. *Hershel and the Hanukkah Goblins*. New York: Holiday House, 1989.

Kimmel, Eric A. *Days of Awe: Stories of Rosh Hashanah and Yom Kippur*. New York: Viking, 1993.

Kimmel, Eric A. *The Chanukkah Guest*. New York: Holiday House, 1988.

King, Elizabeth. *Chile Fever: A Celebration of Peppers*. New York: Dutton, 1995.

Knight, Margy Burns. *Talking Walls*. Gardiner, ME: Tilbury House Publishers, 1992. (S)

Knight, Margy Burns. *Talking Walls: Activity Guide*. Gardiner, ME: Tilbury House Publishers, 1992. (S)

Knight, Margy Burns. *Who Belongs Here? An American Story*. Gardiner, ME: Tilbury House Publishers, 1993. (S)

Knight, Margy Burns. *Who Belongs Here? Activity Guide*. Gardiner, ME: Tilbury House Publishers, 1994.

Kreikemeier, Gregory Scott. *Come with Me to Africa: A Photographic Journey*. New York: Western Publishing, 1993.

Kroll, Steven. *Queen of the May*. New York: Holiday House, 1993.

Kroll, Steven. *Mary McLean and the St. Patrick's Day Parade*. New York: Scholastic, Inc., 1991.

Kroll, Virginia. *Africa Brothers and Sisters*. New York: Four Winds Press, 1993.

Kroll, Virginia. *A Carp for Kimiko*. Watertown, MA: Charlesbridge, 1993.

Krull, Kathleen. *Maria Molina and the Days of the Dead*. New York: Macmillan, 1994.

Kuklin, Susan. *Kodomo: Children of Japan*. New York: Putnam's Sons, 1995.

Kuskin, Karla. *A Great Miracle Happened There: A Chanukah Story*. New York: HarperCollins, 1993.

Lankford, Mary D. *Quinceañera: A Latina's Journey to Womanhood.* Brookfield, CT: Millbrook Press, 1994.

Larrabee, Lisa. *Grandmother Five Baskets.* Tucson: Harbinger House, 1993.

Lawrence, Jacob. *The Great Migration.* New York: HarperCollins, 1992.

Lee, Jeanne M. *Bà-Nam.* New York: Henry Holt, 1987.

Leedy, Loreen. *The Edible Pyramid.* New York: Holiday House, 1994.

Leighton, Maxine Rhea. *An Ellis Island Christmas.* New York: Viking, 1992.

Levin, Carol. *A Rosh Hashanah Walk.* Rockville, MD: Kar-Ben Copies, 1987.

Levine, Ellen. *I Hate English.* New York: Scholastic, Inc., 1989.

Levine, Arthur A. *All the Lights in the Night.* New York: Tambourine Books, 1991.

Levinson, Riki. *Soon, Annala.* New York: Orchard Books, 1993.

Levinson, Riki. *Watch the Stars Come Out.* New York: E.P. Dutton, 1985. (S)

Levy, Janice. *The Spirit of Tio Fernando: El Espiritu de Tio Fernando.* Morton Grove, IL: Albert Whitman & Company, 1995. (E/S)

Lindgren, Astrid. *Lotta's Easter Surprise.* New York: R & S Books, 1991.

Livingston, Myra Cohn, Ed. *New Year's Poems.* New York: Holiday House, 1987.

Livingston, Myra Cohn. *Celebrations.* New York: Holiday House, 1985.

Linden, Anne Marie. *Emerald Blue.* New York: Atheneum, 1994.

Lobel, Anita. *Away from Home.* New York: Greenwillow Books, 1994.

Locker, Thomas. *Family Farm.* New York: Dial Books for Young Readers, 1988.

Lomas Garza, Carmen. *Family Pictures.* San Francisco: Children's Book Press, 1990.

London, Jonathan. *The Sugaring-Off Party.* New York: Dutton Children's Books, 1995.

Lord, Bette Bao. *In the Year of the Boar and Jackie Robinson.* New York: Harper & Row, 1984.

Louie, Ai-Ling. *Yeh-Shen.* New York: Philomel Books, 1982.

Lowry, Lois. *Number the Stars.* Boston: Houghton Mifflin, 1989.

Lowery, Linda. *Earth Day.* Minneapolis: Carolrhoda Books, 1991.

Lutzeier, Elizabeth. *The Wall.* New York: Holiday House, Inc., 1992.

Lyon, George Ella. *Dreamplace.* New York: Orchard Books, 1993.

MacLachlan, Patricia. *Sarah Plain and Tall.* New York: Harper & Row, 1985.

Major, John S. *The Silk Route.* New York: HarperCollins, 1995.

Mandrell, Louise, and Ace Collins. *Runaway Thanksgiving.* Fort Worth, TX: Summit Group, 1992.

Manushkin, Fran O. *The Matzah That Papa Brought Home.* New York: Scholastic, Inc., 1995.

Manushkin, Fran O. *My Christmas Safari.* New York: Dial Books, 1993.

Martin, Bill, Jr., and John Archambault. *Knots on a Counting Rope.* New York: Henry Holt, 1987.

Martin, Rafe. *Rough-Face Girl.* New York: G.P. Putnam's Sons, 1992.

Masters, Nancy Robinson. *The Fabulous Flying Flag Farm.* Abilene, TX: MasAir Publications, 1995.

Mathis, Sharon Bell. *The Hundred Penny Box.* New York: Viking Children's Books, 1975.

McClester, Cedric. *Kwanzaa: Everything You Always Wanted to Know but Didn't Know Where to Ask.* New York: Grumbs & Thomas, 1985.

McDonnell, Janet. *Celebrating Earth Day.* Chicago: Children's Press, 1994.

McGugan, Jim. *Josepha: A Prairie Boy's Story.* San Francisco: Chronicle Books, 1994.

McKissack, Patricia C., and Frederick L. McKissack. *Christmas in the Big House, Christmas in the Quarters.* New York: Scholastic, Inc., 1994.

McLerran, Alice. *The Mountain That Loved a Bird.* New York: Simon & Schuster Books for Young Readers, 1991.

Medearis, Angela Shelf. *Dancing with the Indians.* New York: Holiday House, 1991.

Mennen, Ingrid, and Niki Daly. *Somewhere in Africa.* New York: Dutton Children's Books, 1990.

Miles, Miska. *Annie and the Old One*. Boston: Little, Brown, 1971. (S)

Mills, Lauren. *The Rag Coat*. Boston: Little, Brown, 1991.

Mochizuki, Ken. *Baseball Saved Us*. New York: Scholastic, Inc., 1993.

Mora, Pat. *A Birthday Basket for Tia*. New York: Macmillan, 1992.

Morimoto, Junko. *My Hiroshima*. New York: Puffin Books, 1992.

Morninghouse, Sundaira. *Habari Gani? What's the News? A Kwanzaa Story*. Seattle: Open Hand Publishers, 1992.

Mosel, Arlene. *Tikki Tikki Tembo*. New York: Henry Holt, 1968.

Munsch, Robert. *Love You Forever*. Scarborough, Ont.: Firefly Books, 1986.

Mullins, Patricia. *V for Vanishing*. New York: HarperCollins, 1993.

Murphy, Jim. *Across America on an Emigrant Train*. New York: Clarion Books, 1993.

Myers, Walter Dean. *A Place Called Heartbreak: A Story of Vietnam*. Austin, TX: Raintree Steck-Vaughn, 1993.

Namioka, Lensey. *Yang the Youngest and His Terrible Ear*. New York: Dell Publishing, 1992.

Norrell, Robert J. *We Want Jobs! A Story of the Great Depression*. Austin, TX: Raintree Steck-Vaughn, 1992.

Nunes, Susan Miho. *The Last Dragon*. New York: Clarion Books, 1995.

Oberman, Sheldon. *The Always Prayer Shawl*. Honesdale, PA: Boyds Mills Press, 1994.

Osofsky, Audrey. *Dreamcatcher*. New York: Orchard Books, 1992.

Palacios, Argentina. *Viva México! The Story of Benito Juárez and Cinco de Mayo*. Austin, TX: Raintree Steck-Vaughn, 1993. (S)

Paladino, Catherine. *Spring Fleece: A Day of Sheep Shearing*. Boston: Joy Street Books, 1990.

Paterson, Katherine. *Flip-Flop Girl*. New York: Lodestar Books, 1994.

Paul, Ann Whitford. *Eight Hands Round: A Patchwork Alphabet*. New York: HarperCollins, 1991.

Paulsen, Gary. *The Tortilla Factory*. San Diego: Harcourt Brace Jovanovich, 1995. (S)

Petty, Jo, comp. *Wings of Silver*. Norwalk, CT: The C.R. Gibson Company, 1967.

Pfister, Marcus. *The Rainbow Fish*. New York: North-South Books, 1992.

Pickthall, Marjorie. *The Worker in Sandalwood: A Christmas Eve Miracle*. New York: Dutton Children's Books, 1994.

Pinkney, Andrea Davis. *Seven Candles for Kwanzaa*. New York: Dial Books for Young Readers, 1993.

Pinkney, Gloria Jean. *Back Home*. New York: Dial Books for Young Readers, 1992.

Pitkänen, Matti A. *The Children of China*. Minneapolis: Carolrhoda Books, Inc., 1990.

Polacco, Patricia. *Tikvah Means Hope*. New York: Doubleday, 1995.

Polacco, Patricia. *Pink and Say*. New York: Philomel Books, 1994.

Polacco, Patricia. *Chicken Sunday*. New York: Philomel Books, 1992.

Polacco, Patricia. *Mrs. Katz & Tush*. New York: Bantam, 1992.

Polacco, Patricia. *Uncle Vova's Tree*. New York: Philomel Books, 1989.

Porter, A.P. *Kwanzaa*. Minneapolis: Carolrhoda Books, 1991.

Pryor, Bonnie. *The House on Maple Street*. New York: William Morrow & Company, 1987.

Rabin, Staton. *Casey over There*. New York: Harcourt Brace Jovanovich, 1994.

Raimondo, Lois. *The Little Lama of Tibet*. New York: Scholastic, Inc., 1994.

Random Acts of Kindness. Berkeley, CA: Conari Press, 1992.

Ray, Deborah Kogan. *My Daddy Was a Soldier: A World War II Story*. New York: Holiday House, 1990.

Reddix, Valerie. *Dragon Kite of the Autumn Moon*. New York: Lothrop, Lee & Shepard Books, 1991.

Reeder, Carolyn. *Shades of Gray*. New York: Macmillan, 1989.

Regguinti, Gordon. *The Sacred Harvest: Ojibway Wild Rice Gathering*. Minneapolis: Lerner Publications, 1992.

Rice, James. *Cowboy Night Before Christmas*. Gretna, LA: Pelican Publishing Company, 1990.

Ringgold, Faith. *Tar Beach*. New York: Crown, 1991.

Robinson, Barbara. *The Best Christmas Pageant Ever.* New York: Harper & Row, 1972.

Rodgers, Richard, and Oscar Hammerstein II. "You've Got to Be Carefully Taught." USA: Williamson Music, Inc., 1949.

Rosen, Michael J. *Elijah's Angel.* San Diego: Harcourt Brace Jovanovich, 1992.

Roth, Susan L. *Buddha.* New York: Doubleday, 1994.

Rylant, Cynthia. *An Angel for Solomon Singer.* New York: Orchard Books, 1992.

San Souci, Robert D. *The Talking Eggs.* New York: Dial Books for Young Readers, 1989.

San Souci, Robert D. *N.C. Wyeth's Pilgrims.* San Francisco: Chronicle Books, 1991. (S)

Sandler, Martin W. *Cowboys.* New York: HarperCollins, 1994.

Sandler, Martin W. *Immigrants.* New York: HarperCollins, 1995.

Sathre, Vivian. *Carnival Time.* New York: Simon & Schuster, 1992.

Say, Allen. *Grandfather's Journey.* Boston: Houghton Mifflin, 1993.

Scott, Ann Herbert. *Cowboy Country.* New York: Clarion Books, 1993.

Scott, Geoffrey. *Memorial Day.* Minneapolis: Carolrhoda Books, 1983.

Schwartz, Lynne Sharon. *The Four Questions.* New York: Dial Books, 1989.

Sewall, Marcia. *The Pilgrims of Plimoth.* New York: Atheneum, 1986.

Shalant, Phyllis. *Look What We've Brought You from Mexico: Crafts, Games, Recipes, Stories, and Other Cultural Activities from Mexican-Americans.* New York: Julian Messner, 1992.

Shepard, Aaron. *The Gifts of Wali Dad: A Tale of India and Pakistan.* New York: Scribner's, 1995.

Sheldon, Dyan. *Under the Moon.* New York: Dial Books for Young Readers, 1994.

Siebert, Diane. *Heartland.* New York: HarperCollins, 1992.

Silverman, Maida. *The Glass Menorah and Other Stories for Jewish Holidays.* New York: Four Winds Press, 1992.

Silverthorne, Elizabeth. *Fiesta! Mexico's Great Celebrations.* Brookfield, CT: Millbrook Press, 1992. (S)

Simon, Norma. *Passover.* New York: Thomas Y. Crowell, 1965.

Sing, Rachel. *Chinese New Year's Dragon.* Cleveland, OH: Modern Curriculum Press, 1992.

Singer, Marilyn. *Minnie's Yom Kippur Birthday.* New York: Harper & Row, 1989.

Soentpiet, Chris K. *Around Town.* New York: Lothrop, Lee & Shepard Books, 1994.

Soto, Gary. *Too Many Tamales.* New York: Putnam, 1992.

Spies, Karen. *Our National Holidays.* Brookfield, CT: Millbrook Press, 1992.

Spinelli, Eileen. *If You Want to Find Golden.* Morton Grove, IL: Albert Whitman & Company, 1993.

Stanek, Muriel. *We Came from Vietnam.* Morton Grove, IL: Albert Whitman & Company, 1985.

Steptoe, John. *Mufaro's Beautiful Daughters.* New York: Lothrop, Lee & Shepard Books, 1987.

Stevens, Jan Romero. *Carlos and the Cornfield.* Flagstaff, AZ: Northland Publishers, 1995. (E/S)

Stevenson, James. *Don't You Know There's a War On?* New York: Greenwillow Books, 1992.

Stevenson, James. *Un-Happy New Year, Emma.* New York: Greenwillow Books, 1989.

Stock, Catherine. *Where Are You Going, Manyoni?* New York: Morrow Junior Books, 1993.

Surat, Maria Michele. *Angel Child, Dragon Child.* New York: Scholastic, Inc., 1983.

Suyenaga, Ruth. *Obon.* Cleveland: Modern Curriculum Press, 1994.

Swann, Brian. *A Basket Full of White Eggs.* New York: Orchard Books, 1988.

Swartz, Leslie. *A First Passover.* Cleveland, OH: Modern Curriculum Press, 1992.

Tompert, Ann. *Grandfather Tang's Story.* New York: Crown Publishers, 1990.

Turner, Ann Warren. *Nettie's Trip South.* New York: Macmillan, 1987.

Uchida, Yoshiko. *Takao and Grandfather's Sword.* (Houghton Mifflin Reader)

Uchida, Yoshiko. *The Bracelet.* New York: Philomel Books, 1993.

Van Laan, Nancy. *Buffalo Dance.* Boston: Little, Brown, 1993.

Wallace, Ian. *Chin Chiang and the Dragon's Dance*. New York: Atheneum, 1984.

Waters, Kate, and Madeline Slovenz-Low. *Lion Dancer: Ernie Wan's Chinese New Year*. New York: Scholastic, Inc., 1990.

Wax, Wendy, comp. *Hanukkah, Oh, Hanukkah! A Treasury of Stories, Songs, and Games to Share*. New York: Bantam Books, 1993.

Weedn, Flavia, and Lisa Weedn. *Flavia and the Christmas Legacy*. Italy: Applause, Inc. (New York: Hyperion Books), 1995.

Weisman, Joan. *The Storyteller*. New York: Rizzoli International Publications, Inc., 1993.

Weller, Frances Ward. *Matthew Wheelock's Wall*. New York: Macmillan Publishing Company, 1992.

Wheatley, Nadia, and Donna Rawlins. *My Place*. Brooklyn: Kane/Miller Book Publishers, 1992.

Whipple, Laura. *Celebrating America: A Collection of Poems and Images of the American Spirit*. New York: Philomel Books, 1994.

Wild, Margaret. *Space Travelers*. New York: Scholastic, Inc., 1992.

Williams, Kit. *Masquerade*. New York: Schocken Books, 1980.

Williams, Karen. *When Africa Was Home*. New York: Orchard Books, 1991.

Williams, Karen Lynn. *Galimoto*. New York: Lothrop, Lee & Shepard Books, 1990.

Winslow, Barbara. *Dance on a Sealskin*. Anchorage: Northwest Books, 1995.

Winter, Jeanette. *Follow the Drinking Gourd*. New York: Alfred A. Knopf, 1992.

Winter, Jonah, and Jeanette Winter. *Diego*. New York: Alfred A. Knopf, 1991. (E/S)

Wohl, Lauren L. *Matzoh Mouse*. New York: HarperCollins, 1991.

Wolf, Bernard. *Beneath the Stone*. New York: Orchard Books, 1994.

Yen, Clara. *Why Rat Comes First: The Story of the Chinese Zodiac*. San Francisco: Children's Book Press, 1991.

Yolen, Jane. *Greyling*. New York: Philomel Books, 1991.

Yolen, Jane. *Letting Swift River Go*. Boston: Little, Brown, 1991.

Young, Ed. *Lon Po Po: A Red Riding Hood Story from China*. New York: Philomel Books, 1989.

Zapater, Beatriz McConnie. *Fiesta*. Old Tappen, NJ: Simon & Schuster Books for Young Readers, 1993.

Zapater, Beatriz McConnie. *Fiesta*. Cleveland, OH: Modern Curriculum Press, 1992.

Zolotow, Charlotte. *The Moon Was the Best*. New York: Greenwillow Books, 1993.

Audiovisual Materials (Elementary)

America's Special Days: Arbor Day/Earth Day. Videocassette. Lincoln, NE: GPN, 1994. 14 min.

America's Special Days: Flag Day/Citizenship Day. Videocassette. Lincoln, NE: GPN, 1994. 14 min.

America's Special Days: Independence Day. Videocassette. Lincoln, NE: GPN, 1994. 14 min.

America's Special Days: Martin Luther King, Jr. Day/Black History Month. Videocassette. Lincoln, NE: GPN, 1994. 14 min.

America's Special Days: Memorial Day/Veterans' Day. Videocassette. Lincoln, NE: GPN, 1994. 13 min.

America's Special Days: Native American Day. Videocassette. Lincoln, NE: GPN, 1994. 14 min.

America's Special Days: New Year's Day. Videocassette. Lincoln, NE: GPN, 1994. 14 min.

America's Special Days: Presidents' Day. Videocassette. Lincoln, NE: GPN, 1994. 14 min.

America's Special Days: Thanksgiving Day. Videocassette. Lincoln, NE: GPN, 1994. 14 min.

America's Special Days: Women's History Month. Videocassette. Lincoln, NE: GPN, 1994. 14 min.

Celebrate 1. Videocassette. Columbus, OH: Coronet/MTI Film & Video, 1995. 24 min.

Celebrate 2. Videocassette. Columbus, OH: Coronet/MTI Film & Video, 1995. 23 min.

The Gift of the Sacred Dog. Videocassette. Lincoln, NE: GPN, n.d. 30 min.

Global Celebrations: Authentic Music from Festivals and Celebrations Around the World. 4 audiocassettes. New York: Ellipsis Arts, n.d.

It's in Every One of Us. Videocassette. Wernher Krutein and David Pomeranz. New Era Media, 1987. 5 min.

Holidays for Children: Arbor Day. Videocassette. Bala Cynwyd, PA: Schlessinger Video Productions, 1994. 30 min.

Holidays for Children: Chinese New Year. Videocassette. Bala Cynwyd, PA: Schlessinger Video Productions, 1994. 30 min.

Holidays for Children: Christmas. Videocassette. Bala Cynwyd, PA: Schlessinger Video Productions, 1994. 30 min.

Holidays for Children: Cinco De Mayo. Videocassette. Bala Cynwyd, PA: Schlessinger Video Productions, 1994. 30 min.

Holidays for Children: Easter. Videocassette. Bala Cynwyd, PA: Schlessinger Video Productions, 1994. 30 min.

Holidays for Children: Halloween. Videocassette. Bala Cynwyd, PA: Schlessinger Video Productions, 1994. 30 min.

Holidays for Children: Hanukkah/Passover. Videocassette. Bala Cynwyd, PA: Schlessinger Video Productions, 1994. 30 min.

Holidays for Children: Independence Day. Videocassette. Bala Cynwyd, PA: Schlessinger Video Productions, 1994. 30 min.

Holidays for Children: Kwanzaa. Videocassette. Bala Cynwyd, PA: Schlessinger Video Productions, 1994. 30 min.

Holidays for Children: Rosh Hashanah/Yom Kippur. Bala Cynwyd, PA: Videocassette. Schlessinger Video Productions, 1994. 30 min.

Holidays for Children: Thanksgiving. Videocassette. Bala Cynwyd, PA: Schlessinger Video Productions, 1994. 30 min.

Holidays for Children: Valentine's Day. Bala Cynwyd, PA: Videocassette. Schlessinger Video Productions, 1994. 30 min.

The Lotus Seed. Videocassette. Lincoln, NE: GPN, n.d. 30 min.

Multicultural Celebrations. (Kit with books, audiocassettes, teacher's guides, teacher's resources, and posters) Cleveland, OH: Modern Curriculum Press, 1992.

Multicultural Celebrations II. (Kit with books, audiocassettes, teacher's guides, teacher's resources, and posters) Cleveland, OH: Modern Curriculum Press, 1994.

Teaching in a Multicultural Society. Videocassette. Chappaqua, NY: New Castle Communications, Inc., 1994. 16 min.

TEACHER RESOURCES (Elementary)

Abbott, Marti, and Betty Jane Polk. *Celebrating Our Diversity: Using Multicultural Literature to Promote Cultural Awareness, Gr. K-2.* Carthage, IL: Fearon Teacher Aids, 1993.

Allen, Judy, Earldene McNeil, and Velma Schmidt. *Cultural Awareness for Children.* Menlo Park, CA: Addison-Wesley Publishing Company, 1992.

Andreev, Tania. *Food in Russia.* Vero Beach, FL: Rourke Publications, Inc., 1989.

Anzaldua, Gloria. *Friends from the Other Side: Amigos del Otro Lado.* Emeryville, CA: Children's Book Press, 1993.

Asch, Jan. *Games for Global Awareness.* Carthage, IL: Good Apple, 1994.

Bailey, Donna. *Where We Live: Australia.* Austin, TX: Raintree Steck-Vaughn, 1992.

Bailey, Donna. *Where We Live: Canada.* Austin, TX: Raintree Steck-Vaughn, 1992.

Bailey, Donna. *Where We Live: Germany.* Austin, TX: Raintree Steck-Vaughn, 1992.

Bailey, Donna. *Where We Live: India.* Austin, TX: Raintree Steck-Vaughn, 1992.

Bailey, Donna. *Where We Live: Israel.* Austin, TX: Raintree Steck-Vaughn, 1992.

Bailey, Donna. *Where We Live: Japan.* Austin, TX: Raintree Steck-Vaughn, 1992.

Bailey, Donna. *Where We Live: Kenya.* Austin, TX: Raintree Steck-Vaughn, 1992.

Bailey, Donna. *Where We Live: Mexico.* Austin, TX: Raintree Steck-Vaughn, 1992.

Bailey, Donna. *Where We Live: Nigeria.* Austin, TX: Raintree Steck-Vaughn, 1992.

Bailey, Donna. *Where We Live: Philippines.* Austin, TX: Raintree Steck-Vaughn, 1992.

Bailey, Donna. *Where We Live: Spain*. Austin, TX: Raintree Steck-Vaughn, 1992.

Bahous, Sally. *Sitti and the Cats: A Tale of Friendship*. Niwot, CO: Roberts Rinehart Publishers, 1993.

Barr, Marilynn G. *Patterns for World Cultures: Multicultural Units for Many Lands*. Palo Alto, CA: Monday Morning Books, Inc., 1995.

Baruth, Philip E., ed. *Holiday Cooking Around the World*. Minneapolis: Lerner Publications Company, 1988.

Bauman, Toni, and June Zinkgraf. *Celebrations*. Carthage, IL: Good Apple, Inc., 1985.

Begaye, Lisa Shook. *Building a Bridge*. Flagstaff, AZ: Northland Publishing Company, 1993.

Blackaby, Susan. *One World: Multicultural Projects and Activities*. New York: Troll Associates, 1992.

Braddon, Kathryn. *Cultural Awareness Through Literature: Activities to Accompany 33 Pieces of Children's Literature*. Greensboro, NC: Carson-Dellosa Publishing Company, 1993.

"Bread: Staff of Life." *Faces*. January, 1994.

"Buddhism." *Calliope*. March, 1995.

Burstein, Chaya M. *The Jewish Kids Catalog*. Philadelphia: The Jewish Publication Society, 1993.

Butterfield, Moira, and Nicola Wright. *Getting to Know Britain: People/Places*. Hauppauge, NY: Barron's Educational Series, Inc., 1993.

Caballero, Jane, and Derek Whordley. *Children Around the World*. Atlanta: Humanics Limited, 1984.

Carroll, Joyce Armstrong. *Books for Special Days*. Englewood, CO: Teacher Ideas Press, 1993.

Cerbus, Deborah Plona, and Cheryl Feichtenbiner Rice. *Connecting Social Studies and Literature*. Huntington Beach, CA: Teacher Created Materials, Inc., 1992.

Chaikin, Miriam. *Menorahs, Mezuzas, and Other Jewish Symbols*. New York: Clarion Books, 1990.

"Christianity." *Calliope*. March, 1996.

Cohn, Janice, D.S.W. *The Christmas Menorahs: How a Town Fought Hate*. Morton Grove, IL: Albert Whitman & Company, 1995.

"Coming of Age." *Faces*. February, 1988.

Copage, Eric V. *Kwanzaa: An African-American Celebration of Culture and Cooking*. New York: William Morrow & Company, 1991.

Cuyler, Margery. *Jewish Holidays*. New York: Holt, Rinehart & Winston, 1978.

Dame, Melvina Azar. *Serving Linguistically and Culturally Diverse Students*. New York: Neal-Schuman Publishers, 1993.

DeBoer, Karen. *Multicultural Activities*. Waterloo, Ontario: Roylco Ltd., 1994.

De Saules, Janet. *Getting to Know Spain and Spanish*. Hauppauge, NY: Barron's Educational Series, Inc., 1993.

Edwards, Gerry. *Discovering World Cultures Through Literature*. Glenview, IL: Good Year Books, 1995.

Elder, Pamela, and Mary Ann Carr. *Worldways: Bringing the World into the Classroom*. Menlo Park, CA: Addison-Wesley Publishing Company, Inc., 1987.

Everix, Nancy. *Ethnic Celebrations Around the World*. Carthage, IL: Good Apple, 1991.

"Family Night: Let's Celebrate Mardi Gras." *Pack-O-Fun*. February, 1995: 42-44.

Fitzjohn, Sue. *Festivals Together: A Guide to Multi-Cultural Celebration*. Landsdown Lane, UK: Hawthorn Press, 1993.

Flora, Sherrill. *Multicultural Mini-Units*. Minneapolis: T.S. Denison & Company, Inc., 1993.

Fryar, Maridell, Patty Smith, and Lucinda Windsor. *Celebrations Throughout the Year*. Midland ISD, 1992. (Found in MISD Libraries)

Gaylord, Susan K. *Multicultural Books to Make and Share*. New York: Scholastic Professional Books, 1994.

"Getting Married." *Faces*. June, 1987.

Gomez, Paolo. *Food In Mexico*. Vero Beach, FL: Rourke Publications, Inc., 1989.

Griswold, Verra Jo, and Judith Starke. *Multi-Cultural Art Projects*. Denver: Love Publishing Company, 1987.

"Happy Holidays." *Faces*. December, 1990.

Harlowe, Joyce, and Victoria Saibara. *Holiday Story Play: Costumes, Cooking, Music and More, Pre K-4*. Englewood, CO: Teacher Ideas Press, 1993.

Hayden, Carla D. *Venture into Cultures*. Chicago: American Library Association, 1992.

Heltshe, Mary Ann, and Audrey Burie Kirchner. *Multicultural Explorations: Joyous Journeys with Books*. Englewood, CO: Teacher Ideas Press (Division of Libraries Unlimited, Inc.), 1991.

Hester, Joseph P. *Teaching For Thinking*. Durham: Carolina Academic Press, 1994.

Hester, Joseph P. *Encyclopedia of Values and Ethics*. Denver: ABC-Clio, 1996.

"Hinduism." *Calliope*. March, 1995.

Holiday Cooking Around the World. Photographs by Robert L. and Diane Wolfe. Minneapolis: Lerner Publications Company, 1988.

Hopkins, Lee Bennett. *Hand In Hand, An American History Through Poetry*. New York: Simon & Schuster, 1994.

"Islamic Spain." *Calliope*. November, 1995.

"Judaism." *Calliope*. March, 1994.

Kalman, Bobbie. *We Celebrate Christmas*. New York: Crabtree Publishing Company, 1985.

Kalman, Bobbie. *We Celebrate Easter*. New York: Crabtree Publishing Company, 1985.

Kalman, Bobbie. *We Celebrate Family Days*. New York: Crabtree Publishing Company, 1986.

Kalman, Bobbie. *We Celebrate the Harvest*. New York: Crabtree Publishing Company, 1986.

Kalman, Bobbie. *We Celebrate New Year*. New York: Crabtree Publishing Company, 1985.

Kalman, Bobbie. *We Celebrate Valentine's Day*. New York: Crabtree Publishing Company, 1986.

Kaur, Sharon. *Food in India*. Vero Beach, FL: Rourke Publications, Inc., 1989.

Kollar, Judith. *An Annotated Bibliography of Multicultural Literature*. Huntington Beach, CA: Teacher Created Materials, Inc., 1993.

Linse, Barbara, and Richard Judd. *Fiesta! Mexico and Central America: A Global Awareness Program for Children in Grades 2-5.* Carthage, IL: Fearon Teacher Aids, 1993.

Lipson, Greta, and Jane Romatowski. *Ethnic Pride*. Carthage, IL: Good Apple, Inc., 1983.

Loewen, Nancy. *Food in Germany*. Vero Beach, FL: Rourke Publications, Inc., 1991.

Loewen, Nancy. *Food in Greece*. Vero Beach, FL: Rourke Publications, Inc., 1991.

Loewen, Nancy. *Food in Israel*. Vero Beach, FL: Rourke Publications, Inc., 1991.

Loewen, Nancy. *Food in Korea*. Vero Beach, FL: Rourke Publications, Inc., 1991.

Loewen, Nancy. *Food in Spain*. Vero Beach, FL: Rourke Publications, Inc., 1991.

Lopez, Barry. *Crow and Weasel*. San Francico: North Point Press, 1990.

MacDonald, Margaret Read, Ed. *The Folklore of World Holidays*. Detroit: Gale Research, Inc., 1992.

McElmeel, Sharron L. *Bookpeople: A Multicultural Album*. Englewood, CO: Teacher Ideas Press (Division of Libraries Unlimited, Inc.), 1992.

Meyer, Carolyn, and Kel Pickens. *Multicultural Sing and Learn: Folk Songs and Monthly Activities*. Carthage, IL: Good Apple, 1994.

Milord, Susan. *Hands Around the World: 365 Creative Ways to Build Cultural Awareness & Global Respect*. Charlotte, VT: Williamson Publishing, 1992.

Milord, Susan. *Tales Alive!* Charlotte, VT: Williamson Publishing, 1995.

Myers, Walter Dean. *The Story of the Three Kingdoms*. New York: HarperCollins, 1995.

Nelson, Wayne E., and Henry "Buzz" Glass. *International Playtime: Classroom Games and Dances from Around the World*. New York: Fearon, 1992.

Perl, Lila. *Piñatas and Paper Flowers*. New York: Clarion Books, 1983.

Polon, Linda, and Aileen Cantwell. *The Whole Earth Holiday Book*. Glenview, IL: Scott, Foresman and Company, 1983.

Resnick, Abraham, Margaret Pavol, and Helen Pappas. *Every Day's A Holiday: Value-Based Theme Units For Individual Calendar Days*. Carthage, IL: Fearon Teacher Aids, 1991.

Rochman, Hazel. *Against Borders: Promoting Books for a Multicultural World*. Chicago: American Library Association, 1993.

Rothlein, Liz, and Terri Christman Wild, Eds. *Read It Again: Multicultural Books for the Primary Grades.* Glenview, IL: Good Year Books, 1993.

Rozakis, Laurie. *Celebrate Holidays Around the World.* Santa Barbara: The Learning Works, Inc., 1993.

Rufus, Anneli. *The World Holiday Book.* New York: HarperSanFrancisco, 1994.

Sansone, Emma. *Getting to Know Italy and Italian.* Hauppauge, NY: Barron's Educational Series, Inc., 1993.

Schon, Isabel. *Basic Collection of Children's Books in Spanish.* Metuchen, NJ: Scarecrow Press, 1986.

Schon, Isabel. *Books in Spanish for Children and Young Adults: An Annotated Guide, Series VI.* Metuchen, NJ: Scarecrow Press, 1993.

Schon, Isabel. *Doña Blanca and Other Hispanic Nursery Rhymes and Games.* Minneapolis: T.S. Denison and Company, Inc., 1983.

Sevaly, Karen. *International Children.* Riverside, CA: Teacher's Friend Publications, Inc., 1991.

Smallwood, Betty Ansin. *The Literature Connection: A Read-Aloud Guide for Multicultural Classrooms.* Reading, MA: Addison-Wesley Publishing Company, 1991.

Soleillant, Claude. *Activities and Projects: Mexico.* New York: Sterling Publishing Co., Inc., 1977.

Spann, Mary B. *Literature-Based Multicultural Activities.* New York: Scholastic Professional Books, 1992.

Spann, Mary B. *Literature-Based Seasonal and Holiday Activities.* New York: Scholastic Professional Books, 1991.

Stepanchuk, Carol, and Charles Wong. *Mooncakes and Hungry Ghosts: Festivals of China.* San Francisco: China Books & Periodicals, 1991.

Stevens, Beth Devergsten. *Celebrate Christmas Around the World.* Huntington Beach, CA: Teacher Created Materials, Inc., 1994.

Stull, Elizabeth Crosby. *Multicultural Discovery Activities for the Elementary Grades.* West Nyack, NY: Center for Applied Research in Education, 1995.

Takeshita, Jiro. *Food in Japan.* Vero Beach, FL: Rourke Publications, Inc., 1989.

Tan, Jennifer. *Food in China.* Vero Beach, FL: Rourke Publications, Inc., 1989.

Terzian, Alexandra M. *The Kid's Multicultural Art Book: Art and Craft Experiences from Around the World.* Charlotte, VT: Williamson Publishing, 1993.

Vaughn, Jenny. *Where We Live: Russia.* Austin, TX: Raintree Steck-Vaughn, 1992.

Westridge Young Writers Workshop. *Kids Explore America's African-American Heritage.* Santa Fe, NM: John Muir Publications, 1993.

Westridge Young Writers Workshop. *Kids Explore America's Hispanic Heritage.* Santa Fe, NM: John Muir Publications, 1992.

Westridge Young Writers Workshop. *Kids Explore America's Japanese Heritage.* Santa Fe, NM: John Muir Publications, 1994.

Whipple, Laura. *Celebrating America: A Collection of Poems and Images of the American Spirit.* New York: Philomel Books, 1994.

Wright, Nicola. *Getting to Know France and French.* Hauppauge, NY: Barron's Educational Series, Inc., 1993.

Zaslavsky, Claudia. *Multicultural Math: Hands-On Math Activities from Around the World.* New York: Scholastic Professional Books, 1994.

Zaslavsky, Claudia. *Multicultural Mathematics: Interdisciplinary Cooperative Learning Activities.* Portland, ME: J. Weston Walch, 1993.

Research Base

The Elementary Social Studies Committee of the Midland Independent School District searched for authorities who confirmed their beliefs about what produces quality social studies programs. Although committee members consulted many experts in social studies content and teaching strategies, Walter C. Parker of the University of Washington, Seattle, continues to serve as the guiding light to whom members turn for practical suggestions and insightful solutions.

Committee members eagerly addressed critical issues:

The planning of naturally inclusive, culturally balanced K-6 units about celebrations;

The teaching of an increasingly more diverse population;

The use of writing as a powerful tool for learning;

The phrasing of questions that span the full range of thinking skills; and

The application of multiple intelligence theories to classroom strategies.

Committee members not only concurred with the following authorities but also strove to implement their ideas. At the heart of these curricular efforts rests a genuine commitment to the children of Midland. Through this curriculum, all children will receive opportunities to share their life stories with others as well as feel proud of their various heritages.

Research resources include the following:

Banks, James A. *An Introduction to Multicultural Education.* Boston: Allyn and Bacon, 1994.

Banks, James A. *Teaching Strategies for Ethnic Studies. 5th ed.* Boston: Allyn and Bacon, 1991.

Bower, Bert, and Jim Lobdell. *A Manual for Teaching the Multiple Ability Classroom.* Mountain View, CA: Teachers' Curriculum Institute, 1992.

Bower, Bert, Jim Lobdell, and Lee Swenson. *History Alive! Engaging All Learners in the Diverse Classroom.* MenloPark, CA: Addison-Wesley Publishing Company, 1994.

Carroll, Joyce Armstrong, and Edward E. Wilson. *Acts of Teaching: How to Teach Writing.* Englewood, CO: Teacher Ideas Press, 1993.

Cech, Maureen. *Globalchild: Multicultural Resources for Young Children.* Menlo Park, CA: Addison-Wesley Publishing Company, 1991.

Cohen, Elizabeth. *Designing Groupwork: Strategies for the Heterogeneous Classroom.* New York: Teachers' College Press, 1994.

Curriculum Standards for Social Studies: Expectations of Excellence. Washington, DC: National Council for the Social Studies, 1994.

Gardner, Howard. *Frames of Mind: The Theory of Multiple Intelligences.* New York: Basic Books, 1985.

Hendricks, Robert H., George C. Dawson, Mindy M. Mattila, and Andrew T. Nappi. *Learning Economics Through Children's Stories.* New York: Joint Council on Economic Education, 1989.

Kovalik, Susan. *Teachers Make the Difference.* Village of Oak Creek, AZ: Susan Kovalik and Associates, 1986.

Lazear, David. *Seven Pathways of Learning: Teaching Students and Parents About Multiple Intelligences.* Tucson, AZ: Zephyr Press, 1994.

Lazear, David. *Seven Ways of Knowing: Teaching for Multiple Intelligences.* Palatine, IL: Skylight Publishing, 1991.

Lazear, David. *Seven Ways of Teaching: The Artistry of Teaching with Multiple Intelligences.* Palatine, IL: Skylight Publishing, 1991.

Parker, Walter C. *Renewing the Social Studies Curriculum.* Alexandria, VA: Association for Supervision and Curriculum Development, 1991.

Schug, Mark C. *Economics for Kids: Ideas for Teaching in the Elementary Grades.* Washington, DC: National Education Association, 1986.

Steffey, Stephanie, and Wendy J. Hood. *If This Is Social Studies, Why Isn't It Boring?* York, ME: Stenhouse Publishers, 1994.

Ward, Hiley H. *My Friends' Beliefs: A Young Reader's Guide to World Religions.* New York: Walker and Company, 1988.

A World of Difference. Teacher/Student Study Guide. New York: Anti-Defamation League of B'nai B'rith, 1986.

Zarnowski, Myra, and Arlene F. Gallagher, eds. *Children's Literature and Social Studies: Selecting and Using Notable Books in the Classroom.* Washington, DC: National Council for the Social Studies, 1993.

Nine Core Character Traits

1. Respect

Respect is a part of the inner language we use to explain the real commitments of our lives. It is acknowledging and living a life that views other humans, the environment, and our communities as extensions of ourselves. Respect is a cornerstone of our love and responsibility to others. Respect is the ethical value that recognizes that each person is precious and has intrinsic worth. The value we discover in each other, when respected, becomes the foundation of our character, for dialogue, and for the morally coherent life.

2. Responsibility

Responsibility means that we should take the development of our own lives in hand with the purpose not just of preserving the integrity of human life, but of modifying our lives by improvements of our own doing. The simple recognition of our responsibility to self and others, and to the future that is yet to be, awakens us to the fact that we are not completely our own masters, but rather trustees of a heritage.

3. Compassion

Each person has a value hierarchy, a scale of values, and an ethic that he or she follows as a guide for ordering behavior. Certainly compassion is one of these values as it helps direct behaviors that help others more than they help us. Compassion or sympathy is the human capacity for being affected by the feelings and experiences of others. Sometimes compassion leads us to act altruistically; most of the time it does not. Compassion usually restrains us from acting cruelly. Even if compassion does not cause us to act benevolently, it is still an important source of moral standards, of character, by which we judge both others and ourselves.

4. Diligence (Persistence)

Diligence is a constant and earnest effort to accomplish what is undertaken. It is persistence of both body and mind. By itself, diligence is not a trait of a moral person. One may be diligent is pursuit of morally worthy and morally unworthy goals. Diligence becomes morally significant when we have perseverance, persistence, tenacity, and are resolute and unyielding in following a moral course of action.

5. Courage

Courage is usually considered to be the ability of an individual to sacrifice safety and comfort and to endure hardship for the sake of some noble cause. It may be physical courage or moral courage. The person with moral courage stands for what he or she believes to be right in the face of ridicule and unpopularity, even though it may mean personal loss. Of course, the courage that is displayed by a person may be the means to the attainment of a worthy or an unworthy goal. Thus, courage, loyalty, and intelligence by themselves do not make a person good. These must be considered in the light of the motives and the consequences to which they are related and evaluated by accepted ethical criteria.

6. Fairness

Young children know when things are fair; that is, when they are receiving equitable treatment from their parents, teachers, their friends, or their brothers and sisters. Perhaps the first moral judgment of a child is, "That's not fair!" A fair-minded person who displays critical judgment must be distinguished from a self-serving critical person. The fair-minded critical person is one who has internalized the skills of reason and critical thinking in the service of balanced truth, rationality, autonomy, and self-insight. Fair-mindedness will involve the following behaviors:

CHARACTER EDUCATION THROUGH STORY

Sharing and sociability based on mutual respect and solidarity.

Equity, which means treating others with respect to their needs, their aspirations, and their abilities, and honoring the dignity of their personhood.

Self-control and etiquette for courtesy, an important part of our social lives.

7. Honesty

Morally right conduct is characterized by honesty, that is, fair dealing, reasonable self-control, and personal honesty. Honesty is a moral behavior because it is important to the welfare of other persons; it is community-producing. Generally speaking, moral behavior is composed of three families or areas of consideration:

The effects our actions have on others and ourselves.

Considerations of moral autonomy: a truly autonomous person is one who is in control of his or her life and is morally responsible.

Issues involving the sanctity of life, the unique importance of human life in and of itself.

Morally right (honest) conduct is connected to these three areas because so much of becoming an ethical person in both word and deed is linked to developing a mature self and the choice to honor the significance of other human beings.

8. Integrity

Integrity, more than anything else, means moral wholeness or completeness. It also signifies that one is morally unimpaired or uncorrupted. A person of moral integrity is one who tries to operate on sound moral principles because he or she possesses a character of uncorrupted virtue, especially in relationship to fair dealing, uprightness, honesty, and sincerity. When speaking about our inner character, integrity is the faculty that enables us to tell right from wrong; thus, integrity is not by itself a guide, but it is a guide to being guided: it does not tell us what is right and what is wrong, but it helps us see the truth of right and wrong. A person of integrity is willing to be open to his or her judgment of the right.

9. Citizenship

As used in this manual, citizenship emphasizes the duties and responsibilities of being a citizen. Citizenship is also defined in relationship to civilization, civility, and civil rights. Fundamentally, this implies that citizenship is attached to advanced human societies in which a high level of art, religion, and government has been reached. It also means that in such civilizations, a person will exercise civility or courtesy and behave according to established traditions and law under which he or she has certain liberties and does not consciously violate the rights of others. In this way, citizenship is not a characteristic as such, but the motive to exercise one's citizenship does imply a moral consciousness.

Additional Character Traits Used in This Manual

Although the lessons in this manual are based on the above nine character traits, four other traits or behaviors are used that are related to these nine. For sake of clarification, these four traits have been isolated and defined below.

Friendship

A friend is someone who knows and likes another. Likewise, friendship is liking between persons; it expresses a special moral relationship between persons characterized by trust, honesty, companionship, and a willingness to help the one in need. From earliest times, it was precisely the moral component of friendship that made it the indispensable basis of a good society. This moral component includes:

That friends must enjoy one another's company;
That friends must be useful to one another; and
That friends must share a common commitment to the good.

Love

Love is affection between people. Love may involve the following different forms:

Passion or sexual desire for another person,
A feeling of warm personal attachment or deep affection for a friend;
A benevolent affection for a friend or another human being.

Benevolence is the moral sense of love. It is sometimes called "altruism." Love in this sense lies at the heart of the point of view of morality for it is the uncoerced giving of help, friendship, and love to others when there is no expectation of receiving a reward in any form. Love in the sense of benevolence is an essential part of moral goodness, since it is behavior not only performed for the sole purpose of another's good, but with the sincere desire that a person should have this good.

Appreciation

Appreciation is not generally thought of as a trait of character but a behavior that flows from a person of strong character. To appreciate means to place a sufficiently high estimate on something. In this sense, to appreciate means to exercise wise judgment and delicate insight in realizing the worth of something. Appreciation is related to esteem. To esteem something means to feel respect combined with a warm and kindly feeling.

Cooperation

Cooperation is based on the ability of persons to get along, to attach significance to a larger social entity than themselves. Cooperation is based on collaborative thinking and decision-making that helps one organize his or her self-centered desires by taking other people into consideration. This is why cooperation is usually included among our moral dispositions. As a moral behavior, the purpose of cooperation is to build reciprocal relationships which are founded on mutual exchange, mutual giving and receiving, and powerful feelings of sympathy and fairness.

Character Development Publishing Order Form

TITLE	PRICE	QTY.	$ TOTAL
Advisor/Advisee Character Education LESSONS FOR TEACHERS AND COUNSELORS Sarah Sadlow, 8x11, 120 pages, softcover, ISBN 0-9653163-7-8	$24.95		
America's Pride & Promise Teacher's Kit RELEARNING THE MEANING OF THE PLEDGE OF ALLEGIANCE Rhonda Adams, CD, Sheet Music, Teacher's Guide, Classroom Poster, ISBN 1-892056-16-x	$39.95		
Building Character Schoolwide BUILDING A CARING COMMUNITY IN YOUR SCHOOL R. Bernardo, L. Frye, D. Smith, G. Foy, 8x11, 153 pages, softcover, ISBN 1-892056-10-0	$18.00		
Caring Messages 40 WEEKS OF DAILY DISCUSSION IDEAS ON CHARACTER Sharon L. Banas, 8x11", 56 loose leaf pages, ISBN 1-892056-12-7	$14.95		
Character Education Through Story LESSONS FROM MULTI-CULTURAL LITERATURE K-6 Dr. Joseph Hester, Paul Coble Fellow, 8x11, 488 pages, softcover, ISBN 1-892056-20-8	$39.95		
Cultivating Heart and Character EDUCATING FOR LIFE'S MOST ESSENTIAL GOALS T. Devine, J. H. Seuk, A. Wilson, 6x9, 486 pages, softcover, ISBN 1-892056-15-1	$22.95		
Developing Character for Classroom Success STRATEGIES FOR SECONDARY STUDENTS Charlie Abourjilie, 6x9, 96 pages, softcover, ISBN 1-892056-07-0	$12.00		
Developing Character in Students, 2nd Edition A PRIMER FOR TEACHERS, PARENTS, AND COMMUNITIES Dr. Philip Fitch Vincent, 6x9, 174 pages, softcover, ISBN 1-892-05604-6	$19.95		
Elementary School Guide to Character Education Steve Dixon, 6x9, 120 pages, softcover, ISBN 1-892056-17-8	$15.95		
A Gift of Character: The Chattanooga Story 6x9, 220 pages, softcover, ISBN 1-892056-16-x	$15.95		
Hey, Mr. McRay ANSWERING TEENS ON ISSUES OF JUDGMENT AND CHARACTER Dr. Michael R. McGough, 6x9, 200 pages, softcover, ISBN 1-892056-14-3	$14.95		
Lessons From the Rocking Chair TIMELESS STORIES FOR TEACHING CHARACTER Deb Austin Brown, 6x9, 70 pages, softcover, ISBN 0-9653163-3-5	$8.95		
Life's Greatest Lessons 20 THINGS I WANT MY KIDS TO KNOW Hal Urban, 6x9, 162 pages, softcover, ISBN 0-9659684-4-8	$14.95		
Operating Manual for Character Education Programs 3-ring binder, 9x12, 327 pages, ISBN 1-892056-13-5	$79.95		
Parents, Kids & Character 21 STRATEGIES TO HELP YOUR CHILDREN DEVELOP GOOD CHARACTER Dr. Helen LeGette, 6x9, 180 pages, softcover, ISBN 1-892056-01-1	$15.95		
Promising Practices in Character Education, Vol. 1 NINE SUCCESS STORIES FROM ACROSS THE COUNTRY Edited by Dr. Philip Fitch Vincent, 6x9, 112 pages, softcover, ISBN 0-9653163-0-0	$12.00		
Promising Practices in Character Education, Vol. 2 12 MORE SUCCESS STORIES FROM ACROSS THE COUNTRY Foreword by Dr. Philip Fitch Vincent, 6x9, 148 pages, softcover, ISBN 1-892056-02-4-x	$14.00		
Rules & Procedures THE FIRST STEP TOWARD SCHOOL CIVILITY, 2ⁿᵈ EDITION Dr. Philip Fitch Vincent, 6x9, 96 pages, softcover, ISBN 1-892056-06-2	$14.00		
Rules & Procedures on Video THE FIRST STEP TOWARD SCHOOL CIVILITY (VIDEO) Dr. Philip Fitch Vincent, VHS, 44 minutes, ISBN 1-892056-03-8	$59.95		
BEST SELLER! **Teaching Character...It's Elementary** 36 WEEKS OF DAILY LESSONS FOR GRADES K-5 S. A. Broome, N. W. Henley, 8x11, 232 pages, softcover, ISBN 1-892056-08-9	$27.95		
Teaching Character: Parent's Idea Book A. C. Dotson and K. D. Wisont, 8x11, 84 pages, softcover, ISBN 0-9653163-5-1	$12.00		
BEST SELLER! **Teaching Character: Teacher's Idea Book** A. C. Dotson and K. D. Wisont, 8x11, 160 pages, softcover, ISBN 0-9653163-4-3	$24.00		

CHARACTER DEVELOPMENT PUBLISHING

Pay with credit card or make checks payable to:
Character Development Publishing
PO Box 9211, Chapel Hill, NC 27515
(919) 967-2110, (919) 967-2139 fax
Respect96@aol.com
www.CharacterEducation.com

Subtotal	
(North Carolina residents add 6.5%) Sales tax	
6% SHIPPING WITH A $4 MINIMUM Shipping	
TOTAL	

SHIP TO:

Name _____

Organization _____ Title _____

Address _____

City _____ State: _____ Zip: _____

Phone: ( ) _____ Fax: ( ) _____ PO#: _____

Visa or MasterCard number: _____ Exp. Date: _____

Signature: _____

FAX your order
(919) 967-2139,
call us
(919) 967-2110,
or order from our website:
www.CharacterEducation.com